Woods, Wolds and Groves

The woodland of medieval Warwickshire

Sarah J. Wager

Sarah J. Wager

BAR British Series 269
1998

British Archaeological Reports are published by John and Erica Hedges and by Archaeopress.

This volume has been published by:
John and Erica Hedges
British Archaeological Reports
7 Longworth Road
Oxford OX2 6RA
England
Tel/Fax +44 (0)1865 511560

Enquiries regarding the submission of manuscripts for future publication may be sent to the above address

BAR 269

Woods, Wolds and Groves: the woodland of medieval Warwickshire

© S. J. Wager

Volume Editor: John Hedges BSc(Hons), MA, MPhil, FSA, FSAScot, FRAI, MIFA

Printed in England by Biddles Ltd

ISBN   0 86054 933 X BAR cover edition
ISBN   1 84058 002 X Full colour cover edition

All BAR titles available from:

Hadrian Books
122 Banbury Road
Oxford OX2 7BP
England

The current BAR catalogue with details of all titles in print, prices and means of payment, is available free from Hadrian Books

All volumes are distributed by Hadrian Books Ltd

CONTENTS

List of Figures

Frontispiece: Warwickshire: inferred extent c.1086, with ancient ecclesiastical parishes

*reproduced by kind permission of Warwickshire County Record Office

Conventions common to all maps

.... ancient ecclesiastical parish boundary (taken from tithe maps or, in default of these, old estate maps or Ordnance Survey maps)

...... boundary between townships within parishes (sources as for parish boundaries)

? suggests a site taken not from a map but inferred from other documentary sources

PREFACE

This book is essentially the thesis written under the supervision of Dr. S.R. Bassett of the School of History in the University of Birmingham and accepted for the degree of Doctor of Philosophy in 1996. Dr. Bassett's unfailing help, guidance and interest are most gratefully acknowledged.

A few additions have been made since the thesis was written, in the light of further research and suggestions made by the examiners of the thesis. Responsibility for any errors of fact or interpretation rests with me.

Dr. Rackham's research and books first stimulated my interest in ancient woods. My own study of Hampton Wood and Professor Dyer's research into Pendock (Worcestershire) helped to prompt the questions about Domesday Book's record of woodland which led to the research for this book.

The thesis drew on detailed documentary research in a large number of record repositories and libraries for whose help and advice I am very grateful. Thanks are due specifically to staff of Birmingham Reference Library, the Bodleian Library in Oxford, the British Library, Cambridge University Library, Coventry Record Office, Devon Record Office, Gloucestershire Record Office, Hereford and Worcester Record Office (St. Helen's Branch), the John Rylands University Library of Manchester, King's College in Cambridge, Leicestershire Record Office, Lichfield Joint Record Office, Magdalen College in Oxford, Northamptonshire Record Office, University of Nottingham Library, Nuneaton Public Library, the Public Record Office, The Queen's College in Oxford, the Shakespeare Birthplace Trust Records Office in Stratford-upon-Avon, Staffordshire County Record Office, Walsall Local History Centre, Warwickshire County Record Office, Westminster Abbey, and the William Salt Library in Stafford. Archivists at the Warwickshire County Record Office, the Shakespeare Birthplace Trust Records Office and the Coventry Record Office in particular drew attention to potentially useful sources. The Public Record Office made special arrangements for the production of large numbers of documents. Permission to examine some of the manuscripts at Merevale Hall was kindly given by Sir William Dugdale and arranged by Mrs. M. May.

I am also greatly indebted to the many scholars who have worked on records of medieval Warwickshire previously, editing documents for publication or obtaining microfilms of them and thereby making them more accessible for others, or, in their studies of the topographical, economic and social history of the county, drawing attention to sources of potential use for this study. In addition, I am grateful for advice on the existence and location of various unpublished documents from Professor C.C. Dyer, Dr. N.W. Alcock and the late Mr. Charles Ivin.

Warwickshire County Council's Sites and Monuments Record was helpful in providing information on specific sites and I am grateful to Miss E. Jones, the Sites and Monuments Record Officer. Ms. P. Copson of the Warwickshire Museum kindly gave me access to the Museum's natural history records.

Permission to take and reproduce photographs of documents was kindly given by Warwickshire County Record Office.

The maps were drawn by Mr. H. Buglass.

Mr. R. Sandland kindly gave me permission to visit Walton Wood and Sir Richard Hamilton to visit Thornton Wood.

The work of the Warwickshire Wildlife Trust in conserving some of Warwickshire's remaining medieval woods is acknowledged in the text. I am grateful to the Trust's Director, Dr. Tasker, for his interest in this book.

The interest and encouragement of family and friends have been much appreciated. I am especially grateful to those who welcomed me to Hampton Wood, taught me about its wildlife and management, and encouraged me to write its history, which began the research described in the following pages.

Sarah J. Wager

January, 1998

Abbreviations

BD	Bromley Davenport Manuscripts in the John Rylands University Library of Manchester.
B.L.	British Library.
Book of Seals	*Sir Christopher Hatton's Book of Seals* (ed. L.C. Loyd and D.M. Stenton, 1950).
B.R.L.	Birmingham Reference Library.
C.B.A.	Council for British Archaeology.
C.R.O.	Coventry Record Office.
DB	*Domesday Book. 23. Warwickshire* (ed. J. Morris, 1976) which reproduces the transcription in *Domesday Book* (Record Commission, 1783) and gives the foliation from the original.
Dugdale	W. Dugdale, *The Antiquities of Warwickshire* (revised edition, 1730).
FF	*Warwickshire Feet of Fines*, Vol. I (ed. F.C. Wellstood, Dugdale Society, XI, 1932), Vol. II (ed. F.C. Wellstood, Dugdale Society, XV, 1939), Vol. III (Dugdale Society, XVIII, 1943). These volumes give abstracts in English (with occasional quotations in Latin) of the originals, so where they are cited the English translation is usually given in square brackets.
Formulare	T. Madox, *Formulare Anglicanum* (1702).
HR	Hundred Rolls for 1279-80. Unless otherwise stated, the citations are from the printed edition, ed. T. John, *The Warwickshire Hundred Rolls of 1279-80: Stoneleigh and Kineton Hundreds* (ed. T. John,British Academy Records of Social and Economic History, New Series XIX, 1992).
LC	*The Langley Cartulary* (ed. P.R. Coss, Dugdale Society, XXXII, 1980).
M.MSS.	Middleton Manuscripts in the University of Nottingham.
Ministers' Accounts	*Ministers' Accounts of the Warwickshire Estates of the Duke of Clarence 1479-80* (ed. R.H. Hilton, Dugdale Society Publications XXI (1952), being a transcript of P.R.O., DL29/642/10,421.
Monasticon	W. Dugdale, *Monasticon Anglicanum* (ed. J. Caley, H. Ellis, and P. Bandinel, 1849).
P.R.O.	Public Record Office
n.d.	no date (referring to undated documents)
Reading Abbey Cartularies	*Reading Abbey Cartularies I* (ed. B.R. Kemp, Camden Fourth Series, 31, 1986).
Roll of Justices	*Roll of the Justices in Eyre ... in Gloucestershire, Warwickshire and Staffordshire, 1221, 1222* (ed. D.M. Stenton, Selden Society, LIX, 1940), being a transcript of the eyre rolls in the P.R.O.
R.O.	Record Office.
S	P. Sawyer, *Anglo-Saxon Charters. An annotated list and bibliography* (1968) identifies each charter by a number.
RBW	*The Red Book of Worcester* (ed. M. Hollings, Worcestershire Historical Society, 1934-50).
S.B.T.	Shakespeare Birthplace Trust Records Office, Stratford-upon-Avon.
SLB	*The Stoneleigh Leger Book* (ed. R.H. Hilton, Dugdale Society, XXIV, 1960).
Staffs. R.O.	Staffordshire County Record Office.
TBAS	*Transactions of the Birmingham Archaeological Society.*
TBWAS	*Transactions of the Birmingham and Warwickshire Archaeological Society.*
VCH	*Victoria History of the County of Warwick.*
WA	muniments of the Dean and Chapter of Westminster Abbey.
W.C.R.O.	Warwickshire County Record Office.
Worcs. R.O.	Worcestershire County Record Office (St. Helen's Branch).

Frontispiece: Warwickshire: inferred extent c.1086, with ancient ecclesiastical parishes

Chapter One

INTRODUCTION: "VERY OLD ARE THE WOODS"[1]

The inspiration

This study sprang from a fascination with the theory that ancient woods are amongst the most enduring topographical features in the English countryside[2] and from a personal interest in one of Warwickshire's ancient woods. The history of Hampton Wood,[3] in Hampton Lucy, was seminal to this study because it raised questions about the nature and distribution of the *silva*[4] which was recorded for Warwickshire in Domesday Book and the relationship of that *silva* to later medieval woods. The idea for this study was born when the inadequacy of the Domesday record became apparent. It was fuelled by doubts over the adequacy and accuracy of a number of studies, some of which had been published before developments in English topographical history provided a new context for the history of woodland.

Aims

The first aim of the research was to study the extent and distribution of Warwickshire's woodland in the later medieval period. This was intended to test the assertion that Warwickshire south and east of the Avon was "woodless" in 1086,[5] consider whether much of the woodland allegedly covering large areas of north and west Warwickshire was wood pasture, consider whether there was a general distinction between coppice woods and wood pasture, and trace the history of individual areas of woodland as far as the documentary evidence allowed. The second aim was to examine the implications of this research for later medieval agriculture and settlement, in particular to consider whether the increase in arable land in the twelfth and thirteenth centuries was at the expense of wood pasture rather than coppice woods and to question the use of the word 'colonization' in relation to the expansion of cultivation. These aims are covered in Chapters Two, Three and Four of this study.

The third aim, the subject of Chapter Five, was to examine the evidence for the extent and distribution of woodland in Warwickshire during the early medieval period. In particular it was intended to see how far back the separate traditions of coppice woods and wood pasture could be traced, test the relevance of topographical analysis to the aims of the study, consider the nomenclature of individual areas of woodland, explore interpretation of certain place-name appellatives and other place-names associated with woodland, and attempt to trace the history of individual areas of woodland beyond the documentary evidence in order to compare the extent and distribution of woodland in the early and later medieval periods respectively.

In the course of that comparison it was intended to see whether there were grounds for the theory that coppice woods were relatively permanent features in a changing countryside whose wood pasture, in contrast, might have reverted from arable land or was liable to conversion to agriculture as a result of changes in population levels and other economic factors. It was also hoped to assess the degree of change in the topography of Warwickshire during the medieval period, with particular reference to individual areas of woodland, and to consider how, when and why different traditions of woodland management evolved and the extent to which they coexisted in Warwickshire. It was anticipated that this might involve comparing these traditions in relation to the location of woods on particular soils, the position of woods within land units, the ownership or tenure of woods and the nomenclature of woods.

The final aim was to suggest how the conclusions of the study might be used in topographical studies of other areas of lowland England. This aim is covered largely in relation to the origins of regional variations in topography which are discussed in Chapter Six, and the theme of continuity and change, covered in Chapter Seven.

Definitions of woodland

Woodland is used in this study to cover land on which trees have grown naturally to form the dominant vegetation. It excludes plantations. Trees developed as the natural climax of botanical succession in most parts of Britain from c.10,000 B.C. after the end of the last Ice Age. As different species of tree appeared during climatic changes in succeeding millennia, varieties of woodland grew, initially free from human intervention. It is thought that virtually none of this so-called wildwood survives undisturbed in England.[6] Woods which occupy land which has been continuously wooded since the post-glacial formation of the wildwood but which have been subject to human management are called primary. They retain natural vegetation inherited from prehistory. It is difficult to prove that any particular wood is primary.[7]

Most land in England, if neglected for several decades, will turn into secondary woodland through the natural generation of seed brought by wind or birds or through underground suckers from adjacent trees. Ancient woodland is a deceptive term, for it has been very widely defined to include any semi-natural wood in existence by c.1600, whether primary or secondary.[8] In comparison with primary woods, therefore, some ancient woods may be very young.

The aims set out above often refer to the distinction between coppice woods and wood pasture. The different management traditions which these types of woodland represent are fundamental to this study. They have been carefully described by Dr. Rackham in various works to which this study is indebted.[9]

Coppice woods are managed intensively to produce successive crops of wood and timber.[10] The trees grow naturally and regenerate after they are cut, either by new shoots springing from the stump, which is then known as a stool, or by suckers which spread underground. The regrowth has to be protected from grazing animals, wild or domestic. Therefore coppice woods have to be fenced on a temporary basis for a few years, until the new growth is tough enough to be safe from grazing, or permanently enclosed, generally by a bank and ditch rather than a fence.

The word coppice is thought to come from the Old French *copeiz*, to cut. It does not appear to have been used in England until the thirteenth century,[11] but is now the general term for a much older tradition of woodland management. There is archæological evidence of coppicing in wooden trackways which have been preserved in the Somerset Levels since the fourth millennium B.C.[12] Coppicing cycles may vary from four years upwards, depending upon the size of wood required, tree growth and management practices. They appear to have been much shorter in the medieval than in the modern period.[13] Usually, some trees in a wood are left to grow to maturity before they are felled to provide timber and are replaced by saplings which have grown from seed. This type of management is called coppice with standards. Timber and wood have different uses. Timber posts, beams and planks are used in buildings and other large objects. Wood provides firewood and material for fencing and many other domestic and agricultural purposes.

The term underwood is often used for branches and poles of relatively small size. Trees which produce underwood form the layer of small trees and shrubs which grow above the ground vegetation but below the canopy of timber trees.

The present tense has been used in the foregoing description because there are a few woods in England where coppicing is still practised for commercial purposes.[14] There are others where coppicing is undertaken for nature conservation.[15] However, coppicing is no longer familiar to the majority of the population. Most people rely on electricity and gas to heat their homes and do not look to a local wood for fuel or other needs. Some country-dwellers still burn wood; others may have old memories of coppicing or be aware of the recent development of short-rotational coppicing of willow and poplar planted on former arable land as one kind of modern agricultural diversification.

In wood pasture, the land is shared by trees and livestock. The two are incompatible, because livestock eat young trees or the branches of larger trees and because the shade of trees restricts the growth of grass. Therefore wood is produced from wood pasture either by pollarding, cutting crops of poles which grow from the tree trunk at a level above the reach of grazing animals, or by fencing off areas of young trees or coppice stools until they grow large enough to be inedible. Wood pasture is a less intensive use of land than coppice woods.

Management has a great influence on woodland flora.[16] The ground flora of an ancient coppice wood is distinguished by an abundance of wild spring flowers, particularly in the recently coppiced areas. The flora of wood pasture is usually less spectacular and may be very poor. Some plants are eaten by grazing animals, others are trampled underfoot or shaded out by mature trees. If recently coppiced areas are enclosed for protection of the coppice spring, carefully limited grazing by certain animals can take place without causing undue damage.

There has been confusion between pasture and pannage.[17] Pannage was a payment, in money or kind, which tenants made to their lord in return for fattening pigs on mast from oak or beech trees. It was paid in respect of both coppice woods and wood pasture and presumably also any common pasture by hedges with mature oak or beech. Acorns and beechmast do not crop heavily every year. Pannage is therefore less than seasonal. Its importance has been overrated in relation to the regular grazing provided by wood pasture.[18]

Words for woodland

Woodland is useful as a general term and has been so used in this study. However, such generality obscures not only the variety of woods in the medieval period but also the number of words for woodland which were used in Latin and Old English.

Most medieval documents were written in Latin, which had various words for woodland. *Silva* is the most common in pre-Conquest charters and in Domesday Book. It was used sparingly thereafter. *Nemus* occurs in some pre-Conquest documents. It is not unknown in Domesday Book, but is more common in records linked to the Domesday survey, the so-called 'Domesday satellites'.[19] It is found occasionally in post-Conquest deeds, usually of the twelfth century, less often of the thirteenth century. It has been translated as 'grove',[20] but this is to overlook the existence of the latinized *grava*, often spelt *graua*, from the Old English word *graf*, which appears in the later medieval vernacular as grove, *groue* and, occasionally, *growe*.[21] It also overlooks the Latin *virgultum*, which is open to confusion with *virgulta* (a variant of *virgata*, English virgate,[22] the traditional later medieval peasant's landholding) and which has also been equated with *gardinum* and *ortus* as "a piece of land containing grass, trees and cultivated plants, often surrounded by a wall, hedge, fence or ditch".[23] However, the occurrence of *ortus* and *virgultum* in the same deed (*cum mesuagio & orto et virgulto*)[24] indicates separate, distinct meanings and *virgultum* has been found in a few records with the unambiguous meaning 'grove'.[25] On this basis instances of the term have been included in this study with a note where the meaning is uncertain.[26] *Boscus* is by far the most common word for wood. Like the English word, it means either a topographical feature or the product of trees. The Latin for underwood is usually *subboscus*.

The difference between *silva*, *nemus* and *boscus* may be purely one of fashion and chronology.[27] However, this study will include some evidence which suggests that at some time these words might have reflected different management practices. Parts of the Domesday survey qualify *silva* with the adjectives *pastilis* (pasture) or *minuta* (small), with the latter referring to the underwood of a coppiced wood. However, for most counties, including

Warwickshire, there is no such quali[...] kind of woodland covered by the ter[...] these reasons, the Latin *silva* i[...] ng to the information in [...]

There are some [...] a particular species [...] grove or carr, and [...] hawthorn or blackth[...]

As noted above, the w[...] appearance may be link[...] classes and in a significa[...] thirteenth and fourteenth ce[...] is generally used for wood[...] French word, meaning to gru[...] way into medieval Latin as *ex*[...] and into English as assart. It is [...] 1086, in Domesday Book. It is usua[...] woodland which has been cleared [...] associated with other kinds of land [...] documents relating to Warwickshire [...] during research assarts were almost [...] with woodland.[31] Other words, such a[...] the verb *approware*, were used to refer t[...] improvement of waste ground.[32] The Eng[...] (a cleared piece of ground) and stocking ([...] trees or plants)[33] are usually associated [...] woodland.

There is uncertainty about the precise meani[...] d English words for woodland or features associat[...] with it. The likely meaning of *graf* (modern English grove) will be discussed in Chapters Two and Four. Chapter Five will include a discussion about the significance of the Old English words *leah*, *fyrth*, *holt*, *hyrst*, *shaw* and *wudu*, as well as the compounds which have become the place-names Grafton and Wootton. The English words firebote, haybote and housebote refer to common rights, collectively known as estovers, to gather wood for fuel, fencing and houses.

A known pre-English word for a wood, *ceto*, is mentioned here because it appears that there are two place-names in Warwickshire which included *ceto* and because there was also a wood whose name appears to have included the word as late as the twelfth century.[34] Although there are several place-names in England including *ceto*, there are not many examples of woods whose names included this word, usually corrupted to *chet*. Those which have been identified have been associated mainly with large areas of woodland, rather than with relatively small woods.[35]

This study tries to imagine what Latin and Old English words for woodland might have meant on the ground, and how the medieval realities might have differed, not only from post-medieval woodland management and modern assumptions about the past, but also within the very long period, a thousand years or so, covered by this study.

Chronological terms

The adjective 'medieval' has been used to describe the whole of the period covered by this study, from the collapse of the administrative structure of the western Roman Empire in the fifth century to c.1500.[36] This definition has been widely used in mainland Europe and increasingly so amongst British historians. It avoids the ethnic connotations and the historical assumptions which are implicit in the title Migration Period for the fifth, sixth and early seventh centuries and in the use of the term Anglo-Saxon for the rest of the period up to the Norman Conquest. The possibility of continuity not only in some Romano-British settlements and institutions but also in the majority of the native population [...] the subject of continuing debate and research. Nevertheless, it is still common in England to confine 'medieval' to post-Conquest, or even post-Norman, history. For historians who follow these conventions, the later medieval period equates roughly to the fourteenth and fifteenth centuries. In this study, however, later medieval means after 1066, or, in practice, after 1086, the date of the completion of Domesday Book. Early medieval refers to the centuries before 1066.

In dating documents, historical years starting on 1st January have been used rather than the regnal years generally given in the documents themselves. For convenience, no attempt has been made to follow the later medieval and early modern practice of recording the start of the year on 25th March.[37]

The County of Warwickshire

To talk of Warwickshire at the beginning of the medieval period is an anachronism. Its boundaries were established relatively late in comparison with those of counties in the south of England and even with those of some of the midlands shires. Kent and Sussex, for example, are thought to be based on early medieval kingdoms, even if they do not perpetuate the exact boundaries of those kingdoms.[38] The first surviving documentary reference to the midlands counties or shires appears in the early eleventh century in the Anglo-Saxon Chronicle. It has been argued that the context in which these references appear indicates that the shires were created for military and administrative purposes and were formally established around the towns on which defensive arrangements had been based after the Danish invasions of the late ninth and early tenth century and from which most of the shires took their names.[39] It has been suggested that the area known from the eleventh century as Warwickshire may have been an administrative entity in the tenth century[40] and also that the creation of the midlands shires and the compilation of the document known as the County Hidage may date from the first half of the tenth century.[41] More recently, it has been argued that several of the west midlands shires preserve, in part at least, earlier provincial boundaries and that Warwickshire emerged from a deliberate disturbance of some of these earlier territorial divisions.[42]

By the end of the eighth century the area which later became Warwickshire was part of the kingdom of Mercia. However, only a century earlier the area had been divided politically, with the south-western part being within the kingdom of the Hwicce. That kingdom is thought to have been coterminous, at its fullest extent, with the medieval diocese of Worcester, whose boundary runs through Warwickshire. It is itself likely to have been an amalgamation of smaller political units, one of which, known later as Winchcombeshire, probably included those Warwickshire manors which in 1086 lay south of the river Avon and west of a tributary of the Avon, the river Stour.[43]

Winchcombeshire is unusual in that evidence survives which has enabled its extent to be deduced with some confidence. Other early medieval political territories in the midlands are not so easily defined. The Domesday county of Warwickshire is therefore a well-known and convenient unit on which to base research.

It could be argued that a topographical study should be based on a geographical region. However, the intricate variety of topography in the midlands makes it difficult to define such a region with the precision needed for the research methods adopted in this study. Moreover, the topographical variety within Warwickshire provides an excellent framework within which to pursue the study's aims and objectives. It allows the study to focus on similarities and differences in a way which enhances the interpretation of the evidence. In particular the often quoted contrast between the north and west of Warwickshire and the south and east of the county cries out for consideration in the light of recent research into medieval settlement and topography. For the purposes of that review the river Avon, an easily recognised and defined topographical feature, has been used as a notional dividing line within the county.

The physical background

A topographical history deals with the effects of human endeavour on natural features and vegetation. The latter are originally the products of geology, soils, relief, drainage and climate. Warwickshire, in the centre of the English midlands, is part of a region which has great variety, rather than stark contrasts, in physical features. Its hills are not like the great hills of the Lake District and some other parts of northern England; they are much lower, part of a gentle, rolling landscape. Even the scarp of Edge Hill, on the south-eastern edge of Warwickshire, does not have the height and dramatic impact of, say, the Malvern Hills in adjoining Worcestershire.

The Birmingham Plateau and other high ground in the north of the county contain coal and other minerals whose presence was exploited on a small scale in the later medieval and early modern periods. From the eighteenth century mining and manufacturing transformed large parts of the county. The Black Country stretched westwards from Birmingham over the county boundary, and there was industrial development around the north Warwickshire coalfields. In the twentieth century further urban development greatly increased the area lost to agriculture. Thus the modern contrasts between these industrial and urban areas in the north and the largely rural areas of the south reflect underlying geological differences.[44] These are apparent even in the remaining rural parts of the north, with their sandstone churches and predominantly red-brick or timber-framed houses, contrasting with the picturesque villages of Cotswold limestone in the south-eastern fringe of the county.

Rather than marking the edge of the county, the watershed between the Trent and Severn river-systems lies within it. The courses of Warwickshire's rivers which feed these systems, the Avon and its tributaries in the south, and the Tame and Blythe in the north, post-date the existence of a great pro-glacial lake, known as Lake Harrison, which covered much of the area of the later county during part of the Ice Age.[45] The Avon valley can be seen as a northern extension of the Severn plain. Apart from the middle Avon valley south of Stratford-upon-Avon, the river plain is relatively, and in parts very, narrow.

The soils are very varied. Parts of the county have been covered by relatively recent volumes of the Soil Survey of England and Wales.[46] These show that clay soils were common in south and east Warwickshire. Whilst soil types may be relevant to the incidence of medieval woodland locally, it has recently been acknowledged that on a regional basis there may be little correlation between them.[47]

The physical background to a history of medieval woodland must also take into account the prehistory of woods, as recorded in pollen deposits. Such evidence shows woodland developing gradually after the last Ice Age, with different types of trees succeeding each other in colonising the tundra. Birch was one of the earliest trees. Hazel was widespread and abundant at a relatively early date, probably by c. 6000 B.C., by which time elm and lime were also common. There was diversity of vegetation regionally, and probably locally. It has been argued that the botanical variety of English woods has been inherited from this prehistoric diversity.[48]

Units for the study of topographical history

The information collected during this study is presented and analysed on the basis of ancient ecclesiastical parishes and townships within them. The parish has long been recognised as a unit for the study of local history.[49] Ancient ecclesiastical parishes are usually easy to define, by reference to tithe maps and apportionments or to earlier maps.[50] The ecclesiastical parish boundaries shown on the maps which illustrate this book are taken for the most part from tithe maps and so reflect the ecclesiastical geography of Warwickshire in the first half of the nineteenth century. However, these boundaries are thought to perpetuate not only later medieval bounds, but also early medieval land units, as churches were founded to serve either large territories or subdivisions of them.[51] Some ecclesiastical parish boundaries were changed by the introduction of civil parishes after 1879,[52] but in Warwickshire outside urban areas the adjustments were relatively few.

A township was a sub-division of an ecclesiastical parish, a discrete area identified by its own name. Its inhabitants recognised themselves as belonging to it and it had its own fields. Like a parish, it might be coterminous with a manor. Like a parish, it is thought to represent a unit of land inherited from the early medieval period, although, as will be explained in Chapter Six, there are different views as to when and how land divisions of this size emerged. The difference between townships and small parishes of similar size lay in their respective ecclesiastical status. A township did not have its own parish church. It might have a chapel dependent on the parish church. If that chapel gained its independence from its mother church the township which it served acquired parochial status. There are many instances of such changes in ecclesiastical status in Warwickshire; for example, the churches of Allesley, Leamington Priors and Lillington have been independent since the thirteenth century.[53] Some historians have used township in a different sense, to describe the people living in a community rather than the area which they farmed. Maitland, for example, called the latter a vill rather than a township.[54] This study adopts the geographical definition of township,[55] as used in some tithe awards.

The alternative to parishes and townships as study units would be later medieval or modern manors. The word manor, as used in Domesday Book, is thought to have arisen as a technical term, initially defining a land-holding liable for the national levy called the danegeld, but thereafter associated more with the powers of the lord of the manor over those who held land in the manor. Manors varied greatly in size. Some extended over several parishes or townships, some corresponded to a single parish or township, some consisted of discrete areas or scattered lands intermingled with the lands of other manors within a parish or township.[56] The boundaries of medieval manors were often unknown, as is apparent from the volumes of the Victoria History of Warwickshire. The extents of modern manors may well differ from their medieval predecessors. Many sources of evidence originate from manors rather than parishes or townships, but they usually describe the location of land by reference to parish or township rather than to manor. For all these reasons ancient ecclesiastical parishes and townships are the obvious units for this topographical study.

Documentary evidence

The information on which this study is based comes from various types of document which will be familiar to students of medieval English topography. These sources have been used primarily to establish the existence of individual woods in Warwickshire. The first aim has been to achieve as complete a coverage of the county as possible given the fragmentary nature of the surviving evidence. Additional information about specific woods, their location, size or management, has been sparse, but vital in the task of interpreting the evidence.

The uneven survival of medieval documents means that the picture is incomplete, and for some places blank. It has been said, of medieval history, that "the task of the historian embraces less the skills of selection than those of discovery, detection, and interpretation."[57] This is certainly true for the history of the woodland of medieval Warwickshire. Places for which several types of document survive exemplify the inadequacies of a single source and heighten awareness of the dangers of basing arguments on limited documentation.

The variety of the documentation on which it has been necessary to draw is therefore an asset in itself.

The purpose of the medieval records on which this study is largely based was economic, not topographical. Information about woodland was included only insofar as it was relevant to this purpose. Even when it came to sales of wood, account rolls do not reveal how and where transactions took place nor the destination of the wood (see Fig. 86). Most, though not all, of the documents which have been used share other significant limitations.

Many documents were written and preserved as records of upper and middle class landholdings and the profits to be derived from them. Tenurial units, or manors, did not always form discrete geographical areas; for example, the lands of the manors in Chilvers Coton were intermingled.[58] By the later medieval period manor and ecclesiastical parish were rarely coterminous, although, as indicated above, parishes are thought to reflect early medieval territorial divisions. Manorial fragmentation is apparent in Domesday Book; there were multiple entries for several places in Warwickshire. Consequently, where medieval records of a particular manor survive, they are unlikely to cover all the land in a parish or might even extend into an adjacent parish. Oversley manor, for example, was divided between the parishes of Arrow and Wixford.[59]

Much of the surviving material dates from the last two centuries of the medieval period. Even collections of earlier documents, such as the deeds relating to Middleton[60] and Chilvers Coton,[61] do not pre-date the thirteenth century. The availability of earlier records in a few cases encourages argument by analogy in others. It has been necessary constantly to question the validity of such an argument and to explain in each case why it has been followed.

Some of the primary sources which have been used are available in printed transcriptions or published calendars. The most obvious example of the former is Domesday Book.[62] Examples of the latter are the long series of published calendars of the Patent and Close Rolls in the Public Record Office. Some published transcripts or translations of documents have been used, but with reservations in cases where it can be shown that there have been misinterpretations of the original.[63] Copies of some original documents have been available locally on microfilm.[64] However, the great majority of documents consulted for this study are available only in the original manuscripts. Consequently, this study is greatly indebted to the services provided by record offices, libraries and private archives in preserving these documents and in making them accessible for research.[65]

Three types of evidence, Domesday Book, the Hundred Rolls of 1279, and pre-Conquest or 'Anglo-Saxon' charters, are discussed in Chapters Two, Four and Five respectively, because their deficiencies, as well as their importance, are an integral part of the arguments developed in those chapters.

After the Norman Conquest, charters, the written records of grants, usually relating to land, became a very common type of document. They have been preserved in various public repositories and private collections. They were used by people in lower as well as in upper levels of society. Certain charters were written in such excellent script that they are a delight to read. Sometimes woodland was the subject of grants or leases; some woods were mentioned incidentally, for example as marking the boundary of a piece of land. Many woods discovered during this study are known only from such references. For example, the medieval grove of Songar is known only from grants made to Bordesley Abbey; one grant, recorded on a small strip of parchment in neat writing, stated that the grove was next to the monks' grange of Songar.[66] Deeds are also useful for field-names which are arguably inherited from the early medieval period and which denote former woodland. Although deeds are far from comprehensive in their topographical coverage, they are a valuable supplement to those manorial records dealing principally with demesne lands. For these reasons they have been extensively consulted and have proved extremely useful for this study. Topographical historians with similar experience have echoed these findings.[67]

Frequently religious communities and occasionally important laymen arranged for deeds relating to their lands to be copied into a cartulary. This served to preserve them, unless the cartulary itself was later destroyed, as happened in the case of a cartulary of Coventry Cathedral Priory which was lost in the fire which destroyed the first Birmingham Reference Library.[68] Cartularies could also be used to disguise forgeries from contemporaries. For example, some of the relatively early charters attributed to the earls of Chester have been shown by modern research to be forgeries.[69] Where both original deeds and copies have survived it is possible to check the accuracy of transcription. In the case of Ratley discussed in the following chapter some of the original deeds have survived, so that such a check could be made; the cartulary also included other deeds which supplemented the information gathered from the originals.

Tenants' lands were also recorded in some manorial surveys, but this was more common in the early modern surveys of Warwickshire parishes than in the relatively few medieval surveys. Wroxall and the surveys of Coventry Cathedral Priory's lands contained in the Priory's Register proved to be welcome exceptions. Surveys might not give a full account, even of demesne lands. For example, the history of Hampton Wood which prompted this wider study could be taken back to the late twelfth century through one of a collection of surveys of the bishopric of Worcester, but the bishops' wood in Hampton was mentioned only incidentally in that survey.[70]

Inquisitions post mortem, surveys of the lands of deceased lay tenants in chief of the Crown, are very variable in the information which they offer. Detailed surveys were made only for those manors which had not been sub-infeudated to under-tenants. Consequently, the topographical information provided by the inquisitions is confined to a relatively small number of manors in Warwickshire. As the printed calendars give varying amounts of information about the surveys, the originals in the Public Record Office have been consulted. The calendar has misinterpreted the information about the manor of Wootton Wawen in 1337 which is said to have included "a great wood".[71] The original extent shows the "great wood" to be one of the products of the unnamed demesne wood, not the woodland itself. The "great wood" was distinguished from the underwood.[72] Presumably this distinction was made because tithes were payable on underwood, but not on wood of greater size.[73]

The available manorial extents attached to inquisitions post mortem vary in the details which they include. A few, such as those for Warwick in 1268 and 1316, for Bubbenhall in 1391, and Fulbrook in 1478, named fields and other topographical features.[74] The Fulbrook survey also revealed the location of the adjoining bishops' park in Hampton Lucy (which had been a matter of presumption, based on field-names in eighteenth-century surveys, when the author's history of Hampton Wood was first written). Most extents are less detailed, merely summarising the acreages of different types of demesne land. Only occasionally were woods named, as in Berkswell, Hartshill and Allesley.[75] The two Berkswell extents of 1316 throw some doubt on the accuracy of the inquisitions. Taken in the same year, each extent named three woods, but only one name was common to both. Other records relating to Berkswell testify to the existence of the woods, so each extent was incomplete, presumably including only those woods from which underwood was sold during the accounting period in which the extent was made.

Manorial extents can be usefully supplemented, at least for demesne woods, by manorial accounts. Most of these date from the fourteenth and fifteenth centuries. Sometimes they give details of the management of woods, the amount of underwood cut in them or arrangements to renew their fencing. However, wood sales may be included in the accounts without reference to the source of the wood.

Manorial court rolls are not often of much use for the history of woodland. However, there have been some valuable exceptions. A court roll provides the only medieval reference to Hampton Wood by name. Court rolls gave important information about woodland in Sambourne and the single example of a grove in Hartshill.

The proceedings in various crown courts have also been very useful. The eyre and assizes in particular provided information about the management of a number of woods as wood pasture in the thirteenth century. The records of the proceedings usually lack details such as the sites, sizes or names of woods, although there are some welcome exceptions, such as the case involving a wood at Barton-on-the-Heath, where information about adjoining land was given. In addition, because of their county-wide coverage, they and the records of the court of King's Bench offer the only evidence for the existence of woodland in some places for which few other records have survived, like Barton-on-the Heath.

Where medieval documents give adjacent field-names, or other details about the site of a wood, it may be possible to trace the site, or at least part of it, through modern maps. Tithe maps and estate maps have been used for whichever parishes or manors they were drawn. Often they have been vital tools in the detection of the sites of former woods. Almost as frequently they have been a source of disappointment, either because a map does not exist, or because medieval topographical names were replaced by modern names before the place was first mapped. Coventry has been a particularly frustrating area for that reason. The adjacent parish of Stoneleigh fared much better. For example, a map of 1597 carried the field-names Bradley which presumably indicate the approximate location of the former wood of that name, but on a map of the same area drawn in 1766 the fields had been renamed.[76] If a larger number of sixteenth-century estate maps like those of Stoneleigh and Brailes[77] were available, the task of identifying the sites of former woods would have been much easier.

Whilst the loss of many documents is regrettable, this study has been made possible by the preservation of others, even some that were described as "old writings of no use".[78] The chapters which follow will show how much can be gleaned even from late and fragmentary records, particularly in the context of other evidence for the history of rural topography.

Other sources of evidence

There has been no large-scale archæological fieldwork in Warwickshire which could have complemented documentary records. Much archæological investigation in the county has concentrated on Romano-British urban settlements or on sites threatened by the imminent construction of roads or buildings. Some excavation in Warwickshire has verified the stratigraphy of road and boundary alignments in an area to which topographical analysis has been applied. The results of this technique, which will be described in Chapters Five and Six, have significant implications for the history of rural topography and consequently of medieval woodland in the county.

In addition, the results of fieldwork in other counties have shown how valuable such research can be for topographical history. Awareness of the significance of the results of archæological field survey elsewhere provides a vital context for the interpretation of documentary evidence for Warwickshire. Despite the inadequacies of the available records, the following chapters will show that there is enough evidence, subject to careful interpretation, for an attempt to be made to fulfil the aims and objectives of this study.

1 Walter de la Mare, *All That's Past.*

2 O. Rackham, *The History of the Countryside* (1986), pp. 88-90; idem, *Trees and Woodland in the British Landscape* (second edition, 1990), pp. 62, 77-82; *idem, Ancient Woodland: its history, vegetation and uses in England* (1980), p. 137. This study is greatly indebted to Dr. Rackham's research and writings.

3 For a summary of the author's research on Hampton Wood, see Chapter Three.

4 For the meaning of this Latin word, see the section on words for woodland below.

5 Rackham, *History of the Countryside*, p. 83.

6 For a summary of the development of the wildwood, Rackham, *Ancient Woodland*, p. 6 and Chapter 8, especially pp. 97-9.

7 *ibid.,* p. 6.

8 Rackham, *Ancient Woodland*, pp. 7, viii, and Chapter 8; *idem, History of the Countryside*, pp. 64-8; this definition was applied in R. Lean and D.P. Robinson, *Warwickshire: Inventory of Ancient Woodland* (Nature Conservancy Council, 1989).

9 See note 2 above.

10 This and the succeeding paragraphs draw upon Rackham, *History of the Countryside*, especially pp. 64-7, 87-92, 119-22 and *idem, Ancient Woodland*, pp. 3-5, where more detailed accounts may be found.

11 R.E. Latham, *Dictionary of Medieval Latin from British Sources*, Fascicule II C (1981), p. 487.

12 O. Rackham, 'Neolithic Woodland Management in the Somerset Levels: Garvin's, Walton Heath, and Rowland's Tracks', ed. J.M. Coles, B.J. Orme, F.A. Hibbert, G.J. Wainwright, C.J. Young, *Somerset Levels Papers*, 3 (1977), pp. 65-71; *idem, Ancient Woodland*, pp. 106-7.

13 O. Rackham, *Hayley Wood: Its History and Ecology* (1975), pp. 28-31.

14 Notably the Bradfield Woods in Suffolk - Rackham, *Ancient Woodland*, pp. 26-7.

15 For example, in the Warwickshire Wildlife Trust's reserve at Hampton Wood, where it was resumed in the 1980's after a long period of neglect, and in the privately owned woods of Long Itchington and Ufton.

16 O. Rackham, *Trees and Woodland in the British Landscape* (1976), pp. 7, 126-7.

17 For example, H.C. Darby, *Domesday England* (1977), p. 182, where the Latin phrase *non pastilis* is translated as "without pannage" instead of "without pasture".

18 Rackham, *History of the Countryside*, p. 122.

19 Darby, *Domesday England*, pp. 174, 176, 178.

20 For example, Rackham, *Ancient Woodland*, p. 140 (the Latin text translated into English on that page has *nemus* where the translation grove appears); D. Hooke, 'Pre-Conquest Woodland: its Distribution and Usage', *Agricultural History Review*, 37 (1989), pp. 113-29, see p. 121.

21 For example, in Tanworth-in-Arden c.1500, DR37/74/30 and Newbold on Avon, P.R.O., SC 11/685.

22 R.E. Latham, *Revised Medieval Latin Word List* (1965), p. 514.

23 C. Dyer, *Everyday Life in Medieval England* (1994), p. 113.

24 King's College, Cambridge, WOW/87 refers to a croft and messuage etc. in Ullenhall.

25 For example, in Baddesley Clinton in 1465, *virgultum vocatum Geges Grove*, S.B.T., DR3/793. Gegge Grove was woodland in the later medieval period, see S.B.T., DR3/103, 158. Also in Kenilworth, *cum duabus grauis siue virgultis in villa de Kenelworth*, P.R.O., C 54/200 rot 23d.

26 As in Stretton-on-Fosse and Tysoe, see Gazetteer, Appendix 1.

27 Darby, *Domesday England*, p. 174, suggests that *nemus* and *silva* were interchangeable.

28 *ibid.,* p. 176.

29 *ibid.,* p. 187.

30 *ibid.,* p. 189; Latham, *Revised Medieval Latin Word List*, pp. 33, 180, 420. For the view that an assart was not necessarily taken out of woodland, see Rackham, *Ancient Woodland*, p. 134 (citing J.A., Raftis, *Assart Data and Land Values: Two Studies in the East Midlands* (1974)) and ed. H.E. Hallam, *The Agrarian History of England and Wales, Volume II, 1042-1350* (Cambridge, 1988), p. 227.

31 There is an exception in the calendar of the manuscripts at Merevale Hall, copy in W.C.R.O., MI 211, in which no. 610, a deed dated to the late thirteenth century, includes two asserts on the heath in the territory of Shustoke.

32 See, for example, deeds referring to Allesley and Coundon, C.R.O., BA/B/A/47/3-11 and BA/B/A/55/1-10 and to Stoneleigh, S.B.T., DR18/1/1130, 1147, P.R.O., E 326/6180, E 210/7314.

33 *The Compact Edition of the Oxford English Dictionary* (1971), Vol. II, pp. 2541, 3062.

34 M. Gelling, 'Why Aren't We Speaking Welsh' in ed. W. Filmer-Sankey, *Anglo-Saxon Studies in Archaeology and History 6* (1993), pp. 51-6 for the two place-names; *idem*, personal communication, for confirmation of the distinct possibility of the survival of *ceto* in the name of a medieval Warwickshire wood - see Chapter Three under Binley and also Chapter Five.

35 M. Gelling, *Place-Names in the Landscape* (1984), pp. 190-1; Rackham, *Ancient Woodland*, pp. 132-3.

36 See, for example, the title of the periodical *Medieval Archæology*, also P.H. Sawyer, 'Medieval English Settlement: New Interpretations', ed. P.H. Sawyer, *English Medieval Settlement* (1979), pp. 1-8, especially p. 8.

37 ed. C.R. Cheney, *Handbook of Dates for Students of English History* (Royal Historical Society, London, 1978), pp. 4-5.

38 N. Brooks, 'The creation and early structure of the kingdom of Kent' and M. Welch, 'The kingdom of the South Saxons: the origins', ed. S. Bassett, *The Origins of Anglo-Saxon Kingdoms* (1989), pp. 55-74, 75-83.

39 C.S. Taylor, 'The Origin of the Mercian Shires', ed. H.P.R. Finberg, *Gloucestershire Studies* (1957), pp. 17-51.

40 T.R. Slater, 'The Origins of Warwick', *Midland History*, 8 (1983), pp. 1-13, see p. 3.

41 F.M. Stenton, *Anglo-Saxon England* (third edition, 1971), p. 337; C.R. Hart, *The Hidation of Northamptonshire*, University of Leicester Department of English Local History Occasional Papers, Second Series, Number 3 (1970), pp. 14-5.

42 S. Bassett, 'The administrative landscape of the diocese of Worcester in the tenth century', ed. N. Brooks and C. Cubitt, *St. Oswald of Worcester: Life and influence* (1996), pp. 147-73, see pp. 151-7.

43 S. Bassett, 'In search of the origins of Anglo-Saxon kingdoms', ed. *idem*, *The Origins of Anglo-Saxon Kingdoms*, pp. 3-27, see pp. 6-17.

44 A.E. Trueman, *Geology and Scenery in England and Wales* (revised edition, 1972), Chapter 10, provides a useful layman's guide.

45 G.H. Dury, *The Face of the Earth* (fourth edition, 1976), pp. 187-8.

46 W.A.D Whitfield, *Soil Survey Record No. 19: Soils in Warwickshire I: Sheet SP36 (Leamington Spa)* (1974); W.A.D. Whitfield and G.R. Beard, *Soil Survey Record No. 25: Soils in Warwickshire II: Sheet SP05 (Alcester)* (1975); *idem*, *Soil Survey Record No. 45: Soils in Warwickshire III: Sheets SP47/48 (Rugby West/Wolvey)* (1977); *idem*, *Soil Survey Record No. 66: Soils in Warwickshire IV: Sheet SP29/39 (Nuneaton)* (1980); G.R. Beard, *Soil Survey Record No. 81: Soils in Warwickshire V: Sheet SP27/37 (Coventry South)* (1984); W.A.D. Whitfield, *Soil Survey Record No.101: Soils in Warwickshire VI: Sheet SP 25/35 (Stratford-upon-Avon East)* (1986).

47 T. Williamson, 'Explaining Regional Landscapes: Woodland and Champion in Southern and Eastern England', *Landscape History 10* (1988), pp. 5-13, see p. 7; C. Dyer, *Hanbury: Settlement and Society in a Woodland Landscape*, University of Leicester Department of English Local History Occasional Papers, Fourth Series, Number 4 (1991), pp. 10-11. However, a belief that heavy clay soils influence the regional incidence of woodland persists in, for example, A. Squires and M. Jeeves, *Leicestershire and Rutland Woodlands Past and Present* (1994), p. 30.

48 Rackham, *Ancient Woodland*, pp. 97-9.

49 W.G. Hoskins, *Local History in England* (second edition, 1972), pp. 23-7.

50 J.B. Harley, *Maps and the Local Historian* (1972), pp. 35-6; F.G. Emmison, *Archives and Local History* (1966), pp. 62-4.

51 See C.N.L. Brooke, 'Rural Ecclesiastical Institutions in England: the search for their origins', *Settimane di Studio del Centro Italiano di Studi Sull' alto Medioevo*, XXVIII (1982), Vol. 2, pp. 685-711; G.W.O. Addleshaw, *The Beginnings of the Parochial System*, St. Anthony's Hall Publications No. 3 (third edition, 1970), p.12; G.W.O. Addleshaw, *The Development of the Parochial System from Charlemagne (768-814) to Urban II (1088-1099)*, St. Anthony's Hall Publications No. 6 (second edition, 1970), p. 14.

52 J.B. Harley, *Ordnance Survey Maps: a descriptive manual* (1975), p. 81.

53 *VCH*, Vol. VI, pp. 7, 160, 163.

54 F.W. Maitland, *Domesday Book and Beyond* (1897), pp. 147-50.

55 R. Oliver, *Ordnance Survey Maps: a concise guide for historians* (1993), p. 73.

56 Maitland, *Domesday Book and Beyond*, pp. 107-28.

57 W.B. Stephens, *Sources for English Local History* (1981), p. 5.

58 W.C.R.O., CR136/V122.

59 S.B.T., DR5/2246b; *VCH*, Vol. III, p. 30.

60 M.MSS.

61 W.C.R.O., CR136.

62 A readily available edition is published in county volumes by Phillimore. The volume for Warwickshire, ed. J. Morris, *Domesday Book. 23. Warwickshire* (1976) is referred to in this study by the abbreviation *DB*.

63 As in ed. W.B. Bickley, *Abstract of the bailiffs' accounts of the monastic and other estates in the county of Warwick under the supervision of the Court of Augmentation for the year ending at Michaelmas, 1547*, Dugdale Society Publications, Vol II (1923), a translation of B.R.L., 168,255. On p. 42 it translates "dimid[ia] gran[arum]" as "half a grove", an error which led to a search in vain for 'grove' place-names in Harbury until perusal of another set of monastic accounts, P.R.O., SC 6/Hen.VIII/3738, in which the Harbury entry read "dimid' Granar'", revealed the published misinterpretation.

64 This is the case for most of the Aston MSS. in the British Library, filmed for use with a local history group in Nuneaton, held in Nuneaton Library and consequently of great benefit to this study in saving journeys to London. W.C.R.O. holds microfilm copies of the Beauchamp cartulary (B.L., Add. MS. 28,024, W.C.R.O., MI 177), the Kenilworth cartularies (B.L., Harl. MS. 3650 and Add. MS. 47,677, W.C.R.O., MI 392), the Coventry Cathedral Priory Register (P.R.O., E 164/21, W.C.R.O., MI 409) and various surveys in the Public Record Office. It also has a photostat copy of the cartulary of St. Mary's, Warwick (P.R.O., E 164/22, W.C.R.O., Z251(Sm)).

65 A list of the record offices, libraries and private repositories visited during the author's research is given in the Preface.

66 *BD*.

67 For example, J. Blair, *Early Medieval Surrey. Landholding, Church and Settlement before 1300* (1991), p. 11, describes private deeds as "the most useful written sources".

68 In 1879, see G.R.C. Davis, *Medieval Cartularies of Great Britain: a short catalogue* (1958), p. 33.

69 P.R. Coss, *The Early Records of Medieval Coventry* (1986), pp. 1-10.

70 *RBW*, p. 277.

71 *Calendar of Inquisitions Post Mortem VIII*, no. 126, p. 71.

72 P.R.O., C135/51/7 reads, in the relevant part, *Boscus cuius subboscus nullus quare duobus annis elapsis tam subboscus quam magnus boscus prostratus fuit et pastura ibidem nichil valet propter salvacionem iuvenis bosci ibidem crescentis.*

73 N. Adams, 'The Judicial Conflict over Tithes', *English Historical Review*, LII (1937), pp. 1-22, see pp. 20-21.

[74] P.R.O., C 132/35/13, C 134/49 and 51, E 149/60/16, C 140/67.

[75] P.R.O., C 134/49 and 51, C 133/14/2, C 134/91/27 and DL 43/14/3.

[76] For a copy of the map of 1597, W.C.R.O., Z141/1(U), and of the map of 1766, Z142(L).

[77] W.C.R.O., CR3231, an estate map of Brailes dated c.1585, shows woodland in Upper Brailes, in the area where documentary evidence suggests that the medieval woodland was situated.

[78] This note was found in a box in the Bromley Davenport collection in the John Rylands University Library of Manchester (*BD*).

Chapter Two

THE WOODLAND OF SOUTH AND EAST
WARWICKSHIRE 1086-1500

The topography of Warwickshire south and east of the river Avon in the later medieval period, typically a region of regular open fields and nucleated settlements, has often been contrasted with the countryside in the north and west of the county, where enclosed fields were more prevalent, where settlement was more scattered and where there was much woodland.[1] Such descriptions imply the absence of large areas of woodland south and east of the river Avon. Some scholars have been more explicit and have drawn a starker contrast, describing that part of Warwickshire as "woodless", or virtually so, by the end of the eleventh century.[2] One has gone so far as to claim that the little woodland recorded in Domesday Book was "really located many miles away in the more wooded parts".[3] These claims have been accompanied by detailed analysis and repeated to the point where they have become an accepted view.

It will be argued here that this view of south and east Warwickshire is mistaken. Whilst this part of the county did not have nearly as much woodland as the rest in the period 1086 to 1500, it did have a significant number of woods, certainly enough to belie the adjective "woodless".

Domesday Book

The claim that Warwickshire south and east of the Avon had virtually no woods is based on a largely uncritical acceptance of the information about Warwickshire in the Domesday Book. It overlooks that document's inadequacies and inconsistencies, which have been exposed in relation to the way in which, and the purposes for which, the Domesday survey was undertaken. Domesday Book is particularly inadequate as a record of settlement, churches, pasture, marsh and heath.[4] Its variations and limitations are very apparent in its treatment of woodland.

A summary of some of the research into Domesday Book's records of woodland is presented here in order to consider the implications of that research for the Domesday survey of Warwickshire.

There are about seven thousand references to woodland in Domesday Book, which covers most of England and a small part of Wales.[5] The difficulties in interpreting these references are due largely to the emphasis on manorial income in the Domesday survey; Domesday Book was not a

topographical record.[6] The local variations in the description and measurement of woodland reflect both the county basis of the returns made to the king's commissioners and the extent of the circuits in which they travelled to collect the information.[7]

Most entries in Domesday Book use one of the following formulæ:-[8]

- swine totals, over which there is a difference of opinion as to whether they refer to the estimated number of pigs for pasture or for pannage;[9]

- swine renders or rents, which were apparently related to pannage;

- linear dimensions, usually expressed in leagues and furlongs, presumably being the composite length and breadth of the area(s) of woodland attached to the manor and presumably at the maximum extent without allowing for irregular, indented shapes;

- acres, which provide a reasonably accurate measurement, although there is no indication as to whether the statute acre or a larger acre was used.[10]

There were occasionally entries which departed from the formula which was typical of the particular county or region, or which used terms other than the standard formulæ.[11] Some of these entries make tantalising reading, giving a glimpse of what might have been written if the compilers of Domesday Book had been more interested in woods.[12] Most of the Warwickshire references used linear dimensions, but there are two entries which are completely different from this normal formula. Their significance will be discussed below.

Most of Domesday Book's references to woodland share three deficiencies. Generally, there is no identification or location of woodland within manors, just as fields and meadows are not named or located; only seven entries name woods.[13] It has been shown that the woodland of some manors was detached geographically, perhaps by many miles, from the manorial centre, but Domesday Book gives no indication of this separation.[14] The case normally cited in Warwickshire is Brailes, for which Domesday Book recorded *silva* measuring three leagues by two, all or most of which is thought, following Sir William Dugdale, to have been in Tanworth-in-Arden, over twenty miles to the north. Tanworth was a manorial dependency of Brailes and a parochial dependency of Brailes church and had plenty of woodland in the later medieval period.[15] In many of Domesday Book's entries there is no precise measurement of the quantity or area of woodland. Warwickshire is less deficient in this respect. Most entries make no reference to the management of the woodland; usually we do not know whether it was coppice wood or wood pasture.

In these circumstances it is hardly surprising that studies of Domesday Book's records of woodland have produced conclusions which do not entirely correspond.

Dr. Rackham has claimed that Domesday Book's records of woodland are generally reliable,[16] that there was no random under-recording[17] and that the pattern of wooded and woodless regions revealed in Domesday Book is supported by documentary evidence from the later medieval period and from early medieval charter boundaries.[18] Dr. Rackham's argument has been supported by his detailed study of Lincolnshire.[19] The section of Domesday Book dealing with Lincolnshire is unique in having an explicit distinction between underwood (silva minuta), wood pasture (silva pastilis) and silva pastilis per loca.[20] (The latter phrase has been interpreted variously as wood pastured in places, i.e. coppice woods and wood pasture interspersed within a single area,[21] and as wood pasture in places, i.e. more than one area of wood pasture within the manor.[22]) A study of central Lincolnshire by Dr. G.F. Peterken found that places with records of woods and wood pasture in 1086 matched very closely modern settlements with ancient woods and that in many cases the sizes of these woods were roughly the same as the acreages given in Domesday Book.[23] A similar relationship between eleventh-century and later woods has been claimed for the Lizard peninsula of Cornwall.[24] These studies suggest stability in woodland over at least nine centuries.

It seems scarcely credible that Lincolnshire was the only county in England in which precise distinctions could be drawn between underwood and wood pasture. Dr. Rackham himself has apparently reached this conclusion in respect of Suffolk. His studies of that county, for which Domesday Book's assessment of woodland was in swine totals, conclude that about half the woodland which existed in Suffolk in the late eleventh century was omitted from Domesday Book. He suggests that the numbers of pigs reflected, not the relative nor the absolute size of woods, but their management, because wood pasture could feed more pigs to the acre. Small and wholly coppiced woods were omitted from the record altogether or allotted a few notional pigs.[25] These conclusions about Suffolk's woodland postulate a large under-recording of woods in 1086 which was systematic, not random, and based on a distinction between coppice woods and wood pasture.

Other studies point to under-recording of woods in other counties. Several charters relating to the lands of Abingdon Abbey in the eleventh and twelfth centuries referred to the woods of Cumnor and Bagley; there is no reference in Domesday Book to woodland in either place.[26] The Inquisitio comitatus Cantabrigiensis mentioned woods in two Cambridgeshire manors for which there is no woodland in the entries in Domesday Book.[27]

What are the implications of these conclusions for Domesday Book's references to Warwickshire's woodland? The compilers of Domesday Book used the Latin silva, generally translated as wood, in referring to Warwickshire's woodland and usually gave its linear dimensions. The noun was not qualified by the adjectives minuta and pastilis used in the Lincolnshire entries, so there was no indication as to whether the silva consisted of underwood or wood pasture or a mixture of both. It has been estimated that nineteen per cent of Warwickshire was silva in 1086, but that the proportion in the north and west of the county was over one third, thirty-five per cent. The quantities of silva were individually large; in the county as a whole there were 120 references to silva compared with 432 in Lincolnshire.[28]

It has been calculated that the eleventh-century woods of Lincolnshire, as recorded in Domesday Book, covered approximately four per cent of the land surface.[29] Subject to regional variations in population density and availability of alternative sources of fuel and building materials, it may be reasonable to assume that a broadly similar proportion of woodland would meet local needs elsewhere. On this assumption it would not have been necessary to manage all of Warwickshire's large areas of silva intensively by coppicing, but as the silva was valuable enough to justify entry in Domesday Book it must have been used to some purpose and profit, presumably as wood pasture.

An unusual entry for Offley in Hertfordshire supports this suggested link between silva and wood pasture. It reads Silva cxx porcis. Nemus ad sepes - silva for 120 pigs, nemus for fences.[30] The substitution in other records of silva for nemus has been held to nullify the distinction suggested by the entry for Offley,[31] but for the people who provided the information about Offley there was a difference. Some scholars have translated nemus as grove.[32]

Other evidence suggests that not only much of, but probably all of, Warwickshire's silva as recorded in Domesday Book was predominantly wood pasture. This evidence comes partly from the boundary clauses attached to two of the relatively few pre-Conquest charters which have been preserved for the Domesday county of Warwickshire.[33] Domesday Book itself provides more evidence.

The boundary of Shottery, near Stratford-upon-Avon, is attached to a charter which is attributed to the decade 699-709 and is usually regarded as authentic.[34] The boundary is thought to be of a later date.[35] Its course has not been fully traced in relation to modern maps.[36] However, Billes leah is presumably Billesley on the western edge of Shottery.[37] The next point in the boundary is westgraf, which is thought to correspond to the wood which is called Westgrove today. That wood, which is recorded by name in the sixteenth century,[38] is in Haselor parish, near to, but not at present adjoining, the boundary with Binton and not far from Billesley (Fig. 1).

11

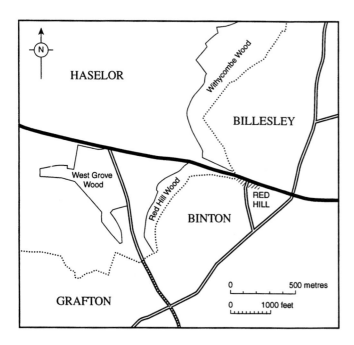

Figure 1: Westgrove

Shottery, which contained thirty-three hides c.700,[39] was a very large territory, which is thought to have included Binton.[40] Shottery is not mentioned in Domesday Book; it is presumed to have been included in the entry for Stratford, of which it was a dependency in the later medieval period.[41] There is no reference to any *silva* in the Domesday Book entries for Stratford, Billesley, Binton or Haselor (although there seems to have been some in Upton township in Haselor parish).[42]

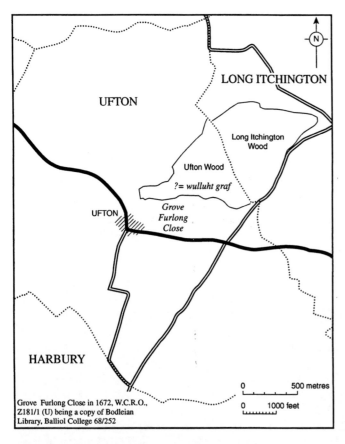

Grove Furlong Close in 1672, W.C.R.O., Z181/1 (U) being a copy of Bodleian Library, Balliol College 68/252

Figure 2: Ufton and Long Itchington Woods

The boundary of Long Itchington, some miles east of Warwick, is described in a clause appended to a charter which is dated to 1001 and is also regarded as authentic.[43] After leaving the river Itchen the bounds refer to a high oak in the middle of *wulluht graf*. The prefix to *graf* contains the same personal name as is found in the place-name of the adjacent parish, Ufton.[44] Woodland straddles the present boundary between Ufton and Long Itchington at a point which corresponds to the *wulluht graf*; each part of the wood is named after the respective parish. A map of 1672 shows a close called Grove Furlong by Ufton Wood.[45] These woods, or the core of them, are thought to be the *wulluht graf* recorded in 1001.[46] However, Domesday Book does not record *silva* for Long Itchington or Ufton,[47] a fact which has been strangely overlooked.[48]

The sites and nomenclature of the later medieval groves of Ufton and Haselor strongly suggest a continuous history with the groves recorded in the charter boundaries. Their absence from Domesday Book may not indicate discontinuity but rather that Domesday Book's record was itself defective. Domesday Book's treatment of woodland elsewhere certainly supports this proposition. The use of the word grove is also a significant factor.

Old English *graf* has become the modern English grove.[49] In the later medieval and early modern periods the noun seems to have been attached to relatively small, private woods.[50] Studies of place-names tend to associate it with woods which were a striking, and therefore presumably isolated, woodland feature, contrasting with open country around. There is no suggestion that *graf* ever meant wood pasture.[51] Unlike some other Old English words for woodland, *graf* may therefore be taken to signify a coppice wood.

The summary entries in Domesday Book could not include all manorial appurtenances. It appears that small areas of woodland were usually omitted. There are only seven alder carrs or groves (Latin, *alnetum*) and two willow beds (Latin, *salictum*) in the whole of Domesday Book.[52] Surely alder carrs and willow beds were far more common in England at that time. It seems reasonable to suggest that for Warwickshire, and presumably for many other counties, the compilers of Domesday Book excluded groves and included a type of woodland which they termed *silva*.

The Warwickshire folios of Domesday Book support this argument with two exceptional entries which seem to prove the rule. These two entries use words other than *silva*. Under Lighthorne a grove, *una grava*, two furlongs long and twenty perches wide, was recorded and in the entry for Weston-under-Wetherley there was a spinney, *spinetum*, two furlongs long and one wide.[53] Here Domesday Book itself distinguished *grava* from *silva*. We know from the two early medieval charter references that Lighthorne is unlikely to have had the only grove in Warwickshire in the eleventh century. It is reasonable to suppose that some other places in south and east Warwickshire which had no *silva* in 1086 had a grove (or spinney) at that time. Evidence of woodland in Warwickshire in the later medieval period supports this conclusion.

Woodland in the later medieval period

It has been argued that woods which appear for the first time in later medieval documents are much older than their recorded history.[54] There are good reasons for this argument, which is an essential premise to the thesis which follows.

It is generally accepted that during the two centuries following the Domesday survey there was a large growth in population, not quantifiable in absolute numbers nor necessarily steady and uniformly distributed but making a great impact on the economy and topography of England.[55] The growth in population stimulated demand for food, especially grain, which encouraged cultivation at the expense of other types of land use, such as marsh, heath and woodland. In parts of Warwickshire there are numerous examples of woodland converted to tillage or pasture.[56] During the twelfth and thirteenth centuries land was not left vacant for long enough to allow secondary woodland to develop. It is therefore logical to postulate that woods whose existence was recorded during that period existed in 1086. Although population is believed to have started to decline early in the fourteenth century, the dramatic fall did not occur until the plague of 1348-9 and, given that it takes some decades for secondary woodland to grow, it is reasonable to assume that a wood recorded before 1350, or even before 1400, was woodland in 1086. (Whether there had been changes in the character of that woodland is another question, which will be discussed in a later chapter.) Several places in Warwickshire for which no *silva* was recorded in Domesday Book had groves or woods before 1350. This study postulates that all these groves and woods existed when Domesday Book was compiled.

This thesis is supported by the name of one of the groves, which was recorded less than a century after the compilation of Domesday Book. *Knicthegraue* (and variants such as *cnihtegraue*) in Ratley seems to include the Old English *cniht*, 'retainer', surely a pointer to a pre-Conquest origin for the grove.[57] Its disappearance in the second half of the twelfth century can be traced through a series of deeds copied into a Stoneleigh Abbey cartulary, of which part has been preserved.[58] Three original deeds have survived elsewhere. A comparison of them with the copies in the cartulary shows that their text was copied accurately (subject to some words being abbreviated or abbreviations extended).[59]

The earliest grants to Stoneleigh Abbey, by Hugh de Arden, included a grove called *cnihtegraue* as *bradewei* divided it.[60] Thomas de Arden, who in another deed described Hugh as his grandfather,[61] confirmed the grant of *Knicthegraue* and allowed the monks to enclose it or assart it at their pleasure.[62] Thomas, or his son of the same name,[63] also granted a meadow in Ratley which was under the wood (*bosco*) called *estlee*,[64] and ten acres and a rood of his grove (*graua*) of *estlee*, of which five acres and one rood were between *bradeweie* and the grove of *estlee* which was of his park.[65] The other five acres of the grove were in *estleeende*. The monks were allowed to assart or enclose this wood also. Confirmatory grants referring to the assarts (*essarta*) of

chnictegraue or *knictegraue* show that the monks chose to clear the wood and suggest that the wood of *estlee* and the grove of *estlee* were synonymous, for in one of these deeds the meadow is described as under the grove rather than under the wood.[66] One of these confirmations[67] was by Waleran, earl of Warwick from 1184 to 1204/5;[68] another confirmatory grant by the same earl referred to the grove rather than to assarts. This points to the assarting of *chnictegraue* during Waleran's earldom, i.e. between 1184 and 1204/5. At least part of the grove of *estlee* seems to have survived to become the Ashley Wood mentioned in a terrier of 1612,[69] and a reference to Nygrove in the same document may preserve the name *chnictegraue*.

Part of the site of Ashley, alias Astley, Wood can be traced through modern deeds and a map of 1808 (see Fig. 3)[70] This site fits other references in a small cartulary of Ratley, where it is stated that ground sloped from *astley grove* towards Hornton (the adjacent parish, in Oxfordshire) and that nearby there was a *swynestemedowe*, which can be linked to the swinstie side allotment of 1808.[71] A map of Ratley Grange[72] includes two fields called Beastwood by fields called park and meadow. Is this name a corruption of the *Prystwood* (presumably Priestwood) of the terrier of 1612 and therefore indicative of the parts of Astley Grove in the park which were granted to the monks of Stoneleigh Abbey?

The references to *bradeweie* in relation to both Astley grove and *chnictegraue* suggest that they were in the same vicinity. Modern maps with field-names cover only parts of Ratley and none includes a name which resembles *chnictegraue*. It has been suggested that the Grove Corner on the first edition of the Ordnance Survey one-inch maps refers to the medieval grove.[73] The identification assumes that the main road along the ridge of Edge Hill was the *bradeweie*, but, given the location of Astley Grove, the road running from west to east to the north of Ashley Wood is a more likely candidate. Grove Corner may take its name from the medieval wood of *doddesgrove* in Radway or the wood called The Grove in the adjoining township of Westcote.[74]

Ratley's groves and the other woods for which documentary evidence has been found before 1350 are listed in Appendix 2. In that list is Lighthorne's grove, six acres in extent in 1316 compared with approximately ten acres in 1086.[75] There is no later medieval record of Weston's Domesday spinney, but there was a wood in Weston in the thirteenth century. Stoneleigh Abbey's *Leger Book* states that the wood of the lord of Weston was in ancient times parcel of Wetherley, i.e. within Stoneleigh parish, so that Weston may have had some *silva* in 1086 which was included in the composite entry for Stoneleigh.[76] There was a grove in Ufton, which is arguably the grove of the pre-Conquest charter. There were also groves or woods in Ettington, Chesterton, Tachbrook, Long Itchington, Cubbington, Bericote in Ashow, Barton-on-the Heath, Tysoe, Radway, Great Wolford, Stretton-on-Fosse, Birdingbury and Long Lawford. The location of a grove associated with Barford is discussed below.

To the groves and woods for which documentary evidence is available before 1350 might be added groves and woods first recorded after that date in Wormleighton, Offchurch, Moreton Morrell, Bascote, Westcote and Burton Dassett, as the lack of earlier references may be due simply to the inadequacy of the documentary record. For example, manorial accounts and court rolls for Wormleighton do not survive before the second half of the fourteenth century.[77] For many places only modern records are available in any detail. A few of these places have woods today. Some of these woods, such as Idlicote Grove, have names which suggest that they may be as old as the groves for which later medieval evidence survives. There was a grove in Idlicote in 1527.[78] For the same reason Moreton Wood in Moreton Morrell may be partly medieval, as there was a grove in Moreton Morrell in the fifteenth century.[79] No documentary evidence has been found to link the medieval grove with the modern wood, but the ecology of the latter, a hazel coppice, which largely survived a modern attempt at replanting, with a fine ground flora of bluebells, celandines and some wood anemones, is consistent with such an identification.[80]

eleventh century at least, the thirteen places in which *silva* was recorded in Domesday Book, Bubbenhall, Ryton-on-Dunsmore, Stretton-on-Dunsmore, Wappenbury, Lillington, Southam, Wasperton, Wellesbourne, Walton, Pillerton Hersey, Brailes, Whichford, Long Compton and Wetherly (*alias* Waverley, in Stoneleigh); details of the amounts of *silva* are given in Appendix 2. Unfortunately, later medieval records for several of these places are scant, so that no evidence has been found for woodland in Southam, Lillington, Wasperton and Pillerton after 1086, and only incidental references for Stretton-on-Dunsmore. It has been claimed that Domesday Book's "woodland entries apparently located in the south of the county are now known to be holdings in the Arden and ... only two small areas of woodland at Ufton and Southam can still be positively located in the Feldon."[81] More recently, doubt has even been cast on the location of Southam's woodland.[82] However, whilst links with places in the north and west of Warwickshire are known for Wasperton, Wellesbourne and Brailes, and the *silva* entered under Brailes in Domesday Book has been attributed wholly or largely to Tanworth-in-Arden, later medieval records show that there was a grove in Brailes and woodland in Wellesbourne.[83] Lillington has a minor place-name, Binswood, which suggests former woodland, which might have disappeared after 1086.[84] It has been suggested that the *silva* of Lillington was the "curious northern extension of the parish containing the Rye Field and the Heath in 1711".[85] Wasperton adjoins Oakley Wood (in Bishop's Tachbrook) of which there are several later medieval records, so it is not implausible to suggest that Wasperton's *silva* might have been part of a larger area of woodland on the boundary between the two parishes.

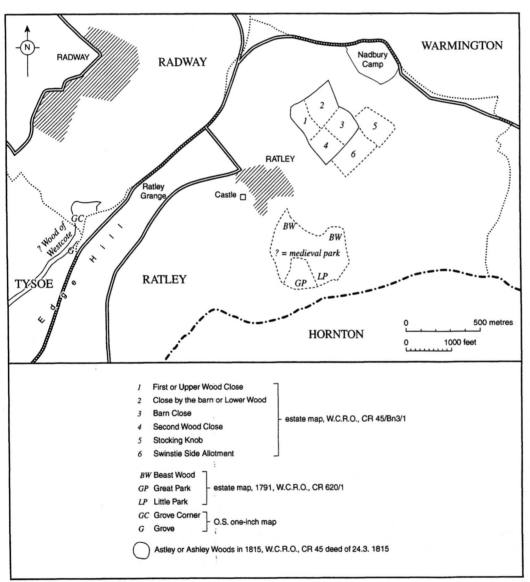

Figure 3: Ratley

1 First or Upper Wood Close
2 Close by the barn or Lower Wood
3 Barn Close
4 Second Wood Close
5 Stocking Knob
6 Swinstie Side Allotment
} estate map, W.C.R.O., CR 45/Bn3/1

BW Beast Wood
GP Great Park
LP Little Park
} estate map, 1791, W.C.R.O., CR 620/1

GC Grove Corner
G Grove
} O.S. one-inch map

○ Astley or Ashley Woods in 1815, W.C.R.O., CR 45 deed of 24.3. 1815

To the woods and groves of south and east Warwickshire found in later medieval records should be added, for the

There are some early modern groves and also some records of fields called grove which probably refer to former woodland. These are also given in Appendix 2. It cannot be assumed that these groves were still woodland in 1086, leave alone in the later medieval period; they may have been converted to tillage or pasture before that date. Whilst the potential significance of such field-names must not be overlooked, care must always be taken in associating them automatically with woodland. In north-east Warwickshire, for example, the modern Grove Farm in Wolvey does not appear in the enclosure award of 1797, but one of the landholders named in the award, though not farming in that part of the parish at the time, had the surname Grove.[86] There is also some doubt about the antiquity of the name of a field called 'Meadow or Grove' in Barford which otherwise could have been associated with an obscure medieval wood called *Perselegrove*.

Perselegrove, which comprised a messuage, a carucate of land and ten shillings rent in 1336, has been so completely forgotten that the editors of the *Calendar of Close Rolls* placed it in Worcestershire and the authors of *The Place-Names of Warwickshire* attributed it to Barston (on the strength of some fields called the Parsley Bed).[87] Sir William Dugdale, who has proved to be remarkably accurate in his topographical references relating to woodland, found a reference to the place in the endowment of a chantry in the church of Stratford-upon-Avon which noted that *Perselegrove* was by Hampton Lucy, a fact confirmed by a case at the assizes in 1316, when the holding in dispute included an acre of wood.[88] None of the parties to that dispute was said to be living in Hampton; Wasperton and Barford, on the opposite bank of the river Avon, were named as local places of residence.

There is an earlier reference to the wood in an undated, but presumably thirteenth-century, deed in which Walter de Bereford granted to Walter d'Eyville (*deiuilla*) all his meadow of Barford which was called the great meadow under the wood of Persele (*totum pratum meum de bereford quod vocatur magnum pratum sub bosco de persele*).[89] The d'Eyville family held part of Walton (hence the name of the manor of Walton Devile) so it seems logical to conclude that the meadow which was granted to Walter d'Eyville became the half of a meadow in Barford which was conveyed with Walton Devile and Walton Mauduit in 1551[90] and was the *walton medow* which was mentioned in describing lands in the vicinity of Westham in 1574.[91] The lords of Walton held a piece of meadow in Barford in the eighteenth century[92] just across the river from the steep, high bank which was part of Hampton Wood in 1736 and possibly in the medieval period.[93] The minor place-name Grove occurs in Hampton Lucy in its simplex form - *Grava* - as early as c.1100[94] and similarly in account rolls for the manor of Hampton in the fourteenth and fifteenth centuries,[95] but the name *Persele* does not appear in any records associated with the manor. A meadow in Hampton Lucy called Parshow is shown on the estate map of 1736 opposite Barford Field; if Parshow has the same first element as *Persele* it may point to the location of the latter across the river. The balance of evidence seems to place *Perselegrove* in Barford, though not necessarily on the site of the field called Meadow or Grove c.1853,[96] for that field was known simply as Long Meadow in 1810.[97]

The sizes of most of the later medieval groves and woods of south and east Warwickshire are unknown. Even where sizes were recorded in inquisitions, the area quoted might have been limited to the wood or underwood ready for sale. Lighthorne's grove was apparently small, the dimensions being given as two furlongs by twenty perches in Domesday Book and six acres being recorded in 1316. Chesterton's grove was said to have included ten acres in 1353, a far cry from the 133 acres in Chesterton Wood in the middle of the eighteenth century.[98] The references to small acreages in woods in the Hundred Rolls of 1279 and related documents[99] can be read as referring not to the size of the wood but to land, possibly assarted, within woods, as with the *boscum continentem x acras terre* in Ufton and the *boscum continentem iij acras terre* in Weston-under-Wetherley.[100] The woods themselves were presumably larger, a probability which is discussed further in Chapter Four.

Woodland may have been more extensive in south and east Warwickshire in 1086 than two or three centuries later. Indeed, there are a few records which indicate woodland clearance during the later medieval period. In that part of Stoneleigh south-east of the river Avon it was extensive. Stoneleigh Abbey's *Leger Book* names the fields which were brought into cultivation from the *bruillum* (arguably an Anglo-Saxon game-park) of Echells and the *bruillum* of Wetherley; several of these fields, as described in the following chapter, can be located on maps.[101] In Birdingbury in the thirteenth century there was an assart by *Stanidelf*, which was by *Le Groue* of Birdingbury.[102] In 1392 there were eight acres of arable land *in le grove infra sepe* - in the grove within the fence or hedge.[103] In 1246-7

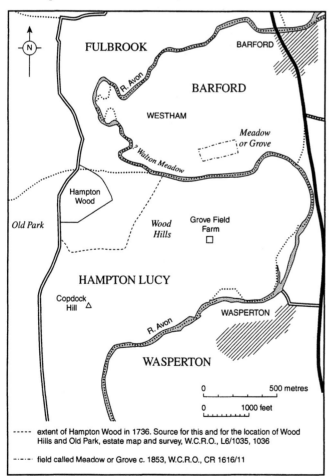

extent of Hampton Wood in 1736. Source for this and for the location of Wood Hills and Old Park, estate map and survey, W.C.R.O., L6/1035, 1036

field called Meadow or Grove c. 1853, W.C.R.O., CR 1616/11

Figure 4: Barford - Westham

15

Walter le frauceys and Aline his wife claimed that Thomas de Bissopesden, lord of Thornton, had deprived them of their common pasture in Thornton in a certain wood containing ten acres.[104] Was this a move to enclose the wood or convert part of it to agriculture? Might the wood in dispute have been part of a larger area of woodland of which the present wood is a remnant? (The present wood is said to have been first planted as a covert between 1822 and 1854, but, if that is the case, it was planted on the same site as a wood shown on a map of 1765.[105]) The wood of 1765, the adjacent Grove Furlong and Rolling Ground, and the fields between them and the brook to the north form a compact area on to which other closes or fields abut, suggesting that they might once have been a single unit. Part of the modern Thornton Farm has a flora associated with ancient woodland.[106]

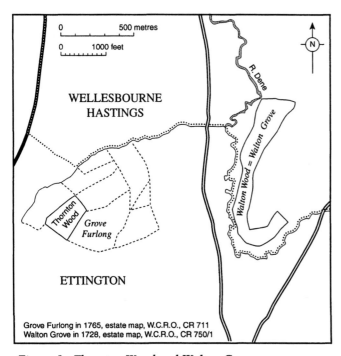

Figure 5: *Thornton Wood and Walton Grove*

There are references to waste in Ufton, Baginton, Lillington and Barford (in Barford's waste there was common pasture in the thirteenth century).[107] Although there is no indication that the waste had formerly been woodland, analogy with waste in north and west Warwickshire (see Chapters Three and Four) suggests that it might have been.

The late eleventh-century distinction between *silva* and groves may have been perpetuated in the nomenclature of later medieval woods in south and east Warwickshire. Most of the places with *silva* in 1086 seem to have had woods instead of, or as well as, groves in the later medieval period. Most, though not all, of the places without *silva* in 1086 had groves rather than woods in the later medieval period. The picture is complicated by changes in terminology during the period. It will be seen from Appendix 2 that Barton had a medieval wood but that the name which has persisted is Barton Grove. Similarly, in the thirteenth century the royal courts referred to a wood in Thornton, whereas the present Thornton Wood is adjoined by a Grove Furlong. *Perselegrove* was a place-name; it had a wood, not a grove,

but the field-name which has survived is grove. Coventry Cathedral Priory called its woodland in Ufton a wood (*boscus*), but the charter of 1001 referred to a grove, and a Grove furlong adjoined the wood in 1672. As will be shown later in this chapter, the terms wood and grove seem to have been used interchangeably in Chesterton.

Where the use of the noun wood appears to have been continuous, as in Whichford, it may indicate an area of former wood pasture. The agreement to impark Whichford Wood allowed pigs in the wood there and in the wood of Long Compton between Michaelmas and Martinmas, presumably the continuation of previous practice.[108] In the last decade of the thirteenth century the wood at Long Compton was being managed principally for wood and timber. In the winter of 1293-4 twelve colts and twenty-four other animals were agisted (pastured) there, but in the following winter there was no agistment because the wood had been cut; in 1296-7 it was recorded that the wood had been enclosed that year (*ponitur in defenso hoc anno*) on account of the regrowth of the wood (*propter successionem bosci*).[109]

It is possible that woods and groves coexisted not only in the county but also within the same manor. However, the only evidence of such coexistence within manors south and east of the river Avon (apart from Stoneleigh) are the faggots *factis de forinceco bosco* in Lighthorne in 1398-9,[110] unless these were made from wood brought in from outside the manor. None of the extents of Lighthorne taken for inquisitions post mortem refers to an outwood and Domesday Book did not include any *silva*.[111]

This study does not claim that there were many woods in south and east Warwickshire in the later medieval period nor in 1086. Certainly there were far fewer than in most of the rest of the county, suggesting some local shortages. Given the importance of wood products in medieval society one is bound to ask how the inhabitants of places with little or no woodland managed without easy access to local woods. Hedgerows and trees around homesteads might have provided enough wood for items of equipment. Tenants, like their lords, might have bought some wood from further afield; Wood Street in Stratford borough suggests a local market. Alternative fuels may have been used, particularly peat. There is evidence of peat digging in Long Lawford; in 1210 the monks of Pipewell had permission to dig turves for fuel in the moor of Long Lawford for their grange there.[112] There is archæological evidence of coal from the vicinity of Nuneaton being used in Chipping Dassett.[113]

Nonetheless, Warwickshire south and east of the Avon cannot be described as woodless, nor virtually so, and its woods were not negligible features in the local topography. The larger woods may have supplied wood for other places, as did Wappenbury Wood in the sixteenth century.[114] Apart from the cluster around Bubbenhall, Ryton, Stretton and Wappenbury, woods and groves were scattered throughout the region. Ufton, Long Itchington, Chesterton, Lighthorne and Moreton Morrell were in the very heart of it (Fig. 6).

Legend

s	*Silva* in Domesday Book
●	Woodland recorded 1086-1350
✕	Woodland recorded 1351-1400
▲	Woodland recorded 1401-1500
○	Groves recorded post 1500

Figure 6: Woodland in Warwickshire south and east of the River Avon, 1086-c.1500

17

Historians have been aware of at least some of these woods,[115] but there has been no attempt, hitherto, to collect all the evidence in order to consider how exceptional, or otherwise, these woods were, or their significance for Domesday studies. Indeed, two types of record may have served to reinforce the impression that there was no woodland worth preserving.

Later medieval timber supplies

The myth of a woodless region may have been perpetuated by an imperfect understanding of the distinction between timber and wood in the manorial economy and of the special arrangements for supplying the former. Timber was an expensive commodity, but was needed in far smaller quantities than wood. Consequently lords or their bailiffs seem to have preferred to transport timber between their estates, often many miles distant from each other, rather than to buy it from local sources. Transport does not seem to have been a problem. This practice has been identified in eastern England.[116] There are examples of it in several manors in Warwickshire where timber procurement and wood sales were distinct.

In 1382-3 timber was carried to Wasperton from Packwood; both manors were held by Coventry Cathedral Priory.[117] Although Wasperton parish bordered on Oakley Wood in Bishop's Tachbrook, the bishops do not seem to have supplied timber to their neighbours. In 1382-3 Wasperton sold faggots and sallows;[118] perhaps the latter came from the banks of the Avon or Thelsford Brook. In 1251 Stephen Bauchan, who had wardship of the lord of Birdingbury, a minor, was allowed housebote and haybote in the wood of Allesley.[119] Timber was sent from Allesley to Birdingbury in 1397-8, when the manors were held by John de Hastings.[120] Brailes and Tanworth were both held by the earl of Warwick. In 1413-4 the park of Brailes provided underwood for sale and the farmer of the site of the manor was allowed two acres of underwood in the grove, yet in the same year thirteen oaks were felled in Tanworth for use in Brailes.[121] Timber which was sent in 1443-4 from the lord's wood in the earl of Stafford's manor of Great Wolford to his manor of Tysoe[122] would probably have passed through Brailes, but was not destined for the earl of Warwick's use. The manor of Sutton-under-Brailes, which belonged to Westminster Abbey, obtained timber from the Abbey's manor of Knowle in 1304-5.[123] However, it obtained timber from the nearby Whichford Park in 1323-4 and bought wood from Whichford in 1377-8.[124]

All these examples are taken from manorial accounts. Few such records have survived from before the fourteenth century. However, it appears that the practice of moving timber between manors in common lordship was current before 1200; c.1196 the earl of Warwick granted with a lease of a mill in Wellesbourne timber from his woods of Claverdon and Tanworth.[125] Although some of the manors involved had been held by the same family or institution since 1086, this did not apply to Allesley or Knowle; Westminster Abbey did not acquire the latter until the end of the thirteenth century.[126] Nor did it apply to the lands of Bordesley Abbey which were scattered amongst several parishes in Warwickshire. When the Abbey leased land in Stretton-on-Fosse in 1537 the tenant was required to rebuild the houses and was granted timber for the purpose from the Abbey's woods in Bordesley in Worcestershire. (The Abbey made similar agreements for supplying timber to Binton, in the Avon valley north of the river.)[127] An arrangement for sending timber from one manor to another should therefore be seen as an aspect of later medieval estate management which might have been, but was not necessarily, derived from earlier links.

Contemporary comments c.1500

Comments which were made in the early decades of the sixteenth century have been used as evidence of the topographical contrast between the north and west, and south and east of Warwickshire. Unfortunately, as far as woods are concerned, the contrast can be exaggerated by selective quotations. This applies to the history of Wormleighton and the *Itinerary* of John Leland.

Amongst the muniments of the Spencer family[128] survive two documents in which John Spencer, lord of the manor of Wormleighton, petitioned the king against an instruction to remove the hedges which had been planted by him and his predecessor, William Cope, when fields were enclosed. John Spencer argued that the hedges supplied much needed wood and timber to the local inhabitants. In a detailed study of the history and topography of Wormleighton various statements have been cited from the first of these petitions, dated to c.1519, including John Spencer's claim that when he came to Wormleighton there was "noo wood nor tymber growing within xij or xiiij myle".[129] The second petition, dated to c.1519, was not cited in the study, but differed from the first in stating that "ther ys very lytill wood growing within xiiij myle of the same".[130] The second claim is more accurate, because, apart from woods which may have existed in the neighbouring county of Northamptonshire, the woods of Chesterton, Long Itchington and Ufton were all within ten, leave alone fourteen, miles of Wormleighton. It may be that these woods were retained for the use of the lord and tenants of those manors, so that there was no local wood or timber available to people in Wormleighton, although in 1385-6 the accounts for the Catesby manor of Ladbroke recorded the cost of sending a man to cut down forty-seven oaks *apud Ichynton Wode*.[131]

The study of Wormleighton also overlooked the existence, or former existence, of a grove in the manor. In 1387 three tenants were presented to the manorial court for taking wood from the lord's grove.[132] Presumably the grove had disappeared by 1500, but the absence of woods in Wormleighton then must not influence the picture in the late fourteenth century and before.

The accounts written by John Leland, the antiquary, of his journeys through England in the years c.1535-43 are said to have made familiar the topographical contrast within Warwickshire.[133] Part of Leland's original manuscript has been lost, but a copy of the whole was made in the sixteenth century.[134] Leland seems to have made two separate sets of notes about Warwickshire, one set serving possibly as the basis for a later, narrative version. The former is known only from the copy of the lost portion.[135] It includes the following statement:- "Such parte of Warwikeshire as lyethe by sowthe on the left hand, or banke, of Avon, is baren of woode, but plentifull of corne."[136] The other version reads, "The othar part of Warwyk-shire that lyethe on the lefte hond or ripe of Avon river, muche to the southe, is for the most parte champion, somewhat barren of wood, but very plentifull of corne."[137] The evidence already discussed in this chapter shows that the second statement was more accurate than the first because it implies the presence of some, if not much, wood.

Leland's statements should also be set in the context of the sense in which he used the word wood. He generally used the noun in the singular, not the plural, implying the product of trees rather than an area covered with trees. This assumption is supported by later sixteenth-century writers who associated woodland with a hedged landscape rather than with woods, although this association was not universal.[138] Seen in this light, Leland's statement that there was little wood in south and east Warwickshire fits the evidence for an open countryside which had few hedges but some woods. However, on occasions Leland noted specific woods adjoining roads on which he travelled, as in his journey between Banbury and Bicester in Oxfordshire.[139]

references in the text which indicate that Leland took a route apparently corresponding to the modern Banbury to Warwick road (the former A41, now the B4100) and the modern editor of the *Itinerary* has assumed that this was the route followed. Leland mentioned Hanwell in Oxfordshire, about half a mile north-east of the road, and, about half a mile from Warwick, a bridge over a brook running into the river Avon.[141] He does not appear to have made a diversion through Kineton, Wellesbourne and Barford, because he described a journey from Warwick to Wellesbourne separately and in some detail.[142] Leland's route is important because the modern Banbury road passes right by Chesterton Wood and divides Chesterton from Lighthorne, as it did on an eighteenth-century map which described it as a turnpike road.[143] It also passes right by Oakley Wood in Bishop's Tachbrook, some three miles south of Warwick.

Chesterton certainly had a wood when Leland travelled through Warwickshire. In 1537 John Peyto, the lord of the manor, leased various lands "and also all thatt his Woode or grove in Chesterton aforeseid callyd Chesterton Grove adioyning to the seid greate fylde."[144] Chesterton Grove was still a wood in 1568 and 1632-3.[145] In deeds of 1322 and 1344[146] the grove was described as near to an unidentified *Axemere* and to the *Syche*, which is probably the stream which is shown on modern maps as flowing alongside the northern edge of Chesterton Wood and which appears to have given its name to land called *Such* in the south-eastern corner of Chesterton, east of the present Chesterton Wood.[147] Later deeds also associate the grove with water courses or leats. Deeds of 1508 and 1520 stated that two pastures called the *over lete* and the *neder lete* adjoined the grove.[148] The lease of 1508 stated that the two pastures also contained wood and with the grove were enclosed within a single fence or hedge (*una sola sepe*). This points to the enlargement of the grove by the development of secondary woodland and may be a consequence of the enclosure of the common fields and their conversion to pasture or other uses, a process which had begun by 1484.[149] An eighteenth-century map shows fields called Wood Furlong on the northern side of Chesterton Wood,[150] pointing to this area for the site of the later medieval woodland.

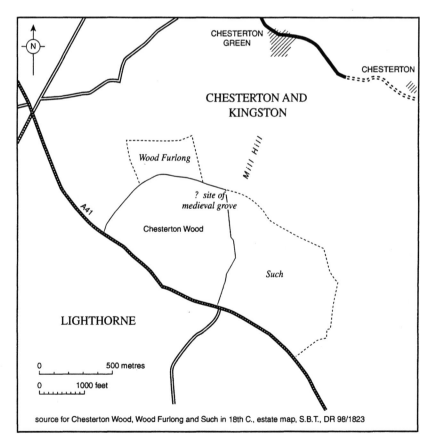

Figure 7: Chesterton Wood

The statement in 1537 that the grove was by the great field is of little help in establishing its location, for in 1538 the great field, containing seventy-nine yards (or yardlands) appeared to cover much of Chesterton; it included minor place-names (*Cleyhill, barnehill*, and the *Syche*) which appear in the north, centre and south-east of Chesterton on the eighteenth-century map.[151] There are later medieval references to a wood in Chesterton; although they never occur in the same documents as the grove the two may have been one and the same. An inquisition post mortem of 1300 included five acres of underwood;[152] another, taken in 1353, referred to an enclosed wood of ten acres (*boscus*

Leland's description of his journey from Banbury to Warwick deserves further attention. He wrote, "I rode from Banbury to Warwik 12. miles by champayne ground, frutefull of corn and gresse, baren of woodde, and 2 miles by some enclosyd and wooddy ground."[140] There are two

19

inclusus continens decem acras) with no underwood but pasture valued at 3s. 4d.[153] An earlier, briefer, inquisition of 1293 referred to part of a wood.[154] (Chesterton was divided manorially, but these inquisitions referred to the same, principal, manor.[155]) In 1441-2 sales of rods and of three weeks' pasture for six bullocks in Sir William Peyto's wood (*boscum*) raised 26s. 4d.[156] In 1474 the *wode* was described as near *Whetffurlonge balke*.[157] The lease of 1520 included, in addition to the grove with its two adjoining pastures, "a pasture called the townre Where the manor place standeth with woodez and grovez therto adioynynge & belongynge"; in a lawsuit in the early seventeenth century this "roughe coppice ground" was said to have been "stocked up" or destroyed by the plaintiff's father.[158] The existence of woodland in Chesterton during the later medieval period and the sixteenth century is certainly well documented, even though it appears to have been much smaller than the modern wood, in parts of which there are traces of ridge and furrow, confirming not only that those parts are secondary woodland but indicating also that they include evidence of medieval ploughing.[159]

Why then did Leland omit Chesterton Grove from his account of his journey from Banbury to Warwick? As indicated above, he may have been interested mainly in the overall impression of the countryside. However, the local topography suggests that the small grove by the stream and the "woodez and grovez" by the manor house could not have been seen from the Banbury road. The ground north of the road, now covered by Chesterton Wood for a substantial length, rises gently before falling more steeply to the Wood's northern edge. From the minor road on the north-eastern side of the Wood the main road is not visible. In short, Leland seems to have overlooked Chesterton Grove simply because he could not look over the hill to see it.

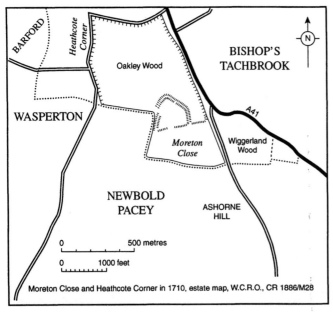

Figure 8: Oakley Wood

There is no doubt about the proximity of Oakley Wood to the Banbury road in the sixteenth century. A deed of 1573 referred to "a certen woode ther lyinge by London wey comonlye called & knowne by the name of Okeley

woodde".[160] The wood (*boscus*) called *Acle* was recorded in a grant by Richard Peche (bishop of Coventry 1161-82) and, under the same name, *Oklie*, was the subject of an agreement between the earl of Warwick and Walter Langton (bishop of Coventry and Lichfield 1296-1321) whereby the bishop was allowed to enclose and impark his wood.[161] As Leland appears to have used a long mile to measure his journeys - the modern distance from Banbury to Warwick by the direct route of the A41/B4100 is some miles in excess of the fourteen miles recorded by Leland - Oakley Wood was probably included in the "enclosyd and wooddy ground" which characterised the last two miles of his journey.

There is no reason to doubt the accuracy of John Leland's account of what he saw, but there was much that he did not see. Whilst he may have travelled along many of the highways in that part of Warwickshire, he seems to have missed most of the byways. He travelled from Marton to Southam and from Southam to Banbury,[162] but he did not take the minor road through Bascote to pass the woods of Long Itchington and Ufton nor, further on, leave the main road to visit the village of Wormleighton a mile or so to the east.

It could be argued that Leland's *Itinerary* shows that woods were a relatively insignificant feature in the topography of south and east Warwickshire in the first half of the sixteenth century. However, John Spencer's roughly contemporary claims about the shortage of wood in Wormleighton confirm that, where they were present, woods and their products must have been important to the local inhabitants. The value attached to them is the obvious explanation for their preservation.

Change and continuity: the preservation of woods

Wormleighton and Chesterton exemplify two extremes in the histories of their respective groves. Wormleighton's grove disappeared towards the end of the medieval period. Chesterton's grove survived and was enlarged; in 1632-3 it supplied wood for sale to people in a dozen surrounding settlements.[163] Both groves appear to have been part of the manorial demesne, so their futures must have been determined by the lords of the two manors.

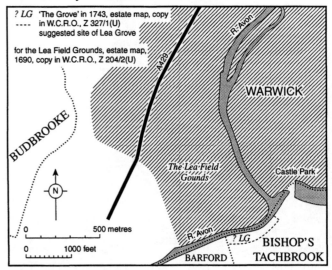

Figure 9: The Lee Grove

The occasion of, and the reasons for, the disappearance of the grove from Wormleighton are unknown. One could speculate that the grove lost its economic importance after enclosure and depopulation. The same fate seems to have befallen Lighthorne's grove. In neither case has grove survived even as a field-name.[164] The Lee Grove in Tachbrook also disappeared. In 1415 the township (*villa*) of *la lee* included open fields, meadows and heath as well as the grove, but by the middle of the sixteenth century the field was a pasture and with the grove was later absorbed into Warwick Castle Park.[165]

Ratley no longer has a grove, but the approximate site of one of the medieval groves is indicated by field-names in wood which can be identified with the former Ashley Wood.[166] Brailes Wood, at the Grove End in 1631, survived until the late seventeenth century.[167]

It has been explained above that there is no surviving evidence of later medieval woodland in four of the places for which *silva* was recorded in 1086. That *silva* may have disappeared relatively soon after 1086. If the argument that *silva* was wood pasture is accepted, it can be suggested that its loss was caused by intensive grazing at a time of rising population and prices.

In the later medieval period woodland in south and east Warwickshire was more commonly preserved than destroyed. The policy of preservation continued into the modern period. Most places which had woods or groves in the later medieval period have woods today. Whilst some areas of woodland disappeared during the later medieval period this did not greatly change the overall pattern of distribution. Woods and groves were scattered unevenly over south and east Warwickshire. It must not be assumed without supporting evidence that the modern wood is the same in site, size or management as the later medieval wood or grove. The history of Chesterton's grove shows how different the medieval and modern woods can be. However, judging from their names, and in some cases from their sites, it does seem that a significant number of these medieval woods and groves survived into the modern period.

Oakley Wood adjoined the main Warwick-Banbury-London road in the sixteenth as in the twentieth century. It is surrounded by a massive wood bank, a relic of its medieval past. The greater part has been replanted with conifers, although some deciduous trees survive in the former Moreton Close and on the margins, including a few small-leaved lime trees.[168] Ettington's medieval grove was in the manor of Lower Ettington; Ettington Grove is shown as the Grove on a map of Lower Ettington c.1795.[169] It too has

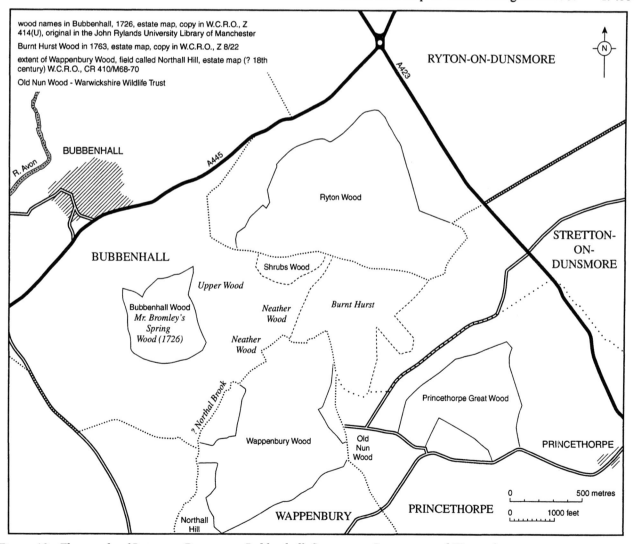

Figure 10: The woods of Ryton-on-Dunsmore, Bubbenhall, Stretton-on-Dunsmore and Wappenbury

been largely replanted with conifers; in outline it is still recognizable as a wood, but even in the deciduous strip on the northern edge there is virtually none of the ground flora associated with ancient woods. The origin of Thornton Wood (in the ancient ecclesiastical parish of Ettington) has been discussed earlier in this chapter; it may be much smaller than the recorded medieval wood.

The wood of Barton was separated by a field from Compton.[170] Barton Grove adjoins the parish boundary with Long Compton and Linch Wood lies a little further west. Whichford Wood, 157 acres in extent in 1817, still has some fine deciduous woodland; it adjoins Long Compton Woods, which have been largely replanted.[171] The present Bericote Wood in Ashow appeared as *Bery Coate grove* on a map of 1597;[172] here conifers reign. Waverley and Weston Woods, which were recorded in the later medieval bounds of Stoneleigh,[173] have also been replanted with conifers; the margins show how fine the woods must have been before replanting. At the time of enclosure Cubbington's woodland, on the site of the present Cubbington Woods, was in the form of various groves. These have not been matched to the surviving later medieval records,[174] but Pryces Grove in Cubbington, on the boundary with Ashow, formed part of the Leigh estates in Stoneleigh and Ashow in 1597,[175] and so may have been Stoneleigh Abbey's Cubbington Grove.

The concentration of *silva* in Ryton-on-Dunsmore, Stretton-on-Dunsmore, Bubbenhall and Wappenbury in 1086 is reflected in the relatively large amounts of woodland in those places in the early modern period (Fig. 10). Documentation is patchy or scant, but there are records of woods in Ryton, Bubbenhall, Stretton, Princethorpe and Wappenbury in the later medieval period.[176] The details of Bubbenhall's enclosure award in 1726[177] suggest that the wood then abutted on to Ryton Wood and that the present Bubbenhall Wood, Mr. Bromley's Spring Wood of 1726,[178] was part of a much larger area of woodland. After a period of neglect Bubbenhall Wood is now to be managed for its wildlife value.[179] Some overgrown coppice has been thinned in the nearby Ryton Wood, which is owned and managed by the Warwickshire Wildlife Trust. Part of Princethorpe's woodland, Old Nun Wood, is also owned by the Trust. Both woods have fine displays of a variety of spring flowers associated with ancient woodland. Princethorpe Great Wood has a magnificent sea of bluebells in the spring, as well as wood anemones, primroses and celandines. Wappenbury Wood, if a petition to Cardinal Morton is to be believed, narrowly escaped destruction threatened at the end of the fifteenth century;[180] its future should be secure following its recent acquisition by the Warwickshire Wildlife Trust.

The woods of Great Wolford and of Long Itchington and Ufton are two of the glories of Warwickshire. Both have been designated Sites of Special Scientific Interest and are largely managed in a tradition which is equally beneficial to nature conservation and historical preservation.[181] The woods of Long Itchington and Ufton are private but skirted in part by a road and a public footpath. They are surrounded by woodbanks and are full of celandines, bluebells, wood anemones, primroses and dog's mercury, with some orchids

and herb paris;[182] the hazel and ash underwood is coppiced and there are many fine, tall, standard oaks.

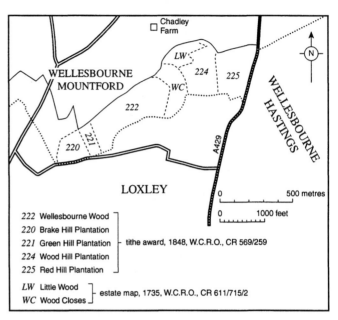

Figure 11: Wellesbourne Wood

During the modern period the woodland of south and east Warwickshire was augmented by some plantations and the development of secondary woodland. For example, the tithe award for Wellesbourne, made in 1848, lists six plantations.[183] Comparison of the tithe map with a map of 1735[184] shows that two of these were already covered with trees in 1735 but that another two had only a few trees by that date. In 1735 a piece of land, which had become part of Wellesbourne Wood by 1848, was called Wood Closes and had a band of trees along one side only. That part of Walton adjoining the Fosse Way had woodland in 1728, but the map gives it names, such as Brake, Compton Peece, and New Copse, which all suggest plantations or secondary woodland.[185] A map of the eastern part of Kineton which was drawn in 1778 shows a clump of six trees in the Great Graves Ground.[186] These trees were presumably the nucleus of Graveground Coppice. The map does not depict any trees on the sites of the woods called Battleton Holt and The Oaks (the former of these woods was removed in 1984).[187] As a result of modern estate management some medieval woods, like that at Wellesbourne, may have become larger than they were in the later medieval period.

The preservation and subsequent development of woodland in south and east Warwickshire suggest that woods in that region were valuable parts of both medieval and modern estates. Their place in manorial demesnes is another indication of the value attached to them. As far as can be ascertained from the surviving records, some of which refer to woods only incidentally, none, except the *moppesgrove* in Bericote, was part of the customary holdings of villeins or freeholders. The Lee Grove in Bishop's Tachbrook was the subject of grants by the earls of Warwick but reverted to their possession.[188] Manorial accounts show that *Wolfordwod* was leased in the fifteenth century[189] and that in the second half of the fourteenth century the abbot of Stoneleigh let Waverley Wood to the Catesby family, who managed it as part of their manor in Bubbenhall.[190] Other records show the groves of Brailes, Lighthorne and Chadley, and Oakley Wood providing the lord of manor with income from sales of wood.[191] It seems, therefore, that not only Chesterton Grove but also most of the later medieval woods of south and east Warwickshire were preserved as a result of the management policies of the lords of the manors concerned.

Conclusions

The history of the later medieval woods and groves of south and east Warwickshire is a lesson in the importance of detailed, critical and informed examination of the documentary evidence. The shortcomings of Domesday Book in relation to topographical features should be known well enough for questions to be asked about the information in it on woodland. Comparison of that information with other evidence has shown suspicions to be well founded. There is documentary evidence (subject to some uncertainties, such as the site of *Perselegrove* in relation to Barford) of woods and groves in at least thirty-five parishes or townships in the region in the period 1100 to 1500 and seven of these seem to have had at least two woods or groves, giving a suggested total of forty-two recorded areas of later medieval woodland.

There are good reasons to believe that most, if not all, of these woods and groves existed when Domesday Book was written. In addition, there was some *silva* recorded in Domesday Book under places for which there is no later evidence of woodland and there were some woods and groves recorded in the first half of the sixteenth century which arguably existed in the later medieval period. The amounts of wood in some places were small, but in other places substantial, and there was enough to contradict the view that this part of Warwickshire was woodless, or virtually so. There was a similar situation in some places north and west of the Avon which will be considered in the following chapters.

Re-examination of the available evidence has been informed by awareness of the different types of medieval woodland. The distinction between wood pasture and coppice wood seems to be the key to the under-recording of woodland in Domesday Book. Whatever changes may have occurred in the management of individual woods subsequently, in 1086 the distinction between *silva* and *grava* was clear. It has important implications for the history of woodland throughout the county. In the light of this distinction the next two chapters will examine the evidence for the woodland of north and west Warwickshire in the later medieval period.

[1] See, for example, R.H. Hilton, *Social Structure of Rural Warwickshire in the Middle Ages*, Dugdale Society Occasional Paper 9 (1950), p. 11.
[2] Rackham, *History of the Countryside*, pp. 81, 83; H.C. Darby and I.B. Terrett, *The Domesday Geography of Midland England* (second edition, 1971), p. 297; B.K. Roberts, *Settlement, Land Use*

and Population in the western portion of the Forest of Arden, Warwickshire, between 1086 and 1350: A Study in Historical Geography (University of Birmingham Ph. D. thesis, 1965), p. 146.
[3] Rackham, *Trees and Woodland in the British Landscape* (second edition), p. 53.
[4] For Domesday Book as a record of settlement, H.C. Darby, *Domesday England* (1977), pp. 15-26; P.H. Sawyer, 'Medieval English Settlement: New Interpretations', ed. P.H. Sawyer, *English Medieval Settlement* (1979), pp. 1-8, see p. 3. For Domesday Book in relation to churches, Darby, *Domesday England*, pp. 52-6; R. Morris, *The church in British archaeology*, C.B.A. Research Report 47 (1983), pp. 68-71; J. Blair, 'Secular Minster Churches in Domesday Book', in ed. P. Sawyer, *Domesday Book: A Reassessment* (1985), pp. 104-142. For Domesday Book in relation to pasture, moor and heath, Darby, *Domesday England*, pp. 149-160.
[5] Rackham, *Ancient Woodland*, p. 112.
[6] P. Sawyer, 'Domesday Studies since 1886', in ed. Sawyer, *Domesday Book: A Reassessment*, pp. 1-4.
[7] Rackham, *Ancient Woodland*, p. 112; Darby, *Domesday England*, pp. 5-6, 171.
[8] Darby, *Domesday England*, pp. 171-87.
[9] For the view that swine totals refer to pasture, *ibid.*, pp. 172-3, that they refer to pannage, Rackham, *Ancient Woodland*, pp. 119-20.
[10] For different sizes of acres see Rackham, *Ancient Woodland*, p. 19.
[11] Darby, *Domesday England*, pp. 187-8.
[12] *ibid.*, pp. 174, 184.
[13] *ibid.*, pp. 186-7.
[14] Rackham, *History of the Countryside*, pp. 79-81.
[15] Roberts, *Settlement, Land Use and Population*, p. 146.
[16] Rackham, *Ancient Woodland*, pp. 112, 115.
[17] *idem.*, *History of the Countryside*, p. 75.
[18] *ibid.*, pp. 75, 79.
[19] Rackham, *Ancient Woodland*, p. 118.
[20] *ibid.*
[21] *ibid.*
[22] Darby, *Domesday England*, pp. 180, 186.
[23] Rackham, *Ancient Woodland*, p. 115.
[24] *ibid.*
[25] *ibid.*, p. 120.
[26] Darby, *Domesday England*, p. 194.
[27] *ibid.*
[28] Rackham, *History of the Countryside*, p. 75; *idem, Ancient Woodland*, p. 114.
[29] Rackham, *Ancient Woodland*, p. 118.
[30] Darby, *Domesday England*, p. 174.
[31] *ibid.*
[32] See, for example, Hooke, 'Pre-Conquest Woodland', p. 121.
[33] For a list of the Warwickshire charters see D. Hooke, *Anglo-Saxon Landscapes of the West Midlands: The Charter Evidence*, British Archaeological Reports (British Series), 95 (1981), pp. 348-352; of the eighteen charters with boundary clauses which are listed, seven refer to places which were outside Warwickshire in 1086. Attention is drawn to the two significant boundary clauses in Rackham, *History of the Countryside*, p. 79.
[34] P.H. Sawyer, *Anglo-Saxon Charters: An annotated list and bibliography* (1968), pp. 86-7; for doubts about the charter's authenticity, B. Yorke, 'The kingdom of the East Saxons', *Anglo-Saxon England*, 14 (1985), pp. 1-36, see pp. 7-8.
[35] B. Cox, 'The Place-Names of the Earliest English Records', *Journal of the English Place-Name Society*, 8 (1975-6), pp. 12-66, see p. 66, cited in D. Hooke, 'Village Development in the West Midlands', in ed. *idem, Medieval Villages: A Review of Current Work* (Oxford University Committee for Archaeology No. 5, 1985), pp. 125-54, see p. 143.

36 D. Hooke, *The Anglo-Saxon Landscape: the kingdom of the Hwicce* (1985), pp. 204, 57, states that "the difficult boundary clause attached to the early grant appears to cover lands in Binton, Luddington and Drayton, which lie to the west of Shottery itself, together with an estate at Ruin Clifford" and also that "whilst the landmarks noted to the south of the river can be readily identified those of the north bank are not so easily identified and the boundaries are not that of a present-day parish".

37 J.E.B. Gover, A. Mawer and F.M. Stenton, *The Place-Names of Warwickshire* (Cambridge, 1936), p. 239, note.

38 As *le Weste Grove* in 1544 (P.R.O., E 318/21/998) and *West grove* in 1534 (P.R.O., E 303/18/502).

39 The charter is printed in W. de G. Birch, *Cartularium Saxonicum*, Vol. I (1885), no. 123.

40 See note 36 above.

41 *VCH*, Vol. III, pp. 259-60; for Stratford-upon-Avon, *DB*, 238c.

42 *DB*, 238c, 242a, 244b, 244b, 243b, 243c, 243d, 244a. There are two places called *Optone* in the Warwickshire folios of Domesday Book; the second is thought to refer to Upton in Haselor.

43 Sawyer, *Anglo-Saxon Charters*, p. 274.

44 Gover, Mawer and Stenton, *Place-Names of Warwickshire*, p. 187.

45 There is a copy of the map in W.C.R.O. at Z181/1(U); the original is in the Bodleian Library (Balliol College 68/252). On the place of *wulluht graf* in the charter bounds, Gover, Mawer and Stenton, *Place-Names of Warwickshire*, p. 134.

46 Rackham, *History of the Countryside*, p. 79.

47 *DB*, 244b, 239a. *VCH*, Vol. VI, p. 125, is in error here, the author having misread the Domesday Book entry translated in *VCH*, Vol. I, p. 341.

48 Rackham, *History of the Countryside*, pp. 79, 81.

49 M. Gelling, *Place-Names in the Landscape* (1984), pp. 193.

50 See Chapters Three and Four and Appendix 1 for groves in Warwickshire.

51 Gelling, *Place-Names in the Landscape*, pp. 189, 192-4.

52 Darby, *Domesday England*, p. 187.

53 *DB*, 243b, 240c.

54 Rackham, *Trees and Woodland in the British Landscape* (second edition), p. 62.

55 A recent and comprehensive summary of research into later medieval population is given in ed. Hallam, *The Agrarian History of England and Wales*, pp 508-93.

56 See Chapter Three.

57 For the Old English *cniht*, see M. Gelling, *Signposts to the Past*, (1978, second, revised edition, 1988) p. 184. The name may be analagous to the *ceorla graf* - the wood of the ceorls (whose social status is uncertain) - recorded in Prestbury in Gloucestershire c.900, see C. Dyer, *Lords and Peasants in a Changing Society: The Estates of the Bishopric of Worcester 680-1540* (1980), p. 34.

58 Now in S.B.T. at DR10/1406.

59 Compare B.L., Harl. Ch. 45 C 47, transcribed in the *Book of Seals*, with S.B.T., DR10/1406, p. 205, P.R.O., E 329/234 with S.B.T., DR10/1406, pp. 211-3 and P.R.O., E 326/11626 with S.B.T., DR10/1406, p. 223 (second charter on that page).

60 S.B.T., DR10/1406, p. 203.

61 ibid., p. 205.

62 ibid., p. 206.

63 ibid., pp. 206-7.

64 ibid., p. 208.

65 ibid., p. 209.

66 ibid., pp. 210-11; P.R.O., E 329/234 and E 326/11626.

67 P.R.O., E 326/11626.

68 For the dates of Waleran's earldom, *Dugdale*, Vol. I, pp. 380-1.

69 B.L., Add. Roll 43,001.

70 W.C.R.O., CR45 contains several uncatalogued deeds relating to Ratley. One dated 3rd June, 1683, refers to "lands, grounds or pastures .. called Ashley alias Asly wood or woods". Another, dated 24th March, 1815, summarises an earlier indenture conveying four parcels of grounds called Astley Woods otherwise Ashley Woods and itself conveys those enclosed grounds called the first Wood Close, the Close by the Barn, the Barn Close and the second Wood Close, stating that they were formerly called Ashly Wood or Woods. The deed gives the acreages of these closes; the names and acreages correspond to four closes on the map of 1808 (CR45/bn3/1). I am indebted to the late Mr. Charles Ivin for these references.

71 S.B.T., DR18/1/596.

72 S.B.T., DR18/25/Bn.38.

73 *VCH*, Vol. V, p. 144.

74 For Radway's grove, S.B.T., DR10/1457; for Westcote's wood, W.C.R.O., microfilm of Castle Ashby MSS., MI 167/1, roll 579.

75 The acreage has been calculated by multiplying the linear measurements in Domesday Book.

76 P.R.O., E 326/6029 and E 315/44/216; *SLB*, p. 102.

77 The surviving rolls are amongst the Spencer MSS. in Northamptonshire Record Office.

78 P.R.O., E 303/17/268.

79 P.R.O., SC 6/1040/7 under *ffirma molendini*. Land called *le lowe* was under the grove (P.R.O., SC 6/Hen VIII/3683; DL 29/642/10,424, DL 29/642/10428-9, but this name has not been traced on the surviving maps of parts of Moreton Morrell (the tithe apportionment covers only part of the parish, W.C.R.O., CR569/171; there is a map of the Warwick lands, copy in W.C.R.O., Z140/2).

80 For the failed replanting in 1956, see P. Murray and S. Carrington, *Flora and Fauna Survey 1979-80* (Warwickshire College of Agriculture); I am indebted to Ms. P. Copson of Warwickshire Museum for sight of this survey.

81 W.J. Ford, *The Pattern of Settlement in the Central Region of the Warwickshire Avon* (M.A. thesis, University of Leicester, 1973), p. 50.

82 D. Hooke, 'Reconstructing Anglo-Saxon landscapes in Warwickshire', *TBWAS*, 100, pp. 99-116, see p. 112.

83 ibid., pp. 42-4, also Roberts, *Settlement, Land Use and Population*, p. 146; Darby and Terrett, *Domesday Geography of Midland England*, p. 297.

84 The enclosure award of 1730, W.C.R.O. QS9/11, mentions Binswood Corner and Binswood Lands End; the sale of Binswood, for £400, is recorded in the accounts of the earls of Warwick for 1664 - W.C.R.O., CR1886/box 411/48.

85 B.K. Roberts, 'Village forms in Warwickshire: a preliminary discussion', ed. T.R. Slater and P.J. Jarvis, *Field and Forest: an historical geography of Warwickshire and Worcestershire* (1982), pp. 125-46, see p. 139.

86 W.C.R.O., CR1124/1.

87 *Calendar of Close Rolls, 1333-37*, p. 693; Gover, Mawer and Stenton, *Place-Names of Warwickshire*, pp. 55-6.

88 *Dugdale*, Vol. II, p. 684; P.R.O., JUST 1/968, rot 14r.

89 B.L., Harl. Ch. 46 A 30.

90 W.C.R.O., CR133/30.

91 W.C.R.O., CR1886/Fifth Shelf/BB.634.

92 W.C.R.O., Z327/2(U).

93 W.C.R.O., L6/1035.

94 *RBW*, pp. 413, 412; for the approximate date of the survey of knights' fees, see Dyer, *Lords and Peasants*, p. 47.

95 Worcs. R.O., 009:1 BA 2636 163 92161 and 92169.

96 W.C.R.O., CR1616/1.

97 W.C.R.O., P30. For this reference and for a discussion about the location of *Perselegrove* in relation to Hampton Wood this paragraph is indebted to Mr. M. Booth of W.C.R.O.

98 P.R.O., C 134/51, C 135/123/5; S.B.T., DR98/1823.

99 A later medieval copy of the entries relating to places in which Coventry Cathedral Priory held lands is in S.B.T., DR18/31/3.

100 ibid. and *HR*, pp. 158, 162; the evidence for woodland in the Hundred Rolls is discussed in Chapter Three.

101 *SLB*, pp. 25, 245; copy of maps in W.C.R.O., Z141(U) and Z414(U). For the meaning of *bruillum*, see Chapter Three under Stoneleigh.

102 B.L., Add. Chs. 53,105 and 48,451.

103 P.R.O., DL 43/14/3.

104 P.R.O., JUST 1/952, rot 4r.

105 For the information on the nineteenth-century covert, see a report prepared in 1982 by the Warwickshire Farming and Wildlife Advisory Group on Thornton Farm; I am indebted to Ms. P. Copson of the Warwickshire Museum for access to a copy of the report.

106 Map of Thornton, W.C.R.O., CR711; information on the flora of Thornton Farm, Ms. P. Copson, Warwickshire Museum.

107 Ufton, P.R.O., E 164/21, f. 212, copy in W.C.R.O., MI 409; Baginton, C.R.O., 39/4; Lillington, S.B.T., DR18/30/15/5; Barford, P.R.O., JUST 1/968, rot 17r.

108 B.L., Egerton MS. 3724, f. 80, copy in W.C.R.O., MI 144.

109 P.R.O., E 352/94, rots 25d-26r.

110 S.B.T., DR98/674a.

111 P.R.O., C 133/100/1 and C 134/49 refer to a *spinetum*, C 134/51 to *i grava* and C 134/90/16 has no woodland at all.

112 B.L., Cotton Caligula A xiii, ff. 145-6.

113 C. Dyer, 'The hidden trade of the Middle Ages: evidence from the West Midlands of England', *Journal of Historical Geography*, 18 (1992), pp. 141-57, see p. 147.

114 N.W. Alcock, *Warwickshire Grazier and London Skinner 1532-1555: The account book of Peter Temple and Thomas Heritage*, British Academy Records of Social and Economic History, New Series, IV (1981), pp. 176-8.

115 See, for example, *Ministers' Accounts of the Warwickshire Estates of the Duke of Clarence, 1479-80* (ed. R.H. Hilton, Dugdale Society, XXI, 1952), footnote to pp. xv-xvi.

116 Rackham, *Ancient Woodland*, pp. 151-2.

117 W.C.R.O., CR2238/1 (reference given by Professor C.C. Dyer); *VCH*, Vol. V, pp. 188, 130.

118 W.C.R.O., CR2238/1.

119 *Calendar of Patent Rolls, 1247-58*, p. 93.

120 Devon Record Office, 248 M/M6; *VCH*, Vol. VI, pp. 4, 38.

121 B.R.L., 167,904.

122 Staffs. R.O., D641/1/2/270.

123 Gloucestershire Record Office, D1099/M31/23.

124 *ibid.*, D1099/M31/40, 44.

125 W.C.R.O., CR133/1.

126 *VCH*, Vol. IV, p. 94.

127 P.R.O., E 303/20/30, 46, 64.

128 The Spencer muniments are now in Northamptonshire Record Office, but the two documents cited here were printed in I.S. Leadam, *Domesday of Inclosures 1517-18*, Volume II (1897), pp. 485-9.

129 H. Thorpe, 'The Lord and the Landscape', *TBAS*, 80 (1962), pp. 38-77, see p. 62.

130 Leadam, *Domesday of Inclosures*, p. 488.

131 P.R.O., SC 6/1041/2.

132 Northamptonshire Record Office, Spencer MSS., roll 216. I am indebted to Professor C.C. Dyer for this reference.

133 *The Itinerary of John Leland in the years 1535-1543* (ed. L. Toulmin Smith, Vol. I, 1907), pp. xxi; Hilton, *Social Structure of Rural Warwickshire in the Middle Ages*, p. 11, footnote.

134 *Itinerary of John Leland*, Vol. I, pp. xxiii-xxiv.

135 *ibid.* and Vol. V (1910), p. vii.

136 *Itinerary of John Leland*, Vol. V, pp. 155-6.

137 *Itinerary of John Leland*, Vol. II (1908), p. 47.

138 Rackham, *History of the Countryside*, p. 189; Williamson, 'Explaining Regional Landscapes', p. 5.

139 *Itinerary of John Leland*, Vol. II, p. 109.

140 *ibid*, p. 40.

141 *ibid*.

142 *ibid.*, pp. 46-47.

143 S.B.T., DR98/1823.

144 S.B.T., DR98/573.

145 S.B.T., DR98/938, 1708.

146 S.B.T., DR98/300, 371.

147 Map in S.B.T., DR98/1823.

148 S.B.T., DR98/540, 551.

149 R.H. Hilton, 'A Study in the Pre-history of English Enclosure in the Fifteenth Century', reprinted in *idem, The English Peasantry in the Later Middle Ages* (1975), pp. 161-73, see pp. 171-2.

150 S.B.T., DR98/1823.

151 S.B.T., DR98/577.

152 P.R.O., C 133/93/24.

153 P.R.O., C 135/123/5.

154 *Calendar of Inquisitions Post Mortem*, Vol. III, no. 137.

155 *VCH*, Vol. V, p. 42.

156 B.R.L., 295,194.

157 S.B.T., DR98/519.

158 S.B.T., DR98/551; B.R.L., 272,820.

159 A. Tasker, *The Nature of Warwickshire* (1990), p. 31; Dr. Tasker (personal communication) cites D. Morfitt as the source of his information on Chesterton Wood.

160 W.C.R.O., CR1908/104/1.

161 B.L., Add. MS. 28,024, f. 63, copy in W.C.R.O., MI 177.

162 *Itinerary of John Leland*, Vol. II, p. 109.

163 S.B.T., DR98/1708.

164 A close called The Grove is shown in the lordship of Stoneton, which was part of the parish of Wormleighton but within the county of Northampton, on a map of 1634 (of which there is a copy in W.C.R.O., Z176/1/1). Stoneton was a separate manor, with a separate set of court rolls, in the fourteenth century, so it is unlikely that trespasses in the lord's grove of Stoneton would have been reported to the Wormleighton court. Four closes with the name Coppice appear on a mid-eighteenth-century estate map of Lighthorne, but there is no grove name on that map, nor in the tithe award; estate map, W.C.R.O., Z228/4(U) and S.B.T., DR98/1821, tithe map, W.C.R.O., CR569/157/2.

165 W.C.R.O., CR26/A/XVI for a detailed deed of 1415; *VCH*, Vol. VIII, p. 471 for the later history of *Lee*.

166 See the account of Ratley's medieval woodland above.

167 B.R.L., 167,910 and 168,204.

168 For the information on the remaining small-leaved lime, Mr. P.A. Pain, personal communication.

169 W.C.R.O., CR229/117/9 and 11.

170 *Curia Regis Rolls*, Vol. XV (1972), no. 910.

171 For map of Whichford Wood in 1817, W.C.R.O., CR1635/410.

172 Copy in W.C.R.O., Z141(U).

173 *SLB*, p. 248.

174 For the enclosure award, W.C.R.O., CR1218/19/1, including Shortley Wood, the Horse Grove, the Foot Grove, and an unnamed wood; a deed of 1750 (B.R.L., 193,175) refers to coppices called Parkers Piece and Town grove otherwise Watery Grove and a deed of 1651 (B.R.L. 86,005) refers to *Billinsgrove* without stating whether or not it was woodland. Medieval records refer both to *Billinsgrove* and simply to the grove (P.R.O., E 210/4582, S.B.T., DR18/31/3 and DR18/1/698).

175 Map of 1597, copy in W.C.R.O., Z141(U).

176 For Ryton, a wood in the twelfth century, Cambridge University Library, Add 3021, f. 238, an outwood in the 1279 Hundred Rolls, *HR*, p. 151, and a reference to *boscum de Ruytone* in 1335, W.C.R.O., CR350/3; for Bubbenhall, an outwood in 1391, P.R.O., E 149/60/16; for Stretton, woodland in 1285, P.R.O., JUST 1/958, rot 1r; for woodland in Princethorpe in 1246-7, P.R.O., JUST 1/952, rot 5r; for Wappenbury, a reference in 1208 in *FF*, Vol. I, no. 190, original in P.R.O., CP 25/1/242/8.

177 W.C.R.O., Z413(Sm.); the originals are in the John Rylands University Library of Manchester.

[178] W.C.R.O., Z414(U); the original is in the John Rylands University Library of Manchester.

[179] L. Barnett and C. Emms, 'Des. Res. to let', *Warwickshire Wildlife*, 97 (Winter 1997), p. 7

[180] B.R.L., Keen 133 (KK114/782/27) is a complaint by Nicholas Catesby that Nicholas Broune, Gerard Danet, Richard Cotes and Robert Belknap had "felled, wasted and distroued" part of the wood, allowed animals to graze in it and were threatening after Epiphany to "felle alle the residue of the seid Wode in so mych that they wolle not leve standyng any thyng that is habull to make a withe to tye a beeste withall And wolle not do the cost to copyse hit to the utter distruicon" thereof. Cardinal Morton, addressed as chancellor of England by the petitioner, held that office from 1493 to 1500.

[181] Some recent planting in Long Itchington Wood does, however, give cause for concern and has been drawn to the attention of the appropriate bodies, Mr. R. Langdon, personal communication.

[182] For the information on orchids and herb paris, Mr. R. Langdon, personal communication.

[183] W.C.R.O., CR569/259.

[184] W.C.R.O., CR611/715/2.

[185] W.C.R.O., CR750/1.

[186] S.B.T., DR98/1825.

[187] For information on the removal of Battleton Holt, Mr. D.E. Solliss, personal communication.

[188] P.R.O., E 326/1917; B.L., Add. MS. 28,024, f. 69, copy in W.C.R.O., MI 177.

[189] Staffs. R.O., D641/1/2/274.

[190] P.R.O., SC 6/1041/12, for 1386-7.

[191] P.R.O., C 134/49; S.B.T., DR98/672a, 672b, 672d, 674; B.L., Add. Roll 44,559; William Salt Library, Salt Roll 335 (1).

Chapter Three

THE WOODLAND OF NORTH AND WEST WARWICKSHIRE

1086-1500: A PARISH SURVEY

Introduction

In recent decades it has been accepted that in 1086, contrary to previous assumptions, woodland did not cover most of Warwickshire north and west of the Avon valley, although many places had plenty of what the Domesday surveyors called *silva*, which must have been an important feature in the local economy and countryside. This acknowledgement replaces popular misconceptions about a region dominated by dense, wild woodland[1] and allows greater flexibility of thought in analysing the evidence for the later medieval period. Just as critical, detailed study has modified traditional views about woodland - or the lack of it - in south and east Warwickshire, a similar study for the rest of the county has proved equally rewarding.

This chapter will summarise the evidence on a geographical basis preparatory to an analysis in the following chapter. An exclusively thematic approach has been rejected. It carries the temptation to illustrate the themes by random examples which may not be representative. Moreover, a detailed description shows both the frequency and distribution of different woodland features and the geographical relationships between them. It ensures that views are modified not by counter-assertions based on generalisations from localised research but by a thorough survey of all available evidence.

The importance of searching for all available evidence cannot be over-emphasised. In a number of places the picture of the later medieval countryside has been changed significantly by a single document, such as the survey of Packwood in Coventry Cathedral Priory's register or the sixteenth-century survey of Berkswell's tenants' holdings. The evidence is limited and unevenly distributed. It is true that there are many records of woodland and woods in the county north and west of the Avon, but the frequency of the references is a reflection of the large number of woods involved and not of the amount of information available for individual woods.

The records share all the deficiencies of the evidence for south and east Warwickshire. Some later medieval woods are known only through a single, incidental reference in a deed which gives no indication of size, management or location. Even the site of a wood to which frequent reference is made may be a matter of conjecture. Where references are more detailed they are not available throughout the period 1086-1500. Twelfth-century records in general, and consequently references to woods in the twelfth century, are rare and usually lack detail. In these circumstances it has not been possible to write a full and precise account of woodland during the period. This is particularly regrettable given the extent of topographical

change which can be inferred for many places by comparing recorded medieval woods with the estimated extent of the Domesday *silva*.

This survey of medieval woodland will start in the Avon valley around Stratford-upon-Avon and move north and then west, before turning south via the valleys of the rivers Tame, Blythe, Alne and Arrow. Parishes for which there is very little or no medieval evidence of woodland have been omitted and confined to the gazetteer at Appendix 1. Ancient ecclesiastical parishes and their constituent townships have been chosen as the units of survey. They were recognised territories in the later medieval period and continued as such well into the nineteenth century, when they formed the basis of the tithe awards whose maps are so useful to topographical historians. Their boundaries are fixed and known, whereas the boundaries of manors are frequently uncertain and the lands of several manors could be intermingled within a single parish or township. The estimated areas of *silva* have been calculated both as a maximum derived from multiplying the dimensions given in Domesday Book (assuming the league to equate to one and a half statute miles) and as about seven tenths of that maximum to allow for irregularities of shape (conveniently, seven tenths of a square league is almost exactly a thousand acres).[2]

Stratford-upon-Avon

The woodland in and around Stratford resembled that of the parishes south and east of the Avon. Few woods were recorded in the later medieval period and there was often no *silva* in the Domesday Book entries. This may explain why William Shakespeare described the flowers of hedgerows, meadows and pastures rather than of woods.

The bishops of Worcester held the manor of Stratford-upon-Avon, although parts of the ancient ecclesiastical parish were enfeoffed to other lords.[3] None of the bishops' records refers to a wood in Stratford or Shottery; Bushwood, meaning bishop's wood, was by Lapworth, where it formed a detached part of the parish of Stratford.[4] Stratford and one of its townships, Clopton, were recorded in Domesday Book but without any *silva*.[5]

The later medieval records of a wood and a grove in Bishopton include a claim in 1231-2 by the Archdeacon of Gloucester of estovers in the wood.[6] A grove produced thorns for sale in 1413-4[7]; whether the wood and grove were one and the same is unknown. There are some modern maps of farms in Bishopton, but they do not include any field-name pointing to the site of the medieval woodland.[8]

Cloptongrove appeared in deeds dated to c.1279-80 as an area which included messuages, land, meadows and pastures,[9] but the reference in 1604 to a grove called Clopton Grove[10] suggests that the thirteenth-century property was indeed named after a wood which was extant and which it adjoined or from which it had been taken by assarting. Fifteenth-century manorial accounts show that *Cloptongrove* adjoined Snitterfield, thus establishing the grove's approximate location.[11] The grove may have become the modern Park Wood.[12]

Binton

Part of the parish was held by Bordesley Abbey, many of whose deeds have survived, but none of these refers to any woodland.[13] The grove or coppice of wood recorded in 1546[14] suggests that there might have been medieval woodland, but none of the four manors recorded in Domesday Book included any *silva*.[15] There are references c.1625 to closes or *grovets* called Townsend grove or Yelvesgrove and Well grove.[16] In 1554-5 twenty acres of wood were included in the manor and in 1588 ten acres.[17] Deeds of Binton Grove in the eighteenth century do not refer to any woodland.[18]

Grafton

There are places called Grafton in ten English counties including Warwickshire. The first syllable in this compound is now thought to be the Old English *graf*, meaning grove.[19] *Silva* was absent from Grafton's manors in 1086,[20] but Grafton had a grove called *Kingesgraue* in 1247, presumably on the site of later fields called Grove. *Kingesgraue* was called a grove, showing that it was woodland rather than just a place-name. The reference was in a transaction involving half an acre of land adjoining the grove.[21] One of Grafton's open fields was called Grove Field on a map of 1740[22] and in the enclosure award of 1814.[23] The latter also reveals the site of the grove itself. Divided into "old enclosures" called The Grove (in Temple Grafton) and Sideless Grove and Meadow Grove (in Arden's Grafton), it was on the western edge of the parish, immediately north of the village of Arden's Grafton and adjoining Grove Hill in Exhall to the west. It seems, therefore, that the hill took its name from the grove in Grafton rather than from a grove in Exhall itself. Exhall (like the neighbouring Billesley) is not well documented in the later medieval period.

Why, of all the groves in Warwickshire, Grafton's grove was the only one to give its name to an ecclesiastical parish is discussed in Chapter Four.

Haselor

As noted in Chapter Two, there was no *silva* recorded for Haselor, but there was *silva* ten furlongs and eighteen perches long by five furlongs wide in Upton,[24] a township within Haselor parish. There were at least sixty acres of wood in Upton in 1314.[25] A dispute over tithes and common rights c.1230 referred incidentally to the wood in Upton, in which Stephen de Upton had common rights

belonging to his land of Upton.[26] In 1364 a deed referred to a wood in Upton Wood called *Rolveswode*. This name is preserved in the modern Rollswood and shows that Upton Wood lay, like others in Haselor, in the south of the parish. Upton Wood was still wood in 1619.[27]

As explained in the previous chapter, the wood called Westgrove in 1534[28] has been identified with the *westgraf* recorded in the boundary of an early medieval charter. It is thought to derive its name from its position in relation to Stratford-upon-Avon and Shottery.[29] This may indicate that Haselor once belonged to a land unit which included those places. Westgrove could, however, be named from its position west of Withycombe and Red Hill Woods, within Haselor itself.

There are also records of woods called *Widecombe*, *Middelgroue* and *Rowheya* in the twelfth century,[30] and a wood called *Maisterswoode* in 1465-6.[31] Withycombe is a wood today. *Maisterswoode* was held by the Knights Hospitallers as part of their manor of Grafton,[32] but was in the parish of Haselor.[33] Masters Wood became known as Red Hill Wood, a name still attached to woodland in Haselor.[34] There is no record earlier than 1534 of wood in Le Hermytage;[35] land of that name was granted to Alcester Abbey in 1158.[36] Woods called Shroud Hill Coppice, Walsingham's Coppice and Alcocks Arbour were recorded in 1619, but may have had different names in 1537, when the Walsinghams acquired part of Rowe Mershe and Clynchames Coppice.[37]

Hampton Lucy

This study began with Hampton Wood and an attempt to make sense of its history. There are tantalising references to the wood of the bishops of Worcester from c.1170,[38] but never in enough detail to explain the relationship between that wood, the square league of *silva* recorded in Domesday Book, recorded assarts, and the significance of the minor place-name Grove.[39]

The bishop's wood was mentioned incidentally in a survey of c.1170.[40] The oxherds (*bovarii*) were to bring timber for their ploughs from the wood with the bishop's wagon and oxen. A tenant held a croft under the wood (*sub bosco*). The bishop had a reeve and woodward (*forestarius*). In surveys of c.1290 and 1299 there was a park.[41] From the reference to an enclosed wood called the park in 1353,[42] it seems that the wood had been imparked. From a late fifteenth-century survey of the manor of Fulbrook to the north[43] it can be deduced that the park adjoined Fulbrook in the area of the present Hampton Wood. The park disappeared between 1549[44] and 1557.[45] At some point before 1736,[46] and possibly in the medieval period, former arable land with ridge and furrow characteristic of ploughing in the medieval period was added to the Wood. In 1736 and as late as 1846 the Wood was just over seventy acres in extent;[47] the present area is about twenty-seven acres. Despite imparkment, the name *Hampton Wode* appeared in a manorial court roll in 1453.[48]

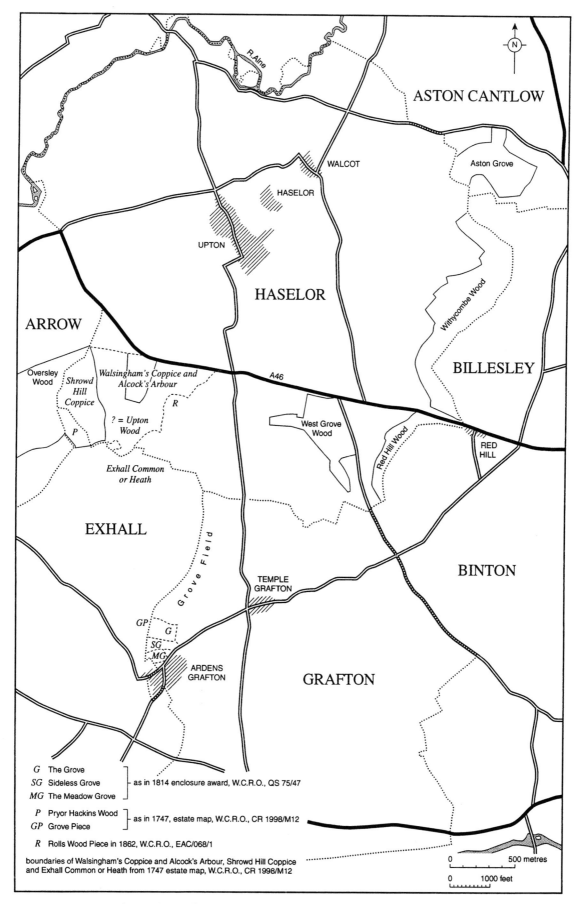

Figure 12: Grafton and Haselor

The minor place-name *Grava* (modern Grove) was recorded in a list of the bishop's knights' fees which was compiled between 1096 and 1112.[49] It appeared as *la grave* in the survey of c.1170 and persisted throughout the later medieval and modern periods, surviving in Grove Farm, which is immediately south of the present Hampton Wood. It is reasonable to assume that a place-name which was well established by c.1100 originated in the early medieval period, when it must have taken its name from a nearby grove. The evidence of place-names[50] and later medieval records points to groves as relatively small, well-defined areas of woodland, not at all like Hampton's large area of *silva* which in 1086 measured a league by a league[51] and therefore probably covered in the order of a thousand acres and possibly up to about 1,400 acres. If the grove and the *silva* coexisted they could have been in close proximity. Alternatively, a seventh- or eighth-century grove could have been enlarged by secondary woodland in times of war or reduced population to become the eleventh-century *silva*. This in turn was presumably reduced by assarting; there was an assart *a la grave* in the survey of c.1170.

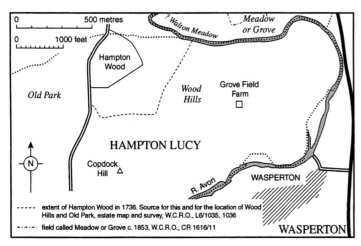

Figure 13: Hampton Wood

The evidence from two other places in Warwickshire for the omission of groves from Domesday Book and the consequent possibility that Hampton's *silva* and grove were separate prompted the author's wider interest in the woodland of medieval Warwickshire.

Warwick and Wedgnock

Early modern maps show that Wedgnock Park contained land from several parishes in and around Warwick.[52] This in itself should be enough to suggest that the development of the park was late and complex. In addition, there are medieval records to show that the original park was very small and that it was enlarged in the fourteenth century to include woods of various places to the north and west of Warwick, those places including at least one deserted medieval settlement.

Sir William Dugdale, following John Rous, stated that the park of Wedgnock was created by Henry, first earl of Warwick, who died in 1123, and that it contained what was called in the fifteenth century Old Park.[53] Under the heading of Wedgnock Park Sir William wrote also that "the tythes of the assarts here, as also of the paunage and venison" were given to the Hospital of St. Michael in the reign of Henry III. It has been assumed elsewhere that this gift was of Wedgnock Park,[54] but references to Wedgnock during the

first half of the thirteenth century show that the place was more than a park. A grant attributed to the period 1213-29 referred to land in Wedgnock, in wood and plain (*in bosco et plano*).[55] A transaction of 1221-2 related to a pasture called Wedgnock, and in 1247 Wedgnock was described as a manor.[56] The park is first mentioned in an inquisition post mortem of 1268,[57] when the earl of Warwick had eighty acres of land at Wedgnock, as well as the park. In 1298 the park was valued at ten shillings and was said to contain twenty acres.[58] Accounts for 1321 included a certain wood (*bosco*) called the park of Wedgnock.[59] In 1321, therefore, the park was still a modest affair. By 1366 there were either two sections to the park, or two separate parks; a commission was ordered to investigate complaints that people had broken into the earl's parks at Sutton Coldfield, Berkswell, *Wegenokwarrewyk*, *Wegenokhastang* and elsewhere.[60] By the end of the fourteenth century the park had almost attained its early modern extent, as is evident from the places named in repairs to the park pale in 1394-5 and 1400-1 and from the record of a later addition in the Budbrooke accounts for 1425.[61] The expansion appears to have begun in the period 1339-42. The Beauchamp cartulary has preserved copies of several charters by which the then earl of Warwick acquired land in Beausale and part of a wood in Hatton called variously *Weggenok Donele*, *Wegenoc Beyvile* and *Weggenok Deyuyle*.[62] The first of these names has been used as evidence that Hatton was the *Donnelie* of Domesday Book,[63] but, as has been recognised subsequently,[64] it was a mistranscription of d'Eyville, the name of a local family which owned land in Hatton.[65] The wood recorded in the Beauchamp Cartulary may therefore have been the forty acres of wood in Hatton a third of which the widow of Roger d'Eyville claimed as part of her dowry in 1247.[66] The references in 1398-9, 1400-1 and 1425-6 to the *Deyvilwode* on the western edge of the park[67] imply that it was in that part of Hatton which lay within Wedgnock Park.

The use of a proper name in *Deyvilwode* is the clue to the origins of at least one other wood in the park. Attempts to locate the park's woods are helped by a list in the cartulary of St. Mary's Church in Warwick of the lands, by parish, within the park,[68] as well as by the park-keeper's accounts. (The list must postdate 1425 as it includes *janyes lesewe* which was not transferred from Budbrooke until that year.[69]) St. Mary's parish itself included *le newewode*, *megurwode*, *Dame Royse grove*, *logge quarter*, *Wodecote poole*, *Botelfeld* and *le meg' launde*. None of these names has survived, but *Megurwode* adjoined *Boseworth Coppice* in Budbrooke,[70] giving an indication of their respective sites. In 1252 Robert le Megre held the wood of *Stokehull*,[71] a settlement located near Warwick which was depopulated by the end of the fifteenth century.[72] The field of *Stokhull* was recorded among the demesne lands of the earls of Warwick in the fifteenth century, so it can be inferred that the wood of *Stokehull* was also acquired by the earls and became the Park's *Megurwode* or *Megrewode*.[73] Stokehill might have been located in that part of the Park which adjoined Saltisford Common in Warwick and where sinuously curved fields lie on either side of Wedgnock Lane.

30

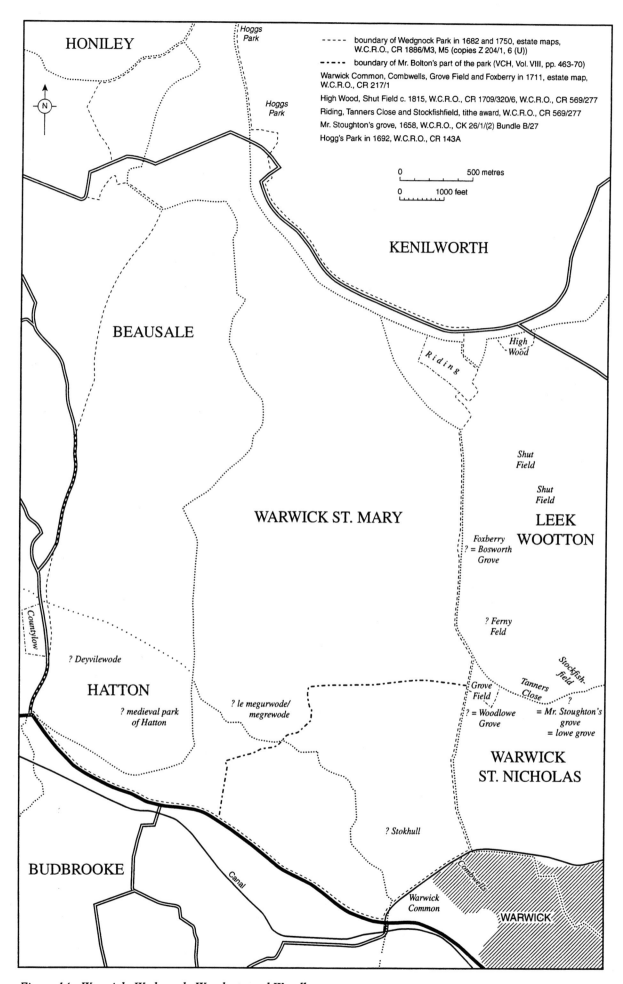

HONILEY

Hoggs Park

Hoggs Park

N

- - - - boundary of Wedgnock Park in 1682 and 1750, estate maps, W.C.R.O., CR 1886/M3, M5 (copies Z 204/1, 6 (U))
- ▪ - ▪ - boundary of Mr. Bolton's part of the park (VCH, Vol. VIII, pp. 463-70)

Warwick Common, Combwells, Grove Field and Foxberry in 1711, estate map, W.C.R.O., CR 217/1

High Wood, Shut Field c. 1815, W.C.R.O., CR 1709/320/6, W.C.R.O., CR 569/277

Riding, Tanners Close and Stockfishfield, tithe award, W.C.R.O., CR 569/277

Mr. Stoughton's grove, 1658, W.C.R.O., CK 26/1/(2) Bundle B/27

Hogg's Park in 1692, W.C.R.O., CR 143A

0 _____ 500 metres

0 _____ 1000 feet

KENILWORTH

BEAUSALE

Riding

High Wood

Shut Field

Shut Field

WARWICK ST. MARY

LEEK WOOTTON

Foxberry
? = Bosworth Grove

? Ferny Feld

Countylow

Stockfish-field

? Deyvilewode

HATTON

? le megurwode/ megrewode

Grove Field

Tanners Close

?

? medieval park of Hatton

? = Woodlowe Grove

= Mr. Stoughton's grove = lowe grove

WARWICK ST. NICHOLAS

? Stokhull

BUDBROOKE

Canal

Combwell

Warwick Common

WARWICK

Figure 14: Warwick, Wedgnock, Woodcote and Woodlow

This south-eastern part of the park was disimparked by 1576. If the area lost then was the same as the area shown as Mr. Bolton's part of the park in 1652, then the *Megurwode* must have been further north and west (though still within St. Mary's parish), because *Magarewoode* was named as being within the park in 1576.[74]

Also to the north of Warwick were Priors Grove, a name which implies a medieval history, and Guy Cliffe Grove, recorded in 1422-3 and 1483.[75] In 1545-6 the first of these, part of the lands of the Priory of St. Sepulchre, was separated from a place called Combwells by Palfrey Meadow; both these places are shown on a map of 1711, but were not at that time adjacent.[76] The site of the latter grove is suggested by the enclosure award for St. Nicholas's parish, which includes Pattens Grove Close near Guyscliff House, and by Sir William Dugdale's reference to "the pleasant Grove" behind Guy's Cliff.[77]

Woodcote and Leek Wootton

Woodcote lay mostly in Leek Wootton and partly in Kenilworth. (Woodcote, Woodlow and Wootton all share the same place-name element, the Old English word for wood, a similarity which is discussed in Chapter Five.) As will be explained in the account of Kenilworth's woodland, part at least of Woodcote's Domesday *silva* seems to have been added to the park of Kenilworth. A sketch map of part of Woodcote drawn c.1815[78] shows High Wood adjoining Kenilworth. A High Wood was named in 1633, but at that time was part of Colewood, further to the south.[79]

The Wedgnock Park example of a medieval wood linked to a former settlement is replicated in Woodlow, Woodcote and Bosworth.[80] The list of lands in Wedgnock Park gave *Wodelowegrove* as the sole item under St. Nicholas parish. The references to *Wodelowegrove* in late fourteenth- and fifteenth-century documents[81] imply that it was next to, rather than within, Wedgnock Park and near to lands in Woodcote. Grove Field, which was formerly called simply Grove, seems the obvious site, adjoining Wedgnock Park and within the parish of St. Nicholas.[82] The relationship between the grove and the twelve acres of woodland in Woodlow which were recorded in the Assize Rolls for 1261-2[83] is unknown. There is also a sixteenth-century record of a wood called the lowe grove, which was part of the lands formerly of St. John's Hospital in Warwick granted to Anthony Stoughton.[84] Mr. Stoughton's grove was mentioned in a deed of 1658[85] from which its site in St. Nicholas's parish, Warwick, can be deduced.

The grove between the two Woodcotes (*inter duas Wudechotes*)[86] was given by William, earl of Warwick, to Godwin the merchant c.1153-84. Its relationship to the groves recorded in a rental of 1458, *Boseworthgrove* and *Pavysgrove*,[87] is unknown. The latter may be equated to the little grove (*paruum Grouetum*) formerly of William Pavy of Warwick recorded in 1412.[88] It was in *fernyfeld*. *Boseworthgrove*, which points to the site of Bosworth (mistakenly identified with Bosworth's Wood in Castle Bromwich[89]) was by *fernyfeld*, but the disappearance of this

and other medieval field-names makes its precise site elusive. Fields called Ridding in the 1458 rental suggest the site of former woodland. Their location can be matched to the fields of that name in the north-west corner of Leek Wootton parish, near to Kenilworth.[90]

Leek Wootton is thought to be the *Optone* which appears in Domesday Book under the land of the king and as a member of the king's manor of Stoneleigh.[91] Apart from the references in the Kenilworth cartulary which indicate that some of Leek Wootton's woodland may have been taken into Kenilworth park in the twelfth century,[92] there is virtually no information on woods belonging to Leek Wootton rather than to Woodcote. In 1537 Kenilworth Priory leased two woods described as groves which adjoined its manor of Cross Grange in Leek Wootton but they were outside the parish.[93] Thickthorn was in Ashow parish and is dealt with in the account of that parish's woodland; Great grove may have become the Bullymore Grove which adjoined Thickthorn on a map of 1597.[94]

Kenilworth

Kenilworth provides good examples of the development of wood pasture into enclosed coppices, of the effect on medieval topography of imparking, both in the later medieval period and subsequently, and of the disappearance of woodland in the early modern period.

In 1086 Kenilworth, held by Richard the Forester, was a member of the king's manor of Stoneleigh.[95] It was credited with *silva* measuring half a league by four furlongs. In addition, the *silva* attached to *Rincele*[96] was arguably related to the later *Rynselcopies*[97] within Kenilworth park. *Rynselcopies* belonged to the manor in the later fourteenth and fifteenth centuries and was adjacent to Wedgnock Park in 1400;[98] it became the *Hoggs Park* and *Runsill Cops* of 1591 and can be traced on a map of Kenilworth in 1692,[99] when it was within Kenilworth parish. Even if it is assumed that the Domesday *silva* was pretty nearly square in shape the maximum area covered would have been about 240 acres for Kenilworth and 120 for *Rincele* and could have been much less.

The wood for which there is the best evidence of location, site and management is the Frith. In 1322 Edward II received a petition claiming that the tenants of Stoneleigh and the free tenants of Kenilworth and Ashow had enjoyed from time immemorial common of pasture for all kinds of animals and agistment for their pigs in the wood called *le ffryth* of Kenilworth and that these rights had been curtailed by Thomas, late earl of Lancaster, who had caused to be enclosed eight hundred acres of that wood and more in divers places and at divers times.[100] The entry in the Hundred Rolls of 1279 is unhelpful. It stated that earl Edmund had two woods, *le ffryth* and *le Parke*, which contained *ccc*[xx] *acras bosci* (*ccc* in a later copy of the document).[101] A figure in the order of three hundred acres is much less than the area attributed to the Frith in 1322, but the strict reading of six thousand is greater than the area of the ecclesiastical parish, which contained about 5,550 acres in the nineteenth century.[102]

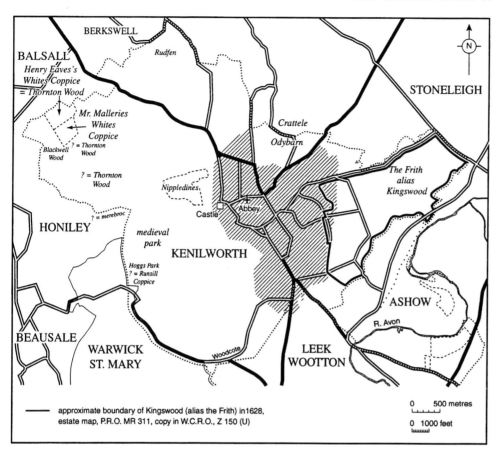

Figure 15: Kenilworth

Map legend:
— approximate boundary of Kingswood (alias the Frith) in 1628, estate map, P.R.O. MR 311, copy in W.C.R.O., Z 150 (U)

0   500 metres

0   1000 feet

One place in the wood of Kenilworth was granted to Stoneleigh Abbey in 1285.[103] In 1324-5 Thomas, late earl of Lancaster, was said to have granted a parcel of the Frith to Kenilworth Priory to hold enclosed.[104] This parcel was called *le Coupiz* and is an early example of the use of the word coppice in Warwickshire.[105] Woods called *Stoneleighness, Knowl hill, Whitemoor* and *Blondel close* were recorded as part of the royal manor in 1383[106] and all four appeared amongst the coppices of the Frith in a survey of 1581.[107] The name Frith comes from an Old English word associated with woodland but of uncertain meaning[108] and suggests early medieval antecedents for the wood. In the later sixteenth century and subsequently Kenilworth's Frith was called Kingswood.[109] Under this name it was shown on a map of 1628,[110] when it consisted of 722 acres enclosed and 170 in common. The Frith can therefore be located with confidence.

As the Frith still contained at least eight hundred acres c.1300, after two centuries during which woodland generally had been subject to clearance rather to expansion, it must have been omitted from Kenilworth's Domesday *silva*, for this is unlikely to have exceeded 240 acres. Either the Frith contained a type of woodland which was not *silva* in 1086, or the land in Kenilworth which Richard the Forester held in 1086 was only part of the area which became the ecclesiastical parish. The size of the Domesday holding

(only three virgates of land and not a large amount of *silva*), its status as a member of the manor of Stoneleigh and the later medieval records of traditional intercommoning with Stoneleigh all point to the second alternative. Further evidence comes from the foundation charter of Kenilworth Priory (later an abbey) and a description of the bounds of the Abbey manor recorded in 1581.[111]

c.1124 Geoffrey de Clinton gave the canons all the land of Kenilworth and wood (*boscum*) and other appurtenances except a part which he retained for the castle and for making his park.[112] The bounds of the Abbey manor in 1581 excluded the Frith, the borough and the western area of Kenilworth with its castle and park. The exclusion of the western area is explained by the exceptions in the foundation charter, but the Frith was nowhere near the castle and park. The logical conclusion is that the Frith did not belong to Geoffrey de Clinton's manor, although it was administered through the castle manor in the fourteenth and fifteenth centuries and in 1322 was called the Frith of Kenilworth. The site and shape of the Frith, which protruded into Stoneleigh parish, suggest that it had once been part of that parish. It therefore seems reasonable to suggest that the Frith was probably part of Stoneleigh's *silva* in 1086 but was linked to Kenilworth when the rest of Stoneleigh was granted to Stoneleigh Abbey in 1204.[113] Kenilworth's other woods are therefore candidates for its Domesday *silva*.

The Priory's foundation charter showed that Geoffrey de Clinton had a number of woods in addition to that which he granted to the Priory. He granted the canons pasture for their animals and pigs wherever the earl's animals and pigs were, both inside and outside the park. The canons' men, however, were restricted to pannage in the earl's other woods (*in aliis boscis meis*) except the hay and the park (*preter haiam et parcum*).[114] Henry I ordered William de Clinton to allow his men of Stoneleigh to have their pasture in the hay which the king had given to Geoffrey de Clinton; the charter referred to the hay as a wood (*boscum*).[115] The hay - called simply *haia* without qualification - was the source of royal gifts of timber in 1238.[116] In 1242 the king granted ten oaks in the wood of Kenilworth outside the hay (*extra haiam*).[117] The hay appears to have been an enclosed wood within an unnamed, larger wood. It was not listed amongst the woods in the sixteenth-century surveys, nor did it appear in the fourteenth- and fifteenth-century accounts for the castle manor. There is no trace of the name on maps of Kenilworth.

The park contained some woodland, forty acres in 1279.[118] The foundation charter for the Priory excepted an unspecified part of Kenilworth for Geoffrey de Clinton's castle and park.[119] Henry II's confirmation stated that land, not wood, was retained for the borough, fishpond and park; wood was retained *ad inforestandum* (presumably meaning for a private chase). The same charter[120] implied that some woodland (*nemus*) from Leek Wootton went into the park, but a papal confirmation in 1126 specified only land from Leek Wootton for the park.[121] The south-western and southern boundary of Kenilworth makes a regular, sweeping curve strongly reminiscent of the course of a medieval park pale. In 1628 this part of Kenilworth included an area of 658 acres called the 'old park'.[122] It appears that the medieval park extended further north, to adjoin Honiley and Rudfen (see below).[123] Little Woodcote was also in the parish,[124] the rest of Woodcote being in Leek Wootton. It has been suggested that the *silva* of one of the two manors of Woodcote which measured one league by half a league was used for the park, being compatible in terms of size.[125] Woodcote, however, is not mentioned in any of the Kenilworth charters, in contrast with the information about Leek Wootton's land and the park.

A foreign wood (*forincecum boscum*) is mentioned in 1237 and appears frequently in accounts for the royal manor which survive from 1388 into the sixteenth century.[126] Wood and timber from it were used for repairs to the castle. It has been assumed by some[127] that the outwood was the Frith. Indeed, the Stoneleigh Leger Book referred to foreign woods in Odybarn and the Frith.[128] Odybarn was certainly not the foreign wood of the Kenilworth castle accounts, as it belonged to the Priory. The accounts refer separately to the foreign wood and the Frith, suggesting that they were distinct. However, one reference to the interests of the tenants of Ashow in the foreign wood certainly points to the Frith, which adjoined Ashow and in which there was inter-commoning; otherwise, the entries referring to the Frith by name deal solely with a commuted render of hens from Stoneleigh and Ashow for herbage.[129] One set of accounts (for 1529-30)[130] refers in consecutive entries to the foreign wood (*in bosco Forinseco*) and the foreign wood of the king (*a Bosco Regis Forinseco*). Given that the name Kingswood replaced that of Frith, this entry could be read as equating the foreign wood with the Frith. More conclusively, a petition to the king c.1322 referred to the Frith as a *forein bois*.[131]

However, another outwood was associated with Kenilworth. Peaches outwood was within the sixteenth-century chase[132] and so in the area north of the castle. Barnet, where rights of common had been secured by the lord of Honiley (who bore the surname Peche) centuries earlier,[133] was in Thornton Wood, also within the chase.[134] Together with these rights of common similar rights had been granted in *merebroc*, arguably the brook which forms the north-eastern boundary between Honiley and Kenilworth parishes in the area of the modern Chase Wood. Thornton Wood, 270 acres in extent in 1591,[135] first appeared in documents in 1581, when it was

stated that the tenants of Kenilworth had surrendered common rights there in exchange for common in Priory Field and other lands.[136] It was separated from the great pool west of the castle by a pasture called Nippledines and was said in 1591 to lie to the north of that pasture. It was separated from a meadow called Cunstable meadow by various pastures. Some of the wood had been taken into a pasture called le Course. Unfortunately, these names did not survive to appear on the estate map of 1692. However, in 1694 "Henry Eaves' Coppice formerly called Thornton Wood" was on the boundary with Balsall[137] and Henry Eaves's Whites Coppice is marked on the map of 1692.[138] The creation of the chase and the subsequent division of the former chase amongst Parliamentary supporters after the Civil War[139] left odd pieces of land called 'wood' on the map of 1692 but no obvious boundary line. However, the association of common woodland with areas which appeared to have adjoined Honiley, the reference to Thornton Wood on the boundary with Balsall in 1694, and the size of the Wood in 1591, suggest that it might have comprised all or part of the woods called Middle Copse and Chase Copse on the map of 1692 and have extended northwards to the boundary with Balsall, adjoining Blackwell Wood.[140] There is no sixteenth-century or earlier reference to woods called Middle Copse, Chase Copse or Henry Eaves's coppice, suggesting that these were new names for old woods. The first two have become Chase Wood. There are no clues to the origin of the name Thornton.

Thornton Wood is another candidate for the foreign wood of the castle accounts. Whilst it may not have been within the manor of Kenilworth in 1086, it may have been part of the Clinton lordship and thus become attached to the manor subsequently. Henry de Clinton had a wood which was near to the canons' wood of Blackwell and to the wood of Robert Franciscus or le Franceis of Langley.[141] Henry de Clinton's wood may have become Thornton Wood. Kenilworth Abbey still held Blackwell Wood at its dissolution[142] and the modern Blackwell Wood is presumably the same wood, or part of it. In 1694 Henry Eaves's Coppice, i.e. part of Thornton Wood, adjoined Blackwell Coppice. There is a fourteenth-century record of a twelfth-century charter which implied that part of Blackwell was within Geoffrey de Clinton's park.[143] Other twelfth-century charters include minor place-names which are associated variously with both *Wridefen* and Kenilworth and show that *Wridefen*, which became Rudfen manor, adjoined the park.[144] The outwood later known as Thornton Wood may therefore have been attached originally to Blackwell or Rudfen, places which are not mentioned in Domesday Book.

Kenilworth Priory also held the wood of Odybarn, arguably the Prior's wood of 160 acres recorded in the Hundred Rolls of 1279.[145] Odybarn can be located as it adjoined the wood of *Crattele* in Stoneleigh and the name survived to appear on the map of 1628,[146] when the area called Odybarn spring, a coppice wood in 1581,[147] and Odybarn heath covered about three hundred acres. *Odybourn sprynge* contained twenty acres in 1545,[148] which suggests that some secondary woodland developed by the early seventeenth century.

There is evidence of some clearance of woodland in

croft, not a grove or a wood, called *le kyngesgraue*, was

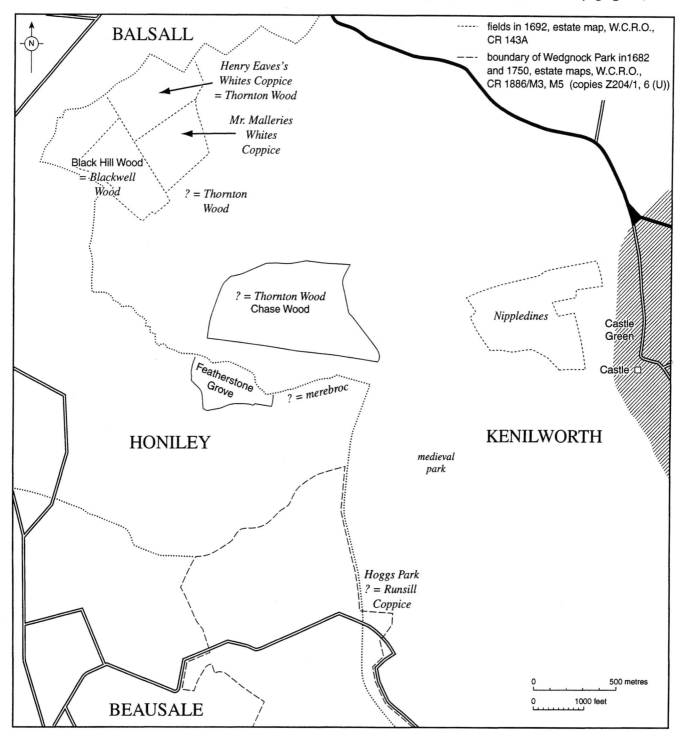

Figure 16: Kenilworth (west)

Kenilworth in the twelfth century. Geoffrey de Clinton granted to one of his officials twelve acres of land for assarting in his wood around *Blachestochehurst*.[149] There were assarts around Henry de Clinton's land called *morham* by the bridge of *Wrydefen*.[150]

The word grove occurs occasionally in medieval records of Kenilworth. The record of the enclosed grove (*gravam inclausam*) in 1279 comes from the Hundred Rolls, which recorded that it was held by a free tenant of the Priory.[151] Two groves (*grauis siue virgultis*), Great Maney and Little Maney, were recorded in the Close Roll for 1362.[152] A

recorded in the accounts for 1438-9[153] and subsequently. The sites of these groves are not known. The survey of 1591 included two groves, Dallies Grove and Gardners Grove, in the tenants' holdings by the borough.[154] The paucity of records for tenants' holdings in the later medieval period may conceal a medieval origin for these groves.

Ashow

The parish of Ashow, like Stoneleigh immediately to the north and Warwick further south, straddled the river Avon. Bericote, the part south-east of the river, was the subject of a separate entry in Domesday Book;[155] as noted in Chapter Two, the manor had no *silva* in 1086, but a wood in the first half of the thirteenth century. In the fourteenth century there was at least one tenant's grove in Bericote, *moppesgroue*, presumably part of the holding called *moppesthynge*.[156]

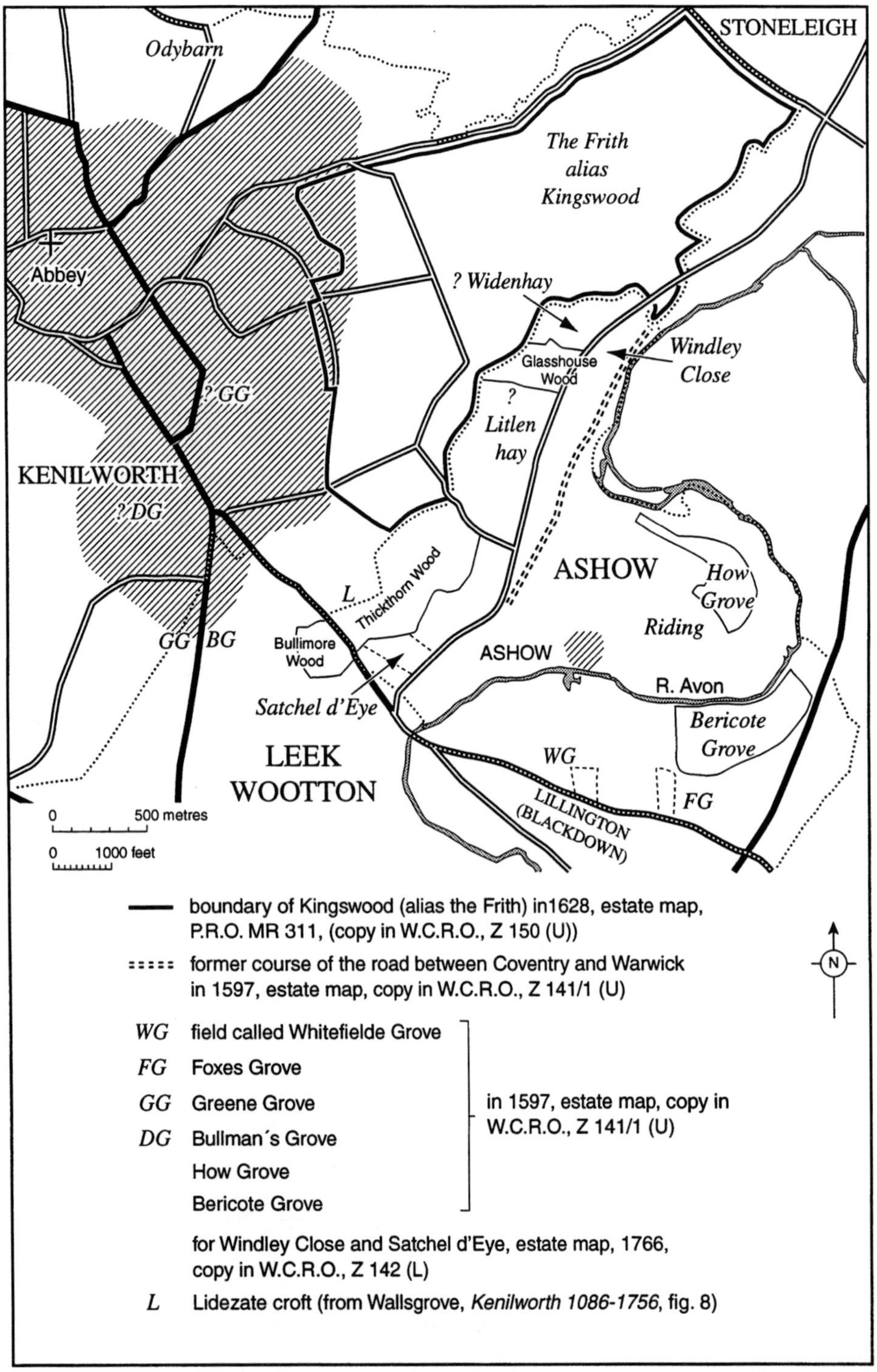

Figure 17: Ashow

Ashow itself had *silva* half a league long by three furlongs wide in 1086[157] - perhaps between 125 and 180 acres - and woods in the later medieval period. In addition, the free tenants of Ashow had common rights in the adjoining Frith of Kenilworth.[158]

In 1200 William de Esseho obtained royal agreement to the division of the wood of Ashow which had been common to him and William de Semilly, on the grounds that the latter had made waste of the whole wood.[159] William de Semilly, his wife and his heir gave to the monks of Stoneleigh a part of the wood of Ashow (*unam partem bosci de esseshou*) which lay between the Warwick-Coventry road and the monks' pool.[160] The 1279 Hundred Rolls attributed an outwood and an enclosed wood to the Semilly lordship (and another wood to Kenilworth Priory).[161] The Semilly wood called *Wydenhaye* was between the Avon and the Frith of Kenilworth.[162] There were new assarts called *Wydenheyewast* in 1340.[163] In 1316 the canons of Kenilworth secured surrender of common rights in a wood called *Thyckethorne* and a pasture called *Littlenhay* which stretched from *Sohochale lidgate* to the hedge or hay (*haiam*) of *Wydenhai* and from the Frith to the fields of Ashow.[164] Sir William Dugdale wrote that in 1301 Geoffrey de Semilly granted to Thomas, earl of Lancaster, all his wastes and woodlands in Ashow, between the river Avon and the Frith of Kenilworth, called *Widenhaye*.[165] In the same year Geoffrey leased all his lands in Ashow to Stoneleigh Abbey, with the express exception of his wood called *Wydenhey*.[166] This wood has been identified tentatively with the modern Windley or Winley,[167] although Windley could also be a corruption of the minor place-name *Quentleye*[168] in *Widenhaye*. Either way the evidence points to *Widenhaye* as the northern tip of Ashow. The field-name Satchel d'Eye and the lidgate in Kenilworth[169] point to the likely site of *Littlenhay*. The present Thickthorn Wood presumably covers all or part of the medieval wood of that name. Thickthorn was given to Kenilworth Priory by John de Simely.[170] The suggestion that the whole area between the Warwick-Coventry road and the north-western boundary of Ashow was once woodland must be tempered by the fact that the course of that road has changed since the eighteenth century and may have undergone other changes at an earlier date.[171]

36

There was more woodland to the east of the road, where How Grove, shown on a map of 1597,[172] presumably occupies the site of the wood (*boscum*) called *le ho* or *la ho* in two thirteenth-century deeds,[173] one of which also referred to assarts by the wood, and in a lease of 1301, when Geoffrey de Symyli also had quarries there.[174]. The Old English *hoh* is found both in the name of the wood called the *Ho* and in the place-name Ashow (medieval *Esse(s)ho*).[175] Next to Ho Hill and divided from it by an assart was another wood called variously *le Birches*,[176] *Nether(e)birches* or *Nethurbirches*.[177] In 1324 Alice, widow of John le Fisher of Ashow, was allowed to cut birches in the wood for her own use and to make faggots of them.[178]

Stoneleigh

Stoneleigh has the best evidence for matching later medieval woodland to the *silva* of Domesday Book. Unusually, and thanks to the traditions preserved by the monks of Stoneleigh Abbey, it is possible to deduce the approximate extent of the twelfth-century woodland and to show that this woodland must have been largely coincident with the *silva*. There is also evidence that much of it was managed as wood pasture and became waste; this makes it reasonable to assume that, in Stoneleigh at least, *silva* was wood pasture. Much of the *silva* appears to have been waste or under cultivation by the late thirteenth century, although the amount which was waste, as distinct from woodland, in 1086 is unknown.

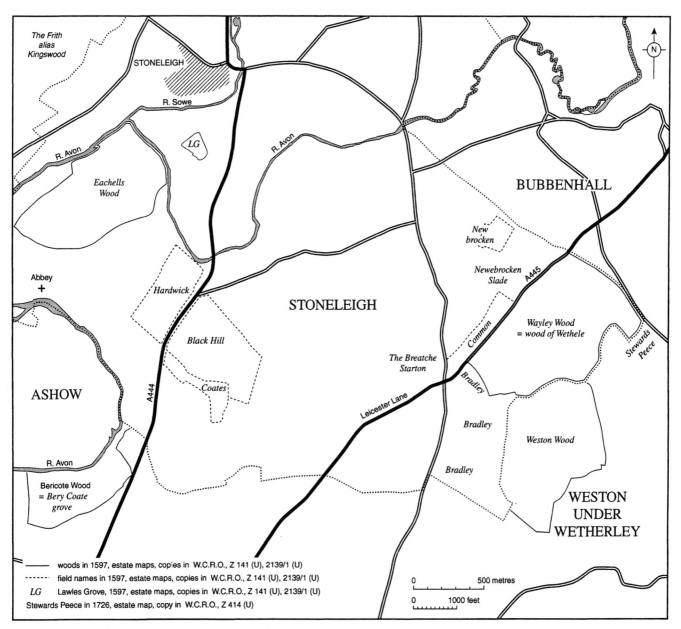

Figure 18: Stoneleigh (south) and Weston Wood

Groves were recorded in Ashow in 1375 and 1431,[179] but their locations are unknown. One may have become the small wood called Cookes grove, the present Glasshouse Coppice, which was shown on the map of 1597.[180]

The large ecclesiastical parish of Stoneleigh straddled the Avon valley. Much of it came to be held by Stoneleigh Abbey in the later medieval period. The Abbey's Leger Book, written c.1392,[181] includes an account of the earlier development of the Abbey's estates. It has been edited and printed with an analysis of its information about later medieval topography.

The grants of arable land which were made to the Abbey and other beneficiaries during the twelfth century gave enough detail for the approximate area of cultivation in the second half of the century to be estimated as 2,040 acres.[182] As the ecclesiastical parish consisted of 9,907 acres,[183] it has been concluded that there were roughly 8,000 acres of uncultivated land, presumably consisting of pasture, heath, marsh etc. as well as wood. The *silva* of Domesday Book measured four leagues by two leagues.[184] Its area might have been between about 8,000 and 11,500 acres. The higher figure exceeds the area of the parish, but, as suggested earlier in this chapter, both the Domesday manor of Stoneleigh and the Domesday *silva* probably included the Frith of Kenilworth.

The foundation charter of the Abbey gave the monks easements in the king's forest, woods and *bruillis*, in the form of both firewood and timber for building.[185] No other details were given; there was no reference to rights to pasture in the woods. Most later documents were more specific, so that separate consideration can be given to the south-eastern and north-western parts of the parish.

The term *bruillum*, apart from one very general reference in relation to the north-west of the parish,[186] was found only in the south-eastern part and nowhere else in Warwickshire. There are some clues to the rare use of this term, which was quite distinct from *boscum*. It has been given three meanings - thicket, covert, and game-park.[187] The third meaning has been taken from Old English glosses of various Latin texts[188] and may relate to Stoneleigh's royal status. Stoneleigh was held by King Edward the Confessor. The tenurial and ecclesiastical links which were recorded partly in Domesday Book and partly in later medieval records show that Stoneleigh was once the administrative centre of a very large territory, which included Kenilworth, Baginton, Bubbenhall, Ryton-on-Dunsmore, and probably Leek Wootton with its ecclesiastical dependencies of Leamington, Milverton, Lillington, Cubbington, and Ashow.[189] It can be suggested that the *bruillum* of Wetherley and Echells was a former Anglo-Saxon game-park attached to the royal administrative centre, an area separate in function, if not in topography, from woods. This suggestion is supported by the possibility that the first element in the place-name Wetherley comes from an Old English word meaning to hunt.[190] If this meaning were certain it would indicate a tradition of hunting much older than the mid-eleventh century.

The Leger Book named the fields which were brought into cultivation from the *bruillum* of Echells and from the whole of the *bruillum* of Wetherley;[191] several can be located on an estate map of 1597.[192] Wetherley extended both west and east of the present Waverley Wood. *Stywardespece* was part of the *bruillum* and *Stewards Peece* appears on a map of 1726.[193] Four fields called *Brounesbreche, Longebreche, Marybreche,* and *Newbrocone* were assarted from the waste of the wood of Wetherley. The last of these four fields can

be traced on the map of 1597. On that map a field called the Breatche was marked as part of Stareton, whereas the medieval fields called *breche* were said not to be part of Stareton.[194] The *bruillum* of Echells included meadows to the north, west and south of the sixteenth-century wood, and fields to the east, of which Hardwick, Black Hill and Coates (presumably the medieval *Cotefurlong*) can also be identified on the map of 1597.[195] The fields must have postdated an agreement between the Abbey and Geoffrey de St. Maur by which the latter recognised his unjust claim to the *bruillum* and surrendered it in return for the right to take wood for fires and fencing or hedging in Cubbington.[196]

The estate map of 1597 also helps to locate the woods of Echells, Wetherley, Bradley and Weston, all recorded in the later medieval period.[197] The Leger Book stated that the monks enclosed the wood (*boscum*) called *Wethele* with its *heiis* and *pasturis* above *Leycestrewey*;[198] the modern map shows a road, called Leicester Lane, skirting the north-western edge of Waverley Wood and continuing through Bubbenhall and Wolston to the Fosse Way. The Leger Book also stated that the wood of Bradley and the wood of the lord of Weston were in ancient times parcel of Wetherley and that the part of Wetherley in which the men of Weston had common was a wood called *Westonwode*, which adjoined the wood of Wetherley.[199] The present Weston and Waverley Woods adjoin. Fields called Bradley on the map of 1597 may mark the site of the medieval wood or of land which was part of a wider area called Bradley, whose wood might have been absorbed into Wetherley Wood. The Echells Wood of 1597 was presumably the wood of *Aceles* recorded in 1245.[200] It was called a "pasture or wode" in 1560.[201]

There were two groves in this south-eastern part of Stoneleigh. One adjoined fields called *Eyresfeldes, Starbruggefeld* and *Grovefeld* in the loop of the river Avon and was called *Eyresgroue*; the lands were held at one time by Robert of Stoneleigh who was called le Eyr.[202] The other was recorded as a boundary point for land near Cloud in a deed attributed to the period 1175-1224.[203] It was in Stareton and was nameless.

Although the Leger Book recorded common rights in Weston Wood, it failed to say whether they were rights to estovers or to pasture or to both. In 1245 Geoffrey de Langley, in virtue of his interest in Stareton, was confirmed in rights of pannage and herbage in the woods of Stoneleigh except for the woods of *Wethele* and *Aceles* and surrendered rights to pasture on the south side of the Avon.[204] The Abbey's policy was to limit if not to abolish wood pasture rights in this part of its estate.

There are many records of pasture and other common rights in Stoneleigh's woods north-west of the Avon. The Hundred Rolls of 1279 stated that the abbot of Stoneleigh had three common woods called *Dolle, Westwode* and *Craccele* (or *Crattele*) which contained a thousand acres of wood and waste.[205] A petition to Parliament in 1290 claimed that the men of the king's ancient demesne in Stoneleigh had estovers in the woods of the manor together with pasture, not only for pigs in pannage but also for other animals (*largam pasturam tam ad porcos in pannagio quam ad alia Animalia*) and the rights to collect nuts, build pigsties and use roads and paths to the church, market and vills of the abbot.[206] Some grants of waste in Westwood specifically obliged tenants to surrender common rights.[207]

that by 1279 other common woods may have disappeared entirely. The Abbey's foundation charter of c.1155[208] referred to assarts in Stoneleigh, Dollesworth and Cryfeld. The Leger Book states that *bosci et bruilli* of Westwood, Cratteley, Dalle and Armeley were for the most part enclosed and assarted by various abbots - i.e. the assarts postdated the Abbey's acquisition of Stoneleigh - and leased to tenants after the trees there had been felled, destroyed by the tenants who had estovers there.[209] The tenants' petition of 1290[210] presents a different view, that the tenants had been deprived of estovers and pasture by the Abbey's assarts.

It is possible to trace, from various medieval records, the likely approximate extents of the common woods and the sites of some other medieval woods.

Westwood seems to have been the largest of the woods. According to the Leger Book, sixty-four acres from the waste of Westwood had been granted to the lord of Allesley and twenty-four of these were included in the park of Allesley[211] which adjoined Stoneleigh parish on its northern edge. Fifty acres of the waste of Westwood called *Tylhull*, presumably the modern Tile Hill in the north-west corner of the parish, were the subject of another grant.[212]

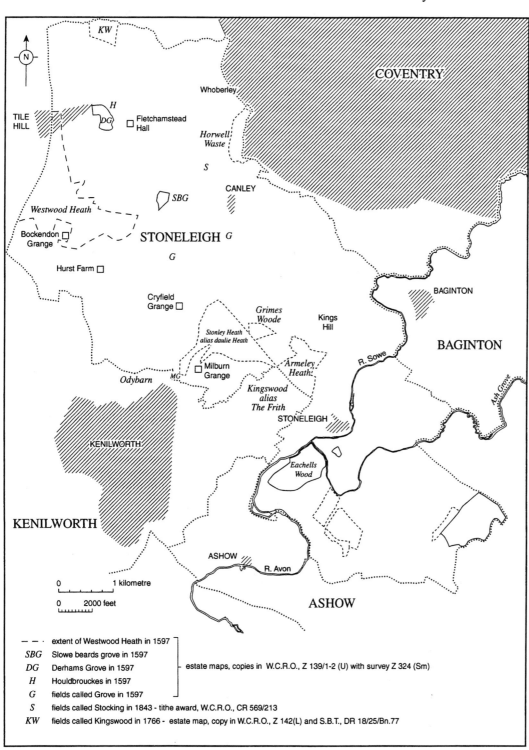

Figure 19: Stoneleigh

The author of the Leger Book stated that Horwell Grange, bordering on Horwell in Coventry, was created from assarts in Westwood.[213] In 1597 the fields on the north-eastern edge of the parish, adjoining Canley Brook and Horwell in Coventry, were all called 'whoreall wast'.[214] Likewise, some

The thousand acres of *Dolle*, *Westwode* and *Crattele* in 1279 are a far cry from the estimated 8,000 acres of *silva* in 1086. However, various references to the boundaries of these woods, in the Leger Book and in deeds, show that the woods must have been much more extensive at an earlier date and of the fields of Hurst were taken out of Westwood.[215] Part of the waste of Westwood adjoined the common field of Canley; another part was above Whoberley.[216] The Knights Templars acquired waste in Westwood specifically to augment their manor of Fletchamstead.[217] It can therefore be deduced that Westwood occupied a very extensive area in the north of the parish, possibly one third of the area north of the river Sowe. The Old English habitative place-name Fletchamstead[218] strongly suggests that Westwood was not a continuous expanse of woodland even before 1086, but the many references to waste suggest that it was largely wood and waste. Westwood had not lost all its trees by the thirteenth century, for there are references to the wood (bosco, Boscum) of Westwood in 1250 and 1290.[219] The relationship between Westwood and the wood (nemore) of Fletchamstead which was mentioned in a deed attributed to c.1130[220] is not clear. Nor is its relationship with an area called Kingswood, whose name suggests a derivation from a time when Stoneleigh was still a royal manor. A deed dated 1326 and another which can be attributed to the period 1293-1310 referred to waste called Kingeswod(e) near the road from Coventry to Berkswell, a description which fits the field-names Kingswood on a map of 1766.[221]

There is no reference to the wood of Hurst in the later medieval period. The royal charter of confirmation to Stoneleigh Abbey in 1204 included assarts of Hurst,[222] but these may have been the part of Hurst which was taken out of Westwood. The minor place-name Hurst survives on modern maps.

The name Crattele is perpetuated in that of Crackley Wood.[223] A map of 1766[224] shows an area of woodland somewhat more extensive than the present wood. At that time it was divided into Great Munkes Hays, Little Munkes Hays, Little Matmakers and Great Matmakers and included an area called Marsh Vatt which is no longer woodland. The name Monkeshay was recorded in 1307, when a tenant surrendered his right to estovers in various enclosures, including a close of Cratteley under the park of Crulefeld (modern Cryfield), namely le Monkeshay.[225] There is a separate reference to the park called Monkeshay.[226] The existence of a Park Field to the east of Munkes Hayes in 1766 provides additional evidence for matching the medieval and modern names. In 1536 the wood called Monkes Heyes contained 95 acres.[227] By 1600 the wood had been divided[228] and in 1639 it was stated that the "twoe great parcells of woodground, woods or Copices of wood" contained an estimated 70 acres.[229] Another wood called Mattmakers contained 24 acres. There are records of sales of wood in all three woods in the late seventeenth century.[230]

Crattele adjoined a wood in Kenilworth called Odybern.[231] Therefore it must have stretched northwards from the parish boundary between Stoneleigh and Kenilworth. Exactly how far it extended east and west along this boundary is uncertain, because the modern name Odybarn is attached to most of the north-east corner of Kenilworth parish. The wood of Crattele might have included either or both of the areas called respectively Crackley Hill Closes and Crackley Heath Closes in 1766.

Kenilworth Priory acquired part of the wood called Crattele in the first half of the thirteenth century, when that part was bounded by a road between Odybarn and the decoy (volatum) of Richard de la Hore.[232] It also included an enclosed pasture called Aumenersclos.[233] Modern field-names do not preserve the location of the medieval decoy or the almoner's close. In 1367 the Priory was said to hold 30 acres of wood called Cratteley Hulles.[234] The Crackley Hill Closes which lay east of Marsh Vatt on the map of 1766 presumably correspond to Cratteley Hulles, but it is not clear whether this area of woodland was the same as that which was granted to the Priory in the thirteenth century. Stoneleigh manor's boundary skirted a wood of the Prior called Pryorisclos by a lane next to the holding called le Holyes.[235] The latter name has survived as Hollies, being attached in 1766 to closes lying west of Matmakers, but it is not clear whether the prior's wood lay north, south, east or west of the Hollies, whether it was an enclosed part of Odybarn or whether it was a separate wood in Stoneleigh. It seems unlikely that it lay to the east of the Hollies, because the name mattemakers was already current in 1477, when mattemakers and holyes were divided by a ditch[236] (a lane now separates the two). There is no evidence that Matmakers was woodland in the late fifteenth century, and in 1581 it was described as a close rather than a wood.[237] However, it may have been wooded in earlier centuries.

The wood of Dolle, or Dalle, can be traced in the same way. In 1271 there was an inquisition into the escape of the abbot's pigs from the wood (boscum) of Dalle to the wood of Kenilworth.[238] Milburn Grange was said to have been taken out of Dalle;[239] the grange was near to the boundary with Kenilworth. In 1277 three acres of meadow under Kyngeshull on the Stivichall side of Stoneleigh were described as next to the wood of Dalle.[240] The Leger Book also recorded forty acres from the waste of the wood of Dalle called Kannoc, a place which became the later Wainbody.[241] In the late thirteenth century a messuage in Canley lay between Locsmythescroft and the wood (boscum) of Dauley.[242] Dalle, therefore, seems to have stretched from Westwood and Canley to Kenilworth.

Although no wood of Armeley was recorded in the Hundred Rolls of 1279, Armeley was described as a foreign wood in the Leger Book.[243] In addition, a deed attributed to the reign of Henry III (1216-72) dealt with pannage in Armeley, Dalle and Westwood.[244] Armeley appears to have been south-east of Dalle. The ditch of Armeley adjoined the Frith of Kenilworth.[245] Armeley Heath is shown on the map of 1597 and in 1526 was described as common pasture adjoining the Frith of Kenilworth.[246] It cannot be assumed that the heath and former wood were coterminous, but the adjoining field-names of Grimes woode and Farr woode on the map of 1597 suggest that much of this area had been woodland. In 1571 land at Kingshill had common of pasture in Armeley, Dalle, Grymswood, Forwood and Sevenhookes.[247]

Forwood may have been part of the wood of Dalle rather than of the wood of Armeley. Forwood was said to be in Milburn, and Milburn Grange was said to have been formed from the wood of Dalle.[248] Forwood was described as

40

cultivated land (*culturis*) in the early thirteenth century, when four of its headlands extended to the close which the monks had made in a decoy (*voleya*).[249] Another charter, ascribed to approximately the same date, c.1235, stated that there was a decoy in *Helwenin* in the wood of the monks.[250] If these decoys were one and the same, the documents show that Forwood adjoined a medieval wood. The field at the southern end of Wainbody Wood, called Upper Grove, may mark the medieval *Harlewyn grove*, whose name looks as if it might be a corruption of *Helwenin*.[251]

Derhams Grove and an unnamed grove in Cryfield.[256] The large field marked Grove on the tithe map south-west of Finham Park[257] is presumably the coppice wood in Finham which in the seventeenth century was said to have been part of Helenhull Grange and called Hellinghall Hill Grove or Gregores Grove alias Graunge Grove.[258] The earliest record of the wood by name is from 1529, when it was described as one of two groves by the side of the Grange, the other being Daniell Grove.[259]

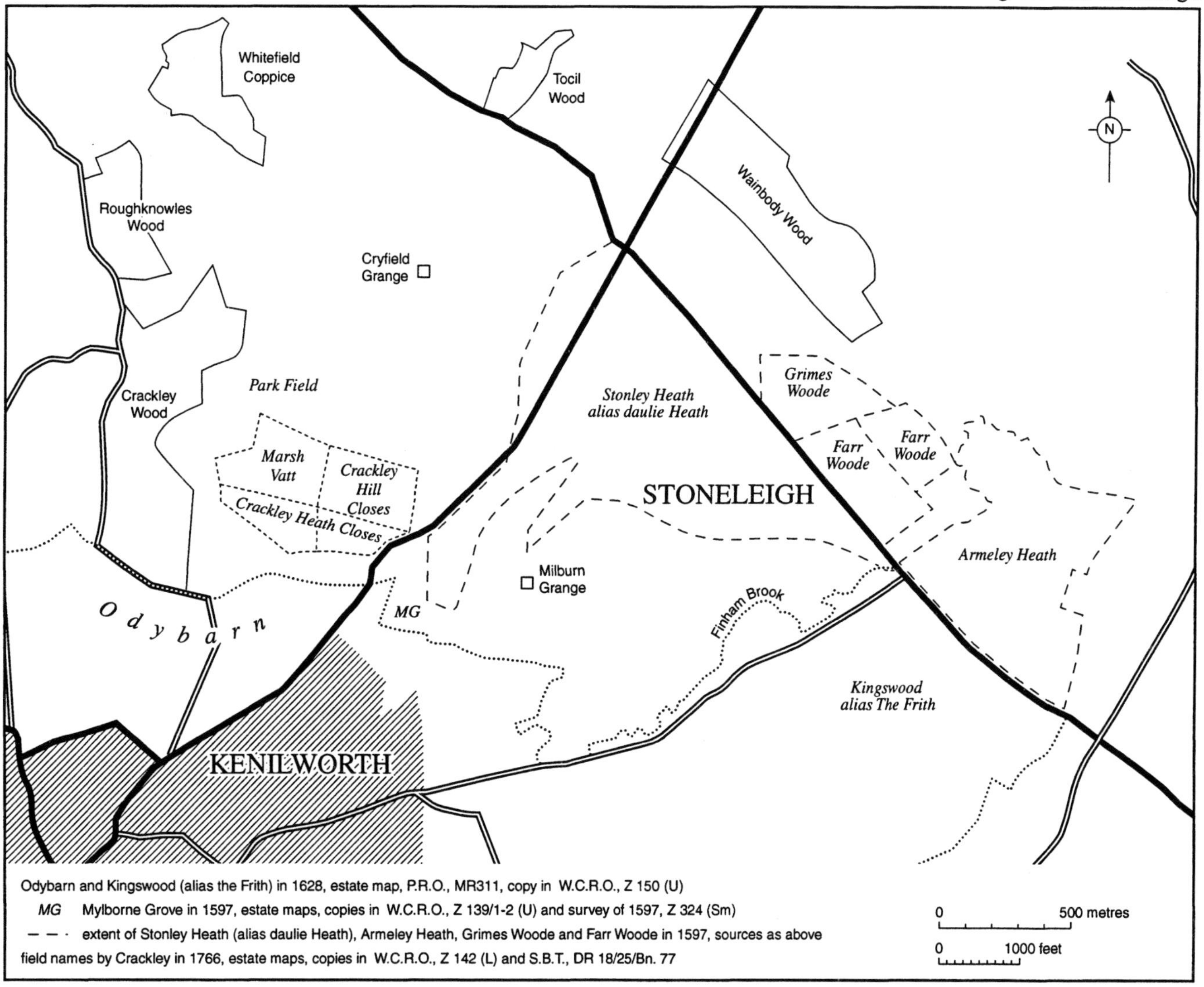

Details of the extensive intercommoning between Stoneleigh

Odybarn and Kingswood (alias the Frith) in 1628, estate map, P.R.O., MR311, copy in W.C.R.O., Z 150 (U)

MG   Mylborne Grove in 1597, estate maps, copies in W.C.R.O., Z 139/1-2 (U) and survey of 1597, Z 324 (Sm)

— — ·   extent of Stonley Heath (alias daulie Heath), Armeley Heath, Grimes Woode and Farr Woode in 1597, sources as above

field names by Crackley in 1766, estate maps, copies in W.C.R.O., Z 142 (L) and S.B.T., DR 18/25/Bn. 77

Figure 20: Stoneleigh (central)

Canley adjoined Westwood and Dalle. It has been claimed that Canley was taken out of Dalle wood, but Canley had its own wood (*bosco*) called *la Lee* in 1270.[252] At least one holding had a grove.[253] There was a place, or a wood, called *schortwode*.[254] The wood of Dalle was next to land in the territory of Canley, but might not itself have been in Canley.

There were a few other groves north-west of the Avon - two in Fletchamstead, one by *Battereswast* in Hurst, one by Hethsale, Guphillfurthe and Whoberley, two in Finbury, and *le Conynger*, of uncertain location.[255] The map of the area drawn in 1597 shows a number of groves, including Mylborne Grove, by Milburn Grange, Slowe Beards Grove,

and several places nearby are given in the Leger Book.[260] Stoneleigh's own tenants had common rights in Hasilwood in Coventry and the woods of Odybarn and the Frith in Kenilworth. The tenants of long-established holdings in Kenilworth and le Hale had common in Westwood, Crackley, Dalle and Armeley. Coventry's tenants, except for cottagers, had common in Hethsale and Stivichall. The Stivichall tenants had common in Dalle. The free tenants of Berkswell had common in Westwood only.

As Stoneleigh's later medieval woods covered the greater part of the parish there must have been a considerable overlap with the Domesday *silva*. The strong traditions of

41

common rights in most of the woods makes it reasonable to assume that, in Stoneleigh at least, *silva* was wood pasture.

seventy-five years of the Domesday survey is more evidence for the omission of groves from Domesday Book and hence for some kind of distinction between groves and *silva*.

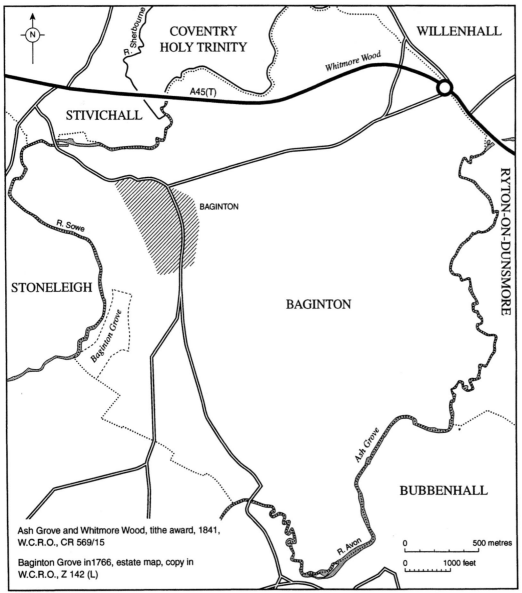

Ash Grove and Whitmore Wood, tithe award, 1841, W.C.R.O., CR 569/15

Baginton Grove in1766, estate map, copy in W.C.R.O., Z 142 (L)

Figure 21: Baginton

Baginton

Baginton lay between the river Avon to the east and the river Sowe to the west. The Kenilworth Priory cartularies have preserved copies of charters attributed to the period c.1130-61 which record two groves in Baginton.[261] *Estgraua*, by the river Avon, was called *Astgrove* by 1423 and *Ashgrove* by the late seventeenth century;[262] it can be located under the last of these names on the tithe map.[263] The tithe map also shows an unnamed grove by the park and the river Sowe, corresponding to the site given for the other twelfth-century grove. In 1766 the unnamed grove of the tithe award was called Baginton Grove and adjoined a mill, so it may have been the *millegroue* of 1469.[264] There is a record of a third grove in 1313 called *Pipilgraue*.[265]

No *silva* was recorded under Baginton in Domesday Book.[266] The record of two groves within fifty or at most

No medieval record has been found of Whitmore Coppice, nor of wood in *kingscliff* and *potters pytts*, all recorded in 1529.[267] There is a record of a dispute over the payment of tithes on wood and timber growing in a close called *crowley yate* in 1447.[268]

An *Estwood* was associated with Baginton in the middle of the twelfth century, but there is no proof of its location there.[269] The first element of the name is shared with *Estgraua*.

Willenhall

The manor of Willenhall was held by Coventry Cathedral Priory, but there is no mention of it in Domesday Book. There are references to the prior's wood of Willenhall from c.1200. From the cartulary of Coombe Abbey we learn that the exit from the wood adjoined a heath called *Wllsched* in Binley and the park of Brandon.[270] Coventry Cathedral Priory's register, compiled in 1411, recorded an enclosed wood (*boscum inclusum*) called *le Wilnehale close*. Between the wood of Willenhall (*boscum de Wilnehale*) and the rabbit warren (*Cunicularium*) of Coombe Abbey was a pasture in wood and plain called *lithewod*, abutting partly on to the park of Brandon and partly on to a croft called *Whitesich* in Binley.[271] These medieval records are corroborated by two separate, sixteenth-century sources, a Coombe Abbey lease of 1538[272] showing that Binley Heath adjoined *Wynall Wood* and a document showing that the wood was by *Woolseyes* heath (?a corruption of *Wllsched*) and Brandon.[273] A map attributed to c.1630[274] shows Brandon park adjoining Binley near to the Willenhall boundary. A later map of Binley[275] shows fields called Whitesich and Conigree west of the boundary with Brandon park.

The Priory's register also stated that the *lythewod* was   Willenhall Wood is now a relatively small wood in the centre

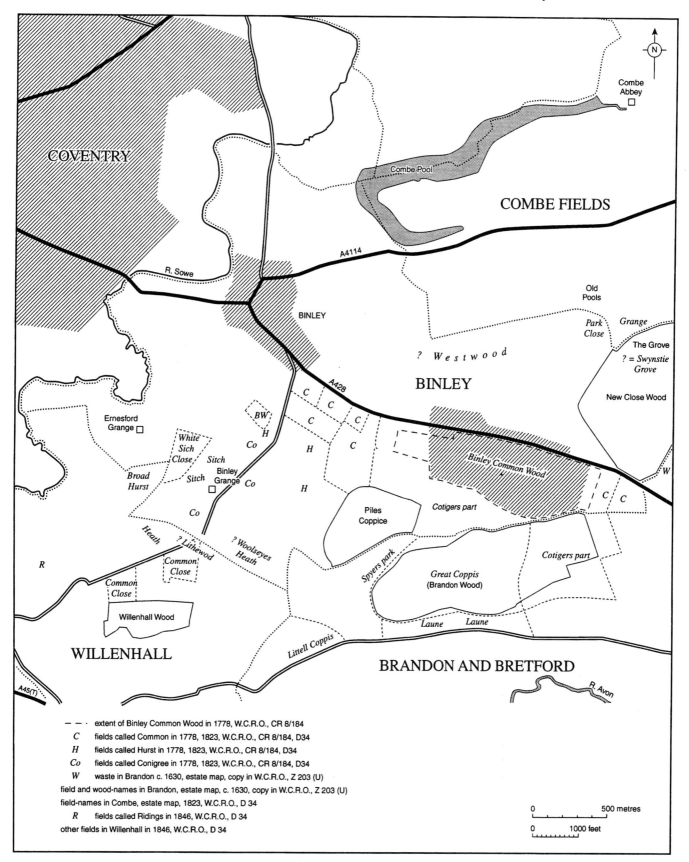

Figure 22: Binley, Brandon and Willenhall

formerly called Horum and Herdewyk;[276] these names are not normally associated with woodland.

of the parish; its flora includes wood anemones, a species associated with ancient woodland. If this was part of the medieval wood, the latter must have been fairly large to stretch to the eastern boundary of the parish.

Binley, Brandon, Brinklow and Coombe

To the east of Coventry the later medieval woods of Binley, Brandon, Brinklow and Coombe appear to have covered a large area around the junction of the four parishes. Tenants from Binley, Brandon and Brinklow inter-commoned with their animals in Westwood in Binley c.1550[277] and probably much earlier. Westwood can be located approximately from references in seventeenth-century documents; part of it was taken into the park of Coombe Abbey.[278]

The *silva* of Binley's two manors in Domesday Book[279] probably amounted to about one hundred acres. By the end of the twelfth century Binley's woodland, called *boscus* or *nemus*, was further divided.[280] It seems reasonable to suggest that Binley Common Wood covered the site of part of the twelfth-century wood. Fields called Common suggest that the wood once extended further westwards and the continuous line on to which field boundaries abut north of the common suggests that the wood may also have extended further north. A deed of 1739 which states that Whitesuch was part of Binley Common suggests that it stretched almost to the boundary with Willenhall.[281] The modern Buttons Wood is the Gardners Wood of 1746;[282] this may have been the wood leased to John Gardener and his wife in 1538, when it was described as "A Grove in Bynley called Comeners Grove".[283] Hints of former ridge and furrow and a relatively poor ground flora suggest that the modern wood, if indeed it has medieval antecedents, may have been a secondary extension to a former medieval grove.

Although field-names suggest that Binley's later medieval woodland was extensive, there is no contemporary evidence of its size. The Hundred Rolls of 1279 stated that the abbot of Coombe had a foreign wood in Binley containing forty-two acres of land and, in a separate entry, eleven acres of land,[284] but these figures probably referred to land taken from the wood rather than to the wood as a whole. Two acres were said to have been taken into the park of Brandon. Since the park of Brandon stretched to the boundary with Willenhall[285] this corroborates the suggested site of the common or foreign wood of Binley.

In the twelfth century Henry de Rokeby gave Coombe Abbey half his wood, which is thought to have been in Binley, called *munechet*,[286] a name which has not been found in subsequent records. By analogy with other names of woods containing the syllable *chet*, it seems that this wood had a name which included the British word for wood, *ceto*.[287] If this is the case, it is the only known later medieval wood in Warwickshire with a British name.[288]

Piles Coppice, of which there is no identifiable medieval record, but which, from its position on the border with Brandon, was presumably the coppice of Lord Harrington recorded in the bounds of Brandon in the sixteenth century,[289] has a large amount of small-leaved lime. This tree is very sensitive to grazing in its early years, so pasture must have been prohibited or carefully managed in the wood. Its proximity to Binley Common Wood suggests that it might have been enclosed from the medieval wood of Binley. Piles Coppice may have been the Binley Coppice recorded in the sixteenth century; in 1746 it contained fifty-one acres.[290]

Domesday Book recorded *silva* four furlongs long and two wide under Brandon[291] probably covering only about fifty to seventy-five acres. A survey of Brandon in 1571[292] recorded a park of 102 acres and coppices containing just over 37 acres and 107 acres respectively using a perch of eighteen feet, i.e. larger than the modern statute acre. In total these figures are three times the estimated area of the Domesday *silva*. A map of c.1630 reflects the survey, and also shows fields called *wast*.[293] The wood (*boscum*) and heath of Brandon were mentioned incidentally in a deed dating from 1226[294] which stated that they were separated by a heath from the enclosed wood of *Burlegh*, a name surviving in Birchley Wood in Brinklow. In 1279 the Hundred Rolls listed a foreign wood in Brandon containing forty acres of wood (not land, as in the case of the entry for Binley) and a park in demesne a league (*leucam*) in length.[295]

Brinklow appeared in Domesday Book only as a hundred name. There are various records relating to the wood of *Burdlege* or *Burhtleia* from the second half of the twelfth century.[296] Part of it (some was assarted) presumably survives in Birchley Wood, because it adjoined the bounds of both Binley and Brandon,[297] as does the present Wood. The twelfth-century assarts also adjoined Brandon,[298] so it can be inferred that they covered land later called Brinklow Heath. There are more records of assarts in 1262, 1272, 1351 and 1384.[299] Fields called Ridding and Birchley on a map of 1838[300] suggest that the medieval wood also extended further east.

In 1501 Coombe Abbey and named freeholders in Brinklow agreed that part of Birchley Wood near the Abbey's grange could be enclosed and made into a coppice[301] - presumably the *Byrtley Copies* recorded a few decades later.[302] Both this agreement and earlier deeds[303] testify to common pasture in Birchley.

Fields called grove suggest the former presence of a grove. On the map of 1838 they were adjoined by Harmley Close. A lease of 1538 included a close or pasture called *Armeley* in Brinklow field "adioynyng unto a grove called morse grove".[304]

Coombe Abbey was in the southern part of Smite, which in 1086 had *silva* measuring half a league by half a league,[305] perhaps covering between 250 and 350 acres. Roger de Moubray endowed the Abbey with all the land of Smite which Richard de Camvill held of him and had given for the foundation of an abbey.[306] There are occasional references to, but no detailed records of, the Abbey's lands in Coombe before the early sixteenth century. The following woods have been identified:-

- *bosco de Cumbe/Combe* in 1261-2 and 1307[307]

- a wood called *Wodegrange* in 1333-5[308]

- wood or coppice called *hill parke* or *hell parke* (=Hill Park Wood) in 1537[309]

- *Swynstie grove* (in Wood Grange in Coombe =?The Grove on a map of 1823) in 1538[310]

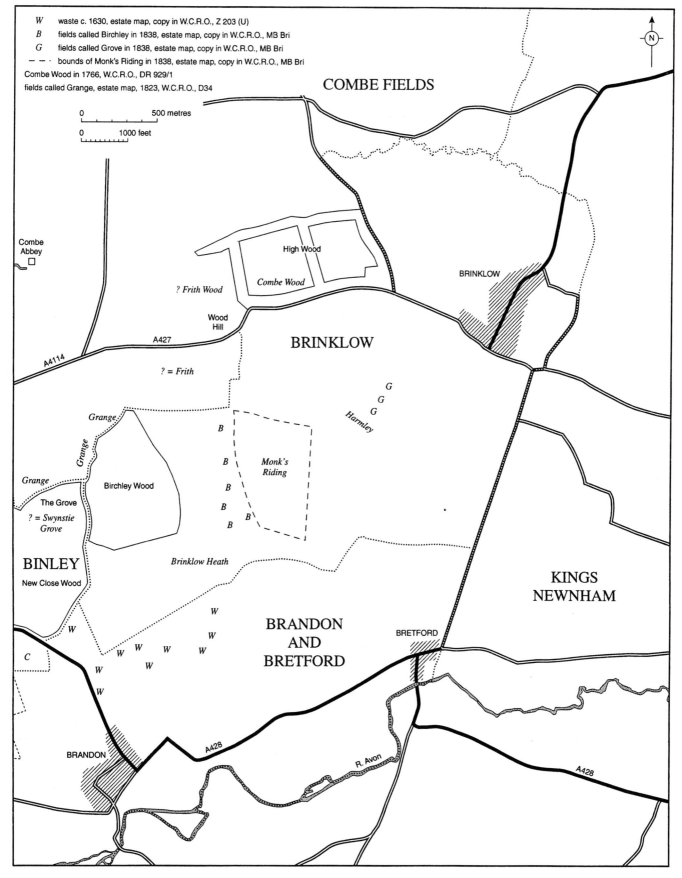

Figure 23: Brinklow and Coombe

- the *Fryth* or *ffrythe* (ground called the Frith was by the ground called the *Parke* and by the grange pool in Wood Grange in 1501 and 1538, but pasture called the Frith was distinguished from the Frith Wood in 1652, so the Wood, which contained 170 acres in that year, could have been further north and, given its size, may well have become the High Wood.[311])

Several of the Abbey's woods seem to have survived into the twentieth century, but much of High Wood has been lost since, only the fringes remaining to show how splendid its spring flowers must have been.

The Coventry area

There have been two detailed studies of the later medieval topography of the area around the city of Coventry, one dealing with the period 1180-1280[312] and the other extending into the fourteenth and fifteenth centuries.[313] Both studies have concentrated on the development of settlement, noting that much woodland and waste were converted to arable and pasture during the later medieval period. They contrast the nucleated settlements and open-field systems of the 'original' or 'old' settlements in and around Coventry with the dispersed settlements and enclosed crofts in areas of former woodland and waste. They see the conversion of woodland to other uses as a deliberate policy promoted by manorial lords who sought to increase their incomes and their social influence in the area.

This account of Coventry's later medieval woodland seeks to complement existing settlement studies by concentrating on the nature and extent of the woodland which existed in 1086 and the woods and wastes recorded subsequently. It will try, subject to the limited survival of minor medieval place-names on modern maps, to locate the woods as precisely as possible, an exercise not attempted hitherto in any published studies. Extensive areas of wood pasture which ceased to be woodland during the later medieval period and a multiplicity of smaller woods and groves were characteristic of the Coventry area as they were of Stoneleigh.

There is relatively detailed documentation for several parts of the area from the thirteenth century onwards and there are also some twelfth-century records. The register of Coventry Cathedral Priory[314] has been especially useful in this study because it includes detailed surveys of demesne and tenants' holdings and descriptions of boundaries of townships and of the manorial wood of Coventry. By the time the register was compiled in 1411 the Priory's interests in the area had expanded far beyond its original eleventh-century endowment to include lands which had been held by laymen in the twelfth and thirteenth centuries, in particular the manor of Coventry itself, once held by the earls of Chester. However, the topography of 1411 could have been very different from that of two centuries earlier. Studies of Coventry's topography can also draw on various charters and deeds, in original form or in cartularies, as well as cases in the royal courts and state documents such as the Hundred Rolls, but these too provide little evidence for the twelfth century.

There has been no attempt in settlement studies to consider the relative proportions of woodland and other land uses in 1086 nor to estimate, for the later medieval period, the relative proportions of woodland and waste within the areas enclosed for conversion to arable, pasture or parkland. There is not enough evidence to achieve the latter estimate, but the attempt raises interesting questions. Most of the recorded grants of land conveyed waste rather than wood. Yet waste did not feature in Domesday Book, which recorded substantial amounts of *silva* in the Coventry area, as shown below.[315] As already explained, waste, like marsh and heath, may have been omitted from Domesday Book or it may have been intermingled with the *silva*. The evidence from the Coventry area strongly supports the theory that there was far more waste in the thirteenth and fourteenth centuries than in 1086 and that it represented degenerated woodland. This appears to have been the case with the woods of Coventry, Sowe and Coundon.

Manor	*silva*	approx. acreage
Coventry	4 square leagues	c.4,000-c.5,750
Sowe	½ league by 4 furlongs (Coventry church)	c.166-c.240
	3 square leagues (shared by Richard the huntsman, the king and the abbot)	c.3,000-c.4,300
Coundon	3 furlongs 30 perches by 3 furlongs (Coventry church)	c.85-c.112
	½ league by 4 furlongs (William Corbucon)	c.166-c.240
Foleshill	-	
Total		c.7417-c.10642

There is some detailed evidence for Coventry's wood in petitions submitted to Parliament in 1336.[316] The dowager queen Isabella, who held the manor of Cheylesmore centred on the park south-west of the city, denied that she had destroyed Coventry's wood and claimed that it had been destroyed by successive priors, who built two manors there and created two thousand acres of arable land out of the wood which Roger and Cecily de Montalt had conveyed to the Priory with the manor of Coventry in 1249.[317] The prior claimed that the wood had become a waste place (*quidam locus vastatus*) destroyed by commoners taking *housbote* and *haybote* and that the wood where the queen now obtained the fuel due to her as part of the agreement of 1249 had been a waste place which had been planted anew (*de nouo plantata*) by the prior's predecessors c.1259-61.[318] The prior's account of the development of Coventry's waste finds a parallel in the statement made in the Stoneleigh Leger Book that the trees of the woods of Stoneleigh had been destroyed by tenants taking *fuyrbote*, *heybote* and *housbote*.[319] Both the religious houses thought the alleged cause plausible; neither referred to common pasture rights as the cause of the destruction.

(There was common pasture in the earl's wood of Coventry[320] just as there was in the woods of Stoneleigh.) The growth of population and house building in the city of Coventry certainly provides a context for the argument that excess estovers were to blame. The queen's claim is also credible, supported by evidence from the Priory's own records.

According to the register, the Priory's park of Whitmore and manor of Newland were created from wood and waste.[321] A royal grant in 1332 gave the Priory permission to impark wood and waste in Whitmore.[322] The register did not attribute the wood and waste in question to the wood of Coventry; indeed, it specifically excluded Whitmore from Hasilwood.[323] However, it is plain from the petitions to Parliament that the citizens of Coventry regarded Whitmore as part of their wood, for they destroyed the fences around the new enclosures.[324] The evidence for the manor of Newland, which was not named in the proceedings of 1336, is not so sound. The register includes two spurious charters giving the bounds of Newland and stating that it was created from 280 acres of woodland and waste in Keresley and Exhall.[325] The truth about the disappearance of much of Coventry's later medieval woodland may combine the accounts given by both sides. Assarting by successive priors must have reduced the amount of woodland available to the local population for pasture and estovers, thereby intensifying demands on the wood which remained at a time when the local population was increasing.

The allegations made to Parliament in 1336 implied that Coventry's wood was very large. It was treated as an entity not only in the proceedings of 1336 but also in thirteenth-century charters which used phrases such as in bosco meo (1204-8), bosco de Couentre (1249), forinseco bosco de Couentre (1243 and 1249).[326] Deeds relating to adjoining land in Keresley and Exhall also refer simply to the wood of the earl (bosco domini Comitis) or Erleswode.[327] However, the Priory's register said that the wood conveyed to the Priory by the earl in 1249 was in two parts, the inwood of Hasilwood and the outwood or foreign wood of Bernet (boscum intricecum de Hasilwod & boscum forincecum de Bernet), and gave the bounds of each part.[328] Many of the minor place-names in the boundary descriptions have disappeared, but enough remain to give some indication of the extent of these woods.

The outwood called Bernet began at the horeston on the road to Nuneaton under the Bechewast and ran along various streams to Tackford. This, with Sydenhale, Bedworth Rectory and Cattescroftlane, can be traced on modern maps; the Rectory appears on the tithe map for Bedworth and the lane was also part of the boundary of Exhall.[329] Together with the statement that the rest of Exhall was within the manor of Newland, these place-names suggest that the western boundary of Bernet followed the road running southwards through Ash Green and Neal's Green. Bernet therefore seems to have included the eastern half of Exhall and a large part of Foleshill. Hasilwood began at Cowderey in the corner beyond Stoke called Calowdonlane, and

included the whole vill of Stoke, which might correspond to the area of the ecclesiastical parish of Stoke, and Bisshopwast, Erdeswyk (which adjoined Bernet and may be the modern Edgwick) and Harnalewast. It adjoined Whitmore Park. Foleshill's boundary touched it in the area where Foleshill took in Henley lordship.[330] A pasture called le dalbylesowe was near to Hasilwood; Dalby's Leasowe survives in the tithe award.[331]

The bounds copied into the Priory's register in 1411 appear to date from the thirteenth century; they refer to lands and woods of local lords such as Ernald de Bosco. Presumably they reflect the extent of the earl's wood at that time. The division into Hasilwood and Bernet may be no older than this, especially as there are no independent records of the latter name. Hasilwood itself is mentioned incidentally in a deed of 1297.[332] The register only records two lost charters of earl Ranulph III (?c.1200) which dealt with assarts adjacent to the earl's wood of Bernet.[333] The wood of Hasilwood appeared in a letter of doubtful authenticity attributed to earl Hugh II (1153-81).[334] However, the Stoneleigh Leger Book, compiled c.1392, preserved an independent tradition that the tenants of Stoneleigh had rights of common in Hasilwood.[335] Bernet, if it has the same derivation as Barnet in Middlesex, is an Old English word meaning burning or burnt place; as deciduous woodland is difficult to burn, the name may refer to charcoal burning.[336] Hasilwood is self-explanatory and could be equally of Old English or Middle English derivation. In the later medieval period Hasilwood and Bernet formed a common wood, much of which became waste. The adjectives intrinsecus and forinsecus may refer to the positions of the two parts in relation to the city of Coventry.

Although the woods of Hasilwood and Bernet must have once covered thousands of acres they do not give a full picture of the extent of the woodland of Coventry before the losses of the later medieval period. From the accounts of the manors of Newland and Whitmore and from the information about other woods in and around Coventry, such as the wood of Sowe, it appears that a large proportion of the area was wooded. The nature, and in particular the density, of that woodland remains an open question. Hasilwood, for example, was said to include the whole vill of Stoke, a place which has an Old English name associated with some kind of habitation in the early medieval period, implying that the pre-Conquest woodland was open enough for some settlement. The sheer size of the later medieval wood of Coventry makes it reasonable to suggest that it formed a significant part of the silva.

The wood of Sowe, or part of it, also had a proper name. The wood (boscum) of Sowe was mentioned in some thirteenth-century documents and, according to the Hundred Rolls of 1279, contained 120 acres of outwood.[337] A deed of c.1300 referred both to the waste of Sowe and to the wood called Schortwode.[338] The Priory's register said that the alternative name of the waste of Sowe or Sowe Woodewast was Schortwod and described tenants' holdings in the waste of the wood of Sowe (in vasto bosci de Sowe).[339]

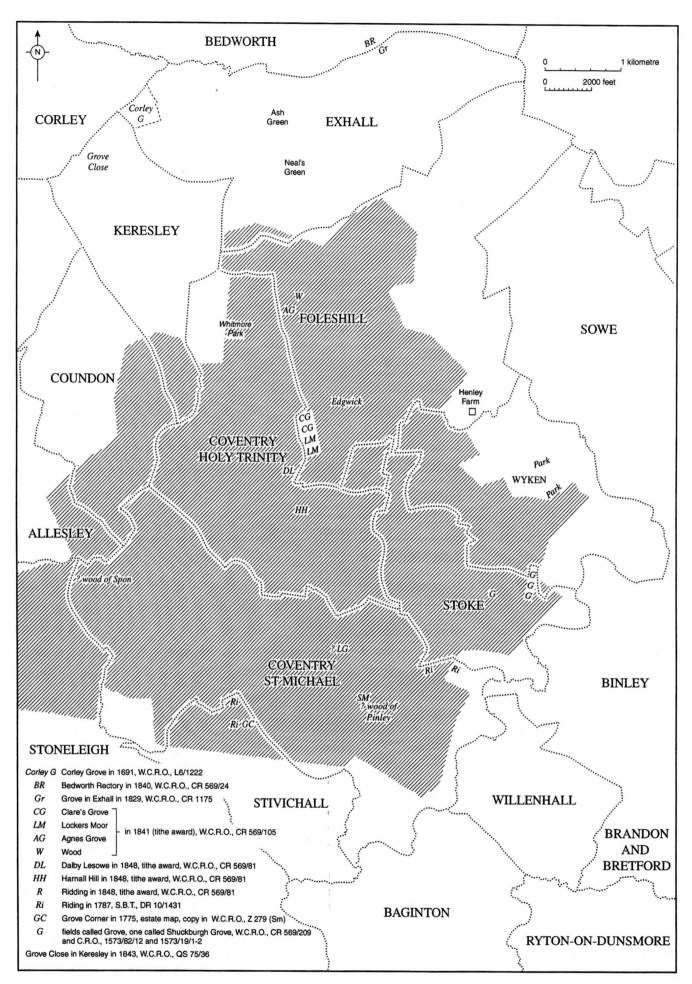

BEDWORTH

CORLEY *Corley G*

Grove Close

Ash Green

EXHALL

SOWE

KERESLEY

Neal's Green

W
AG FOLESHILL

Whitmore Park

COUNDON

Edgwick

Henley Farm

CG
CG
LM
LM COVENTRY HOLY TRINITY

DL

Park WYKEN
Park

HH

ALLESLEY

? wood of Spon

G
G
G
G

STOKE

LG

COVENTRY ST MICHAEL

Ri *Ri*

BINLEY

Ri

SM
? wood of Pinley

STONELEIGH

Ri
Ri GC

Corley G Corley Grove in 1691, W.C.R.O., L6/1222
BR Bedworth Rectory in 1840, W.C.R.O., CR 569/24
Gr Grove in Exhall in 1829, W.C.R.O., CR 1175
CG Clare's Grove ⎤
LM Lockers Moor ⎥ in 1841 (tithe award), W.C.R.O., CR 569/105
AG Agnes Grove ⎥
W Wood ⎦
DL Dalby Lesowe in 1848, tithe award, W.C.R.O., CR 569/81
HH Harnall Hill in 1848, tithe award, W.C.R.O., CR 569/81
R Ridding in 1848, tithe award, W.C.R.O., CR 569/81
Ri Riding in 1787, S.B.T., DR 10/1431
GC Grove Corner in 1775, estate map, copy in W.C.R.O., Z 279 (Sm)
G fields called Grove, one called Shuckburgh Grove, W.C.R.O., CR 569/209 and C.R.O., 1573/82/12 and 1573/19/1-2

Grove Close in Keresley in 1843, W.C.R.O., QS 75/36

STIVICHALL

WILLENHALL

BRANDON AND BRETFORD

BAGINTON

RYTON-ON-DUNSMORE

Figure 24: The Coventry area

The register also recorded that the heir of Richard de Loges (who held part of Sowe in the second half of the thirteenth century[340]) had in the waste of Sowe 160 acres of land formerly wood.[341] This record and the list of tenants' holdings point conclusively to the development of substantial parts of Sowe wood into waste.

field-names in Foleshill in 1841, tithe award, W.C.R.O., CR 569/105

field-names in Sowe in 1844, tithe award, W.C.R.O., CR 569/207

Cliffords Waste in 1778, W.C.R.O., CR 8/184

Mr. Petoes Waste and Ansty Waste Field c. 1600, W.C.R.O., CR 285/56

Welsh Woods in 1778 and 1823, W.C.R.O., CR 8/184, D34

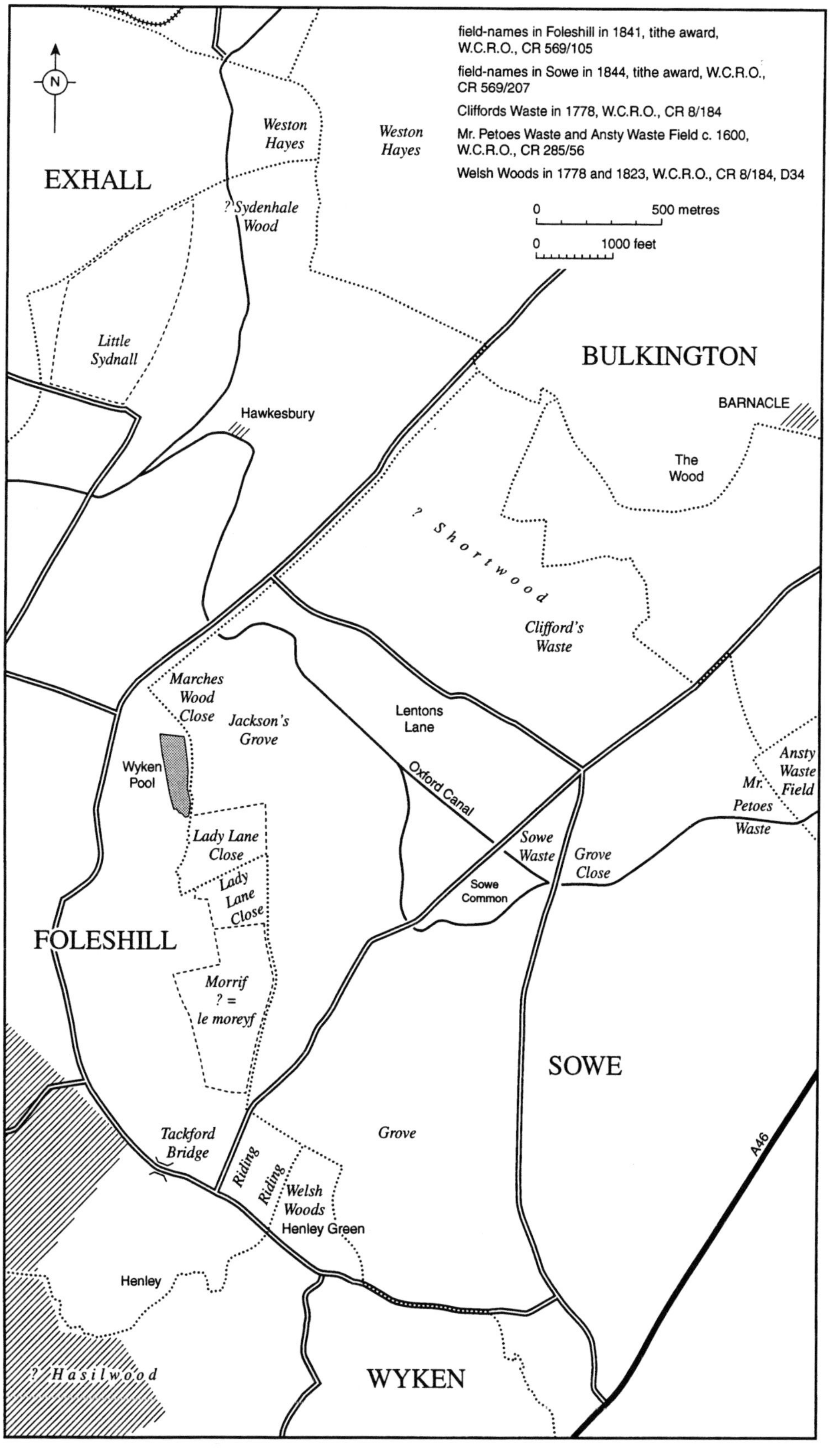

Figure 25: Sowe and Foleshill

The full extent of Sowe's later medieval wood and waste is not evident from the surviving records, which relate mainly to the Priory's holding. The limits to the Priory's lands are reflected in a survey of 1302-3 copied into the register and recording the right to enclose the outer waste of Sowe called *Schortewod*;[342] this implies that there was an inner waste beyond the Priory's control. The register included details of all the Priory's demesne and tenant land created out of the waste and calculated the total arable acreage as 514; the manor as a whole included 758 acres of land and waste.[343] However, the total area of the ecclesiastical parish of Sowe was about 2,500 acres.[344] In 1262 at least part of the wood of Sowe was still held jointly by the Priory and two laymen;[345] the Segrave part of Sowe waste adjoined Barnacle in Bulkington.[346] Shortwood also adjoined an assart of Barnacle.[347] The legal disputes in 1262 and earlier years, the Hundred Rolls and the Priory's register all show that the wood of Sowe was a common wood.[348]

The tradition that Coundon waste was formerly Coundon wood was also recorded in the Priory's register.[349] It also stated that between the waste, formerly wood, and the waste of *holifast* were two wastes called *Herneiswast* and *Bradnokkwast* and an unnamed waste of fifty acres all lying together. This information, matched with field-names on maps of Coundon and Allesley (see Fig. 28) and a survey of lands in Coundon c.1600, enables the waste to be located fairly precisely. In the survey Coundon waste was said to adjoin Keresley Heath;[350] crofts called Waste adjoined Keresley Heath in the early nineteenth century.[351] Holifast was in the north-eastern corner of Allesley, adjoining Coundon.[352] Various grants of new land were made in Coundon wood and waste.[353]

If it is difficult to suggest how the woods of Coventry, Sowe and Coundon matched the *silva* of Domesday Book, it is impossible to say how the other later medieval woods in the area related to the *silva*; however, it is valuable to consider the issues raised by the question. There is good reason to believe that the entry in Domesday Book for Coventry subsumed several other settlements. When the total area of the constituent ecclesiastical parishes and townships - about 22,000 acres[354] - is compared with the estimated extent of the *silva* (c.7,500-10,500 acres) it can be seen that less than half the area, and possibly only one third, was *silva* in 1086. There was certainly enough land to support a number of settlements. Although the sizes of those settlements and of lands attached to them are unknown, it is going too far to state that "most of the district was woodland and waste" until the thirteenth century.[355] Coundon, Sowe and Foleshill were identifiable places by 1086, but they were the subject of separate entries in Domesday Book for reasons which need not have been connected with their size. Coundon and Sowe were entered separately because they were not in the king's hands, Foleshill because it and Ansty were in a different hundred from Coventry. The single entry for Coventry can therefore be attributed simply to tight royal control of the lands formerly held by Countess Godiva; there was no reason to record all the settlements within the manor separately. Most of them were recorded as being in existence by the middle of the twelfth century,[356] less than seventy years after the Domesday survey. If most of the principal later medieval settlements within the Coventry area were identifiable settlements by 1086 they could have had their own woodland as well as fields, meadows and pastures by that date. Some of that woodland might have taken the form of groves.

There were many groves, even allowing for apparent changes in name of some of them. Only a few of their sites can be located. Some, such as those situated south-west and south-east of the city, were outside the main common woods and carried the names of local settlements or manors such as Asthill, Horwell, Shortley and Harnall.[357] Some were associated with minor place-names which are arguably of Old English origin, Bigging, Attoxhale and Hawkesbury.[358] Several were tenants' groves, such as that held by Henry Wolf in Foleshill, by *Dame agnes grove* and Whitmore park, the groves which were part of *Erneysplace* and *Bagotplace* in Sowe and, from their names, presumably three groves belonging to the Drapers' Company in Stoke.[359] The sites of these three groves can be suggested thanks to the preservation of a long series of records of the property of the Drapers' Company, which in 1379 leased a piece of land and three groves of wood called *Harperesgrove*, *corbynsgroue* and *Shukkeburghgroue*, by the Netherplace in Stoke.[360] The name Shuckburgh Grove survived into the eighteenth century, but has been identified with two different fields called Grove, both in Stoke, but one adjacent to Wyken and the other further south.[361] The former field may be the more likely site, because it was divided into three, thus corresponding to the three groves.

Once there is a hint as to the origin of a grove. Permission was given to enclose the alder-grove at Pinley called *Plategrove* and all common rights in it were surrendered.[362] This could be read as confirming the separation and

enclosure of a group of alders in common land or wood. It cannot be assumed that all groves had so recent an origin, but the association of a grove with a holding formed wholly or largely from waste certainly points to the later medieval period for the definition of that grove as a distinct area of woodland. For example, the manor of Hawkesbury was said to be in the waste of Sowe and its grove may therefore have been enclosed from the wood of Sowe before or as that wood became waste.[363]

The groves of Asthill and Horwell may have had a similar origin, for they and the wood called Middlewood were situated in an area from which other woodland was cleared during the later medieval period. There are several records of assarts associated with Asthill.[364] The Gregory Leger Book preserved a rental which included the assarts of Asthill and Horwell, equating them with the site of the manor, laund and park.[365] Successive changes in field-names have hindered identification of the sites of the later medieval settlements, the assarts, and the woodland which remained in the fourteenth and fifteenth centuries. However, some medieval field-names survived into the eighteenth century to be recorded in a deed of 1729, when several had alternative names, and some of these remained in use by the time of the tithe award in 1846.[366]

In 1439 three fields, a meadow and a grove were situated between the common pasture called *hethsale* (Hearsall Common on early modern maps) and a pasture called *middelwode*.[367] They can be matched to five fields on an eighteenth-century estate map[368] and point to the location of Middlewood immediately to the south of those fields. Middlewood was recorded as a wood in an earlier, undated and presumably thirteenth-century deed, but was a field by the fourteenth century, if not earlier.[369] It is not clear which of the five nineteenth-century fields had been Horwell grove; Horwell was described as a "decayed hamlett" in 1593 and the grove had become a field by 1598-9.[370] A deed of 1373 which describes abuttals of fields called *Littelhorwell*, *Atkynscroft* and *Phelippesfeld* suggests some subdivision of land between 1373 and 1439 and refers to a place of wood (*placea bosci*) instead of to a grove.[371] According to the Hundred Rolls, however, there was a grove in Horwell in 1279.[372] Horwell extended further south and west. A field adjoining Canley Brook which was called *Waydursfeld* and *Spencersfeld* after successive owners and which adjoined land of the earl of Lancaster called *Potterscroft* was in Horwell, and in the parish of Stoneleigh the land to the west of Canley Brook was called Horwell waste.[373]

In 1555 a field or pasture called Lodge Field was described as part of the king's demesne belonging to Asthill Grove.[374] Lodge Field appears to have included the field in the south-western corner of Asthill which was called Moat Close in the tithe award and which is shown on the first edition of the six-inch Ordnance Survey map with earthworks at its western edge. In the sixteenth century Lodge Field seems to have extended beyond the area of the nineteenth-century Moat Close, for in a dispute over tithes it was described as adjoining another field and part of Horwell Lane to the north and the wood of Asthill to the east and south.[375] Moat Close is in the right position for the site of the former Asthill park. In 1279 land at *Swetebrugge*, acquired by Stoneleigh Abbey from Thomas de Canele and presumably lying in Stoneleigh parish, was described as under the park of Asthill.[376] It is possible, of course, that the Lodge Field absorbed the site of the former settlement at Asthill.

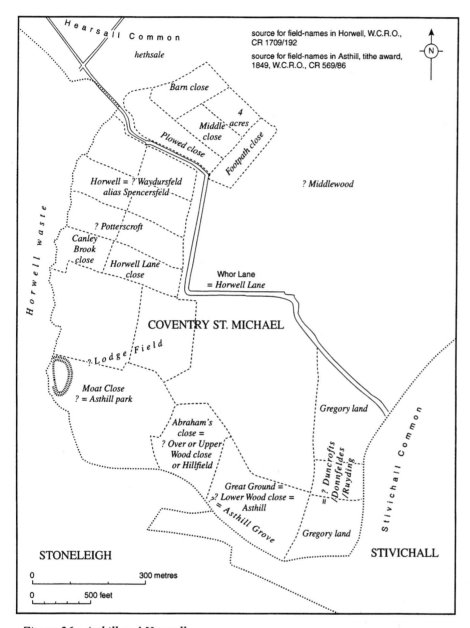

Figure 26: *Asthill and Horwell*

The wood of Asthill which lay to the east and south of Lodge Field in the sixteenth century was arguably Asthill Grove, possibly enlarged since the thirteenth century. A survey of Stivichall dated to c.1580-90 included the "woods and pastures that lye within the hamlett of Astell" and named them as "the grounds called middlewoods, the two duncrofts and Johns Crofte, Crosse Close, Lodge feild...four other closes which lie betwen horwell laine and horr waste.. seaven other closes which lye betwen myddlewoode and hershole... also a grove called Astell Grove".[377] In 1573 and 1620, when they were leased by the Gregory family, the Duncroftes were also called Dunfeildes and Dunrydinges.[378] In 1388, 1396, and 1488 two crofts called *Donnfeldes* and *le*

Ruydyng were described as lying between the Grove of Asthill and the highway leading to *Hethsale* (presumably Hearsall Common).[379] It seems reasonable to suggest that these fields corresponded to the Gregory lands in Asthill in 1787 and at the time of the tithe award.[380] They were on the western side of Stivichall Common. They adjoined fields which can be identified with the fields described in a deed of 1729 as Upper Wood Close alias Hillfield and Lower Wood Close, formerly "Astell Grove".[381] It has been possible, therefore, to suggest the sites of both Middlewood and Asthill Grove.

The woodland of Asthill and Horwell shows not only how completely some medieval woodland vanished from field-names as well as on the ground but also how close the medieval city of Coventry was to woodland. That woodland might have been far more extensive in the twelfth than in the fifteenth century. Middlewood became the name of a field. The name of the field called Ruyding also implied former woodland. It can be suggested that both Hearsall Common and Stivichall Common were once woodland and that Middlewood derived its name from its position between them.

There was woodland to the south-east of Coventry as well as to the south-west. Medieval deeds and some surviving medieval field-names allow the sites of Langley Grove and the wood of Pinley to be suggested with some confidence, although the multiplicity of mills, whose names were changed over the centuries, complicates the identifications.

In 1347 a grove called *Luttelgroue*, which belonged to the Langley family, was described as by the river Sherbourne, and in 1351 as not only by the river but also between *Bussheleymulne* and *Neuwemulne*.[382] In 1357 the small grove which had belonged to Alice de Langley was separated by three pieces of arable land from the garden of the Carmelites.[383] In 1368 the grove next to *Busheleymulne* was called *Langeleygrove*.[384] In 1393 *Longgeley grove* was said to be by St. Anne's Chapel; the site of St. Anne's Carthusian Priory is now called the Charterhouse.[385] Deeds referring to the little grove have been endorsed to the effect that the grove was next to the chapel.[386] The name *Sent Anne grove* was recorded in 1423, but the name *Langeley Grove* reappeared in 1487, when it was separated by fields called *Wriggesden* and *Parkefeld* from *Baronsfeld*.[387] The first two field-names have disappeared, but Baronsfield and the site of

51

Charterhouse are on the tithe map[388] and it therefore seems that Langley Grove, formerly Little Grove, lay somewhere between them. The grove might also have been known as the grove of Shortley, which was said to be by the wood of Coventry in 1262 and whose timber was the subject of indentures in 1350, because Charterhouse was founded in Shortley field.[389]

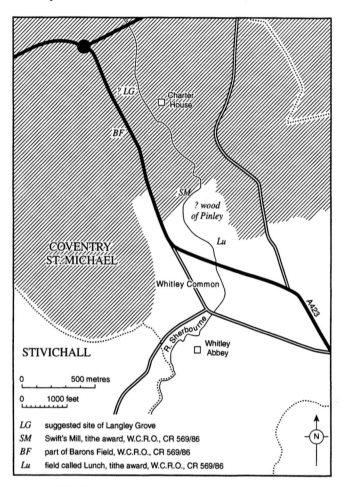

Figure 27: Pinley

The wood of Pinley (to be distinguished from the Pinley Wood between Rowington and Claverdon) was originally a common wood; Geoffrey de Langley's tenants at Pinley surrendered their common rights in the wood of Pinley in 1237.[390] In 1251 Geoffrey was granted a licence to enclose a way between his houses in Pinley and his wood there for the enlargement of his park and to make a park from his wood.[391] It has been claimed that the wood or park was only five acres in extent,[392] but the entry in the Hundred Rolls of 1279-80 from which this figure is taken stated that there were five acres of land[393] and therefore could have referred to arable land within the wood. The mill of Stifford was under the wood of Pinley.[394] Stifford Mill has been identified variously with Dilcock's Mill and Swift's Mill.[395] If the latter identification is taken, the site of Stifford Mill can be derived from Swift's Mill on the tithe map. That map also preserves the name Lunch,[396] arguably a corruption of *Linch/Lynche*, which in 1383 reached to a new ditch under the park of Pinley.[397] The wood presumably lay between the mill and the Linch. In 1317 there was also a grove by *Stiffordesmulne*; in 1343 it was called a small grove

(*Grouetum*).[398] In 1610 parcels of land near Swift's Mill were described as former groves of wood.[399]

Another grove in the area was called *Plategrove*, associated with part of the Linch and situated towards the southern part of *Alruneford* and between the bridge of *Alreneford* and the croft of Whitley Mill; in one deed it was called an alder-grove (*alnetum*) and may therefore have been the unnamed alder grove in Pinley in 1241.[400] It may have been the grove next to Alderford Mill in 1476.[401] Whitley itself had a grove in the middle of the thirteenth century; it was held by Juel Belinger of Walter de Daivilla.[402]

The existence of tenants' groves is an additional dimension to Allesley's later medieval woodland. Allesley, once part of Coventry parish,[403] was not recorded separately in Domesday Book. It has been said of Allesley that in 1279-80 it was "perhaps the nearest to a 'classical manor' that the locality produced", being "entirely coincident with the vill" and having a wood of forty acres and a park.[404] The evidence for Allesley's later medieval woodland shows that this picture of one manor, one wood, was false. There were several demesne woods, namely *asshawe, holifast, Bolewellshauwe, Estendmor, Suffagegrove* and *Orchard*. The first was recorded as early as 1208, the second in 1305, and these two and the next three in a survey of 1325.[405]

Deeds dating from 1300 show the lord of the manor obtaining surrender of common rights in wastes and woods from tenants.[406] In 1305 he and the prior of Coventry agreed to the mutual surrender of their and their tenants' common rights in the woods, wastes, moors, alder-groves etc. of Allesley and Coundon.[407] Grants of waste land were made in 1298-1300.[408] The loss of woodland is also suggested by a separate, demesne field called *Allesleywaste* in a survey of 1392.[409]

The sizes of Allesley's demesne woods were given in surveys of 1325 and 1392,[410] which show variations in acreages, but there is no information on the extent of thirteenth-century woods, leave alone twelfth- or eleventh-century woodland. The woods were not concentrated in one part of Allesley, although the number of early modern woods in the north-eastern corner suggests the presence of a large area of woodland in the medieval period. As noted in the description of Coundon's woodland above, the adjoining *Holifast* was presumably in the area of Allesley marked Hollyfast on nineteenth-century maps.[411] The wood called *Asshawe* adjoined Coundon on one side and Whoberley on another. The boundary of Coundon is said to have run through the middle of *Asshawe*. The wood must therefore have occupied the south-eastern corner of Allesley.[412]

Allesley's manorial surveys give no hint of the woodland beyond the demesne. The manorial accounts of 1467-8 mentioned *hunygrove*.[413] The chance survival of a document dating from 1441-2 and listing the lands held by William Nilder shows that the holding of this tenant included two groves.[414] A survey of Allesley in 1626 reveals a countryside full of small woods and groves,[415]

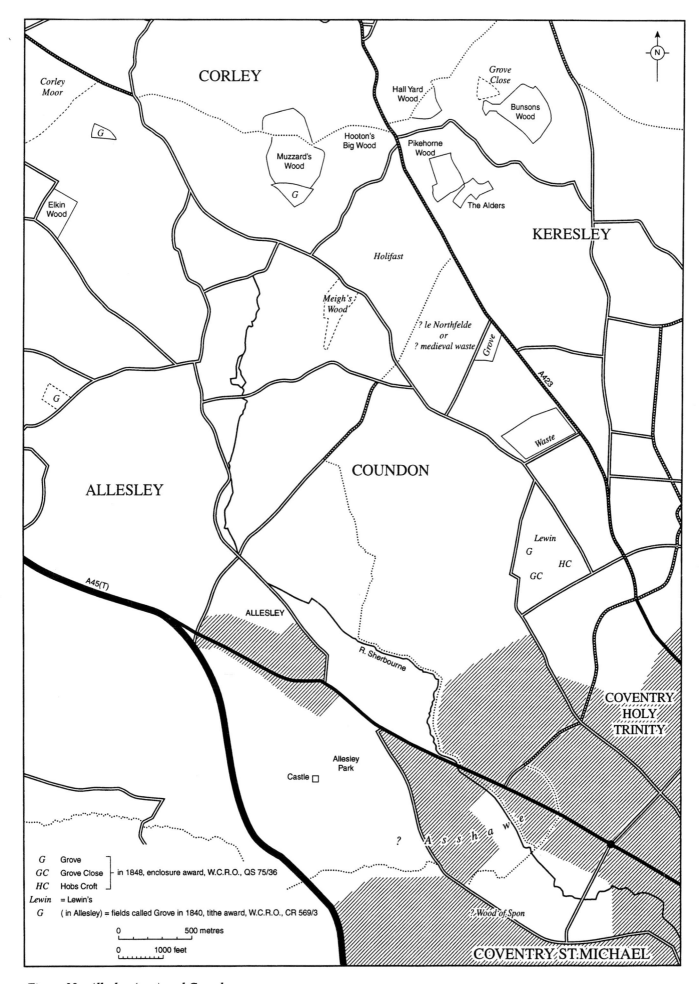

Figure 28: Allesley (east) and Coundon

which may have been a legacy of the later medieval period. Few medieval field- and wood-names seem to have survived to be recorded on modern maps, so it is not possible to suggest locations for the recorded medieval woods and groves other than *Asshawe* and *Holifast*, although fields called grove are likely sites.

Keresley seems to exemplify the way in which the development of secondary woodland can obscure the nature and extent of later medieval woods. Most of the later medieval deeds which deal with land in Keresley fail to mention woodland. There are references to the *Erleswode*,[416] but this adjoined Keresley to the east, being in Exhall or Whitmore. In 1411 the Priory's register stated that part of Keresley's waste was below the park of Whitmore.[417] Spurious deeds in the register refer to the tradition that 280 acres of wood and waste in Keresley and Exhall were given to the Priory and formed the manor of Newland.[418] The shape of the north-eastern boundary of Keresley certainly makes the claim plausible (Fig. 28).

Robert Scraptoft[420] may have formed the nucleus of *gret bonson* and *lytyll bonson copy* which were recorded in a survey of Keresley's demesne woods dated to 1520-26.[421] It may be significant that the proper names of those woods did not include the words wood or grove; some were called coppices or *copy*. Secondary woodland is suggested by an acre of wood and underwood called *le longeacre* in 1411;[422] in the survey of 1520-6 there was a wood called simply long acre containing twelve acres. In 1411 William Northcroft held an acre and a rood called *le Northcroftished* which was enclosed and planted with wood (*inclusam & cum bosco plantatam*) and in or near the waste of Keresley.[423] The shapes of the modern woods in the west of Keresley,[424] with sinuous lines reminiscent of the curve of arable furlongs (see Fig. 28), suggest that some of them were, in part at least, secondary woodland. In 1411 there were three groves in Keresley in lands called *le harselhull*, *le Bernecroft* and *le Wesyndenthyng*,[425] but there is no record of them subsequently. Grove Close may mark the site of one of them.

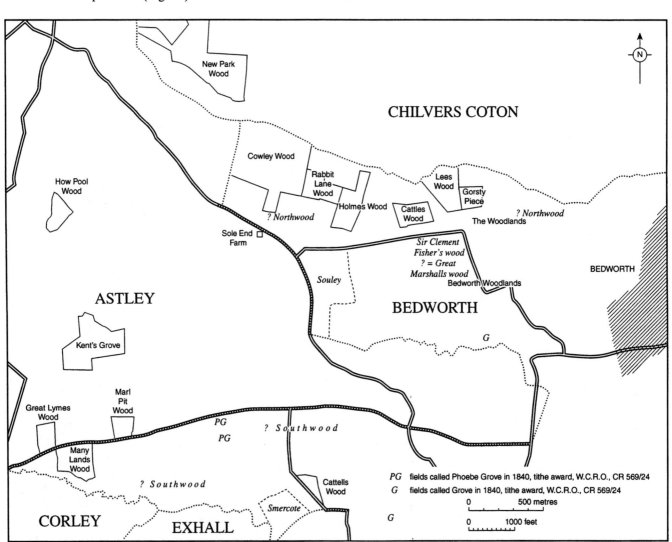

Figure 29: Bedworth

In the thirteenth century Richard Bounce of Keresley received an acre of new assart by the prior's waste.[419] The Bounce family may have given their name to Bunson's Wood. The grove given to the Priory by Elias Buns' and

Bedworth

Domesday Book attributed to Bedworth *silva* measuring one league by half a league and a similar amount in total to

Smercote and *Soulege*.[426]   These two places can be identified with the parts of Bedworth parish which protrude westwards and which were arguably the sites of the two later medieval woods which were called *le Northwode* and *le Suthwode* in 1270.[427] Smercote survives as a minor place-name in the south-west of the parish. *Soulege* is the name of fields in the north-west, near to Sole End in Astley with which the Domesday entry has normally been identified.[428] A reference in 1240 to land in Chilvers Coton in the field towards *souleg*[429] supports the link with Bedworth, for Chilvers Coton adjoins Bedworth but not Sole End in Astley. Both Domesday entries use the phrase *cum oneratur*, which is discussed in Chapter Four.

The suggested site for the Northwood is supported by several pieces of documentary evidence. Part of the Northwood lay towards the wood of the prior of Arbury;[430] the priory held much land in Chilvers Coton and its wood may have been *Herewardeshay*, part of which seems to have been destroyed and part of which might have been taken into the modern park, which is near to Bedworth. The endorsement of another deed refers to a wood called the Hook, which the deed itself describes as land in the wood of Bedworth. The name seems to have survived in the Towns end Hook which was part of Cattels Wood in 1702; Cattles Wood appears on modern maps.[431] In 1315 land in Northwood in the fields of Bedworth was said to adjoin *Foukeruydyngg*,[432] a name which also survived to appear on maps of Chilvers Coton. Land in Northwood Field in 1696 belonged to a family called Jephcott; Jeffcoats land is shown on a contemporary sketch map of the Bedworth Woodlands area.[433]

Although Northwood was described as a wood (*quodam bosco*) in 1440, earlier deeds show that there was land within it which was not wooded; one deed, dated 1270, stated specifically that parts of it had been assarted and, by reference to all the assarts in Bedworth, implied that there were assarts elsewhere.[434] There was common pasture in both Northwood and Southwood.[435] No deeds have survived relating to grants of land within the Southwood, but there is a reference to assarts in Smercote.[436]

Other woods in Bedworth might originally have been part of the Northwood. A deed of 1275-6 referred to the wood called *Calue'croft* next to the wood of Thomas son of Peter de monte on the one side and the wood formerly of Robert michel on the other.[437] The name michel may have been preserved in the name of Great Marshalls Wood, which in 1633-4 belonged to Robert Fisher;[438] a map of 1696 shows Sir Clement Fisher's wood in Bedworth.[439] The land around was the subject of enclosure shown on a rough sketch map in 1695,[440] but the wood on the map of 1696 is arguably Great Marshalls Wood and so also gives the approximate site of the wood called *Calue'croft*. The area called Bedworth Woodlands on modern maps therefore reflects the location of medieval woods. The Hospital of St. John the Baptist in Coventry held the wood called *le Oxewodde*, which appears to have been near to Smercote ford and Corley Brook.[441] Independent confirmation of the existence and location of this wood can be found in the Register of Coventry Cathedral Priory, which includes in its detailed description of the bounds of Corley an *Oxewodwey* near to Smercote.[442]

Two groves were recorded in the sixteenth century,[443] but no earlier reference to them has been found.

Chilvers Coton

In 1086 Chilvers Coton had a large area of *silva* measuring one and a half leagues by a league and probably covering between 1,500 and 2,150 acres.[444] The area of the ecclesiastical parish of Chilvers Coton was 4,180 acres[445] and included Arbury and Griff, neither of which was mentioned in Domesday Book.

Most later medieval records relating to lands in the parish date from the thirteenth century and subsequently. From the thirteenth century onwards there are records of a foreign wood, several named and unnamed woods and six groves.[446] The evidence suggests that most of the woodland was in the western part of the parish.

A wood called the *hudells* was mentioned in the twelfth century, when half of it was granted to Arbury Priory.[447] Land and wood called *Hudells* - perhaps the other half? - were granted to William de Sees and may therefore have become the later Seeswood.[448] *Herewardeshay* incorporated the name of another local family. It was the subject of deeds dated 1234 and 1253-4 and of a lawsuit in 1341.[449] It was next to *mulnefeld* and not far from the road to Astley,[450] but its name did not survive to appear in early modern surveys or maps, nor did the wood appear in a survey of Priory lands taken at the Dissolution.[451] Part of it might have become New Park Wood and part might have been the wood of the prior which a thirteenth-century deed described as by Bedworth.[452] New park was in existence by 1491 and adjoined Windmill Field (=?the medieval *mulnefeld*) on early modern maps.[453]

Chilvers Coton provides evidence for matching the English noun outwood with the Latin *boscus forinsecus* - foreign wood - and equating both with common woodland. The Priory's wood called *le kedyng* was near to the foreign wood of John de Sudeley, lord of Griff.[454] *Cesewode* was near to the *Owtewode* in 1468, when the latter was said to be in Griff.[455] Both Spring Kidding Wood and Seeswood, which presumably preserve the names of these two medieval woods, appear on early modern maps by Coton Outwoods.[456] There are records of Coton Outwoods as a common in 1601-2, 1606 and 1685.[457] Two deeds refer to the wood of the lord of Griff which was next to *Horselebrok*; Horseley brook was by *Abellspeese*, which in turn is shown as by Seeswood and the outwood.[458] It seems, therefore, that this wood and the foreign wood were the same. Arbury Priory was granted land there for a piggery.[459]

There are no clues to the origins of the six groves recorded in the later medieval period. Seven others which are named in sixteenth-century documents may have existed in earlier centuries or may include some of the recorded medieval groves under new names.[460] The wood (*bosco*) called

Nythtynggalegrove,[461] if it does not take its name from a person, must owe its name to nightingales, which like thickets of underwood of several years' growth.

5,000 acres. In the later medieval period the ecclesiastical parish also included the townships of Stockingford, Attleborough and Horston; in the nineteenth century it covered 6,112 acres.[463] These figures suggest that more

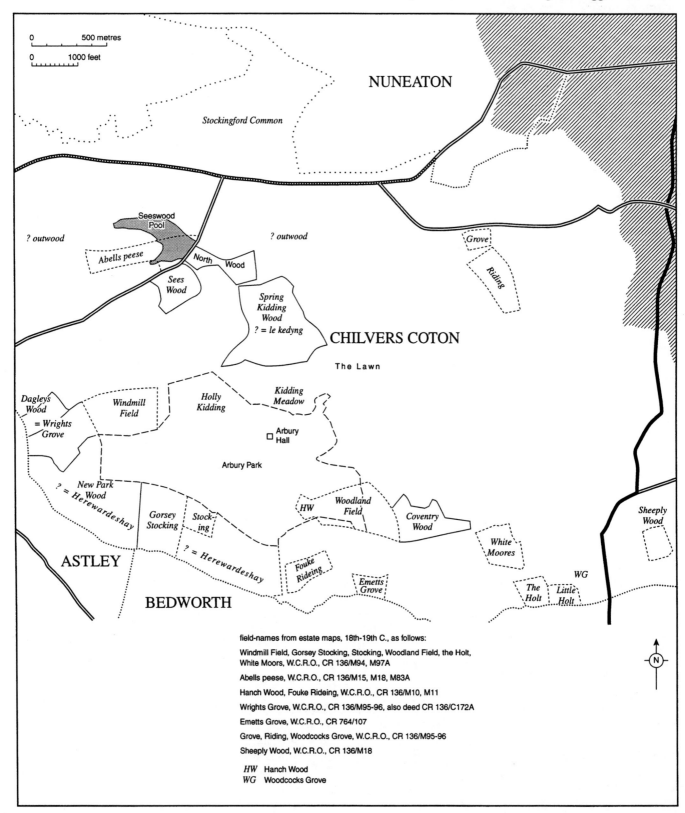

Figure 30: Chilvers Coton

Nuneaton

In 1086 there were about three and half square leagues of *silva* in Nuneaton,[462] amounting, say, to between 3,500 and

than half the area was wooded in 1086.

From the late fourteenth and early fifteenth centuries there are some detailed records for Nuneaton Abbey's woods. Accounts record sales of wood and timber and the cost of fencing or refencing woods.[464] Although most of those woods seem to have been enclosed by the late fourteenth century, there was an earlier tradition of wood pasture. In 1330 it was claimed that William Jabet had been deprived of his common pasture in eighty acres of wood in Nuneaton and Stockingford.[465]

With the exception of Horston Wood most of the Abbey's recorded woodland was concentrated in the western part of the parish. Many of the medieval woodland names have disappeared, but enough remain to point to the approximate locations of the named woods. Information in the Abbey's accounts about juxtaposed woods or other topographical features has been used together with sixteenth-century surveys, eighteenth-century maps and the tithe map to estimate the position of the woods.

The starting points have been the Hanch and John's Wood and the extent of Nuneaton and Stockingford Commons on the enclosure award of 1806.[466] If these commons were the remains of medieval common woodland and waste they would have been outside the Abbey's enclosed woods. The *Hanch* or *Haunch* was a wood in 1368-9 and in 1842, when the nearby closes called John's Wood presumably marked the site of the later medieval wood called *Joniswode*.[467] The wood called *Hanchemor* was next to the *Hanch*. John's Wood was separated from a close called *Haunche* by another close called *mussepole*.[468] The *Outwode*, arguably corresponding to the modern Nuneaton Common, was by John's Wood, *merilindewode* and *hardecnol* and *heathfield*; *merilindewode* also adjoined a wood called *Hacking*.[469] As the Dugdale family owned land called *Murlyne* in Stockingford in 1644, it can be suggested that the part of the Dugdale lands which adjoined Nuneaton and Stockingford

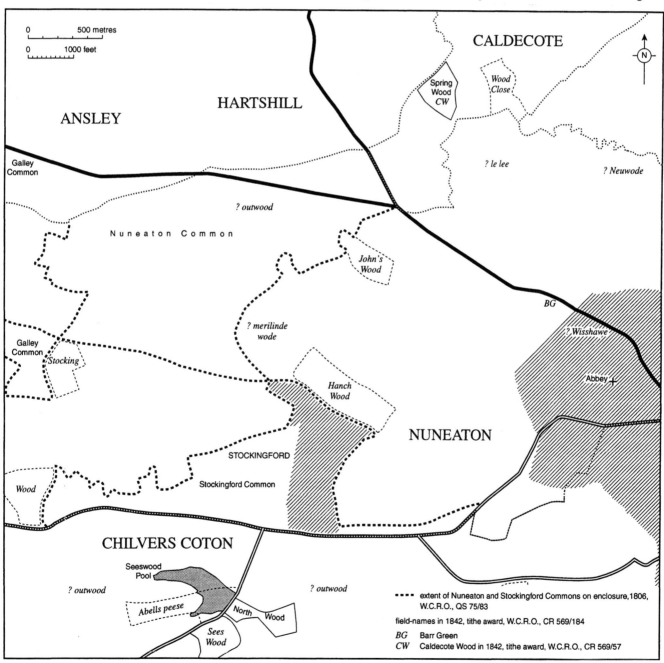

Figure 31: *Nuneaton and Caldecote Wood*

Common in the tithe award included the site of the former *merilindewode*.[470] *Hardecnol* was between the park of Hartshill and *le lee*[471] and therefore on the northern boundary of Nuneaton. Part of *le lee* abutted directly on to the park of Hartshill; it also adjoined *Neuwode* and *Caldecotewode* (presumably in Caldecote to the north), and in the thirteenth century was divided from the river Anker by an assart.[472] Presumably *Nethurle*, *Overle*, *Middelle* and perhaps also the wood called *Neusonle* were parts of *le lee*; *middelle* adjoined *le Whitefurlong*.[473] By the sixteenth century the great ley was east of the outwood and of a road leading from Hartnall gate to Atherstone.[474]

There was a gate called *Blakewatergate* by the *Hanch* and by a wood called *Neutakenhyn*; *Blakwater* was itself a wood.[475] *Neutakenhyn* adjoined a meadow called *le Stocking*, *Blacwater* field and the outwood.[476] The *Neuwode* was not only by *le lee* but also not far from Weddington bridge[477] and presumably therefore to the north of the borough of Nuneaton. A wood called *Wisshawe* in 1400-2 may have become the pasture called *Wyshawe* which in 1543 was within the precinct of the court of the Abbey up to *barre grene*.[478] The wood called *le Clos* was under the vill of Nuneaton.[479] The wood called *Allers* was in Stockingford field under the *Closwal* towards *Wickaycross*.[480] *Haliwellesiche* was by John's Wood and the middle pool, which in turn was by Blackwater field.[481] The *Hywod* or *Hiwode* has not been located; it was at *le merehukus*.[482]

Stockingford formed a large area in the west of the ecclesiastical parish, and the absence of detailed records of land there, even for the fourteenth and fifteenth centuries, further limits the information on the history of Nuneaton's woodland. Woods in Stockingford called *Newhay* and *Nettlebeddesmoor*[483] did not belong to Nuneaton Abbey.

There is evidence of the conversion of both wood and waste to agriculture. In the sixteenth century pastures called *Countes Wood* and *Hyrdmanys grove* presumably marked the sites of medieval woods; the former was within the close of the monastery and was separated from Hanch Wood by Blackwaterfield.[484] Some thirteenth-century charters refer to a field or cultivated land in woods called variously *silva Jocelini*, *bosco Jocelini* and *Godsalmes Wood*.[485] Robert fitz Jocelin was one of the early benefactors of Nuneaton Abbey; woods were included in his gifts,[486] but the location of the land taken out of the *silva Jocelini* and *bosco Jocelini* is not known. There were assarts between the river and the wood called *le lee*.[487] In a rental of 1335[488] under the heading of *Eton citra aquam* - Nuneaton this side of the water - there were twelve tenancies which included increments of waste (*cum incremento vasti*), twenty-eight free tenancies of waste anciently ploughed (*libere tenentes de Vasto antiquato arrento*) and another thirteen tenancies of similarly ancient waste. Some tenants for life also held pieces of waste. There was no reference to woodland within any of these tenancies. Some waste was left uncultivated. In the sixteenth century the various named parts of a wood called the *wastewood* amounted to two hundred acres.[489]

This could have been secondary woodland which had regenerated on the waste.

Caldecote

The ecclesiastical parish of Caldecote covered just over 686 acres,[490] an area far too small to contain the three square leagues of *silva* entered under the bishop of Chester's manor of Caldecote in Domesday Book. That amount of *silva* could have covered nine or ten thousand acres. Other parishes in the vicinity had their own entries in Domesday Book and the other two manors held by the bishop, Farnborough and Tachbrook, contained in total about four and a half thousand acres. The only plausible explanation for the entry under Caldecote was a scribal error in attributing to it the *silva* from another manor or in writing leagues for furlongs. An area of woodland roughly three furlongs square would have covered up to 120 acres, a reasonable size in view of the area of the parish. In 1839 Caldecote Wood, called Spring Wood on the later Ordnance Survey maps, was less than twenty acres in extent,[491] but in the later medieval period the wood of Caldecote adjoined the northern edge of Nuneaton parish.[492] There was a tradition of wood pasture, as shown by a legal dispute heard in 1261-2.[493] However, the wood recorded in an inquisition post mortem in 1364 was enclosed.[494]

Atherstone, Oldbury and Mancetter

The Domesday Book entry for Atherstone included four square leagues of *silva*,[495] which arguably belonged also to Mancetter and Oldbury (places within the same parish as Atherstone but omitted from Domesday Book) and to Hartshill and Ansley. They had no *silva* in 1086[496] but woodland was recorded there in the later medieval period and they too were townships within the parish of Mancetter.

Records of medieval woodland in Atherstone, Oldbury and Mancetter are sparse, but are useful for establishing a link between outwoods and commons. Legal proceedings recorded in 1231 referred to the wood of Mancetter.[497] A deed of 1234 referred to the outwood of Mancetter, the wood of *Crumpeleg* and the parks of *Armele* and *Morleg* and stated that there was common pasture in the lord's woods and parks.[498] The locations of the woods and parks of Mancetter are uncertain (there is no estate or tithe map of the whole township), but it can be suggested that the area called Mancetter park in 1775[499] preserved one of the medieval parks. The wood of *Crumpeleg* was between *Merestrete* and *Warlauwesmede* and Coventry way and the meadow of the villeins of Mancetter. *Merestrete*, the boundary street, appears in a deed relating to Oldbury (see below) and was presumably the road which marks the eastern boundary of Mancetter and Oldbury and the western boundary of Hartshill. The references to meadows suggest that the wood was not far from a river; Woodford Bridge over the River Anker may therefore take its name from the wood of *Crumpeleg*.

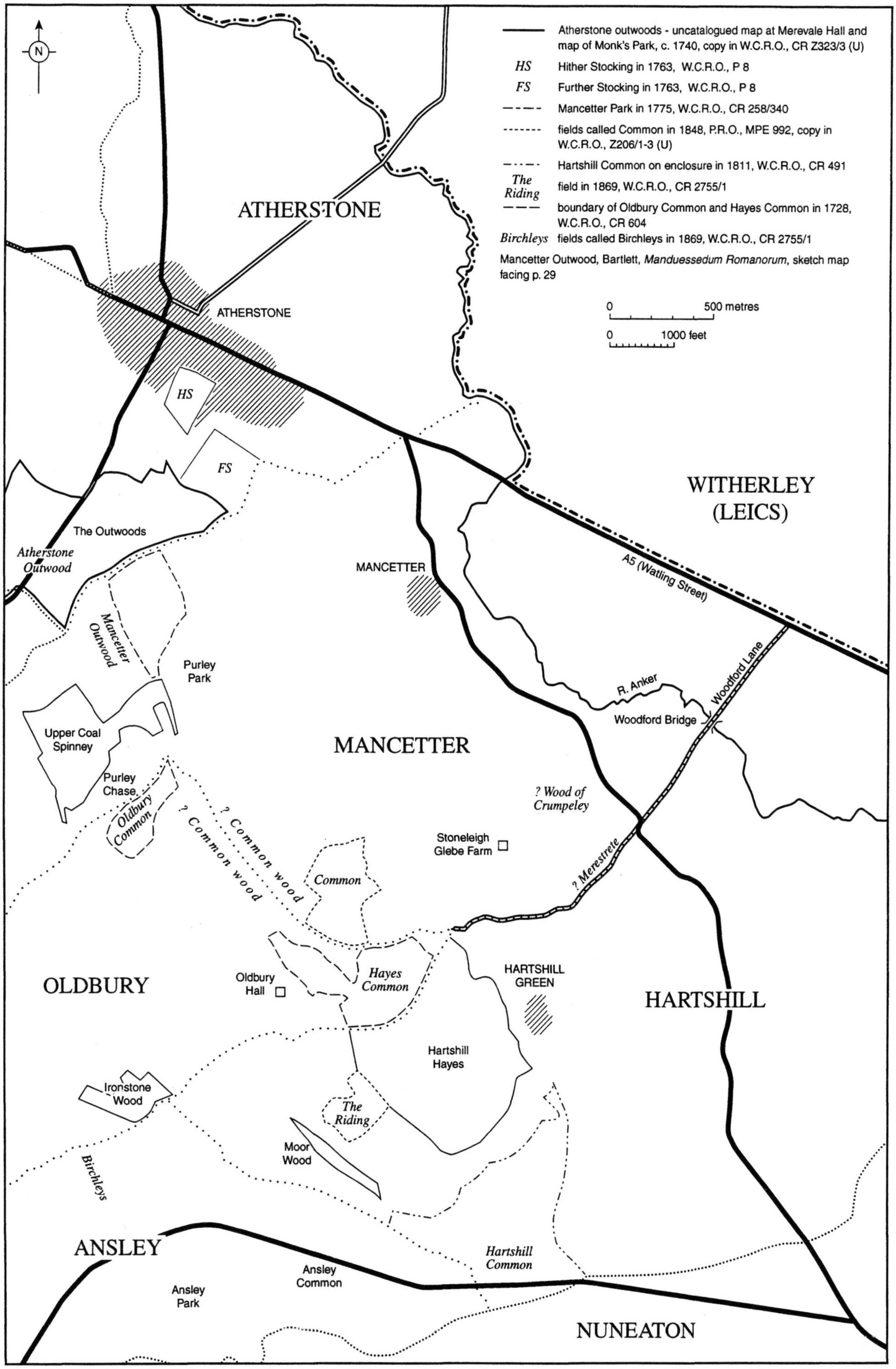
N
Atherstone outwoods - uncatalogued map at Merevale Hall and map of Monk's Park, c. 1740, copy in W.C.R.O., CR Z323/3 (U)
HS Hither Stocking in 1763, W.C.R.O., P 8
FS Further Stocking in 1763, W.C.R.O., P 8
Mancetter Park in 1775, W.C.R.O., CR 258/340
fields called Common in 1848, P.R.O., MPE 992, copy in W.C.R.O., Z206/1-3 (U)
Hartshill Common on enclosure in 1811, W.C.R.O., CR 491
The Riding field in 1869, W.C.R.O., CR 2755/1
boundary of Oldbury Common and Hayes Common in 1728, W.C.R.O., CR 604
Birchleys fields called Birchleys in 1869, W.C.R.O., CR 2755/1
Mancetter Outwood, Bartlett, Manduessedum Romanorum, sketch map facing p. 29
0 500 metres
0 1000 feet
ATHERSTONE
ATHERSTONE
HS
FS
WITHERLEY (LEICS)
The Outwoods
Atherstone Outwood
MANCETTER
A5 (Watling Street)
Mancetter Outwood
Purley Park
R. Anker
Woodford Lane
Woodford Bridge
Upper Coal Spinney
MANCETTER
Purley Chase
Oldbury Common
? Common wood
? Common wood
? Wood of Crumpeley
Stoneleigh Glebe Farm
Common
? Merestrete
OLDBURY
Oldbury Hall
Hayes Common
HARTSHILL GREEN
HARTSHILL
Hartshill Hayes
Ironstone Wood
The Riding
Moor Wood
Birchleys
ANSLEY
Hartshill Common
Ansley Common
Ansley Park
NUNEATON

Figure 32: Atherstone, Oldbury, Mancetter, Hartshill

The outwood and the outwoods of the other townships are easier to locate. Atherstone Outwoods were recorded in 1547.[500] The extent of the eighteenth-century Atherstone outwood, and the location of fields called Stocking[501] suggest that most of the manor south of Watling Street was once woodland and that some of the woodland was cleared in the later medieval period. The customs of Atherstone manor (recorded no later than 1248) referred to a wood which bore nuts for collection and mast for pannage.[502]

Two leases of a parcel of wood in the outwood of Oldbury in 1538[503] establish that the outwood of Mancetter adjoined the outwood of Oldbury and Hartshill park. In the late eighteenth century it also adjoined Atherstone Outwood.[504] Matched against a map of Oldbury drawn in 1728[505] and the first edition of the Ordnance Survey one-inch maps, the leases show that part of the sixteenth-century outwood of Mancetter and the outwood of Oldbury became the eighteenth-century commons. The name Common survives in Mancetter. The location of the woods suggests that they once stretched across most of the ridge of high ground running from north-west to south-east across the parish.

A charter describing the location of land and wood in Oldbury has been attributed to the reign of Henry I (1100-35).[506] It recorded a grant by Walter de Hastings to Polesworth Abbey of the site of Oldbury and all Stipershull, including fields and woods, down to the midst of the valley on that side of Mancetter, also part of the wood south-east of Oldbury extending to the brook coming down from Hartshill and grounds called Calvecroft and Birchley between Mere street and Birchley street to Hugh's wood in circumference. The Hugh was Hugh de Hardreshull, but the location of Calfes croft and Birchley on a map of Oldbury dated 1728 and of Birchleys on a map of Ansley dated 1869-70[507] suggests that Hugh's wood was in Ansley rather than in Hartshill. The Hardreshull family held land in Ansley.[508]

Hartshill and Ansley

Hartshill had three demesne woods in 1276, called *suthhaye*, *le Hokehaie* and *le Neuhaye*; there was pasture in all three, although only in *le Neuhaye* was it common pasture, and all were subject to pannage.[509] The description in 1403 of the wood called *Hardreshull Hay* as next to the manor and vill of Hartshill[510] fits the site of the modern Hartshill Hayes.

Some of Hartshill's woodland was common and had become waste by the end of the thirteenth century. In 1296 William de Harderdeshull granted to Henry Ynge three acres of land in the common of his waste (*in common' de Wasto meo*) in the wood of Hartshill.[511] The grant reserved mineral rights in the event of coal (*carbo maris*) being found on the land and promised recompense to the grantee. Hartshill Common, shown on the enclosure map dated 1808,[512] adjoined Hartshill Hayes. The services of customary tenants included collecting nuts for one day.[513]

Hartshill park was to the south-east of Oldbury, whose outwood it adjoined in 1538.[514] It stretched to the boundary of Nuneaton, as shown by accounts kept by Nuneaton

Abbey; there was a hedge between the Abbey's wood called *le lee* and the park of Hartshill in 1401-2.[515] In 1372-3 there was a hedge between a wood of Hartshill and a wood of Nuneaton,[516] suggesting that the park was wooded. If the park had originally been woodland, there must have been an extensive block of woodland in the south of Hartshill stretching into Nuneaton.

A court roll of 1376 recorded under Hartshill a fine for cutting down trees in a certain grove (*in quadam Groua*).[517] The document gives no indication of the site, size or ownership of the grove, but as it also referred to trees in *le hay* and *le sowthay* it implied that the grove was distinct from these woods.

A tradition of common pasture in at least some of Ansley's woodland is apparent from a dispute recorded in 1246-7.[518] There is a separate record of the wood of Ansley in the same year (murder had been committed there).[519] A wood in Ansley granted to Henry de Lilleburne in the thirteenth century was still woodland in 1413; it lay between two fields and was near to the highway leading to Coventry.[520] The relationship between the wood of Henry de Lilleburne and the hundred acres of woodland which were attributed to Ansley in the late thirteenth century[521] is not known. A thirteenth-century grant of two assarts (totalling seven acres)[522] shows that there was some clearance of woodland in Ansley. The reference to woodland adjoining Calvecroft and Birchley in Oldbury (see above) suggests that at least some of Ansley's woodland was on the northern boundary of the later parish west of the modern Ansley Common. Mineral rights were reserved in a grant of land in the waste of *Bircheley* in Ansley,[523] presumably in the vicinity of the modern Birchleys. One of the two woods recorded in 1411 called *Astonestray* and *Monewod*[524] can be located approximately in the south-western corner of Ansley, by Monwood Lea.

As suggested above, an explanation for the absence of *silva* from Hartshill and Ansley in Domesday Book is that all the *silva* for the five townships of Mancetter parish was entered under Atherstone. The areas of Ansley (2,694 acres) and Hartshill (1,465 acres),[525] when added to those of Mancetter, Oldbury and Atherstone, give a total of just over seven thousand acres, against which four or five thousand acres of *silva* is a more realistic figure than when it is set against any lesser combination. It is also a figure which suggests that a large proportion of Mancetter parish was wooded in the eleventh century.

Merevale

The pattern of extensive woods and the tradition of wood pasture were continued further west. There were at least one hundred acres of wood pasture in Merevale in 1260,[526] perhaps the *meryvall outwode* of 1437-8.[527] Despite the existence of Merevale Abbey there are few records of woodland in Merevale in the later medieval period; no cartulary for the Abbey has been located and the surviving account book, including a rental for 1497-8, dates from the very end of the period.[528] Domesday Book did not mention

Merevale. Although the medieval records give no clues to the location of woodland, it seems reasonable to suggest that the outwood may have occupied part of the area south of the modern Merevale Hall, adjoining Atherstone outwood and Bentley Common.

Grendon

Domesday Book attributed a square league of *silva* to Grendon.[529] The wood of Grendon was mentioned in 1221-2 and 1261-2.[530] In 1273 the widow of Robert de Grendon sued Ralph de Grendon for a third of a messuage, four carucates of land, a water mill, fifty acres of park, three hundred acres of wood, a fishery and £10 of rent in Grendon.[531] In the thirteenth century there were assarts in the wood, between Watling Street and the watercourse or channel (*doetum*) descending from *haselhurst*.[532] Other assarts were near to the wood by Watling Street and there was common pasture in the adjoining waste.[533] The present Grendon Common, now a rare survival of lowland heath in Warwickshire, was separated from Watling Street by fields called Ridding,[534] so it seems likely that the Common marks part of the site of the medieval wood. Both the tithe award and an earlier estate map[535] include fields with wood, common and waste names. There were also assarts in the township of Whittington, presumably marked by fields called stocking in the tithe award.[536]

Grendon provides another example of the link between outwoods and commons. A court roll of 1564 referred to the common of Grendon called *Grendon outewoddys*.[537] In 1571 an arbitration award included common rights in Grendon Wood.[538]

Polesworth, Freasley and Baddesley Ensor

References to later medieval woodland are very sparse for much of Polesworth parish, which also included the townships of Baddesley Ensor, Bramcote, Dordon, Freasley, Pooley and Warton. Polesworth was omitted from Domesday Book and the entry for *Bedeslei*[539] could refer either to Baddesley Ensor or to Baddesley Clinton. For Polesworth Abbey, like Merevale Abbey, no cartulary is known.[540]

Sir William Dugdale found references to assarts of wood in Polesworth, a wood in Pooley which included St. Edith's Well and was imparked in 1506, and wood in Dordon.[541] There were separate records of woods in Pooley and Polesworth in 1285 and in Dordon c.1300.[542] A survey of Polesworth Abbey's woods in 1545[543] included three coppices, *Newe taken in, Sheldon* and *lytwood*, also *parke wood, Bearley wood*, and *Echells Common*. A map of Dordon drawn in 1722 shows several waste names;[544] there are medieval deeds referring to waste in Dordon[545] which might have been former woodland.

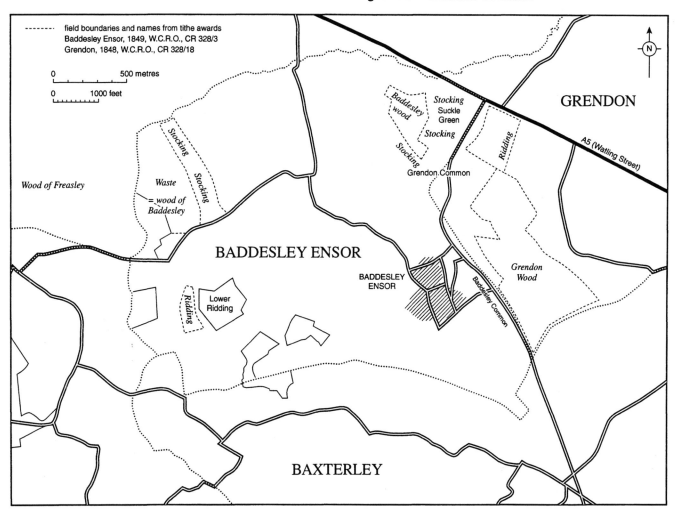

Figure 33: Grendon Wood and Baddesley Ensor

From this very limited information Polesworth's woodland seems to have shared with neighbouring parishes characteristics such as woods, coppices, assarts, commons and waste. The detailed information about Freasley's wood, recorded during a protracted legal dispute in the thirteenth century, amply confirms this impression and throws more light on the disappearance of woodland from this part of Warwickshire.

that medieval woodland was not confined to the part by Freasley.

There was another wood in Freasley called *Stodfoldhay*, whose enclosure was the subject of a deed in the Lilleshall Abbey cartulary and which was said to be in the vicinity of the manor's court (*curie sue vicino*).[549]

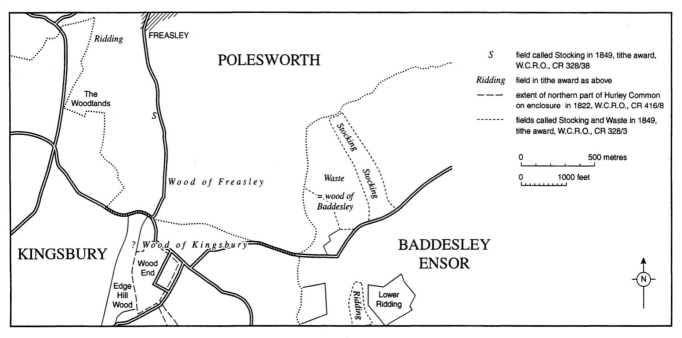

Figure 34: Freasley

Assarts had been created in the wood before 1240 and Lilleshall Abbey turned part of another forty acres over to cultivation. The original grant gave the Abbey and the Abbey's tenants estovers and pannage and allowed the Abbey common pasture for all its animals in the wood. It defined the bounds of the land which was granted to the Abbey by assarts, crossways and simply a line drawn through the middle of the wood, which did not appear to have any internal enclosures or coppices. Some of the assarts were held by tenants with woodland in neighbouring parishes. It was alleged that initially the disputed forty acres were not enclosed with ditches and hedges so that the bounds were confused and the wood and waste had become a kind of waste land (*fuerunt quasi quoddam wastineum*). By 1292 a description of the bounds showed that the wood had become waste and that the parts of the woods of Baddesley and Kingsbury which adjoined that of Freasley when the grant was made had also become waste.[546]

Freasley's tithe award covers part of the township only, but includes fields called Ridding and Stocking by Freasley Green,[547] suggesting that the area had been woodland. The bounds of Freasley's medieval wood confirm this inference and also give the sites of two other adjoining woods, in Kingsbury (see below) and Baddesley Ensor. Waste names on the tithe map for Baddesley Ensor[548] presumably mark part of the medieval wood and waste, although fields called stocking and common in the east of the township suggest

Tamworth

Tamworth, like Polesworth, was omitted from Domesday Book and there are few records of its woodland in the later medieval period. Two townships, Amington and Wilnecote, were recorded as manors in Domesday Book and both had some *silva*.[550]

The bounds of one third of Amington's wood were described in 1213.[551] It extended towards Alvecote in Shuttington. Amington's waste adjoined Glascote and there was waste in its wood.[552] By the early thirteenth century there was at least one assart by the wood.[553] In 1304 forty acres of common wood were under threat; John de Clinton claimed that he had been deprived of his common pasture there.[554] In 1366 Great Amington adjoined *Aucote* (=Alvecote) Wood in Shuttington;[555] in the late sixteenth century it was estimated that Alvecote wood contained one hundred acres.[556] This suggests that there was a large area of woodland in the Amington/Alvecote area. None of the field-names on a nineteenth-century estate map matches the boundary points of Amington's wood in 1213, although, from its name, the Frith Wood on that map may have existed in the medieval period.[557] The place-name Wood-house appears on Ordnance Survey maps north of Glascote; the Frith Wood, when mapped in the nineteenth century, adjoined Glascote Heath.

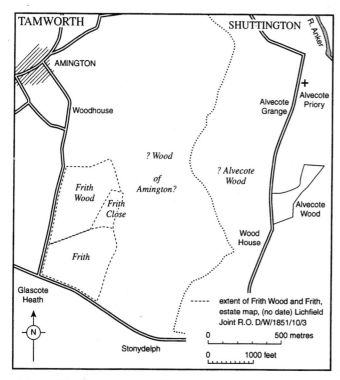

Figure 35: Amington and Alvecote

Burton Abbey had land and wood in a wood called *Kyngeswode* c.1281-1305.[558] A wood called Kingswood was shown on Yates's map of Warwickshire in the late eighteenth century,[559] when it adjoined Polesworth to the north of Watling Street. There is also a medieval record of the waste of Kingswood, which referred to *Farleybroc*, *Deepmoor* and the road from Wilnecote to Alvecote.[560]

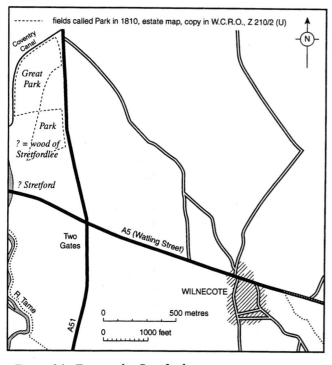

Figure 36: Tamworth - Stretford

The wood of *Stretfordlee*, mentioned in a court roll for the manor of Tamworth in 1446,[561] presumably belonged to the township of Stratford, which appears to have been in the vicinity of the modern Two Gates[562] and therefore presumably took its name from a road-crossing by means of a ford over the river Tame to the west. In 1673 the manor of Tamworth included Lea Wood park.[563] If this preserved the wood of *Stretfordlee* and if it corresponded to the fields called park on an estate map of 1810,[564] then it provides the clue to the site of the medieval wood and shows that the wood must have been situated north of Watling Street immediately east of the river Tame.

Kingsbury

For many places in north and west Warwickshire the loss of woodland can be inferred from references to assarts. Seldom are there accounts of woods becoming assarts. Seldom also is there contemporary evidence of the exact boundary of a wood. Kingsbury is an exception in both respects, thanks to records of a long dispute over a wood in an adjacent parish. It also throws some further light on the relationship between woodland and waste.

Domesday Book recorded *silva* one league square - say between 1,000 and 1,400 acres - under Kingsbury.[565] and a much smaller amount - perhaps thirty to forty acres - under Dosthill,[566] a township within the ecclesiastical parish. With 6,591 acres in the parish[567] it seems that about one sixth of the area was *silva* in 1086.

From detailed records of a dispute over woodland in Freasley to the north we know that the wood of Kingsbury and later the waste of Kingsbury[568] adjoined Freasley and that its northern edge must therefore have coincided with the parish boundary at that point. The present Kingsbury Wood is further south and the northern part of that wood lies on marked ridge and furrow, albeit with masses of wood anemones, plants characteristic of ancient woodland. The northern tip of Edge Hill Wood adjoins Freasley and the area called Wood End to the east of this wood was common land on enclosure in 1822[569]. It seems therefore that part of the medieval wood and waste of Kingsbury was on the site of the present Edge Hill Wood and adjacent common, but it is not certain how far south the wood extended at different points in the later medieval period. Before it became waste it might have been contiguous with the wood of Hurley to the south. The area of ridge and furrow in Kingsbury Wood may mark medieval assarts which reverted to woodland possibly even before the end of the medieval period.

The word common suggests that in Kingsbury tenants had rights of common pasture. This was certainly the case in Hurley's wood. In a case at the assizes in 1261-2 it was claimed that John de Bracebridge, lord of Kingsbury, had deprived Walter de Hurley of his common pasture.[570] Walter maintained that, during the reign of the present king (Henry III, 1216-72), his father had commoned with all kinds of animals in a certain wood which contained about sixty acres. John had made an assart of that wood and brought the land into cultivation so that Walter could no longer common as his father had. In his defence John de Bracebridge said that he had a great waste in Hurley and

63

cited the Statute of Merton as giving him the right, as lord of Hurley, to approve from his wood and assart the place in which Walter had commoned because he had compensated Walter with pasture elsewhere. This case is notable not only as a record of a substantial assart but also in the apparent interchangeability of the terms waste and wood.

The area of Hurley Common, as enclosed in 1822,[571] and adjacent closes called in the tithe award waste or ridding, seem the obvious site for the medieval wood of Hurley. This likelihood is strengthened by a reference in a court roll of 1419 to encroachment on the common of Hurley, namely *le Newelane* and *Hurleywod*.[572]

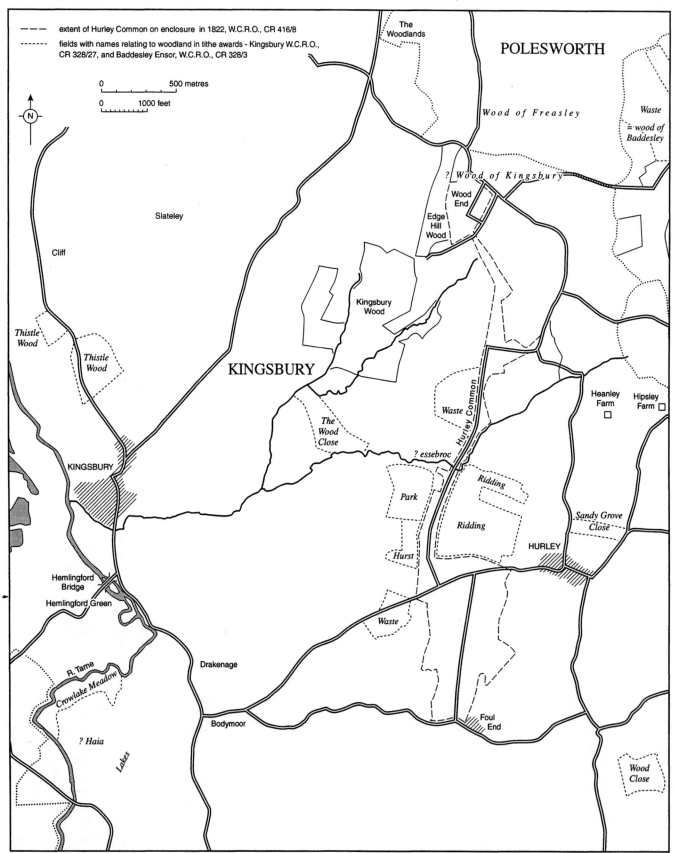

Figure 37: Kingsbury

Various deeds refer to land which was arguably former woodland, suggesting loss of woodland during the later medieval period. It included waste by Edgehill and a field called *Slaughtleywaste* in 1331,[573] pastures called *Freseleyewaste*, *Spencerwaste*, *le hyewaste* and *Blomereswaste* in a rental of apparent fifteenth-century date,[574] Kingsbury Waste in 1332,[575] waste at *Gledenhurst* in 1300[576] (on the eastern side of Hurley), a carucate of assarts at *essebroc* in the early twelfth century,[577] assarts in Kingsbury and Hurley in 1240-1,[578] and newly assarted land by the park of Kingsbury c.1200.[579] The extent of Hurley Common on enclosure and the location of fields called waste, ridding and stocking on the tithe map suggests that a large area of medieval woodland ran from north to south through the middle of the parish.

However, the reference in 1419 to the wood of the lord at *le Clyfe* (modern Cliff), combined with field-names in Thistlewood from the tithe award and pasture called *fistlewoode* recorded in the early sixteenth century,[580] suggests that there was a significant area of woodland in the west of the parish. Records of a dispute over intercommoning between Halloughton and Whitacre also indicate woodland in the Halloughton area, perhaps reflected in the Wood Croft in the tithe award south-west of Halloughton Hall and adjoining the parish boundary with Whitacre.[581]

Kingsbury had a hay, but its nature was not described. It was between the river Tame and two places called *lacum & sippelac*.[582] The tithe award and map for Kingsbury show a place called Lakes by Coton Farm; Crowlake Meadow was a little further north, by the river Tame.[583]

Middleton

Neither of the two entries in Domesday Book which have been attributed to Middleton referred to any *silva*.[584] However, there were several distinct areas of woodland in Middleton in the later medieval period and the wood of Middleton was extensive.

The wood of Middleton was mentioned frequently in cases heard before the justices in eyre, in 1221-2, 1231-2 and 1247.[585] The entry for 1247 is the most informative, for the attorney of Philip Marmion, lord of Middleton, declared that Philip had a wood between his park and the chase of Ela, countess of Warwick, and that the wood was not part of the chase. The wood must have been in the area of the modern Middleton Wood Farm. The first edition of the Ordnance Survey one-inch map called the area to the east of the Farm 'The Wood'. The chase of the earls of Warwick was presumably Sutton Chase, which was said to include Middleton.[586] The location of the former park around Middleton Hall is confirmed by various references. A survey of demesne lands in 1605 listed a new park and an old park "wherein the manore howse standes".[587] The inquisition post mortem into Philip Marmion's lands stated that there was a pool in the park under the courtyard.[588] An area of land called Middleton Pool appears on the first edition of the Ordnance Survey six-inch map immediately adjoining Middleton Hall, whose medieval stone hall survives, and near to Park-gate Farm. There may be remnants of the wood of Middleton in the centre of New Park Wood, but the western part of the latter wood is on ridge and furrow.

That the medieval wood was extensive may be inferred from a deed dated 1249 in which Philip Marmion and the countess reached agreement over their respective assarting activities, including eighty acres in the wood of Middleton, and a dowry settlement in 1292 including ninety acres of wood and waste which were within the chase of Sutton in the common of the neighbourhood (*patrie*).[589] Adding the wood and waste of 1292 to the wood lost to cultivation half a century earlier gives at least 170 acres of woodland.

The relationship between the wood of Middleton and other woods which were recorded by name is nowhere explained. It could be suggested that they had been parts of a single wood but were later separated from the main part of the wood by intervening assarts. Certainly two of them appear to have been in the same vicinity, in the north-west of the parish. The longevity of Philip Marmion[590] and the absence of dates from his deeds make it difficult to prove or disprove this theory. Philip Marmion had woods called *le Lindes*[591] and *sokone*.[592] The former was presumably by waste called *Le Lyndes* which was on the heath of *Turteleye* in 1333.[593] *Sokone* was near *drybrok*, which in turn was near to *le spires*; the field called The Spires east of Trickley (?a corruption of *Turteleye*) Coppice places the wood in the north of Middleton. A late eighteenth-century map showed Middleton Heath in this area.[594] The Breeches, also near Trickley Coppice, may represent *le Brech* by *Turteley heth*,[595] which was also by *Le Lindes*. Neither *sokone* nor *le Lyndes* was included in the list of woods in the manorial survey of 1419-20.[596] As both names were attached to waste as well as to woods[597] it can be suggested that both woods had become partly waste and partly arable land by the early fifteenth century.

The list of 1419-20 included the wood of *lytylpark*, one outwood called *Wodyshurst*, two parcels of outwood called *le Wallehede*, two parcels of wood called *Swarthale*, and one wood recently felled called *Sharpenok*. Of these only *Wodyshurst* appeared in earlier deeds. In 1301 it was described as *silvam que vocatur Wodehurst* next to the heath called *sebenhale* and not far from the road to Lichfield;[598] this suggests that it was in the west of the parish. A lease of the wood in 1385 excepted oaks, maples and crabtrees from the sale of wood there.[599] Surviving deeds show that there were assarts, presumably of woodland, in other parts of the parish. Two deeds refer to assarts on the boundary with Moxhull in Wishaw[600] and another to an assart by Stoke;[601] Stoke End is in the south of the parish. In its association with wastes and assarts Middleton's woodland resembled woodland elsewhere in the region. The presence of a common, foreign wood (*boscus forinsecus*) suggests a tradition of wood pasture. No record has been found of a medieval grove to suggest the origin of the field-name Meer Grove. There is no apparent explanation for the absence of *silva* from the entries in Domesday Book.

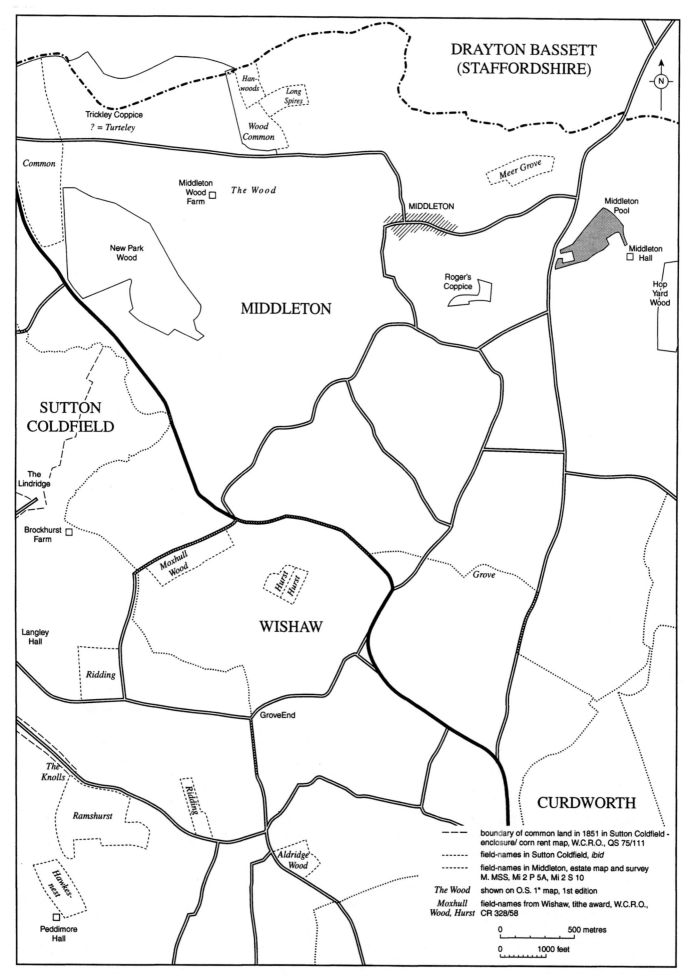

Figure 38: Middleton, Sutton Coldfield (east) and Wishaw

Sutton Coldfield

Sutton Coldfield illustrates well the distinctions between a medieval chase, park and woodland. It provides another twelfth-century example of a hay, showing that, as in Kenilworth, a hay was different from a park or wood.

In Sutton Chase, which earl Thomas called his forest (*foresta mea*),[602] the earls of Warwick enjoyed special hunting rights, though without the benefits of royal forest law. The Chase was not a wood, but included woods. It covered a very large area, not only Sutton itself but also Middleton, Wishaw, Minworth, Curdworth and Erdington in Warwickshire and Perry Barr, Great Barr, Shenstone, Weeford, Hints and Drayton Bassett in Staffordshire.[603] Its extent was similar to that of a royal forest. Indeed, an account of the customs of the manor in 1309 recorded a tradition that when the manor of Sutton was in the king's hands (i.e. before the manor was granted to the earls of Warwick) the whole chase was afforested.[604] Given its extent, the earls' rights in their chase had to be reconciled with the interests of other local landholders, particularly in relation to woodland.[605] Sir William Dugdale recorded that in the reign of Henry VIII Bishop Vesey, who secured the royal grant of Sutton Park for the town, "destroyed the Chase for the benefit of the Poor", who for "xxd. per an. had keeping for their Cows". This account is corroborated by John Leland, who recorded that Bishop Vesey "obtayned licence to deforest the chace there; whereupon he builded dyvars praty howsys of stone in the forest".[606] A few of these stone houses, and Sutton Park itself, survive.

The original medieval park is thought to have been much smaller than the later park. A study of the surviving earthworks in Sutton Park, which covers much of the west of the parish, suggests that the original park was immediately west of the manor house and was enlarged during the later medieval period.[607] This enlargement has a parallel in another of the medieval parks belonging to the earls of Warwick at Wedgnock (see under Warwick above). Sutton Park was large enough to include five fishponds by 1479-80; John Leland, writing fifty to sixty years later, recorded a tradition that they had been made in the reign of Henry V and stated that all five were within the park. He described one of them as adjoining the west end of the parish church, which stands on a ridge outside the present boundary of Sutton Park. He added that the other pools had been drained as a matter of policy and were good meadow ground. However, the names of three of the medieval pools, *Wyndle*, *Kepers* and *Bracebridge*, are attached to pools which are within the Park today, suggesting that the sites of the medieval pools may have been flooded again to form the present pools.[608]

Sutton Park now has a mixture of woodland (with much birch and holly), grassland and heath, but the ecology of the medieval park is unknown. It could well have included some woodland or absorbed woodland as it was enlarged to the present 2,400 acres. In the north and east of the Park are woods with names typical of medieval woods - Nuthurst, Hollyhurst, Darnel Hurst, Streetly Wood. However, it seems

probable that some parts, particularly in the west, were heath, marsh or moor, for not only are there peat deposits which have been the subject of some scientific analysis, but a colony of marsh fritillary butterflies survived there until the 1950's. These rare butterflies are extremely intolerant of shade, reluctant to move over natural barriers when breeding and consequently very localised in distribution and susceptible to changes in habitat. Their disappearance from Sutton Park has been attributed to a decline in grazing and consequent growth of scrub and woodland.[609]

Some of the Chase's woodland lay within Sutton. Domesday Book recorded *silva* measuring two leagues by one league under Sutton.[610] The *silva* amounted to perhaps between 2,000 and 2,800 acres, in comparison with nearly 12,500 acres in the ecclesiastical parish of Sutton Coldfield.[611] Roger, earl of Warwick (who died in 1153[612]) acquired the manor from the crown. It was agreed that he and his heirs should have a park and a free hay enclosed (*unum parcum & unam liberam Hayam in defensione*) and an outwood.[613] Of the hay there is no further record, unless it can be associated with one of the three place-names with the element hay recorded in later centuries. There was a close (*clausum*) called *Sidehaleheye*, recorded in an inquisition post mortem in 1316,[614] which presumably became the coppice called *Sydenhalehey* in 1433-4, *Syndenhamhey* in 1481[615] and *Sydnall haye* in 1581, when it contained thirty acres of pasture, land, wood, furze and vert.[616] It seems reasonable to suggest that the name survives in Signal Hayes in Walmley. The lord's coppice at *Gleodenhurstheye* was recorded in 1415[617] and *le Oldehey* c.1500;[618] the latter was part of the manor of Newhall. Sir William Dugdale recorded that Bishop Vesey "inclosed all the Coppices called the seaven Heys and set up Gates and Locks to them....appointing the Coppices to be for Fewell to the Inhabitants".[619] It has been assumed that the hays were within Sutton Park,[620] but Sir William Dugdale's account, which is taken from a manuscript which he had seen but whose present whereabouts is not known, suggests the contrary, for the seven hays are described quite separately from the Park. Moreover, this interpretation is consistent with the Bishop's deforestation of the Chase, for he would presumably have wished to preserve any surviving woodland in the area of the Chase.

The unspecified number of outwoods (*bosci forinseci*) recorded on earl Guy's death in 1316[621] may represent the scattered remnants of the twelfth-century outwood, as in the meantime there had been some clearance or assarting in Sutton's wood. There is a reference to the wood of Sutton as late as 1306,[622] when there was also a separate wood of Peddimore.[623] Deeds of Thomas, earl of Warwick from 1228-9 to 1242,[624] refer to a single wood of Sutton. Earl Thomas was a prominent figure in the local assarting movement. He granted land for assarting *in Nemore meo de Sutton*[625] and *in Bosco de Suttona*.[626] The land conveyed by the latter deed was in *Rommeshurst*, which can be matched to Ramshurst in the enclosure award[627] and thereby shows that Sutton's wood was in the east of the parish. The deed also refers to adjacent land of Augustine of Wishaw and to the assart of Nicholas of Curdworth. These two were involved in a legal dispute in 1261-2,[628] when Nicholas claimed common pasture in Sutton and Augustine, with another local landholder, Walter de Berford, asked the judge if it was possible to claim common for a holding which had been assarted and which had also been common to all in the neighbourhood and common pasture. Nicholas conceded the argument and admitted that his holding had been part of the earl of Warwick's demesne.

Haucksnest, nor *Langley Knolles*, and gave Henry his assart in *Burhale* between the two great roads to Langley. Langley, Brockhurst, Bleakmoor, Wheatmoor (near Ashfurlong) and Hawksnest (north of Peddimor Hall and not be confused with Hawkesnest near Reddicap Heath) are readily identifiable from the enclosure award of 1851[630] and confirm that Sutton's wood occupied a large part of the east of the parish. Blakemore's location, near to Middleton, is confirmed independently in a medieval deed.[631]

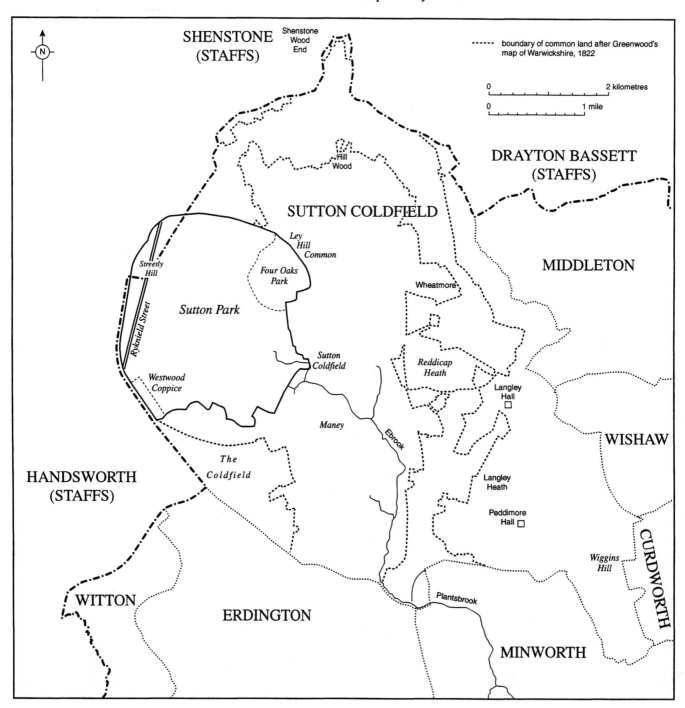

Figure 39: Sutton Coldfield

The locations of some assarts are given in an agreement which earl Thomas made in 1240 with Henry de Ascellis,[629] who quitclaimed his rights in assarts in *Brechurste* and in *Blakemor*, between Langley and *Hauckesciestrete*, and in *Wyttemor*. The earl agreed not to assart from *Wylnerdesleye* to *Ravennsley* between Wishaw and the far side of

Whilst Sutton's wood was regarded as a single wood in the thirteenth century and was of considerable extent, it cannot have been an undifferentiated, impenetrable expanse of woodland, as the existence of well-known minor place-names within it shows. The deed of 1240 and the legal dispute show that it was common wood pasture. Common rights also included fuel. In 1246-7 Henry, parson of Wishaw (a witness to the deed referring to *Rommeshurst* and guaranteed his common rights in the agreement of 1240) brought a writ against earl Thomas's widow, countess Ela, for his estovers in her wood in Sutton.[632]

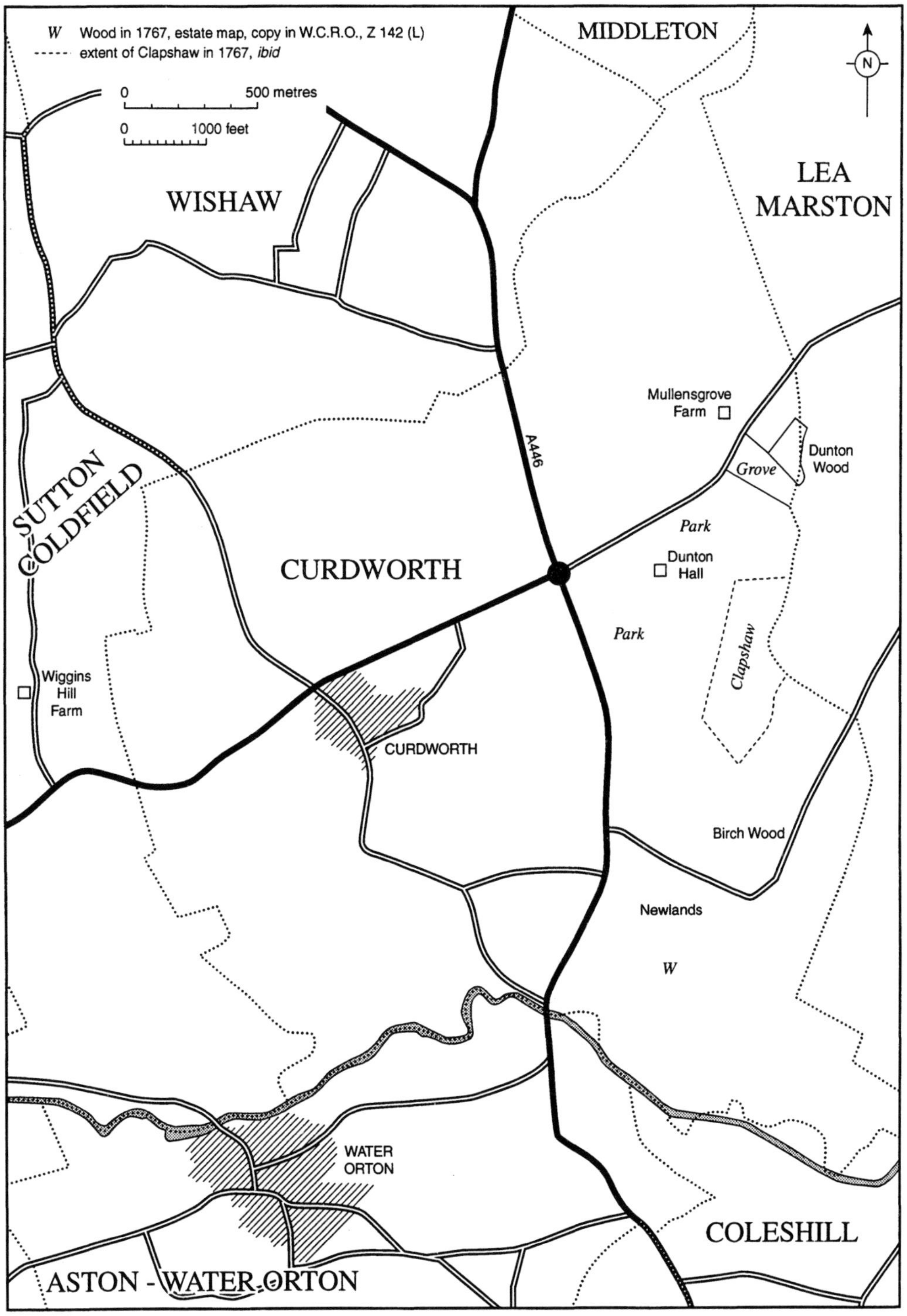

park in 1316.[637] The wood does not occur in later records, but it may have become Ley Hill Common, which was near the north-eastern edge of the park.

The commons which were enclosed in the nineteenth century are shown both on the map which accompanied the enclosure award[638] and on Greenwood's map of Warwickshire published in 1822.[639] On enclosure in 1851 they covered over three thousand acres. They were therefore presumably more extensive than the *silva* of Domesday Book. They may point to the existence of a more extensive area of common woodland in the early medieval period, or they might have comprised waste, heath or moor, as well as wood, throughout the medieval and modern periods. They may also have included land used for medieval agriculture.

Wiggins Hill, between Curdworth and Minworth, was already a separate manor in 1086 and had four square furlongs of *silva*.[640] Deeds dating from 1331 and 1339 refer respectively to the wood of Geoffrey Gamell and the wood of John Gamel called *Greueokus* which bordered on the field of Wiggins Hill by *la Greue lydyate*.[641]

Wishaw and Moxhull

Wishaw had three square furlongs of *silva* in 1086,[642] (probably no more than twenty to thirty acres, against an area of 1,161 acres for the ecclesiastical parish[643]) and a foreign wood with common pasture in 1326.[644] There was a common with oak trees in 1507.[645]

Figure 40: Curdworth

Most of the late fifteenth-century demesne woods were in the east of the parish - *Reddeweycoppes, Sydenhalehey, Hawkesnest* and *Lyndrich Copies*,[633] but Hill Wood was in the north and Echelhurst Wood in the south.[634] Pasture in *Lyndrich Copies* was let in 1479.[635] A wood called *La Lee* in 1298 contained fifty acres[636] and was associated with the

An undated deed described land in Middleton as being towards the wood of Moxhull,[646] but most records of Moxhull's woodland concern its disappearance. In the second half of the thirteenth century local lords were parties to cases involving assarts and waste in Moxhull.[647]

Fifteenth-century documents recorded a pasture called Moxhull Wood.[648] Closes called Moxhull Wood in the Wishaw tithe award[649] presumably mark parts of the former wood.

Curdworth and Minworth

The ecclesiastical parish of Curdworth may be divided into four parts, Curdworth itself, Dunton to the east, Minworth, detached, to the west, and, beyond Minworth, Berwood. Only Curdworth and Minworth are named in Domesday Book. Both had *silva*, measuring respectively half a league in length and breadth, and half a league long and three furlongs wide.[650]

Berwood was an established place-name in the middle of the twelfth century. The cartulary of St. Mary's Abbey, Leicester, recorded that Hugh de Arden, whose gift was confirmed by Henry II, gave the place (*locum*) of Berwood to the Abbey, including all that part of his wood (*nemoris*) which was between the *Ebroc* and the river Tame as far as the boundary with Erdington.[651] These boundaries enable the area to be located. Ebrook is an alternative name for Plants Brook, although the cartulary included other gifts of land *cum nemore* next to the old or ancient Ebrook,[652] thus implying that two streams, or two branches of the same water-course, bore the same name.

The cartulary recorded gifts of land and wood by Thomas de Arden and William de Arden and that the manor of Berwood

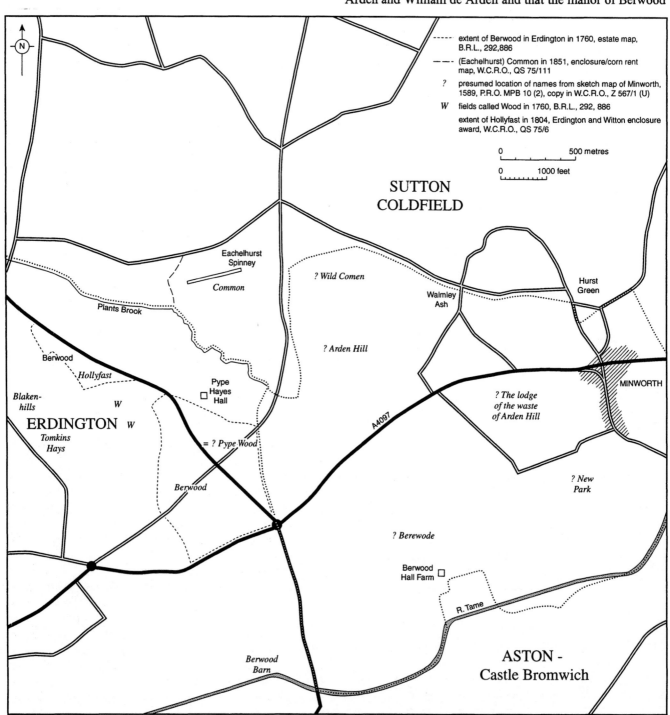

Figure 41: Minworth and Berwood

70

included three hundred acres of wood.[653] The Arden family retained woodland in Curdworth; c.1242 Ela, dowager countess of Warwick, confirmed that Thomas de Arden could exploit his wood of Curdworth between the land of Margery, countess of Warwick, and his own land.[654] Thomas de Arden had a wood at *hullesmor*.[655] William de Arden leased twenty-four acres of wood in Berwood, between *Ebroc* and *Bredestrete* as far as *Goseforth*.[656]

Berwood extended westwards into the neighbouring manor of Erdington and also eastwards into Minworth. An exceptionally early map of Minworth, drawn in 1589,[657] shows three areas west of the New Park called *parte of Berewode*. The same map shows the waste of Arden Hill; this may have been the wood called *Ardernewode* which was mentioned in a deed dated to c.1300.[658]

In 1290 Ralph de Gorges was said to have cut trees in the wood of the abbot of Merevale at Dunton, perhaps the tithe-free part of Dunton Wood.[659] Ralph had a manor in Dunton with a wood of his own called *Clapshawe*, presumably on the site of the fields of that name.[660] There was a grove called *Dernshawe* in 1514; this proper name has not survived, but the woodland which in the tithe award of 1846 was called 'part of Dunton Wood' was called in 1767 'The Grove' and so may mark the site of *Dernshawe*.[661]

Erdington

In 1086 Erdington had *silva* measuring one league long and half a league wide *in defenso regis*; this has been translated as "in the king's enclosure".[662] Royal interest in the woodland may be related to the medieval Sutton Chase, which included Erdington and which, as explained in the foregoing account of woodland in Sutton Coldfield, apparently originated as a royal forest. Erdington's *silva* might have covered about five hundred acres. Its medieval wood and waste were divided between the three manors into which Erdington had been partitioned by 1218.[663] There is enough evidence to infer that the wood was part of Berwood, named with *hollyfast* as one of the lord's woods in 1541.[664]

There was an outwood, arguably Berwood, in that part of Erdington which was held by Henry de Erdington in 1282.[665] In 1309 the wood of Henry's younger son, another Henry, was near to the wood of the Abbey of Leicester, i.e. Berwood in Curdworth parish which is known to have been woodland in the twelfth century.[666] In 1433 the manor, which had descended to Thomas de Erdington, contained one hundred acres of wood.[667] *Pypewode*, next to *le ffoxholen in Berewode*, was presumably the woodland attached to the manor of Pype, a manor which was held by Walter Maunsel in 1218 and which contained sixty acres of wood in 1303.[668] Walter Maunsel enclosed his part of the waste of Erdington for cultivation.[669] Some wood remained, for firewood was taken from the separate (*separale*) wood of William Maunsel in 1247.[670] The link with Berwood is confirmed by records of the earldom of Warwick, which acquired the manor of Pype.[671] Account rolls of the earl for 1413 and 1417 referred to the lord's wood of *Berewode*.[672] Roger de Erdington was the lord of the third manor, which

also included waste and which was also linked with Berwood; he granted two acres of his waste in Berwood to William son of Guy de Assarto.[673] In the light of the records of waste and assarting it is reasonable to suggest that Berwood in Erdington could have extended as far as Wood End, a minor place-name recorded in 1462-3 and marked on a map of 1760.[674]

Hollyfast, the other demesne wood in 1541, was presumably in the area of the Hollyhurst or Hollyfast of the enclosure award[675]. To the south of it Blakenhills may mark the edge of Henry de Erdington's assart which lay between *Blakenhale* and *Thacherco*.[676] In 1462-3 Blakenhale included *le Newlond* and *Tomkynsshey*; the latter can be found on the map of 1760.[677] *Olifast* was called a waste in 1525.[678] There was also waste adjoining Witton to the south.[679]

Erdington had the same association of wood pasture, assarts, waste, modern commons and greens as is found elsewhere in north Warwickshire, and woodland in a few tenants' holdings.[680] In 1350 a tenant's holding included an acre of wood; in 1462 a grove called *dwerffholes* was part of a holding.[681] *Dwerffeshole* was between Erdington Slade and Witton Slade.[682] The grove adjoined a blade mill in 1543,[683] so it was probably next to the river Tame or the Hawthorn Brook.

Aston

To Aston Domesday Book attributed *silva* three leagues by half a league.[684] This could have been distributed throughout the area which became the ecclesiastical parish, although Erdington and Witton were already separate manors in 1086, or concentrated in certain parts of it. Aston's *silva* may have covered between about 1,500 and 2,100 acres and Erdington's between 500 and 700 acres; Witton had no *silva*.[685] The ecclesiastical parish contained 10,898 acres.[686]

There are few records for Aston itself and no record of woodland before the sixteenth century. A close of the wood of *Lozdgynssehul* (?= the eighteenth-century Lozells Wood) was recorded in a rental of Thomas Holt's lands in 1532.[687] There was a grove of wood (*grauam Bosci*) at *holebrok* in Castle Bromwich in 1331.[688] Two medieval place- or field-names include Old English words for wood, but surviving deeds do not say whether *Brechurst* and *Bockenholt* still had woodland in the thirteenth and fourteenth centuries. There is the same lack of evidence for *Washwood* in Saltley.[689]

There is evidence of a considerable amount of assarting in various townships within Aston parish. A legal dispute dealt with common pasture in one hundred acres of newly ploughed land (*terre de novo frussate*) in Bordesley, as a result of which Thomas de Maydenheth secured permission to approve his own wastes in Aston and Duddeston, provided that Roger de Somery could do the same in Bordesley and Bromwich.[690] An inquisition post mortem into Roger's lands in 1291 recorded seventy-eight free tenants holding lands of new assart and rendering £12 15s. 3¼d.[691] There was a dispute over common pasture in forty acres of waste in

Castle Bromwich and Bordesley belonging to a freeholding in Little Bromwich and another over common pasture in thirty acres of heath in Wood Bromwich which belonged to a freeholding in Water Orton.[692] There was waste in Water Orton, some of which was 'approved'.[693] Adam Bacon held a wood there in 1261-2.[694]

There were wood and waste in Witton, with common rights recorded in the former in 1469.[695] They may have been on the site of the later Witton common, which adjoined Erdington.[696]

Sheldon

The fragmentary and scant evidence of medieval woodland in Sheldon is supplemented by helpful enclosure and tithe awards. It is thought that Sheldon is represented in Domesday Book by the manor of *Machitone*, which became the minor place-name Mackadown. If this is the case there was *silva* measuring one league by half a league in Sheldon in 1086.[697] An assart called *monelond*, the subject of a thirteenth-century deed, has been located in Sheldon, in the north-east of the parish, by land called Holifast in the tithe award.[698] Fields called wood and ridding in the tithe award suggest that there was once a large area of woodland in this

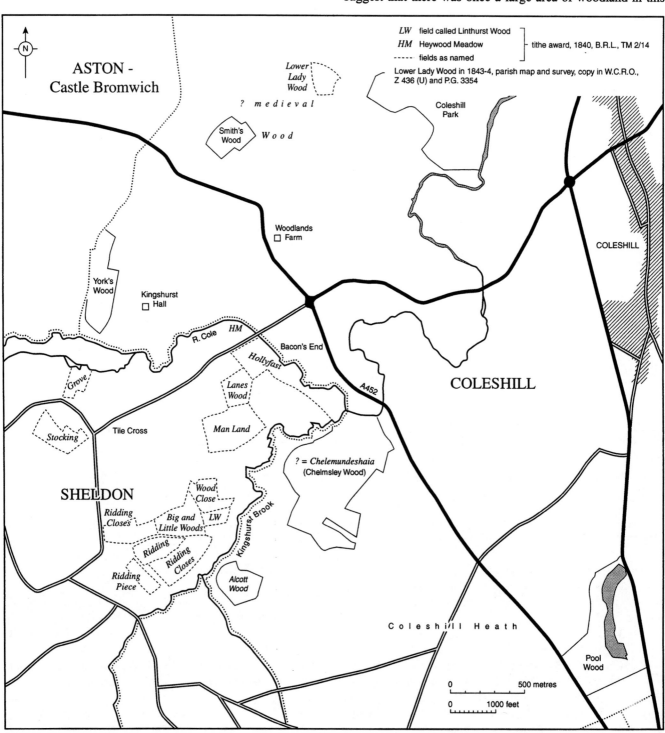

Figure 42: Sheldon and Coleshill (west)

part of Sheldon. Another medieval deed referred to the wood of John Haumond by a meadow adjoining the river Cole and near the lord's waste.[699] Common pasture in a piece of waste was the subject of a legal dispute in 1288.[700] The enclosure award[701] shows an area called the Outwoods, presumably marking a former medieval wood. The field-name Grove on the tithe map may mark the site of the medieval *Gerardsgrove* by Newland.[702]

Bickenhill and Marston Culy

The ecclesiastical parish of Bickenhill contained several manors during the later medieval period, including Lyndon and Kineton in a detached area adjoining Sheldon and Solihull.[703] It was already divided into three manors by 1086, when Domesday Book recorded no *silva* for Marston, but *silva* both for the manor called Bickenhill (four furlongs square) and for the 'other' Bickenhill (twelve furlongs by

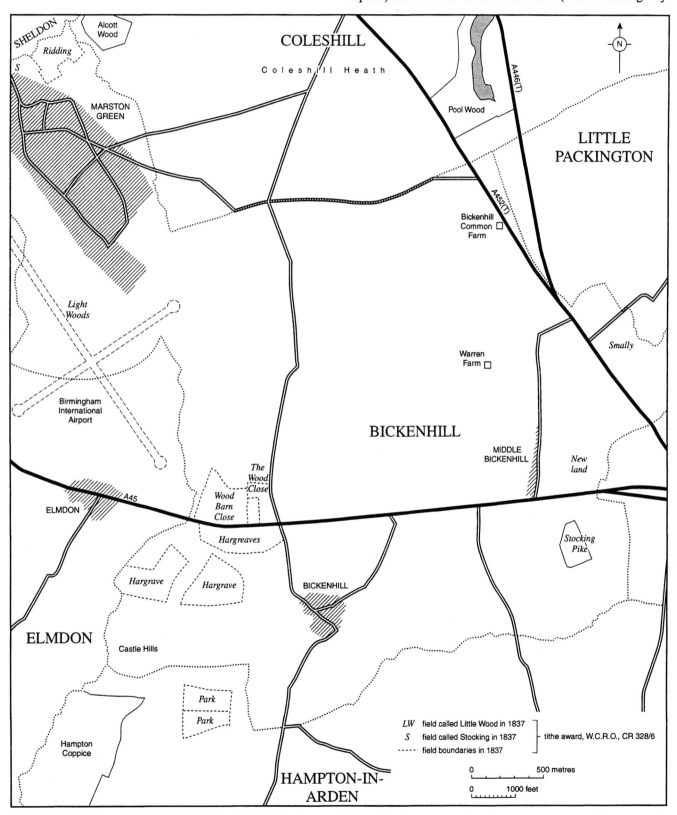

Figure 43: Bickenhill

73

six).[704] In total there could have been over six hundred acres of *silva*. If the ecclesiastical parish comprised the Domesday manors, the area of the latter would have amounted to 3,771 acres including Lyndon and 2,837 excluding it.[705]

A collection of deeds dating from the thirteenth century has provided much information about the later medieval manors called Bickenhill.[706] What is lacking for the most part is evidence that the minor place- and field-names derived from woodland marked places which were still wooded in or after 1086. There is some evidence for *Hargrave*, which extended to the boundary with Elmdon and which appears from field-names to have straddled the boundary between Church Bickenhill and Wavers Marston, unless the fields in the one were named simply from their proximity to the grove in the other.[707] In 1240 it was recognised that Sir Hugh de Ardern had the right to assart land in *Hargrove*.[708] Woodland clearance further east is suggested by the field-name Stocking Pike. A thirteenth-century deed associates the family of Corbison, holder of Stockyngs, with land in *La Lee*, in which common pasture rights were surrendered, and, whilst it is never stated that *La Lee* was woodland, it was a distinct area which was associated with *Hargrave* in that a tenant was specifically excluded from both.[709] The presence of Bickenhill Common in the north-east of the parish may indicate former woodland; if so, it could be suggested that woodland once extended along the whole of the eastern edge of Bickenhill.

Despite the absence of *silva* from Marston in 1086, not only was *Hargrave* apparently at least partly in Wavers Marston but there was a wood in Marston Culy in 1272 called *Echles* or *Ethles*.[710] The tithe map shows fields called stocking and ridding in the north of the manor, adjacent to the presumed site of medieval woodland in Sheldon, and closes called Light Wood or Light Woods in the south (the letter 's' appears to have been added since 1642, when a deed referred to Lightwood).[711] In the late thirteenth century Henry de Sheldon claimed that he had been disseised of common pasture for his pigs and other animals in land and wood in Marston Culy; the Marston Culy defendants claimed that there was an agreement between them and the free tenants of Sheldon whereby each of them could approve their waste.[712] This reference supports the suggested location of adjacent medieval woods in Sheldon and Marston Culy.

The tithe map included several wood names in Lyndon and Kineton, particularly Ladywood in the north-east corner by Lyndon Green. A court roll recorded the removal of *whypstokkes* and *evylstaves* from *lyndon wode* in 1464 and the earl of Stafford owned a pasture of the same name.[713]

Coleshill

Domesday Book recorded a substantial amount of *silva* under Coleshill, three leagues by half a league,[714] which would have covered perhaps between 1,500 and 2,100 acres. In 1200 the widow of Osbert de Clinton claimed one third of the wood of Coleshill as dower and then quitclaimed to Osbert's heir woodland called *Chelemundesheia*, *Witemore*

and *Hoppele*, and, beyond the water, an unnamed area of wood stretching from the oak called the oak of Castelli to *Lutleshaie Vuerende*, *Wirsetemede* and *Bromwiche Blakeleg'*.[715] The agreement of 1200 showed that there were named woods in Coleshill by that date. It implied that these were not the only woods in Coleshill, for if all the woods had been the subject of the quitclaim it would have been unnecessary to identify them separately. It also gave a relatively early record of a hay which was a wood. Some thirteenth-century deeds referred to the lord's woods in general.[716] More in the same series referred to named assarts.[717] There are records of woods called *Chelmondeshay*, *Lanediwode*, *Rokesleyschawe*, *Beltesley* and the Lady Wood[718] and of an unnamed grove in 1367.[719]

Most of the minor place-names in the agreement over the dower of Osbert de Clinton's widow in 1200[720] have disappeared, but it is possible to infer (Fig. 42) the site of the unnamed area of woodland, on the other side of the water (presumably the river Cole) from *Chelemundesheia*. Chelmsley Wood, now a housing estate, survived into the twentieth century. A family called Castello held part of a knight's fee in Castle Bromwich;[721] this and the reference to *Bromwiche Blakeleg'* suggest that the dowager's wood adjoined Castle Bromwich. Later references to Ladywood, arguably the third of the wood received in dower by the widow of Osbert de Clinton, can be linked to a field called Lower Ladywood in 1845;[722] that field is some distance to the east of the boundary with Castle Bromwich, suggesting that the wood was very extensive. However, as Ladywood was called an arable field in 1520,[723] it appears that some, if not much, of the wood had disappeared by c.1500. Beltesley was in *Aldecotenhale*, but whether it became the modern Alcott Wood is questionable.[724] There is no clue as to the location of the tenant's grove.

Shustoke

There was *silva* in Shustoke in 1086,[725] probably over five hundred acres in extent. Several thirteenth-century deeds refer to the wood of Shustoke, which adjoined land in *Brograve*, described in one deed as the wood of *Broggraue*.[726] Braggary Field has been associated with *Brograve*[727] and its site certainly matches the location inferred from medieval records; the wood of *Broggraue* was near to the field of Blythe and some land in it was by the park of Shustoke.[728] The approximate site of the park can be inferred from the description 'Old Park' on a map of 1793 and the field-name Park Pale on the tithe map.[729] Part of the wood may have been imparked and part allowed to become waste, for waste adjoined *Whatecroft*, a name which also survived to appear as Wheatcroft near to Braggary Field on the tithe map.[730] The wood was probably extensive, for land by it is described as towards the fishpond (*vivarium*); three fields called Fish Pool (?part of the fifteenth-century *ffysshepolfeld*) are nearly a mile to the east of Wheatcroft.[731]

There might have been more medieval woodland at the eastern end of the parish; there were fields called upper and nether wood by the church in the seventeenth century, presumably represented by the Over Wood on the tithe map,[732] and woodland in the eastern tip of the parish in the eighteenth century, by fields called Birch Grove.[733]

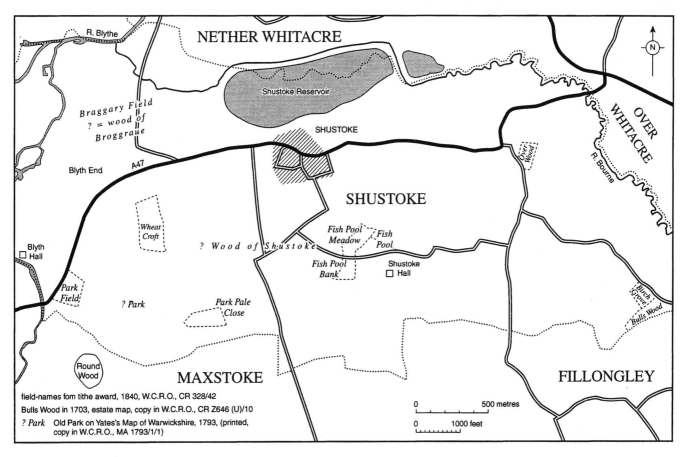

Figure 44: Shustoke

Bentley

Bentley was a detached part of the ecclesiastical parish of Shustoke which adjoined Merevale. It was a separate manor in 1086, when Domesday Book recorded *silva* measuring half a league by three furlongs,[734] perhaps 180-250 acres.

Monks Park and Bentley Park Woods covered over five hundred acres in the eighteenth and nineteenth centuries, Hoar Park about seventy acres.[735] There were other woods and field-names associated with wood, including Bentley Common.[736] They were much more extensive than the inferred area of Domesday *silva*. The first two parks, if not all three, originated in the later medieval period. Bentley Park was already divided in 1265 and Monks Park may have been formed from that part of Bentley's woodland which was given to Merevale Abbey in the twelfth century. The monks' park was described as a wood or a park in 1399.[737]

Maxstoke

There is no entry for Maxstoke in Domesday Book.[738] Sir William Dugdale's attribution of *Machitone* to Maxstoke has been dismissed in favour of Mackadown in Sheldon (see above).[739]

An inquisition post mortem into the lands of William de Oddingeseles in 1295 recorded a park which produced income from pasture, pannage and underwood, also a foreign wood (*unus boscus forinsecus*) with similar sources of income.[740]

In 1336 land in Maxstoke was given to a newly-founded house of Austin canons and in 1344 John de Clinton gave them the manor house within the park, together with lands which included 145½ acres of wood and pasture and thirteen acres of underwood.[741] The grant seems to have been confirmed in 1347, when the canons acquired the whole of the park and other lands in Maxstoke, including the two areas of woodland called *Byrchenemor* and *Oldfeld*.[742] Both minor place-names suggest secondary woodland. The former may have survived in the wood called Birchmoor Stump, which was in the southern part of the parish called the Priory lordship in 1767[743].

William de Clinton obtained a licence to crenellate in 1345 and built his castle in *le Outewood*, which was common to all the freeholders of Maxstoke, enclosing and imparking that wood and granting common of pasture in *Le Brodfield* to the freeholders.[744] On the tithe map the Old Park was around the castle[745] and presumably approximates to the area of the outwood, although later accretions and subtractions are possible. Red campion, a characteristic flower of ancient woodland, grows in uncultivated areas near the castle.

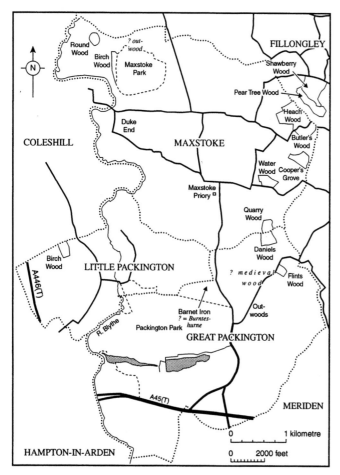

Figure 45: Maxstoke and Packington

In 1419 there was an unnamed grove, of land and wood, which adjoined the highway leading from Coventry towards Maxstoke and Coleshill.[746] A rental of c.1344 included one grove held by a tenant.[747]

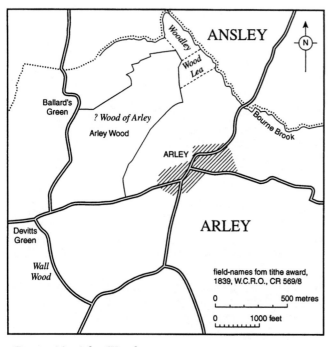

Figure 46: Arley Wood

References in accounts of the earls of Stafford to fields or pastures called *Erleswode, halmonswode* and *riddyng*[748] suggest the loss of woodland during the medieval period, although some of the lands attached to the Stafford manor lay outside Maxstoke.

Arley

Bounds of Arley are attached to an Anglo-Saxon charter dated to 1001. They make no reference to a wood, unless *hwitan lege* was a wood as well as a minor place-name.[749] Domesday Book credited Arley with *silva* measuring one and a half leagues by a league,[750] possibly over 1,500 acres. There is a record of *Arleyheth* in 1394-5,[751] but the various names ending in -ley in the tithe award[752] do not include a Whitley which could be matched to the *hwitan lege* of the Anglo-Saxon charter. Fields called *Wodleg* and *Chutheleia* were specified, with the wood, in a division of Arley manor in 1202.[753] A field called Far Wood Lea adjoined Arley Wood on the north-east in the tithe award. There was common pasture in at least part of Arley's woodland in 1285,[754] but no evidence of the woodland's extent at that date. The present wood includes some heath.[755]

Fillongley

There were four manors called Fillongley in 1086.[756] Each was assessed at half a hide and each contained some *silva*. However, only two of the four entries gave both the length and breadth of the *silva*, so that it is even more difficult than usual to estimate the approximate extent of it in 1086. As one manor had *silva* measuring two leagues by one it is reasonable to assume that Fillongley had at least two thousand acres of *silva* towards the end of the eleventh century. The total acreage of the ecclesiastical parish was 4,731,[757] so it seems possible that half the area of the parish, or even more, consisted of *silva* in 1086. The later medieval manorial history of the parish is complex.[758]

A list of named woods and groves is given in an undated memorandum in the Warwick Castle manuscripts[759] stating that "that these be the wooddes In olde ffylingley & the ffaules of them". The handwriting is of the fifteenth or early sixteenth century, so the document reflects the position at the end of the medieval period in one manor only, a manor which also included part of Alspath in Meriden parish. The list included *Birchleyhey, Fauke Woodd, Albones groue, Cotterells groue, a lytle woodd cauled pertre groue, ii smale Groues in Alspade, sladen groue, the herst in marbrokes, lawrance Cookes Woodde, the Water Woodd, the Shetthawnce, Carters Woodde, Hesell hurst in Wrechboulls lande* and *a lytle Groue cauled Hye Asche groue*. Some of these names match woods or field-names in the tithe award.[760] Old Fillongley Hall was north of Birchley Hays Wood, separated from it by two fields called Stocking, a name suggesting former woodland. Forke Wood Field adjoined fields called Falkwood in Corley presumably the site of *ffauke woodd*. The name *Water Wood* survives; perhaps the modern Pear Tree Wood is *pertre grove*.

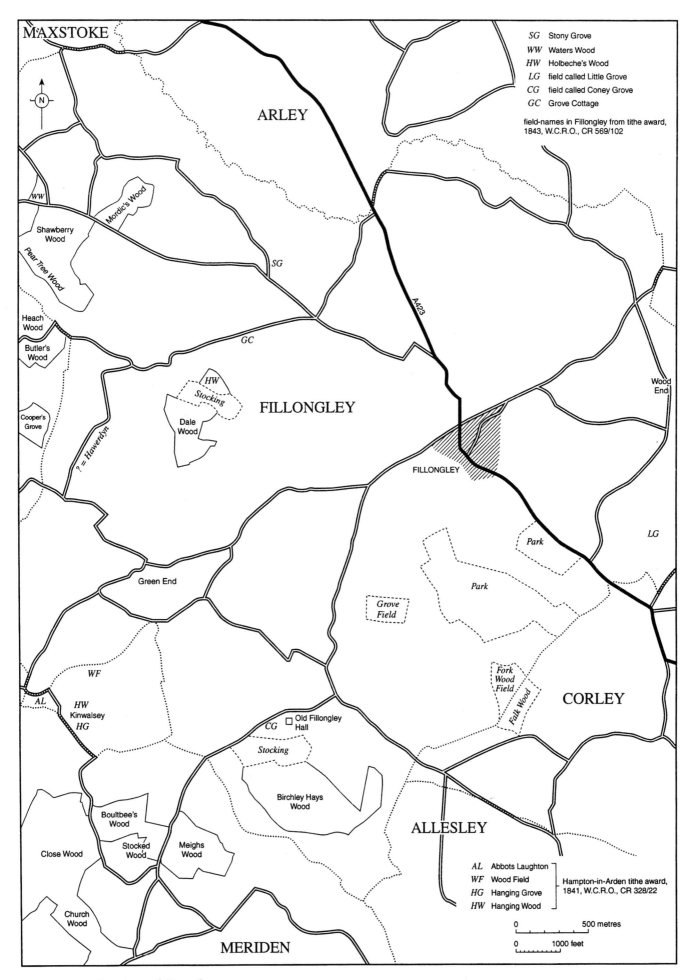

Figure 47: Fillongley and Kinwalsey

There is little other information about Fillongley's later medieval woodland. Inquisitions post mortem of members of the Hastings family, lords of Bergavenny, referred to an enclosed wood in 1313,[761] a park in which a little fort was situated (*quidem parcus in quo situm est unum fortelettum*) in 1325,[762] an enclosed park in 1392,[763] and a park in 1436.[764] If the Hastings manor in Fillongley included any woods other than the park they must have been held by tenants and not in demesne. The names of some of the woods in the list referring to Old Fillongley suggest that these too had been held by tenants. Two surviving deeds refer to tenants' groves, the grove of William Snelle in 1485[765] and a grove of John son of John de Rutone of Fillongley called *le Holowegreuen* in the fee of Old Fillongley in 1317.[766] There may have been other groves which were unrecorded.

Wallehawinge.[768] The great grove once of John de Filungele adjoined land which contained a little grove and which was given to Coventry Cathedral Priory by Henry Gaumbe or Jaumbe; the Priory had granted the land, with a ploughland and wood growing on the ploughland, to Robert Falke.[769] Did the ploughland become the *Jaumbe Wode* named in deeds of 1323 and 1435,[770] and the grove remain a grove? In 1429 *Geambe Wood* was near to *dawefelde* and in the tithe award of 1839 Daw Field was by Jane Wood.[771] It seems reasonable to assume that *Jaumbe Wode* became Jane Wood.

One member of the Falke family presumably gave his name to the *Falke Wood* which straddled the boundary between Corley and Fillongley in 1411[772] and was marked by fields called Fawke Wood in 1839.[773] Even where other woods and groves had proper names there are problems in

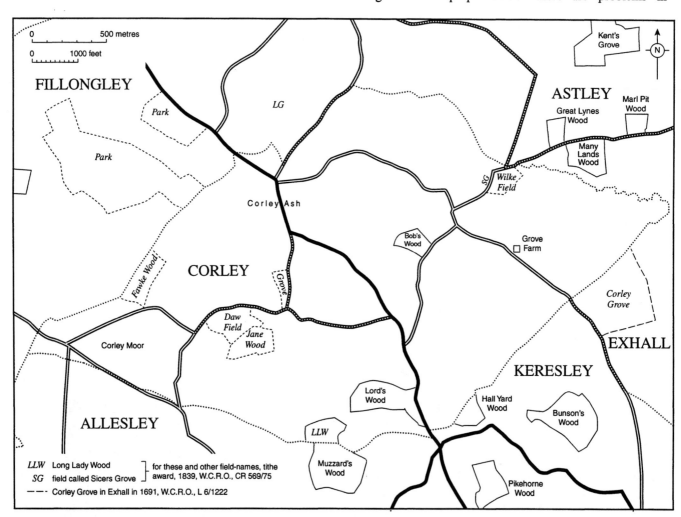

Figure 48: Corley

Corley

Corley had a relatively small amount of *silva* in 1086,[767] probably between thirty and forty acres. The recorded later medieval woodland was scattered throughout the parish and cannot be matched to the Domesday *silva*.

One deed shows that three groves were in close proximity to each other, namely the grove of John de Filungele, a grove of Radulf Wodecot (?or Wodecoc) and a grove called

identifying their locations. It may seem reasonable to suggest that the Lord's Wood of the tithe award was the *maysterswod* (master's wood) on the southern boundary of Corley in 1411.[774] However, the *maysterswod* was then west of groves called *Wodcokksgrove* and *moserddeswod*, whereas on the tithe map the Lord's Wood is east of Woodcock Hill and land, including plantations, called Muzzards (which adjoined Muzzards Wood in Allesley). Long Lady Wood further west is in the correct position for *maysterswod*. The wood of Joanna Catesby called *le Tacheley* was on the northern edge of Corley.[775] This must have been distinct from the grove called *Thacheley* in 1261[776] which was part of Corley glebe,[777] but presumably the two were in the same vicinity. The priory had a small, unnamed grove in two fields called *le monkesfeld*.[778] The grove in Corley next to *Syserslone* in 1418-9[779] is presumably the Sycers Grove of 1688,[780] and the meadow of that name in 1839,[781] as both it and Sycers Lane were near to Wilke Field. Confusingly, the grove called *Corley grove* was not in Corley, but in the manor of Newland in Exhall by Coventry to the east.[782]

There was a hay in Corley in the middle of the thirteenth century which included land;[783] we do not know whether it had once been a wood.

Alspath and Meriden

The ecclesiastical parish of Meriden included the township of Alspath, which was recorded in Domesday Book as a manor with *silva* one and a half leagues long by one league wide,[784] probably over 1,500 acres. The total area of the parish was 2,931 acres,[785] so *silva* may have covered at least half of this area in 1086.

There are references to the wood of Alspath in several medieval deeds.[786] There is evidence that Alspath's wood either was not the only wood in Alspath in the thirteenth century or had been subdivided, and that some of it had already been lost to assarting.[787] Four acres and two holdings in the wood (*bossco*) of Alspath extended to the bounds of the wood (*nemoris*) of Richard de Kinton.[788] Matilda, widow of Richard de Kinton, confirmed to Richard Walduyve of Alspath lands which the latter held in Alspath including some by the common wood (*commune boschum*),

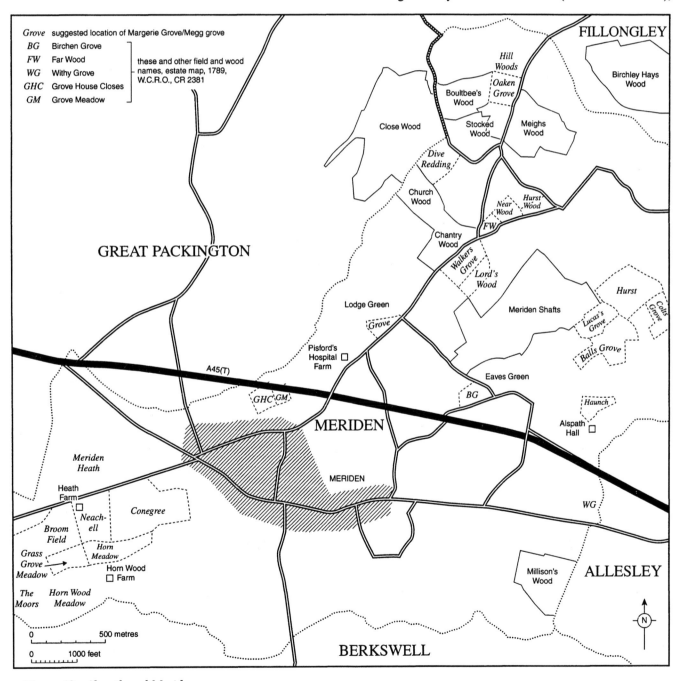

Figure 49: Alspath and Meriden

79

kingweisford, *fenniwey* and *fastuluussiche*;[789] Richard de Kinton made a grant in the same area to Richard Walduyve's son.[790] This common wood and the wood of Alspath were either identical or adjacent, because *fastoluussiche* was also mentioned in one of the deeds referring to the wood of Alspath[791] and *fenniwey* in another.[792] *Kyngeweye* was said in a later deed to lead towards Packington, but as many roads lead from Meriden into the adjacent parish of Packington to the west this is not of much help in locating the common wood.[793] The wood called *Shutehauunch*, which was described as part of the wood,[794] may have been in the area of the modern Haunch. Late eighteenth-century maps[795] show a variety of woods and groves concentrated north of the modern A45, including the wood called Lord's Wood, a name suggestive of a medieval demesne wood. Meriden Shafts has been described as a common wood and identified with at least part of the medieval common wood.[796] It may be identical with the grove called *shafts sprynge woods* c.1523-7.[797]

There are records of several medieval groves which cannot be traced on modern maps. The eighteenth-century Balls Grove, Lucas's Grove, Birchen Grove, Colts Grove, Walkers Grove and Oaken Grove may have been renamed since the later medieval period. Ballis Grove was recorded in 1531.[798] Half a grove called *Ormesgreva* was mentioned in a deed of 1323-4.[799] *Chirchegrove* by *Oldworthyng*[800] may have become the later Church Wood. The grove held by Coventry Cathedral Priory in 1411 was unnamed,[801] as was the wood which belonged to the Buckmore family at about the same time.[802] *Whittgrove*, which was held by John and Margaret Brayles in 1452, may have become firstly the *margerie grove* which was conveyed with a messuage called *Breylles* in 1528 and then the Megg/Magg Wood or Grove which was associated with the tenement called *Braylis*.[803] Meggrove and Chantry Wood contained eight acres when they were leased in 1656, 1668 and 1688; they were described as lying north of the lane from Meriden to Fillongley.[804] However, they were probably not contiguous. *Margerie grove* was bought by William Pisford[805] and on a map of 1789 the Pisford lands included a field called Grove to the south of Lodge Green.[806] Magg Grove and Megge Wood were described as near Lodge Green in the seventeenth century.[807] *Dyve ruddyng*, which was called a close of wood in 1454,[808] never included the word 'grove' in its title, although it was described as a grove in 1550.[809] The name *ruddyng* suggests that it had at one time been cleared before reverting to secondary woodland by 1454; the name survived to mark its site on the map of 1789.

Horn Wood in Meriden[810] can be located approximately from modern maps. It was still a wood in 1513, when the wood within it and within two other woods called the *reught lesue* and *benetts spryng* was sold to Thomas Weggewod and John Whaburley of Meriden,[811] but much, if not all, of it had been cleared by 1614.[812]

Packington

Domesday Book recorded *silva* one league square under Packington,[813] making no distinction between the later manors and parishes of Great and Little Packington. Great Packington (known as Packington Priors) was granted to Kenilworth Priory in the twelfth century.[814] Little Packington was divided manorially in the later medieval period.[815]

The wood of Packington Priors is relatively well documented. It adjoined the hermitage,[816] whose name survives in Little Packington. Some waste adjoined the wood and the hermitage.[817] Corners of the wood were called *Wellehurne* and *Burnteshurne*.[818] The latter name also survives, as Barnet Iron. All this information, together with an area called the Outwoods on a map of 1777,[819] helps to locate the medieval wood (Fig. 45). The wood of Packington Priors [820] was a foreign wood in which residents of Kinwalsey to the east surrendered rights to pasture and pannage as parts of it were enclosed and assarted,[821] though not without a dispute in 1260.[822] Other parts of the wood were called *Waterslademore* and *Ailyhmehey*,[823] but these names have not survived. There were woods called *Newe parke wood* (36 acres) and *Oldeparke wood* (20 acres) in 1544, and woodland on Packington Common.[824]

Two and a half acres of land in the wood of Little Packington were the subject of a thirteenth-century deed.[825] The manor's waste adjoined Coleshill waste and some of its common land the wood of the prior of Kenilworth, i.e. Great Packington.[826] Worcester Cathedral Priory had a waste called *Holwaste* belonging to its hermitage in Little Packington.[827]

Hampton-in-Arden

Domesday Book attributed nine square leagues of *silva* to the manor of Hampton-in-Arden,[828] an area possibly between 9,000 and 12,000 acres, far larger than the townships of Hampton, Diddington and Kinwalsey (2,318 acres in the tithe award).[829] However, Nuthurst, Knowle and Balsall, which were not mentioned in Domesday Book and which were part of the ecclesiastical parish of Hampton in the later medieval period,[830] are thought to have been part of the Domesday manor for those reasons; the same may apply to Baddesley Clinton. It is not known how the *silva* was divided between the several places which are presumed to have existed within the Domesday manor.

Woodland in Hampton itself is well attested from the second half of the twelfth century. By combining evidence from a series of charters[831] with later information, particularly a very detailed survey made in 1649,[832] and a map from 1812,[833] the approximate sites of some of the areas of woodland have been identified.

The twelfth-century charters referring to land in Hampton held by Robert, Archdeacon of Lisieux, vary in detail. Some include the land and little area of woodland of Birchley and Aspley and the little area of woodland of the Lee and the workable wood at Chadwick (in Balsall) and all hays which belonged to the lordship of Hampton (*terram & siluulam de bircheleia & hespelea & siluulam de la lea & Nemus operabile apud Chedleswich & Omnes haias que pertinent ad dominium de hamtona*).[834] These charters seem to differentiate between *silva* and *nemus*. The adjective workable (*operabile*) qualifying *nemus* suggests the cutting of wood and timber rather than wood pasture. In contrast the *silva* might have been wood pasture. The naming of specific woods implies that there were other woods in Hampton at that time; otherwise the charters could have referred simply to all the woods of Hampton. Indeed, one charter recording a grant by Archdeacon Robert of Lisieux of all his land of Hampton dealt in generalities and referred to *boscum*.[835] A deed of 1109-14 referred to Burnulf's wood (*nemus*) of Hampton.[836]

There are at least two records of an alder-grove near the bridge of *Bradeford*.[838] There was a wood called *Parkersmor* in 1376.[839]

Solihull

It has been assumed[840] that in Domesday Book the ecclesiastical parish of Solihull was represented by the manors of Ulverley and Longdon. Both manors had *silva*; it measured four leagues by half a league in the former and one league by half a league in the latter,[841] in total probably between 2,500 and 3,500 acres. This was a substantial area.

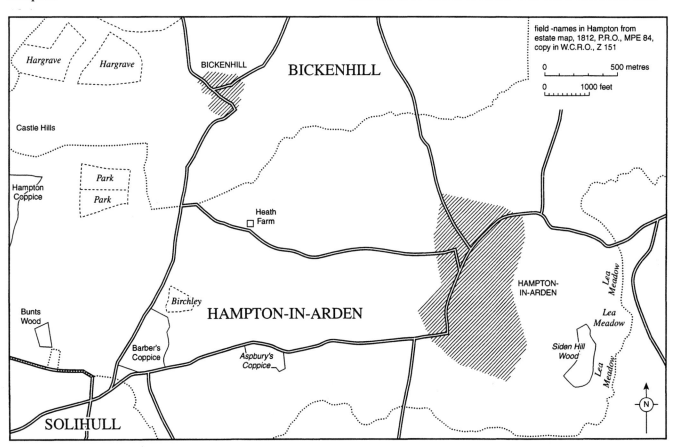

Figure 50: Hampton-in-Arden

The charters show that Birchley and Aspley were partly wooded in the late twelfth century. In 1649 Aspleys Coppice lay west of the medieval village and Birchleyes Coppice further west. The present Aspbury's Coppice may retain, in a corrupted form, both the name Aspleys and the medieval *hespelea*. It cannot be assumed that the modern coppices were medieval woodland; they may have grown up on land which had been cleared of woodland during the medieval period or on land which adjoined the medieval woodland.

Leywode, presumably the wood of *la lea*, was pasture in 1612 and 1649.[837] The name is not on modern maps, but the name Lea Meadow is, and the relationship of this meadow to Lea Wood in the 1649 survey, and to moorland to the north, points to the location of the medieval wood in the oval area of fields in the east of the parish. The modern Siden Hill Wood postdates the map of 1812.

It could be suggested that the long arm of the parish stretching south-westwards matched the shape implied by the measurements of the *silva* and that much of Solihull's eleventh-century woodland ran along the north and west of the parish. In relation to the size of the parish itself (11,296 acres)[842] and in comparison with the adjoining parish of Tanworth, much of Solihull's rural topography is not well documented. However, such records as there are do indeed point to the location of some of Solihull's medieval woodland in this area.

The names of Row Wood[843] and Lee Wood[844] survived into the modern period, so pointing to their approximate locations in the north of the parish. Deeds referring to land in Tanworth[845] confirm the site of the enclosed wood (*clauso bosco*) of Sir Nicholas de Oddingeselles in the area of the modern Clowes Wood adjacent to Tanworth parish.

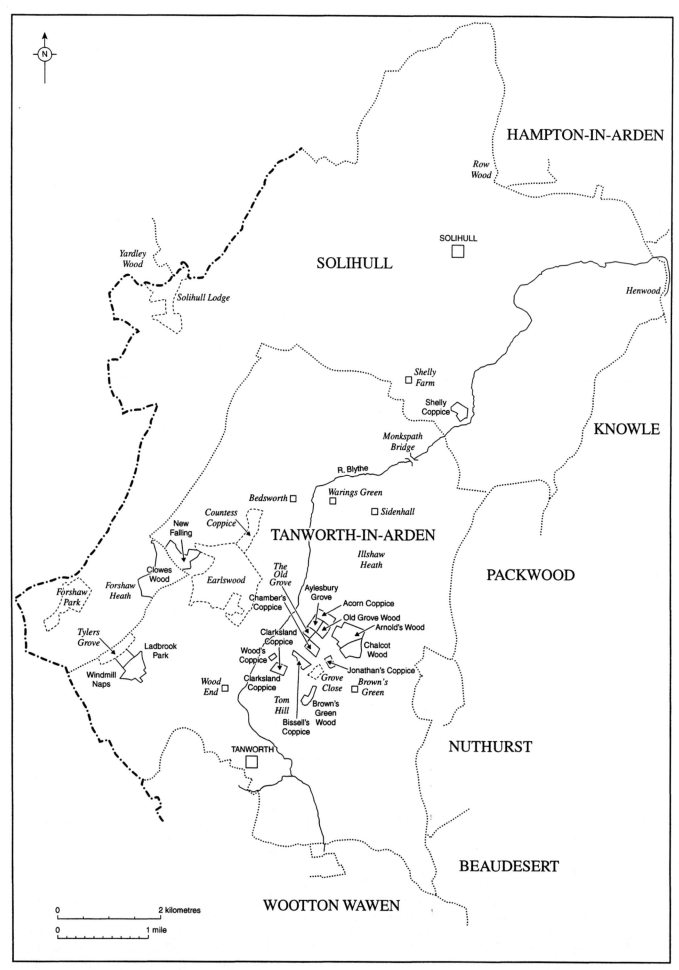

Figure 51: Solihull and Tanworth-in-Arden

In 1652 the wood was one of three demesne woods in the manor of Forshaw and adjoined land also called Clowes.[846] It has been suggested that the name of the wood comes from a local family.[847] The reverse is also possible, as both land and wood called *le clos* (i.e. the close) were recorded in Forshaw in 1310.[848] The name of Clouse Wood in Morton Bagot may have a similar derivation. The medieval wood called *Colmoreswod*[849] has so far defied location.

was not *deepwall grove* and Parish Coppice was formerly Painswell Croft.[857]

Firebote and haybote in the common of Solihull were recorded in 1373.[858] Solihull Wood was recorded as a common wood in 1495, when the parish (and county) boundary ran between it and Yardley Wood,[859] c.1600, when it contained four hundred acres,[860] and in 1606.[861] From its proximity to Yardley Wood, it appears to have been

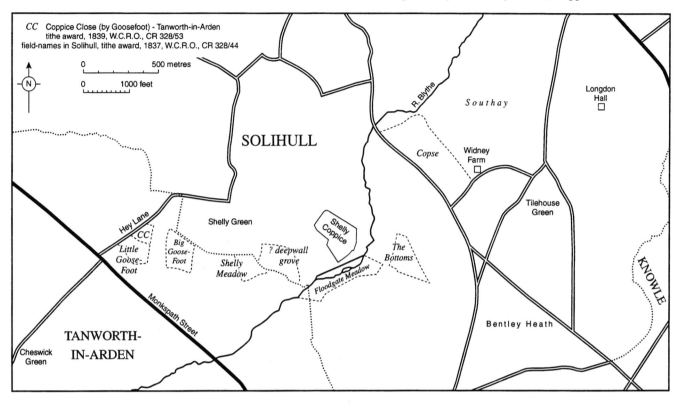

Figure 52: Solihull - Shelley and Southay

The tithe award of 1837[850] included twenty-eight coppices, two copses and ten groves. These, and field-names indicative of former woodland, were mainly in the north and west of the parish. The Archer family of Tanworth held land in Solihull and their papers record some groves. *Herynggesgrove*[851] was presumably attached to lands called *Herryngs* in Olton.[852] *Deepwall grove* was situated just east of Shelley Green; its site can be inferred from a survey made c.1500 and from later deeds. It was further west than the modern Shelley Coppice, formerly called Bottoms Coppice.[853] There was an unnamed grove adjacent to Southay,[854] possibly on the site of fields called coppice in the tithe award. There was a grove in *copperedyng*[855] in Longdon, presumably in the area called Cop Ridding in the tithe award. A grove of uncertain name (due to a torn manuscript), possibly *Chircheyardesgroue* (after its owner - there was a Churcheyarde Coppice in 1585), was by Whitefield in Solihull.[856] Minor place-names mark the site of *Herryngs* and *copperedyng* on the tithe map, but no fields called grove are associated with them. As these medieval groves have disappeared without trace it is possible that others met a similar fate. The ten fields called grove on the tithe map may be the remnants of a larger number of medieval groves. It cannot be assumed that the modern coppices are medieval groves renamed; Shelley Coppice

in the area of Solihull Lodge,[862] the largest area of common land shown in the Solihull enclosure award of 1843.[863]

The twelfth-century foundation charter of Henwood Priory referred to the wood of Longdon; land and wood called *Havekeseard* formed a later gift.[864] Modern maps show a field called Hawkshead by Henwood and other features in the boundary of the original grant can be traced.[865] Henwood Greaves was a common in 1544.[866]

Barston

In 1086 the Domesday survey recorded *silva* half a league by three furlongs in the duplicate entries for Barston.[867] This may have covered between 125 and 180 acres. Much of the parish was held by the Knights Templars in the late twelfth century,[868] but a survey of the Knights' lands in 1185 seems to have omitted all demesne lands, including woods, from their Warwickshire manors.[869] The lands of this religious order were granted c.1312 to the Knights Hospitallers, who were already in possession of other land in Barston.[870] Barston was not mentioned in the survey of the Knights' estates in 1338;[871] it might have been included under Balsall. Park and wood were recorded in 1199, so it seems reasonable to infer that the common woods called Barston Park and Escott Wood recorded in 1538 and 1540[872] were medieval woods. The sites of these woods can be traced through enclosure and tithe maps.[873] Escott Wood was arable land by 1842; the modern woodland was planted subsequently. An area of woodland appears on a map of Eastcote Hall in 1720 west of Escott Green,[874] but there is no known medieval record of it, nor of the area called The Wood which on the tithe map was separated from Escott Wood by land called Kettles.

outwoods, *Chessetwod* and *Knolleoutwode*, which provided pasture, pannage and underwood.[876] Parts of these woods can be traced. The name Chessetts Wood survives. It adjoined Kingswood (another common wood) in Lapworth.[877] Knowle outwood (sometimes called simply the wood of Knowle) was in the area of the modern Knowle Common, which in 1816 adjoined former waste in Longdon.[878] In 1542 *Clubbeland* was described as lying towards the wood of Knowle;[879] in 1816 closes called

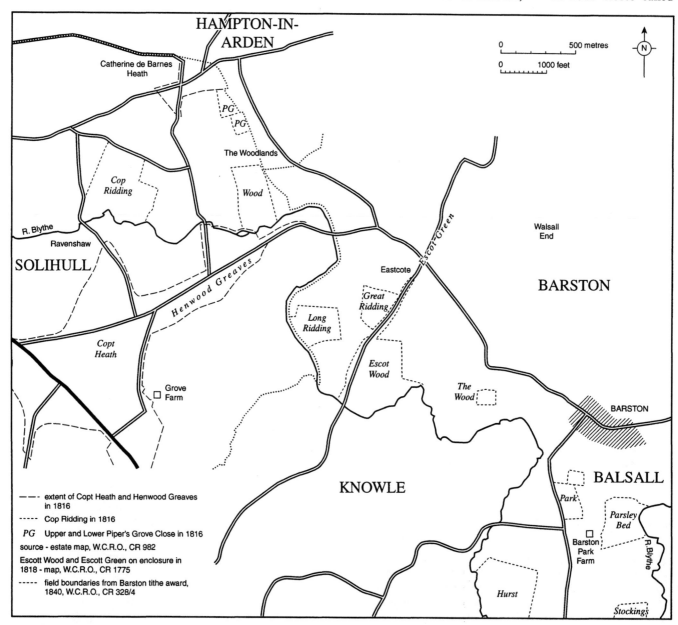

Figure 53: Barston and Henwood

A place called *Perselegrove* has been attributed mistakenly to Barston because of fields there called Parsley Bed;[875] that grove is discussed in Chapter Two.

Knowle

Knowle, not mentioned in Domesday Book but probably part of the manor of Hampton-in-Arden (see above), had relatively detailed records from the late thirteenth century revealing a strong tradition of wood pasture. There were two

Clubland were situated north-east of Knowle Common.[880] Yates's map of Warwickshire carried the legend Knowle Wood by Knowle Common.[881]

Both woods and the park had small-leaved lime trees - *lyndes* - whose bark, called bast, was sold in the 1290's by manorial officials.[882] *Croppes* of lime trees were sold in 1400-1 and subsequent years.[883] Pollarded and coppiced limes are very long-lived, but young lime trees are sensitive to grazing.[884] There were lime trees in Knowle Wood and Chessetts Wood in 1605,[885] which suggests that they had been successfully conserved since the medieval period.

The surviving manorial accounts do not refer to pasture or pannage in relation to the wood which was called *Derrech*

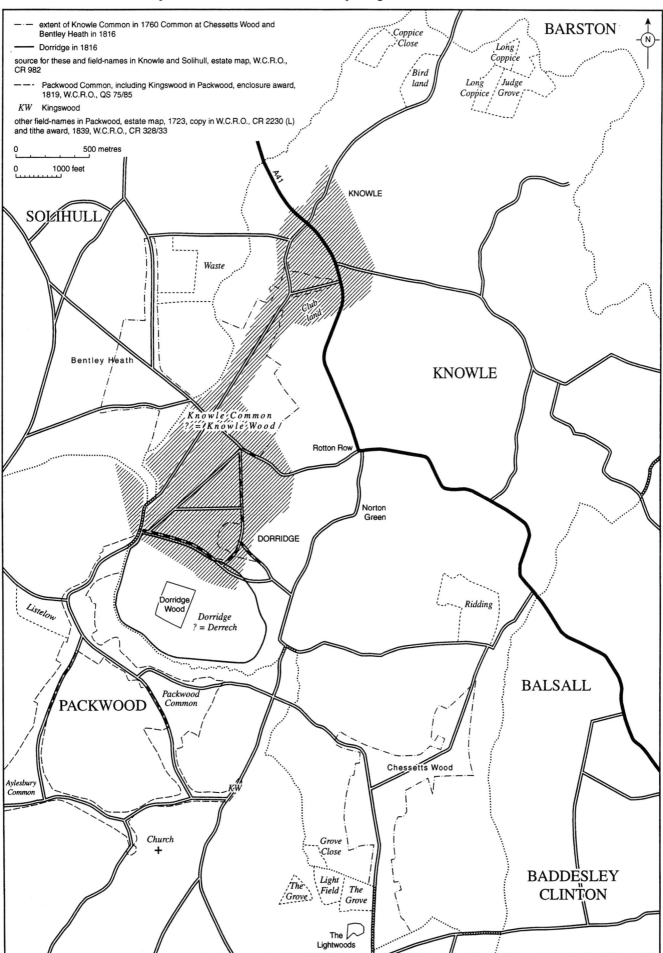

Figure 54: Knowle

(modern Dorridge). However, a case heard at the assizes shows that there was common pasture in the wood which was available to a tenant of land in Widney in Solihull.[886] The name *Derrech* means deer-ridge.[887] The likely site of the wood, which contained fifty acres in 1556, can be inferred from the large, oval area of Dorridge, divided into closes by 1820.[888] The modern Dorridge Wood has grown up on Thistley Close since 1820.

There was a park, in which pannage was allowed in 1301-2.[889] Westminster Abbey asserted land in the park (and in *Wyteslade* in Longdon in Solihull) soon after it acquired the manor in 1292.[890] Accounts for 1293, 1294-5 and 1298-9 recorded payments for assarting roots of trees and making a ditch to enclose a new assart, and the sale of oaks and underwood from asserted land.[891] Such detailed records of assarting are rare.

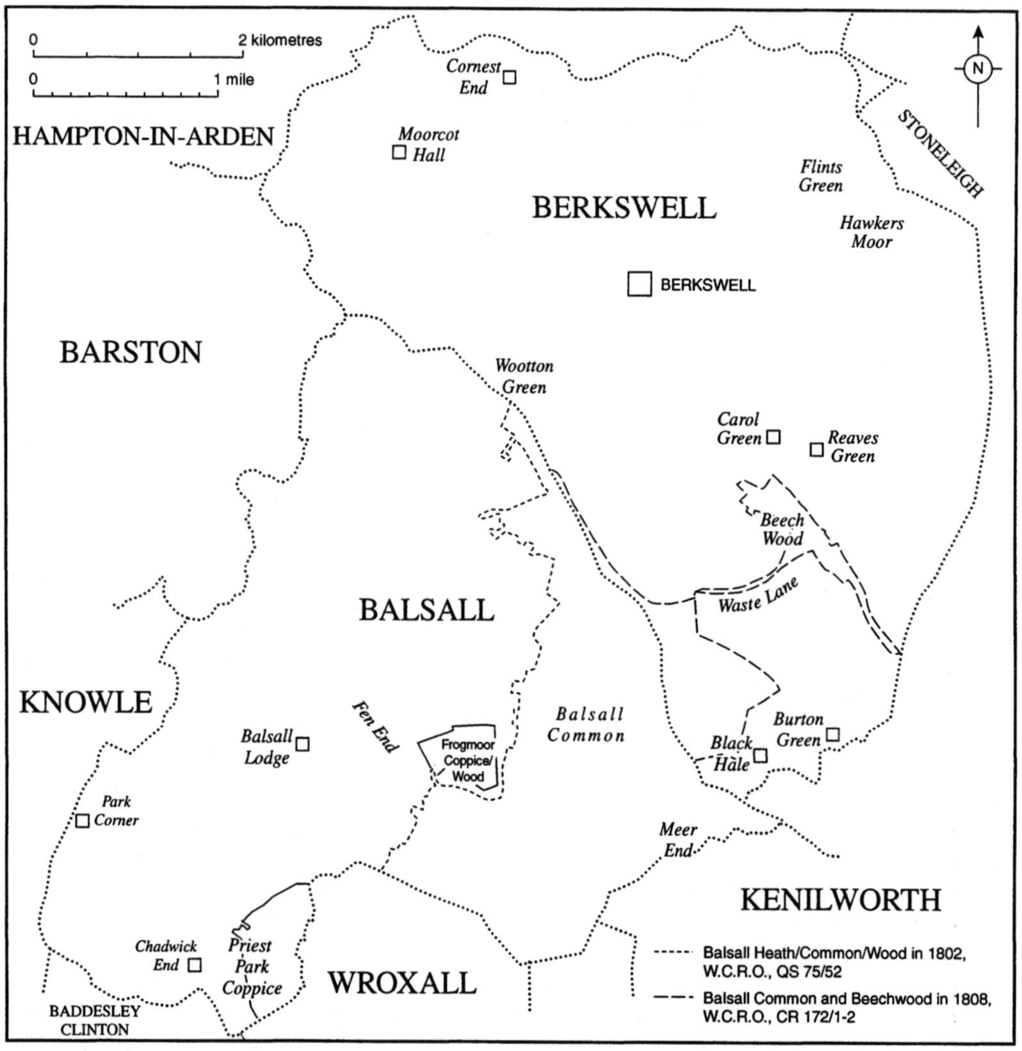

no groves at all. Two groves were mentioned in a survey of 1542.[896] Most of those in the survey of 1605[897] were in Longdon (in Solihull) or other parts of the manor beyond the township of Knowle. The earliest record found of a grove dates from 1276, when William de Arderne was murdered in his grove called *Briddesmor* next to the priory of Henwood.[898] William held land in Hampton-in-Arden and Solihull as well as in Knowle, but the location of fields called Birdsland (Birds being a possible corruption of *Briddes*) in Knowle across the river from Henwood Hall suggests that the grove was in Knowle.[899]

Balsall

Balsall's manorial records are strangely silent about woodland. Surveys of lands held by the Knights Templars[900] and subsequently by the Hospital of St. John of Jerusalem[901] do not include woodland. The former survey, made in 1185, omitted demesne lands altogether; the nature of customary services described in the survey suggests that there was land in demesne at the time.[902] The latter survey, made in 1338, included the profits from underwood without specifying the source of supply.[903] However, there are some records of Balsall's woodland in the later medieval period.

A fourteenth- or fifteenth-century copy of a deed, to which Alan Martell, master of the Templars in England in the early thirteenth century, was a party, concerned tithes of pannage and of assarts in the Templars' wood of Balsall (*in bosco nostro de Belesale*).[904] In 1322 it was recorded that in 1320 John de Moubray had sold trees in his park of Fennypark and his wood called *Le Merewod* near Balsall.[905] Modern place-names suggest that

Figure 55: Balsall and Berkswell

Three groves were recorded separately in the manorial records. Accounts for 1386-7 included *Bromlesgraue*,[892] accounts for 1400-1 the grove called *Newcloswode*,[893] and a rental of 1448-9 an unnamed grove of wood which was held by John Hogges.[894] An earlier, detailed rental[895] contained

Le Merewod was that part of Balsall's wood in Meer End. The name Fennypark may survive in the modern Fen End. The Templars' wood should presumably be linked to the woodland described in the sixteenth-century survey of Balsall below.

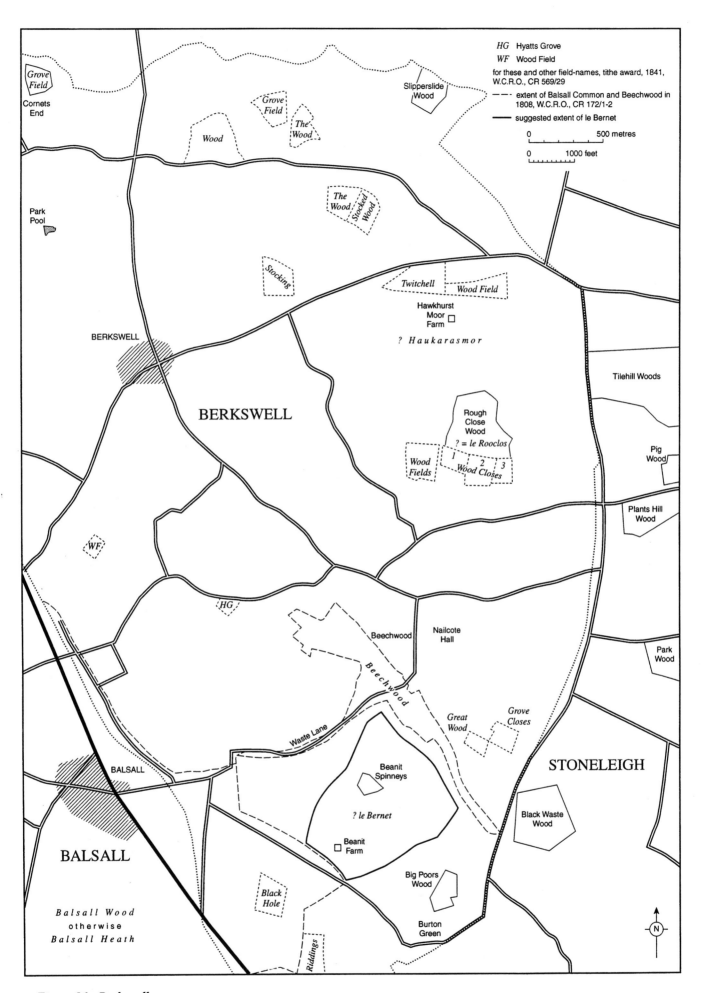

Figure 56: Berkswell

87

A dispute over common pasture belonging to the lord of Berkswell, which adjoins Balsall to the east, was recorded in 1288; eight acres of wood and heath in several places were at issue.[906] The dispute suggests that part of Balsall's wood adjoined Berkswell and that the Templars had been actively enclosing parts of their woodland. Despite this, the "great comen woodd called Balsall Wood" contained 350 acres in 1538,[907] when there was also a "yong wood" called Frogmore, presumably part of the modern Frogmore Coppice. A similar survey in 1540[908] recorded a park of 277 acres, 157 acres of which were oaks and three acres of which were underwood, and *prestys parke* of about 41 acres. The former is presumably marked by numerous fields or closes called park on a map of 1759[909] and the latter by the extant Priests Park Wood. Balsall Wood became Balsall Heath,[910] otherwise Balsall Common,[911] a name now attached to the settlement in the north of the former wood.

There are no records of groves in the later medieval period, but dopkins grove was mentioned in the survey of 1538 and Datkins Grove appears with a few other grove names on modern maps. It may be, therefore, that there were a few tenants' groves in Balsall in the later medieval period.

Berkswell

Medieval records of woodland in Berkswell refer overwhelmingly to demesne woods. The apparently large amount of woodland in the later medieval period is in line with the square league of *silva* which was recorded in Domesday Book.[912] It seems to have covered much of the eastern part of the parish. A deed which has been attributed to the second half of the twelfth century[913] suggests that the separate, named woods identified from c.1300, together with the park, had been parts of a single, large wood of Berkswell. Nigel de Mandeville granted to the canons of Kenilworth the right to take two cartloads of dead wood in his wood (*bosco*) of Berkswell, wherever they wished in the whole wood outside his park and the part called *Bernet*. *Le Bernet* was a separate wood in 1316, listed with other demesne woods called *le Rooclos, Rounderuding, Broderedyng* and *yesterhuyrne*.[914] The park was west of the church and of the modern village; part of its pale can be traced today,[915] assuming, that is, that this and fields called park do not reflect extensions to the park after Nigel de Mandeville's grant. *Bernet*, whose name became attached to the modern Beanit Farm, can be traced through seventeenth-century court rolls which refer to the lord's wood called *Bernett* or *Bearnett* in Nailcote End near fields called Cottams,[916] eighteenth-century deeds which record how this wood came to the Dugdale family,[917] and the self-contained area which was owned by Dugdale and Lant in 1808.[918] This area is now a large, coherent block of modern fields, on to which other field boundaries abut. Even if the twelfth-century park did not extend as far west as later field-names suggest, the location of *Bernet*, the commons enclosed in 1808 and the likely sites of other later medieval demesne woods described below point to an extensive area of woodland in the eastern half of the parish, where most of Berkswell's greens were also located. However, the exact coincidence of the later

medieval woodland and the Domesday *silva* cannot be presumed.

There are also records of woods called *Haukarasmor, Blakenhale* and *Lee Wood*.[919] *Blakenhale*, presumably *le Blakehale* of 1480-1, was described, with *Bechewode*, as a common wood in 1553.[920] It may have been in the vicinity of the fields called Black Hole in the tithe award[921] and the modern Blackhales Farm south of the area of waste called Balsall Common in the 1808 enclosure award. *Bechewode* can be easily identified from that award.[922] The name Balsall Common may reflect the intercommoning between Balsall and Berkswell which was the subject of a court case in 1289.[923] *Lee Wood* has not been located. *Haukarasmor* seems to have become Hawkhurst Moor Farm, where two Wood Fields and a hedge of small-leaved lime suggest the former presence of a wood.[924] A deed of 1758 stated that "a newly-erected Messuage or Tenement" with enclosed land called Hawkers Moore Farm "was theretofore a Coppice or Wood Ground".[925]

There has been some confusion between Hawkers Moor Wood and Rough Close Wood, arising from lack of access to available evidence about them.[926] Both were listed as demesne woods at the end of the survey of 1553.[927] Rough Close Wood is the obvious candidate for the medieval wood called *le Rooclos* and the identification has been made unquestioningly by place-name scholars.[928] It has been disputed on the grounds of a reference to the destruction of Rough Close Wood,[929] but this interpretation overlooks the existence of two adjacent parts of Rough Close in separate ownership. The glebeland was developed as a coppice wood in the seventeenth century,[930] becoming part of the Parsons Wood, which is now represented by the Wood Fields to the south-west of the modern Rough Close Wood (Fig. 56).[931] Rough Close Wood itself seems to have remained both as woodland and under the control of the lord,[932] and survives, albeit damaged.[933]

Three of the woods listed in the inquisitions post mortem of 1316,[934] *Rounderuding, Broderedyng* and *yesterhuyrne*, have not been located, but land called Ridding appears on the tithe map adjacent to Balsall Common. The first was still wood in 1553.[935] The *Wastewode* recorded in 1455-6 and 1553[936] may have been the same as the *Westwode* mentioned in the main part of the 1553 survey. If so, it was presumably by Westwood Heath, which adjoined Westwood in Stoneleigh.

As far as woodland is concerned, the most striking feature of the 1553 survey is the appearance of at least twenty-nine groves amongst the tenants' holdings. Only a few were named, but some were associated with named tenements or described by approximate location. They appear to have been more widely distributed than the demesne woods, although some were in the east of the parish near to those woods. They included Ryders Grove, several groves in Cornest End, one in Taylors on Trogarshill, one at Colersfeld, one in goodyge, Colyerswell between Beachewoode and Westelane, four in Blakesend, one in hukyns place, three by Twychelbrok, one in palescroft, four in Nailcote End, one on Readhill and one in Oldnall End.

that the groves were at least as old as the fifteenth century. A deed of 1486 referred to two groves in Berkswell called *Walsall groves* and two fields with two groves called the

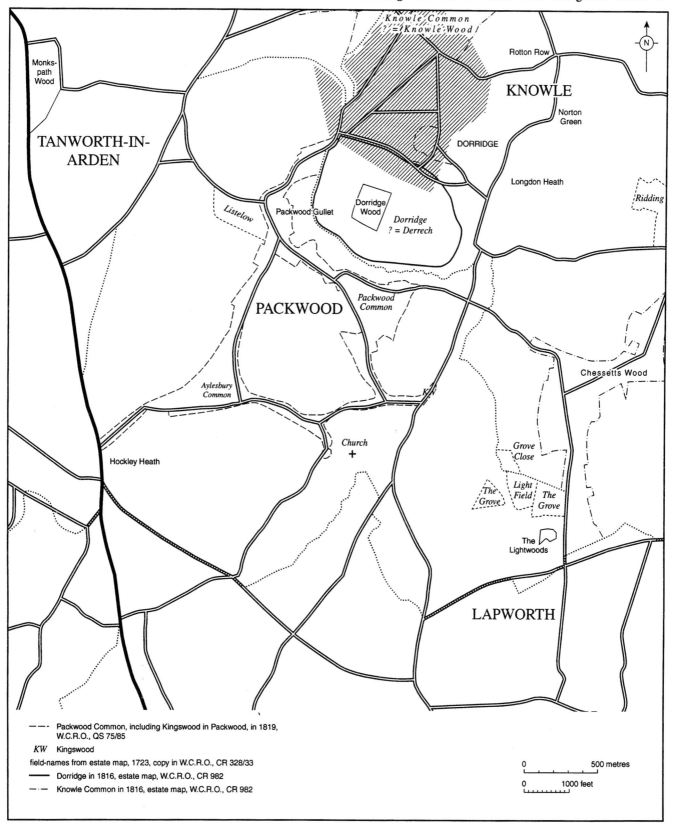

Figure 57: Packwood

A few field-names including the word grove in the tithe award presumably mark the sites of some of these groves. There are hints within earlier records relating to Berkswell

neder and *over Fenn*.[937] A grove by the pasture called *Twynchefeld* was recorded in 1480-1.[938] Analogy with other parishes in the region suggests that this pattern of small tenants' groves was older still.

Packwood

The very name suggests a wooded place. Packwood was not mentioned in Domesday Book. Sir William Dugdale attributed Wasperton's *silva* to Packwood, for Packwood was attached to the manor of Wasperton and its church was dependent on the church of Wasperton.[939] If this attribution is correct (and it is suggested in Chapter Two that the *silva* could have been in Wasperton itself) there was not much *silva* in Packwood in 1086, perhaps 85 to 120 acres at the most within the dimensions of half a league and two furlongs.[940]

A deed confirming lands to Coventry Cathedral Priory c.1183 included the wood of Packwood and the church built there (*nemus de pacwda cum ecclesia illic constructa*).[941] Did "there" refer back to Packwood in general or to the wood in particular? Packwood church, whose earliest surviving fabric has been dated to the late thirteenth century,[942] is situated towards the south of the parish. It was within the lands held by the Bishop of Coventry and Lichfield in 1819[943] which may equate to the Priory's lands.

A survey of Packwood in 1410-11 recorded three groves in demesne, called *le lusterley grovis*, and sixteen groves held by a total of eleven of the Priory's tenants.[944] The management of the tenants' groves was regulated by the lord of the manor; the tenants could not fell trees or timber in the groves and fields which they held of the lord, since all groves and woods were reserved to the lord and his successors, but the tenants might have pasture and underwood of the groves. Unfortunately, the survey does not describe the location of the tenants' holdings. They took the form of enclosures (*clausuras, clausuris*), crofts, moors, pieces of waste land and meadow, and an odd field or two (*monelande* and *le Ruydynge*); there was no indication of any common fields. The tithe award[945] has only two fields called grove. It shows that listelowe, presumably a corruption of *lusterley*, was in the north of the parish and that Packwood Common was in the middle. The medieval name *Lyhtewode*[946] presumably survived in the name Light Fields, shown on a map of 1723,[947] in the south-eastern part of the parish, adjacent to Chessetts Wood in Knowle and to Kingswood in Lapworth. Part of Packwood's common was called Kingswood, but it did not adjoin Kingswood in Lapworth.

Tanworth-in-Arden

There is no specific reference to Tanworth in Domesday Book. Tanworth is thought to have been surveyed as an unnamed member of Brailes, for it was a chapelry of Brailes parish in the later medieval period.[948] In 1086 Brailes had *silva* measuring three leagues by two leagues,[949] a total area of between perhaps 5,000 and 7,000 acres. It has been claimed, following Sir William Dugdale,[950] that this *silva* was in Tanworth. Certainly later medieval records show many woods in Tanworth and only one wood in Brailes.

Dr. Roberts, in his detailed study of these records, concluded that in the second half of the thirteenth century the earls of Warwick "jealously reserved for their own purposes the west of the manor which was still heavily wooded"[951] whilst following a deliberate policy of granting pieces of waste land to both freeholders and villeins.[952] He assumed that woodland "must have been present in some quantity" in other estates in Tanworth, but found that "little can be learnt" about it.[953] For the purposes of this study the most striking feature of the surviving deeds and rentals is the large number of woods and groves in Tanworth outside the earls' demesne. They are listed in Appendix 1.

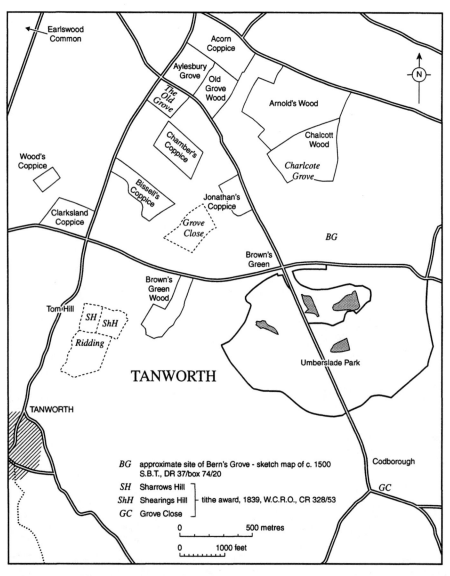

Figure 58: Tanworth-in-Arden - south

Tanworth could almost be called the parish of tenants' woods and groves, but the demesne woodland should not be overlooked.

c. 1196 Waleran, earl of Warwick, referred to his wood of Tanworth in a grant of the mills of Walton and Barford.[954] There are some references to the wood of the lord (*bosco domini*) or the wood called *Erleswode* in deeds and in the earls' account rolls, which survive intermittently from 1377[955] and, for woodland, record the use or sale of timber rather than underwood, although the latter was mentioned in the inquisitions post mortem of 1316. Between 1268 and 1298 John le Archer quitclaimed to earl William his right to both estovers and common pasture in the earl's wood of Tanworth.[956] Inquisitions post mortem into the lands of earl Guy in 1316 referred to a foreign wood which included thirteen acres of pasture of new assart which were common for part of the year.[957] Pasture as well as wood was sold in *Newefalling* in the later fourteenth century.[958] Neither *Newefalling* nor another source of wood, *Countessclose*, was called a wood or a grove in the earls' records; in the early modern period they were called coppices.[959] Three groves appear in the accounts, *Wawmondes grove* in 1395-6,[960] *Rankegrove* in 1418-9,[961] and *ffulvordesgroue* in 1429-30.[962] The names of the first and last of these groves suggest that the people concerned had at one time held them of the earl.

There are no records of the sizes of the demesne woods. Earlswood and Sarehurst jointly contained 308 acres in 1544,[963] but this is not a reliable indication of their extent, say, three centuries earlier. Nor was the type of land use in 1544 necessarily the same as in earlier centuries; 21 of the 308 acres were meadow, 167 "Waste & fedyngs" and 120 described as "resydue".[964] It has also been suggested that the earls' park was formed from woodland.[965]

As most of Tanworth's woods and groves were outside the demesne there is little evidence to show how they were managed. (The Archer family, which built up a large estate in Tanworth from the lands of other families, appears to have let its lands; a few leases of groves survive from 1495 to 1516.[966]) It could be suggested that, despite their numerical superiority, they were smaller in their overall extent than the earls' woods, but there is no evidence for this. Indeed, there was one great wood (*magno bosco*), held by the Fulford family[967] and apparently situated in the eastern part of Tanworth.[968] It must also be emphasised that, relatively plentiful though the Archer muniments are, they did not cover the whole parish. The surviving documents give only a partial picture of Tanworth's topography; still less do they indicate the nature and extent of changes in land use between, say, c.1100 and c.1500. Consequently, there is no direct evidence of when and how the various tenants' woods and groves acquired their separate identities.

It has been argued that at least some of the tenants' holdings which included groves, such as Warners and Brouns, had been created from waste land.[969] This implies that the groves had been formed either as secondary woodland, or by enclosing small patches of woodland which had survived on

the waste. The records do show a distinction between woods and groves which is at least as old as the twelfth century. *Lutlegroveshei*, recorded c.1200,[970] was presumably named after a grove which was little in comparison with other groves. The records show also that the tenants' woods and groves were widely scattered throughout Tanworth

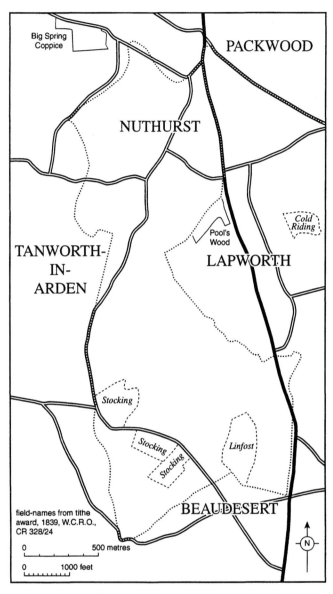

Figure 59: Nuthurst

The presence of groves in tenants' holdings suggests that most of the groves were not large. Rare sketch maps of c.1500 amongst the Archer papers show both *Charlecote grove* and *berns grove*.[971] The former seems to be roughly the same shape and size as the modern Chalcot Wood, but the grove of c.1500 could have been larger than that of, say, c.1300. The modern Tylers Grove, presumably a corruption of the later medieval *Tylhous Grove*,[972] certainly includes some secondary woodland; part of it lies on ridge and furrow.[973] The *berns grove* of c.1500 was very small, only about two acres in extent. Due to the disappearance of many of the groves and of their names, the sites of most other groves cannot be given precisely, but some surviving field-names indicate approximate locations. In relatively close proximity to *Charlecote Grove* and *berns Grove* were

91

Wattelonde grove and two groves in the chantry lands. The northern edge of the parish, in and around Monkspath, affords several more examples. In addition to the groves in *Warners* and *Brouns*, there was another, little, grove in *brouns* on the side next to *Warners*. The grove called *goosfoot* was presumably in or by the closes called Big and Little Goosefoot in the tithe award; perhaps it became the adjacent Coppice Close. The *spon growe (sic)* was near to the river Blythe. *Moorrs growe* and *archers growe* were adjacent and near to *smiths pool*. *Cheswykus growe* was by *Whyteffeylde* and *lyghts fordrowe* (there is a Whitefield by Light Hall in the tithe award) and presumably near to Cheswick Green.[974]

Nuthurst

The place-name Nuthurst is recorded as *Hnuthyrste* in an Anglo-Saxon charter considered to be authentic and attributed to the decade 699-709.[975] The place-name implies that not only was a type of woodland called hurst to be found there before the eighth century but also that it was distinguished from other hursts by the production of nuts.[976] This deduction is supported by the use of hurst in minor place-names in the parish, *Hadingehurst/Hodenghurst*, *Stanihurst* and, in deeds dated 1349, 1360 and 1594, a field called *Linthurst*.[977] The name Lindhurst is said to have survived into the twentieth century, attached to fields in Nuthurst Farm adjoining the Stratford Road.[978] The tithe award includes two field called Linfost.[979] Other examples of Lindhurst have been interpreted as referring to a hurst of linden or small-leaved lime trees.[980] There was a tradition of lime trees in Nuthurst, where there was a medieval lane called *le Lindes*.[981] There is no indication that any of the hursts was woodland in the later medieval period.

There were at least two groves of wood in Nuthurst, called *Gunnild grove* and *Systeleyes grove* respectively.[982] Another grove, *le Hulgrave*, was described as moor instead of wood.[983] In 1331 William Trussell was licensed to impark his wood in Nuthurst.[984] There was a wood (*boscum*) called *le yondrewode*.[985]

Lapworth and Bushwood

The identification of the ancient ecclesiastical parish of Lapworth with manors recorded in Domesday Book is so uncertain as to make an estimate of the area of the Domesday *silva* even more tentative than usual. If *Lapeforde* was written in error for Lapworth, then there were probably more than 2,000 acres of *silva*, which measured two leagues by one league.[986] It has been suggested that the *silva* which was entered under the royal manor of Kineton and Wellesbourne was Kingswood,[987] which was described as belonging to the manor of Kineton in 1279, when tenants of Wellesbourne had rights to fuel, pannage and pasture there,[988] and which lay partly in Lapworth parish.[989] However, as explained in Chapter Two, there was woodland in Wellesbourne itself in the later medieval period. The presence of the minor place-name Kingswood in nearby parishes suggests that royal interest in local woodland may

have extended well beyond the Kingswood of the enclosure award.[990]

Lapworth parish also included part of Bushwood. The name Bushwood is a corruption of the bishop's wood.[991] When enclosure and tithe awards were made the greater part of Bushwood was a detached portion of the parish of Stratford-upon-Avon; the rest was divided between the parishes of Lapworth and Rowington.[992] By 1252,[993] if not long before, Bushwood was an appurtenance of the manor of Stratford-upon-Avon, which was held then, in 1086, and for centuries previously, by the bishops of Worcester.[994] The ecclesiastical relationship suggests an early tenurial link, but there is no record of this in the Domesday Book entry for *Lapeforde*.[995] There is an eleventh-century tradition that Lapworth had belonged to the church of Worcester but had been alienated before the Norman Conquest.[996] Perhaps Bushwood was then within Lapworth. The line of the parish boundaries suggests that the area belonging to Stratford parish had been detached from Lapworth. Bushwood may have been the wood of Lapworth, with that part which became parochially dependent on Stratford escaping the pre-Conquest alienation. This may be why Bushwood was called the wood of Lapworth in 1197, when Fraericus de Bissopesdun quitclaimed to the bishop the whole wood of Lapworth called Bishopswood.[997] In 1299 six of the bishop's tenancies included assarts,[998] suggesting that part of Bushwood had been cleared in the later medieval period.

There was another named wood in Lapworth. Two thirteenth-century deeds refer respectively to land in the assart of *Wulvurenewode* and in the waste of *Wulvernewode*.[999] In 1350 the name was attached to two fields and a meadow and in 1446-7 to a close.[1000] Unlike Kingswood and Bushwood the name has not survived. It is possible that some of Lapworth's woodland became parkland. There was a park in 1299 which featured in various later deeds.[1001]

Luke Sorel held woodland in Lapworth in 1221.[1002] There was a large family of Sorels,[1003] so it cannot be assumed that the field called *Sorelesfeld* in Lapworth in 1375[1004] was Luke Sorel's land or near his wood.

There is no indication as to which wood was the wood of Lapworth mentioned in a gift to Reading Abbey[1005] which was probably made in the later twelfth century.

There were some groves in Lapworth. One adjoined a field called le *Harperesfeld* in 1364,[1006] in 1407 there was a grove called *Stikmonesmor*,[1007] and in 1408 another adjoined land called *Neuewast*.[1008] A grove called *Bromon grove* in Brome manor in 1501 was described as land (*terram*) adjoining Rowington in 1509.[1009] There was a *Heye grove* in 1569.[1010] Groves were mentioned amongst the general appurtenances of the manor when it was divided in 1369.[1011] Some grove names appear in the tithe award[1012] and presumably mark the sites of former medieval groves. There do not appear to have been groves amongst the bishop's lands in 1299.[1013]

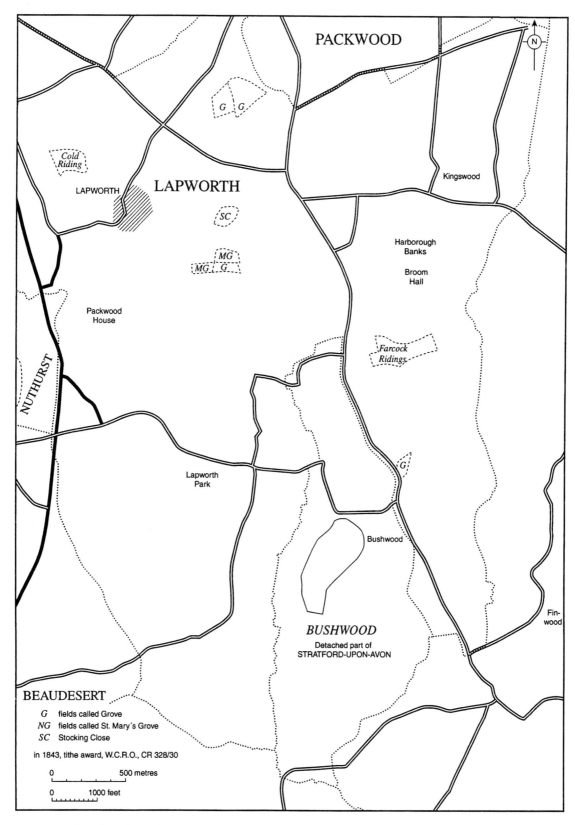

Figure 60: Lapworth and Bushwood

Baddesley Clinton

The entry for Baddesley in Domesday Book may refer to Baddesley Ensor rather than to Baddesley Clinton,[1014] so that any attempt to match the later medieval woodland to the *silva* of Domesday Book must be uncertain. Baddesley Clinton is another, and well-documented, example of a countryside of little groves and great woods, commons and parks. Numerous deeds, accounts and court rolls, a fifteenth-century survey and a map of 1699[1015] all help to locate most of the known medieval woods and groves. They include rare documentary evidence of secondary woodland formed in the later medieval period.

93

There appear to have been three woods. The Outwood was mentioned only once by that name, c.1300,[1016] but by analogy with places elsewhere and by comparing names associated with the outwood and with lands in the waste of Baddesley[1017] it may be equated to the common wood (communi bosco) mentioned in a manorial court in 1429[1018] and to the common (communem) of Baddesley recorded in the fifteenth-century survey and in 1593-4.[1019] This was in the area of Baddesley Green, common or waste land enclosed in 1812[1020] and shown on the map of 1699 on the northern edge of Baddesley.[1021] The waste called Kingswood, which was also in this area,[1022] presumably approximated to the "Roxall Kingswood" shown on the map of 1699 on the north-eastern edge of Baddesley.

Haywood was the subject of a deed c.1200 in which it was called a *defensa*. Already enclosed, it was nonetheless available for pasture and wood. Later it was called a park.[1023] In 1329 twenty-one acres of land in the park, with wood growing on them, were leased to Isabel, widow of Philip de Chetewinde; a grant of two acres was made at the same time.[1024] In 1415 there was separate pasture in Haywood.[1025] By the fifteenth century at least some parts of the wood were managed as coppice, substantial wood sales being recorded in three of the relatively small number of account rolls which have survived for the manor.[1026] Haywood was presumably the separate wood (*separali bosco*) of the lord mentioned in the court rolls,[1027] and there is a reference to repairs in its boundary fence.[1028] It could not have contained a great deal of timber, as timber was brought from Honiley park to repair the manor house in 1457-8.[1029] Haywood contained some small-leaved lime before it was replanted with conifers in the twentieth century. In 1491 a tenant was presented to the manorial court for unauthorised removal of bast (from the bark of lime trees) from the wood of the lord,[1030] so it appears that small-leaved lime had been long established in the wood. Significant amounts of small-leaved lime in Baddesley at an earlier date are suggested by the field-name *Lindhurste* recorded in 1275 and 1318.[1031] The deed of 1275 is endorsed in a later hand 'Wales rent', so the field may have been in the area of the fields called Wallis in 1699.

Baddesley's medieval groves were held originally by tenants, but had become part of the manorial demesne by 1503.[1032] Most of them were in the vicinity of Haywood. *Gegge Grove* survived as a minor name in 1699; it was still wood in 1620[1033] and was added to Haywood between 1699 and 1847.[1034] Other groves cannot be precisely located by surviving field-names, but their location can sometimes be deduced or suggested from the names of fields which were adjacent to, or associated with, them. *Dodsgrove* extended to *Geggesgrove* and was by a close called *Chetewyns*,[1035] which became the closes called Chatings in 1699. Was *Dodsgrove* the grove described as formerly belonging to Roger Chetwynde in 1376?[1036] There were three groves in *Gilberdeslond* in 1336;[1037] did they merge to become the single *Gilberdesgrove* of 1503[1038] and did this become the Gilberts Coppice by land called Gilberts in 1699? Two adjacent groves conveyed to John Mayell in 1429[1039] were presumably in the vicinity of land called Males in 1699 and

may therefore have become the wood then called Sides Coppice, now Nunnery Coppice and in 1606-7 Long Grove.[1040] As the Tilehouse was also called Heywood house and was associated with land called Clepittes in 1628,[1041] the *tylhous grove* of 1478[1042] may have become the Clay Pitts grove of 1639[1043] and the Clay Pitts Coppice of 1699 which, like Gilberts Coppice, survives today. Whitleys grove, presumably the *Whitlesgrove* of 1456-7,[1044] was near to the common of Baddesley.[1045]

One of the groves adjoining Haywood originated as secondary woodland between 1330 and 1422, when John Brome of Baddesley leased a small grove (*grovettum*) in Baddesley which was formerly two crofts and part of a croft, namely *Bromcroft*, *Pappeley croft* and part of *Lediscroft*, between Haywood and the road from Baddesley to Warwick.[1046] These crofts were not described as wood in 1330,[1047] when their location was more precisely defined by the statement that they also lay between *Grenefeld* (shown on the map of 1699) and *Reufeldes* (probably the croft which was called Four Fields in 1699[1048]). This grove was called *Bromesgrove*, which was described as adjacent to Haywood in 1444-5, to *Grenefeld* in 1457-8 and to *ffoaresfeld* (=Four Fields) in the fifteenth-century survey.[1049] Like Gegge Grove, it is within the present Haywood.

Three groves were situated in or around Newland in the west of Baddesley. *Birchengrove* belonged to the duchy of Lancaster[1050] and was recorded as a wood in the accounts for the duchy's lands in the area.[1051] Part of *Birchengrove* was called *Barlowes grove*[1052] and was presumably the grove at *morreylane* which was held by Robert Barlowe in 1491.[1053] There was a grove in a field called *Newlond* in 1339[1054] which may have been the *Newenhamgrove* associated with *le Newelond* in 1347.[1055] One of these groves may have been the grove of Henry Somerlane which was in the same area in the fifteenth century.[1056]

One grove was between the manor and the millpond in 1451-2[1057] and is presumably represented by the field-name The Grove on the tithe award by the pool of Baddesley Clinton Hall.[1058] There was another field called Grove a little further to the west which had trees in 1699 but was pasture in 1847. The latter may have been the grove by *le Sprynges* through land called *magyndey* by the manor in 1451-2.[1059]

Of Rowington Coppice, carpeted in bluebells in the spring, no record earlier than 1593 has been found[1060] and there is no hint of a possible earlier name. It is in Baddesley Clinton, but named after the adjacent parish.

Wroxall

Wroxall was not mentioned in Domesday Book. It is less well documented than Baddesley, but a rental and court rolls show that it too had tenants' groves in addition to demesne woods, a park and a hay. There is some detailed topographical information about Wroxall's woodland in confirmations of the endowments of Wroxall Priory, which was founded in the middle of the twelfth century.[1061]

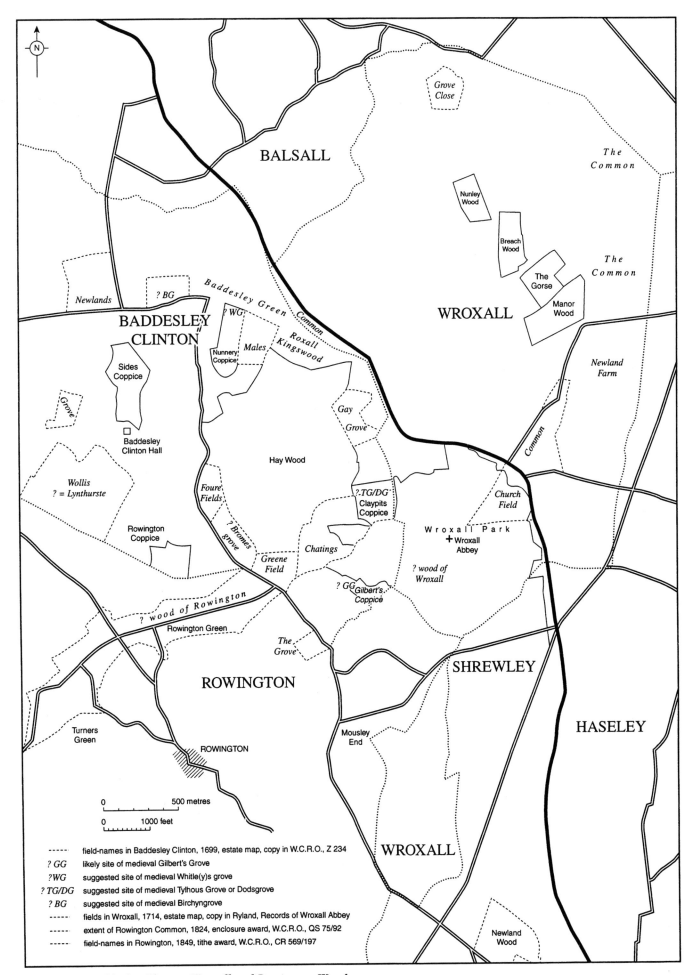

N

BALSALL

Grove Close

The Common

Nunley Wood

Breach Wood

The Common

WROXALL

The Gorse

Manor Wood

Newlands

? BG

Baddesley Green   *Common*

BADDESLEY CLINTON

?WG

Roxall Kingswood

Nunnery Coppice

Males

Newland Farm

Grove

Sides Coppice

□ Baddesley Clinton Hall

Gay Grove

Common

Wollis
? = Lynthurste

Hay Wood

?.TG/DG Claypits Coppice

Church Field

Foure Fields

W r o x a l l   P a r k
✚ Wroxall Abbey

Rowington Coppice

? Bromes grove

Chatings

? wood of Wroxall

Greene Field

? GG Gilbert's Coppice

? wood of Rowington

Rowington Green

The Grove

SHREWLEY

ROWINGTON

HASELEY

Turners Green

Mousley End

ROWINGTON

0   500 metres

0   1000 feet

WROXALL

Newland Wood

---- field-names in Baddesley Clinton, 1699, estate map, copy in W.C.R.O., Z 234

? GG   likely site of medieval Gilbert's Grove

?WG   suggested site of medieval Whitle(y)s grove

? TG/DG   suggested site of medieval Tylhous Grove or Dodsgrove

? BG   suggested site of medieval Birchyngrove

---- fields in Wroxall, 1714, estate map, copy in Ryland, Records of Wroxall Abbey

---- extent of Rowington Common, 1824, enclosure award, W.C.R.O., QS 75/92

---- field-names in Rowington, 1849, tithe award, W.C.R.O., CR 569/197

Figure 61: Baddesley Clinton, Wroxall and Rowington Wood

The bounds of Wroxall's wood touched Rowington and included two minor place-names, *Wyteley* and *Bernet*.[1062] The latter name has not been traced, but the former seems to have survived as Whitley Gate in the bounds of Rowington which were recorded in 1605.[1063] Wroxall's wood therefore adjoined Rowington. This location corresponds to the information given in the legend attached to the foundation of the Priory, whose founder, earl Hugh, was taken prisoner in the Holy Land and, on vowing to establish a Benedictine nunnery, was reportedly miraculously transported home, to find himself in his wood, at the place where the east end of the priory's church later stood.[1064] The Priory was in the southern part of Wroxall, near to Rowington. In 1482-3 woods of the Priory were by *Churchfelde*, north-east of the church according to a map of 1714.[1065]

The Priory's woodland was extensive. Two petitions to the king c.1322 claimed that Sir John de Moubray had deprived the Priory of one hundred acres and three hundred acres of wood respectively; the latter referred also to one hundred acres of waste.[1066] Some of the Priory's woodland may have been in Beausale (see below), at Shortwood, which it claimed as part of Wroxall parish, or in the detached part of Wroxall parish adjoining Shrewley.[1067] There was more than one wood in Wroxall itself. Kingswood was named in thirteenth-century deeds which dealt with adjoining land in Baddesley Clinton[1068] and was presumably on the site of the Roxall Kingswood shown on the edge of a map of Baddesley manor drawn in 1699.[1069]

Confirmations of the Priory's endowments[1070] stated that earl Hugh had a park and hays, in which the nuns were quit of pannage; this statement and the grant of hedging for *Nonneley* from earl Hugh's hay (*haya*) indicate that these places had trees. Creation of a park might explain the loss of minor place-names such as *Bernet*.

It is only through the survival of some court rolls and a rental that we learn about the tenants' woodland. In 1327-8[1071] eight tenants each held a grove. All except one held in bondage, the eighth at the lady's will. At the manorial court of Wroxall in May, 1335, it was reported that Henry Wodecock had cut down a tree in the grove of Thomas de Kylcote,[1072] one of the tenants listed as holding a grove in 1327-8. None of the groves has a proper name in the medieval records. Three grove names appear in a survey of 1542,[1073] but one was then described as a toft. The relationship between the medieval groves and the coppices which were included in the map and survey of 1714 is unknown.

Rowington

Under Rowington Domesday Book included *silva* measuring one and a half leagues by eight furlongs,[1074] covering an area of perhaps between 1,000 and 1,400 acres, which might have extended into Wroxall. This suggestion arises from Wroxall's absence from Domesday Book and the joint tenure of the later medieval manors. Wroxall was held in the mid-twelfth century by Hugh, son of Richard, who claimed part of the land and wood of Rowington in 1150.[1075] This and other references to woodland in Rowington survive in the cartulary of Reading Abbey, to which the vill of Rowington was granted c.1133.[1076]

The cartulary records a tenacious tradition of wood pasture. A deed of c.1155-8 confirmed that the Abbey and its tenants in Rowington had common of wood and plain (*de bosco et de plano*) in the reign of Henry I (1100-35).[1077] A deed of 1150 confirmed rights of common for the men of Shrewley in the abbot's wood of *Aspele* and for the tenants of Rowington in the wood of Shrewley.[1078] Common of pasture in the wood of Rowington called *Inwode* was the subject of a quitclaim in 1252.[1079] In 1221 Reading Abbey claimed common of pasture in lands which had been assarted from a wood called *Eweruge*.[1080] In 1606 tenants had pasture rights in Rowington Green (thirty acres), Aspley Wood (sixteen acres), *Busshops* Wood (some of which was in Rowington, some in Lapworth and the rest of which formed a detached part of Old Stratford parish) and Turners Green.[1081] The same survey stated that one copyhold tenant had common pasture in Rowington Wood. Common in a "Wast or Comon called Pynneley" was recorded in 1536-7.[1082]

From an early date there were distinct, named woods in Rowington, but, despite the survival of these names into the sixteenth century, the woods are not easy to locate. A published reconstruction of the medieval topography of Rowington carries many question marks, including one against Aspley Wood, and does not mark *Eweruge* or Rowington Wood at all.[1083] In 1543-4 *Asple* Wood was described as adjoining the township of Pinley;[1084] this places it in south-east Rowington (rather than on the western edge as shown in the published reconstruction). There it might have adjoined the wood of Pinley which was recorded c.1220.[1085] In 1481 the waste called *Pinley Wodde* was separated from land called *Colmesay* by land called Pinley Rudding.[1086] *Colmesay* is thought to have become the Cumsey shown on modern maps;[1087] on the tithe map of Rowington a close called the Ridding separated Cumsey from Pinley Green.[1088] This association of medieval wood with later green is found elsewhere in Rowington.

The approximate location of Rowington Wood may be inferred from medieval court rolls and accounts relating to Baddesley Clinton. In 1491 a lane ran between the wood (*boscum*) called Rowington Wood and the church of Baddesley.[1089] In 1457-8 a gate was made in the lane leading from Rowington Wood to Wroxall called *Chetwynneslane*.[1090] Land called *Chetewyns* was situated in the south-east corner of Baddesley. These references show that Rowington Wood was in the north of Rowington parish, probably including Rowington Green. Endwood End, situated to the north-east of Finwood Green,[1091] may mark the edge of a wood. Finwood is thought to be a corruption of *Inwood*,[1092] which appears to have been in the vicinity of *Eweruge*, alias *Overruge*. Two crofts in *Overruge* called Packwoods which were recorded in 1491 and subsequently[1093] came to Wroxall Charities; in 1707 the crofts were said to be in Inwood End.[1094] This location corresponds to the information given in the Reading Abbey cartulary to the effect that *Eweruge* adjoined Luke Sorel's land in Lapworth.[1095]

It is not clear whether the foreign wood which was mentioned in one deed[1096] was in Rowington or Pinley. Parts of Kingswood and Bushwood were in Rowington, but neither was part of the Abbey's manor.

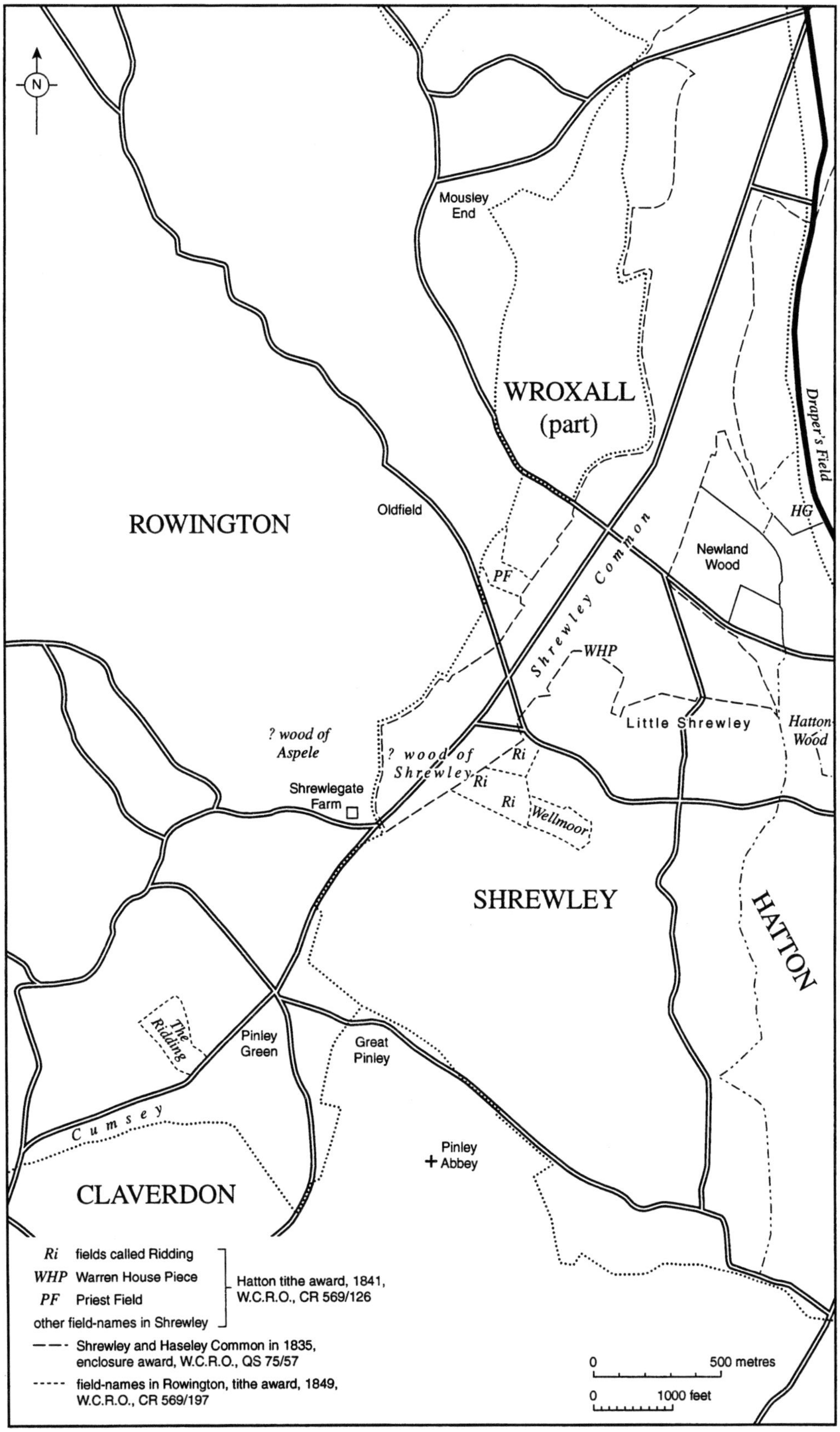

Shrewley

Shrewley was part of the ecclesiastical parish of Hatton but the subject of a separate entry in Domesday Book which included *silva* measuring one league by half a league.[1097] It is tempting to equate Shrewley's eleventh-century *silva* with Shrewley Common as it appeared on the first edition of the Ordnance Survey one inch map, stretching the full length of the long north-western edge of the township and reaching across to the present Newland Wood. Surviving medieval and early modern records, compared with field-names in the tithe award,[1098] appear to refer mainly to land in the central area of Shrewley. They do indeed suggest that the later medieval woodland occupied at least part of the area covered by Shrewley Common in the early nineteenth century, but they also show that there was not a uniform development from wood to common.

As explained in the account of Rowington's woodland, the cartulary of Reading Abbey preserved a record, dated to 1150, that the men of Rowington should have common of pasture everywhere in the wood of Shrewley where the men of Shrewley had common. By the early fourteenth century the pasture rights of the abbot and men of Rowington were exercised in the waste of Shrewley.[1099] Either the wood pasture had lost many of its trees during the two intervening centuries or the wood had been enclosed or otherwise become unavailable and pasture in the waste allocated in compensation. These records suggest that the wood of Shrewley adjoined Rowington. Part of the modern Shrewley Common forms the south-western boundary of Shrewley with Rowington and, when Rowington's commons were enclosed in 1824, they

Figure 62: Aspley and Shrewley Woods

included a few pieces of land on Shrewley Common.[1100]

References in medieval deeds to the wood, waste and heath of Shrewley indicate that these areas were in close proximity and that the waste may have encroached upon the wood during the thirteenth and fourteenth centuries. A field called *le kyngesfeld*, near to the house of John Brocschaw, lay between *le middelfeld* on one side and the wood (*boscum*) of Shrewley on the other.[1101] In 1341 and 1346 a messuage by John Brokeschawe's curtilage lay between *le kyngesfeld* and the waste (*vastum*) of Shrewley.[1102] The name *kyngesfeld* did not survive to appear on modern maps, but a sixteenth-century document offers both an explanation for the name's disappearance and clues to its former location and thence to the site of the wood.

In setting out his case for ownership of the trees on Shrewley Heath, Clement Throckmorton (*ob.* 1573),[1103] recorded that "a greate parte of the heathe was called & knowne by the name of kingsfeld & hath bin tilled".[1104] Shrewley Heath does not appear in the enclosure award for Hatton and Haseley, nor on the tithe map.[1105] However, there are references to it in later medieval and early modern documents which give an approximate location. The *kyngesfeld* did not form the whole of the sixteenth-century heath and was presumably added to an existing heath, which was recorded as early as 1304.[1106] Deeds of 1412 and 1434 recorded the conveyance of a croft called *Whyteleynewlonde*, which was between *Edmundusnewlond*, *Halle newlond* and *Shyreuesleyheth*.[1107] In 1664 there was a cony warren "now planted" upon Shrewley Heath;[1108] on the tithe map there is a Warren House Piece to the south-west of Newland Wood. It appears, therefore, that the heath extended westwards from the modern Newland Wood (which was woodland by 1627 if not long before[1109]). This evidence, together with the information in another medieval deed that the wood of Shrewley was near to a lane leading from Rowington to Warwick,[1110] suggests that the medieval wood lay to the west of Newland Wood. The wood may of course have extended further north and south, as did Shrewley Common. It is also possible to speculate that the *kyngesfeld* had been created from wood or waste or heath, as presumably was the case with the areas called *newlond*. Newland Wood may have taken its name from adjacent new land or have grown up as secondary woodland on some of that new land.

An unnamed grove was associated with the *kyngesfeld* in several medieval deeds. It might have been the same grove as that next to *dounescroft*, which was once held by Adam le king, whose family presumably gave its name to the *kyngesfeld*.[1111] The name *dounescroft* does not appear in the tithe award. A grove called *ffylylode grove* was near *Welmorefeld* and *Couzmorefeld* in the fifteenth century;[1112] Wellmoor is the name of a close in the tithe award. A grove called Shrewley Grove in 1594[1113] may have had a medieval origin, but there is no clue to its site.

In proceedings in the king's court in 1205-6[1114] the abbot of Reading claimed common pasture in Shrewley, but not in eight acres of assart nor in the wood (*bosco*) called *le Frith*

which contained twelve acres according to the perch of wood. This name has vanished.

Haseley

In the adjoining parishes of Haseley and Hatton (the latter included Shrewley and Beausale) later medieval manorial boundaries crossed those of parishes. For example, the Warwick earldom's manor of Haseley included lands in Beausale, such as *Gannowstokkyng*.[1115] Haseley's park extended into Beausale and adjoined Wedgnock Park.[1116] If it is assumed that the ecclesiastical parish reflected the manor of 1086 rather than the later medieval manor, then the Domesday *silva*, which measured one league by two furlongs and matched the elongated shape of Haseley parish, would have occupied no more than about 250 acres out of the 1,152 acres in the parish.[1117]

Surviving records locate one of Haseley's demesne woods in the centre of the parish. A map of 1728[1118] shows closes called Wood Closes, Hither Wood and Further Wood north-west of Haseley Green. It can be deduced that these mark the site of the medieval wood called *Le clos*. To the north-east of them the tithe map shows lands called Soleys.[1119] This name perpetuated the name of a holding in the vill and fields of Haseley which in 1431 was called *Cokeyesrudyng* alias *Sloley*; a deed dated 1312 stated that *cokgesredinge* adjoined the wood of *Le clos*.[1120] In 1351 land which had belonged to John de Sloleye adjoined the wood called *Haseleye Clos*.[1121] Haseley Close (not a wood) was rented to tenants of the earl of Warwick in the late fourteenth and fifteenth centuries[1122] and appears in a sixteenth-century valuation of the Warwick lands, together with Haseley Close Coppice,[1123] otherwise Haseley Close Wood in 1526-7.[1124] This wood may well have been the enclosed wood which was recorded in an inquisition post mortem of the lands of the earl of Warwick in 1316.[1125] In 1627 the wood contained a hundred acres,[1126] but it had disappeared by 1728.

Demesne woods called *luscomgrove* (a coppice within the park) and *Birchgroue* (called a wood, *boscum*) appeared in accounts for 1392-3 and a grove called *le Conynger* in accounts for 1394-5 and 1423-4.[1127] *Birchgroue* was in Beausale (see below). Luscomb field-names on the tithe map suggest the approximate location of *luscomgrove* and a field called Horns Grove adjoining Hatton presumably marks the small grove of wood called *Horne grove* which appeared under Hatton in a sixteenth-century survey of the earl of Leicester's woods, together with a coppice called *Lynen Draperes* in Haseley.[1128] There is a single, fourteenth-century reference to *Russelegrove* in or by the field of Haseley.[1129]

There is no direct evidence that any of these woods and groves was managed as wood pasture. However, modern records of a common in Haseley[1130] suggest, by analogy with better documented commons elsewhere, that Haseley Common had been a medieval common wood or waste and that the nearby wood called *Le Clos* was enclosed from it.

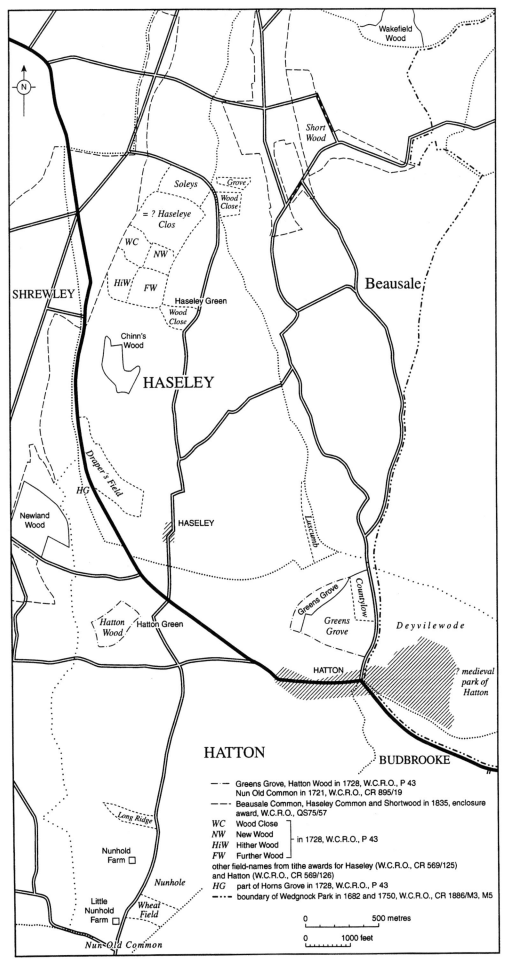

Figure 63: Haseley, Beausale and Hatton

Legend:

—·— Greens Grove, Hatton Wood in 1728, W.C.R.O., P 43
····· Nun Old Common in 1721, W.C.R.O., CR 895/19
— — — Beausale Common, Haseley Common and Shortwood in 1835, enclosure
    award, W.C.R.O., QS75/57

WC   Wood Close
NW   New Wood
HiW Hither Wood   } in 1728, W.C.R.O., P 43
FW   Further Wood

other field-names from tithe awards for Haseley (W.C.R.O., CR 569/125)
and Hatton (W.C.R.O., CR 569/126)

HG   part of Horns Grove in 1728, W.C.R.O., P 43
—··— boundary of Wedgnock Park in 1682 and 1750, W.C.R.O., CR 1886/M3, M5

0   500 metres

0   1000 feet

Beausale

Beausale, in Hatton parish, had *silva* of two furlongs.[1131] Both Wroxall Priory and the earls of Warwick had an interest in the medieval Shortwood. Several medieval deeds describe adjoining land. In one *sortwode* appears simply as a minor place-name;[1132] another refers to the waste of Shortwood and deeds of 1320, 1328 and 1351 refer to the heath called Shortwood.[1133] The earls of Warwick were receiving rent *pro vasto de Shortwode* in the thirteenth century.[1134] However, Shortwood was described as a wood in a dispute over common rights in 1572.[1135] It seems either that Shortwood consisted of distinct areas of woodland, waste and heath, of which only the latter two adjoined land for which later medieval records have survived, or that the waste had some scattered trees, or that woodland regenerated in the waste between the mid-fourteenth and later sixteenth centuries. The later medieval wood was apparently more extensive than the common of 1714 and 1841,[1136] for in the early thirteenth century Shortwood adjoined Honiley.[1137]

Much of the eastern part of Beausale, including its park, seems to have been taken into Wedgnock Park c.1339.[1138] Beausale's park produced wood for fuel.[1139]

A deed dated 1636[1140] stated that *Birch groue* was in Beausale and there are medieval records of land in *askelushull* adjoining *birchusgrove* or *birchesgraue*.[1141] Two areas are candidates for *Birchgroue*. Closes called

99

Stockings and Wood Close are shown on the tithe map north of Kites Nest Farm. A coppice or grove of wood was recorded as being in this area in 1569, by a lane leading from Beausale to Henbrook on the west and Megge meadow to the north.[1142] In addition, on the western edge of Beausale there is a small wood adjoined by a Grove close. Whether this is medieval or post-medieval woodland is unknown.

Honiley

Shortwood adjoined untilled land or waste (*landa*)[1143] in Honiley. There was wood in Honiley in the early thirteenth century on half the land from *yarkedich* through *Wetecroftssich* to the ditch of the park of Kenilworth, also a wood called *Nuthurst* following boundaries between the wood of Hugh son of William and the ditch of the earl of Warwick.[1144] Another deed referred to the wood between the park of the earl and the old *Haia*, together with half the foreign wood of the fee of Hugh son of William, namely that half towards *jarkedich*.[1145]

The references to the park of Kenilworth and the ditch of the earl of Warwick suggest that the woods mentioned in the medieval deeds adjoined Kenilworth and land incorporated into Wedgnock Park, but tithe award for Honiley does not include any minor names which might help to locate these woods more precisely. A park called Mountfort's park is said to have been in the extreme east of the parish.[1146]

Hatton

It is uncertain whether Hatton was the subject of a specific entry in Domesday Book or, if it was, under which name it appeared. Sir William Dugdale thought that it was not mentioned at all and concluded that it was associated with Wroxall, also omitted.[1147] More recently, the entry for *Altone* has been attributed to Hatton.[1148] *Altone* had no *silva* in 1086. The identification of Hatton with the *Donnelie* of Domesday Book should be disregarded for the reasons explained in relation to the *Deyvilwode* of Wedgnock Park (see above under Warwick).

A twelfth-century deed[1149] recorded a grant by Hugh, lord of Hatton, to the Priory of St. Sepulchre in Warwick of full common of his wood for constructing hedges and buildings in the priory's lands in Hatton. The location of this wood and its relationship to woods recorded in subsequent centuries are unknown. Did it become the *Deyvilwode* or the common of Hatton?

In 1439 land called *Nether Countelowe* was described as within the common of Hatton and adjoining a little grove (*Grouiculum*) belonging to Robert Agrene of Hatton.[1150] The tithe map for Hatton[1151] shows a piece of land called Countylow by Greens grove and the road from Warwick to Haseley; the road was mentioned in several deeds referring to *Countelowe*.[1152] The earliest surviving reference to Greens grove by its modern name dates from 1516, when it was said to have belonged to Symond and Robert Grenes.[1153] In 1504 *Nether Countelowe* itself was described as a grove.[1154] The evidence points to enlargement of the little grove of 1439 until, as the modern Greens Grove, it contained over forty acres in the eighteenth and nineteenth centuries.[1155] Part of this enlarged wood survives.

The grove of the prior of Studley was mentioned in deeds dating from 1319 and 1324.[1156] It adjoined *Grovecroft* and *vernycroft*, but these names have not survived to identify the site of the prior's grove. It may have been renamed as Rutters Grove or Porters Grove, woods

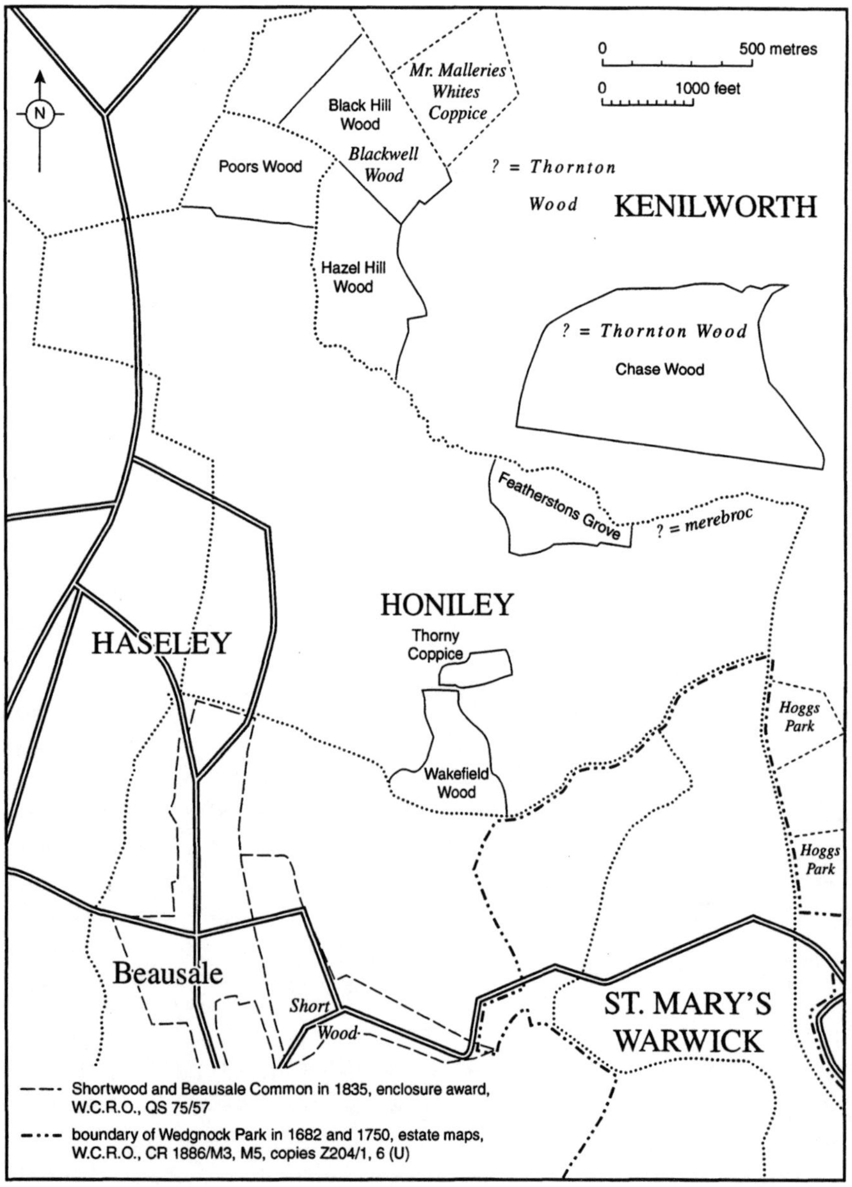

Figure 64: Honiley

which contained seventeen and sixteen acres respectively in 1627,[1157] but they have proved equally elusive. Was one of them renamed Hatton Wood, shown on a map of 1728 (and surviving in part), or is this the remnant of the wood of Hugh of Hatton?[1158]

Richard de Boreford had a grove in 1309, which, like Greens Grove, was near to *Redhulfeld*.[1159] Did it become Greens Grove, or perhaps Rutters Grove or Porters Grove, or was it distinct from all of these?

Hatton had an area of waste called the *nonwolde*,[1160] but this was not associated with any known area of later medieval woodland. The name survives in the modern Nunhold Farm.

Hampton,[1163] but a careful reading of the copy deed suggests that the reference was to Budbrooke.

If the twelfth-century possessions of the Curly family can be equated to the manor of *la Grave (Curly)*[1164] or *kurleysgrove*[1165] then the twelfth-century wood may be one of the two woods mentioned in an inquisition post mortem conducted in 1316. Unusually, the inquisition recorded the site of one wood, a grove next to the manor house (*unum capitale mesuagium....cum graua adiacente*) and the name of another wood (*alius boscus qui vocatur Wegenok*).[1166] This wood does not appear in any later records of the manor, which was amalgamated with the manor of Budbrooke during the fourteenth century.[1167] However, in the fifteenth century that part of Budbrooke parish which was within

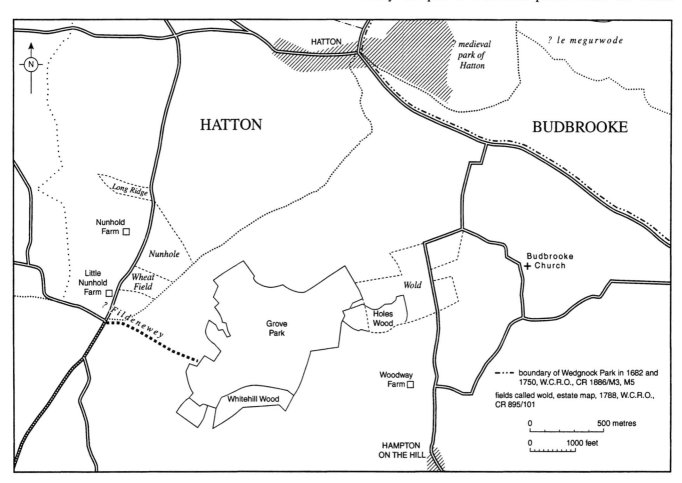

Figure 65: Budbrooke

Budbrooke and La Grave

Domesday Book attributed *silva* measuring one league by three furlongs to Budbrooke,[1161] perhaps between about 250 and 350 acres. There is a twelfth-century record of woodland in the parish which could have been in the township of Hampton-on-the-Hill rather than in Budbrooke itself. Robert de Curly granted to the church of St. Mary in Warwick tithes and land in Budbrooke and Hampton and confirmed the local priest's ancient customary rights in the wood of the same vill (*in nemore eiusdem ville*).[1162] Sir William Dugdale assumed that the same vill was

Wedgnock Park included the old park of Budbrooke (as well as *Boseworth coppice*).[1168] One could suggest that the wood called *Wegenok* became the old park of Budbrooke. The grove next to the manor house of *la Grave* presumably disappeared into Grove Park, which was not mentioned in 1316 but which had been created by 1403-4[1169] and had acquired its modern name by 1434-5.[1170] The site of the medieval manor house is uncertain, although a timber-framed house did precede the nineteenth-century mansion of Grove Park.[1171]

The manor of Budbrooke had a separate, unnamed wood in 1290-1.[1172] There was a grove called variously *Blesardsgrove*, *Blysardesgrove* and *Blusardesgrove*,[1173] but references to it ceased abruptly after 1425-6, for no obvious reason. In that year *Janynslesewe* and *Stokhullefeld* were taken into Wedgnock Park; the grove might have shared the same fate, but it did not appear in later accounts for the Park. There was also a "grove called the parsonage grove", which was recorded in a survey of 1589-90 as next to the church of Budbrooke;[1174] it may have been a medieval grove of wood. It was called a pasture in that survey. The survey also recorded The Grove of five acres which was part of "Parkers holding at the wold" and was a coppice.

In 1221-2 Walter of Norton was party to a case involving a messuage next to a spinney (*iuxta spinetum*),[1175] but it is not clear whether he lived in Norton Curlieu in Budbrooke parish or in Norton Lindsey, for which little or no later medieval topographical information has been found.

The size of the ecclesiastical parish of Wootton reflects the former status of its church as an early medieval minster, which served several places which later attained independent parochial status.[1176] At the time of the tithe award, in 1842, Wootton parish included the Domesday manors which can be identified as Wootton itself, Offord, Edstone, Whitley and Ullenhall..[1177]

There was a great deal of *silva* in Wootton Wawen and surrounding manors in 1086. Wootton's *silva* was two leagues long by one wide, possibly over two thousand acres. Offord had *silva* one league long and half a league wide, perhaps at least five hundred acres, Edstone half a league by half a furlong, Whitley half a league by two furlongs, and Ullenhall half a league by one furlong.[1178]

Land in the area to the west of Wootton Wawen village was held by the Montfort family of Beaudesert or their successors in the Freville family for much of the later medieval period. A survey of Freville lands made in 1419-20 recorded that the wood (*boscus*) called *fforwod* contained twenty acres, and that there were parcels of wood, amounting to five acres, in *mayowes*.[1179] The same survey included a pasture called *mayowesforwode*. The association of *mayowes* and *forwod* and the proximity of the modern Mays Wood to Forwood Park suggest that Mays Wood might have developed from the parcels of wood recorded in 1419-20. However, a Five Acre Wood, which contained over thirty-one acres in 1736,[1180] is another candidate for those parcels of wood which amounted to five acres in 1419-20. The presence of the field-names Riddings and Stubbs[1181] suggests former woodland.

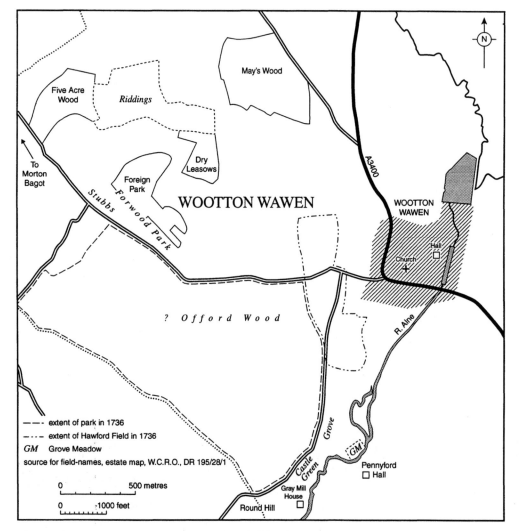

Figure 66: Wootton Wawen - Forwood and Offord

Wootton Wawen

The documentary evidence for the early medieval topography of the area and the significance of the place-name Wootton are discussed in later chapters. Evidence for later medieval woods in the area will inform that discussion as well as contribute to the parish survey in this chapter.

The wood of *Halestoue* (variously *haluestou*, *holewestowe*) by Kington was mentioned in at least two thirteenth-century deeds,[1182] which show that the wood became, or formed the nucleus of, the modern Austy Wood, which adjoins Kington and Edstone (Fig. 69). One deed recorded that the abbot and convent of St. Peter Castellione (of which Wootton Priory was a dependency) had surrendered their custom in the wood;[1183] this suggests that they had common rights there. In the fifteenth century the earls of Stafford sold faggots of firewood from the wood.[1184] A road from Edstone to the parish church of Wootton ran through or by (*per*) the wood of *halewestowe*.[1185]

It has been suggested that *Halestoue* or Austy, whose name is Old English for 'holy spot',[1186] may be associated with the church of Wootton Wawen.[1187] As explained above, the church was an early medieval minster, recorded in an early eighth-century charter, with the earliest parts of the present fabric dated to the tenth or eleventh centuries.[1188] The nature and location of the 'holy spot' are unknown, but the existence of a wood of *Halestoue* indicates that the place was important enough to name an area of woodland.

The site of Offord has been located traditionally towards the southern edge of the parish of Wootton Wawen. Earthworks typical of later medieval settlement sites have been found in land on the edges of Grey Mill and Pennyford Hall Farms.[1189] This location is confirmed by matching field-names on a map of 1736[1190] to places in Offord which were named in later medieval and early sixteenth-century documents. In 1736 Hawford (i.e. Offord) Field stretched from the north-east edge of Wootton Park towards the village of Wootton, but it was of such an elongated, disjointed shape that one suspects that its western portion had disappeared into the park. On the park's south-eastern edge was Castle Green, mentioned in accounts of the earls of Stafford.[1191] In the southern tip of the park Round Hill matches another Offord name.[1192]

mentioned in the same entry in accounts for 1487 and 1506-7.[1194] The site of Offord Grove was presumably the field called the Grove shown on the map of 1736. A court roll of 1386 referred to trespasses in Offord Wood and in the *lytulgrove*;[1195] the latter may have been an earlier name for Offord Grove. The presence of both demesne wood and demesne grove is rare in Warwickshire.

The township of Aspley, in the north-west of the parish, was not recorded separately in Domesday Book. The tithe map of 1842 shows three closes with Oldborough Wood in their names, but these presumably refer to the adjacent parish of Oldberrow, which was in Worcestershire. A deed of 1285 described a stream which ran from the wood of the lord of Oldberrow across the moor of *Elye* to the ditch of Mockley (presumably the same stream which runs to the north of the present Mockley Wood).[1196] On the western edge of Aspley a Grove Close on the tithe map probably marks the site of Elys Grove, which in 1565 was described as a "grove of greate timber & wood" containing one acre and bordered by *Uluebarrowe Woodsyde*.[1197] Aspley included Mockley Wood. The leases of *Molkelewode* dating from 1401 and 1415 refer to *espringes*, showing that at the beginning of the fifteenth century at least part of it was managed as a coppice wood.[1198] There was underwood and pasture in the park of Aspley in 1372.[1199] The location of the park is presumably marked by various park names on the tithe map.

The wood of Ullenhall belonged to the earldom of Stafford in the twelfth century. Land and assarts under *Hortselewelle*

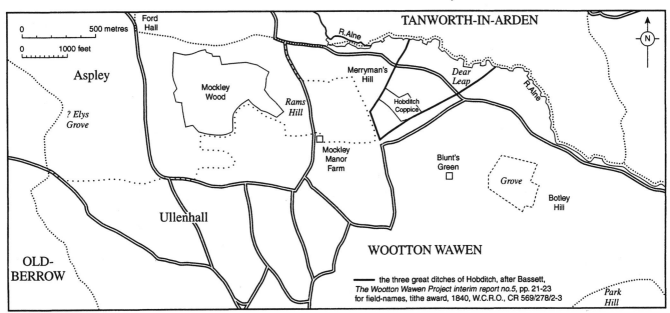

Figure 67: Wootton Wawen - Aspley, Mockley and Ullenhall

Sir William Dugdale saw a record of a grant made during the reign of Henry II (1154-89) which involved all the land in Offord except that held by three freeholders and all the wood on the left hand side of the road from Wootton Wawen to Morton Bagot.[1193] This hardens the suspicion, roused by the absence of any field-names suggestive of the location of Offord Wood, that the Wood, with part of Offord field, was absorbed into Wootton Park. *Offordgrove* was not an alternative name for Offord Wood, because both woods were

(a similar minor place-name is associated with woodland in Spernall) were granted to Stone Priory by Robert de Stafford and sixty acres of assarted land were recorded in a deed of 1194.[1200] Part of the site of Ullenhall's wood is known from a copy of a twelfth-century charter in the cartulary of Stone Priory.[1201] The grant gave the bounds of part of the wood. Some of the minor place-names, such as *Stanieta*, have not survived to appear on modern maps,[1202] but the boundary of Botley serves to give the general location and the three great ditches which the part of the wood comprehended (*cum tribus magnis fossatis*) must be the massive earthwork called Hobditch with two connected banks and ditches. These are no later than the centuries immediately following the Romano-British period and possibly of Iron Age date.[1203] Much of the modern Merryman's Farm was therefore within the medieval wood of Ullenhall. The earthworks show that part of the wood must have been secondary woodland.

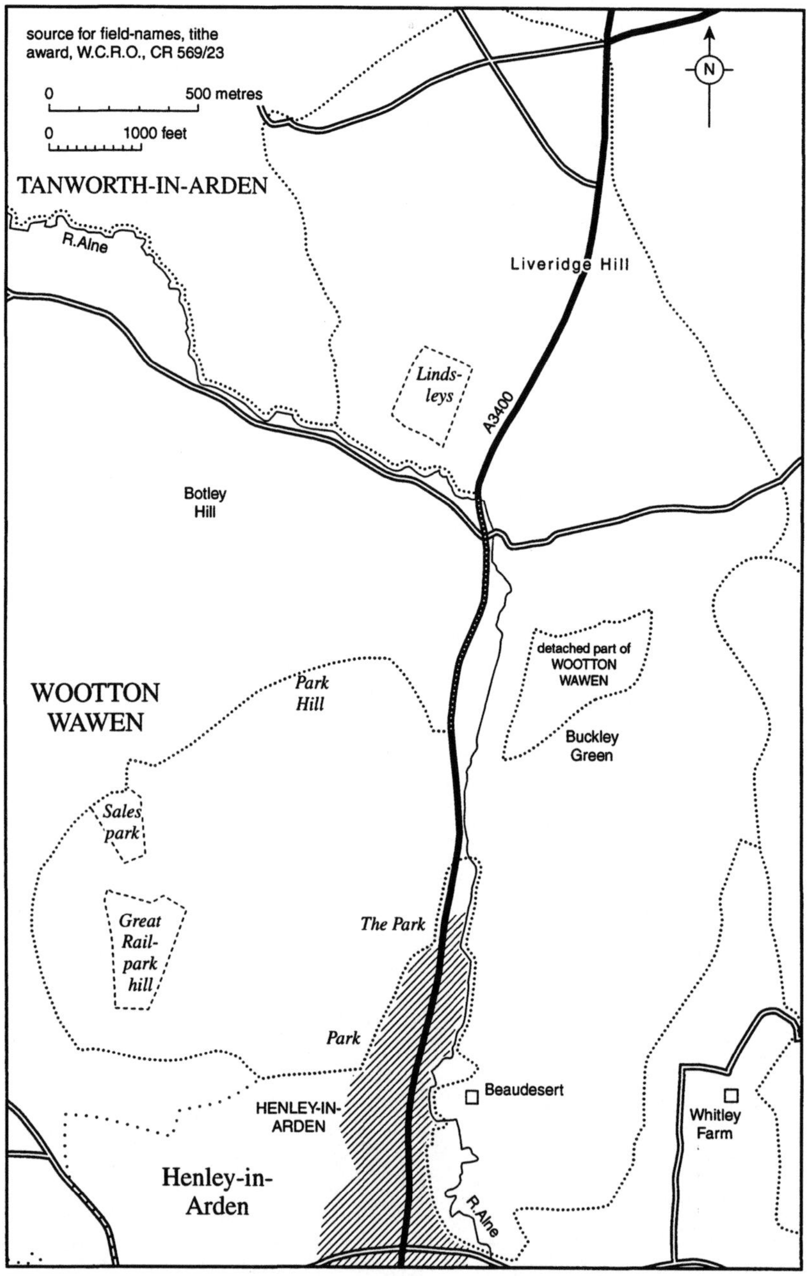

Figure 68: Beaudesert

Four acres of wood and assart (*bosci et essarti*) were recorded for Whitley in 1212.[1204] Despite the preservation of various deeds relating to Whitley, no records of medieval woodland have been found. There was a furlong called the shaw (*culturam vocatam le Schawe*), a name presumably derived from an Old English word for woodland.[1205]

Most of the surviving medieval deeds dealing with land in Edstone refer to holdings distributed in small parcels in the

fields there and to woodland in Songar (see below under Claverdon) but not to any wood or assarts explicitly situated in Edstone itself. There is a record of common pasture in land in Edstone, from *chelewelesiche* to *huturel* under *foxhole* and then to the spring called *Wodewelle*, various assarts and the corner of *Birchurste* (which was in or adjoining Langley - see below under Claverdon); other deeds also refer to *Birchurst*.[1206] It may be that the rest of the deeds covered only the southern part of Edstone and that there was woodland to the north in the area of the modern Short Grove (arguably the Short Grove recorded in 1449-50[1207]), Ashen Coppice and Knowles Wood. The shape of that northern part matches the long, narrow measurements of the Domesday *silva*.

A grove in Henley was held by John Golafre c.1275.[1208]

Beaudesert

Although there was no *silva* in the manor of 1086 which became the later Beaudesert,[1209] there are records of woodland in Beaudesert in the later medieval period. As drawn on the tithe map and first edition of the Ordnance Survey Beaudesert included an area of land which protruded into Ullenhall and was surrounded by Ullenhall on three sides.[1210] This prominent deviation in the boundary line suggests that the land within it had some particular value and had been detached from Ullenhall for some purpose. The land was the site of Beaudesert's great park (there was a little park, too, beside the river) which contained three hundred acres of wood in 1326.[1211] There were two groves in Beaudesert in 1463.[1212] One of them was in a close called 'the manor of lymseys', the other in a close called Penkes. The field called Lindsleys in the tithe award[1213] may correspond to the fifteenth-century close called *lymseys*, but there is no field called grove to mark the site of either medieval wood.

Preston Bagot

The *silva* of the manor of Preston Bagot measured one league by half a league in 1086.[1214] The shape of the parish, whose southern portion was a rectangular area joined to the rest of the parish by a narrow neck of land, suggests that the parish boundaries were drawn to include a particularly valuable or useful area. To the south-east are similar appendages to Kington in Claverdon and Edstone in Wootton Wawen. As far as Kington is concerned (see below under Claverdon) there is evidence to indicate that the value of this area lay in its woodland. Few medieval records give minor place-names in Preston Bagot which can be matched with names on the tithe map and a map of Wootton Wawen drawn in 1736.[1215] The name of Eggwell Wood, called Hagwell Coppice in 1736, may come from the medieval *Egge*, which occurs in two thirteenth-century deeds relating to Preston Bagot and seems to have the same derivation and meaning as the *Egge* which became the modern Edge Hill in south-east Warwickshire.[1216] However, Eggwell Wood and the Edge above Beaudesert are some distance apart.

Of the two deeds in the Reading Abbey cartularies referring to woodland in Preston Bagot one, attributed to 1226-38, mentions a grove but gives no indication of its location.[1217] Another, possibly from 1221-38, refers to wood by the land held of Geoffrey Chimbel and associates the land with a mill.[1218] A late sixteenth-century survey of lands formerly belonging to Reading Abbey in this area includes Chellombis meadow by the brook to the north of the lord's land called *foxley* (which may be matched to the Foxley on modern maps) and south of the road from Preston to Henley.[1219] An alder-grove in Preston was granted to Bordesley Abbey c.1231-58;[1220] it was presumably on wet land, but there are no further clues to its location.

It has been suggested that *Heselholt*, an area in the north of the parish which produced rent for the lord of Beaudesert in 1265,[1221] was a manor created by post-Conquest assarting.[1222] The place-name itself appears to contain the Old English *holt*, translated as wood, possibly a wood with a single or main species of tree.[1223] This is no proof that the area was woodland in the later, as distinct from the early, medieval period or even in 1086.

Claverdon

The parish of Claverdon included Langley, Kington and Songar. Only one dimension, a league, was given for Claverdon's *silva* in Domesday Book; Langley's measured one league by half a league and that in Kington was worth ten shillings a year.[1224]

There are references to the earl of Warwick's wood of Claverdon in some twelfth-century deeds, the earliest of which has been dated to 1123.[1225] Thirteenth-century deeds relating to *Birchurst* in Langley (see below), a reference to *Armeley* (a name which survived into the modern period) as an assart,[1226] and the context of one of the twelfth-century grants suggest that the wood was in the west of Claverdon, north of Langley and Edstone. The grant of common pasture in the wood of Claverdon to Reading Abbey and its tenants in Rowington[1227] would have been much more convenient in a wood adjoining their own lands than in one situated further east. In the late sixteenth century the modern Barnmoor Green was known as Claverdon Common, a name suggestive of former woodland.[1228] The similarly suggestive minor place-names of Ridding and Redding were located in the north and west of the parish in the tithe award.[1229] Thomas, earl of Warwick, is said to have granted to Pinley Priory an assart between the wood of Claverdon and the Priory's lands,[1230] but as the Priory is said to have held land in

Claverdon as well as in Pinley this deed does not provide conclusive evidence for the site of the wood.

There were other assarts in Claverdon. An inquisition post mortem of 1325 recorded thirty acres newly assarted as part of the demesne.[1231] Claverdon's present woods cannot be regarded as the remnants of medieval woodland, for Hanging Wood, known as Hadley Kings Coppice and Armley Coppice in the eighteenth and nineteenth centuries, includes ridge and furrow, showing that it is at least in part secondary woodland.[1232]

There are records of assarts on the high ground south-west of Kington Grange which lies between Preston Bagot and Edstone and extends to Austy Wood. This must be the site of *Chyrholt* alias *Sirhoulte*. Hugh de Burleia granted to Wootton Wawen Priory part of his assarts in Claverdon between *halwestowe* (Austy) and *Sirhoulte* together with thirty-six selions in *Sirhoulte* itself, which was described as being in Claverdon.[1233] Like *Heselholt* in Preston Bagot the name *Sirhoulte* seems to preserve the Old English *holt* meaning wood.

Another deed referring to *Sirhoulte* dealt with land in Kington by the road from Austy Wood (*bosco de haleustou*) towards *Piriford*.[1234] This minor place-name seems to survive in the field-names Perryford Close and Perryford Keynton and the ditch associated with the land may be reflected in the name of the field called Moated Keynton.[1235] The land adjoined a marlpit belonging to the priory by *Kinghemegraue*. The first two elements of this name appear to be king (as in Kington) and the Old English *haeme* (people of).[1236] The same elements appear in *Kingemewolde* in Kineton by Wellesbourne.[1237] The use of the word *haeme* suggests a pre-Conquest history for the grove of the people of Kington. In 1575 the Throckmorton lands in Kington included a wood called Grove Wood.[1238] This wood-name has not been traced on any modern map or document but by matching field names in the survey of 1575 with names on the tithe map it has been deduced that the site of the sixteenth-century grove was probably Little Meadow Coppice; the medieval grove probably extended to the parish boundary[1239].

Surviving evidence suggests that much of Langley's woodland had been cleared by c.1300. In that year *Birchurste* was described as a tenement belonging to Bordesley Abbey between the road leading from Kineton towards Langley and the common field of Edstone.[1240] A deed dealing with land in Edstone included an assart and *Birchurst* as boundary points.[1241] Another referred to assarts in Langley by *Chellewellesiche* and the bounds of Edstone.[1242] Reading Abbey held land in Langley next to *Birchurst*.[1243] A late sixteenth-century survey of lands attached to the Abbey's manor of Rowington included Langley Moor in Claverdon.[1244] It seems reasonable to infer that Langley Moor was held by the Abbey in the later medieval period and that its site, near to Edstone, helps to locate *Birchurst*.

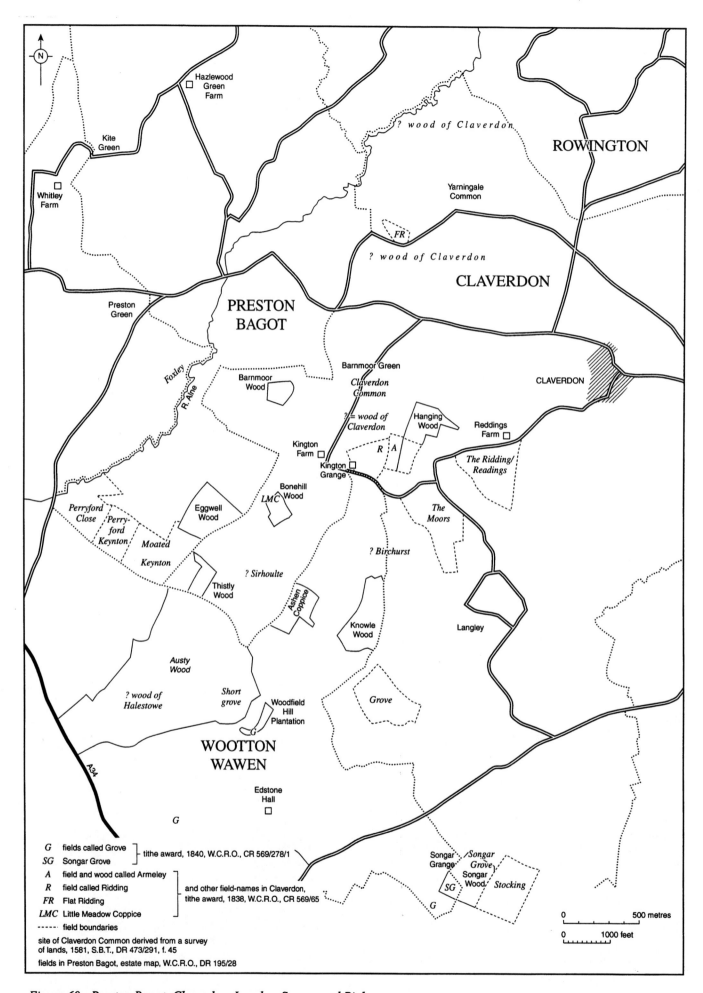

N

Hazlewood
Green
Farm

Kite
Green

ROWINGTON

? wood of Claverdon

Whitley
Farm

Yarningale
Common

FR

? wood of Claverdon

CLAVERDON

Preston
Green

PRESTON
BAGOT

Foxley

R. Alne

Barnmoor Green

Barnmoor
Wood

Claverdon
Common

CLAVERDON

?= wood of
Claverdon

Hanging
Wood

Reddings
Farm

Kington
Farm

R A

The Ridding/
Readings

Kington
Grange

Perryford
Close

Bonehill
Wood

LMC

Eggwell
Wood

Perry-
ford
Keynton

The
Moors

Moated

Keynton

? Birchurst

Thistly
Wood

? Sirhoulte

Ashen Coppice

Knowle
Wood

Langley

Austy
Wood

? wood of
Halestowe

Short
grove

Grove

Woodfield
Hill
Plantation

G

A34

WOOTTON
WAWEN

Edstone
Hall

G

G   fields called Grove
SG   Songar Grove

tithe award, 1840, W.C.R.O., CR 569/278/1

A   field and wood called Armeley
R   field called Ridding
FR   Flat Ridding
LMC   Little Meadow Coppice

and other field-names in Claverdon,
tithe award, 1838, W.C.R.O., CR 569/65

------- field boundaries

site of Claverdon Common derived from a survey
of lands, 1581, S.B.T., DR 473/291, f. 45

fields in Preston Bagot, estate map, W.C.R.O., DR 195/28

Songar
Grange

Songar
Grove

Songar
Wood

Stocking

SG

G

0   500 metres

0   1000 feet

Figure 69: Preston Bagot, Claverdon, Langley, Songar and Pinley

106

Langley Grove was recorded in the sixteenth century.[1245] Presumably it occupied the area marked by Grove names on the enclosure and tithe maps.[1246] In 1383 a court roll for Langley included a grant of land in a field called *Groffeld subtus hayic de Edston* (Grove Field under the hedge of Edstone) so it is reasonable to infer the existence of the grove in the fourteenth century.[1247] Some deeds mention *Snellesgrove*, near to a marlpit, but there are no other clues to this grove's location.[1248]

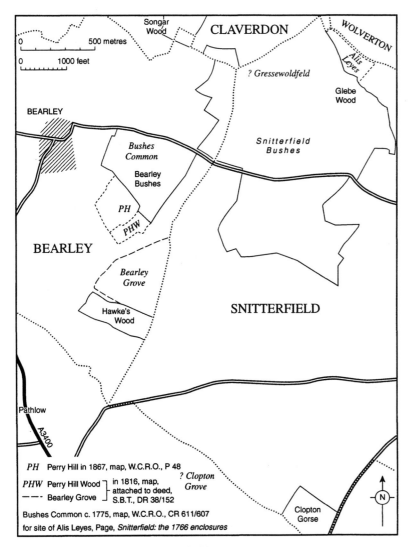

Figure 70: Bearley and Snitterfield

References to the grove of Songar occur in several thirteenth-century deeds which recorded gifts to Bordesley Abbey of adjacent land in Edstone.[1249] One deed recorded the grant of the grove itself. Ralph, son of Hugh of Edstone, gave the monks all his grove next to the monks' Songar Grange (*totam grauam que mea fuit iuxta suhangra grangia eorundem monachorum*), explaining that he had done this for the soul of his lord Thurstan de Montfort, who had given him the same grove for his service.[1250] Thurstan de Montfort II, father of Peter de Montfort who was a witness to the grant, died in 1216,[1251] so the grant was probably made shortly afterwards. A wood (sadly recently replanted) adjoins the present Songar Grange in Claverdon. In the early nineteenth century it was called Nut Wood.[1252] It is now called Songar

Wood, but abuts on to a small piece of woodland in Edstone called Songar Grove.[1253] All early modern references to Songar Grove locate it in Claverdon,[1254] so the adjoining woodland in Edstone is probably a secondary extension of the original grove which retained the name grove when the original grove acquired a new name. In 1545 a survey stated that Songar grove, in Claverdon, set with oak and ash of ten years' growth, contained five acres; there was a separate valuation of the *sprynge* or underwood.[1255] Fields called Stocking to the south of the wood in 1826[1256] suggest that the grove was part of a larger area of woodland which was partially cleared at some point.

Wolverton

There is little information on the later medieval topography of Wolverton. There are no clues to the disappearance of the small area of *silva* (a furlong in length and half a furlong in width - a maximum of four acres) recorded in Domesday Book under the larger of Wolverton's two manors.[1257] Nor is there any record of a grove which would have matched the enclosure called The Grove which was shown on a map of 1820 at the north end of the village.[1258] A few medieval deeds do refer to field-names which can be traced on the map of 1820, but these are of interest principally in relation to the early medieval, rather than to the later medieval, period.[1259]

Bearley

Neither of Bearley's two manors had *silva* in 1086,[1260] but there was a grove in the thirteenth century. Richard, son of Geri, granted to William de Burle all the grove (*totam grauam*) which lay between the land of the monks of Bordesley and Pathlow and all the croft lying between the same grove and Pathlow.[1261] Robert, son of William de Burleia, granted to Bordesley Abbey land and all his grove which his father had acquired from Geri in a plea in his lord's court (*totam grauam meam quam pater meus adquisiuit de geri in curia domini mei placito*). Bordesley Abbey would hold from Robert's lord, William Cumin.[1262] Robert's grant was the subject of at least three other deeds.[1263] John de Burleia made another grant to the Abbey of land in the field of Bearley extending from the assart of the monks to the forks (*furcas*) of Pathlow next to the path from the grove of *Burleia* towards Clopton.[1264] Other grants referred to the waste under the grove of John (presumably John de Burle), a grove abutting on *Stoniewei* and the assart between *le Stanwei* and land towards Pathlow.[1265] These deeds give the grove's approximate location, suggest that it could have been named after either the place or the family of Bearley and show that it had been part of a larger area of woodland.

Bearley grove appears to have reverted to the lord of the manor, unless it was divided between the lord and the

107

Abbey, for in 1317 Sir John Cantilupe, lord of Snitterfield and of part of Bearley, granted to his son and heir the whole of his grove called *Burleye groue* in his lordship of Snitterfield.[1266] Bearley Grove was still part of Snitterfield manor in 1816, when part of it was shown on a map of the estate.[1267] The suggestion that the lord held only part of the grove is supported by manorial accounts for 1439 and 1461, in which it was stated that the demesne lands were out to farm, including all that part of the underwood in *Burleygrove* which belonged to the manor.[1268] The woodland which was mapped in 1816 may not have been part of the original grove, because there are records of the grove's enlargement. Accounts of 1461 stated that a croft called Newlond, which used to render 2s. 6d. per annum, had been enclosed within the grove called *Burley grove* on the orders of Thomas Huggeford and Nicholas Rodey, executors of the late Richard, earl of Warwick.[1269] This is a clear, and rare, record of the establishment of an area of secondary woodland towards the end of the later medieval period. The inclusion of *Newland crofte* in *Burleygrove* was mentioned in accounts for 1480-1[1270] and the new area of woodland still had a separate identity in 1545.[1271] By 1668 land called *Bearly Grove* contained 160 acres and in 1692 two coppices called Bearley Grove contained 120 wood acres.[1272] Presumably the parts of the early modern wood towards Pathlow were the original medieval grove, but the exact boundaries of that grove and of the wood which was assarted are unknown. There is no evidence to associate the medieval waste with the Bushes Common of c.1775.[1273]

Three explanations can be suggested for the absence of *silva* from the Domesday record of Bearley's manors. Firstly, a scribe may have omitted *silva* accidentally. Secondly, the Domesday manors may have excluded the eastern part of the ecclesiastical parish where the later medieval woodland seems to have been situated. Snitterfield manor might have extended into Bearley in the eleventh century as it did in the fifteenth; however, Snitterfield had no *silva* in Domesday Book either.[1274] Thirdly, Bearley's woodland in 1086 might have differed in some way from the *silva* of other manors in the Wootton area. The nomenclature of Bearley's grove points to the third of these possibilities, analogous with the groves of south and east Warwickshire. There was no hint of pasture rights in the medieval grove of Bearley. However, the records of assarts and the single reference to waste are reminiscent of many other places in north and west Warwickshire for which *silva* was recorded in Domesday Book. There is no apparent solution to the problem.

Snitterfield

There was no *silva* in the manor of Snitterfield in 1086.[1275] There was a wood called *Coldwellhull* in 1306[1276] which may be matched to the *Cawdell als. Heads hill ffeild* of 1672, which was part of Hunger hill field in the extreme east of the parish in 1765, and to the modern wood called Caldwell Spring Wood.[1277]

Snitterfield offers an example of the formation of secondary woodland on land which was cultivated in the later medieval period. It has been stated that both Snitterfield Bushes and

the once adjacent Bearley Bushes in Bearley were formerly areas of permanent cow pasture, which became redundant following improved agricultural rotations in the eighteenth century and reverted to scrub and woodland.[1278] This statement presents a problem in historical ecology, for Snitterfield Bushes contain species of plants, particularly herb paris, which are associated with ancient woodland rather than with comparatively late secondary woodland.

Snitterfield Bushes are first mentioned in manorial documents dated 1560,[1279] so they antedate their alleged eighteenth-century origin by at least one hundred and fifty years. In the second half of the sixteenth century they were used for grazing sheep at certain, prescribed times of the year.[1280] The evidence that the Bushes were arable land in the later medieval period is as follows. A croft called *Alse leys* appears on a modern map by Snitterfield Bushes.[1281] In 1309 a deed described ploughed land (*cultura*) called *Alis leyen* as between land of Robert Morin and land of John le Caus and extending in length from the king's highway up to the ploughed land of Wolverton.[1282] In manorial accounts for 1461 uncultivated land (*terre friste*) called *Alis leys* was next to Songar in *Gressewoldfeld* and was in the lord's hands through lack of tenants.[1283] Lands called Greswolds lay to the south of Snitterfield Bushes in the modern period and Greswold was meadow land in 1461, but *Gressewoldfeld* as such does not reappear.[1284] This documentary evidence suggests that the field was withdrawn from cultivation in the fifteenth century and became the Bushes. Manorial accounts for 1430-1 recorded thirty selions of uncultivated land next to Bearley and another twenty selions next to Bearley field. The herbage of this land produced nothing because it was being pastured by the cattle and animals of the manor.[1285] It is not clear whether this land lay north or south of the modern road running east to west through Snitterfield Bushes. However, given the amount of woodland in the eastern part of Bearley in the modern period, together with the presence there of medieval woodland in the form of Bearley Grove (see above, under Bearley) it can be suggested that plants characteristic of ancient woodland spread from Bearley's woodland into Snitterfield over the centuries. It could also be suggested that at some stage in their development the Bushes were augmented by some saplings from a wood in which herb paris grew and that the plant came with the trees in the soil around them.

Aston Cantlow

The parish of Aston Cantlow included Wilmcote, Shelfield and Newnham.[1286] Domesday Book recorded *silva* measuring one square league under Aston, but no *silva* under Newnham or Wilmcote.[1287] There was no separate entry for Shelfield.

There seems to have been woodland in Shelfield in the later medieval period. In the thirteenth century William de Canteloupe granted to Studley Priory all his assarts outside the park there as bounded by the road between Spernall and Aston.[1288] Park names in Shelfield therefore point to the approximate location of the assarted woodland.[1289] Inquisitions post mortem in 1254, 1273, 1345 and 1436 did not refer to any woodland outside the park.[1290] However, accounts for the year 1467-8 dealt not only with the lack of sale of wood from the park of Shelfield but also with the sale of thorns from *Astongrove*.[1291] The present Aston Grove is the same shape as in 1776, when it contained nearly thirty-five acres, but that shape suggests that at some time closes had been added to or taken out of it.[1292] The grove is on the southern edge of the parish, adjoining Withycombe Wood in Haselor.

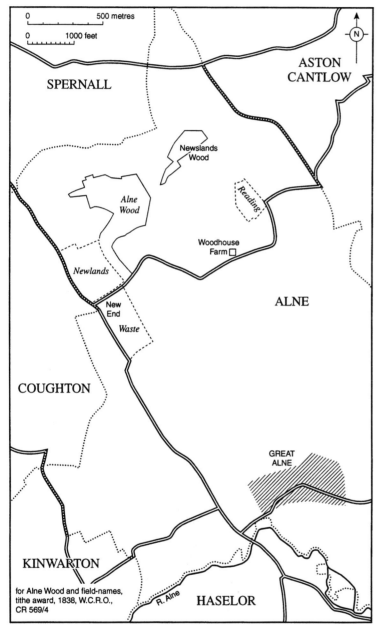

Figure 71: Alne

Alne

Domesday Book recorded *silva* measuring half a league by four furlongs under Alne, which was held by Winchcombe Abbey.[1293] In the second half of the twelfth century the Abbey acquired all the land, in wood and plain, between Alne and Aston (Cantlow) on condition that it should remain uncultivated and common rights maintained as in the rest of the wood and plain of Alne.[1294] Nonethless, the Register of Winchcombe Abbey referred to forty-one acres of assarts in Alne c.1240 and to tithes from eighty acres of assarts in 1220.[1295] In 1272 the abbot and others were said to have deprived Simon of Kinwarton of common pasture for his animals in forty acres of wood and land in *Rounalne*.[1296] Some tenants held by custom of assart (*consuetudinem assarti*) in 1361-2.[1297] It is hardly surprising that land called *Newelond* adjoined the wood of Alne in 1316.[1298] The modern Alne Wood presumably contains some remnants of the medieval wood which were not cleared; land called Newlands adjoined it on a map of c.1695.[1299] There is a single record of a tenant's grove,[1300] but no clue as to its site

Morton Bagot

In 1086 the manor of Morton had *silva* measuring half a league by one furlong.[1301] The probable location of Morton Bagot's wood (*bosco*) recorded in 1227[1302] must be inferred by analogy with better documented woods. The proximity of Clouse Wood to Morton Common, alias Morton Wast in 1695, suggests that Clouse Wood was the enclosed wood separated from the common wood.[1303] The name is similar to that of Clowes Wood in Forshaw, Solihull, which is arguably derived from the French or Latin for close. Morton Bagot is poorly documented in respect of minor medieval place-names, so it is not possible to say whether the modern Bannams Wood, much of which is demonstrably secondary woodland,[1304] and Pools Wood have medieval antecedents.

Spernall

Domesday Book's entry for Spernall included *silva* measuring three furlongs by one, no more than thirty acres out of the 1,090 acres which formed the ecclesiastical parish.[1305] There are records of both wood pasture and enclosed woods in the later medieval period with enough detail to suggest the site of one of those woods in the north of the parish, but no information on the area covered by wood.

Common in the wood (*bosco*) of Spernall was surrendered by Robert Bagod (lord of Morton Bagot) to John Durvassal (lord of Spernall).[1306] The deed specified the bounds within which those common rights were exercised, including the wood which John had from Robert de Offewrth, *hortsole* and *arab-le*. Another thirteenth-century deed referred to common pasture in the woods and lands of John Durvassal and his son Roger.[1307]

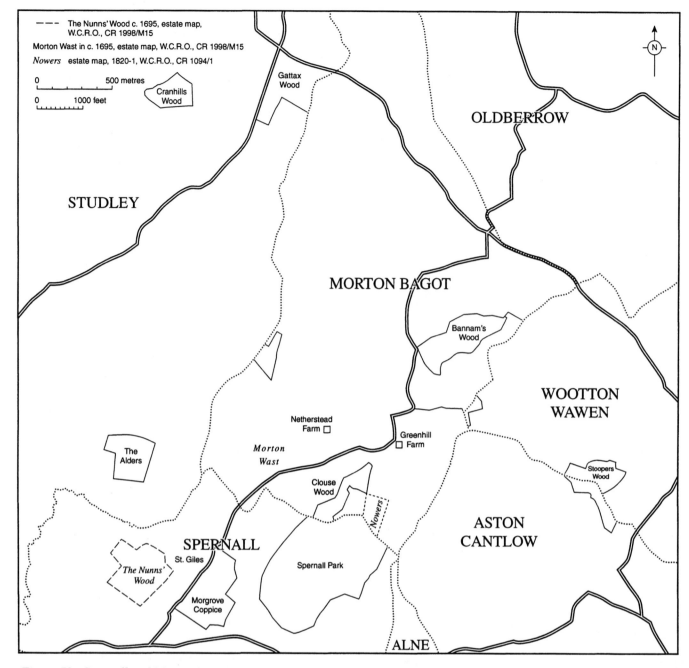

Figure 72: Spernall and Morton Bagot

A deed in which John granted specific woods and lands in Spernall to Roger can be dated to 1238-9 because it described one of the witnesses, Philip de Assellis, as sheriff of Warwick.[1308]   John conveyed not only named lands but also his whole wood of Spernall as it was enclosed which was called *Les oueres* and *la meregrave*, with a certain part of the land which was within the wood and the meadow within the same.   Morgons, alias Moregroves, Coppice, recorded on seventeenth- and eighteenth-century estate maps, preserves the latter name, not only in the wood but also in the adjoining Grove Butts.[1309] The character of the wood has certainly changed; it is now a conifer plantation. On the supposition that *Les oueres* was near, if not contiguous with, *la meregrave* and given the pasture rights in John Durvassal's wood which were surrendered by the lord of Morton Bagot, it is reasonable to suggest that the wood of Spernall adjoined Morton Bagot. *Nowers*, a field-name on the southern edge of Morton Bagot,[1310] adjoining Spernall park, bears enough resemblance to *oueres* to prompt the suggestion that *Les oueres* disappeared into Spernall park. The creation of a park could also explain the disappearance of the names *hortsole* and *arab-le*.

The Durvassal wood and the wood of Robert of Offord were apparently not the only woods in Spernall. The land called St. Giles's, formerly of Cookhill Priory, included a coppice wood called *Nunwoode* containing fifteen acres at the Dissolution.[1311] On a map of c.1695 the Nuns Wood was shown as twenty-five acres in extent.[1312] The same map attributed over thirty-one acres to Morgons Coppice. The modern size cannot be used as a guide to the size of the medieval woods, although the apparent increase in size of the Nuns Wood may be attributable to the use of wood acres, larger than statute acres, at the Dissolution.

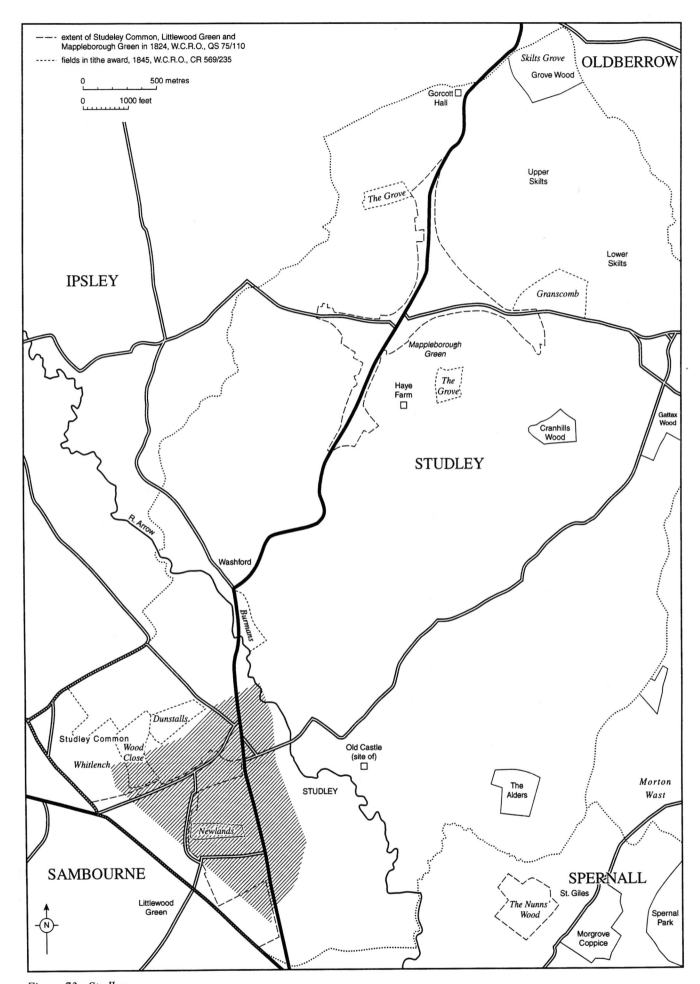

Figure 73: Studley

extent of Studeley Common, Littlewood Green and
Mappleborough Green in 1824, W.C.R.O., QS 75/110

fields in tithe award, 1845, W.C.R.O., CR 569/235

0   500 metres

0   1000 feet

OLDBERROW

Skilts Grove

Grove Wood

Gorcott
Hall

Upper
Skilts

Lower
Skilts

The Grove

Granscomb

IPSLEY

Mappleborough
Green

Haye
Farm

The
Grove

Cranhills
Wood

STUDLEY

Gattax
Wood

R. Arrow

Washford

Burmans

Dunstalls

Studley Common

Wood
Close

Whitlench

Old Castle
(site of)

STUDLEY

The
Alders

Morton
Wast

Newlands

SAMBOURNE

Littlewood
Green

N

The Nunns'
Wood

SPERNALL

St. Giles

Spernal
Park

Morgrove
Coppice

Studley

Studley, a large parish of some 4,110 acres,[1313] was divided into three separate manors in 1086. All three had *silva*, measuring respectively one league by half a league, three furlongs by two furlongs and, for Mappleborough, one furlong square.[1314] There were more manors in subsequent centuries.[1315] None is well documented, but the dimensions of the largest area of *silva* in 1086 approximate to the extent of Studley Common in 1824 together with the area called Whitlench and Wood Closes in the tithe award.[1316] Whitlench was a wood in 1719 and 1640,[1317] when it lay to the west of land called dunstalls, a name which appeared in that position on the tithe map. In 1330 it was recorded that King John had afforested within the Forest of Feckenham the vill of Studley with the wood this side of the river Arrow (*cum bosco citra Riueram de Arewe*) which the prior of Studley and the Master of the Templars held.[1318] This was the corner of the parish which includes Studley Common and Whitlench.

A confirmation in 1328 of a twelfth-century charter referred to an alder-wood and two other areas of woodland.[1319] The former lay between *Stretford* and *Washford* and the deed implies that the meadow called *Brunham* (thought to equate to the Burnam of the tithe award[1320]) was in the area. Washford can be found on the tithe map and modern Ordnance Survey maps. The deed also refers to the wood next to the land of Aschetill and the wood between the land of Alan and the land of Roger de la Haye, but these descriptions do not enable the woods to be located on modern maps.

Another deed, dating from 1201, referred to two woods, the wood of *Haia* and the wood of Robert son of William.[1321] From its name, Haye Farm may point to the site of the wood of *Haia*. The wood (*boscum*) of Mappleborough was acquired by Peter de Montfort from Peter de Corbyson in the fourteenth century; Mappleborough Green here provides a suggested site for the wood.[1322] Gorcot had a wood recorded in the thirteenth century, and a grove, called *Ladigrove*, which was in a field called *Hayfeld*.[1323] In 1605 Ladygrove and Hayfield were in Skilts Park.[1324] The modern Grove Wood is a candidate for Ladygrove. Graingecumb Wood (Graungecombe Wood in 1560[1325]) was in Skilts Park in 1596 and 1605[1326] and may have been on the site of fields called Granscomb on the tithe map.

Sambourne

Sambourne was part of the ecclesiastical parish of Coughton.[1327] It was the subject of a separate entry in Domesday Book which showed it to be a manor of Evesham Abbey and to include *silva* measuring one league by half a league,[1328] perhaps five hundred acres or so. The Abbey continued to hold the manor throughout the later medieval period. The abbot and his tenants were said to have enclosed a considerable area of the royal Forest of Feckenham (in Worcestershire) which had been extended by King John to include Sambourne. In 1280 the abbot recovered his wood of Sambourne which had been seized following disputes between his bailiffs and those of the queen.[1329]

There are no records to show where the medieval wood of Sambourne was situated. The names 'Sarts' which appear on a map of 1746 south of New Diggins Coppice[1330] suggest at first sight that these were fields originally called assarts and cleared from woodland in the medieval period. However, there is a record that "the Diggins and Sart were parcell of Samborne Heath and enclosed by Thomas Throckmorton Esquire" in the sixteenth century.[1331] Whether, like part of Shrewley Heath, they had been arable land in the later medieval period is not known. The fine flora of Rough Hill Wood suggests that this might have been part of the medieval wood, but the earliest known record of Rough Hill Wood by name is from 1574, when Pilsors Wood was said to adjoin it.[1332] Part of Rough Hill Wood is on ridge and furrow, pointing to the growth of secondary woodland towards the end of the later medieval or during the early modern period, before the map of 1764 was drawn.

The chance survival of a few court rolls from the period 1472-1516 throws a new light on Sambourne's woodland.[1333] Court rolls for 1480, 1482, 1487, 1489, 1490, 1505, and 1516 show that several of the tenants held coppices, *copecia*. Some tenants were fined for not enclosing their coppices after felling, and for the consequent destruction of new growth from the trees. In some cases the locations of the coppices were described by reference to minor place-names which appear to survive in field-names on a map of 1746.[1334] Three coppices were in *Tomefeld*, *hyckfelds* and *Parkefylds* respectively, although on the map of 1746 there was no woodland in the various closes called Great and Little Tom Field, Hick Field and Park Field. *Pighell* in *Pullesore* was presumably in or adjacent to one of the several closes called Pilzer in 1746 which were to the south-east of Rough Hill Wood. That wood and Pilsors Wood adjoined each other in 1574.[1335] It seems reasonable to suggest that the large, compact area on the map of 1746 which looks as if it was taken out of Sambourne Heath was the former *Newlond* with its *hethlane ende*. In 1746 this area included five small coppices. (Two of those coppices survive, but there is little if any underwood in them; their ground flora includes some bluebells, but lacks the fine display of spring flowers which characterises many ancient woods.) Sambourne differs from other manors in north and west Warwickshire in that its tenants' woods were called coppices instead of groves or woods.

A second interesting feature of the court rolls is the evidence for hedges as a source of wood; they were enclosed in the same way as coppices to protect regrowth.[1336] The map of 1746 marks a hedge belonging to the sixteen houses; there is a record of "the sixtene hedge" in 1598.[1337]

Coughton

Coughton had *silva* measuring six furlongs by four; the Domesday Book entry also included pasture for fifty pigs,[1338] which was presumably in the *silva*. Woods and minor place-names associated with woodland or former woodland were mentioned in medieval deeds relating to Coughton, but not all of them have been located on modern maps. Manorial fragmentation in the later medieval period makes it difficult to identify and locate areas of woodland which were held by different families or branches of those families.[1339] In particular there is doubt about the site of the wood of Coughton itself, which may or may not have been distinct from Wyke Wood.

The two families between which the Domesday manor seems to have been divided[1340] both granted Alcester Abbey a place in the wood (*bosco*) of Coughton in which to make a piggery (*unam placeam in bosco meo de coctun in qua sibi unam porcheriam faciant*) and a wagon load of wood for the Abbey's kitchen every week in the wood (*nemore*) of Coughton (*qualibet ebdomada in nemore meo de coctun unam quadrigatam bosci ad coquinam suam*).[1341] The use of two different words for wood, *boscus* and *nemus*, in the same document may reflect a distinction between wood pasture, used for grazing animals, and an enclosed wood for underwood. Any such distinction was lost on the clerk who recorded Henry III's confirmation of the grants in 1241 at Woodstock; he wrote *quandam placiam in bosco de cocton ad quandam porcheriam faciendam et unam carectatam busce singulis septimanis in bosco de cocton*.[1342] A medieval deed would not normally have repeated the phrase *in bosco de cocton*; it would have used a phrase such as *in eodem bosco* or *in bosco predicto* - in the same wood, or in the aforesaid wood - and that is indeed how this grant has been interpreted by modern editors.[1343] The original deeds, however, suggest the possibility of two separate woods of different types.

The medieval manor of Beauchamp Court, which became part of the Warwick earldom, was in King's Coughton in Alcester parish.[1344] A pasture called Coughton Grove on a map of 1754, was in King's Coughton.[1345] Earthworks have been mapped for 'The Grove'.[1346] There was also an area of waste called Priors Wood, which was by Alcester Warren.[1347] Lands formerly of Alcester Abbey were acquired by Fulke Greville in 1544,[1348] but whether the two medieval deeds refer to Abbey lands which came to the Grevilles or simply to rights in a wood which continued to be held by laymen is a nice question.

The site of the wood held by the Bruilly family can be identified approximately as within Coughton Park. In the thirteenth century Simon de Bruly and his son Robert had a wood in Wyke next to a place called *trenthia*, i.e. Trench, a name which occurs in several documents.[1349] A deed of 1430 described furlongs south of *le Wykewode* adjacent to *le Billesleystrench, le lordestrench, Oldenhale, Canneclos, Cannecroft, Dykyngs* and *pekescroft*.[1350] A manorial rental of 1500 stated that pastures called *Belyngsborough, Dykyng, prioursfeld* with a virgate called *priours Grove, Wykyng* with pasture in *le Wykewode*, and *Trench hull* were in the park, whereas in 1483-4 they had been merely pastures.[1351] A deed of 1569 also located Wyke Wood within Coughton Park.[1352] These references confirm Sir William Dugdale's statement that Wyke had been "totally depopulated and included within Coughton Parke".[1353] The deed of 1569

referred to both the old and new parks of Coughton, explaining that they adjoined each other. Their proximity is presumably reflected in the field-names on maps of c.1695 and 1746 on which closes with park names and *Billingsborrough* were shown to the south and east of the area known today as Coughton Park.[1354] On the earlier map that area was covered with trees and divided into "The hither sides ye Wood" and "The further sides ye Wood" amounting to 164 acres. In 1600 wood was sold out of "A copise called neither weeke Copise conteyninge by estimacon xxx^t Acres" within Coughton Park.[1355] It seems reasonable to conclude that the medieval Wyke Wood, possibly enlarged by secondary woodland, survived within the modern Coughton Park until the Park was turned into a conifer plantation.

The minor place-name *Billesleystrench* presumably preserves the name of John de Bilesle, who was said to hold a wood in 1270-1.[1356] This suggests that the wood, which he held jointly with Reginald de Buteller, might have been in the vicinity of Coughton Park, but the trench might have surrounded land other than woodland.

In 1300 William de Spineto was said to hold that part of the vill of Coughton, in wood and plain, on the side of the river Arrow towards the west (*cum bosco et plano que est citra Riveram de Arewe versus occidentem*).[1357] This statement corresponds to references in thirteenth-century deeds to waste held by William de Spineto; the waste was between Icknield Street and another highway leading to Wyke.[1358] These references suggest that the waste was east of the later Coughton Park.

A reference to a green called the hay (*viride qui vocatur le heye*) may be reflected in the field-name Haywood on the map of 1746, north of Coughton Park and on the boundary with Sambourne.[1359] Other medieval minor place-names indicative of woodland or former woodland include *longa greva* near *Rowmersse, scorthurst* or *ssorta hursta*, described as a furlong, and *Bradegrauam*.[1360] None of these has been located on modern maps. A treeless close called The Grove and Tims Grove, which had trees in 1746, are candidates for the site of a medieval grove.

The field-name *le frith* in a deed of 1339 may preserve the Old English word *fyrhth* or *fyrhthe*, meaning wood or land overgrown with brushwood, scrub on the edge of woodland.[1361] That meaning is indicated by the spelling *ffyrthe*,[1362] found in a deed of 1355; *le ffyrthe* was near Billingsborough and Clapper Hill, south of the modern Coughton Park.[1363]

Alcester

There is no entry for Alcester in Domesday Book. There is a reference, in a confirmation of grants to Alcester Priory, to the wood of Alcester in 1241.[1364] In 1262 the Priory had the right to estovers in the woods (*boscis*) of Alcester by gift of William Botereux and Peter son of Herbert.[1365] Later medieval records also indicate several separate woods rather than a single area of woodland.

113

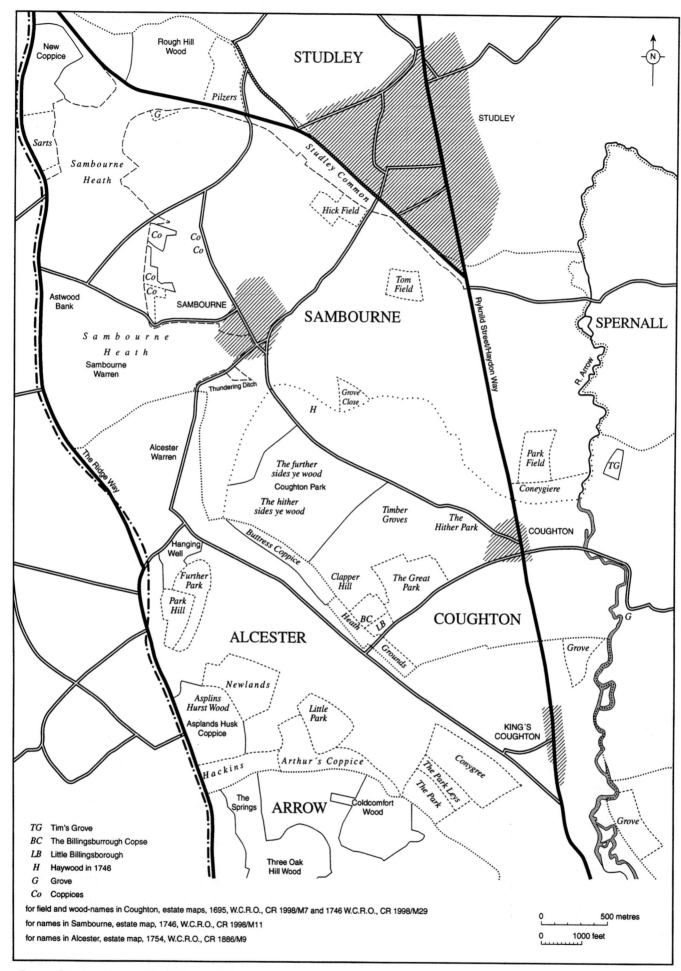

STUDLEY

New Coppice

Rough Hill Wood

Pilzers

G

Sarts

STUDLEY

Sambourne Heath

Studley Common

Hick Field

Co

Co
Co

Tom Field

Co

Co

Astwood Bank

SAMBOURNE

SAMBOURNE

SPERNALL

S a m b o u r n e
H e a t h

Sambourne Warren

R. Arrow

Thundering Ditch

Grove Close

H

Ryknild Street/Haydon Way

Alcester Warren

Park Field

TG

The further sides ye wood

Coughton Park

Coneygiere

The hither sides ye wood

Timber Groves

The Hither Park

The Ridge Way

COUGHTON

Hanging Well

Buttress Coppice

Clapper Hill

The Great Park

Further Park

Park Hill

Heath

BC
LB

COUGHTON

G

ALCESTER

Grounds

Grove

Newlands

Asplins Hurst Wood

Little Park

KING'S COUGHTON

Asplands Husk Coppice

Conygree

Arthur's Coppice

The Park Leys

Hackins

The Park

The Springs

ARROW

Coldcomfort Wood

Grove

Three Oak Hill Wood

TG   Tim's Grove

BC   The Billingsburrough Copse

LB   Little Billingsborough

H   Haywood in 1746

G   Grove

Co   Coppices

for field and wood-names in Coughton, estate maps, 1695, W.C.R.O., CR 1998/M7 and 1746 W.C.R.O., CR 1998/M29

for names in Sambourne, estate map, 1746, W.C.R.O., CR 1998/M11

for names in Alcester, estate map, 1754, W.C.R.O., CR 1886/M9

0   500 metres

0   1000 feet

Figure 74: Sambourne, Coughton and Alcester

A claim to estovers in four hundred acres of wood in Alcester which was heard in 1398 gives some indication of the extent of woodland in the later medieval period, although much of it may have disappeared by 1398.[1366] However, most of the recorded medieval woods have not been located, so it is not possible to show whether the medieval, like the eighteenth-century, woodland was concentrated in a particular part of the parish. A map of 1754 shows Alcester Common along most of the north-eastern boundary with Coughton, and Buttress Coppice adjacent to the modern Coughton Park.[1367] (On modern maps the Park and Coppice form a single area of woodland owned and replanted by the Forestry Commission.) To the south-west of the Common were closes carrying park names and, around them, Hanging Well Coppice, Asplins Hurst Wood and Arthur's Coppice.

Buttress Coppice was, in core at least, a medieval wood, whose site can be confirmed by a deed of 1569 which described it as adjacent to Coughton Park.[1368] The deed also named places and described measured pieces of land which correspond largely with the agreement of 1355 between Alexander Buttras (presumably a corruption of Botreaux, the name of the lords of one of the manors of Alcester)[1369] and Guy Spyney (the Spineys held part of Coughton)[1370] for extinguishing and preserving common pasture rights.[1371] Alexander Buttras was allowed to enclose all his wood called *Buttras Coppyes*. The use of the word coppice in the name of the wood strongly suggests that the agreement confirmed an existing enclosure.

The Beauchamp family had woodland in Alcester. In 1291 Walter de Beauchamp was given permission to bring into cultivation sixty acres of his wood in Alcester which was within the Forest of Feckenham.[1372] The assarted woodland may have become the pastures of *Luttulwodefeld* and *Buldewode* by 1466-7, in which year the Beauchamp accounts also recorded sales of wood in *Brokehulle cowpyce* and *kyttevalettelowe*.[1373] The name of the latter may have become corrupted to *kyt ferret coppice* in a deed of 1578.[1374] (The element *valette*, presumably derived from the Latin *valletum*,[1375] is found also in relation to woodland in the Wedgnock Park accounts of 1401-2 - *quodam valetto vocato Kylyngworthurne*.[1376] It is a rare term, but not peculiar to Warwickshire.[1377]) Accounts for 1504-5 state that timber was taken out of a wood called *le Waste*.[1378]

By the Dissolution the Priory held woodland of its own. A Crown survey in 1544, after the Priory's dissolution, helps, with later maps, to locate two of the Priory's woods.[1379] The *priors hacking*, a parcel of waste ground of six acres, adjoined Sambourne Heath. The *hckyng*, a common wood of two acres, may have been part of the later Hackins which adjoined Ragley. (Confusingly, there was another *priors hackyng*, a pasture, not wood, in Upton in Haselor, which adjoined Oversley Park and which had become partly wooded by 1747.[1380])

In 1257 Robert de Baginton had a wood described as being below Alcester.[1381]

Some later medieval deeds refer to *le Hurstweye* and one described half an acre of land as *super Hurstam* but none of them indicates whether the Hurst was wood at that time.[1382] The existence of Asplins Hurst Wood in 1754 may reflect the site of the medieval Hurst. A deed of 1563 shows that it was known formerly as Astlyns Hurst and also that the wood further to the east, called Arthur's Coppice in 1754, was, in part at least, known as the *parke coppice* in the middle of the sixteenth century.[1383]

Arrow and Oversley

Domesday Book recorded *silva* measuring one league by two furlongs under Arrow (say between about 175 and 235 acres) and three furlongs by one furlong under Oversley.[1384] The parish of Arrow is on the whole poorly documented for the later medieval period. In 1229 it was reported that William de Camville had cut down his wood of Arrow which was within the forest (of Feckenham) without the king's agreement. There was a wood to which a murderer fled in 1262. In 1326 Robert Burdet's wood of Arrow was said to have been taken into the forest of Feckenham without warrant and Robert had licence to impark his wood in 1333.[1385] Forty-four acres of old assart were attributed to Arrow in 1280,[1386] so there had presumably been some clearance before the wood was imparked. Presumably the Arrow Park which was shown on a map c.1800 marks the approximate site of the wood which Robert Burdet had licence to impark, or of part of it.[1387]

The relationship between Ragley Park's eighteenth-century woods and any medieval woodland is unknown.[1388] Ragley was not the subject of a separate entry in Domesday Book.

A survey c.1320 recorded three woods in the manor of Oversley, *Calwohull, Budeleye* and *Hoghw'grove*.[1389] Oversley manor included Wixford in 1287[1390] and by the mid sixteenth century, if not before, also extended into Exhall and parts of Grafton and Broom.[1391] This complicates the search for the sites of the three woods, but there are useful clues to the sites of two of them. Three fields or groups of fields are called grove on maps of Oversley manor.[1392] None of them is obviously next to a highway. However, in the middle of the northern half of the presumed area of the medieval park a field called Highway Ground straddles the line of the Roman road which runs through the park. The field called Grove, a short distance to the east and also on the line of the Roman road, may therefore have been the site of the medieval *Hoghw'grove*. *Budeleye* was by the field of Oversley.[1393] A seventeenth-century tradition equates *Budeleye* with Moor Hall in Wixford.[1394] North of Wixford Town Meadow in 1747 was a close called Little Grove which adjoined Castle Hill, otherwise called Betley, in Oversley.[1395]

The modern Oversley Wood is the southern half of Oversley Park, whose full extent of about 380 acres can be estimated from the shape of field boundaries and the field-name Durlip - deer-leap.[1396] The survey of c.1320 stated that the park contained 387 acres, a figure so remarkably close to the sum derived from modern field acreages as virtually to confirm the exact site of the medieval park. How much of the park was formed from woodland is unknown. The *silva* recorded in Domesday Book could hardly have exceeded thirty acres. Certainly the park cannot be equated to a tract of primary woodland; the line of a former Roman road can be traced across the northern half of the park's site.

Weethley

No *silva* was entered under Weethley in Domesday Book.[1397] A little is known of Weethley's later medieval woodland through some legal disputes, including two claims to estovers in woodland there.[1398] From the second we learn that there were at least fifty acres of wood. In 1315 there

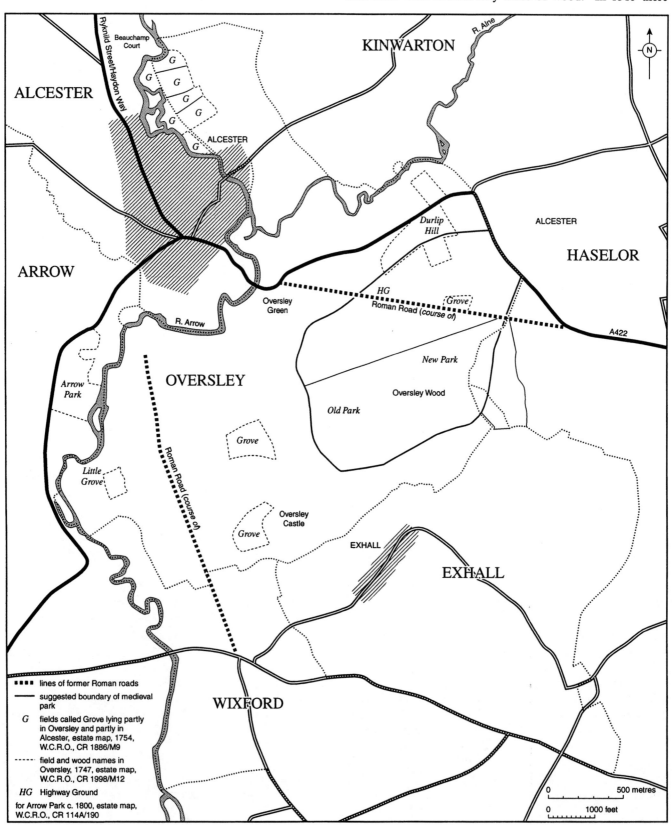

Figure 75: Arrow and Oversley

were at least forty acres.[1399] There was common pasture in waste in Weethley in 1288.[1400] In 1543-4 *Whetheley coppice* contained eighty acres.[1401] The site of the wood is not given in surviving medieval records, but some correspondence with the modern Weethley Wood seems likely.

Of the two manors in Salford in 1086, that which belonged to Evesham Abbey (Abbots Salford) had no *silva*.[1402] although there was some woodland recorded there (*cum bosco*) in 1300.[1403] The manor which became Salford Priors had a small amount of *silva*, measuring two furlongs by half a furlong.[1404] The later medieval manor of Salford Priors included the hamlets or townships of Wood Bevington, Cock Bevington and Dunnington.[1405] Domesday Book recorded Bevington under Worcestershire, with three acres of *silva*.[1406]

In 1326 it was claimed that the prior of Kenilworth's wood of Wolvedon, belonging to his manor of Salford, had been taken into the Forest of Feckenham (in Worcestershire) without warrant.[1407] In 1433 there was a dispute over part of the wood of Wolvedon. Halesowen Abbey claimed that the disputed area was in Atch Lench in Worcestershire.[1408] From this and from the references to Abbots Morton and Church Lench in the location of the woodland it can be deduced that the wood of Wolvedon occupied the area of the present Rough Hill Wood. In 1580 a lease of the former monastic woods in Salford Priors stated that three of them, Old Close Coppice, Roughehill Coppice and Coldepittes Coppice, were surrounded by a single hedge.[1409] It seems that the wood of Wolvedon had been divided into coppices. These coppices contained 134 acres. Given the much smaller area which would have been covered by the *silva* recorded in Domesday Book it is possible that the Domesday survey was incomplete, or that the coppices of 1580 included secondary woodland which had developed since the Domesday survey, or that in 1086 the wood of Wolvedon was in Worcestershire and was only later attached to the manor of Salford Priors.

The last of these possibilities is supported by a study of the origins of medieval hundreds in the diocese of Worcester. The parish of Salford Priors has been identified with the site of a minster church which served an early medieval territory including not only Bevington in Esch Hundred in Worcestershire but possibly also the six manors called Lench in the same Hundred.[1410] The disturbance of territorial boundaries in the area provides a context in which the wood of Wolvedon could have become attached to Kenilworth Priory's manor of Salford.

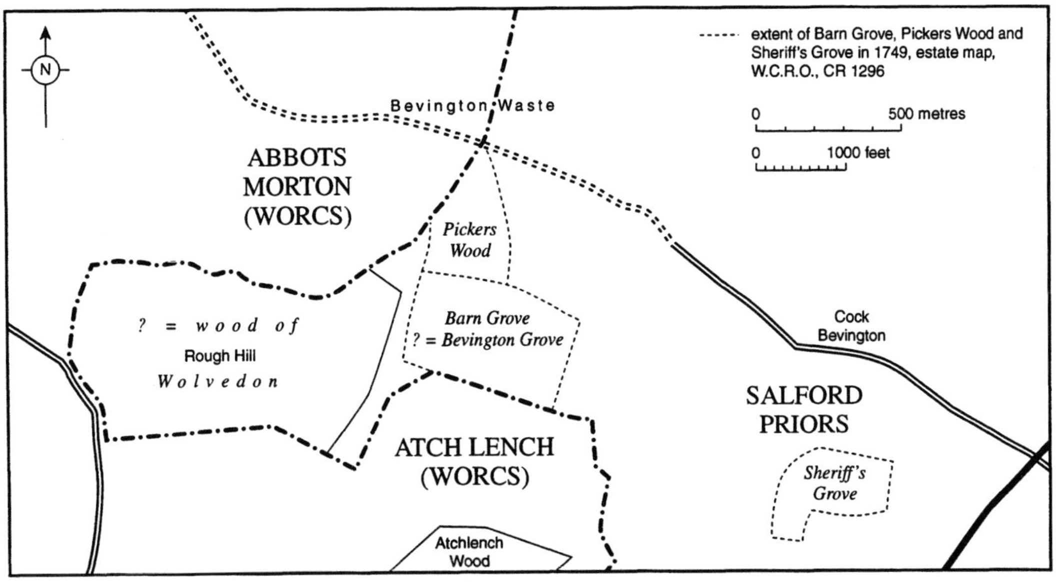

Kenilworth Priory sought to 'approve' land from wood and waste in Salford.[1411] There was an assart in *Biuintonesgrave*, whose name suggests that it was a wood in Bevington.[1412] The assart extended into *pikaresh[ale]*, a name

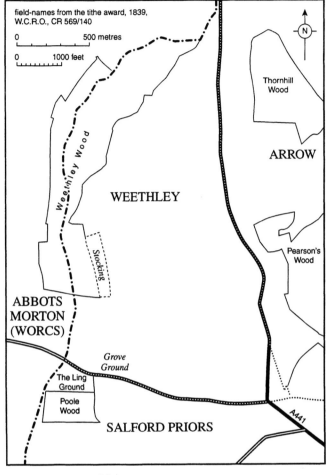

Figure 76: Weethley

Salford

Figure 77: Salford Priors

117

which arguably survives in the sixteenth-century Pickersale Coppice, which may have become Pickers Wood.[1413] If this is the case, then it points to the former Barn Grove as the possible site of the medieval grove of Bevington.

The identification of the site of Wolvedon and of the probable site of Bevington's grove suggests the existence of a large area of woodland which in the later medieval period was shared between the parishes of Salford in Warwickshire and Atch Lench and Abbots Morton in Worcestershire.

Bidford

Bidford stands out amongst the manors of the Avon valley below Warwick in the exceptionally large amount of *silva* which was recorded in Domesday Book under the king's manor there.[1414] *Silva* four leagues long by one league wide must have covered in the order of four thousand acres or more. The bishop of Bayeux held a manor with a much smaller amount of *silva*, measuring two furlongs by one furlong.[1415] The ecclesiastical parish of Bidford covered only 3,184 acres.[1416] No woodland was recorded in Bidford itself during the later medieval period. Either Domesday Book was in error, perhaps mistaking furlongs for leagues, or the *silva* disappeared without trace soon after 1086, or the king's manor may have included other places outside Bidford. The Domesday *silva* of Bidford, as of several other places in north and west Warwickshire, is a mystery.

[1] Darby and Terrett, *The Domesday Geography of Midland England*, p. 297; C. Dyer, 'The Retreat from Marginal Land: The Growth and Decline of Medieval Rural Settlements', in ed. M. Aston, D. Austin, and C. Dyer, *The Rural Settlements of Medieval England* (Oxford, 1989), pp. 45-57, see p. 57.

[2] For this method of calculation see Rackham, *Ancient Woodland*, pp. 113-14. The equation of a league with one and a half statute miles is also followed by Darby, *Domesday England*, p. 178.

[3] *RBW*, p. 244.

[4] See under Lapworth below.

[5] *DB*, 242d.

[6] P.R.O., JUST 1/951A, rot 9d.

[7] W.C.R.O., CR1911/14.

[8] W.C.R.O., CR2433/31/125 and EAC/138 are sale particulars including Bishopton Hill Farm.

[9] S.B.T., ER3/235/1-6, 236-8, 240.

[10] S.B.T., DR150/2/1; this reference was drawn to my attention by Dr. R. Bearman.

[11] S.B.T., DR10/2429, DR38/1429; B.L., Egerton Roll 8624.

[12] R. Bearman, personal communication.

[13] P.R.O., under E 315 - e.g. E 315/37/213; E 315/40/21, 193; E 315/41/88, 149; E 315/44/218, 223; E 315/45/5, 39, 177, 201; E 315/46/156; E 315/47/233, 259; E 315/48/209; E 315/49/135; E 315/50/111, 125, 261; E 315/52/245.

[14] W.C.R.O., CR114A/104/1.

[15] *DB*, 243b, 243d, 244a.

[16] W.C.R.O., CR2776/1, pp. 187, 429.

[17] *ibid.*, pp. 182-3.

[18] W.C.R.O., CR912.

[19] Gelling, *Place-Names in the Landscape*, p. 193. This view is different from that in Gover, Mawer, and Stenton, *Place-Names of Warwickshire* p. 209.

[20] *DB*, 243b, 244a.

[21] *FF*, Vol. I, no. 662.

[22] B.R.L., 247,148-9.

[23] W.C.R.O., QS75/47.

[24] *DB*, 243c; There were two places called *Optone* in Domesday Book, but the first (*DB*, 238b), amongst the lands of the king and a member of Stoneleigh, is thought to refer to Leek Wootton - *VCH*, Vol. VI, p. 167.

[25] *FF*, Vol. II, no. 1409.

[26] Cartulary of St. Mary's Warwick, P.R.O., E 164/22, f. cxxiii, copy in W.C.R.O., Z251(Sm).

[27] *Calendar of Close Rolls, Edward III, 1364-68*, pp. 71-2; W.C.R.O., CR1998/box 71(1).

[28] P.R.O., E 303/18/502.

[29] Gover, Mawer and Stenton, *Place-Names of Warwickshire*, p. 212.

[30] *ibid.*, ff. cxxv, cxxiiij.

[31] B.R.L., 168,238.

[32] P.R.O., E 318/20/999.

[33] W.C.R.O., D19/475, and QS75/56.

[34] W.C.R.O., CR114/114A.

[35] P.R.O., E 303/18/502.

[36] *VCH*, Vol. III, p. 110.

[37] W.C.R.O., CR1998/box 71(1) and CR1998/box 45/GG7/1-6.

[38] For the survey of c.1170, *RBW*, pp. 276-8.

[39] *DB*, 238c; for the record of assarts and the first record of *la grave* c.1096-1112, *RBW*, pp. 276-8, 412; for the dates of the latter record, Dyer, *Lords and Peasants*, p. 47.

[40] *RBW*, pp. 276-8.

[41] *ibid.*, pp. 263, 274-5.

[42] P.R.O., E 152/91.

[43] P.R.O., C 140/67.

[44] P.R.O., C 54/463 includes the name park.

[45] P.R.O., E 318/41/2191 includes wood only.

[46] A map of this date (accompanied by a survey), W.C.R.O., L6/1035-6, shows the wood with its present western boundary, which includes the area of ridge and furrow.

[47] Tithe award in W.C.R.O., CR569/122.

[48] Worcs. R.O., 001:9 BA 2636 164 92178a.

[49] *RBW*, p. 412; for the dates of the list of knights' fees, Dyer, *Lords and Peasants*, p. 47.

[50] Gelling, *Place-Names in the Landscape*, p. 194.

[51] *DB*, 238c.

[52] E.g. W.C.R.O., CR1886/M24A.

[53] *Dugdale*, Vol. I, pp. 272, 379; see also P.R.O., C 137/27.

[54] *The Beauchamp Cartulary Charters 1110-1268* (ed. E. Mason, Pipe Roll Society, New Series Vol. XLIII, 1971-73), p. 166.

[55] *ibid.*

[56] *FF*, Vol. I, pp. 63-4.; *ibid.* pp. 139-40.

[57] P.R.O., C 132/35/13.

[58] P.R.O., C 133/86/1.

[59] P.R.O., SC 6/1040/24.

60 *Calendar of Patent Rolls 1364-67*, p. 367.

61 W.C.R.O., CR1886/474, 475 and CR895/8/14.

62 The original of the cartulary is B.L., Add. MS. 28,024, with a microfilm copy in W.C.R.O., MI 177. See ff. 68-70.

63 Roberts, *Settlement, Land Use and Population*, pp. 143-4.

64 *VCH*, Vol. VIII, p. 467.

65 Coss, *Lordship, knighthood and locality*, pp. 181-3.

66 P.R.O., KB 26/176, rots 4d, 27r.

67 W.C.R.O., CR1886/481, 475, 487.

68 P.R.O., E 164/122, f. cccxxix, copy in W.C.R.O., Z251(Sm).

69 W.C.R.O., CR895/8/14.

70 W.C.R.O., CR1886/481.

71 *FF*, Vol. I, no. 705.

72 W.E. Tate, 'Enclosure Acts and Awards relating to Warwickshire', *TBAS*, LXV (1943, 1944) pp. 45-104, see pp. 58, 60.

73 W.C.R.O., CR1886/482; CR1886/487 for spelling *Megrewode*.

74 *VCH*, Vol. VIII, pp. 468-70.

75 A grove at *Gybbeclyfe* was recorded in 1422-3, W.C.R.O., CR1886/485 and *Gyclyff Grove* in 1483, P.R.O., DL 29/643/10439.

76 P.R.O., SC 6/Hen VIII/3745; this is repeated in a deed of 1588, concerning the site of the former Priory of St. Sepulchre's, S.B.T., DR37/2763. For the map of 1711, W.C.R.O., CR217/1.

77 Copy of enclosure award of 1773 made in 1787, B.R.L., 353,352; *Dugdale*, Vol. I, p. 273.

78 W.C.R.O., CR1709/320/6.

79 S.B.T., DR3/534; for Colewood, map of 1711, W.C.R.O., CR217/1.

80 For the former settlements Tate, 'Enclosure Acts and Awards', pp. 58, 60.

81 In 1398-9, W.C.R.O., CR1886/481; in 1430, W.C.R.O., CR26/W16-17; in 1437, W.C.R.O., CR26/1(1) bundle A/W18; in 1458, W.C.R.O., CR26/XXXII.

82 For the field-names, deed of 1658, W.C.R.O., CR26/1(2) bundle B/27; for the location of Grove Fields, map of 1711, W.C.R.O., CR217/1.

83 P.R.O., JUST 1/954, rot 20d.

84 For a lease of the grove in 1573, W.C.R.O., CR1886/4849; the owner was Anthony Stoughton, to whom the hospital lands had been granted in 1540 (*VCH*, Vol. VIII, p. 444).

85 W.C.R.O., CR26/1(2) bundle B/27.

86 W.C.R.O., CR26/A/I.

87 W.C.R.O., CR26/XXXII.

88 P.R.O., E 326/5441.

89 Tate, 'Enclosure Acts and Awards', pp. 58, 60

90 For the field-names, see Leek Wootton tithe map, W.C.R.O., CR569/277 and estate map of 1750, W.C.R.O., CR1886/M5, copy at Z204/6(U).

91 *VCH*, Vol. VI, p. 167. This attribution is not followed in *DB*, 238b, which is based on Gover, Mawer and Stenton, *Place-Names of Warwickshire*, p. 212, where *Optone* is said to refer to Upton in Haselor.

92 S. G. Wallsgrove, *Kenilworth 1086-1756* (1991), ch. 2 and fig. 3, but see B.L., Add. MS. 47,677, ff. ccclix, xcii, copy in W.C.R.O., MI 392/2, the latter entry referring to land rather than to wood.

93 P.R.O., E 303/17/285.

94 W.C.R.O., Z141/1(U).

95 *DB*, 238b.

96 *DB*, 239d.

97 *John of Gaunt's Register, 1379-1383*, Vol. II (ed. J.C. Lodge and R. Somerville, Camden Third Series, LVII, 1937), pp. 278-79; P.R.O., DL 29/643/7545; W.C.R.O., CR1886/475.

98 ed. Lodge and Somerville, *John of Gaunt's Register*, pp. 278-9; P.R.O., DL 29/643/7545; W.C.R.O., CR1886/475.

99 W.C.R.O., CR576/1, f. 17; *ibid.*, CR143A.

100 S.B.T., DR10/516; P.R.O., SC 8/161/8023.

101 *HR*, p. 44.

102 As the tithe map covers only a small part of the parish, this figure has been taken from the 1865 edition of the year-book *County of Warwick*, p. 44.

103 *SLB*, p. 42.

104 P.R.O., SC 8/55/2750 and C 81/129/7129 appear to be duplicates; the former is damaged.

105 Rackham, *Ancient Woodland*, p. 5, gives the date of the earliest known example from eastern England as 1331, but R.E. Latham, *Dictionary of Medieval Latin from British Sources*, Fascicule II C (1981), p. 487, gives several examples from the thirteenth century.

106 *John of Gaunt's Register, 1379-1383*, Vol. II (ed. J.C. Lodge and R. Somerville, Camden Third Series, LVII, 1937), p. 278.

107 P.R.O., LR 2/185, copy in W.C.R.O., MI 295.

108 Gelling, *Place-Names in the Landscape*, p. 191.

109 P.R.O., LR 2/185, copy in W.C.R.O., MI 295; W.C.R.O., CR576/1.

110 P.R.O., MR 311 S/0777, copy in W.C.R.O., Z150(U).

111 P.R.O., LR 2/185, copy in W.C.R.O., MI 295.

112 B.L., Harley 3650, f. 2, copy in W.C.R.O., MI 392/1.

113 *SLB*, p. 26.

114 B.L., Harley 3650, f. 2, copy in W.C.R.O., MI 392/1.

115 B.L., Add. MS. 47,677, f. cxxiii, copy in W.C.R.O., MI 392/2.

116 *Calendar of Close Rolls, Henry III, 1237-42*, p. 50.

117 *ibid.*, p. 78.

118 *HR*, p. 44.

119 B.L., Harley 3650, f. 2, copy in W.C.R.O., MI 392/1.

120 B.L., Add. MS. 47,677, f. ccclix, copy in W.C.R.O., MI 392/2.

121 *ibid.*, f. xcii.

122 P.R.O., MR 311 S/0777, copy in W.C.R.O., Z150(U).

123 For Honiley, see B.L., Cott. Ch. xxiii 15.

124 W.C.R.O., CR569/139.

125 Wallsgrove, *Kenilworth*, ch. 2 and fig. 3.

126 For 1237 reference, *Calendar of Close Rolls, Henry III, 1237-42*, p. 502; for the later accounts, P.R.O., DL 29/463/7539-7563.

127 *VCH*, Vol. VI, p. 134.

128 *SLB*, p. 101.

129 e.g. P.R.O., DL 29/463/7540.

130 S.B.T., DR18/30/15/11.

131 P.R.O., C 81/129/7129. This is one of a series of petitions relating to the Frith, having mainly similar contents to the damaged petition P.R.O., SC 8/55/2750.

132 W.C.R.O., CR576/1.

133 *Dugdale*, Vol. I, pp. 247-8.

134 W.C.R.O., CR576/1.

135 *ibid.*

136 P.R.O., LR 2/185, copy in W.C.R.O., MI 295.

137 W.C.R.O., Z421(Sm).

138 W.C.R.O., CR143A.

139 Wallsgrove, *Kenilworth*, ch. 8.

140 *ibid.*, figures 7, 13 and 15 locates Thornton Wood further east, apparently unaware of the reference in 1694 and offering no explanation for the origins of the Middle Copse and Chase Copse of 1692. It also suggests (in Chapter 13) that the wood belonged to Kenilworth Abbey, simply on the basis that the Abbey enjoyed common rights there, but the Abbey's woods in Kenilworth parish were listed in a survey of 1545 (P.R.O., E 318/16/743) and did not include Thornton Wood.

141 B.L., Harley 3650, ff. 9-10, copy in W.C.R.O., MI 392/1.

142 P.R.O., E 318/16/743.

143 P.R.O., JUST 1/1400, rot 126d.

144 B.L., Harley 3650, ff. 61, 62, copy in W.C.R.O., MI 392/1.

145 *HR*, p. 48.

146 P.R.O., MR 311 S/0777, copy in W.C.R.O., Z150(U).

147 P.R.O., LR 2/185 copy in W.C.R.O., MI 295.

148 P.R.O., E 318/21/1143.

149 B.L., Add. MS. 47,677, f. primo, copy in W.C.R.O., MI 392.

150 *ibid.*, f. xiii.

151 *HR*, p. 49.

152 P.R.O., C 54/200, m. 23d.

153 P.R.O., DL 29/463/7540.

154 W.C.R.O., CR576/1; Wallsgrove, *Kenilworth*, fig. 8 gives suggested sites for these two groves inferred from the detailed survey.

155 *DB*, 241d.

156 For *moppesgroue*, P.R.O., SC 2/207/77 (court roll of 1389); for *moppesthynge*, P.R.O., SC 2/207/79.

157 *DB*, 241c.

158 S.B.T., DR10/516.

159 *VCH*, Vol. VI, p. 13.

160 P.R.O., E 210/3697.

161 *HR*, p. 110.

162 *Dugdale*, Vol. I, p. 266.

163 P.R.O., E 315/47/115.

164 B.L., Add. MS. 47,677, f. clv, copy in W.C.R..O., MI 392/2.

165 *Dugdale*, Vol. I, p. 266.

166 P.R.O., LR 14/229.

167 Gover, Mawer and Stenton, *Place-Names of Warwickshire*, p. 361; for the location see the tithe map of Ashow in W.C.R.O., CR569/13 and the estate map of 1766, copy in W.C.R.O., Z142(L).

168 P.R.O., E 315/51/73.

169 W.C.R.O., Z142(L); Wallsgrove, *Kenilworth*, fig. 8.

170 B.L., Add. MS. 47,677, f. cxlii, copy in W.C.R.O., MI 392/2.

171 Compare modern maps with the estate map of 1766, copy in W.C.R.O., Z142(L).

172 Copy in W.C.R.O., Z 141/1(U).

173 S.B.T., DR18/1/54; P.R.O., E 315/51/73.

174 P.R.O., LR 14/229.

175 Gover, Mawer and Stenton, *Place-Names of Warwickshire*, p. 155.

176 P.R.O., E 315/51/73.

177 P.R.O., E 210/5693, 6517; E 326/497, 459, 3471.

178 P.R.O., E 210/5693.

179 P.R.O., E 210/5451; S.B.T., DR18/1/59.

180 Map of 1597, copy in W.C.R.O., Z 141/1(U); for the identification with Glasshouse Coppice see map of 1766, copy in W.C.R.O., Z142(L).

181 *SLB*, p. ix.

182 *SLB*, pp. xliv-lvii.

183 W.C.R.O., CR569/213.

184 *DB*, 238b.

185 *SLB*, pp. lix, 15-6.

186 *ibid.*, p. 26.

187 R.E. Latham, *Dictionary of Medieval Latin from British Sources*, Fascicule I (1975), p. 219.

188 A.H. Smith, *English Place-Name Elements*, Part I (1956), p. 146.

189 See *DB*, 238b for Kenilworth and *Optone* (?Leek Wootton); *SLB*, p. 9 for Ryton; B.L., Harley 3650 (Kenilworth Cartulary) ff. 36-7, copy in W.C.R.O., MI 392/1, for Leek Wootton and its dependencies and Baginton; S.B.T., DR10/258 for Bubbenhall as a chapelry of Ryton c.1183.

190 Gover, Mawer and Stenton, *Place-Names of Warwickshire*, p. 185.

191 *SLB*, pp. 25, 245.

192 Copy map in W.C.R.O., Z 141/1(U).

193 *SLB*, p. 248; map of Bubbenhall and surroundings of 1726, original in the John Rylands University Library of Manchester and copy in W.C.R.O., Z 414(U).

194 *SLB*, p. 245.

195 *ibid.*, p. xlix.

196 P.R.O., E 326/6228.

197 *boscum de Wethele* (S.B.T., DR18/1/705); *bosco de Bradley* (S.B.T., DR18/1/698); *Weston Wode* (*SLB*, pp. 248, 102).

198 *SLB*, p. 25.

199 *ibid.*, p. 102.

200 *FF*, Vol. I., no. 618, pp. 224-5; for original, P.R.O., CP 25/1/243/20.

201 S.B.T., DR18/1/745.

202 *SLB*, pp. 126, 135-36, 138.

203 B.L., Add. MS. 47,677, f. cxxxix, copy in W.C.R.O., MI 392/2.

204 *FF*, Vol. I., no. 618, pp. 224-5; for the original, P.R.O., CP 25/1/243/20.

205 *HR*, p. 73 has *Craccele*. Careful examination of documents emanating from Stoneleigh Abbey itself, for example, S.B.T., DR18/1/926, confirms the reading *Crattele/Crateley*.

206 *Rotuli Parliamentorum*, Vol. I, p. 46, cited in J. Birrell, 'Common Rights in the Medieval Forest: Disputes and Conflicts in the Thirteenth Century', *Past & Present*, 117 (1987), pp. 22-49, see pp. 48-9.

207 S.B.T., DR18/1/1137-44.

208 *SLB*, pp. lix, 15-6.

209 *ibid.*, p. 26.

210 *Rotuli Parliamentorum*, Vol. I, p. 46; P.R.O., SC 8/269/13404.

211 *SLB*, p. 175.

212 *ibid.*, pp. 178-79.

213 *ibid.*, p. *l*.

214 W.C.R.O., Z139/2(U).

215 *SLB*, p. liii.

216 S.B.T., DR18/1/1131; P.R.O., E 326/6180.

217 S.B.T., DR18/1/1127, 1133.

218 Gover, Mawer and Stenton, *Place-Names of Warwickshire*, p. 183.

219 *Calendar of Close Rolls, Henry III, 1247-51*, p. 339; S.B.T., DR18/1/705.

220 B.L., Add. MS. 47,677, f. cccxli, copy in W.C.R.O., MI 392/2.

221 S.B.T., DR18/1/696 and P.R.O., E 210/8066 (the date of the latter deed has been derived from the approximate dates when John was Abbot of Stoneleigh, see *VCH*, Vol. II, p. 81); for the map of 1766, copy in W.C.R.O., Z142(L).

222 *SLB*, pp. 23-4.

223 The name has been read as *Craccele* rather than *Crattele* in the original manuscript of the Hundred Rolls, ed. T. John, *The Warwickshire Hundred Rolls of 1279-80: Stoneleigh and Kineton Hundreds*, British Academy Records of Social and Economic History, New Series, XIX (1992), p. 73. There is a similar reading by editors of the *Calendar of Patent Rolls*, see volume for 1354-58, p. 184. Careful examination of documents emanating from Stoneleigh Abbey itself, for example the Leger Book, and a deed in S.B.T., DR18/1/926, confirms the reading of *Crattele*. Such documents are more likely than national records to preserve the correct pronunciation.

224 Copy in W.C.R.O., Z142(L).

225 *SLB*, p. 127.

226 *ibid.*, p. 220.

227 S.B.T., DR18/1/733.

228 W.C.R.O., CR561/2, no. 26.

229 S.B.T., DR18/10/27/1.

230 S.B.T., DR18/3/28/4; DR18/3/52/24, 26, 30, 31; DR18/25/Bn.72.

231 B.L., Add. MS. 47,677, ff. cxxvii, cxxx, copy in W.C.R.O., MI 392/2.

232 *Formulare*, pp. 377-8.

233 *SLB*, p. 211.

234 *Calendar of Inquisitions Miscellaneous*, Vol. III (1937), p. 238.

235 *SLB*, p. 246; also B.L., Add. MS. 47,677, f. cxxxvi, copy in W.C.R.O., MI 392/2, which seems to confuse Odybarn and *Crattele*.

236 S.B.T., DR18/30/24/13.

237 P.R.O., LR 2/185, copy in W.C.R.O., MI 295.

238 *SLB*, p. 39.

239 *ibid.*, p. liii.

240 *ibid.*, p. 42.

241 *ibid.*, p. 201; S.B.T., DR18/3/45/2.

242 S.B.T., DR10/1017.

243 *SLB*, p. 101.

244 B.L., Add. MS., 47,677, f. 76, copy in W.C.R.O., MI 392/2.

245 *SLB*, p. 247.

246 S.B.T., DR10/1459.

247 S.B.T., DR10/1212.

248 S.B.T., DR10/1299; *SLB*, p. l.

249 S.B.T., DR10/1300.

250 S.B.T., DR10/1079.

251 For Upper Grove, the estate map of 1766, copy in W.C.R.O., Z142(L); for *Harlewyn grove*, *SLB*, p. 217.

252 *SLB*, p. liv; S.B.T., DR18/1/838.

253 S.B.T., DR18/1/850.

254 S.B.T., DR18/1/847.

255 B.L., Lansdowne 200, ff. lxiv-lxv for Fletchamstead; S.B.T., DR18/1/850 for Canley; *SLB*, p. 214 for Hurst; S.B.T., DR10/1189 for Hethsale etc.; *SLB*, p. 121 for Finbury; *ibid.*, p. 150 for *le Conynger*.

256 W.C.R.O., Z139/2(U).

257 W.C.R.O., CR569/213.

258 S.B.T., DR10/1762.

259 S.B.T., DR10/1194.

260 *SLB*, p. 101.

261 B.L., Harley 3650, ff. 19, 29-30, copy in W.C.R.O., MI 392/1; for the dates, see C. Watson, *The Kenilworth Cartulary* (Ph.D. thesis, University of London, c.1968), p. 321.

262 S.B.T., DR10/2119b; *BD* under Baginton.

263 W.C.R.O., CR569/15.

264 For the map of 1766, see the Stoneleigh Abbey estate maps of 1766 (map 2), copy in W.C.R.O., Z142(L); for the medieval *millegroue*, S.B.T., DR10/2220.

265 C.R.O., 39/19.

266 *DB*, 241c.

267 P.R.O., E 303/18/519.

268 P.R.O., Sta.Cha. 2/XX152.

269 *SLB*, pp. 8, lviii.

270 Coombe Abbey cartulary, B.L., Cotton Vitell. A i, f. 165.

271 P.R.O., E 164/21, f. 70v, copy in W.C.R.O., MI 409.

272 P.R.O., E 303/16/80.

273 M.MSS., Mi M 232.

274 B.L., Add. MS. 48,181, PS5/1804, copy in W.C.R.O., Z 203(U).

275 W.C.R.O., D34, map no. 14.

276 P.R.O., E 164/21, f. 73r, copy in W.C.R.O., MI 409.

277 S.B.T., DR37/box 114.

278 Bodleian Library, Craven 6, 78.

279 *DB*, 238d, 241c.

280 B.L., Cotton Vitell. A i, ff. 42-45.

281 W.C.R.O., D34; W.C.R.O., CR8/47.

282 Bodleian Library, Craven 320.

283 P.R.O., E 303/16/57.

284 *HR*, pp.128, 129.

285 See above, under Willenhall.

286 B.L., Cotton Vitell. A i, f. 44; one of the witnesses to the deed transcribed into the cartulary was Laurence, Prior of Coventry c.1144-79 (*VCH*, Vol. II, p. 58).

287 Dr. M. Gelling, personal communication, has confirmed that *munechet* "looks a distinct possibility for a *ceto* name."

288 There are two place-names including -*chet* (see Chapter Five), but this is no indication that the woods from which these place-names were derived were extant in the later medieval period. For examples elsewhere in England of woods with names containing -*chet*, Rackham, *Ancient Woodland*, pp. 132-3.

289 M.MSS., Mi M 232.

290 Binley Coppice was listed as one of the woods of Coombe Abbey c.1550 (S.B.T., DR37/box 114), with eight acres, but this may have referred to the area of wood ready to cut; for Piles Coppice in 1746, Bodleian Library, Craven 320.

291 *DB*, 241c.

292 M.MSS., Mi Da 94.

293 B.L., Add. MS. 48,181, PS5/1804, copy in W.C.R.O., Z 203(U).

294 *FF*, Vol. I, no. 427; original in P.R.O., CP 25/1/243/15.

295 *HR*, p. 52.

296 S.B.T., DR10/37-42, 48-49, 117; B.L., Cotton Vitell. A i, ff. 37-41.

297 *ibid.*

298 *ibid.*, ff. 40-41; S.B.T., DR10/38, 41, 42.

299 S.B.T., DR10/48, 49; B.R.L., Keen 40A.

300 W.C.R.O., MB Bri.

301 S.B.T., DR10/117.

302 S.B.T., DR37/Box 114.

303 e.g. S.B.T., DR10/49 and B.L., Cotton Vitell. A i, f. 37.

304 P.R.O., E 303/16/86.

305 B.L., Cotton Vitell. A i, f. 37; *DB*, 239c.

306 B.L., Cotton Vitell. A i, f. 37.

307 P.R.O., JUST 1/954, rot 58d; JUST 1/966, rot 10d.

308 *Book of Seals*, no. 499, p. 344.

309 P.R.O., E 303/16/55.

310 P.R.O., E 303/16/36.

311 S.B.T., DR10/117; P.R.O., E 303/16/36; see also S.B.T., DR37/Box 114; for the survey of 1652, Bodleian Library, Craven 6.

312 Coss, *Lordship, knighthood and locality*, *passim*.

313 *VCH*, Vol. VIII.

314 P.R.O., E 164/21, copy in W.C.R.O., MI 409.

315 *DB*, 239c, 239a, 244c, 238d, 243b.

316 *Rotuli Parliamentorum Anglie Hactenus Inediti MCCLXXIX-MCCCLXXIII*, (ed. H.G. Richardson and G. Sayles, Camden, Third Series, LI, 1935), pp. 240-66.

317 *ibid.*, pp. 259, 249-53.

318 *ibid.*, 259, 242.

319 *SLB*, p. 26.

320 *The Charters of the Anglo-Norman Earls of Chester c.1071-1237*, (ed. G. Barraclough, The Record Society of Lancashire and Cheshire, CXXVI, 1988), no. 366a, p. 363.

321 P.R.O., E 164/21, ff. 3r, 12r, copy in W.C.R.O., MI 409.

322 *ibid*, f. 3r; for the date, *VCH*, Vol. VIII, p. 76.

323 P.R.O., E 164/21, ff. 52v-53r, copy in W.C.R.O., MI 409.

324 *Rotuli Parliamentorum Anglie Hactenus Inediti*, pp. 242-3.

325 P.R.O., E 164/21, f. 76v, copy in W.C.R.O., MI 409.

326 Coss, *Early Records*, pp. 23-4; for the 1243 reference, *Calendar of Close Rolls, Henry III, 1243-7*, p. 46.

327 Bodleian Library, Queen's College, 2339, 2348; M.MSS., Mi D 4007.

328 P.R.O., E 164/21, ff. 52v-53r, copy in W.C.R.O., MI 409.

329 Bedworth tithe award, W.C.R.O., CR569/24; boundary of Exhall, P.R.O., E 164/21, f. 18r, copy in W.C.R.O., MI 409.

330 *ibid.*, f. 24r. Some of the bounds given for Foleshill, such as *ladylane*, *le moreyf* and *le Ruydyng*, can be matched to points on the parish boundary in the tithe award (see Fig. 25) suggesting similarity of the medieval and ancient ecclesiastical boundaries.

331 *ibid.*, f. 3v; for the tithe award of Holy Trinity parish, W.C.R.O., CR569/81.

332 C.R.O., BA/D/H/26/2.

333 Coss, *Early Records*, pp. 25-6, citing P.R.O., E 164/21, f. 173r, copy in W.C.R.O., MI 409.

334 Coss, *Early Records*, pp. 32-3.

335 *SLB*, p. 101.

336 E. Ekwall, *The Concise Oxford Dictionary of English Place-Names* (fourth edition, 1960), p. 27; Rackham, *History of the Countryside*, pp. 72, 84.

337 e.g. P.R.O., E 315/41/219, E 315/45/18; *HR*, pp. 141, 143.

338 C.R.O., BA/H/H/344/2.

339 P.R.O., E 164/21, ff. 54v, 198v, copy in W.C.R.O., MI 409.

340 Coss, *Lordship, knighthood and locality*, pp. 136-42.

341 P.R.O., E 164/21, f. 64v, copy in W.C.R.O., MI 409.

342 *ibid.*, f. 198v.

343 *ibid.*, unnumbered folio after f. 202.

344 Tithe award, W.C.R.O., CR569/207.

345 Coss, *Lordship, knighthood and locality*, p. 142.

346 P.R.O., E 326/10026.

347 C.R.O., BA/H/H/344/1.

348 Coss, *Lordship, knighthood and locality*, pp. 140-42; P.R.O., E 164/21, f. 198v, copy in W.C.R.O., MI 409; S.B.T., DR18/31/3, f. 121.

349 P.R.O., E 164/21, f. 4r, copy in W.C.R.O., MI 409.

350 S.B.T., DR91/2.

351 W.C.R.O., QS75/36.

352 W.C.R.O., CR569/3.

353 P.R.O., E 164/21, f. 187r, copy in W.C.R.O., MI 409.

354 The total of c.22,000 is derived from the tithe awards for the parishes of St. Michael and St. John - 3,665 (W.C.R.O., CR569/86); Holy Trinity - 1,825 (W.C.R.O., CR569/81); Sowe - 2,505 (W.C.R.O., CR569/207); Stoke - 921 (W.C.R.O., CR569/209); Foleshill - 2,594 (W.C.R.O., CR569/105); Allesley - 4,225 (W.C.R.O., CR569/3); from the enclosure awards for Coundon and Keresley - 1,046 and 1,058 (W.C.R.O., QS75/36); from a map of part of Stivichall - 732 (copy in W.C.R.O., Z279 (Sm.)) and a map of Willenhall - 750 (W.C.R.O., D34); and, in default of maps and surveys, from the year-book *County of Warwick* for 1865, giving 2,033 acres for Exhall and 787 for Wyken.

355 This statement is made in *VCH*, Vol. VIII, pp. 40-2.

356 Coss, *Lordship, knighthood and locality*, p. 31; *VCH*, Vol. VIII, *passim*.

357 W.C.R.O., DR564/I(a)/418 and 419, also C.R.O., 468/350 and 361 and P.R.O., DL 29/463/7551 for Asthill's grove; *HR*, p. 123 for Horwell's grove; S.B.T., DR18/31/3, p. 108, *LC*, no. 257 and *FF*, Vol. I, no. 791 for the grove in Shortley; C.R.O., 468/360 for *harnale Groue*.

358 C.R.O., 468/15 and 215 for *Byggyng Grove*; P.R.O., E 164/21, ff. 45v, 199v, and 58r, copy in W.C.R.O., MI 409, for groves in Attoxhale and Hawkesbury.

359 P.R.O., E 164/21, ff. 19r, 45v, 199v, 58v, copy in W.C.R.O., MI 409, for the grove held by Henry Wolf and the groves in *Erneysplace* and *Bagotplace*; C.R.O., 468/87 for *Harperesgrove, Corbynsgroue* and *Shukkeburghgroue* in Stoke.

360 C.R.O., 468/87. For other deeds in the series, 468/59, 139.

361 C.R.O., 1573/19/1-2, plan XII, and W.C.R.O., DR929/2, plan 13, place Shuckburgh Grove by Wyken, whereas C.R.O., 1573/19/3-4 attributes the name to the site further south, whose

location can be identified from the information about Drapers' Company lands in the tithe award.

362 *LC*, no. 305.

363 P.R.O., E164/21, f. 58r, copy in W.C.R.O., MI 409.

364 S.B.T., DR10/457; Coss, *Early Records*, p. 9; *idem, Lordship, knighthood and locality*, pp. 37-8.

365 S.B.T., DR10/1409, f. 59.

366 For the deed of 1729, C.R.O., 101/1/262; tithe award of 1846-9, W.C.R.O., CR569/86.

367 W.C.R.O., DR564/I(a)/437. The fields came to the Holy Trinity Guild, which preserved records of them.

368 W.C.R.O., CR1709/192; the five fields are Barn Close, Plowed Close, Middle Close, Four Acres and Footpath Close.

369 W.C.R.O., DR564/I(a)/403, 405, 428.

370 W.C.R.O., DR564/I(a)/440, 441.

371 W.C.R.O., DR564/I(a)/429.

372 *HR*, p. 123.

373 W.C.R.O., DR564/I(a)/424, 429, 430, 434; for Horwell waste, see under Stoneleigh and in particular the map of 1597, copy in W.C.R.O., Z139/2(U).

374 S.B.T., DR10/781.

375 C.R.O., 17/10/2.

376 S.B.T., DR10/459.

377 S.B.T., DR10/1786.

378 S.B.T., DR10/421, 439-40.

379 C.R.O., 468/350, 169, 361.

380 For the survey of 1787, S.B.T., DR10/1431, accompanying map in S.B.T., PR63, being a copy of B.L., Add. MS. 41,477; for the tithe award, W.C.R.O., CR569/86.

381 C.R.O., 101/1/262.

382 C.R.O., BA/B/P/439/7 and BA/B/P/137/13.

383 C.R.O., BA/B/P/441/1.

384 C.R.O., BA/B/P/440/5.

385 C.R.O., BA/B/P/432/1.

386 *VCH*, Vol. VIII, p. 331.

387 C.R.O., BA/A/A/3/1 for *Sent Anne Grove*; *ibid.*, BA/B/A/86/1 for *Langeley Grove*.

388 W.C.R.O., CR569/86.

389 For the grove of Shortley, *FF*, Vol. I, no. 791 and *LC*, no. 257; for the site of Charterhouse, *Calendar of Close Rolls, 1381-85*, pp. 65-6.

390 *LC*, no. 379.

391 *Calendar of Patent Rolls, 1247-58*, p. 100.

392 Coss, *Lordship, knighthood and locality*, p. 108.

393 *HR*, p. 148.

394 *LC*, no. 439 (early 13th century), C.R.O., BA/B/P/431/5-6 (deeds dated 1347 and 1357).

395 *VCH*, Vol. VIII, pp. 192-3; C.R.O., BA/B/P/432/1.

396 W.C.R.O., CR569/86.

397 S.B.T., DR10/479.

398 C.R.O., BA/H/H/375/2 and BA/B/P/431/4.

399 C.R.O., BA/G/D/1/1.

400 *LC*, nos. 527, 350, 415 and 305.

401 S.B.T., DR10/489.

402 *Calendar of Inquisitions Miscellaneous*, Volume I, p. 159; for the date, Coss, *Lordship, knighthood and locality*, p. 70.

403 *VCH*, Vol. VIII, p. 316.

404 Coss, *Lordship, knighthood and locality*, pp. 119-20.

405 *FF*, Vol. I, no. 174 for the wood of *Asshawe*; C.R.O., BA/B/A/47/10 for the wood of *holifast* in 1305; P.R.O., C 134/91/27 for the survey of 1325.

406 C.R.O., BA/B/A/47/5, 7 and 9.

407 C.R.O., BA/B/A/47/10.

408 P.R.O., SC 11/679, date in P.R.O., *Lists and Indexes*, XXV, p. 327.

409 P.R.O., DL 43/14/3.

410 P.R.O., C 134/91/27 for the survey of 1325; P.R.O., DL 43/14/3 for the survey of 1392.

411 See Ordnance Survey, first edition of one-inch map and six-inch map.

412 Several deeds refer to land adjoining *Asshawe* - C.R.O., BA/B/A/19/1-2, BA/B/A/54/1, 11, and 12, BA/B/A/107/4, BA/B/P/260/1, BA/B/P/357/1, BA/B/P/401/2, BA/B/P/451/8; the Coundon boundary reference comes from the Register of Coventry Cathedral Priory, P.R.O., E 164/21, f. 6r, copy in W.C.R.O., MI 409.

413 W.C.R.O., CR623/box 1.

414 S.B.T., DR98/699c.

415 W.C.R.O., CR623/box 14.

416 Bodleian Library, Queen's College, 2339, 2348.

417 P.R.O., E 164/21, f. 7r, copy in W.C.R.O., MI 409.

418 *ibid*, ff. 76v, 12r and, for the dubious authenticity of the deeds, Coss, *Early Records*, pp. 1-2.

419 Bodleian Library, Queen's College, 2376.

420 P.R.O., E 164/21, f. 44r, copy in W.C.R.O., MI 409.

421 Queen's College, Oxford, 4 F 12a.

422 P.R.O., E 164/21, f. 9r, copy in W.C.R.O., MI 409.

423 *ibid.*, ff. 8v, 10v.

424 W.C.R.O., CR569/84 for the tithe map of Keresley and QS75/36 for the enclosure map.

425 P.R.O., E 164/21, ff., 8v, 10r, 7r, copy in W.C.R.O., MI 409.

426 *DB*, 240c.

427 P.R.O., E 326/388.

428 For the field-names, tithe award, W.C.R.O., CR569/24; for Sole End, *Dugdale*, Vol. I, p. 122.

429 P.R.O., E 315/38/89.

430 W.C.R.O., CR136/C126.

431 P.R.O., E 326/3608; for survey W.C.R.O., CR432/box 29.

432 P.R.O., E 326/11652.

433 For deed, W.C.R.O., CR299/83/1, and map, W.C.R.O., CR764/104/4.

434 W.C.R.O., CR136/C107 for the deed of 1440; for other deeds, W.C.R.O., CR136/C126, C111a, P.R.O., E 326/388, 10773, 11257B, 11652; P.R.O. E 326/388 contains the specific reference to assarts in the Northwood.

435 P.R.O., JUST 1/954, rot 23r; P.R.O., E 326/388.

436 Bodleian Library, Ms. Top A Warwick C8, p. B6d.

437 P.R.O., E 326/11258; the wood called variously *Kaluecroft* and *calvercroft* is mentioned in other deeds - P.R.O., E 326/10790, 12950.

438 P.R.O., E 178/5689.

439 W.C.R.O., CR136/M9.

440 W.C.R.O., CR764/104/4.

441 P.R.O., E 326/10778.

442 P.R.O., E 164/21, f. 11v, copy in W.C.R.O., MI 409.

443 P.R.O., E 303/17/219; *VCH*, Vol. VI, p. 29.

444 *DB*, 244a.

445 In the absence of a tithe map this figure has been taken from the year-book *County of Warwick*, (1865), p. 39.

446 The six groves with medieval records are a grove of wood in *modymannyslond* in 1332 (W.C.R.O., CR136/C756a, C777); a grove called *holemore* in 1375 (*ibid.*, CR136/C776); a grove of wood next to *le jolassche* in 1373 (*ibid.*, CR136/C775); *Nythtynggalegrove* in 1392 (*ibid.*, CR136/C786); a grove called *Odenegreven* in 1296 (*ibid.*, CR136/C739, C744a); and a grove in *le Gryue* (Griff) in 1356 (P.R.O., E 326/3731). In addition, seven groves were mentioned in the sixteenth century, *woodcocks grove*, *temple park grove*, the *kyngesffeld grove*, *schypeleys grove*, *lez haunche*, *Emmetts grove*, and *Wrights grove* (W.C.R.O., CR440/12, CR136/C798, CR136/C313, CR136/C309, CR136/C341; and P.R.O., E 315/404). It is of course possible, if not probable, that due to changes in name the later records duplicated the earlier.

447 *Dugdale*, Vol. II, p. 1074 and confirmatory charter in P.R.O., E 315/39/17.

448 W.C.R.O., CR136/C716; for Seeswood W.C.R.O., CR136/C150 and C744a.

449 The surname appears in P.R.O., E 315/35/232, a deed relating to Bedworth; for *Herewardeshay* W.C.R.O., CR136/C145, C717, C760, C761.

450 W.C.R.O., CR136/C734.

451 P.R.O., E 315/400.

452 W.C.R.O., CR136/C126.

453 W.C.R.O., CR136/C126; for New Park P.R.O., E 303/17/241, maps in W.C.R.O., CR136/M94, M97A.

454 W.C.R.O., CR136/C410.

455 W.C.R.O., CR136/C420a.

456 W.C.R.O., CR764/107.

457 W.C.R.O., CR136/C1030, CR136/C1098, CR136/V13, ff. 20-21.

458 W.C.R.O., CR136/C300; B.L., Add. Ch. 48,068; W.C.R.O., CR136/C1139; maps, W.C.R.O., CR136/M18, M83A.

459 W.C.R.O., CR136/C300.

460 The six groves with medieval records are a grove of wood in *modymannyslond* in 1332 (W.C.R.O., CR136/C756a, C777); a grove called *holemore* in 1375 (*ibid.*, CR136/C776); a grove of wood next to *le jolassche* in 1373 (*ibid.*, CR136/C775); *Nythtynggalegrove* in 1392 (*ibid.*, CR136/C786); a grove called *Odenegreven* in 1296 (*ibid.*, CR136/C739, C744a); and a grove in *le Gryue* (Griff) in 1356 (P.R.O., E 326/3731). The seven groves mentioned in the sixteenth century were *woodcocks grove*, *temple park grove*, the *kyngesffeld grove*, *schypeleys grove*, *lez haunche*, *Emmetts grove*, and *Wrights grove* (W.C.R.O., CR440/12, CR136/C798, CR136/C313, CR136/C309, CR136/C341; and P.R.O., E 315/404).

461 W.C.R.O., CR136/C786.

462 *DB*, 239c, 241d.

463 W.C.R.O., CR569/184.

464 For example, B.L., Add. Rolls 49,759, 49,760, 49,762, 49,763, 49,765 (copies of most of the B.L. documents used for Nuneaton are in Nuneaton Library); for Horston Wood, B.L., Add. Rolls 49,715, 49,760, 49,403.

465 P.R.O., JUST 1/970, rot 5r.

466 For the enclosure award, W.C.R.O., QS75/83; the extent of Nuneaton and Stockingford Commons on enclosure in 1806 was about 660 acres.

467 B.L., Add. Roll 49,711; W.C.R.O., CR569/184; B.L., Add. Roll 49,720.

468 B.L., Add. Roll 49,760; W.C.R.O., Z364(Sm.).

469 *ibid.* and B.L., Add. Rolls 49,762, 49,765, 49,759, 49,763.

470 For the deed of 1644, catalogue of Merevale MSS. in W.C.R.O., no. 1902; tithe map, W.C.R.O., CR569/184.

471 B.L., Add. Roll 49,763.

472 B.L., Add. Rolls 49,760, 49,721, 49,715; B.L., Add. Ch. 48,491.

473 B.L., Add. Roll 49,760.

474 B.L., Add. Ch. 48,806.

475 B.L., Add. Roll 49,765.

476 B.L., Add. Ch. 48,918.

477 B.L., Add. Rolls 49,715, 49,765.

478 B.L., Add. Roll 49,760; W.C.R.O., Z364 (Sm.).

479 B.L., Add. Roll 49,721.

480 B.L., Add. Roll 49,765.

481 B.L., Add. Roll 49,715; P.R.O., E 303/17/383 and 388.

482 B.L., Add. Rolls 49,727, 49,719.

483 *The History and Antiquities of the County of Leicester*, Vol. I, Part II (J. Nichols, 1815, republished 1971), Appendix XVII, p. 82; P.R.O., E 326/1882.

484 W.C.R.O., Z364(Sm.); P.R.O., E 303/17/400; B.L., Add. Ch. 48,806.

485 B.L., Add. Chs. 49,071, 49,070, 49,069.

486 *Dugdale*, Vol. II, p. 1066.

487 P.R.O., E 326/8008.

488 B.L., Add. Ch. 49,466.

489 B.L., Add. Roll 49,457.

490 See tithe award, W.C.R.O., CR569/57.

491 *ibid.*

492 B.L., Add. Ch. 49,721, 49,760.

493 P.R.O., JUST 1/954, rot 10d.

494 P.R.O., C 135/181/16.

495 *DB*, 239c.

496 *ibid.*

497 *Curia Regis Rolls*, Vol. XIV, nos. 1,105 and 1,630.

498 *FF*, Vol. I, no. 447; original in P.R.O., CP 25/1/243/18.

499 W.C.R.O., CR258/340.

500 W.C.R.O., L2/86.

501 For the outwood, an undated, uncatalogued map in the Merevale MSS., kindly drawn to my attention by Mrs. M. May; for the fields called Stocking in 1716, W.C.R.O., P7.

502 *Select documents of the English lands of the Abbey of Bec* (ed. M. Chibnall, Camden, Third Series, LXXIII, 1951), p. 103.

503 P.R.O., E 303/18/431, 444.

504 B. Bartlett, *Manduessedum Romanorum: Being the History and Antiquities of the Parish of Manceter [including the hamlets of Hartshill, Oldbury, and Atherstone], and also of the adjacent parish of Ansley, in the County of Warwick* (1791), map on p. 29. Mr. Bartlett seems to have had access to documents, including some medieval deeds, whose location is not now known.

505 W.C.R.O., CR604.

506 *Dugdale*, Vol. II, p. 1082. For the Latin text, *Monasticon*, Vol. II, pp. 365-6.

507 W.C.R.O., CR604 for the map of Oldbury, *ibid.*, CR2755/1 for the map of Ansley.

508 Bartlett, *Manduessedum Romanorum*, p. 48 equates the wood of Hugh with Hartshill Hayes. For the Hardredeshull family and Ansley, see the deeds appended to Bartlett's work, also *VCH*, Vol. IV, p. 6 (which seems to draw on the same material as was available to Bartlett).

509 P.R.O., C 133/14/2.

510 Bartlett, *Manduessedum Romanorum*, p. 149.

511 *ibid.*, p. 137.

512 W.C.R.O., CR491.

513 B.L., Cott. Ch. iv 52.

514 P.R.O., E 303/18/431.

515 B.L., Add. Roll 49,760.

516 B.L., Add. Roll 49,715.

517 B.L., Harl. Roll Y 13.

518 P.R.O., JUST 1/952, rot 9r.

519 *ibid.*, rot 40r.

520 P.R.O., E 315/41/20 for the thirteenth-century grant; P.R.O., E 212/93 for the deed of 1413.

521 P.R.O., JUST 1/1245, rot 31r.

522 Bartlett, *Manduessedum Romanorum*, p. 137.

523 *ibid.*, pp. 138, 148.

524 *ibid.*, p. 141.

525 *County of Warwick* (1865) gives 2,694 acres for Ansley and 1,465 for Hartshill.

526 P.R.O., JUST 1/953, rot 4r.

527 Staffs. R.O., D641/1/2/269.

528 A. Watkins, 'Merevale Abbey in the late 1490s', *Warwickshire History*, IX, No. 3 (1994), pp. 87-104, is based largely on the manuscript in the P.R.O., E 315/283.

529 *DB*, 242b.

530 *The Roll of the Justices in Eyre in Gloucestershire, Warwickshire and Staffordshire, 1221, 1222* (ed. D.M. Stenton, Selden Society, LIX, 1940), p. 373; P.R.O., JUST 1/954, rot 51d.

531 *Collections for a History of Staffordshire*, Vol. VI, Part I (William Salt Archaeological Society, 1885), p. 61, citing Banco Roll no. 6, Trinity Term, first year of Edward I.

532 M.MSS., Mi D 4022, 4027, 4028.

533 William Salt Library, H.M. Chetwynd, Bundle 3.

534 W.C.R.O., CR328/18.

535 *ibid.*; Staffs. R.O., D1176/A/39/11.

536 M.MSS., Mi D 4021; tithe award, W.C.R.O., CR328/18.

537 B.R.L., 193,151.

538 W.C.R.O., CR762/35.

539 *DB*, 241a.

540 There is no entry in Davis, *Medieval Cartularies of Great Britain: a short catalogue*.

541 *Dugdale*, Vol. II, pp. 1102, 1117, 1121, 1118.

542 P.R.O., C 133/41/5; P.R.O., JUST 1/958, rot 31d; P.R.O., JUST 1/1320, rot 10d and see also William Salt Library, H.M. Chetwynd Bundle 3 for a copy of a final concord dated 1302.

543 P.R.O., E 318/11/499.

544 Staffs. R.O., D1176/A/39/11.

545 Worcs. R.O., calendar of MSS. at Madresfield Court, nos. 11, 12.

546 *Select Cases in the Court of King's Bench under Edward I*, Vol. II (ed. G.O. Sayles, Selden Society, LVII, 1938), pp. 97-112; part of a cartulary of Lilleshall Abbey, Staffs. R.O., D593/A/1/10/10.

547 W.C.R.O., CR328/38.

548 W.C.R.O., CR328/3/1.

549 Staffs. R.O., D593/A/1/10/10.

550 *DB*, 240a, 243a.

551 *FF*, Vol. I, no. 212.

552 Staffs. R.O., D593/A/1/22/3, 10.

553 *FF*, Vol. I, no. 212.

554 P.R.O., JUST 1/965, rot 1d.

555 Staffs. R.O., D593/A/1/23/4.

556 P.R.O., LR 2/185, copy in W.C.R.O., MI 295.

557 For the estate map, Staffs. R.O., D/W/1851/10/3; for the significance of Frith, see Chapter Three under Kenilworth and Chapter Four.

558 *Collections for a History of Staffordshire* (William Salt Archaeological Society, Part I, Vol. V, 1884), p. 88.

559 *A Map of Warwickshire Drawn from an Actual Survey taken in the Years 1787-1788-1789 by Willm. Yates & Sons* (1793), copy in W.C.R.O., MA 1793/1.

560 B.R.L., 480,682.

561 B.R.L., Norton MSS. 67.

562 See Beighton's map of Hemlingford Hundred, in *Dugdale*, Vol. II, also "An Accurate map of the County of Warwick ...by Thomas Jefferys", copy in W.C.R.O., MA 1787.

563 S.B.T., DR76/2/21.

564 A copy of the map is in W.C.R.O., Z 212/2.

565 *DB*, 239c.

566 *DB*, 241a.

567 W.C.R.O., CR328/27.

568 *Select Cases in the Court of King's Bench*, p. 105.

569 W.C.R.O., CR416/8.

570 P.R.O., JUST 1/954, rot 21r.

571 W.C.R.O., CR416/8.

572 B.L., Egerton Roll 8621.

573 M.MSS., Mi D 4091.

574 B.L., Egerton Roll 8618.

575 M.MSS., Mi D 4094.

576 M.MSS., Mi D 4020/1.

577 B.L., Cott. Ch. xxii 3. Coss, *Lordship, knighthood and locality*, p. 221, associates *essebroc* with Foul End in the south of Kingsbury parish and claims (p. 281) that the name has been lost. However, the enclosure award for Hurley (W.C.R.O., CR 416/8) records a stream called Nassers Brook on the north-western edge of Hurley Common. If the initial letter of Nassers Brook is dropped, the name resembles *essebroc*. Moreover, assarts by the park of Kingsbury, which field-names suggest lay west of Hurley Common, were held by Hugh de essebroc c.1200 (M.MSS., Mi D 4054).

578 M.MSS., Mi D 4070 and 4071.

579 M.MSS., Mi D 4054.

580 B.L., Egerton Roll 8621 for the wood, M.MSS., Mi M 130/47B for the pasture.

581 P.R.O., JUST 1/964, rot 7r and JUST 1/1279, rot 4d for the medieval record, W.C.R.O., CR328/27 for the tithe award.

582 B.L., Cott. Ch. xxv 25; B.L., Cott. Ch. xxii 2.

583 W.C.R.O., CR328/27.

584 *DB*, 242a, 244c-d.

585 *The Roll of the Justices in Eyre 1221-2*, p. 373; P.R.O., JUST 1/951A, rot 6r; P.R.O., JUST 1/952, rot 27r, for which last see a copy in M.MMS., Mi Da 84/4.

586 For Sutton chase, see the account of Sutton Coldfield below.

587 M.MSS., Mi M 237/1.

588 P.R.O., C 133/62/5.

589 M.MSS., Mi D 4310; *Close Rolls of the reign of Edward I*, Vol. III (1904), p. 269.

590 *Dugdale*, Vol. II, pp. 1133-4.

591 M.MSS., Mi D 4255.

592 M.MSS., Mi D 4277, 4291, 4328.

593 M.MSS., Mi D 4384.

594 M.MSS., Mi 2 S10, Mi 2 P5A; for Yates's map of 1787-9, W.C.R.O., MA 1793/1.

595 M.MSS., Mi D 4413.

596 M.MSS., Mi M 124.

597 M.MSS., Mi D 4328, 4384.

598 M.MSS., Mi D 4325.

599 M.MSS., Mi D 4525/2.

600 M.MSS., Mi D 4271, 4300.

601 M.MSS., Mi D 4306.

602 B.L., Add. Ch. 20,468.

603 P.R.O., C 134/49 and B.L., Add. MS. 28,024 (Beauchamp cartulary), ff. 100-105, copy in W.C.R.O., MI 177.

604 *Dugdale*, Vol. II, p. 912.

605 B.L., Add. MS. 28,024 (Beauchamp cartulary), ff. 100-105, copy in W.C.R.O., MI 177.

606 *Dugdale*, Vol. II., p. 913; *Itinerary of John Leland*, Vol. II, p. 98.

607 M. Hodder, 'Earthwork Enclosures in Sutton Park, West Midlands', *TBWAS*, 89 (1978-79), pp. 166-70. Dr. Hodder (personal communication) has since revised his conclusions about successive enlargement of the original park, preferring to regard the earthworks within the present Park as subdivisions of it, although he agrees from the archaeological evidence that the curving enclosures below the site of the manor around Wyndley could have preceded the pale around the present Park.

608 *Ministers' Accounts of the Warwickshire Estates of the Duke of Clarence 1479-80*, p. 34; *Itinerary of John Leland*, Vol II, pp. 97-8. I am indebted to Dr. Hodder for a discussion about the medieval pools.

609 For the information about peat deposits I am grateful to Dr. Hodder. On the habitat of marsh fritillary butterflies in general, ed. A.M. Emmet and J. Heath, *The Moths and Butterflies of Great Britain and Ireland*, Volume 7, part I (1990), p. 236; on marsh fritillary butterflies in Sutton Park, I am indebted to Mr. M. Slater.

610 *DB*, 238b-c.

611 The figure of 12,477 is given in the year-book *County of Warwick*, (1865), p. 35.

612 *Dugdale*, Vol. I, p. 379.

613 *Dugdale*, Vol. II, pp. 909-10.

614 P.R.O., C 134/49.

615 S.B.T., BRT1/3/180; *Ministers' Accounts of the Warwickshire Estates of the Duke of Clarence 1479-80*, p. 35.

616 M.MSS., Mi Da 87.

617 M.MSS., Mi M 134/3.

618 M.MSS., Mi Da 84/41.

619 *Dugdale*, Vol. II, p. 913.

620 Birmingham City Council Planning and Architecture Department, *Archaeology in Sutton Park* (leaflet, no date).

621 P.R.O., C 134/49 and C 134/51.

622 P.R.O., JUST 1/966, rot 3r.

623 *ibid*., rot 4r.

624 *Dugdale*, Vol. I, pp. 382-3.

625 B.R.L., 348,037.

626 B.R.L., 348,039.

627 For the enclosure award, W.C.R.O., QS75/111, copy in Sutton Coldfield Library. See also ed. R. Lea, *Scenes from Sutton's Past* (Sutton Coldfield, 1989), pp. 22, 25, in which, unfortunately, the wrong reference number - 348,038 instead of 348,039 - is attached to the deed and the date given in the catalogue, 1237, mistranscribed as 1207; Thomas did not become earl until 1228-9.

628 P.R.O., JUST 1/951A, rot 15r.

629 The deed was copied into the Beauchamp cartulary, B.L., Add. MS. 28,024, f. 101, copy in W.C.R.O., MI 177.

630 W.C.R.O., QS75/111, p. 86, copy in Sutton Coldfield Library.

631 M.MSS., Mi D 3949/1.

632 P.R.O., JUST 1/952, rot 32d.

633 *Ministers' Accounts of the Warwickshire Estates of the Duke of Clarence 1479-80*, pp. 30-44.

634 *ibid*., p. 32; M.MSS., Mi M 134/9.

635 *Ministers' Accounts of the Warwickshire Estates of the Duke of Clarence 1479-80*, p. 37.

636 P.R.O., C 133/86/1.

637 P.R.O., C 134/49.

638 W.C.R.O., QS75/111.

639 M.W. Beresford, 'The economic individualism of Sutton Coldfield', *TBAS*, 64 (1941-42), pp. 101-8, see sketch map on p. 103 and plate facing p. 108.

640 *DB*, 241a.

641 Staffs. R.O., D1287/6/19/54 and 53.

642 *DB*, 243a, 243b.

643 *County of Warwick* (1865), p. 35.

644 P.R.O., C 134/102/6.

645 W.C.R.O., MR2/Folder 13.

646 M.MSS., Mi D 4300.

647 P.R.O., JUST 1/952, rot 27d; JUST 1/1228, rot 29r; JUST 1/1283A, rot 9r; JUST 1/1283B, rot 4d.

648 W.C.R.O., MR1/Folder 1; B.R.L., 488,765.

649 W.C.R.O., CR328/58.

650 *DB*, 240d-241a.

651 Nichols, *County of Leicester*, Vol. I, p. 79.

652 Beresford, 'The economic individualism of Sutton Coldfield', p. 102; Nichols, *County of Leicester*, Vol. I, p. 79.

653 *ibid*.

654 *Book of Seals*, no. 51, p. 35.

655 Staffs. R.O., D1287/6/18/5.

656 *The Roll of the Justices in Eyre 1221-2*, p. 223.

657 Original in P.R.O., MPB 10(2), copies in Sutton Coldfield Library and W.C.R.O., Z 567/1(U).

658 B.R.L., Wingfield Digby MSS., A101.

659 *VCH*, Vol. IV, p. 62, citing *Calendar of Patent Rolls, 1281-92*, pp. 406-7.

660 Beauchamp cartulary - B.L., Add. MS. 28,024, ff. 103-4, copy in W.C.R.O., MI 177.

661 W.C.R.O., CR328/13/1 for the tithe award and Z142(L) for a copy of the map of the Leigh estate in Dunton in 1767.

662 *DB*, 243a.

663 *VCH*, Vol. VII, p. 63.

664 M.MSS., Mi M 129/1, 3.

665 P.R.O., C 133/32.

666 Staffs. R.O., D1287/6/20/21; for Berwood in Curdworth, see under Curdworth; for the relationship between the two lords called Henry, *VCH*, Vol. VII, p. 63.

667 P.R.O., C 139/63.

668 B.R.L., 347,860; *VCH*, Vol. VII, pp. 63-4.

669 P.R.O., JUST 1/952, rot 32 (two *rotuli* are numbered 31; the case cited here is on the second of the two, before that numbered 33).

670 *ibid.*, rot 14d.

671 *VCH*, Vol. VII, p. 64.

672 M.MSS., Mi M 129/1, 3.

673 P.R.O., JUST 1/952, rot 32; *The Manuscripts of the late Reginald Rawdon Hastings*, Vol. I (Historical Manuscripts Commission, 1928), p. 150.

674 B.R.L., 347,913 and 292,886.

675 W.C.R.O., QS75/6; copy also in B.R.L., MS. 1382/1, 3.

676 Beauchamp Cartulary, B.L., Add. MS. 28,024, f. 100, copy in W.C.R.O., MI 177.

677 B.R.L., 347,913 and 292,886.

678 B.R.L., 347,876.

679 Beauchamp Cartulary, B.L., Add. MS. 28,024, f. 100, copy in W.C.R.O., MI 177.

680 See a survey of 1655, B.R.L., 349,825; for tenants' woods, B.R.L., 347,854 and 347,913.

681 B.R.L., 347,854 and 347,913.

682 B.R.L., 349,825.

683 B.R.L., 347,879.

684 *DB*, 243a.

685 *ibid.*

686 *County of Warwick*, p. 35; this figure includes Erdington, as no separate figures are given for the constituent townships.

687 B.R.L., 371,055 for map showing Lozells Wood, 413,517 for rental.

688 B.R.L., 19,836.

689 The Castle Bromwich deeds are in B.R.L., 19,801-74; for Washwood, Staffs. R.O., D1287/6/15/36.

690 P.R.O., JUST 1/958, rot 13d.

691 *Calendar of Inquisitions Post Mortem*, Vol. II, no. 813, p. 493.

692 P.R.O., JUST 1/1283A, rot 6r; JUST 1/1245, rot 55d.

693 Staffs. R.O., D1287/6/19/11; P.R.O., JUST 1/1279, rot 14r; JUST 1/954, rot 28d.

694 P.R.O., JUST 1/958, m. 13d; *Calendar of Inquisitions Post Mortem*, Vol. II, no. 813, p. 493; Staffs. R.O., D1287/6/19/11; P.R.O., JUST 1/1279, rot 14r and JUST 1/954, rot 28d.

695 B.R.L., 347,863; P.R.O., JUST 1/955, rot 4r.

696 B.R.L., 347,863; P.R.O., JUST 1/955, rot 4r; maps in B.R.L., 305,520 and 1382/1, 3.

697 *VCH*, Vol. IV, p. 201; *DB*, 240d-241a; for field-names, tithe award, B.R.L., TM2/14.

698 B.R.L., 431,122; V.H. Skipp, *Greater Birmingham* (1980), p. 15 and tithe map in B.R.L., TM2/14.

699 B.R.L., 431,125.

700 P.R.O., JUST 1/1278, rot 1r.

701 B.R.L., MS. 1382/6.

702 B.R.L., TM2/14; Staffs. R.O., D641/1/2/269.

703 V.H.T. Skipp, *Discovering Bickenhill* (1963), map on p. 8.

704 *DB*, 241a, 240d.

705 W.C.R.O., CR328/6.

706 Skipp, *Discovering Bickenhill*, pp. 15-6, using W.C.R.O., CR593.

707 P.R.O., C 146/2025 for boundary with Elmdon; tithe map at W.C.R.O., CR328/6 for field-names.

708 *FF*, Vol. I, no. 575; original in P.R.O., CP 25/1/243/19.

709 W.C.R.O., CR593/47/1 and CR593/30.

710 *FF*, Vol. I, no. 869 has *Ethles*, but the original, P.R.O., CP 25/1/244/29 can be read either as *Ethles* or *Echles*.

711 W.C.R.O., CR328/6; B.R.L., 193,194.

712 P.R.O., JUST 1/1228, rot 39r; JUST 1/1231, rot 19r; JUST 1/1237, rot 25d.

713 W.C.R.O., CR1911/12; Staffs R.O., D641/1/2/269, 270, and 274.

714 *DB*, 238b.

715 The abstract in *FF*, Vol. I, no. 73 refers to the castle oak, but the original in P.R.O., CP 25/1/242/4 reads *quercus Castelli*, suggesting that the oak belonged to the local family of that name, for which see *VCH*, Vol. IV, p. 44.

716 B.R.L., Wingfield Digby MSS., A21, A24/1, A47, A72.

717 B.R.L., Wingfield Digby MSS., A30, A31, A38, A45, A51, A76, A91.

718 *ibid.*, A46, A92, A108, A519, A589; P.R.O., JUST 1/954, rot 53r; for the Lady Wood, P.R.O., SC 11/683 and M.MSS., Mi D 3980.

719 B.R.L., Wingfield Digby MSS., A388.

720 *FF*, Vol. I, no. 73, original in P.R.O., CP 25/1/242/4.

721 *VCH*, Vol. IV, p. 44.

722 For the medieval wood called Ladywood, P.R.O., SC 11/683; for the field of 1845, parish survey, copy in W.C.R.O., P.G. 3354 and accompaning map, *ibid.*, Z436(U).

723 M.MSS., Mi D 3980.

724 For the location of Beltesley in Alcott, P.R.O., E 326/10722; deed of 1557, B.R.L., 324,104.

725 *DB*, 243c-d.

726 W.C.R.O., Z551(Sm); P.R.O., E 40/9877; B.R.L., Keen 54, 118 for the wood of Shustoke and *Brograve*; for the wood of *Broggraue*, see the catalogue of the manuscripts at Merevale Hall, copy in W.C.R.O., MI 211, numbers 1326, 1371. Both these documents, seen at Merevale Hall, are later copies of the same, presumably thirteenth-century, deed of which the original has not been located.

727 Gover, Mawer and Stenton, *Place-Names of Warwickshire*, p. 350.

[728] Merevale Hall, nos. 1326, 1371; the park is also mentioned in B.R.L., 429,351 and Keen 118, and in P.R.O., C 135/5/5.

[729] Map of Warwickshire in 1793 by Yates, copy in W.C.R.O., MA 1793/1; tithe award, W.C.R.O., CR328/42.

[730] Staffs R.O., D593/A/1/24/1 and B.R.L., 429,351 for the waste.

[731] B.R.L., Keen 118; B.L., Cott. Ch. xii 33 for *ffysshepolfeld*.

[732] W.C.R.O., CR1184/box 1 (deed dated 20 March, 1661); tithe map, W.C.R.O., CR328/42.

[733] W.C.R.O., Z646/10(U) and tithe map, W.C.R.O., CR328/42.

[734] *DB*, 243d.

[735] See copy maps in W.C.R.O., Z323/2, 3(U), and tithe map, W.C.R.O., CR328/42.

[736] W.C.R.O., CR1169/36.

[737] *VCH*, Vol. IV, pp. 210-11.

[738] *ibid.*, p. 201.

[739] *ibid.* and *DB*, 241a.

[740] P.R.O., C 133/73/2.

[741] *VCH*, Vol. IV, p. 138; *Calendar of Patent Rolls, 1343-45*, p. 369.

[742] *Calendar of Close Rolls, 1346-9*, pp. 80, 414.

[743] For a copy of the map of 1767 see W.C.R.O., Z149(L).

[744] *Calendar of Close Rolls, 1346-9*, p. 139.

[745] W.C.R.O., CR328/31.

[746] P.R.O., E 210/621 and B.R.L., Keen 92.

[747] Bodleian Library, MS Trinity College 84, copy in W.C.R.O., MI 272.

[748] For example, Staffs. R.O., D641/1/2/269, 270, 271, 272.

[749] Gover, Mawer and Stenton, *Place-Names of Warwickshire*, p. 123.

[750] *DB*, 244b.

[751] W.C.R.O., CR136/150.

[752] W.C.R.O., CR569/8.

[753] *FF*, Vol. I, no. 123.

[754] P.R.O., JUST 1/958, rot 2r.

[755] Mr. P. Thompson, personal communication.

[756] *DB*, 238d, 242d, 244c.

[757] W.C.R.O., CR569/102.

[758] *VCH*, Vol. IV, pp. 69-72.

[759] W.C.R.O., CR1886/3370.

[760] W.C.R.O., CR569/102.

[761] P.R.O., C 134/13/1.

[762] P.R.O., C 134/91/27.

[763] P.R.O., DL 43/14/3.

[764] P.R.O., C 139/76.

[765] S.B.T., DR18/10/46/3/1.

[766] Northamptonshire R.O., Th.1495.

[767] *DB*, 244c.

[768] Bodleian Library, Queen's College, 2337.

[769] S.B.T., DR10/217-222, especially 222.

[770] B.R.L., 348,005 and 348,009.

[771] For the deed of 1429, C.R.O., BA/D/D/49/5; for the tithe award, W.C.R.O., CR569/75.

[772] P.R.O., E 164/21, f. 11v, copy in W.C.R.O., MI 409.

[773] W.C.R.O., CR569/75.

[774] P.R.O., E 164/21, f. 11v, copy in W.C.R.O., MI 409.

[775] *ibid.*

[776] S.B.T., DR10/223.

[777] P.R.O., E 164/21, f. xi, copy in W.C.R.O., MI 409.

[778] *ibid.*

[779] W.C.R.O., CR136/153.

[780] W.C.R.O., CR1371.

[781] W.C.R.O., CR569/75.

[782] P.R.O., E 164/21, f. 12r, copy in W.C.R.O., MI 409, for the medieval grove; for its location, see map of 1690-1 in W.C.R.O., L6/1222.

[783] S.B.T., DR10/215-216.

[784] *DB*, 239c.

[785] *County of Warwick*, p. 38.

[786] S.B.T., DR10/531 and 534; S.B.T., ER1/63/293; B.R.L., 608,879, 608,881, and 608,882; C.R.O., BA/D/K/10/1-2.

[787] S.B.T., DR10/534; B.R.L., 608,881.

[788] S.B.T., DR10/534.

[789] B.R.L., 608,881.

[790] S.B.T., DR10/531.

[791] S.B.T., DR10/534.

[792] B.R.L., 608,882.

[793] B.L., Add. Ch. 8398.

[794] B.R.L., 608,881.

[795] For maps see W.C.R.O., CR2381, also Z309/2(U) and survey, MI 367/4.

[796] D.M.K. Agutter, *Meriden: Its People and Houses* (1990), p. 5.

[797] S.B.T., DR10/1777.

[798] For the locations of these groves, W.C.R.O., CR2381; deed of 1531, W.C.R.O., CR299/207.

[799] S.B.T., ER1/63/294.

[800] W.C.R.O., CR669/bundle G.

[801] P.R.O., E 164/21, f. 48v, copy in W.C.R.O., MI 409.

[802] P.R.O., E 315/31/235.

[803] C.R.O., 54/27, 9/1, BA/A/A/2/2, 54/69, BA/D/K/10/26.

[804] W.C.R.O., list no. 2 of Finch-Knightley deeds at Packington, nos. 3/3/11-13.

[805] C.R.O., 9/1.

[806] W.C.R.O., CR2381.

[807] C.R.O., 54/69 (deed of 1630-1), BA/D/K/10/26 (deed of 1652).

[808] P.R.O., E 326/8944.

[809] B.R.L., 249,976

[810] S.B.T., ER1/63/297.

[811] William Salt Library, H.M. Chetwynd, bundle 8.

[812] W.C.R.O., CR669/bundle G.

[813] *DB*, 241a.

[814] B.L., Harley 3650, f. 6, copy in W.C.R.O., MI 392/1.

[815] *VCH*, Vol. IV, pp. 183-4.

[816] B.L., Add. MS. 47,677, f. xxiij, copy in W.C.R.O., MI 392/2.

[817] *ibid.*, f. xx.

[818] *ibid.*, f. xxvij.

[819] W.C.R.O., Z301/1(U).

[820] B.L., Add. MS. 47,677, f. xxiij, copy in W.C.R.O., MI 392/2.

[821] *ibid.*, ff. xxiij-xxv; P.R.O., JUST 1/953, rot 3d.

[822] P.R.O., JUST 1/953, rot 3d.

[823] B.L., Add. MS. 47,677, ff. xxiij-xxv, copy in W.C.R.O., MI 392/2.

[824] P.R.O., E 318/10/434.

[825] Staffs. R.O., D1287/6/18/28.

826 W.C.R.O., list of Finch-Knightley deeds at Packington Hall, Bundle J, nos. 2/71 and 2/88.

827 B.L., Add. MS. 47,677, f. xx, copy in W.C.R.O., MI 392/2.

828 *DB*, 243c.

829 W.C.R.O., CR328/22.

830 S.J. Wager, *Early Medieval Land Units in the Birmingham Area: An Historical Study* (University of Birmingham M. Phil. thesis, 1988), pp. 153-4 and *passim*.

831 B.R.L., Wingfield Digby MSS., and D.E. Greenway, *Charters of the Honour of Mowbray 1107-1191* (1972), pp. 212-8, which appears to have overlooked the collection in B.R.L.

832 B.R.L., 511,984.

833 W.C.R.O., Z151, being a copy of P.R.O., MPEE/84.

834 B.R.L., Wingfield Digby MSS., A1/2, A3, A4, A5.

835 B.L., Cott. Ch. xi 35.

836 *Charters of the Honour of Mowbray 1107-1191* (D.E. Greenway, British Academy Records of Social and Economic History, new series, i, 1972), p. 9.

837 P.R.O., LR 15/2/68 for a lease of 1612; B.R.L. 511,984 for the survey of 1649.

838 B.L., Add. Ch., 21,416; S.B.T., DR37/2170.

839 P.R.O., SC 2/207/31.

840 V. Skipp, *The Origins of Solihull* (second edition, 1984), *passim*.

841 *DB*, 244b, 240d-241a.

842 W.C.R.O., CR328/44.

843 P.R.O., C 146/996.

844 S.B.T., DR37/147.

845 S.B.T., DR37/147, 1420.

846 W.C.R.O., CR645/19.

847 Gover, Mawer and Stenton, *Place-Names of Warwickshire*, p. 63; my attention was drawn to this by Mr. R. Hill.

848 P.R.O., E 326/3642.

849 P.R.O., C 146/2960.

850 W.C.R.O., CR328/44.

851 S.B.T., DR37/box 116.

852 *ibid*.

853 For the survey, S.B.T., DR37/74/30 and for deeds, S.B.T., DR37/2574 and W.C.R.O., CR299/288/2, CR299/195/1A.

854 S.B.T., DR37/box 76.

855 *BD* under Longdon.

856 P.R.O., C 146/10192 for the medieval grove, B.R.L., 324,101 for the coppice in 1585.

857 For Shelley Coppice, see above, for Parish Coppice, W.C.R.O., CR1291/100/1-6.

858 Westminster Abbey muniments 607.

859 B.R.L., 427,740.

860 S.B.T., DR37/box 116.

861 *ibid*.

862 V. Skipp, 'The Evolution of Settlement and Open Field Topography in North Arden down to 1300', in ed. T. Rowley, *The Origins of Open-Field Agriculture* (1981), pp. 162-83, see p. 168.

863 W.C.R.O., QS75/102.

864 *Dugdale*, Vol. II, pp. 949-50.

865 Map of 1816, W.C.R.O., CR487; tithe map, W.C.R.O., CR328/44; for the suggested boundary of the land granted, an undated sketch map, W.C.R.O., CR1886/2372.

866 P.R.O., E 318/4/121.

867 *DB*, 242d, 241a.

868 *VCH*, Vol. IV, p. 23.

869 *Records of the Templars in England in the Twelfth Century* (B.A. Lees, 1935), p. cix.

870 *VCH*, Vol. IV, p. 23.

871 *The Knights Hospitallers in England* (ed. L.B. Larking, Camden Society, LXV, 1857).

872 W.C.R.O., CR112/Ba.188/2 and P.R.O., E 315/361; for 1199, *VCH*, Vol. IV, p. 23.

873 W.C.R.O., CR1775, CR328/4.

874 W.C.R.O., CR1498.

875 Gover, Mawer and Stenton, *Place-Names of Warwickshire*, pp. 55-6. The grove was in or by Barford - see Chapter Two.

876 Westminster Abbey 620.

877 W.C.R.O., QS75/70, enclosure award.

878 W.C.R.O., CR487.

879 P.R.O., LR 2/185, copy in W.C.R.O., MI 295.

880 W.C.R.O., CR487.

881 W.C.R.O., MA1793/1.

882 P.R.O., SC 6/1039/22 and Westminster Abbey 27,692.

883 P.R.O., SC 6/1039/21, 22 and SC 6/1040/1-2 clearly refer to *lyndes*; in P.R.O., SC 6/1040/3-6, also SC 6/Hen VII/875 (1500-1) the word has been misunderstood by the scribe and written as *byndes*.

884 Rackham, *Ancient Woodland*, p. 243.

885 P.R.O., LR 2/228.

886 P.R.O., JUST 1/1245, rot 7r.

887 Gover, Mawer and Stenton, *Place-Names of Warwickshire*, p. 63.

888 Deed of 1556, W.C.R.O., CR1886/2252; map of 1820, W.C.R.O., CR487.

889 Westminster Abbey 27,699.

890 Westminster Abbey 3,246.

891 Westminster Abbey 27,692, 27,694, 27,695.

892 Westminster Abbey 27,711.

893 P.R.O., SC 6/1039/21.

894 Westminster Abbey 621.

895 Westminster Abbey 63,959.

896 P.R.O., LR 2/185, copy in W.C.R.O., MI 295.

897 P.R.O., LR 2/228.

898 *Calendar of Inquisitions Miscellaneous*, Volume I, p. 589.

899 *VCH*, Vol. IV, pp. 94, 222; for Birdsland, W.C.R.O., CR 487.

900 Lees, *Records of the Templars in England*.

901 Larking, *The Knights Hospitallers in England*.

902 Lees, *Records of the Templars in England*, pp. xvii, cix.

903 Larking, *The Knights Hospitallers in England*, p. 179.

904 P.R.O., E 210/5586.

905 *Calendar of Close Rolls, 1318-1323*, p. 588.

906 P.R.O., JUST 1/1278, rot 1d.

907 W.C.R.O., CR112/Ba.188/2, p. 41.

908 P.R.O., E 315/361, copy in W.C.R.O., Z146/3.

909 W.C.R.O., CR621/5.

910 W.C.R.O., QS75/52.

911 W.C.R.O., CR621/5-6.

912 *DB*, 224a-b.

913 B.L., Harley 3650, f. 27, copy in W.C.R.O., MI 392/1.

914 P.R.O., C 134/49, 51.

915 D. Tracey, 'Within the Pale - the story of Berkswell Park', *Berkswell Miscellany*, Vol. IV (1988), pp. 7-9.

916 W.C.R.O., MR21/2.

917 Manuscripts at Merevale Hall (catalogue in W.C.R.O., MI 211), numbers 895 (dated 1710), 1494 (dated 1722), 1901 and 1945 (dated 1708) state that the wood contained about sixty-six acres of customary woodland measure. Wood acres are much larger than statute acres, so the area of about 164 statute acres calculated from the tithe award for the presumed site of the wood (see below) is consistent with the identification.

918 Marked on the enclosure map, W.C.R.O., CR172/1-2.

919 B.L., Add. MS. 28,024, ff. 80-1, 82, copy in W.C.R.O., MI 177.

920 P.R.O., E 36/167, folio at the end of the volume.

921 P.R.O., DL 29/642/10422; W.C.R.O., CR569/29.

922 W.C.R.O., CR172/1-2 and QS75/12/4-8.

923 P.R.O., JUST 1/1283A, rot 7d.

924 D Morfitt, 'Ecology of the Moor; A Threatened "Ancient" Landscape - Hawkhurst Moor and Rough Close Wood', *Berkswell Miscellany*, Vol. III (1987) (no page numbers).

925 Merevale Hall, number 1962A&B.

926 Morfitt, 'Ecology of the Moor' was written at short notice in response to a mining application.

927 P.R.O., E 36/167.

928 P.R.O., C 134/49; Gover, Mawer and Stenton, *Place-Names of Warwickshire*, p. 58.

929 D. Morfitt, personal communication.

930 W.C.R.O., DR72A/1, 2, 5-6, 7-9, 13-29.

931 W.C.R.O., CR569/29.

932 A manorial wood called Rough Close Wood was the subject of a deed of 1706 (W.C.R.O., CR299/136/1A-B) and came to the Greswolde Lewis family in 1782 (W.C.R.O., CR299/80), hence the name Lewis with the word Wood on the enclosure map of 1808 (W.C.R.O., CR172/1-2).

933 D. Morfitt, 'Ecology of the Moor'.

934 P.R.O., C 134/49, 51.

935 P.R.O., E 36/167.

936 P.R.O., SC 6/1038/2; P.R.O., E 36/167.

937 S.B.T., DR10/394.

938 P.R.O., DL 29/642/10422.

939 *Dugdale*, Vol. II, p. 784.

940 *DB*, 239a.

941 S.B.T., DR10/258.

942 *VCH*, Vol. V, p. 231.

943 Packwood enclosure award, W.C.R.O., QS75/85.

944 P.R.O., E 164/21, ff. 204r-206r, copy in W.C.R.O., MI 409.

945 W.C.R.O., CR328/33.

946 Gover, Mawer and Stenton, *Place-Names of Warwickshire*, p. 291.

947 W.C.R.O., Z230(L), original at Packwood House.

948 Ford, *Pattern of Settlement*, pp. 42-3.

949 *DB*, 238b.

950 *Dugdale*, Vol. II, p. 774; Ford, *Pattern of Settlement*, pp. 42-3.

951 Roberts, *Settlement, Land Use and Population*, p. 146.

952 *ibid.*, pp. 176-8.

953 *ibid.*, p. 318.

954 W.C.R.O., CR133/1.

955 S.B.T., DR37/box 107/8 and DR37/box 108/8, 34, 36, 40, 45.

956 B.L., Add. MS. 28,024, f. 98, copy in W.C.R.O., MI 177.

957 P.R.O., C 134/49, 51.

958 S.B.T., DR37/box 107/1, 3, 4, 8.

959 S.B.T., DR37/1277, 1322.

960 S.B.T., DR37/box 107/6.

961 S.B.T., DR37/box 108/31.

962 S.B.T., DR37/box 108/41.

963 S.B.T., DR37/1277; P.R.O., E 318/21/1124.

964 P.R.O., E 318/21/1124.

965 Roberts, *Settlement, Land Use and Population*, p. 148.

966 *ibid.*, pp. 287-319; leases of groves, S.B.T., DR37/1057, 1071, 1084, 1086, 1090, 1091.

967 S.B.T., DR37/593.

968 Roberts, *Settlement, Land Use and Population*, p. 322.

969 Roberts, *Settlement, Land Use and Population*, pp. 407, 410 and Fig. 39A.

970 S.B.T., DR37/24.

971 S.B.T., DR37/74/19-20, see also B.K. Roberts, 'North-West Warwickshire: Tanworth-in-Arden', in R.A. Skelton and P.D.A. Harvey, *Local Maps and Plans from Medieval England* (1987), pp. 317-28.

972 P.R.O., E 40/6610, copy in S.B.T., DR37/box 82.

973 Tasker, *The Nature of Warwickshire*, p. 30; the information about Tylers Grove was provided for the book by Mr. D. Morfitt (A. Tasker, personal communication).

974 S.B.T., DR37/74/30, which has the spelling *growe* rather than grove. For the tithe award, W.C.R.O., CR328/53.

975 Sawyer, *Anglo-Saxon Charters*, no. 64.

976 Gelling, *Place-Names in the Landscape*, pp. 198, 302.

977 S.B.T., DR37/2285a/8, 9, 22, 50, 52; B.R.L., 277,430.

978 J.J. Belton, *The Story of Nuthurst cum Hockley Heath, Warwickshire* (1948), p. 33.

979 W.C.R.O., CR328/24.

980 Gelling, *Place-Names in the Landscape*, pp. 197, 222.

981 S.B.T., DR37/2285a/1.

982 S.B.T., DR37/2285a/73, 69.

983 S.B.T., DR37/2285a/23.

984 *VCH*, Vol. IV, p. 99, citing *Calendar of Patent Rolls, 1330-4*, p. 174.

985 S.B.T., DR37/2285a/36.

986 *DB*, 242a.

987 Ford, *Pattern of Settlement*, p. 44.

988 *HR*, pp. 165-7, 169, 280.

989 W.C.R.O., CR328/30.

990 W.C.R.O., QS75/70.

991 Gover, Mawer and Stenton, *Place-Names of Warwickshire*, p. 232.

992 W.C.R.O., QS75/92 (enclosure award), CR328/30 (tithe award); Ordnance Survey, Index to the Tithe Survey.

993 *RBW*, p. 471.

994 *DB*, 238c; Dyer, *Lords and Peasants*, p. 11.

995 *DB*, 238c, 242a.

996 H.P.R. Finberg, *The Early Charters of the West Midlands* (second edition, 1972), p. 186.

997 *The Great Roll of the Pipe for the Ninth Year of the Reign of King Richard The First. Michaelmas 1197. (Pipe Roll 43)* (ed. D.M. Stenton, Pipe Roll Society, new series, VIII, 1931), p. 178.

998 *RBW*, pp. 254-5.

999 P.R.O., E 40/4660, 4264.

1000 P.R.O., E 40/4655; P.R.O., SC 11/819.

1001 P.R.O., C 133/88/6 for the reference in 1299; see also P.R.O., E 40/4360, 4366 and S.B.T., DR37/2247.

1002 *Reading Abbey Cartularies*, Vol I, p. 430.

1003 B.L., Harl. Ch. 86 E 27.

1004 B.L., Add. Ch. 14,006.

1005 *Reading Abbey Cartularies*, Vol. I, pp. 458-9.

1006 P.R.O., E 40/4246.

1007 P.R.O., E 40/4384.

1008 P.R.O., E 40/4416.

1009 B.R.L., 437,896; W.C.R.O., CR1008/43.

1010 P.R.O., E 40/12374.

1011 S.B.T., DR37/2247.

1012 W.C.R.O., CR328/30.

1013 *RBW*, pp. 254-5.

1014 *VCH*, Vol. I., p. 320; Gover, Mawer and Stenton, *Place-Names of Warwickshire*, p. 14.

1015 The records are in S.B.T. at DR3 and DR422, except for the map of 1699, which is still at Baddesley Clinton Hall; there is a copy in W.C.R.O. at Z234.

1016 S.B.T., DR3/13.

1017 S.B.T., DR3/14, 16-19.

1018 S.B.T., DR3/785.

1019 S.B.T., DR3/807, 336.

1020 S.B.T., DR422/34-35.

1021 W.C.R.O., Z234.

1022 S.B.T., DR3/48.

1023 S.B.T., DR3/11, 50, 203, 204.

1024 S.B.T., DR3/48, 50.

1025 S.B.T., DR3/783.

1026 S.B.T., DR3/802, 803, 805.

1027 S.B.T., DR3/781, 785.

1028 S.B.T., DR3/800.

1029 S.B.T., DR3/805.

1030 S.B.T., DR3/795.

1031 S.B.T., DR3/5, 21.

1032 S.B.T., DR3/289, 290; C.C. Dyer, 'A Small Landowner in the Fifteenth Century', *Midland History*, Vol. I, no. 3 (Spring, 1972), pp. 1-14, see pp. 4, 12.

1033 S.B.T., DR3/380.

1034 Compare the map of 1699 with the tithe map, W.C.R.O., CR328/2.

1035 S.B.T., DR3/801 and 184.

1036 S.B.T., DR3/111.

1037 S.B.T., DR3/66, 67.

1038 S.B.T., DR3/289, 290.

1039 S.B.T., DR3/203, 204.

1040 S.B.T., DR3/354, 357. On the early two and a half inch Ordnance Survey map the name Sides Coppice was transferred to a wood west of Baddesley Clinton Hall.

1041 S.B.T., DR3/391.

1042 S.B.T., DR3/794.

1043 S.B.T., DR3/395-97.

1044 S.B.T., DR3/804.

1045 S.B.T., DR3/807.

1046 S.B.T., DR3/183.

1047 S.B.T., DR3/51.

1048 S.B.T., DR3/40.

1049 S.B.T., DR3/800, 339, 807.

1050 S.B.T., DR3/241, 245.

1051 P.R.O., DL 29/463/7551.

1052 S.B.T., DR3/302-4.

1053 S.B.T., DR3/795.

1054 S.B.T., DR3/71.

1055 S.B.T., DR3/80.

1056 S.B.T., DR3/807.

1057 S.B.T., DR3/803.

1058 W.C.R.O., CR328/2.

1059 S.B.T., DR3/803.

1060 S.B.T., DR3/334.

1061 On the foundation date, see R. Dace, 'The Foundation and Endowment of Wroxall Priory', *Warwickshire History*, Vol. VII, No. 3 (Summer, 1991), pp. 75-9, especially pp. 75-6.

1062 *Monasticon*, Vol. IV, p. 92 and *Records of Wroxall Abbey and Manor, Warwickshire* (J.W. Ryland, 1903), p. 19.

1063 P.R.O., LR 2/228.

1064 Ryland, *Records of Wroxall Abbey*, pp. 214-6.

1065 *ibid.*, p. 89 and map (no page number).

1066 *ibid.*, p. 19; the originals are in the P.R.O., SC 8/68/3357 and SC 8/152/7586 and use the French word for wood, *boys*.

1067 *VCH*, Vol. III, p. 115.

1068 S.B.T., DR3/48, 50.

1069 W.C.R.O., Z234, being a copy of the original at Baddesley Clinton Hall.

1070 *Monasticon*, Vol. IV, p. 92.

1071 Ryland, *Records of Wroxall Abbey*, p. 21; original in P.R.O., SC 11/697.

1072 Ryland, *Records of Wroxall Abbey*, p. 31.

1073 W.C.R.O., CR113/Wr3.

1074 *DB*, 242a.

1075 *Reading Abbey Cartularies*, pp. 455-6.

1076 *ibid.*, p. 448.

1077 *Reading Abbey Cartularies*, pp., 451-2.

1078 *ibid.*, pp., 451-2, 456-7, 462, 430.

1079 *ibid.*, p. 462.

1080 *ibid.*, p. 430.

1081 P.R.O., LR 2/228.

1082 *Records of Rowington*, Vol. I (J.W. Ryland, 1896), MS 39.

1083 J. Woodall, *From Hroca to Anne* (1974), map entitled 'Medieval Period' in the folder at the back; on p. 19 it is stated that Aspley Wood was by Inwood End in the west of the parish. For the wood probably to be associated with Inwood, see below.

1084 P.R.O., E 315/457.

1085 W.C.R.O., CR284/1.

1086 W.C.R.O., CR1008/32.

1087 W.C.R.O., CR2310/1, f. xxviii.

1088 W.C.R.O., CR569/197.

1089 S.B.T., DR3/795.

1090 S.B.T., DR3/805.

1091 W.C.R.O., QS75/92.
1092 Woodall, *From Hroca to Anne*, p. 19.
1093 W.C.R.O., CR1008/36, 43, 45.
1094 W.C.R.O., CR1008/107.
1095 *Reading Abbey Cartularies*, p. 430.
1096 *ibid.*, pp. 459-60.
1097 *DB*, 242a.
1098 Many of the records are amongst the Bromley Davenport MSS. (hereafter *BD*), where they are kept in boxes in alphabetical order by place but have no catalogue numbers; for the tithe map W.C.R.O., CR569/126.
1099 Ryland, *Records of Rowington*, Vol. I, p. 3.
1100 Rowington Manor and Bushwood enclosure award, W.C.R.O., QS75/92.
1101 *BD*, box 160.
1102 *ibid.*
1103 *VCH*, Vol. III, p. 106.
1104 *BD*, box 161.
1105 W.C.R.O., QS75/57 and CR569/126.
1106 *BD*, box 160.
1107 *ibid.*
1108 *BD*, box 138.
1109 *ibid.*
1110 *BD*, box 160.
1111 *ibid.*
1112 *ibid.*
1113 *ibid.*
1114 *Curia Regis Rolls*, Vol. IV, p. 228.
1115 *BD*, box 137.
1116 W.C.R.O., CR1886/481.
1117 W.C.R.O., CR569/125 (tithe award) for the size of the parish.
1118 W.C.R.O., P43.
1119 W.C.R.O., CR569/125.
1120 B.R.L., Keen 72.
1121 B.R.L., 304,288.
1122 *BD*, box 137.
1123 *ibid.*
1124 P.R.O., SC 12/16/47.
1125 P.R.O., C 134/49.
1126 *BD*, box 138.
1127 *BD*, box 137; only odd years are covered by the surviving accounts.
1128 *ibid.*
1129 B.L., Add. MS. 28,024, f. 69, copy in W.C.R.O., MI 177.
1130 Tithe award, W.C.R.O., CR 569/125.
1131 *DB*, 238d.
1132 B.R.L., Keen 26 (see KK60/782/83) under Haseley.
1133 *ibid.* (KK78/782/63, KK40/782/85, KK86/782/59, KK71/782/71).
1134 *The Beauchamp Cartulary Charters 1100-1268*, p. 182.
1135 *VCH*, Vol. III, p. 115.
1136 See map in Ryland, *Records of Wroxall Abbey* and tithe map of 1841, W.C.R.O., CR569/126.
1137 B.L., Cott Ch. xxiii, 15 and 16, also *FF*, Vol. I, no. 169, original in P.R.O., CP 25/1/242/8.
1138 *VCH*, Vol. VIII, p. 467.
1139 Cartulary of St. Mary's Church, Warwick, P.R.O. E 164/122, ff. clxxiv-clxxv, ccxix, copy in W.C.R.O., Z251(Sm.).
1140 *BD*, box 137.
1141 B.R.L., Keen 26 (KK63/782/82, KK69/782/73); S.B.T., DR10/33.
1142 *BD*.
1143 For the meaning of *landa*, Latham, *Revised Medieval Latin Word-List*, p. 269; *FF*, Vol. I., no. 169.
1144 B.L., Cott. Ch. xxiii 15.
1145 B.L., Cott. Ch. xxiii 16; see also *FF*, Vol. I, no. 169, original in P.R.O., CP 25/1/242/8.
1146 *Dugdale*, Vol. II, p. 643; *VCH*, Vol. III, p. 120.
1147 *Dugdale*, Vol. II, p. 650.
1148 *DB*, 244b and note.
1149 P.R.O., E 315/47/129.
1150 S.B.T., DR37/2183.
1151 W.C.R.O., CR569/126.
1152 *BD*, also S.B.T., DR37/2183, 2190.
1153 P.R.O., E 40/3952.
1154 S.B.T., DR37/2190.
1155 See the map of 1728 in W.C.R.O., P43, also the accompanying survey at CR611/214 and the first edition of the Ordnance Survey one-inch map.
1156 *BD*.
1157 *ibid.*, box 138.
1158 W.C.R.O., P43.
1159 P.R.O., E 40/8284.
1160 *BD*.
1161 *DB*, 243a.
1162 P.R.O., E 164/22, f. ix, copy in W.C.R.O., Z251(Sm).
1163 *Dugdale*, Vol. II, p. 661.
1164 *VCH*, Vol. III, p. 66.
1165 P.R.O., E 40/6377.
1166 P.R.O., C 134/47/18.
1167 *VCH*, Vol. III, p. 66.
1168 P.R.O., E 164/22, f. ccxxx, copy in W.C.R.O., Z251(Sm). See also the account of Wedgnock above.
1169 W.C.R.O., CR895/8/2.
1170 W.C.R.O., CR895/8/19.
1171 *VCH*, Vol. III, p. 65.
1172 P.R.O., SC 12/14/87.
1173 W.C.R.O., CR895/8/4, 5, 10, 11, 12, 13 and 14.
1174 W.C.R.O., CR895/80/1.
1175 *The Roll of the Justices in Eyre 1221-2*, pp. 284-5.
1176 Bassett, 'In search of the origins of Anglo-Saxon kingdoms', p. 18.
1177 For the Wootton Wawen tithe map, W.C.R.O., CR 569/278.
1178 *DB*, 242c, 242d.
1179 M.MSS., Mi M 124.
1180 W.C.R.O., DR195/28.
1181 Tithe map and award, W.C.R.O., CR569/278.
1182 W.C.R.O., CR712/2; P.R.O., E 315/38/41.
1183 Cartulary of Wootton Wawen Priory, copy in W.C.R.O., MI 332, f. 2.
1184 Staffs. R.O., D641/1/2/272, 273, 276, 277; B.R.L., 168,236.
1185 W.C.R.O., CR712/2.

1186 Gover, Mawer and Stenton, *Place-Names of Warwickshire*, p. 243.

1187 S.R. Bassett, personal communication.

1188 *idem*, 'In search of the origins of Anglo-Saxon kingdoms', p. 18, and *The Wootton Wawen Project: interim report no. 3* (University of Birmingham, 1985), pp. 13-14.

1189 *ibid.*, p. 9.

1190 W.C.R.O., DR195/28.

1191 Staffs. R.O., D641/1/2/269, 270 and D641/1/2/3.

1192 P.R.O., E 318/3/81.

1193 *Dugdale*, Vol. II, p. 832.

1194 W.C.R.O., CR2981 (Maxstoke Castle MSS., not yet catalogued) for 1487, P.R.O., SC6/Hen VII/868 for 1506-7.

1195 Staffs. R.O., D641/1/2/3.

1196 For the tithe map for Aspley, W.C.R.O., CR569/278/3; deed of 1285 in King's College, Cambridge, WOW/52 (the list of these deeds in W.C.R.O. gives the old number S8&9/25 and mistakenly attributes the wood to Ullenhall).

1197 W.C.R.O., MI 176, for a copy of a King's College survey numbered S53.

1198 W.C.R.O., CR569/278/3; King's College, Cambridge, WOW/56, 128.

1199 P.R.O., C 135/224/4.

1200 For the wood of the Staffords and the assarts, William Salt Archaeological Society, *Collections for a History of Staffordshire*, Vol. VI (1885), p.2 and Vol. II (1881) pp. 274-6; for the deed of 1194, *Descriptive Catalogue of the Charters and Muniments...at Berkeley Castle* (I.H. Jeayes, Bristol, 1892), p. 19. The original of the latter is kept at Berkeley Castle but has been seen by the author by kind permission of the County Archivist for Gloucestershire, Mr. D. Smith.

1201 B.L., Cotton Vespasian E xxiv, f. 4.

1202 However, *Stanieta* may have become the sixteenth-century *Stannyerde* on the boundary between Mockley manor and Ullenhall, and *molebroc* may be the river running eastwards from Oldberrow north of the present Mockley Wood, S.R. Bassett, personal communication, citing D. Graham.

1203 For the age and course of the Hobditch earthworks, S.R. Bassett, *Wootton Wawen Project: interim report no. 4* (University of Birmingham, 1986) pp. 21-3; *idem, Wootton Wawen Project: interim report no. 5* (University of Birmingham, 1987) pp. 21-5.

1204 *Curia Regis Rolls Richard I and John, 11-14 John*, p. 368.

1205 For some Whitley deeds, King's College, Cambridge, WOW/90, 95; for *le Schawe*, P.R.O., E 315/41/99; for the meaning of the word shaw see Chapter Four.

1206 The deed cited at length is in the *BD* MSS. Other deeds dealing with land in Edstone and also referring to Birchurst are in S.B.T., DR37/3012-14. For other deeds relating to Edstone, P.R.O., E 326/5809, E 315/48/125, E 315/49/41; W.C.R.O., CR712; *BD*.

1207 King's College, Cambridge, WOW 223(ii).

1208 S.B.T., DR37/2199.

1209 *DB*, 240d. On the identification of the two Domesday manors called *Prestetone* with the later medieval manors and townships of Preston Bagot and Beaudesert, see S.R. Bassett, *The Wootton Wawen Project: interim report no. 7* (University of Birmingham, 1989), p. 3.

1210 W.C.R.O., CR569/278/2.

1211 For the site of the little park, P.R.O., E 315/41/99; for the wood in 1326, *VCH*, Vol. III, p. 208.

1212 P.R.O., E 40/9087.

1213 W.C.R.O., CR569/23.

1214 *DB*, 240a.

1215 S.R. Bassett, *The Wootton Wawen Project: interim report no. 8* (University of Birmingham, 1990), p. 12.

1216 B.L., Cott. Ch. xxvii 134 and King's College, Cambridge, WOW/94; for the place-name element, Gover, Mawer and Stenton, *Place-Names of Warwickshire*, p. 12; for Hagwell Coppice, W.C.R.O., DR195/28.

1217 *Reading Abbey Cartularies*, p. 445.

1218 *ibid.*, p. 444.

1219 S.B.T., DR473/291, f. 45.

1220 P.R.O., E 326/2953.

1221 *VCH*, Vol. III, p. 143.

1222 Bassett, *The Wootton Wawen Project: interim report no. 7*, p. 12.

1223 Gelling, *Place-Names in the Landscape*, pp. 196-7.

1224 *DB* 240a, 242d.

1225 Cartulary of St. Mary's Church, Warwick, P.R.O., E 164/22, f. xiii, copy in W.C.R.O., Z251(Sm.) for the deed dated to c.1123; W.C.R.O., CR133/1 (in the name of Waleran, earl of Warwick 1184-1204); *Reading Abbey Cartularies*, pp. 426, 429, 435-6.

1226 Gloucestershire Record Office, catalogue of Berkeley Castle MSS, GC1888.

1227 *Reading Abbey Cartularies*, p. 426.

1228 S.B.T., DR473/291, f. 45.

1229 W.C.R.O., CR569/65.

1230 W.C.R.O., CR2310/1, f. xlvii.

1231 P.R.O., C 134/90/16.

1232 S.B.T., DR473/28; for ridge and furrow in Hanging Wood, personal observation, confirmed by D. Morfitt, 'Oliver Rackham views Warwickshire Woodland', *Warwickshire Wildlife*, 74 (Warwickshire Nature Conservation Trust, September, 1990), p. 9.

1233 King's College, Cambridge, WOW/110; P.R.O., E 315/38/41, E 326/1107 and E 326/11416.

1234 King's College, Cambridge, WOW/110.

1235 For the field-names, W.C.R.O., DR195/28.

1236 For another example of *haeme* in Warwickshire, see M. Gelling, 'The place-name volumes of Worcestershire and Warwickshire: a new look', in ed. T.R. Slater and P.J. Jarvis, *Field and Forest: an historical geography of Warwickshire and Worcestershire* (1982), pp. 59-78, see p. 70.

1237 Magdalen College, Oxford, Westcote MSS. 23 and Gover, Mawer and Stenton, *Place-Names of Warwickshire*, p. 282.

1238 S.B.T., DR18/3/23.

1239 I am indebted to Dr. S.R. Bassett for sharing his deduction with me.

1240 *BD*.

1241 *ibid.*

1242 *ibid.*

1243 *Reading Abbey Cartularies*, p. 429.

1244 S.B.T., DR473/291, f. 45.

1245 W.C.R.O., CR895/18.

See enclosure map, W.C.R.O., QS75/28 and tithe map, W.C.R.O., CR569/65.

[1246] See enclosure map, W.C.R.O., QS75/28 and tithe map, W.C.R.O., CR569/65.

[1247] S.B.T., DR18/30/18/1.

[1248] *BD*; P.R.O., E 315/49/43. If the initial letter of the grove's name is dropped, the name of Knowles Wood might preserve the medieval *Snelles*.

[1249] *BD*; P.R.O., E 326/4883 and E 315/39/13.

[1250] *BD*.

[1251] *VCH*, Vol. III, p. 43 and *Dugdale*, Vol. II, p. 799.

[1252] W.C.R.O., CR569/65 and CR449/1/3.

[1253] Ordnance Survey two and a half inch maps.

[1254] P.R.O., E 318/21/1121; *BD*.

[1255] P.R.O., E 318/21/1121.

[1256] W.C.R.O., CR449/1/3.

[1257] *DB*, 243b.

[1258] S.B.T., ER103/2.

[1259] See Chapter Five under the wolds of Warwickshire.

[1260] *DB*, 242d, 243b.

[1261] *Formulare*, no. DCLX, p. 369.

[1262] P.R.O., E 326/8453.

[1263] P.R.O., E 315/41/265, E 210/7462, E 326/772.

[1264] P.R.O., E 315/43/155.

[1265] P.R.O., E 315/45/106, E 326/772, E 326/4566.

[1266] S.B.T., DR98/786.

[1267] S.B.T., DR38/152.

[1268] S.B.T., DR10/2429 and DR38/1429.

[1269] S.B.T., DR38/1429.

[1270] P.R.O., DL 29/645/10464.

[1271] *Calendar of Letters and Papers of Henry VIII*, Vol. XX, Part 2, p. 123, no. 266 (32).

[1272] S.B.T., DR38/44-5, 56, 65.

[1273] W.C.R.O., CR611/607.

[1274] *DB*, 240a.

[1275] *DB*, 240a.

[1276] Gover, Mawer and Stenton, *Place-Names of Warwickshire*, p. 224.

[1277] S.B.T., DR38/1477, and ER1/140 for the location of Caldwell and the Ordnance Survey 25 inch map (second edition) for Caldwell Spring Wood.

[1278] B.K. Roberts, 'Field Systems of the West Midlands', in ed. A.R.H. Baker and R.A. Butlin, *Studies of Field Systems in the British Isles* (1973), pp. 181-231, see p. 206.

[1279] S.B.T., DR38/1434-1436.

[1280] *ibid*.

[1281] C. Page and R. Page, *Snitterfield: the 1766 enclosures* (typescript, 1977, copies in W.C.R.O., CR 1784, and S.B.T., 87.2), Appendix 16.

[1282] S.B.T., ER2/396.

[1283] S.B.T., DR38/1429.

[1284] S.B.T., DR38/1429 and W.C.R.O., CR1784.

[1285] S.B.T., DR38/1477.

[1286] *VCH*, Vol. III, pp. 31, 42.

[1287] *DB*, 244a, 239a.

[1288] *VCH*, Vol. III, p. 34.

[1289] Map, W.C.R.O., CR882.

[1290] P.R.O., C 132/17/15, C 133/2/7, C 135/41/19, C 139/76.

[1291] W.C.R.O., CR623/box 1.

[1292] Map, W.C.R.O., CR882.

[1293] *DB*, 239a.

[1294] *Landboc sive registrum monasterii beatae mariae virginis et sancti cenhelmi de Winchelcumba* (ed. D. Royce, Vol. i, 1892), p. 184.

[1295] Royce, *Landboc*, Vol. ii, pp. 530-31, 553.

[1296] P.R.O., JUST 1/955, rot 6r.

[1297] Gloucestershire Record Office, D678/99.

[1298] W.C.R.O., CR1886/292.

[1299] W.C.R.O., CR1998/M15.

[1300] Royce, *Landboc*, Vol. ii, pp. 562-3 (a deed of February, 1435).

[1301] *DB*, 242d.

[1302] *Curia Regis Rolls*, Vol. XIII, no. 273.

[1303] W.C.R.O., CR1094 for map of 1820-21, CR1998/M15 for map of Spernall of c.1695.

[1304] D. Hooke and D. Marshall, *The Arrow Valley Project 1. Morton Bagot, a parish survey, Part 1. The Landscape, a topographical survey* (University of Birmingham, Department of Geography Occasional Publication Number 24, 1987), pp. 20-21. Compare also the maps in W.C.R.O., CR1094 with twentieth-century maps to see the increase in the size of the wood.

[1305] *DB*, 243c; W.C.R.O., CR569/208.

[1306] For the deed, W.C.R.O., CR1998/box42/AA2. For the identification of the lords of the two manors, *VCH*, Vol. III, pp. 135, 172.

[1307] W.C.R.O., CR1998/box 42/AA5/1-3.

[1308] W.C.R.O., CR1998/box 42/CC2; for Philip de Ascellis as sheriff, *Dugdale*, Vol. II, p. 1149.

[1309] W.C.R.O., CR1998/M15, M10 and M20.

[1310] W.C.R.O., CR1094.

[1311] *VCH*, Vol. III, p. 173; P.R.O., E 318/10/446 for the survey at the Dissolution.

[1312] W.C.R.O., CR1998/M15.

[1313] *County of Warwick*, p. 35.

[1314] *DB*, 243b, 243c (to include *Mapelberge*).

[1315] *VCH*, Vol. III, pp. 175-83.

[1316] W.C.R.O., QS75/110 for the enclosure award of 1824, W.C.R.O., CR569/235 for the tithe award.

[1317] S.B.T., DR36/2, DR33/16.

[1318] P.R.O., E 32/255, rot 3.

[1319] *Calendar of Charter Rolls, 1327-41*, Vol. IV, pp. 60-61.

[1320] D. Hooke and R. Taylor, 'The Augustinian priory of Studley, Warwickshire', *TBWAS*, 98 (1993-94), pp. 73-90, see p. 74.

[1321] S.B.T., ER1/61/19.

[1322] *Dugdale*, p. 742; P.R.O., E 41/375.

[1323] *BD*.

[1324] B.R.L., 167,405.

[1325] B.R.L., 167,486.

[1326] B.R.L., 167,446, 167,405.

[1327] *VCH*, Vol. III, p. 86.

[1328] *DB*, 239b.

[1329] *VCH*, Vol. III, p. 87; for the afforestation of Sambourne see also P.R.O., E 32/255, rot 3.

[1330] W.C.R.O., CR1998/M11.

[1331] S.B.T., DR5/1047.

[1332] S.B.T., DR5/2368.

1333 S.B.T., DR5/2357-2363.

1334 W.C.R.O., CR1998/M11.

1335 S.B.T., DR/2368.

1336 For example, S.B.T., DR5/2358. There is a sixteenth-century parallel in south-east Essex in the use of wide hedges as areas of woodland; see O Rackham, *The Ancient Woodland of England: The Woods of South-East Essex*, (1986), pp. 21-2.

1337 S.B.T., DR5/2387.

1338 *DB*, 241d.

1339 For the manorial history, *VCH*, Vol. III, pp. 79-82.

1340 *VCH*, Vol. III, pp. 79-81.

1341 W.C.R.O., CR1886/15 and 62.

1342 P.R.O., C 53/34.

1343 *Calendar of Charter Rolls, 1226-57*, p. 256.

1344 *Dugdale*, Vol. II, p. 766.

1345 Coughton Grove is described as part of the manor in deeds of 1678, 1706, and 1724, W.C.R.O., CR1886/box417/92; it was also recorded in manorial accounts of 1614-15, W.C.R.O., CR1886/TN1. The map is in W.C.R.O., CR1886/M9.

1346 See plan in D. Hooke, 'Village Development in the West Midlands', in ed. *idem, Medieval Villages: A Review of Current Work* (1985), pp. 125-54, on p. 150.

1347 W.C.R.O., CR1886/box 108/1688 (dated 1598), CR1886/box 416/37/2 (dated 1614) and CR1886/box 416/3 (also dated 1614).

1348 *VCH*, Vol. III, p. 17.

1349 W.C.R.O., CR1998/J2/32 for the Bruly wood; W.C.R.O., CR1998/B2, CR1998/J2/34, for other medieval references to *trenthia*.

1350 W.C.R.O., CR1998/bundle K.

1351 S.B.T., DR5/2192 and 2191.

1352 W.C.R.O., CR1886/1582.

1353 *Dugdale*, Vol. II, p. 756.

1354 W.C.R.O., CR1998/M7, M29.

1355 W.C.R.O., CR1998/box 61/folder4/16.

1356 P.R.O., E 32/229; John de Billesle is said to have married one of the daughters of the lord of one of the manors - *VCH*, Vol. III, p. 79.

1357 *ibid.*, p. 80; P.R.O., E 32/255, rot 3.

1358 W.C.R.O., CR1998/F1, G3 and G7.

1359 W.C.R.O., CR1998/B6.

1360 W.C.R.O., CR1998/A1/3, CR1998/A4/3, CR1998/B2, CR1998/B3.

1361 W.C.R.O., CR1998/G7; Gelling, *Place-Names in the Landscape*, p. 191.

1362 Smith, *English Place-Name Elements*, Vol. I, p. 190.

1363 W.C.R.O., CR1998/bundle K.

1364 P.R.O., C 53/34, m.5.

1365 *Close Rolls Henry III, 1261-1264*, p. 58.

1366 P.R.O., JUST 1/1508, rots 4d-5r.

1367 W.C.R.O., CR1886/M9.

1368 W.C.R.O., CR1886/1582.

1369 *VCH*, Vol. III, p. 15.

1370 *ibid.*, p. 80.

1371 W.C.R.O., CR1998/box35/bundle K.

1372 *VCH*, Vol. III, p. 16.

1373 W.C.R.O., CR1886/166a.

1374 W.C.R.O., CR1886/box 106/1649.

1375 Latham, *Revised Medieval Latin Word-List*, p. 504, questions whether this word meant 'mound'. In the context of woodland it might therefore have referred to a woodbank or to a wooded bank.

1376 W.C.R.O., CR1886/482.

1377 See, for example, a coppice called *wolronsvalet* in Inkberrow in 1539-40, P.R.O., SC 6/Hen VIII/ 5694.

1378 W.C.R.O., CR1886/183.

1379 P.R.O., E 318/19/984 for the survey, W.C.R.O., CR1886/M9 and M12 for maps.

1380 W.C.R.O., CR1886/M12.

1381 *Calendar of Patent Rolls, 1247-58*, pp. 585, 594.

1382 W.C.R.O., CR1886/28, 81, 61.

1383 W.C.R.O., CR1886/box 417/96.

1384 *DB*, 238d.

1385 *Calendar of Close Rolls Henry III, 1227-31*, p. 187; P.R.O., JUST 1/954, rot 48d; *Calendar of Close Rolls, 1323-27*, p. 55; *Calendar of Patent Rolls, 1330-34*, p. 406.

1386 P.R.O., E 32/231.

1387 W.C.R.O., CR114A/190.

1388 W.C.R.O., CR114/RagIII/6/ii and iii for a map showing the eighteenth-century woods.

1389 S.B.T., DR5/2246b.

1390 P.R.O., C 133/49/3.

1391 *VCH*, Vol. III, p. 30.

1392 W.C.R.O., CR1998/M9 and M12.

1393 S.B.T., DR5/2255.

1394 B.L., Harley 3650, f. 77, copy in W.C.R.O., MI 392/1, see marginal annotation.

1395 G.E. Saville, *Oversley: Some of its History: Part I*, Alcester and District Local History Society Occasional Paper No. 28 (1982), p. 9.

1396 *ibid.*, p. 8.

1397 *DB*, 239b.

1398 P.R.O., JUST 1/954, rot 9r (1261-62), JUST 1/1278, rot 2r (1288).

1399 P.R.O., JUST 1/968, rot 1r.

1400 P.R.O., JUST 1/1278, rot 1r; JUST 1/1279, rot 12r.

1401 P.R.O., E 318/15/683.

1402 *DB*, 244b; *VCH*, Vol. III, p. 158.

1403 P.R.O., E 32/255, rot 3.

1404 *DB*, 244b; *VCH*, Vol. III, p. 158.

1405 *ibid.*, p. 155.

1406 *DB*, 175d.

1407 *VCH*, Vol. III, p. 158, citing *Calendar of Close Rolls, 1323-27*, p. 557.

1408 B.L., Add. MS. 47,677, ff. clxix-clxxi, clxxxvii-clxxxviii, copy in W.C.R.O., MI 392/2.

1409 B.R.L., 167,733.

1410 Bassett, 'The administrative landscape of the diocese of Worcester', p. 163.

1411 For the use of the verb 'approve' see Chapter One; B.L., Add. MS. 47,677, f. clxv, copy in W.C.R.O., MI 392/2..

1412 *ibid.*, ff. clxiiii, clxxii.

1413 For Pickersale Coppice and Barne Grove in 1576, B.R.L., 167,733 and for Pickers Wood, map of 1749, W.C.R.O., CR1296.

1414 *DB*, 238b.

1415 *DB*, 238d.

[1416] *County of Warwick*, p. 35.

Chapter Four

THE WOODLAND OF NORTH AND WEST WARWICKSHIRE

1086-1500: AN ANALYSIS

Introduction

The reader who has followed patiently the perambulation through north and west Warwickshire in the previous chapter may recall with relief the promise that this chapter will be analytical. The journey was long but it should have been illuminating. It should have impressed the reader with the quantity and variety of woods in north and west Warwickshire and the recurrence of certain themes. These themes, such as the varying quantities of *silva* recorded in Domesday Book, the disappearance of large areas of woodland, the prevalence of wood pasture, common rights, wastes and assarts, and the uneven distribution of hays and groves, have significant implications for commonly held views about the woodland of north and west Warwickshire.

This chapter will consider questions arising from these themes. It will try to decide what the *silva* of 1086 was like, how it was managed, whether it was wood pasture as suggested in Chapter Two, what impact it made on the local topography and economy and how it related to the woods which were recorded in subsequent centuries. Were later medieval woods formed from remnants of the *silva* or did they have separate identities within the *silva* when Domesday Book was compiled? Did the apparent distinction between wood pasture and coppiced woodland in south and east Warwickshire in 1086 also exist in north and west Warwickshire? Were there changes in the management of woodland during the later medieval period? Was there a shift from wood pasture to coppices? In particular, what were the histories of the groves of north and west Warwickshire found in records of the thirteenth, fourteenth and fifteenth centuries but almost, though not entirely, absent from twelfth-century records?

Despite the deficiencies in evidence discussed in preceding chapters, the large amounts of *silva* recorded in Domesday Book and the sheer number of woods which were recorded in the four succeeding centuries are impressive.[1] After 1086 the extent of woodland can rarely be measured in anything approaching absolute terms and even then not before the thirteenth century. However, from the more detailed records then available, not only about woods themselves but also about land which had been woodland, a rough picture of the distribution of woodland can be obtained for the better documented parishes and townships. There is certainly enough information to improve upon the general statements which have been made about the woodland of north and west Warwickshire and to develop the argument about the distinction between different types of woodland.

The reader is invited to stand back and, pardoning the pun, try to see the wood for the trees.

The *silva* of Domesday Book and later medieval woodland

Warwickshire north and west of the Avon has long been renowned for the amount of *silva* recorded in Domesday Book. The Latin noun *silva* has been quoted deliberately from Domesday Book because of uncertainty about the kind of woodland which it represented; an English word might give a misleading impression. The nature of the Domesday *silva* may be obscure but the existence of large amounts of it is indisputable. The very concentration of *silva* in the region offers an opportunity to define it and relate it to later medieval woodland.

The problems involved in trying to match the *silva* with later medieval woodland were outlined in Chapter Two. Domesday Book does not give the location of the *silva*. It does not say whether the *silva* attached to a manor was a single block of woodland or a composite total of several distinct areas which may or may not have been contiguous. Most manors had some *silva* in 1086, but manors which had very large amounts were often the centres of extensive areas with other, dependent settlements, which were not mentioned in Domesday Book. As explained in the introduction to Chapter Three, it is not even possible to calculate the exact areas of *silva* involved, because the linear dimensions given in the entries for Warwickshire may have been taken at the longest and widest parts of the *silva* without any allowance for irregularities of shape. Changes in some manorial boundaries after 1086, such as appear to have occurred in Kenilworth, further complicate attempts to match the *silva* of Domesday Book to the woodland of later medieval parishes or townships.

There is one parish in which the Domesday *silva* and the later medieval woodland each formed such a large proportion, perhaps four fifths, of the area that the two must have overlapped considerably. For Stoneleigh, in short, it is possible to conclude that some of the *silva* and later medieval woodland not only probably coincided but must have done so. The later medieval woods of Stoneleigh shared with many of the woods of north and west Warwickshire a tradition of wood pasture. The inference is that Stoneleigh's *silva* was wood pasture. This conclusion is compatible with the theory that the distinction between *silva* and groves lay in their management.

Domesday Book itself includes information which can be interpreted as evidence that *silva* was wood pasture. The phrase *cum oneratur*, combined with a value, qualifies the *silva* in twelve entries for Warwickshire. It has been translated in one commentary as "when it bears mast" and in another commentary as "when exploited".[2] A third translation of the verb related specifically to Domesday Book is "to stock".[3] Following this meaning the phrase would be translated as "when stocked" (with livestock). The phrase is associated with livestock in only one of the entries in the whole of Domesday Book, that for Adderbury and Bloxham in Oxfordshire, and in that entry the livestock in question were pigs, so that the phrase could be related to pannage as well as to pasture.[4] None of the sources from which the three translations have been taken recognises the possibility of a different meaning. Yet each meaning is distinct and each has different implications for the use of the *silva*. Mast can be found in any wood, coppice or pasture, which has mature oak or beech trees; pannage is not the same as pasture.[5] Exploitation of a wood could be through the sale of underwood, timber and bark from a coppice or by leasing grazing in wood pasture. To stock a wood with animals is to use it for pasture. If the third translation, which appears to be the least considered, were correct it would be conclusive evidence that the *silva* of Sutton Coldfield, Fillongley, *Rincele*, Claverdon, Preston Bagot, Smercote and *Souleg*, Bedworth, Packington, Ulverley (in Solihull), Arley and Astley[6] was wood pasture.

In two entries in the Warwickshire folios of Domesday Book, for Stoneleigh and Coughton, the amount of *silva* was followed immediately by a statement about pasture for a specified number of pigs.[7] It has been assumed that the pasture was provided by the *silva* rather than being distinct from it.[8] In some parts of the country *silva* was measured in terms of swine totals or swine renders, but these formulæ were not used in Warwickshire. The textual juxtaposition of *silva* and pasture in the entries for Stoneleigh and Coughton is therefore circumstantial, rather than conclusive, evidence that the *silva* of these two manors provided pasture for pigs. It is supported by later evidence. In the thirteenth century the monks of Alcester Priory were allowed a piggery in the wood (*bosco*) of Coughton. By the same deed they were granted a wagon-load of firewood every week from the wood (*nemus*) of Coughton.[9] A parallel distinction between *nemus* and the diminutive of *silva* is implied by some twelfth-century deeds relating to Hampton-in-Arden.[10] The Hampton-in-Arden deeds are remarkable not only for this distinction but also for the existence in the twelfth century of separate areas of woodland within one township, and for the relatively late use of the noun *silva*. (*Nemus* too was used less often after the twelfth century; *boscus* became the common word for wood.)

The apparent coincidence of Domesday *silva* with wood pasture answers one of the questions posed above. It also has implications for the impact of the *silva* on the local topography. Even in places where the *silva* was so extensive that it was the dominant feature of the countryside it need not have presented a densely wooded aspect. As explained in Chapter One, the density of trees in wood pasture was lower than in coppice woods. The more intensive the grazing, the more open the woodland was likely to be. The history of wood pasture in Warwickshire in the later medieval period, in particular the reasons for its disappearance, is therefore relevant to the nature of the *silva* of 1086.

Later medieval wood pasture

There was a very strong tradition of wood pasture in north and west Warwickshire. There are contemporary records of it in over thirty places. The references are almost invariably to pasture exercised as a common right and are relatively frequent because of moves by many lords to restrict that right to a smaller area of woodland or even to replace it by pasture elsewhere, for example over arable land after harvest. The frequency of the restrictions and the sense of grievance which they often engendered are reflected nationally in the Statute of Merton of 1236 and locally in several legal disputes, in a few of which the defendant quoted the statute,[11] as well as in deeds which reflect local agreements to eliminate common rights in parts of Stoneleigh, Allesley, Coventry, Coundon and Packington.[12]

The limitations which some lords sought to place on common rights in woodland and waste often accompanied the intended conversion of woodland to arable cultivation. There are no records of extending pasture rights over woods. In these circumstances it is plausible to argue that any wood in which rights of common pasture were exercised represented the survival of a traditional custom rather than its introduction or extension. On this basis it could be suggested that the tradition extended back for centuries. Indeed, the antiquity of the tradition is generally assumed.[13]

Woods called outwood (*boscus forinsecus*) or, less frequently, common wood are, where evidence of their management is available, invariably associated with wood pasture. This association is consistent with an interpretation of outwood as meaning a wood outside the lord's exclusive control. There are records of over two dozen outwoods in north and west Warwickshire.[14] There are some well documented examples - in Chilvers Coton, Balsall, Grendon and Oldbury[15] - of outwoods which became modern commons. These examples, together with other modern commons which appear to be on the site of later medieval woodland, for example in Shrewley and Kingsbury, suggest that modern commons hold the clue to the sites of later medieval woods whose location is otherwise unknown or uncertain. The association should not be used as a precise or infallible guide, because part of Shrewley Common had been heathland and, before that, arable land. On enclosure in 1851 Sutton Coldfield's commons covered over three thousand acres,[16] a higher figure than the maximum estimate for the area of the *silva* recorded in 1086. However, given the prevalence of common pasture in woodland in north and west Warwickshire in the later medieval period, an association between medieval common pasture and modern commons is plausible. In certain cases it is demonstrable. In the absence of any contemporary evidence for the site of a medieval wood, it is certainly worth arguing by analogy with other, demonstrable examples. In this way it has been possible to suggest sites for the woods of Morton Bagot and Claverdon. In the case of the latter the suggestion was subsequently confirmed by documentary evidence.

A topographical association between greens and woods is apparent from the history of woodland in Rowington, Pinley, Baddesley Clinton, Haseley, Hatton, Offord, Freasley, Baddesley Ensor, Erdington, Exhall, Foleshill, Coundon, Keresley and Berkswell.[17] Greens could be found in other parishes with large amounts of woodland, such as Tanworth-in-Arden and Solihull. This feature of north and west Warwickshire has been compared with the pattern of settlement around the greens and commons of the Suffolk claylands, although in many of the Suffolk examples greens were associated with moorland rather than with woodland in later medieval records.[18] However, Domesday Book implies large amounts of woodland in parts of the Suffolk claylands. It may be that the Domesday *silva* of Warwickshire survived longer than that of Suffolk to appear in the historical record. A better comparison chronologically may be the Chilterns, where small areas of common woodland are thought to have been reduced to open greens during the later medieval period.[19] Large greens in eastern England generally have been associated with former woodland.[20]

Sometimes pasture can be shown to have existed in contiguous woods which belonged to neighbouring parishes and to have been shared by the tenants in the respective manors, as in Rowington and Shrewley, Stoneleigh, Kenilworth and Ashow, and Binley, Brandon and Brinklow.

As wood pasture is a less intensive way of using woodland than coppicing, its association with large amounts of woodland is not surprising. It may also have been a significant factor in the disappearance of much of that woodland.

The disappearance of woodland

It is a commonplace amongst historians and historical geographers that large areas of woodland in north and west Warwickshire became arable land or virtually treeless pasture during the twelfth and thirteenth centuries.[21] Just as the large amounts of *silva* recorded in Domesday Book are indisputable, so it is obvious from early modern surveys, if not from medieval records, that much of this *silva* had disappeared by the end of the medieval period, if not long before. For most places there is simply not enough evidence to show exactly why, when and how that happened. A general picture has to be inferred from what evidence there is, and the lack of precision inevitably carries a danger of misinterpreting that evidence.

The reasons which are generally advanced for the disappearance of much of the Domesday *silva* are compatible with the chronology of that phenomenon in Warwickshire. The loss has been attributed to the incentives of rising prices for land and produce associated with an increase in population which led to an extension of arable cultivation at the expense of other types of land use.[22] Prices of grain were not recorded often enough for price trends to be discernible before the second half of the twelfth century, but there is enough evidence to show that they rose thereafter and particularly sharply at the beginning of the thirteenth century.[23] The national population may have risen quickly during the twelfth century, although figures for Warwickshire are available only for three manors. Overall population in the north and west of the county is thought to have risen three and a half times between 1086 and 1350.[24] Even with a smaller increase there would have been a demand for more arable land. It was arguably this demand which led to clearance or assarting of woodland.

It has been claimed that the number of recorded cases of assarts in England and the acreages involved are so small as to amount to no more than a tiny fraction of the lost *silva* of Domesday Book.[25] However, the surviving records for Warwickshire do point to a great deal of assarting in woods. The nature of these records differs between the twelfth and thirteenth centuries. The disputes which reached the king's courts in the thirteenth century and for which records have been preserved may have been the tip of the proverbial iceberg. How much assarting had already taken place in the twelfth century? How many cases were referred to local courts whose records have not survived? How many grievances went unheard? How much woodland clearance took place without antagonising tenants? If a lord could remove common rights from part of his woodland or waste without provoking a legal challenge, either by limiting the removal to a specified area or by granting land in compensation, it was in his interest to do so. Examples occur in Stoneleigh, Coventry, Allesley, Coundon and Packington.[26]

For the twelfth century, as noted in the previous chapters, records generally are much sparser. However, the tradition of the development of the Stoneleigh estate by assarting, as recorded in the Abbey's *Leger Book*,[27] suggests that similar activity may have taken place elsewhere in the twelfth century. For example, in the early twelfth century Osbert de Arden granted a carucate of assarts in *essebroc*[28] and there were at least sixty acres of assarted land in Ullenhall by 1194.[29] The Statute of Merton of 1236, rather than marking the height of lords' activities in restricting or extinguishing freeholders' common rights and in enclosing or assarting woodland and waste, may have been prompted by the level of protest. Assarting in the twelfth century may have left an acceptable amount of common pasture and thereby avoided disputes; later activities may have involved smaller amounts of woodland but have increased the pressure on the remainder to a point where assarting was no longer acceptable. This is admittedly speculation, but it serves to warn that the evidence must be assessed in relation to the lack, survival or loss of records.

Consideration of the nature of the woodland which was converted to arable or pasture during the later medieval period is crucial to an understanding of the process of conversion. The existence of two different traditions of woodland management,[30] a constant theme of this study, is highly relevant to this process.

Popular views about the disappearance of woodland in north and west Warwickshire are reflected in questions such as "Who wielded the axes, burned off the undergrowth, hedged the new fields, and gave them their first rough ploughing?"[31] Elsewhere, whilst acknowledging that there is no contemporary account of the techniques used during the period 1150-1350, it has been implied that derelict woodland or 'virgin' woodland were the types to be cleared.[32] There is an indirect reference to the process of woodland clearance in Warwickshire; the accounts of Westminster Abbey for the manor of Knowle record workers being paid for removing tree roots.[33] Despite the lack of direct evidence, it has been assumed not only that Warwickshire's lost woodland was cleared chiefly by felling and ploughing but also that much of it was dense and overgrown.

The association of assarting with wood pasture and common rights provides important evidence to counter such an impression, at least for the thirteenth century. There were several recorded cases in which tenants were deprived of their common pasture rights in their lord's wood in order that their lord might assart all or part of the wood. For example, the eyre roll for 1261-2 included six such cases, in Caldecote, Hurley in Kingsbury, Bedworth, Foleshill, Griff in Chilvers Coton, and Coventry.[34] The association between assarting and wood pasture may be no more than the simple consequence of the large amount of wood pasture in the region. However, it implies that the techniques of woodland clearance used in assarting were those appropriate to wood pasture rather than to coppice woods.

There is no contemporary description of wood pasture, so we do not know to what extent it resembled the modern forms of parkland, wooded commons or places such as the New Forest. However, woodland which is pasture must be open enough for animals to move about freely as well as to obtain suitable grazing. If it is grazed constantly or for large parts of the year the ground flora will be quite different from that of a coppice.

The tools, techniques and time needed to clear wood pasture are different from those used in coppices. To clear a coppice, especially one which is overgrown and has hawthorn and blackthorn thickets amongst the coppice stools of hazel, ash, elm or lime, entangled with rampant brambles, honeysuckle and briars, is very hard work, which takes much time and effort, even with modern tools. To fell timber trees which are well spaced over a grazed sward is quite a different exercise and, given the value of timber for building and other special purposes,[35] one which would have been more profitable for the land owner. From a practical viewpoint it is therefore wholly logical that assarting seems to have concentrated on wood pasture.

However, assarting was far from being the only, or possibly even the main, way in which woodland disappeared. It seems that in large parts of north and west Warwickshire many woods were not carefully managed to achieve a permanent balance between trees and grass. The development of modern, largely treeless, commons shows that trees could disappear without assarting and with common rights remaining. There are some places, such as Stoneleigh, Coventry, Freasley, Kingsbury and Coundon, for which there are explicit records of woods degenerating into waste.[36] Other woods, such as that in Shrewley, and *le sokon* and *le lindes* in Middleton,[37] disappeared silently from the historical record to be replaced by references to waste, from which it may be inferred that similar degeneration had occurred.

How did woods become wastes and why was such degeneration a feature of the period? Why had the woodland

which was lost not turned into waste centuries earlier? It is possible that some woodland became waste before 1086, with the *silva* of Domesday Book being the fortuitous record of the stage reached by the late eleventh century. There is no hint in Domesday Book of an association of waste with woods. There the word waste was used to describe whole manors which yielded no income following the subduing of local resistance to the Norman king.[38] However, like marsh and heath, waste in one of its later medieval senses, approximating to modern, largely treeless commons, may have been omitted from Domesday Book or even have been combined with the *silva*.

Surviving contemporary views on the development of waste in medieval woods are rare. The priors of Coventry and the abbots of Stoneleigh attributed the degeneration of their woods to local tenants' abuse of the right of common estovers. Significantly, neither mentioned over-grazing.[39] Was this because the rising population had created a greater demand for common fuel than pasture? Or had grazing long since excluded coppicing in favour of a few pollards and the resultant delicate balance between grass and trees become all too susceptible to over-felling of the remaining trees? In the case of Stoneleigh, the views of some of the tenants have survived to supplement the official account. In a petition to the king dated to c.1290[40] they claimed that the abbot had deprived them of their estovers by assarting and selling woodland, also that he had destroyed their pigsties (*porcherier*), stopped up paths into the wood, and reduced the amount of pasture available to them. If the tenants are to be believed, the abbot's account was less than the full story.

However, the contemporary emphasis on excess estovers as the reason for the loss of woodland in Stoneleigh and Coventry can be matched to an interpretation of archaeological evidence. Excavations of dwellings on various sites in other parts of the country have revealed cases where, during the thirteenth century, the practice of setting the posts of timber-framed buildings directly into the ground was replaced by the building of low walls or footings on which a timber superstructure was erected.[41] Rather than reflecting climatic change, this new building method may have been a consequence of an increasing shortage of timber and an attempt to make timber-framed dwellings last longer.[42] It has also been noted that the timbers of most surviving medieval buildings were made from large numbers of small trees (usually oaks) and that even in large and important buildings outsize timbers were rare by the fourteenth century.[43]

The development of waste in Warwickshire's later medieval woods may have a parallel in changes in woodland elsewhere. In the New Forest, for example, soil pollen records suggest that hazel, now very uncommon in the Forest, was relatively abundant in the thirteenth century.[44] This decline in hazel has been attributed to an intensification of grazing or a failure to maintain the presumed practice of temporarily enclosing parts of the Forest to protect the growth of underwood from animals. Once the underwood had been lost, continual heavy grazing and the felling of timber trees would have produced treeless commons. A recent study of the early modern period in Whichwood

Forest, Oxfordshire concluded that misuse, over-use and lax regulation undermined the delicate ecosystem of Whichwood before disafforestation and conversion to agriculture in the nineteenth century.[45]

Whatever the exact combination of circumstances in particular woods, the marked growth in population is the obvious cause of the pressure on common woodland, which was usually wood pasture. Wood pasture has been described as "less inherently stable" than coppice woods.[46] Common woods, in which lords could limit common rights but only, in accordance with the Statute of Merton, within reason, were vulnerable to increased demand from larger numbers of tenants, whether for pasture or for fuel.

Woods within woods: medieval coppices

Woods became wastes in the absence of effective measures taken to preserve them, or parts of them. Enclosure for coppicing enabled part of a wood to be managed more intensively so that another part could be assarted or grazed heavily without causing the lord any shortage of wood or timber. It was an arrangement which became common in royal forests.[47]

Coppicing of demesne woods is said to have become the norm in most English woods by c.1250.[48] If that is so, Warwickshire seems to have been exceptional in the amount of wood pasture which still existed in the second half of the thirteenth century and subsequently. However, treatises on estate management dating from c.1276-c.1285 assumed that most estates would have access to wood pasture and made recommendations for its use.[49] There are some records which imply the introduction of coppices into Warwickshire's woods during the later medieval period. Certain coppices or enclosed woods were associated with other woods, wastes or commons in a way which suggests that they had been enclosed from the latter. There is also some explicit evidence of such enclosures.

Part of the wood of Berkswell was called *Bernet* in the twelfth century; in 1316 there was no record of the main wood but there was a separate wood called *Le Bernet*, which produced underwood.[50] In 1285 Stoneleigh Abbey was granted a place in the *Frith*, a wood of several hundred acres in which tenants from Stoneleigh, Kenilworth and Ashow had common rights. Tenants complained that their pasture rights had been curtailed by enclosures. In 1324-5 the prior and convent of Kenilworth claimed that Thomas, Earl of Lancaster, had granted them in the wood called the Frith a parcel which was called the Coppice (*Coupiz*).[51] By 1383 there were at least four coppices in the *Frith*; one of them was called *Stoneleighness*, surely the place granted to the Abbey in 1285. In 1591 there were twelve coppices and two areas not yet coppiced; a map of 1628 showed 722 acres as enclosed and 170 in common. The army of the English Commonwealth, not medieval lords and tenants, destroyed Kenilworth's woods.[52] Buttress Coppice in Alcester was surrounded on three sides by Alcester Common. In 1355 an agreement between the lords of Alcester and Coughton included a provision for Alexander Buttras to enclose all his

wood called *Buttras Coppyes*.[53] The name of the wood showed that the agreement recognised an existing enclosure.

These examples point to the origins of coppices as enclosed portions of common woods. The enclosures may have been older than the first record of them. They may be derived from a long-standing practice of dividing the woods concerned into separate areas reserved, perhaps temporarily, for common grazing and common estovers respectively, but there is no direct evidence of such temporary subdivision in Warwickshire.

As explained in Chapter One, the word coppice is thought to come from the Old French *copiez* (to cut). It has not been found in use in eastern England before the fourteenth century, but there are several examples from other parts of the country in the thirteenth century.[54] The earliest examples of the word in Warwickshire found during this study date from the early fourteenth century.[55] Coppices may therefore represent a particular phase in the development of Warwickshire's later medieval woodland which coincided with a period when French was in common use amongst the upper classes of later medieval society.[56] They were associated with the restriction of common rights. That they were not a universal practice even when woods were divided is illustrated by the fate of Freasley's common wood. When forty acres of it were granted to Lilleshall Abbey in 1240 the bounds were described as if there had been no previous division of the wood. The Abbey did not develop its portion as a coppice and did not even fence it off. Before protracted legal disputes over the grant were resolved much of the wood had become a waste.[57]

This is not to say that places without coppices had no woods which were managed principally for wood and timber. Their enclosed woods had other names which may indicate different histories. Ralph, abbot of Lilleshall, agreed, as part of a general understanding over assarts and pasture in Freasley, to the enclosure of a wood called *Stotefoldeshay*.[58]

The hays of north and west Warwickshire

Hays were recognised features in the Warwickshire countryside by 1086. There was one in the unidentified Domesday manor of *Donnelie* which measured half a league by half a league.[59] Domesday Book gives more information about hays in some other counties, stating that deer were kept in them and that certain hays were in woods.[60] There were several woods with names including hay, but also medieval hays which were not described as woods (see Appendix 5).

Two separate, albeit related, meanings have been attached to the medieval Latin *haia* - hedge, and enclosure in a forest.[61] The dictionary definition gives Old French *haie* as the origin of the Latin word, but a study of English place-name elements has linked the latinized *haia* with the Old English *(ge)haeg* and offered a more elaborate definition of its use in the medieval period: "a part of a forest fenced off for hunting".[62] Dr. Rackham has modified this definition by stating that the hays of Domesday Book "were not parks but corrals or other devices for catching wild deer".[63] This would explain why some hays were described as fixed, thereby implying that others were moveable, and why some manors had more than one hay.[64] A study of pre-Conquest woodland has suggested links between pre-Conquest hays and areas which were later designated royal forests by the Norman kings.[65]

No document relating to Warwickshire defines a hay; its nature is taken for granted. However, records relating to Warwickshire's hays are compatible with Dr. Rackham's definition. They distinguish hays from woods and parks. In one twelfth-century deed the hay of Kenilworth was described as a wood, but later records referred to it simply as a hay, distinct from Kenilworth's park and outwood.[66] The hay of Kingsbury, not described as a wood, was mentioned in the same deed as the park of *Brochelai*; it was near the rive Tame.[67] The free, enclosed hay (*liberam Hayam in defensione*) of Sutton Coldfield was granted to the earls of Warwick as part of the manor together with Sutton's park and outwood.[68] It will be seen from Appendix 5 that several of Warwickshire's hays were recorded in the twelfth century, a remarkable fact given the relative paucity of documents for that century. Several hays were described as woods in the later medieval period; others, known only from a single reference which gives no detail of their vegetation, may have been woods. There was a tradition of wood pasture in *Stotefoldeshay* but not in the hay of Kenilworth.

Overall, Warwickshire's hays were strongly associated with demesne woods in the north and west of the county. Their Domesday credentials and twelfth-century prevalence suggest pre-Conquest origins. The need for hays was presumably overtaken by the later medieval fashion for creating parks and stocking them with imported, captive, fallow deer. In time hays became indistinguishable from other enclosed woods in function if not in nomenclature.

Groves

Warwickshire's groves offer much clearer evidence than do hays for the diversity of the county's woodland in the later medieval period. They are crucial to any consideration of the nature of the *silva* of Domesday Book. They pose fundamental questions about the history of the countryside to which they belonged. Groves were presumably formed either by enclosing portions of hitherto unenclosed woodland or by allowing or encouraging secondary woodland to develop on pieces of enclosed land. The real problems lie in defining the chronology of their formation and in analysing the reasons for their distribution.

The history of woodland in south and east Warwickshire shows that groves were distinct from woods by 1086. It also suggests that groves which were recorded before 1350 in places for which there was no *silva* in Domesday Book nonetheless existed in 1086 and were omitted as being different from *silva*. A similar picture emerges in that part of the middle Avon valley immediately north-west of the river.

Like the groves of south and east Warwickshire, the groves of Grafton, Haselor, Bishopton and Clopton were part of the lord's demesne. The boundaries associated with the charter

of 699-709 for the territory then known collectively as Shottery[69] show that there was at least one grove in the area in the early medieval period (although, as the boundaries are thought to be later than the charter,[70] not necessarily by c.700). Its name, *westgraf*, is the same as that of the wood in the south-east corner of the ecclesiastical parish of Haselor, in the vicinity of other identifiable points in the charter bounds. It is arguable that the modern Westgrove Wood is a remnant of the early medieval grove or has developed from that grove through changes in size and shape caused by loss or expansion of woodland. Some of the manorial groves in the Avon valley, such as the two groves in Baginton c.1130-61[71] and the grove between the two Woodcotes (to the north of Warwick) recorded between 1153 and 1184,[72] were documented early enough to suggest that they were in existence in 1086. Yet there was no *silva* in Baginton according to the Domesday survey.

Grove was used as a minor place-name in three parishes north-west of the river Avon in or adjoining the river valley, Stratford-upon-Avon, Budbrooke, and Hampton Lucy. *Cloptongrove* in Stratford was first recorded in the late thirteenth century and referred, at least in part, to arable land, but later records of a wood of that name suggest that the arable land took its name from an adjacent grove.[73] *La Grave* in Budbrooke was first recorded c.1185; in 1316 a grove which was described as a wood adjoined the manor house of *La Grave*.[74] In Hampton Lucy the name appears to be of pre-Conquest origin, because *la Grave* was well enough established as a minor place-name to appear in a list of knights' fees created by the bishop of Worcester between 1096 and 1112.[75] Throughout the later medieval period and up to the present day the name was attached to land south of the present Hampton Wood, which is arguably the remnants, supplemented by some secondary woodland, of the wood which the bishops of Worcester imparked in the thirteenth century.[76] There is no record of the bishops' wood being called a grove in the later medieval period.

There is evidence for the pre-Conquest origin of another grove in the name *Kinghemegrave* in Kington by Wootton Wawen.[77] By the early thirteenth century, if not earlier, there was a grove in Songar and another in Bearley, which also lacked *silva* in Domesday Book.[78] These places are well beyond the Avon valley, but there is no evidence to contradict the theory that these groves too were of pre-Conquest origin. Moreover, three places in the Tame/Blythe valley - Bickenhill, Lea Marston and Shustoke - each had a grove which was such a significant feature of the local topography that its proper name survived the disappearance of the grove. *Haregrove* in Bickenhill or Marston Culy, *Blacgrava* in Lea Marston and *Brograve* in Shustoke may all have been demesne groves.[79] Most demesne groves did not have proper names. Like other groves further south several groves around Coventry were identified by the manors to which they belonged; the groves of Asthill, Harnall, Hawkesbury, Horwell, Shortley and Whitley were first recorded in the thirteenth century.[80]

The demesne groves to the north and west of the Avon valley may therefore have been similar in nature to the groves south and east of it. Their presence may have been obscured by

142

other medieval woodland, by the amounts of *silva* in Domesday Book and by the attention paid to woodland clearance. Their origins, however, may be different. The manors to which many of them belonged were not manors in Domesday Book. Unless some large manors, such as Coventry, had several groves in demesne in 1086, the groves attached to manors in and around Coventry in the thirteenth and fourteenth centuries may have been the groves of substantial freeholdings which were promoted to demesne status as manors proliferated. Whatever their original tenurial status, the chronology of their formation is obscure, for the widespread occurrence of *silva* in 1086 inhibits the development of the argument which was applied to the woodland of south and east Warwickshire in Chapter Two.

Even more obscure are the tenants' groves of Warwickshire. The multitude of tenants' groves concentrated in certain parishes is a phenomenon which has been largely overlooked; even where it has been noted, its full extent has not been discovered hitherto.[81] This may be a consequence of the relative scarcity of documents giving details of tenants' lands.

The records known as the Hundred Rolls of 1279-80 are in some respects a remarkable exception. However, although they name tenants and give the size of individual holdings, they do not give full details of those holdings, being concerned mainly with the dues attached to each virgate, messuage or cottage.[82] The surviving records relate to the returns of inquisitions in Stoneleigh and Kineton Hundreds. They include demesne woods for Stoneleigh itself, Kenilworth, Brandon, Allesley, Bubbenhall, Bericote, Ashow, Willenhall, Coundon, Binley, Sowe, Pinley (by Coventry), Ryton-on-Dunsmore, Ufton, Weston-under-Wetherley, Kingswood, Packwood, Whichford and Long Compton, and demesne groves for Baginton, Horwell (by Coventry), Cubbington and Chesterton.[83] They refer to only one tenant's grove, in Kenilworth.[84] As the earliest surviving record of the tenants' groves in Packwood dates from 1411[85] (apart from a record of one of the groves in 1398[86]), it could be argued that Packwood's groves were formed after 1279. Yet there were tenants' groves in the neighbouring Tanworth-in-Arden in the thirteenth century. As the Hundred Rolls did not regularly record other appurtenances, such as meadow,[87] the reference to a grove in Kenilworth may be analogous to the stray grove in Lighthorne in Domesday Book.

Furthermore, when the Hundred Rolls are read alongside other documents they appear deficient in their record even of demesne woods. For example, only four acres of land, and none of wood, were attributed to the wood of Bubbenhall.[88] Given the apparent extent of this wood in the fourteenth century,[89] it seems unlikely that this figure referred to the size of the wood in 1279. The information given about the wood of Weston-under-Wetherley was that it contained three acres of land enclosed to the damage of the community without warrant and that those acres used to be common pasture.[90] The sizes of woods are given only for Stoneleigh, Kenilworth, Brandon and Sowe. The Rolls even omit the demesne woods of Bishop's Tachbrook, Offchurch, Wellesbourne (as distinct from Kingswood), Ettington and

Thornton.[91] All these woods lay south of the river Avon and, Thornton's wood apart, had no known common rights.[92] If coppiced demesne woods could be omitted from the Hundred Rolls, tenants' groves were presumably even more irrelevant to the inquisition. The Hundred Rolls of 1279 give a false impression of woodland in the late thirteenth century.

Even where records of tenants' groves are available, they have attracted little interest. For example, a detailed study of Tanworth-in-Arden concentrates on grants of waste which were made in the thirteenth century and claims that little can be learnt of the groves and woodland on the Archer estate, which was an amalgamation of several tenants' lands.[93] Yet Tanworth was remarkable for the very existence of tenants' groves. The lack of interest in these groves may be a consequence of their virtually complete disappearance, apart from a few, possibly enlarged, exceptions, such as Chalcot Wood and Tylers Grove in Tanworth and probably the coppices of Baddesley Clinton. This too is a striking phenomenon, especially when one realises how numerous the groves once were.

The distribution of tenants' groves was uneven and apparently confined to a relatively small number of parishes. A comprehensive survey of Stoneleigh Abbey's lands, including those held by tenants, reveals a few.[94] At the end of the fifteenth century there were two in the Knights Hospitallers' manor of Fletchamstead in Stoneleigh parish.[95] Three occur in late sixteenth-century surveys or rentals of Kenilworth.[96] Several emerge from the records relating to Coventry and its environs, particularly the Priory's register of 1410-11.[97] There were a few in Chilvers Coton.[98] Single examples are recorded for Coleshill, Castle Bromwich, Erdington, Hartshill and Alne.[99] Most were concentrated in a few parishes between Coventry and the western boundary of Warwickshire. They are recorded in later medieval deeds and rentals for large parts of Tanworth-in-Arden, a survey of Packwood, deeds and a survey of Baddesley Clinton, a rental for Wroxall, and odd fifteenth-century documents dealing with tenancies in Berkswell supplemented by a detailed survey of 1553.[100] There are no comparable surveys of Allesley, Corley, Fillongley, Meriden or Solihull, but references in medieval deeds confirm the presence of some groves there and later wood- and field-names hint strongly at the former presence of more.[101] There were a couple in Nuthurst, one in Henley, two in Beaudesert and possibly one in Ullenhall, places to the south and east of Tanworth, but otherwise tenants' groves, as distinct from demesne groves, appear to have been absent from the whole of the Wootton Wawen area.[102]

In some places the absence of groves may be more apparent than real. For example, Packwood's tenants' groves are revealed only in the survey. However, there are fifteenth-century rentals of Middleton, fourteenth-century rentals of Nuneaton, and very detailed late sixteenth-century or early seventeenth-century surveys of Rowington, Hampton-in-Arden, Warwick and Kenilworth, but none of these reveals a concentration of groves such as that in Packwood.[103]

The survey of Packwood gives rare information about the management of tenants' groves. In addition to showing that groves were held by both freehold and copyhold tenants, the survey explained that the tenants could not fell trees or timber in either their groves or their fields, since all groves and woods were reserved to the lord. Tenants' rights were limited to underwood and pasture.[104] If underwood grew in these groves it must have been protected against grazing for some years after cutting, forcing pasture to take second place in at least part of each grove. Some of the Packwood tenants held more than one grove, three in one instance, but this may have been a consequence of the reorganisation and amalgamation of holdings when population fell after the plagues of the fourteenth century. None of the Packwood groves, except the Lusterley Groves held by Coventry Cathedral Priory and not by tenants, had a proper name. Tenants' groves elsewhere for the most part lacked proper names or were called after their tenants or former tenants; exceptions included *Wallhawinge* in Corley[105] and some of the groves in Tanworth-in-Arden.

It is difficult to link the distribution of tenants' groves to any circumstances which were peculiar to the places concerned. They were all in areas for which Domesday Book recorded much *silva* (although Domesday Book did not have specific entries for Tanworth, Packwood or Wroxall), but other places with large amounts of *silva* do not seem to have had tenants' groves. They were found in the manors of lay and ecclesiastical lords alike, but the same lords held other manors in which groves were not present or prevalent. Both Tanworth and Berkswell were held by the earls of Warwick, but other manors of the Warwick earldom, such as Warwick itself, Claverdon and Sutton Coldfield, do not seem to have had tenants' groves. Coventry Cathedral Priory had held Sowe and Willenhall, like Packwood, for centuries, but these two manors did not share Packwood's multiplicity of groves. Later medieval lordship does not seem to have been the decisive factor in the distribution of groves.

The only apparent common feature in the distribution of groves is geographical propinquity. Solihull, Tanworth and Packwood were contiguous, whilst Baddesley Clinton and Wroxall adjoined each other only a little further east. Berkswell, Fillongley, Meriden, Allesley and Corley formed another group of adjoining parishes.

In an attempt to explain the distribution of Warwickshire's tenants' groves parallels have been sought elsewhere. Medieval cartularies and deeds contain examples of groves in several counties.[106] Dr. Rackham's studies of the historical ecology of ancient woodland concentrate on extant woods where ecological evidence is available and on those whose management is relatively well documented. He acknowledges that tenants' groves fail him on both counts,[107] but this acknowledgement at least shows that such groves are familiar to him from his studies, which concentrate on eastern England.[108] Some groves are included in Dr. Rackham's study of the woods of south-east Essex, but they are not described specifically as tenants' groves.[109] A study of Wychwood in Oxfordshire referred briefly to groves but deliberately omitted them from analysis of the Domesday and later medieval woodland.[110] In only one area, the Chilterns, do they seem to have been the subject of special attention.

In a study of part of the Chilterns where Great Missenden Abbey had extensive estates, E.C. Vollans noted that some groves were associated not only with areas of woodland but also with adjacent arable land to which they gave their name. She called them cultivated groves and believed that they were formed during the subdivision and partial clearance of woodland in the twelfth and thirteenth centuries.[111] This belief is understandable in view of the juxtaposition of pieces of woodland held by various tenants in the Missenden area, where woodland appears to have been granted, purchased, exchanged and leased in the same way as other types of land.[112] Dr. Roden's study of field systems revealed a similar situation throughout the Chilterns. Groves were held by free and unfree tenants alike. Some adjoined houses or gardens, others were within arable fields. They were usually situated on valley slopes, rather than alongside larger woods and common woods on the plateaux.[113] Dr. Roden followed Dr. Vollans in suggesting that subdivided woods were probably formed through the enclosure of waste by a number of individuals, but did not offer any example of a grove recorded as having been created in this way.[114]

Did the tenants' groves of Warwickshire have a similar origin and is that the explanation of their distribution? It has long been recognised that many parts of north and west Warwickshire were characterised by dispersed settlement and field systems where tenants held small fields or crofts in severalty and where common fields were confined to a small area, as in the south of Tanworth,[115] or were absent altogether, as in Packwood.[116] In Warwickshire, as in the Chilterns, the settlement pattern has been attributed to a gradual clearance of woodland and waste during the medieval period, particularly after the Conquest.[117] However, recent research in other regions of England has led historians to think that many dispersed settlement patterns have much earlier origins.[118] This is not to deny that there was change and expansion at the expense of woodland during the later medieval period. Existing settlements could have been enlarged through grants of wood, waste and moor, and some new tenancies created in the same way.

Some groves were associated with former woods. In Stoneleigh there were groves in Hurst and Fletchamstead; some of them may be shown, after changes in name, on a map of the north-west of the parish drawn in 1597.[119] That area is thought to have corresponded to the medieval woods of Westwood, Hurst and Crackley, which were not converted to arable, pasture or waste until the later medieval period. The manor of Hawkesbury, which had a grove, was described as being in the waste of Sowe.[120] The manor of Asthill, to the south-west of Coventry, also had a grove and was said to have been formed from assarts.[121] Circumstantial evidence of this kind suggests that at least some of the groves in Stoneleigh and the Coventry area were formed during the later medieval period.

The juxtaposition of woods and groves on a late eighteenth-century map of Meriden suggests that the wood of Alspath was divided during the later medieval period and that Alspath's groves also had a later medieval origin. The surviving medieval deeds do not afford any proof. They refer to assarts in the wood and to other unnamed woods.[122]

Gerard de Waldeyue gave an unnamed grove in Alspath to Coventry Cathedral Priory, but there is no evidence to link this grove with part of the wood of Alspath called *schutehaunch* which was granted to William Waldwyue by the widow of Richard de Kinton.[123] About two centuries separate the records. The Waldeyue family lands could have included both wood and grove and could have changed in composition during this period.

We know the origin of one grove in Warwickshire. *Bromesgrove* in Baddesley Clinton developed as secondary woodland between 1330 and 1422 in two crofts and part of a croft.[124] This grove, although it was by Haywood, was certainly not a piece of woodland which was preserved and set aside during twelfth- or thirteenth-century assarting on the lines postulated for the groves of the Chilterns. However, its chronology and origins cannot be taken as typical because many tenants' groves were recorded well before 1350 in economic circumstances which were not propitious to the formation of secondary woodland. It seems that tenants' groves might have had a variety of different chronologies.

Some groves of secondary woodland may have been formed by allowing hedges to expand into adjoining crofts. There is one record of such a grove or *hegerao* in Kingsbury in 1514.[125] Exactly the same terminology occurred in a survey of Plumberow in south-east Essex in 1579, when the manor included eighteen groves or hedgerows, which could be up to one hundred yards wide.[126] A survey of Budbrooke in 1590 included a tenancy with one coppice and three hedgerow springs which were all subject to the same arrangements for felling wood.[127]

Tenants' groves were not recorded in quantity until the thirteenth century, but this may be due simply to the fact that the relatively scarce records of the twelfth century concentrate on demesnes, rather than on tenants' holdings. Once records of the latter are available (the earliest Tanworth deeds date from c.1200) groves are in evidence. Apart from the deeds from which the development of *Bromesgrove* in Baddesley Clinton can be inferred, no record hints at the formation of a grove. The negative evidence is nonetheless important. Not one of the many deeds by which wood or waste was granted to tenants gave permission for all or part of it to be enclosed as a grove. No account of assarting of demesne or common woods states that the lord replaced his tenants' rights to estovers by substituting other areas of woodland for them to develop as groves within their holdings. Had such an allocation been made it is likely that the groves would have been situated together in one part of the manor. In Tanworth and Solihull the scattered distribution of the groves shows the opposite to have been the case. In Packwood field-names have not perpetuated the memory of former groves, so their sites are unknown. There are examples in Tanworth and Corley of two or three groves which adjoined each other.[128]

At first sight the record of a demesne grove in the Hundred Rolls of 1279 seems to support the notion that some groves were formed by enclosing a piece of common woodland during the later medieval period. A grove in Allesley belonging to Sir John de Hastings was said to include a rood of land enclosed from common pasture.[129] However, the record is more likely to refer to land added to an existing grove than to the formation of a new one. As explained above, several entries in the Hundred Rolls deal with land, presumably assarted, within woods and ignore the woods themselves.[130] The commissioners for the hundredal surveys were interested in any infringement of rights, so the enclosure of common land without proper authority would have claimed their attention.

The nomenclature of groves is a strong argument for proposing that there was something distinctive in their nature or origins. Some of the Tanworth tenants held woods, not groves.[131] The survey of Allesley made in 1626 suggests that there was an historical distinction between groves and woods. Two coppice woods were called groves in the copyhold record of the tenancy.[132] The potential significance of the different terminology is further highlighted by the tenants' coppices (*copecia*) of Sambourne. These were never called groves. Moreover, unlike Tanworth's scattered groves, they do appear to have been concentrated in two parts of Sambourne - Newland, where five coppices were shown on a map of 1746,[133] and an area further north. Their existence is known only from a surviving series of court rolls for certain years between 1480 and 1516; tenants were presented to the court for not keeping their coppices in order.[134] None of the adjacent townships and parishes appears to have had a similar pattern of tenants' coppices; there are plenty of records for Coughton and Great Alne which should have given at least a hint of such a pattern but which, apart from one grove in Alne,[135] are silent on the subject. The coppices of Sambourne may have been formed by enclosing parts of woods at a relatively late date after the word coppice had become fashionable in the fourteenth century.[136]

The nomenclature of groves may be an important clue to the period when they became an established feature of the countryside, if not to the chronology of individual groves. The newly formed *Bromesgrove* in Baddesley Clinton was presumably called a little grove (*grovettum*)[137] because it resembled existing groves in the neighbourhood. The linguistic evidence suggests that groves were so well established when the word coppice came into popular use as to preempt widespread adoption of the new word in the medieval period, although coppices were common amongst demesne woods by the sixteenth century. It could be suggested that tenants' groves were imitations of demesne groves in both function and name. However, the lords of the manors of Tanworth, Baddesley Clinton, Wroxall, Nuthurst and Berkswell did not have groves amongst their demesne woods.

As later medieval evidence offers no obvious reason for the erratic distribution of tenants' groves, the question of their origins will be discussed further in Chapter Six in relation to regional variation in the early medieval period. As far as the later medieval period is concerned, the very existence of these groves modifies the traditional view of medieval woods. Groves show that woodland was not necessarily either common or restricted to the lord. Studies of woodland elsewhere in England do not prepare the researcher for the diversity of the woodland in Warwickshire. This diversity has important implications for views about the later medieval topography of the county.

Woodland clearance and the myth of colonization

Far from being covered with large tracts of dense woodland broken by scattered, small settlements, by 1086 Warwickshire north and west of the Avon had many areas of land which were not wooded. In those places which had plenty of woodland, the clearance of woodland in the twelfth and thirteenth centuries reduced the amount of wood. By the thirteenth century, from which more detailed records are available, this part of the county had many woods, large and small, intermixed with fields, pastures, meadows, moors and heaths. There was already variety in types and sizes of woods in the twelfth century and arguably earlier.

As has been pointed out, we do not know the density of trees in most medieval woods, and certainly not in the eleventh and twelfth centuries,[138] but the widespread existence of wood pasture must have lowered the density of tree cover. Woods which were grazed were either full of clearings or had fewer trees to the acre than coppice woods. Where wood pasture had degenerated into wastes or commons trees were even fewer. The small groves which characterised some places, at least from c.1200, may have consisted mainly of underwood which was cut in a short coppicing cycle and did not grow to any great height. The countryside had plenty of trees, but not in the form of large areas of dark, forbidding, unused woodland.

In such a countryside, the description of the conversion of woodland and waste to cultivation as colonization[139] gives a false impression of the social and topographical history of the region. Since the 1950's the use of the word colonization in relation to later medieval settlement has promoted the view that there were many areas of untouched woodland or other unsettled land in north and west Warwickshire.[140] There is now some belated recognition that the word is a misnomer.[141]

This study should reinforce that recognition. The *silva* of Domesday Book was extensive in places, but not in others. It was nowhere impenetrable, for it was measured for separate manors in 1086. There were certainly some very large areas of woodland still in the twelfth and thirteenth centuries, but all the evidence suggests that they were used by local inhabitants, particularly for pasture and fuel, and were therefore accessible and familiar. The conversion of woodland to arable, pasture, or coppices during the later medieval period should not be compared to the colonization of uninhabited wilderness or prairie. It was more akin to the enclosure of commons in the eighteenth and nineteenth centuries, a process which was also associated with an increasing population and which also caused bitterness amongst some of those affected by it.

Misconceptions about Warwickshire's woodland also include popular views about medieval parks and forests.

Parks

Most parks were a specialised form of wood pasture, as they had to provide food and shelter for deer.[142] There is direct evidence that some woods in Warwickshire were imparked, as in Arrow, Maxstoke, Nuthurst and Pinley by Coventry.[143] However, some parks also contained former arable land, especially, though not exclusively, if they were created or enlarged after c.1350. Wedgnock Park is an example.[144] That being accepted, it is indisputable that Warwickshire's medieval parks were concentrated in the north and west of the county and that the circumstantial evidence associating many of them with woodland is strong.

The claim that imparkment was a method of woodland preservation[145] is an unfortunate generalization. The chronological development of each park, including its post-medieval history, should be considered individually. The action of the priors of Coventry in imparking their wood at Whitmore may well have saved it from the destruction which was apparently the fate of the main wood of Coventry.[146] However, it is arguable that the woods which were taken into Wedgnock Park in the fourteenth century had already been preserved from assarting in the thirteenth century; imparkment did not save them from subsequent destruction in the sixteenth century.[147] It has been suggested that the wood of *Les oueres* in Spernall became Spernall Park;[148] even if this were so, the wood was already enclosed before it was imparked. The same may have been the case with *Herewardeshay* in Chilvers Coton.[149] *Wykewode* was not taken into Coughton Park until the late fifteenth century. It will be seen from some of the examples cited that there is a case to be made for parks as the agents of the destruction of woodland as well as of its preservation. In addition, wherever parks were formed, subsequent field-names tended to reflect the existence of the park and to replace most previous names; fields called park eliminated even the names of former woods, as is seen in eighteenth-century maps of Wedgnock Park.[150]

Forests

Accounts of Warwickshire's topography which refer to forests use the word in its modern sense of an extensive area of wild and dense woodland. In the later medieval period the meaning was very different. A medieval forest was land where special privileges or the king's forest law protected deer and their habitat.[151] Most of Warwickshire was not a royal forest area. One exception was the south-west corner, which belonged to the royal Forest of Feckenham in Worcestershire.[152] There were three private forests, or chases, connected with Sutton Coldfield, Kenilworth and Merevale; the first of these seems to have originated as a royal forest.

Sutton Chase, called a forest in at least one deed,[153] illustrates well the distinction between forests or chases, parks, and simple woods. Its boundaries extended far beyond the manor and parish of Sutton to include several places in Staffordshire as well as in Warwickshire. In 1309 an account of the customs of the manor of Sutton Coldfield recorded a tradition that the Chase was afforested when the manor was held by the Crown, i.e. before it was granted to Roger, earl of Warwick, in the twelfth century. As the Chase included Erdington, it is arguable that Erdington's *silva*, which was recorded in Domesday Book as being within the king's enclosure (*in defenso regis*), was even then part of a royal forest.

Although some of the woodland of north and west Warwickshire was afforested by the Norman kings, or by nobles with royal permission, the region as a whole was neither a wild expanse of woodland nor a forest in the medieval, legal sense. For that reason, the term 'Forest of Arden' as applied to the region is a misnomer which will be discussed further in the following chapter.

Conclusions

The role of woodland as an important but, with local exceptions, by no means dominant feature of the local economy and topography in north and west Warwickshire has been amply demonstrated. The northern part of the Avon valley below Stratford-upon-Avon resembled south and east Warwickshire in the nature and distribution of its woodland, suggesting that the river Avon did not form a regional divide in the later medieval period. The variety of the woodland further north and west, not fully appreciated hitherto, should also be apparent.

Some large areas of woodland were converted to other uses between 1086 and the end of the thirteenth century, but many woods remained. The statement that "Arden in Warwickshire ... became no more wooded than the rest of the country" by 1350[154] is not substantiated by the evidence, although it may be true of north and west Warwickshire in the late twentieth century. A strong tradition of wood pasture persisted throughout the later medieval period. However, this was not the only form of woodland management; woods called coppices, groves and hays appear to have been enclosed and managed for wood and timber. Evidence suggests that this diversity in types of woodland may predate the later medieval period.

1 For the amounts of *silva* see the descriptions of individual parishes and townships in the previous chapter. A glance at the gazetteer which forms Appendix 1 will give an immediate impression of the large number of woods of which there is some medieval record.
2 For "when it bears mast" see *VCH*, Vol. I, p. 292 and Darby and Terrett, *Domesday Geography of Midland England*, p. 294. For "when exploited" see *DB, passim*, e.g. 238b for Sutton Coldfield.
3 Latham, *Revised Medieval Latin Word-List*, p. 322.
4 Darby, *Domesday England*, p. 184; ed. H.C. Darby and E.M.J. Campbell, *The Domesday Geography of South-east England* (1962), pp. 212-3; *Domesday Book. 14. Oxfordshire* (ed. J. Morris, 1978), f. 154d.
5 Rackham, *Ancient Woodland*, p. 155; *idem, History of the Countryside*, p. 122.
6 Darby and Terrett, *Domesday Geography of Midland England*, p. 294, footnote 2.
7 *DB*, 238b, 241d.
8 Darby and Terrett, *Domesday Geography of Midland England*, p. 294.
9 W.C.R.O., CR1886/15 and 62.
10 B.R.L., Wingfield Digby MSS., A1-A10; Greenway, *Charters of the Honour of Mowbray*, pp. 215-218.
11 For an English translation of the Statute of Merton see *English Historical Documents Volume Three 1189-1327* (ed. H. Rothwell, 1975), pp. 351-4 (p. 352 for the relevant clause). For the implications of this particular clause see Coss, *Lordship, knighthood and locality*, pp. 104-5, and the royal writ relating to it in *Bracton on the Laws and Customs of England*, Volume Three (S.E. Thorne, 1977), p. 180. For examples of cases relating to Warwickshire in which the statute was cited in relation to woodland or waste, see P.R.O., JUST 1/954, rot 21r, JUST 1/955, rot 4r, JUST 1/958, rot 2r, JUST 1/969, rot 2d, JUST 1/970, rot 5r, JUST 1/1245 rot 35r, JUST 1/1279, rot 14r.
12 *SLB*, p. 26; C.R.O., BA/B/A/55/1-9 and BA/B/A/47/3-11; S.B.T., DR18/1/1127, 1130, 1137-44, 1147; and P.R.O., E 326/6180.
13 For example, Hooke, *Anglo-Saxon Landscapes of the West Midlands*, p. 149.
14 There were outwoods in Allesley, Ashow, Atherstone, Baddesley Clinton, Binley, Brandon, Bubbenhall, Weston in Bulkington, Chilvers Coton, Caludon in Coventry, Coleshill, Coundon, Coventry, Erdington, Grendon, Kenilworth, Knowle, Mancetter, Maxstoke, Merevale, Middleton, Nuneaton, Oldbury, Great Packington, Packwood, Newton Regis, Sheldon, Sutton Coldfield, Sowe, Willenhall, and Wishaw. For details, see Appendix 1 and Chapter Three.
15 See the descriptions of woodland in these places in Chapter Three.
16 W.C.R.O., QS75/111.
17 See the detailed accounts of woodland in these places in Chapter Three.
18 P. Warner, *Greens, Common and Clayland Colonization: The Origins and Development of Green-side Settlement in East Suffolk*, University of Leicester Department of English Local History Occasional Papers, Fourth Series, Number 2 (1987), pp. 45-6 and Chapter 2.
19 D. Roden, 'Woodland and its Management in the Medieval Chilterns', *Forestry*, 41 (1968), pp. 59-71, see p. 68.
20 Rackham, *Trees and Woodland in the British Landscape* (second edition), p. 149.
21 J.B. Harley, 'Population Trends and Agricultural Developments from the Warwickshire Hundred Rolls of 1279', *Economic History Review*, second series, xi (1958), pp. 8-18, see p. 12; Rackham, *History of the Countryside*, p. 88; B.K. Roberts, 'A Study of Medieval Colonization in the Forest of Arden', *Agricultural History Review*, 16 (1968), pp. 101-13, see p. 101; Coss, *Lordship, knighthood and locality*, pp. 24, 32.
22 See previous footnote.
23 ed. Hallam, *The Agrarian History of England and Wales II: 1042-1350*, pp. 716-33.
24 *ibid.*, pp. 509-12, 529.
25 Rackham, *Trees and Woodland in the British Landscape* (second edition), p. 56.
26 *SLB*, p. 26; C.R.O., BA/B/A/55/1-9 and BA/B/A/47/3-11; S.B.T., DR18/1/1127, 1130, 1137-44, 1147; and P.R.O., E 326/6180.
27 *SLB*, p. 26.
28 B.L., Cott. Ch. xxii 3. From other land mentioned in the charter, *essebroc* seems to have been in vicinity of Kingsbury. As explained above, Coss, *Lordship, knighthood and locality*, p. 221, associates it with Foul End in the south of the parish, but if the initial letter of the modern Nassers Brook is removed the similarity with the name *essebroc* suggests that the streams were one and the same and that *essebroc* flowed westwards from the north-west side of Hurley Common, where Nassers Brook was recorded in the enclosure award for Hurley (W.C.R.O., CR416/8).

29 Berkeley Castle muniments, SC 38; the help of Mr. D.J.H. Smith, County and Diocesan Archivist for Gloucestershire, in arranging access to this deed is gratefully acknowledged.

30 See Chapter One and the references given there.

31 Skipp, *The Origins of Solihull*, p. 21.

32 Roberts, *Settlement, Land Use and Population*, pp. 163-5.

33 Westminster Abbey, 27,692 and 27,699; for the sale of roots, *ibid.*, 27,693, 27,695, 27,704.

34 P.R.O., JUST 1/954, rots 10d, 21r, 23r, 23d, 27d, 31r.

35 Rackham, *Ancient Woodland*, pp. 145-7, 151-3.

36 See the accounts of woodland in these places in Chapter Three.

37 See the accounts of these woods in Chapter Three.

38 Darby, *Domesday England*, pp. 234-59.

39 *Rotuli Parliamentorum Anglie Hactenus Inediti* (Richardson and Sayles), pp. 240-66; *SLB*, p. 26.

40 P.R.O., SC 8/269/13404.

41 C. Dyer, 'English Peasant Buildings in the Later Middle Ages (1200-1500)', *Medieval Archaeology*, 30 (1986), pp. 19-45, see pp. 35-36.

42 S.R. Bassett, personal communication.

43 Rackham, *History of the Countryside*, pp. 86-7.

44 P. Colebourn, *Hampshire's Countryside Heritage: Ancient Woodland*, (Hampshire County Council, 1983) pp. 24, 26, 30.

45 M. Freeman, 'Whichwood Forest, Oxfordshire: An Episode in its Recent Environmental History', *Agricultural History Review*, 45 (1997), pp. 137-48.

46 Rackham, *Ancient Woodland*, p. 173.

47 *ibid.*, pp. 173-4, 185-6.

48 *ibid.*, p. 135.

49 *Walter of Henley and other treatises on estate management and accounting* (ed. D. Oschinsky, 1971), pp. 5-6, 75 (for dates), 285, 424-5. The treatises include references to a piggery (*porcherie*) in a wood and to feeding cattle in wood pasture (*en pasture de boys*).

50 B.L., Harley 3650, f. 27, copy in W.C.R.O., MI 392/1; P.R.O., C 134/49, 51.

51 P.R.O., SC 8/55/2750 and C 81/129/7129, the latter being a better-preserved copy of the same petition.

52 For the disappearance of the Frith, Wallsgrove, *Kenilworth*, chapter 10, and for the Park and Chase, *ibid.*, chapter 12.

53 W.C.R.O., CR1998/box35/bundle K.

54 Rackham, *Ancient Woodland*, pp. 3-5.

55 P.R.O., SC 8/55/2750 and C 81/129/7129 date from 1324-5.

56 L.C. Hector, *The Handwriting of English Documents* (second edition, 1966, reprint, 1988), p. 21.

57 See the account of Freasley's woodland under Polesworth in Chapter Three.

58 Staffs. R.O., D593/A/1/10/10.

59 *DB*, 240a.

60 Darby and Terrett, *Domesday Geography of Midland England*, pp. 32, 89, 136-40, 247.

61 R.E. Latham, *Dictionary of Medieval Latin from British Sources*, Fascicule IV (1989), p. 1130.

62 Smith, *English Place-Name Elements* Vol. I, pp. 214-5.

63 Rackham, *Ancient Woodland*, pp. 188, 191.

64 Darby and Terrett, *Domesday Geography of Midland England*, pp. 32, 89, 136-40, 247.

65 D. Hooke, 'Pre-Conquest Woodland: its Distribution and Usage', Agricultural History Review, 37 (1989), pp. 113-29, see pp. 123-29.

66 B.L., Add. MS. 47,677, f. cxxiii, copy in W.C.R.O., MI 392/2; *Calendar of Close Rolls, 1237-42*, pp. 385, 50, 78 and *Calendar of Patent Rolls, 1216-25*, pp. 360-2.

67 B.L., Cott. Ch. xxii 2 and Cott. Ch. xxv 25.

68 *Dugdale*, Vol. II, pp. 909-10.

69 Sawyer, *Anglo-Saxon Charters*, no. 64; Birch, *Cartularium Saxonicum*, Vol. I, pp. 178-79; Gover, Mawer and Stenton, *Place-Names of Warwickshire*, p. 212.

70 Cox, 'The Place-Names of the Earliest English Records', p. 66, cited in Hooke, 'Village Development in the West Midlands', p. 143.

71 B.L., Harley 3650, f. 19, copy in W.C.R.O., MI 392/1.

72 W.C.R.O., CR26/A/I.

73 See the account of Stratford-upon-Avon's groves in Chapter Three.

74 See under Budbrooke in Chapter Three.

75 *RBW*, pp. 413, 412, and for the date, Dyer, *Lords and Peasants*, p. 47.

76 See under Hampton Lucy in Chapter Three.

77 See under Wootton Wawen in Chapter Three.

78 See under Claverdon and Bearley in Chapter Three.

79 For records of these minor place-names, Gover, Mawer and Stenton, *Place-Names of Warwickshire*, pp. 59, 85, 350.

80 See under Coventry in Chapter Three.

81 Dyer, 'English Peasant Buildings', p. 27 refers briefly to tenants' groves, without giving examples; A. Watkins, 'The Woodland Economy of the Forest of Arden in the Later Middle Ages', *Midland History*, XVIII (1993), pp. 19-36 mentions groves on p. 26, citing Bordesley, Coleshill, Castle Bromwich, Wroxall, Tanworth-in-Arden, Baddesley Clinton, Kingsbury, Maxstoke and Chilvers Coton. The incompleteness of this list will be apparent. The place of pasture and wood in Castle Bromwich is not called a grove in the document cited in the article (B.R.L. 19,862), although there was a grove of wood at *holebrok* in Castle Bromwich in 1331 (B.R.L., 19,836).

82 *HR, passim.*

83 *ibid.*, pp. 66-7, 69, 73, 44, 48, 52, 85, 90, 106, 110, 121, 126, 128-9, 141, 143, 148, 151, 158, 162, 165-7, 169, 180, 280, 297, 318 for demesne woods and pp. 55, 123, 154, 235 for demesne groves.

84 *ibid.*, p. 49.

85 P.R.O., E 164/21, ff. 204r-206r, copy in W.C.R.O., MI 409.

86 C.R.O., 54/40.

87 There were occasional entries referring to meadow, for example *HR*, pp. 211, 222, 265. No meadow appeared under Weston by Cherington, yet tenants were obliged to mow meadow there - pp. 241, 243.

88 *HR*, p. 90.

89 For a survey of 1391, P.R.O., E 149/60/16, and a lease of 1371, P.R.O., E 42/219.

90 *HR*, p. 162.

91 *ibid.*, pp. 187-9, 78-80, 165-9, 280-2, 285-6.

92 See Chapter Two.

93 Roberts, *Settlement, Land Use and Population*, pp. 318, 287-319.

94 *SLB*, pp. 126, 207, 214, 217, 150.

95 B.L., Lansdowne 200, ff. lxiv-lxv.

96 Gover, Mawer and Stenton, *Place-Names of Warwickshire*, p. 174; P.R.O., SC 12/27/36, copy in W.C.R.O., MI 295.

97 P.R.O., E 164/21, copy in W.C.R.O., MI 409.

98 See the description of Chilvers Coton's woodland in Chapter Three.

99 B.R.L., Wingfield Digby MSS., A333; B.R.L., 19,836; B.R.L., 347,913; B.L., Harl. Roll Y 13; Royce, *Landboc*, Vol. ii, pp. 562-3.

100 See the descriptions of woodland in these places in Chapter Three, also the Gazetteer in Appendix 1.

101 See the descriptions of woodland in these places in Chapter Three.

102 See the descriptions in Chapter Three.

103 Middleton rentals: M.MSS., Mi M 124, 175, 206 and 207. Nuneaton rentals: B.L., Add. Rolls 49,464, 49,466 (copies in Nuneaton Library). Survey of Rowington: S.B.T., DR473/291. Survey of Hampton-in-Arden: B.R.L., 511,984. Survey of Warwick: W.C.R.O., CR1886/Cupboard 4/18. Surveys of Kenilworth: W.C.R.O., CR576/1 and P.R.O., LR2/185.

104 P.R.O., E 164/21, ff. 204r-206r, copy in W.C.R.O., MI 409.

105 Bodleian Library, Queen's College 2337.

106 Examples from printed documents include *Registrum sive Liber irrotularius et consuetudinarius Prioratus Beatae Mariae Wigorniensis* (ed. W.H. Hale, Camden , 91, 1865), ff. 46b, 51a; 'Some Records of Northill College, No. II' (C.G. Chambers, Bedfordshire Historical Record Society, Vol 2, 1914), pp. 111-125, see p. 114; *Medieval deeds of Bath and District* (ed. B.R. Kemp, Somerset Record Society, 73, 1974), pp. 155, 167, 190, 192, 205; *Chertsey Cartularies* (Surrey Record Society, Vol II, part 1, 1958), pp. 70, 80-82, 120, 197, 243, 245-46, 317-327; *Registrum Malmesburiense*, (ed. J.S. Brewer and C.T. Martin, Rolls Series, Vol II, 1880, reprinted 1965), pp. 97, 98, 142, 143, 212, 221, 269; *Calendar of Close Rolls, 1302-7*, p. 269; *Calendar of Close Rolls, 1346-49*, p. 541; *Calendar of Close Rolls, 1374-77*, pp. 218, 531; *Calendar of Close Rolls, 1377-81*, p. 467; *RBW*, pp. 2, 235, 339, 380; *Calendar of Charters and Documents relating to Selborne and its Priory preserved in the Muniment Room of Magdalen College, Oxford* (ed. W.D. Macray, Hampshire Record Society, 1891), pp. 6, 37-38, 62, 110; *The Cartulary of the Knights of St. John of Jerusalem in England, Part 2 Prima Camera Essex* (ed. M. Gervers, British Academy Records of Social and Economic History, New Series, 23, 1996), pp. xc-xcv.

107 Rackham, *Ancient Woodland*, p. 137.

108 *ibid.*, p. 26.

109 Rackham, *The Ancient Woodland of England: The Woods of South-East Essex*, see especially pp. 17-8.

110 B. Schumer, *The Evolution of Wychwood to 1400: Pioneers, Frontiers and Forests*, University of Leicester Department of English Local History Occasional Papers, Third Series, no. 6 (1984), pp. 16, 18.

111 E.C. Vollans, 'The Evolution of Farm-Lands in the Central Chilterns in the twelfth and thirteenth centuries', *Transactions of the Institute of British Geographers*, 26 (1959), pp. 197-238.

112 Roden, 'Woodland and its Management in the Medieval Chilterns', pp. 59-71, see p. 63.

113 D. Roden, *Studies in Chiltern Field Systems*, (University of London Ph. D. thesis, 1965), see especially pp. 182-3, 255, 314, 350, 354, 358, cited here by kind permission of the Librarian of the University of London.

114 *ibid.*, pp. 351, 354.

115 Roberts, *Settlement, Land Use and Population*, fig. 48.

116 P.R.O., E 164/21, ff. 204r-206r, copy in W.C.R.O., MI 409.

117 See, for example, Hilton, *Social Structure of Rural Warwickshire in the Middle Ages*, p. 11.

118 T. Williamson, 'Explaining Regional Landscapes', pp. 8-10.

119 For groves in Hurst, Fletchamstead and Crackley, P.R.O., E 210/201; *SLB*, pp. 207, 214, 217; B.L., Lansdowne 200, ff. lxiv-lxv; P.R.O., SC 2/207/79. For the map of 1597, W.C.R.O., Z141/1(U).

120 P.R.O., E 164/21, f. 58r, copy in W.C.R.O., MI 409.

121 For the assarts, S.B.T., DR10/1409, f. 59. For the grove, W.C.R.O., DR564/I(a)/418, 419; C.R.O., 468/350, 361; P.R.O., DL 29/463/7551.

122 B.R.L., 608,882; S.B.T., ER1/63/293; C.R.O., BA/D/K/10/1, 2.

123 P.R.O., E 164/21, f. 48v for the grant of the grove; B.R.L. 608,881 for the grant of *schutehaunch*.

124 S.B.T., DR3/183, 51, 800, 339, 807; for a detailed account, see Chapter Three under Baddesley Clinton.

125 M.MSS., Mi M 130/2.

126 Rackham, *The Ancient Woodland of England: The Woods of South-East Essex*, pp. 21-3.

127 W.C.R.O., CR895/80, f. 7v.

128 For Tanworth, S.B.T., DR37/185; for Corley, Bodleian Library, Queen's College 2337.

129 *HR*, p. 85.

130 This appears to have been the case with the woods of Baginton, Bericote, Ashow, Ryton, Ufton, Weston, Willenhall, Coundon, Binley and Pinley near Coventry - *HR*, pp. 14, 38, 40, 44-5, 48-50, 53, 54, 55, 64.

131 S.B.T., DR37/720.

132 W.C.R.O., CR623/box14.

133 W.C.R.O., CR1998/M11.

134 S.B.T., DR2357-2363, in particular 2358, 2360 and 2361.

135 Royce, *Landboc*, Vol. ii, pp. 562-3.

136 For a discussion of the word coppice, see above under 'Woods within woods: medieval coppices'.

137 S.B.T., DR3/183.

138 Rackham, *Ancient Woodland*, p. 111.

139 As in B.K. Roberts, 'A Study of Medieval Colonization in the Forest of Arden', *Agricultural History Review*, 16 (1968), pp. 101-13; *idem.*, *Settlement, Land Use and Population, passim*, especially pp. 183-6, 425-6, 553; K.P. Witney, 'The Woodland Economy of Kent', *Agricultural History Review*, 38, Part I (1990), pp. 20-39, see p. 35; Warner, *Greens, Commons and Clayland Colonization, passim*, e.g. pp. 13, 24-5; A.M. Everitt, 'The making of the agrarian landscape of Kent', *Archaeologia Cantiana*, XCII (1976), pp. 1-31, see pp. 11, 22-3; *idem, Continuity and Colonization: the evolution of Kentish settlement* (1986), for example, pp. 6-7, 12, 41, 53.

140 W.G. Hoskins, *The Making of the English Landscape* (1955), chapter 3, entitled 'The Colonization of Medieval England'.

141 Schumer, *The Evolution of Wychwood to 1400*, pp. 5-6, 35-36, 59; Dyer, 'The Retreat from Marginal Land', pp. 53-4; T. Williamson and L. Bellamy, *Property and Landscape* (1987), p. 75.

142 For a general account of medieval parks with specific reference to woodland see Rackham, *Ancient Woodland*, pp. 188-199.

143 See the descriptions of woodland in these places in Chapter Three.

144 See under Warwick and Wedgnock in Chapter Three.

145 Roberts, *Settlement, Land Use and Population*, p. 148.

146 See under Coventry in ChapterThree.

147 W.C.R.O., CR1886/2593 shows the state of Wedgnock Park in the late sixteenth century.

148 See under Spernall in Chapter Three.

149 See under Chilvers Coton in Chapter Three.

150 For Wedgnock, map of 1682, W.C.R.O., CR1886/M3, map of 1760, W.C.R.O., CR1886/M312, map of 1774, W.C.R.O., CR1886/M4, and map of 1788, W.C.R.O., CR1886/M24A.

151 For a general account of medieval forests with specific reference to woodland Rackham, *Ancient Woodland*, pp. 175-88.

152 J. West, *The Administration and Economy of the Forest of Feckenham during the Early Middle Ages*, (University of Birmingham thesis, 1964), pp. 322-68.

153 See under Sutton Coldfield in Chapter Three.

154 Rackham, *History of the Countryside*, p. 88; *idem, Ancient Woodland*, p. 134.

Chapter Five

THE WOODLAND OF WARWICKSHIRE IN THE EARLY

MEDIEVAL PERIOD

Introduction

The topographical division of Warwickshire between a well wooded region in the north and west and a region with much less woodland in the south and east was apparent not only in the later medieval period but already in 1086. How much older was this regional diversity? When did it originate? How sharp was the difference in earlier centuries and how varied was woodland, in its types as well as its distribution, within each of the regions? In seeking answers to these questions this chapter will review the evidence for the nature and distribution of woodland in Warwickshire in the early medieval period.

The inadequacies of the evidence for the later medieval period, especially for the twelfth century, have been amply demonstrated. For the early medieval period the evidence is far less and what there is requires even more careful interpretation. There are virtually no documentary records for the fifth and sixth centuries.[1] The traditions relating to these centuries which were preserved in the Anglo-Saxon Chronicle are a much later record and have been shown to be unreliable; in any case they do not refer to large parts of England in the fifth and sixth centuries. Bede's *Ecclesiastical History* is a generally accurate account of certain kingdoms in the seventh century, but draws on unreliable sources for earlier centuries.[2] Charters do not appear until the seventh century. They usually survive only in later copies and may be forgeries, albeit based on legitimate claims. They are also unevenly distributed geographically and chronologically.[3] Archaeological evidence for the fifth and sixth centuries still concentrates largely on Germanic, pagan burial customs and grave goods. The real contrast between the physical remains of Romano-British settlement and the very different material culture of the early medieval period has been reinforced by the limitations of the aims and techniques governing the nature and extent of archaeological survey in many areas.[4] Place-names are plentiful and accordingly much reliance has been placed upon them, but they are difficult or impossible to date and easy to misinterpret.[5]

Until even a couple of decades ago, it was widely thought that the settlement pattern of 1086, at least in certain regions including the west midlands, had been achieved only after centuries of woodland clearance during the early medieval period. Put crudely, it was thought that during the fifth and sixth centuries people of Germanic origin conquered a thinly populated country, drove the British-speaking inhabitants westwards into Wales and then began to clear large areas of dense woodland in order to establish settlements. The evidence of archaeology and place-names and the traditions

of the Anglo-Saxon Chronicle were used to support this view.[6]

The mass of archæological evidence collected in recent decades has shown that lowland Britain was densely settled during the Romano-British period.[7] A good example of such archæological investigation is the Worcestershire parish of Hanbury, where field-walking has revealed that most of the parish was cultivated in the Romano-British period.[8] In the light of this research it has been claimed that English-speaking people may have become politically and socially, rather than numerically, dominant, with their language being adopted by the rest of the population.[9] This view is not universally accepted. Some scholars still maintain that the dominance of the Old English language must have been consequent upon a significant level of immigration during the fifth and sixth centuries.[10]

Apart from pagan cemeteries the archæological record for the west midlands in the early medieval period is a virtual blank. However, at Wasperton in Warwickshire the physical juxtaposition of burials according to different cultures and the tendency of later graves not to intersect earlier interments both suggest peaceful coexistence and even integration.[11] Post-Roman buildings and artefacts were much less durable than Romano-British remains and, even if they have been preserved, are difficult to date, but other evidence shows that settlement and cultivation continued, if not so intensively, after the collapse of Roman rule in the first half of the fifth century. Topographical analysis of roads and field boundaries, a technique to be considered in more detail in the following chapter, shows that land use over much of the Wootton Wawen area has been continuous since at least the Romano-British period, even though the type of use may have changed within that framework.[12] The particular road and field systems in that area have not been traced much further north, but topographical analysis has been used to extend the pattern southwards and if applied elsewhere might reveal road and field systems on a different axis but demonstrably of similar antiquity.[13] In addition, there is now evidence of institutional continuity in the west midlands in the form of some British churches and the territories which they served.[14]

In the light of these recent developments in archæological and topographical research, the evidence for the amount and nature of woodland in Warwickshire in the centuries before 1086 should be reassessed. This chapter will deal at length with two traditional types of evidence, early medieval charters and place-names. It will extend the latter to cover minor place-names and the names of regions and territories, drawing on the multi-disciplinary techniques used to identify those territories. It will also explore the use of later medieval evidence for links between territories in relation to the distribution of woodland.

Early medieval charters

There are fewer early medieval charters for Warwickshire than for the adjoining county of Worcestershire, largely because many of the charters of the cathedral church of Lichfield were destroyed by fire in the seventeenth century.[15] However, there are enough to throw some light on the nature and distribution of woodland c.700 and in the tenth and early eleventh centuries. Moreover, the charters relating to Worcestershire provide a west midlands context in which it is plausible to argue for a corresponding variety of early medieval woods and groves in the adjacent county of Warwickshire. The Worcestershire charters, and their boundary clauses in particular, have been the subject of detailed study.[16] They show that both woods and groves[17] were distinct features in the Worcestershire countryside by the tenth century. One boundary even ran between two woods.[18] A charter dated 866 referred to a wooded common (*in commone illa siluatica*).[19]

Leaving aside charters which are deemed spurious or of doubtful authenticity - the products of churches which wanted written proof of a claim which might well have been genuine - there are copies and in a few cases original manuscripts of more than two dozen charters dealing with places in Warwickshire. They refer to Shottery, Nuthurst, Ingon in Hampton Lucy, Hampton Lucy itself, Stratford-upon-Avon, including Bishopton, Clopton, Luddington and possibly Ruin Clifford, Wootton Wawen, including Aspley and an unidentified *Teodeces leage*, Warwick, Duddeston in Aston, Austrey, Wormleighton, Shipston-on-Stour, Alveston, including Tiddington, Bickmarsh in Welford-on-Avon, Kineton, Southam, Ladbroke, Radbourn, Long Itchington, Arley, Little Compton, Farnborough, Myton, Coventry and Weston-on-Avon.[20] There is also a spurious charter for Oldberrow in Worcestershire which shared a boundary with land in Warwickshire; the boundary clause, of a later date, is thought to be authentic.[21] Most of the charters relating to Warwickshire south and east of the Avon date from the tenth and eleventh centuries, but for a few places north and west of the Avon there are earlier records.

Boundary clauses attached to some of the charters are potentially of particular help to this study because of the noticeable propensity of ancient woods to lie on boundaries between parishes or townships. There are bounds for Shottery, Bishopton, Luddington, Aspley, *Teodeces leage*, Wormleighton, Shipston-on-Stour, Alveston, Kineton, Southam, Ladbroke, Radbourn, Long Itchington, Arley, Farnborough and Myton. They illustrate the drawbacks to this kind of evidence. The boundary of Arley followed rivers or streams for much of its course, and on those stretches would have omitted any features which adjoined the river.[22] Any woods which did not lie on the boundary had no chance of a mention and even those which were near to it could be ignored. Most features described cannot be identified with certainty or have disappeared without trace, even in the form of minor place-names. Despite much effort, scholars have been unable to do more than guess the limits of

several of the places for which boundary clauses have survived.[23] Even where an identification can be made with some confidence, it must be remembered that the boundary clause may not be contemporary with the charter and cannot therefore be dated with certainty. Nonetheless, charter bounds do provide some very important evidence.

Most of the charters which deal with places in south and east Warwickshire give no hint of any woodland. However, the bounds of Long Itchington, attached to a charter dated 1001, were cited in Chapter Two as evidence for the existence at the beginning of the eleventh century of a grove on the boundary between Long Itchington and Ufton in the area of the present Long Itchington and Ufton Woods.[24] One of the Alveston charters, dating from 966, is another notable exception; the grant included part of a wood (*wudu*) of which there is no known post-Conquest record.[25] An earlier grant of land in the Stratford area referred to some wood hills which are thought to have been situated on the western boundary of Alveston.[26]

The charters dealing with places north and west of the Avon are fewer in number. Those for Ingon and Hampton Lucy give only the hidages (the early medieval equivalent of a tax assessment) attached to those places, but even this information shows that they were established settlements in the eighth century.[27] The hidages are the same as those given in a late twelfth-century survey.[28] There is no detailed information on Warwick, Duddeston or Austrey.[29] However, four of the charters are very useful.

That which deals with land in Shottery and Nuthurst is exceptionally early, being attributed to the decade 699-709, although the boundaries which appear in the surviving copy are in all probability later than the original charter.[30] The boundaries have not been fully solved but suggest that in the early medieval period Shottery was a much larger territory than in the later medieval period, apparently including lands in Binton, Drayton, and Luddington to the north of the Avon and also Ruin Clifford to the south.[31] They show that there were groves in the Avon valley in the early medieval period; the *westgraf* discussed in Chapters Two and Three was presumably distinguished by the epithet west from other groves in the area. The boundaries also refer to *billes leah*, a name which has survived as the modern Billesley, and, south of the river Avon, to the wood hills which may match the wood in the tenth-century Alveston charter. Shottery was a valuable territory, assessed at thirty-three *cassatorum*. The charter did not give boundaries for Nuthurst, but, by conveying a wooded place at Nuthurst, it showed that the area had much woodland. The woodland had a value, so it must have been productive. People knew it by name, a name which implied a distinction from other hursts in the neighbourhood.

A few decades later, c.716-37, the land given to a nobleman called Æthelric by King Æthelbald of Mercia for the founding of a church at Wootton Wawen comprised twenty hides of land in the district anciently called *Stoppingas* in the place called Wootton (*Uuidutuun*), next to the river Alne (*Æluuinnae*).[32] The charter survives only in a copy, but is regarded as an authentic record of a genuine grant.[33] The grant conveyed the land according to its ancient bounds and with *campis et saltibus et pratis*. The first and third of these appurtenances are easily translated as fields and meadows, but the second has been the subject of at least three different interpretations. In one of these *saltibus* is translated as "pastures", in another as "glades" and in a third as "wooded uplands".[34] Evidence from Kent supports the last of these. The noun *saltus*, in the form of the ablative singular *saltu*, appears in a few eighth-century and early ninth-century charters relating to the Weald of Kent. In one case (*in saltu Anderedo*) the editor translated *saltu* simply as "wood", in another (*in saltu qui dicitur Andred*) the word "woodland" was used.[35] A third example (*in commune saltu*) has been translated as "in the common wood".[36] The form of the ablative singular indicates that the ablative plural is *saltibus*. A related adjective, *saltosus*, has been translated as "growing in upland woods".[37] It seems therefore that in the first half of the eighth century Wootton Wawen had some upland woods, at least in that part which was the subject of the charter. The twenty hides of the grant are thought to have become the later Domesday manors of Wootton, Whitley and Preston (two manors carried the latter name meaning the estate of the priests).[38] It has been suggested that the southern parts of Preston Bagot and Kington, which are on high ground, were once wooded; Austy Wood (the later medieval wood of *Halestowe*) is also on high ground.[39] At the beginning of the eighth century, therefore, the territory had a variety of natural resources, with woodland apparently confined mainly to higher ground.

The charter of 963 dealing with Aspley and the unidentified *Teodeces leage* can be usefully considered together with that for Oldberrow. The latter, attributed to the year 709, is regarded as a forgery, but is thought nonetheless to incorporate boundaries genuinely dating to the period 840-52.[40] Some points on the boundary appear to match certain of those in the bounds of Aspley and *Teodeces leage*. An attempt has been made to identify the various boundary points with modern topographical features, but this is admittedly tenuous.[41] However, the boundary clauses show that, when they were written, the lands to which they referred were not dense, overgrown, impenetrable woodland but places whose boundaries could be perambulated and recorded, *inter alia*, by reference to streams, a spring, marshy ground, roads, pools, a valley, a barrow, five oak trees, a smooth meadow and the edge of a wood. It has been suggested that the wood was on the boundary of Oldberrow and Ullenhall.[42] Woods in this area were distinct features in a varied countryside. One of the roads mentioned was called *scir holtes weg*, which appears to include the Old English *holt*, a type of wood.[43] In 1410 land called *Shyrewolt* was described as lying near the highway from Brown's Green in the south of Tanworth-in-Arden.[44] A more precise location has been suggested in fields called Sharrows Hill and Shearings Hill in the tithe award (see Fig. 58).[45]

Evidence relating to the ninth and tenth centuries does not necessarily reflect the position in earlier centuries. The evidence from Nuthurst, a few miles to the north, suggests that there might have been rather more woodland c.700. In spite of, or because of, its woodland, Nuthurst was an economically valuable place by c.700. A century before the Norman Conquest the area around Oldberrow and Tanworth-in-Arden might not have been so very different in its topography from the later medieval period, subject to variations in the proportions of agricultural land cultivated and used as pasture. From the scanty evidence for north and west Warwickshire it is reasonable to suppose that there could have been at least as much woodland in the ninth and tenth centuries as there was at the time of the Domesday survey. The presence of a wood in Alveston suggests that in the Avon valley there was more woodland in the tenth century than in the later medieval period. Was there also more woodland in south and east Warwickshire during the early medieval period and, if so, how much more? Can the evidence of place-names supplement that of charters?

Place-names as topographical evidence

Place-names have been used by historians for two distinct, but related, purposes. Much has been written about them as evidence for the political and social process whereby Old English became the language of the inhabitants of the country which became known as England. New thinking about this process, outlined earlier in this chapter, has influenced the interpretation of place-names, particularly those containing habitative elements.[46] It has also ensured that the search for a relationship between place-names and the chronology of anglicization has remained an important theme in place-name studies. This theme has influenced the interpretation of place-names as topographical evidence.

Place-names have been used as evidence of physical settlement in both its wider and narrower senses, the use of the land and a site of habitation.[47] As dwellings accompany the exploitation of natural resources and affect the natural topography, the two meanings of the word are inextricably linked. However, studies of topographical place-names have been dominated by an interest in habitation sites to the point where, until relatively recently, the significance of place-names in relation to natural topography was neglected.[48] Topographical place-name studies have still not assimilated fully recent developments in archæological research and interpretation. In some cases sound philological evidence has been set aside in favour of certain preconceptions about early medieval topography which the place-names themselves ought to have brought into question; an example is given below in relation to the name *Dercet*.

For much of its course the debate about the significance of English place-names was influenced by the belief that large numbers of immigrants from the Germanic-speaking areas of northern Europe settled in Britain in the fifth and sixth centuries and that the successive stages of their settlement were reflected in different types of place-name. This belief is at odds with the more recent claim that the numbers of Germanic immigrants were small and that Old English was the language of socially and politically dominant groups of people which was adopted by native British speakers in a period of social and political change. For many decades scholars thought that habitative names ending in -*ingas*, and -*ingaham*, names referring to pagan worship and names containing certain personal names marked the earliest English settlements. When the location of pagan burials was used to discredit this theory it was suggested that some types of topographical place-name might well have been those most commonly used by the earliest settlers. The assumption that characteristic types of place-name marked immigrant settlements was not questioned until very recently. However, the concept of relative chronology in place-names persists in relation to allegedly later phases of place-name formation. In particular it is considered that the elements *leah* and *tun* were not common in place-name formation until a relatively late date.[49] This argument will be considered in the discussion about the place-name *leah* later in this chapter.

Place-names which preserve Latin or British elements, or contain Old English words for British-speaking people, are now accepted as evidence that there must have been coexistence of people who spoke British and those who spoke English.[50] In Warwickshire several river names - Avon, Leam, Itchen, Alne, Arrow, Anker, Tame and Cole - are in all probability pre-English.[51] Coundon is thought to contain such a name.[52] The two places called Exhall, one by Alcester and one by Coventry, include the British word for church (*ecles*).[53] Chadshunt retains the Latin *funta*, 'spring'.[54] Walcote in Grandborough and Walcote in Haselor may mark settlements of British-speaking people.[55]

Three recorded place-names are thought to include the British word for a wood, *ceto*. Two of them, Dassett in south Warwickshire and Dosthill in the north, have medieval forms (*Dercet*) consistent with a derivation from British words meaning oak wood. This derivation was accepted only after other research suggested the presence of early medieval woodland in parts of south and east Warwickshire.[56] The name of the wood associated with Binley called *munechet* also seems to have included *ceto*, but the name did not survive beyond the medieval period.[57]

The relative scarcity of British place-names is now thought to have been a consequence of social and political change, for the archaeological evidence of Germanic culture in Warwickshire is confined to relatively small numbers of burials in accordance with Anglo-Saxon customs.[58] The surviving pre-English place-names indicate co-existence and therefore allow for a degree of continuity in settlement and use of the land.[59]

The interpretation of Old English topographical place-names is fraught with difficulty. Crucial to their significance for the early medieval countryside is an appreciation of when and how they were formed and their subsequent development. When a description of a topographical feature becomes a permanent place-name it loses its contemporary relevance, because the feature which the name originally described may change or disappear so that the name becomes an anachronism.

Both major and minor topographical place-names must have originated in the same way, as descriptions of a place. The problem lies in determining their chronologies. This is difficult even for major place-names. The first surviving record of most of them is in Domesday Book, but enough appear in pre-Conquest records for early medieval origins to

be postulated for most major place-names.[60] For the mass of minor place-names and field-names which first appeared in post-Conquest documents it is much more difficult to suggest a date of origin. It has even been suggested that, as a rule, they should be regarded as later in origin than major place-names.[61] However, early medieval records include examples of minor place-names which persisted as well as of some major place-names which disappeared. The difficulties encountered in trying to match early medieval charter boundaries, or even later medieval field-names, to modern maps,[62] suggest that minor place-names were more prone to disappear than major place-names. However, enough survived for it to be arguable that a minor place-name containing a distinctively Old English element is early medieval in origin. Indeed, the names of some later medieval furlongs which contain Old English habitative elements have been used as evidence of early medieval settlement.[63] This leaves open the question of when in that period particular names, or types of name, were formed. Moreover, if a word was used in place-names over several centuries it might have changed its meaning during that period. This is thought to be the case with -*tun* (usually modern -ton), applied to both a small farmstead and a large territory.[64]

When a topographical feature gives its name to a nearby dwelling or group of dwellings the potential for confusion is even greater, for the place-name may have followed the inhabitants if they moved the site of their dwellings. Archaeology has shown that the phenomenon known as settlement shift was prevalent throughout the medieval period.[65] The name of a settlement site may also become attached to the whole of a territory controlled by the inhabitants of that site. It is also conceivable that some British place-names were translated into English, having become anachronisms even before the English name was formed.[66]

Place-names do not necessarily mark settlement sites. They may refer to landmarks alongside routes, or to topographical features which were familiar because they were tilled or grazed or because they adjoined fields, pastures, meadows and woods.

The few surviving early medieval charters illustrate the difference nicely. They show that some place-names attached to settlements or settlement areas, such as Shottery, Nuthurst and Wootton, have persisted from the early eighth century to the present day. They do not indicate whether *billes leah* referred to an extant topographical feature called a *leah* or whether it had already achieved the status of the place-name Billesley. Some of the boundary points in the charter for Aspley and *Teodeces leage* may have been contemporary descriptions, others minor place-names which were already centuries old in the tenth century. As already noted, few of these boundary points can be traced in modern minor place-names. This may indicate that they described actual features which have since disappeared, but could also be a consequence of changes in landholding arrangements. Many minor names from the later medieval period have also disappeared.

It is possible, therefore, that a name associated with woodland ceased to refer to a wood and became attached to a place, inhabited or otherwise, as early as the seventh century. This may diminish the value of topographical place-names, but it does not render them useless. Whether a place-name recorded in the medieval period denotes an extant wood or marks the site of a former wood, it says something about the history of the countryside. It shows that, when the name was formed, the place was woodland which was known and accessible and differentiated by the local inhabitants from surrounding land or from other areas of woodland. If the name refers to a site of former woodland it testifies to loss of woodland. The problem then becomes one of chronology.

There is, however, a further problem. Despite careful research into the "vast and subtle topographical vocabulary" of Old English, the meanings of several words remain uncertain.[67] Of no words is this more true than those associated with woodland.[68] This will be apparent in the ensuing discussion about the contribution of place-names, major and minor, to a history of woodland in Warwickshire in the early medieval period. First amongst them, in number and in the significance attached to them by historians, are place-names which include the element *leah*.

Place-names including *leah*

Much has been written about the topographical significance of place-names ending in *leah*, but on the whole discussion has not kept pace with the changes in thinking about early medieval settlement. When that thinking is applied to both major and minor place-names in Warwickshire it raises very interesting possibilities.

The place-name element *leah* has often been used as evidence of settlement in wooded areas in the early medieval period. Place-names ending in *leah* have been held to indicate woodland clearings which Anglo-Saxon immigrants made for their settlements.[69] This view has influenced place-name studies in the past and still serves to encourage the presumption of a habitative sense, whereas the names may have originated simply as a description of an area of land rather than the site of dwellings.

The Old English word has been translated as "forest, wood, glade, clearing", later "pasture, meadow". It is believed to be related to a word meaning light, hence the meaning "glade" or "clearing" which is supported by some documents in which *leah* is regarded as the equivalent of a field. The evidence which has been used to support the meaning wood is capable of other interpretations. Where *leah* was used in the name of a place which was described as wooded in the eighth century the name need not have come from the wood but from some other feature associated with the wood. Eighth-century woods called *leah* might not have been woods two or three centuries earlier. Despite this possibility, the meaning "clearing" has been deemed inappropriate for places in areas where very few examples of names including *leah* occur and where there is thought to have been little woodland to be cleared, and in such areas of presumed open country the meaning "wood" is preferred.[70]

It has been suggested that in areas where the word occurs frequently, as in parts of north Warwickshire, such place-names "may contain the word in a quasi-habitative sense, used by English speakers to denote sites where settlements in forest clearings were flourishing when they arrived." This suggestion sits uneasily with the statement that "forest" was probably the earlier sense of *leah* in place-names.[71] Nor does it address the practical difficulties of having two contrasting meanings - wood and clearing - for the same word at the same time. That the word generally might have changed its meaning is wholly credible and a common phenomenon in the English language. That it had two separate meanings concurrently in the same region is less so. What happened in areas which were neither open countryside nor heavily wooded? How did people interpret *leah* when they read it in bounds attached to a charter granting land with which they were not familiar? Which meaning prevailed and where was the linguistic boundary drawn? It is unsatisfactory to leave the choice of meaning to the local historian.[72] Specifically, the translation of Ratley in Warwickshire as 'red wood' on the basis that it is desirable to find a meaning other than 'clearing' for isolated names including *leah*[73] overlooks the fact that some of Ratley's woodland was cleared in the twelfth century.[74] There could have been clearings in Ratley centuries earlier. Moreover, apart from the fact that English woods are not red, one of the most striking features of the modern topography of Ratley is the reddish colour of the ploughed soil, which would have been exposed in a clearing.

It has been suggested that *leah* was a particular type of woodland, namely wood pasture. A translation of wood pasture reconciles the apparently divergent meanings of *leah*.[75] As discussed in Chapters One and Four, wood pasture has less tree cover than a wood which is managed principally to produce wood. Animals must either be able to graze freely amongst the trees or they must be confined to clearings. Wood pasture is therefore open and light, at least in parts, and fits the meaning which has been traditionally attached to *leah*. The meaning also fills a gap in place-name elements which are derived from topographical features; at present (apart from *denn*, which is confined to parts of south-east England[76]) these elements contain no word specifically for wood pasture. Wood pasture could have existed in countryside which was predominantly arable as well as in areas with a much greater proportion of woodland and pasture, so there is no need to suggest different meanings for *leah* according to regional geography. Its prevalence in north and west Warwickshire could be explained by the strong tradition of wood pasture there. However, the proponent of this argument subsequently reverted to the duality of meaning discussed above, possibly in recognition of the weakness in the argument which is described below.[77]

Wood pasture is generally regarded as a practice which dated at least from the early medieval period.[78] However, records of it, which because of the paucity of early medieval documents are available mainly from the later medieval period, are not confined to places or woods with names including *leah*. In Stoneleigh, for example, there was pasture in the great wood of Westwood as well as in the woods of *Crattele*, *Armele* and *Dolle*. The Frith of

Kenilworth was wood pasture, but Kenilworth had no names ending in *leah*. Chapter Three provides numerous other examples to illustrate the point. Later in this chapter it will be argued that the wolds of Warwickshire were wood pasture. If *leah* was the Old English word for wood pasture it has to be asked why the word was not used to name these areas of woodland. It could be argued instead that pasture was the norm in early medieval woodland and did not require a special term. What then was the distinctive characteristic of a *leah* which gave it that name rather than one of the other Old English words for woodland? Why was it so common, and yet not universal?

It has been pointed out that, rather than being the result of colonising activities by the Anglo-Saxons, a "clearing can arise as easily by the retreat of agriculture, by the surrounding fields becoming woodland".[79] This possibility certainly fits the archæological and topographical evidence for the early medieval period which suggests continuity of land use in some areas, probably accompanied by less intensive agriculture, some retreat from marginal land and changes in some sites of habitation. Perhaps *leah* should be associated with secondary woodland in the process of formation, the fifth- or sixth-century equivalent of the "set-aside" agricultural policies of the 1990's. If circumstances changed before the tree cover became dense, this land might have been the first to be converted to agriculture once more. This theory might also help to explain why *leah*, which is so common in major place-names, is not so prominent amongst place-names which were first recorded before 730.[80] Settlements associated with marginal land were unlikely to serve as administrative or ecclesiastical centres and less likely to be coveted as gifts by powerful churches; hence there were fewer reasons for them to appear in the historical record at an early date.

Some of the words compounded with *leah* indicate open, even cultivated, land rather than woodland, referring to crops such as barley, wheat and flax.[81] The occurrence of *leah* in minor place-names in Warwickshire also lends support to a meaning associated with open land or clearings. In studying the records of later medieval woods in the county it is remarkable how few of them had names ending in *leah*. There were woods called simply *lea* or *lee*, without the suffix 'wood', in Hampton-in-Arden, Sutton Coldfield, Nuneaton, and Canley in Stoneleigh. *leah* was compounded with other words to name woods called *Le Thacheley* in Corley, *Aclea* or *Ocle* in Bishop's Tachbrook, *Bradlegh* in Offchurch, and *Armele*, *Crattele* and *Dolle* in Stoneleigh; none of these names had the suffix 'wood' during the later medieval period, although Oakley Wood acquired it in the sixteenth century.[82] Many names including *leah* became major place-names; many minor place-names ending in ley appear in later medieval documents without obviously referring to woods. Was this because *leah* as a word for woodland was replaced in later centuries by the word 'wood' and survived in place-names, major and minor, only where it was transferred to settlements or other features? Or did *leah* refer from the outset to features which were associated with woodland rather than to woods themselves? The few woods incorporating *leah* but without any suffix might have been originally open land by woodland whence encroaching

secondary woodland absorbed the *leah* and turned it into a wood. In Stoneleigh, for example, it can be suggested that *Armele*, *Crattele* and *Dolle*, which were all on the southern or south-eastern side of Westwood, between it and the later medieval village, had been open land on to which Westwood's trees spread at some time during the early medieval period.

Until the meaning of *leah* can be resolved by further philological research it does little to advance our knowledge of how much woodland there was at different times during the period c.500 to 1086. A clearing implies the disappearance of woodland, encroachment of secondary woodland the opposite. Neither interpretation allows for the stability of woodland. The absence of place-names ending in *leah* from a region may indicate that the amount of woodland in that region remained static during the period when *leah* was used to form place-names. *leah* therefore cannot be regarded as the only indicator of woodland or former woodland and is an unreliable guide to its overall distribution. For north and west Warwickshire it is therefore far from satisfactory for the purposes of this study to conclude simply that *leah* was associated with woodland. The existence of woodland in north and west Warwickshire is not in dispute. However, the theory that it referred in some way to changes in amounts of woodland at least matches current thinking about early medieval settlement history. It also links *leah* with land use rather than with the establishment of settlement sites.

For south and east Warwickshire the association of *leah* with woodland is more rewarding. Alongside the statement that place-names associated with woodland, such as *leah*, are "thick on the map" in north and west Warwickshire it has been accepted that the south and east of the county has "few or no such place-names".[83] This belief is true only insofar as major place-names are concerned. Loxley and Ratley, the two examples, are both on the fringes of the area. The picture is different when minor place-names are taken into account. Figure 78 and Appendix 3 set out the evidence for place-names which probably include *leah* in south and east Warwickshire. Some of the names have been taken from modern sources and may not include *leah*. For example, Hockley in Milverton may be analogous with Hockley in Lapworth further north; the medieval forms of the latter show that it does not derive from *leah*.[84] It could be suggested that all the names in south and east Warwickshire use *leah* in the later sense of "meadow, pasture", but, as at least three of them - *Ocle* in Bishop's Tachbrook, *Bradlegh* in Offchurch, and *Yerdeley* in Long Compton - were attached to later medieval woods, such a suggestion would be perverse. Regardless of the dichotomy in the other two meanings of *leah* - and there is no reason why wood pasture or secondary woodland should not have developed south of the Avon to allow less intensive use of land - the conclusion must be that there was more woodland in that region in the early medieval period than there was in the later medieval period. Even so *leah*, whether or not it is associated specifically with either the retreat or expansion of woodland, cannot give the full picture, for it says nothing about the size of the wood with which it is associated.

Figure 78: Minor place-names probably including leah and hyrst south and east of the river Avon

Similar drawbacks apply to other minor place-names. Nonetheless, for an area which has been characterised by a lack of woodland, the evidence of these minor place-names is important.

Place-names including *hyrst*

As with *leah*, the meanings of *hyrst* - modern hurst - are ambiguous. It has been translated as both hillock and wood. "Wooded hill" may be the "best rendering" in the circumstances,[85] but there is no certainty in this compromise. *Hyrst* has not attracted the same level of debate as *leah*, because it does not have the meaning "clearing" and the corresponding connotation with settlement and because it occurs much less frequently in major place-names. There is a well authenticated early example of it in a major place-name in Warwickshire. Nuthurst was used as a place-name in a charter dated to the decade 699-709. As already pointed out, there were presumably other hursts in the neighbourhood when the name was formed; other compounds including hurst are documented for the parish in the later medieval period. In minor place-names *hyrst* is potentially as old as in major place-names.

Hyrst occurs in minor place-names in north and west Warwickshire. In Sutton Coldfield, for example, Echelhurst, Brockhurst, Ramshurst and Langleyhurst, when added to minor names in *leah* - Wyndley, Roughley, Langley, Walmley, *Wytele*, *la Lee*, *Ravennsley* and *Wylnerdesleye* - suggest a combination of hilly areas of woodland and pieces of open land nearby, each with a distinct identity.[86] *Hyrst* also occurs in minor place-names in south and east Warwickshire. If *hyrst* can indeed be taken to denote woodland, then it provides further evidence of woodland south and east of the Avon in the early medieval period. The evidence is shown in Figure 78 and Appendix 4. The places which had hursts were widely dispersed. In Stretton-on-Dunsmore the name Burnthurst was attached to a wood which survived into the modern period.

The wolds of Warwickshire

Uncertainty about the meaning of *wald* and its variant *wold* in place-names is related to the chronology of individual names. All the examples in Warwickshire come from later medieval sources. However, it is widely accepted that major place-names are much older than the earliest surviving records of them, and this study has argued that the same applies to minor place-names which incorporate Old English elements. A study of *wald* and *wold* strengthens this argument.

The topographical significance of *wald* and *wold* has been discussed on various occasions. In relation to Kent, west Cambridgeshire, Yorkshire, Lincolnshire, Leicestershire and the Cotswolds it has been suggested with greater or lesser conviction that *wold* signified an extensive upland area which had been wooded at some time in the early medieval period but which had been largely or wholly cleared of woodland subsequently, certainly by the later medieval period if not centuries earlier.[87] More recently, it has been argued that in Northamptonshire, Leicestershire, and Warwickshire "*wald* implied countryside which was ...distinguished by small isolated stands" of woodland and that regional names for densely wooded tracts used *wudu* instead of *wald*.[88]

All studies have addressed the fact that *wold*, at least from c.1205, has another meaning - open upland.[89] This is generally regarded as a secondary meaning which arose from topographical changes. As large areas of woodland disappeared people came to associate *wald* or *wold* with a bare, hilly terrain better suited to pasture than to arable land. The Weald of Kent was a notable exception. Some scholars argue that, once the meaning changed, *wold* was then applied to other tracts of upland pasture, but others maintain that *wold* was always associated with land which had been wooded when the name was first given.[90] For example, it has been stated unquestioningly that *wold* used as a minor place-name in Yorkshire "designates one community's share of the upland pasture" and that such minor place-names "are not relevant to any discussion of woodland".[91] In contrast, there has been no hesitation in asserting that a medieval field-name (Moor Old) in Pendock, Worcestershire, "preserved the memory of former woodland".[92] A similar line has been taken in relation to field-names including wold in Northamptonshire in relation to research into the origins of open fields there.[93] The alternative spellings have not been linked to any difference in meaning during the medieval period, but *wold* has become the modern form and now carries the meaning open, upland pasture.

No area of Warwickshire has acquired the title of the Warwickshire Wolds, but Sir William Dugdale certainly saw a parallel with wolds elsewhere when he wrote under Coton in Churchover, which had been called *Coton super Waldas* in the thirteenth century, of "these hilly parts being then, and after, called Wouldes as many other of that kind are to this day in other Counties".[94] In the only published study of wolds in Warwickshire the high altitude noted by Dugdale has been emphasised by describing them as "the upland wolds which form the eastern fringe of Warwickshire".[95]

There were nearly forty places in Warwickshire which had a wold. They are listed in Appendix 5. This number is much larger than has been recognised hitherto. Moreover, contrary to the impression given in the published study,[96] there are later medieval records for all except two of them. Some wolds, usually corrupted to holt instead of wold, have survived into the modern period and serve as place-names today; Wolvey Wolds, Southam Holt, Napton Holt, Itchington Holt and Kington Holt are all marked on modern Ordnance Survey maps.[97]

The geographical distribution of Warwickshire's wolds is remarkable. It is wider than has been thought hitherto, even taking into account the recent interpretation of the minor place-name wold at Compton Verney as meaning former woodland.[98] Wolds occur not only along the north-eastern fringe of the county but also south of the river Avon, singly and in clusters, and there are a few examples in the Avon valley north of the river (Fig. 79).

N

0 _____ 10 kilometres
0 _____ 5 miles

Newton
Regis
Seckington
Austrey
Shuttington
Tamworth
Polesworth
Lea
Marston
Grendon
Middleton
Kingsbury
Baddesley
Ensor
Mere-
vale
Atherstone
Baxterley
Sutton
Coldfield
Wishaw
Bentley
Mancetter
Caldecote
Oldbury
Hartshill
Weddington
Minworth
Curdworth
Nether
Whitacre
Over
Whitacre
Ansley
Nuneaton
Stretton Baskerville
Copston
Magna
Birmingham
Aston
Coleshill
Shustoke
Arley
Astley
Bedworth
Bulkington
Wolvey
Wibtoft
Edgbaston
Sheldon
Maxstoke
Fillongley
Corley
Exhall
Shilton
Withybrook
Willey
Little
Packington
Great
Packington
Bickenhill
Meriden
Allesley
Foleshill
Walsgrave
on
Sowe
Anstey
Monks Kirby
Elmdon
Hampton
-in-Arden
Solihull
Barston
Berkswell
Coventry
Wyken
Combefields
Harborough
Magna
Churchover
Knowle
Balsall
Stoneleigh
Stoke
Binley
Brinklow
Kings
Newnham
Newbold
on
Avon
Avon
Packwood
Willenhall
Brandon & Bretford
Church
Lawford
Long
Lawford
Clifton
upon Dunsmore
Tanworth
Nuthurst
Baddesley
Clinton
Honiley
Kenilworth
Baginton
Ryton on
Dunsmore
Wolston
Rugby
Hillmorton
Bushwood
Beaudesert
Lapworth
Preston
Bagot
Wroxall
Haseley
Beausale
Leek
Wootton
Ashow
Stretton on Dunsmore
Bourton
on
Dunsmore
Dunchurch
Bilton
Ipsley
Studley
Rowington
Shrewley
Warwick St. Mary
Milverton
Lillington
Cubbington
Wappenbury
Weston
under
Wetherley
Princethorpe
Frankton
Willoughby
Morton
Bagot
Hatton
Budbrooke
Hunningham
Marton
Birdingbury
Leamington
Hastings
Grandborough
Sambourne
Spernall
Claverdon
Leamington
Spa
Offchurch
Long
Itchington
Wolfhampcote
Coughton
Alne
Wootton
Wawen
Norton
Lindsey
Warwick
St. Nicholas
Radford
Semele
Stockton
Lower
Shuckburgh
Alcester
Wolverton
Sherbourne
Barford
Whitnash
Ufton
Southam
Napton
on the Hill
Upper
Shuckburgh
Kinwarton
Haselor
Bearley
Snitterfield
Fulbrook
Bishop's
Tachbrook
Harbury
Ladbroke
Radbourne
Priors
Marston
Arrow
Oversley
Billesley
Stratford
on Avon
Hampton Lucy
Avon
Wasperton
Newbold
Pacey
Chesterton
and
Kingston
Chapel
Ascot
Bishops
Itchington
Priors Hardwick
Weethley
Exhall
Temple
Grafton
Binton
Old Stratford
Charlecote
Moreton
Morrell
Lighthorne
Gaydon
Fenny
Compton
Wills Pastures
Stoneton
Hodnell
Wixford
Salford
Priors
Bidford
Alveston
Wellesbourne
Hastings
Compton
Verney
Chadshunt
Burton
Dassett
Wormleighton
Watergall
Bickmarsh
Milcote
Loxley
Combrook
Kineton
Avon
Dassett
Mollington
Atherstone-
on-Stour
Wellesbourne
Mountford
Butlers
Marston
Radway
Warmington
Shotteswell
Whitchurch
Stour
Ettington
Oxhill
Ratley
and Upton
Halford
Tysoe
Pillerton Hersey
Pillerton Priors
Ilmington
Idlicote
Whatcote
Honington
Compton
Wynyates
Stretton
on Fosse
Barcheston
Brailes
Sutton
under Brailes
Burmington
Wolford
Cherrington
Whichford
Barton on
the Heath
Long
Compton
Little Compton

• Places with wolds

Figure 79: Warwickshire's wolds

158

The wolds which have been traced through surviving minor place-names on modern maps were usually on or near parish or township boundaries and often adjoined other wolds. Superficially, they seem to belong to the classification of minor names denoting a share of upland pasture. Indeed, several of them, *Chaddesdon Wold* and *Gaydon Wold* in 1495,[99] Kingston Wold in 1310,[100] *Walda* in Napton in 1411,[101] and *le Waud* in Southam in 1262 alias *Southam Wolde* in 1481,[102] were specifically described as common pasture in medieval documents. Does this indicate the secondary meaning of upland pasture or was it a legacy of former areas of wood pasture? Although there is no early medieval record of the word *wald* or *wold* in Warwickshire, there is indirect evidence that, in this county as elsewhere, minor place-names were formed from *wold* in the early medieval period, before the change in meaning to upland pasture.

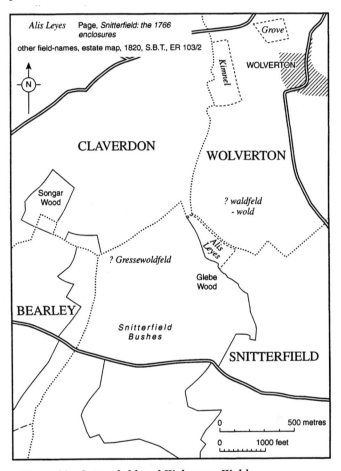

Figure 80: *Snitterfield and Wolverton Wolds*

Tenth-century charters with boundary clauses survive for several places, Southam, Radbourne, Ladbroke, Kineton and Wormleighton, in which the minor name *wald* or *wold* was recorded in the later medieval period, but neither element appears in the boundary clauses.[103] However, the eighth-century charter conveying land in Wootton Wawen is unique to the west midlands in using the Latin *saltibus* (upland woods) in its list of appurtenances.[104] The noun *saltus* has been found in a few Kentish charters in which it refers to the Weald of Kent.[105] In addition, the place-name *Kingemewold* in Kineton suggests an early medieval origin because in it *wold* was compounded with the Old English *haeme*, meaning "people of".[106]

The parts of Wootton Wawen which seem to have been covered by the charter had upland woods in the later medieval period as well as in the eighth century.[107] These woods were not far from the wolds of Snitterfield and Wolverton. From the location of later field-names, the wolds of these two parishes were arguably adjacent to each other in the thirteenth century. In Chapter Three it is argued that the northern part of the modern Snitterfield Bushes was the medieval field called *Gressewoldfeld*. Wolverton's medieval *Waldfeld* included a furlong called *kemenhul*; in 1820 closes called Kimnel were near to the boundary with Langley, suggesting that the field occupied the south-western part of the parish, by Snitterfield.[108] There is no later medieval record of woodland on the wolds of Snitterfield and Wolverton.

It can be suggested from this evidence that the distribution of wolds in Warwickshire reflects the early disappearance of woodland before use of the word *wald* or *wold* gave way to *wudu*. It has been suggested independently of this study that the use of *wald* was influenced by chronology rather than by meaning.[109] This argument would explain why forests and districts elsewhere in England which were well wooded in the later medieval period carried names including wood rather than wold.[110] (The minor place-name *Sherwold* in Tanworth-in-Arden seems at first sight to be an isolated example of *wold* in the north of the county, but it appears as *Shyrewolt* in 1410 and is presumably derived from the *scir holtes weg* of a tenth-century charter, showing that the Old English word was *holt* not *wold*.[111])

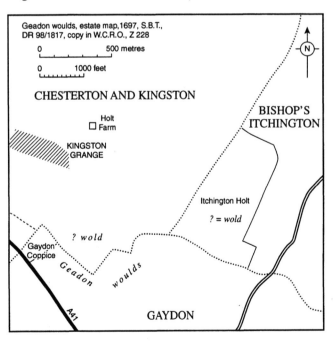

Figure 81: *Bishop's Itchington, Kingston and Gaydon Wolds*

The local topography of Warwickshire's wolds may present a conclusive argument for their history. Whilst the secondary meaning of *wald* or *wold* is invariably given as upland open space or pasture, the primary meaning was not necessarily restricted to woodland which was on high ground.[112] This was noted in a study covering wolds in Warwickshire but was not recognised as pertinent to the county because of an assumption that all Warwickshire's wolds were uplands.[113]

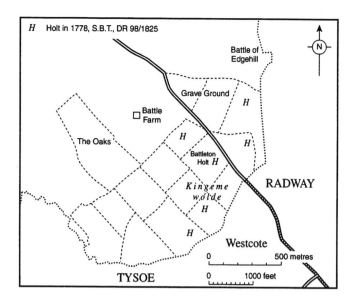

H Holt in 1778, S.B.T., DR 98/1825

Battle of
Edgehill

Grave Ground

□ Battle
   Farm

The Oaks

H

H

Battleton
Holt *H*

*Kingeme
wolde*
H

H

RADWAY

Westcote

0   500 metres

0   1000 feet

TYSOE

Figure 82: Kineton's wold

None of Warwickshire's wolds appears to have been on low ground, but some were not upland areas in relation to the surrounding terrain. The wolds of Snitterfield, Budbrooke and Hatton were all on higher ground but not dramatically so. Itchington Holt, Kingston Holt and Gaydon Wolds were similarly situated. One could give these places the benefit of the doubt, as with Southam Holt, which lies on a small ridge, but the nearby Ladbroke and Napton Holts are relatively level land overlooked by the steep Napton Hill to the north and the hills of Priors Marston to the east. Wibtoft's wold does not stand out from the surrounding terrain. By no stretch of the imagination can Kineton's wold, by the site of the battle of Edge Hill (commemorated in Battleton Holt) in the plain below the steep escarpment of Edge Hill, be described as upland. On philological and topographical grounds the evidence for Kineton's wold having been woodland at some time in the early medieval period is very strong. The evidence for the origins of the other wolds is inconclusive, but it certainly does not allow them to be dismissed unquestioningly as upland pasture with no tradition of former woodland.

If Warwickshire's minor place-names of wold and holt date from the centuries before c.800 they almost certainly mark the sites of former woods. Such woodland must have disappeared during the early medieval period, although some of it may have remained to be called wood rather than wold. There are records of later medieval woodland in several places which also had wolds - Hatton, Budbrooke and Pailton.[114] Southam had *silva* in 1086 and both a *Waldwei* and a *Wudewei* at the beginning of the thirteenth century.[115]

There were several other later medieval woodways in places with no known woodland at the time - Farnborough, Grandborough, Hodnell, Napton, Newton and also Cawston and Thurslaston in Clifton-on-Dunsmore, Priors Marston, Shuckburgh, Willoughby, Wolfhampcote and Withybrook (the latter also had a *would weye*).[116] It has been claimed that a medieval *Wodewei* led from the medieval village of Stretton-on-Fosse to an area called Hurst Quarter and must therefore refer to a period when the Hurst was woodland,

although other examples of such a road-name in Worcestershire and Oxfordshire have been related to regional rather than local links.[117] Did the roads called *Wodewei* in Warwickshire once lead to local woodland which remained after the noun *wald* was replaced by *wudu* but which disappeared a few centuries later?

One of Warwickshire's wolds belonged to a township for which there is no record of a wood or grove in the later medieval period, but where the lord of the manor collected pannage from the tenants. The sum of eighteen pence was collected in the manor of Chadshunt, belonging to the bishop of Coventry and Lichfield, in 1305-6.[118] This sum might have been rendered in respect of acorns from oak trees scattered in hedges, or even a few odd trees on Chadshunt Wold itself, but pannage is an ancient customary payment which is likely to reflect a time when trees were more plentiful in Chadshunt.

Was the disappearance of trees from the wolds linked to the formation of groves? As grazing or clearance threatened the trees of the wolds, did lords enclose portions of the woodland as groves? There is no strong evidence to suggest that this was the origin of the groves of south and east Warwickshire. No grove whose exact site can be suggested adjoins a known wold. Although groves and wolds could have coexisted, they are seldom found in the same townships. Ufton and Budbrooke (the latter north-west of the Avon) are exceptions. In 1590 the wold of Budbrooke was in the same area as some groves and near to Grove Park. The absence of any obvious relationship between wolds and groves means that it was possible that they represented separate traditions of woodland management which pre-dated the disappearance of trees from the wolds.

Woodland disappeared from the wolds in unknown circumstances. It has been suggested that the Scandinavian place-names characteristic of wolds in some other counties "may represent new colonization between the end of the ninth century and the eleventh" accompanied by "the development of a mature common-field system in the vales" below the wolds.[119] In the neighbouring county of Northamptonshire the reorganisation of fields attached to various settlements seems to have started in the ninth century.[120] It is therefore reasonable to suggest a similar chronology for the development of Warwickshire's open fields and for the transformation of wooded wolds into woodless pastures. The possibility of a link between these changes in rural topography is discussed in the following chapter.

Warwickshire's later medieval wolds and modern holts are crucial to the history of early medieval woodland in the county. Potentially the names are as old as the adoption of the Old English language in this part of England. The evidence for the early medieval origins of Kineton's wold allows similar origins to be proposed for the other wolds. If they were indeed woodland at one stage, they put the topographical history of south and east Warwickshire into a new perspective.

160

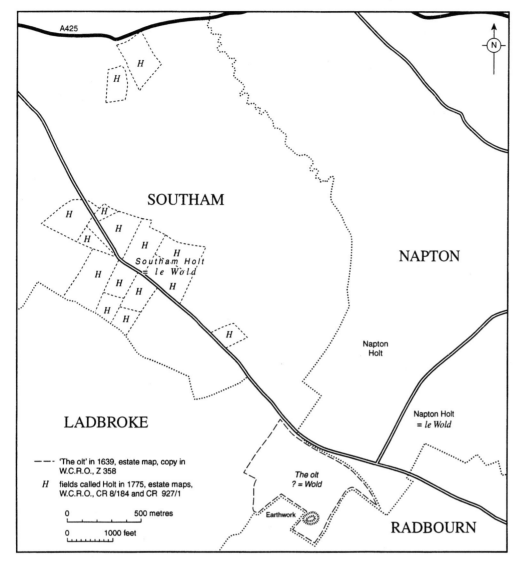

Figure 83: Southam, Ladbroke and Napton Wolds

Key on map:

— · — 'The olt' in 1639, estate map, copy in W.C.R.O., Z 358

H   fields called Holt in 1775, estate maps, W.C.R.O., CR 8/184 and CR 927/1

0   500 metres

0   1000 feet

This region would have had large areas of woodland up to perhaps c.800, for the wolds extend over many acres on modern maps. For example, field-names in Southam containing the word holt covered about two hundred acres and their disposition suggests that Southam's wold was once more extensive. When agreement was reached on its enclosure in 1620, Southam "Wolde alias Waude ...and of late commonly called by the name of the Olte" was estimated as 560 acres in extent.[121] Southam Holt adjoins Ladbroke Olt, 83 acres in 1639.[122] The woods which can be presumed to have covered them might have resembled in their extent the concentration of woodland on the boundaries of Ryton-on-Dunsmore, Stretton-on-Dunsmore, Wappenbury and Bubbenhall which, as explained in Chapter Two, is suggested by the *silva* of Domesday Book, later medieval records and modern maps.

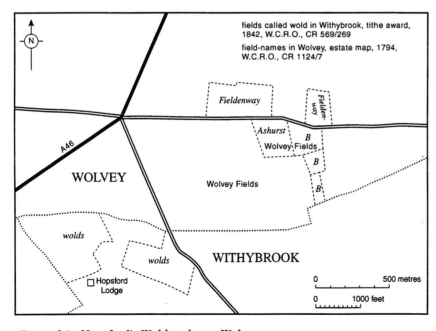

fields called wold in Withybrook, tithe award, 1842, W.C.R.O., CR 569/269

field-names in Wolvey, estate map, 1794, W.C.R.O., CR 1124/7

0   500 metres

0   1000 feet

Figure 84: Hopsford's Wold and west Wolvey

Large as the acreages of the wolds may be, they are less than the estimated thousands of acres of Domesday *silva* attached to many places in north and west Warwickshire. It is therefore reasonable to suggest that even in the early medieval period south and east Warwickshire did not have as much woodland as appears to have existed further north and west. It seems that Warwickshire's wolds were the sites of former woods which were not extensive or concentrated enough to give their name to a region like the wolds of Lincolnshire, Yorkshire or the Cotswolds. Whilst not of regional importance they were nonetheless locally significant.

The existence of wolds is significant not only for the region south of the Avon but also for the north-east of the county, an area largely neglected hitherto in this study because there is so little evidence of woodland there in the later medieval period. It makes plausible the meaning of the place-name Wolvey, the early spellings of which are thought to perpetuate the Old English words for "wolf island" or "wolf enclosure", names which have been described as "surprising" in view of the later absence of woodland from the area.[123] The wolds in and around Wolvey suggest that there could have been plenty of woodland providing suitable habitats for wolves. The position of the wolds on the eastern edge of Wolvey and Withybrook and of fields called holt in Wibtoft and Willey suggest that these places, together with Monks Kirby and Copston Magna, each had a portion of a single area of woodland centred on Cloudesley Bush and covering several hundred acres.

the Avon, for the former region had fewer woods than the latter in the later medieval period.

The minor nature of place-names with the element wold in Warwickshire may explain why their topographical significance has not been appreciated fully hitherto. Some other Old English words for wood are also mainly confined to minor place-names in Warwickshire.

Old English words for wood in minor place-names

There are some Old English words for wood which occur only or mainly in minor place-names and then infrequently. The word frith (Old English *fyrhth* or *fyrhthe*) has usually

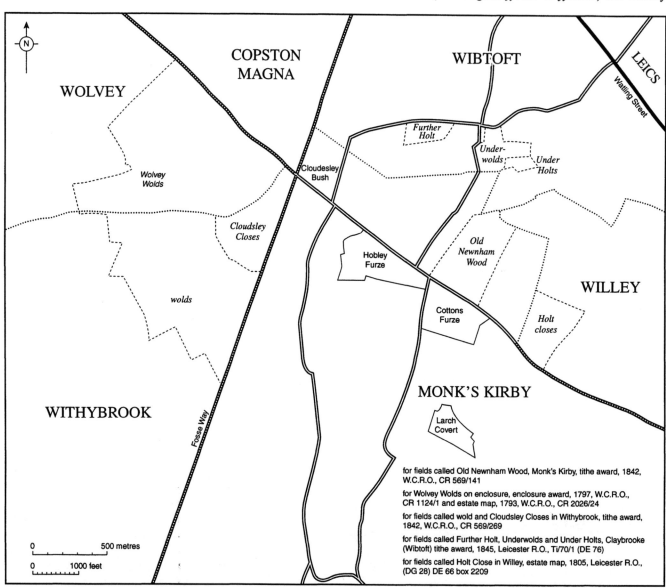

Figure 85: Wolds in Wolvey, Withybrook, Wibtoft and Willey

for fields called Old Newnham Wood, Monk's Kirby, tithe award, 1842, W.C.R.O., CR 569/141

for Wolvey Wolds on enclosure, enclosure award, 1797, W.C.R.O., CR 1124/1 and estate map, 1793, W.C.R.O., CR 2026/24

for fields called wold and Cloudsley Closes in Withybrook, tithe award, 1842, W.C.R.O., CR 569/269

for fields called Further Holt, Underwolds and Under Holts, Claybrooke (Wibtoft) tithe award, 1845, Leicester R.O., Ti/70/1 (DE 76)

for fields called Holt Close in Willey, estate map, 1805, Leicester R.O., (DG 28) DE 66 box 2209

Further west, wolds in the north-western corner of Withybrook parish belonging to the township of Hopsford and the nearby field called Ashurst in Wolvey point to another area of former woodland (Fig. 84). The change from a countryside with plenty of woodland to one which was characterised by open fields and pasture was even more marked in the north-east of the county than south and east of

been translated as wood, but may be better translated as "land overgrown with brushwood, scrub on the edge of forest".[124] The latter translation implies secondary woodland. Scrub could have developed into mature woodland long before woods called Frith were recorded in the later medieval period. Of the eight examples of the name found in Warwickshire, those in Kenilworth and Shrewley were certainly woods; part of Coombe Abbey's Frith was a wood.[125] There is only a modern record of Frith Wood in

Amington (in Tamworth), and only incidental references to the *Frithbrok* on the boundaries of Coundon and Whoberley, *Frid* in Tanworth-in-Arden, *Fyrthe* in Coughton and *frith* in Wolvey.[126] From their names, however, it is reasonable to presume that they referred to woods, or former woods, with a pre-Conquest history.

There seem to have been few shaws (*sceaga* - Old English for 'small wood') in Warwickshire. The major place-name Wishaw probably means willow shaw.[127] Woods called shaw included *Clapshawe* and *Dernshawe* in Dunton in Curdworth, *le Shawe* in Monkspath, *Wisshawe* in Nuneaton and *Rokesleyschawe* in Coleshill.[128] There was a furlong (*cultura*) in Whitley by Wootton Wawen called *le Schawe*.[129]

Holt too is rarely found. It occurs in the *scir holt* of the *Teodeces leage* charter, in *Haselholt* in Preston Bagot, and possibly in Holt in Kingsbury.[130] Its rarity may be a consequence of botanical factors; Warwickshire may have had mixed deciduous woods rather than woods dominated by a single species of tree.

It could be suggested that these words were seldom used because, once wold had fallen out of use, the words wood and grove were found more appropriate to describe Warwickshire's woodland in the early, as well as in the later, medieval period.

graf and Grafton, *wudu* and Wootton

As shown in Chapter Three and Appendix 1, most later medieval woodland was called a wood or a grove. However, few woods and groves gave their names to settlements. In particular these words are rare as the first element in a place-name. A place-name which includes grove or wood therefore points to something very distinctive about that woodland.

The three cases of *Grave* (in Budbrooke, Clopton and Hampton Lucy) were discussed in Chapter Four. There is a single example of Grafton in Warwickshire, in the Avon valley north of the river. Only recently has it been accepted that Grafton may have included the Old English word for grove, rather than another word of similar spelling but different pronunciation meaning pit or trench.[131] The place-name occurs in several other counties, but in no case are there more than two examples in a county. It has been suggested that "these settlements derived special advantages from the grove."[132] In Warwickshire the record of a grove in Shottery or Haselor in the early medieval period and the large number of groves known from later medieval sources imply that the place-name was prompted by more than the mere existence of a grove. Nor is Arden's Grafton unique in the apparent proximity of the later medieval settlement to the site of a grove.[133] Moreover, to use such evidence is also to overlook the possibility of settlement shift. A translation of "farm by the grove" or "grove settlement" is therefore not entirely satisfactory. Rather it might be relevant to relate the name to the management of the territory to which the grove belonged. It could be suggested that most groves formed part of the demesne or home farm, where they were not

exceptional, but that occasionally separate arrangements were made to manage the grove, which then gave its name to a subsidiary farm within a larger territory. The appellative Wootton may have a similar relationship to early medieval territorial organisation.

wudu - "wood" - has been described as "probably the most colourless of Old English terms for a collection of trees".[134] It has been used so commonly in the later medieval and modern periods that of itself it gives no indication of the age of a wood. It is difficult to suggest, for example, when the *Wyldewode* which gave its name to one of Stratford's two fields (recorded in a survey in 1299)[135] lost its trees. Packwood became a major place-name and is also unusual in combining wood with a personal name.[136] The nearby Kingswood and Bushwood were proper names used primarily to describe woods rather than settlements in the later medieval period, although Bushwood included assarts by the end of the thirteenth century and could be regarded as a place-name by then if not earlier.[137] Kingswood and other woods of the same name in Wroxall, Tamworth and Stoneleigh (and from the sixteenth century the Frith of Kenilworth) were primarily woods.[138]

Wootton Wawen, Leek Wootton, Woodcote and Woodlowe are indubitably the names of places rather than of woods. In each of them *wudu* is the first element rather than the last and qualifies another topographical term.[139] The presence of two places called Wootton in a county which is thought to have had many woods requires explanation.

The place-name Wootton combines the Old English *wudu*, earlier *widu*, with *tun*, a very common place-name element meaning variously "an enclosure, farmstead, estate, village"[140] or a settlement "in open country".[141] The form in King Æthelbald's charter of 716-37 referring to Wootton Wawen, *Uuidutuun*, shows this derivation clearly.[142] The compound occurs in thirty-three major settlement names in England,[143] but as yet no study of them has been undertaken.[144] The tentative translation "settlement which performs some function in relation to a wood" has been offered as a hypothesis.[145]

There must have been something noteworthy about the wood(s) of Wootton to prompt the name. The suggestion that settlements called Wootton "had a special function in relation to the wood and its products"[146] seems plausible by analogy with other appellatives referring to the particular feature or product of a dependent settlement within a larger economic unit, such as Barton (barley, corn or demesne farm)[147] or Hardwick (herd farm),[148] or, as suggested above, Grafton (grove farm). For example, the four Woottons in Shropshire were all dependent townships within larger parishes[149] and might have fulfilled a special function within an early medieval territory.

At first sight Wootton Wawen and Leek Wootton do not fit the analogy with the appellatives Barton and Hardwick. They were quite the opposite of minor, dependent settlements. Each had a later medieval church with numerous dependent chapels serving other places.[150] In the case of Wootton Wawen certainly, and in the case of Leek

Wootton probably, the ecclesiastical importance was established in the early medieval period. A central role was a feature of at least three other Woottons in England which were the centres of medieval hundreds.[151]

The minster church at Wootton Wawen served a large *parochia* which is thought to have been approximately co-extensive with the *regio* of the *Stoppingas* named in King Æthelbald's charter. The nature of this *regio*, and of many similar territories, has been explored in recent studies of the origins of Anglo-Saxon kingdoms.[152] The territories have been defined as "distinct polities" or "embryonic kingdoms" in the fifth and sixth centuries. When amalgamated into the larger Anglo-Saxon kingdoms, which were the subject of historical record, they became "typically the land units on which minster churches were set up in the seventh and eighth centuries".[153] Consequently, they can be traced where later medieval parochial links survived. The coalescence of these regions into small kingdoms probably involved both conquest and intermarriage.[154] By the early eighth century the *regio* of the *Stoppingas* was part of the kingdom of the Hwicce, whose territory is thought to have corresponded approximately to the area of the medieval diocese of Worcester.[155] There were probably several stages in the formation of the kingdom.

This political context offers an explanation for the association of the place-name Wootton with known or inferred early medieval territories. Detailed study of the area around Wootton Wawen suggests that Wootton, although it was the site of the minster church, was not the administrative centre of this once independent territory.[156] The status of Leek Wootton in relation to early medieval territories is far from clear, but there is enough evidence to suggest that it too, with its ecclesiastical dependencies, once lay within a larger territory.

Leek Wootton is thought to be the *Optone* which is entered in Domesday Book under the land of the king and immediately before Kenilworth. *Optone* had two priests, who presumably ministered to a large parish.[157] *Optone* contained three hides; the Domesday manors which in the later medieval period were served by the chapels dependent on Leek Wootton church brought the taxable value of that area to twenty-seven and a half hides in 1086.[158] This was only just over half the hidage of the presumed *regio* around Wootton Wawen. Moreover, Leek Wootton itself did not occupy a central position in relation to the places which were linked with it.

In Domesday Book *Optone* and Kenilworth were described as members of the king's manor of Stoneleigh. It could therefore be suggested that the area which was ecclesiastically dependent on Leek Wootton church was a subdivision of a larger territory based on Stoneleigh. Stoneleigh was a royal manor before 1066 and the centre of the Domesday, and later medieval, hundred of that name. However, there was no ecclesiastical link between Stoneleigh and Leek Wootton in the later medieval period. The cartulary of Kenilworth Priory recorded links between Stoneleigh church, which was appropriated to the Priory, and chapels in Baginton and Newnham Regis,[159] so presumably

it would have recorded any similar links with the church of Leek Wootton had such links existed. A pre-Conquest tenurial link between *Optone* and Stoneleigh is undeniable, but it may not have been as old as Leek Wootton's other apparent early medieval connections.[160] The Domesday hundred of Stoneleigh may be an agglomeration of various early medieval territories, for it includes places which belonged originally to other territories. For example, Bishop's Itchington, in the extreme south of the hundred, must have belonged, from its name, to the same administrative unit as Long Itchington in the hundred of Marton.

The place-names Woodcote and Woodlowe are important clues to the territorial affiliations of Leek Wootton. Leek Wootton was bordered by Kenilworth to the north, Ashow and Milverton (its presumed dependencies) to the east and Warwick to the south. Woodcote was divided between the ecclesiastical parishes of Leek Wootton and Kenilworth, but this division may have accompanied the creation or enlargement of the park of Kenilworth and therefore have taken place in the twelfth century.[161] The place-name could denote a cottage settlement which was part of Wootton rather than cottages which were adjacent to a wood. Similarly, the name Woodlowe might refer to the barrow or tumulus of Wootton rather than the tumulus which adjoined a wood.[162] The settlement of Woodlowe, however, was in the parish of St. Nicholas, Warwick, immediately adjacent to Woodcote in Wootton. Indeed, it has even been claimed that Woodlowe lay in both Wootton and Warwick.[163] Were the settlement and tumulus named merely from their proximity to Wootton or were they once part of Wootton? Was Wootton itself once part of the same territory as Warwick?

Leek Wootton and Warwick were in two different dioceses. It has been suggested that this need not be a strong argument against an early territorial link between them.[164] It has been recognised that elsewhere the diocesan boundary may not reflect the exact boundary of the Hwiccan kingdom.[165] For example, the church of Aston in the diocese of Coventry and Lichfield made persistent claims on Yardley church in the diocese and county of Worcester to the point where it can be concluded that, as Yardley was a manor of Pershore Abbey in the diocese of Worcester, ecclesiastical influence had diverted the boundary at that point to take Yardley into the Worcester diocese.[166] There is no evidence of cross-border ecclesiastical or tenurial links in the vicinity of Warwick and Leek Wootton. However, the early medieval territorial affiliations of Warwick are even more obscure than those of Leek Wootton.

It is uncertain whether Warwick's initial importance derived solely from the establishment there of a fortified *burh* in the early tenth century, presumably "to control the north-eastern gateway into the Hwiccan province", or whether Warwick had an earlier history as a royal administrative centre with its own minster church.[167] If Warwick were the administrative centre of an independent territory in the sixth or seventh century, its geographical position on the edge of that territory would have been unusual. It also seems a remarkable coincidence that two places, both with important churches and both on the edges of their presumed territories rather than in the centre of them, were immediately opposite to each other across the diocesan boundary. This juxtaposition and the location of Woodlowe suggest that Leek Wootton may have been a subsidiary part of an early medieval *regio* which included Warwick.

This conclusion leaves two questions unanswered. What was so special about the woods of Wootton to prompt the use of the name in these two places and nowhere else in Warwickshire? Why were both places the sites of important churches?

The relative amounts of woodland in Leek Wootton and in other places in the surrounding area in, say, the sixth and seventh centuries are unknown. Wootton Wawen does not seem to have had a topography which was significantly more wooded than most other places in the early medieval territory. The charter of 716-37 refers to high woods (*saltibus*), but also to fields and meadows; the area was not exclusively, perhaps not even predominantly, woodland. In 1086 places outside the area which is thought to equate to the twenty hides conveyed by the charter, such as Offord and Claverdon, had plenty of *silva*. It may be that places called Wootton exploited woodland for more than local use, with the word *wudu* or *widu* referring to the product of woods rather than to the woods themselves.

This discussion about the significance of *wudu* as a place-name element is inconclusive. It fails to throw much light on the nature or distribution of woodland in the early medieval period.

The distribution of woodland

The distribution of place-name elements denoting, or associated with, woodland, has long been used as evidence of the presence of woodland in the early medieval period.[168] Such names give no indication of the size of the woods to which they referred. Moreover, the words wood and grove have been in apparently continuous use since the adoption of the Old English language and therefore mask the history of woods to which they became attached. This study has also suggested that *leah* was characteristic of retreating or encroaching woodland and that its absence from the nomenclature of a particular locality may indicate that the amount of woodland in that area remained stable during the period when *leah* was used in place-names. Thus the many names including *leah* in north and west Warwickshire, in both major and minor place-names, may indicate plenty of woods but do not indicate how large, or small, the woods were. Whilst minor place-names in south and east Warwickshire reveal unsuspected early medieval woodland they too fail to quantify it. A *leah* by a ten-acre wood may be part of a very different countryside from one in which a *leah* was associated with a hundred-acre wood.

Despite these reservations, place-names provide important evidence for the distribution of woodland in Warwickshire in the early medieval period. The numbers of minor place-names which include the elements *leah*, *hurst* and *wald* and the major place-name Dassett suggest that there were significant quantities of woodland south and east of the river Avon at the time when those names were formed. The situation in the later medieval period, when large parts of this region had only small woods or groves or no woods at all, cannot be projected back to, say, the eighth century. The evidence for this hitherto unsuspected and widespread distribution of woodland is of fundamental importance for the history of the topography of the region.

Words which certainly describe woodland - *frith*, *shaw* and *holt* - tend to be concentrated in north and west Warwickshire. The place-name element *leah*, though its precise significance is uncertain, is nonetheless to be associated with woodland. Together with the place-name Wootton and the charter evidence for woods in Wootton Wawen and Nuthurst, the evidence of place-names does suggest that the region was at least partially wooded and that it had more woodland than the region which became the south and east of the county.

There is other evidence which has been used to argue that woodland was present in large quantities north of Wootton Wawen in contrast to places with little or no woodland further south. This evidence requires critical examination, not only because the argument overlooks the evidence for some woodland south and east of the Avon but also because it does not take account of recent thinking about the formation of Anglo-Saxon kingdoms.

It has been claimed that "a block of woodland situated near the headwaters of the rivers Arrow and Alne"[169] resembled tracts of woodland and pasture elsewhere in England which were originally used for communal, seasonal grazing by the inhabitants of a large territory but were "gradually appropriated to regions, then particular individual settlements".[170] This claim is based on known tenurial and ecclesiastical links between places in the Arrow and Alne watershed and places south of the Avon. The former were invariably dependent in some way on the latter. The church of Tanworth-in-Arden was a chapel of Brailes church twenty-five miles to the south-east.[171] Bushwood was part of the parish, and manor, of Stratford-upon-Avon.[172] Packwood chapel was dependent on the church of Wasperton.[173] The Hundred Rolls of 1279 stated that the tenants of Wellesbourne had common in Kingswood involving cartloads of wood, pannage and pasture.[174] It has been assumed that Nuthurst was linked to Shottery and Arley to Long Itchington in the same way.[175] The explicit record of Wellesbourne's tenants' common rights in Kingswood, the name Kingswood and the names of three of the other places involved, Packwood, Bushwood and Nuthurst, together with the tradition of dependence, certainly suggest that the links involved the exploitation of woodland resources by places to the south. The links have been thought to pre-date the Norman Conquest. Indeed, the grant of Nuthurst to the church of Worcester was recorded c.700. However, the status of Nuthurst does not support the theory that it was separated by the grant from a block of common woodland which had originally been used for transhumance by the people of the Hwicce.

This theory is based on an explicit assumption that each of the known links was between places in the same Anglo-

Saxon kingdom. It has even been stated that none of the links crossed the diocesan boundary, which is presumed to represent the boundary of the kingdom of the Hwicce. However, they did cross in at least two cases. Shottery was in the diocese of Worcester, but Nuthurst chapel was dependent on the church of Hampton-in-Arden, which was in the diocese of Coventry and Lichfield.[176] An attempt has been made to explain away the discrepancy as a later transfer to Hampton-in-Arden from a fragmenting land unit based on Shottery.[177] The opposite is equally possible, if not more likely. Nuthurst could have been detached from a territory based on Hampton-in-Arden as a gift to the church of Worcester. The fact that Packwood, which was not mentioned in the *Taxatio Ecclesiastica* of 1291, was also in the diocese of Coventry and Lichfield in 1535[178] has been overlooked.

Given the theory that the kingdom of the Hwicce was formed by the accretion of formerly independent territories it is possible to formulate quite a different theory for the links. As the Hwiccan kingdom expanded from its apparently original centre around Winchcombe the territories on its northern edge would have been the last to be acquired. Any area of common woodland on that boundary could not have been part of the original kingdom.

By the end of the seventh century the kingdom was a province of Mercia.[179] The Hwiccan royal dynasty seems to have accepted its demotion, presumably as the price of a continuing, albeit subservient, role. It could be suggested that the kings of Mercia used grants of land to encourage such acquiescence amongst the Hwiccan princes, the Hwiccan church and the Hwiccan nobility. This land need not have been within the Hwiccan kingdom. In these circumstances Packwood could have been given to a prominent Hwiccan layman whilst Nuthurst was given to the church of Worcester. Whether Tanworth, Kingswood and Bushwood were within the Hwiccan border or not is uncertain; it is theoretically possible that in these places existing ecclesiastical links were broken and a new link with the diocese of Worcester formed. Yardley in Worcestershire has already been cited as an example of the influence of the churches in that diocese in trying to break earlier ecclesiastical links and form new ones. A study of hundreds in the diocese of Worcester has concluded that this was a "common occurrence" in the west midlands.[180] The link between Long Itchington and Arley, though not found in any surviving record before 1001, may have followed a similar process of political aggrandizement in north Warwickshire; as already noted in the discussion about early medieval charters, there is very little information about the area covered by the diocese of Coventry and Lichfield in comparison with that of the diocese of Worcester.

Whilst there is no evidence to support the theory that Nuthurst, Kingswood, Bushwood, Packwood and Tanworth had been part of a wood which was common to the people of the kingdom of the Hwicce, there is no reason to dispute the suggestion that transhumance, the movement of livestock from one region to another, was practised by laymen or churches who held, or had access to, land in north and west Warwickshire or that this practice was linked to the

distribution of wood pasture.[181] There does not appear to be any reason to disbelieve the evidence for a substantial amount of woodland in the area north of Wootton Wawen, at least from the end of the seventh century. The evidence suggests that the traditional topographical division between Arden and Feldon pre-dates the Norman Conquest.

Arden, Feldon and Woodland

The topographical distinction between Arden and Feldon is a commonplace in modern historical and geographical studies of Warwickshire. A broad distinction has been drawn between the wooded region of the Arden in the north of the county and the virtually woodless Feldon in the south.[182] These regional names have not been used in this study hitherto, because aspects of the early modern countryside which have been associated with them may obscure the evidence for the early medieval period and because their boundaries are unknown. However, they should be considered in any discussion of regional topography in the early medieval period, because Feldon is an Old English word and Arden may be even older and of pre-English origin.

The evidence for the existence and partial extent of these regions comes mainly from later medieval and early modern sources, but is arguably a reflection of a pre-Conquest distinction which persisted into the later medieval period. The later medieval evidence is not plentiful. It is largely in the form of place-names and road-names. On the assumption that later records maintained medieval traditions, the later medieval evidence may be amplified by references in some sixteenth-century surveys and by the comments in topographical and historical accounts of Warwickshire which were written in the sixteenth and seventeenth centuries. By combining the evidence from these sources a few regional boundary points can be located fairly precisely.

Travelling through Warwickshire between c.1535 and 1543[183] John Leland learned "that the most parte of the shire of Warwike, that lyeth as Avon river descendithe on the right hand or rype of it, is in Arden (for soe is auncient name of that parte of the shire)".[184] Arden is probably, though not certainly, derived from a pre-English word meaning high or steep.[185] In the later medieval period it was suffixed to Hampton (by Solihull), Henley (by Wootton Wawen), Morton (Bagot), Coleshill, Stoneleigh, Dunton (in Curdworth), and Weston (in Bulkington).[186] There are a few references to Arden as a district independently of place-names, such as that in Stoneleigh c.1290.[187] Customary land measures of Arden were used in Solihull and Chilvers Coton.[188] The church of Arden, mentioned in 1130, is thought to have been the church of Coleshill in the ecclesiastical deanery of Arden.[189] Two documents associate Yardley in Worcestershire with Arden.[190]

The geographical distribution of these references is compatible with the information collected by John Leland and shows that the Arden extended over much of the area north and west of the river Avon. However, there is not enough evidence for the region's exact boundary to be deduced. It extended at least as far as the river Avon at

Stoneleigh, but further west it is not certain whether Morton Bagot and Henley-in-Arden marked the southernmost limit. Consequently it is not possible to say whether the early medieval territory of Wootton Wawen was wholly or only partly within the topographical region of the Arden.

The common association of Arden with large areas of woodland may reflect later medieval evidence. At a popular level it has been attributed to the poet Michael Drayton, who was born in Warwickshire and who in 1612 described Arden as a forest which had once stretched from the river Trent to the river Severn.[191] The popular view may also be attributable to the imaginary Forest of Arden made famous by Shakespeare's 'As You Like It'. In the later medieval period people did not use the phrase Forest of Arden, even when referring to the custom of Arden in relation to woodland.[192] Historians who are sensitive to the true meaning of 'forest' in the later medieval period have referred simply to the Arden,[193] following medieval and sixteenth- and seventeenth-century usage. Regrettably, in view of both the medieval and modern meanings of the word, not all scholars have been so careful.[194] Even when omitting the word forest, some have assumed that the Arden was originally the name of an area of woodland.[195]

Frequent use of the term Forest of Arden has helped to perpetuate the mistaken belief that the region was a vast tract of largely uninterrupted woodland. There is a single known medieval reference to a forest of - more probably in - Arden.[196] It has been claimed that this reference supports the popular view of the medieval forest.[197] However, it is obvious from the context that when, in 1148, Robert, earl Ferrers, gave Merevale Abbey his whole forest of Arden (*totam forestam meam de Ardena*)[198] he must have been conveying a relatively small private chase in the vicinity of Merevale. The phrase *de Ardena* distinguished the location of the chase from the earl's lands beyond the Arden, such as the manor of Orton-on-the-Hill in Leicestershire, also granted to Merevale Abbey in 1148,[199] and later called Orton *subtus Ardern*.[200] The earl's forest probably resembled the private forest which Geoffrey de Clinton was permitted to establish in Kenilworth.[201]

The word Arden was used as a district-name, without any special connotation with woodland. Moreover, there is evidence that it was not used to denote woodland in the later medieval period. Contemporaries who were conscious of the wooded nature of parts of county used the very word woodland as a regional name. Camden, in his *Britannia*, and Sir William Dugdale, writing half a century later, used it instead of Arden.[202] In the preface to *The Antiquities of Warwickshire* Sir William explained that the river Avon divided "the Woodland (for so that part of the Countie lying North thereof is called) from the Feldon".[203] Camden stated that the Avon "doth after a sort sever one from the other."[204] Sir William used the name also in his main text, from which we learn that the Woodland extended from just north of Warwick to the environs of Tamworth, and included specifically Hampton-in-Arden, Atherstone by Mancetter and Astley.[205]

Woodland was a regional name in the later medieval period and, unlike Arden, was used in some sixteenth-century manorial surveys. In the thirteenth century and later two places in Warwickshire were given the suffix Woodland, *Hatton in le Wodeland* in 1272 (also in other thirteenth-century deeds and in 1324, 1411 and 1457)[206] and *Preston in Wodeland* (Preston Bagot) in 1311.[207] In a survey made in 1547 Atherstone by Mancetter was described as standing "in the greate hye way called Wattling strete on the border of the felden Countrey joyning to the Woodlannde".[208] In a survey of c.1545 Kenilworth was described as "in the wooddland countree".[209] In 1590 a detailed survey of Budbrooke referred to "the Queenes high waye called Musewaie leading from Barford into the woodland" and "the Queenes high waye leading from Hampton into the woodland".[210] It implied that both Barford and Hampton-on-the-Hill (in Budbrooke parish) were outside the Woodland. As Hatton, the adjoining parish to the west, was in the Woodland, the boundary of the Woodland can be located fairly precisely at this point.

In Chapter Two it was explained that in the later sixteenth century some writers used the term woodland to refer to a hedged countryside which had much wood but may have had few woods. Later medieval records show that the greater parts of north and west Warwickshire had both. Camden associated the Woodland with woods.[211] There is not an obvious contrast, at many centuries distance and with sparse documentation, between the later medieval topography of Budbrooke and Hatton, but there are marked differences, in terms of the number of woods, between places to the north of these two parishes on the one side and places to the south on the other.

Feldon, unlike Arden and Woodland, was not used in place-names. John Leland does not seem to have been aware of it as a local name. However, it appeared in the sixteenth-century surveys of Atherstone - where it applied to south-west Leicestershire - and Kenilworth, which lay within three miles of the "felden Countre".[212] Today it is used by historians and historical geographers to describe Warwickshire south and east of the river Avon, although it is accepted that the area has never been defined precisely.[213]

Feldon is derived from the Old English *feld*, interpreted as 'open country' in contrast with woodland, hills or marsh. For most of the early medieval period *feld* was used irrespective of cultivation and apparently did not acquire the modern sense of field until the tenth century. It has been suggested that in settlement names it probably means 'open land previously used for pasture'.[214] The district name Feldon may be a corruption of the dative plural *feldum*, in which case it would mean 'at the open lands'.[215] However, it is in a different form that it is found in an early medieval charter and some later medieval deeds.

The element *felden(e)* or *fildene* appeared in various Warwickshire road-names and crossing points in the later medieval period. It is thought to be an Old English word meaning 'of the dwellers in open country' rather than an adjective of later origin describing land attached to a particular settlement.[216] A charter dating from 1016 referred to a *feldene straet* on the boundary of Bishopton, a township within the parish of Stratford-upon-Avon. The street is thought to have become the modern A34 (now demoted to the A3400).[217] That road passes through Stratford and across the river into south Warwickshire. The *fildenestrete* which was mentioned in a thirteenth-century deed relating to Edstone in Wootton Wawen[218] and the road called *Feldon way* in Wilmcote in 1464[219] were presumably the same road; the former A34 passes through both places. This road-name was obviously well-established by the early eleventh century and appears to have been of regional rather than local significance.

Other examples of *fildene* can all be linked to three other long-distance routes, two of which led from north to south Warwickshire and the third of which, like the *Feldenbrigg* of Atherstone,[220] led into Leicestershire.

The *fildeneford* of Pinley near Rowington[221] was near the south-west part of Hatton, where a road called variously *Vildeneweye*, *Netherefildeneway* and *le fildenewey* [222] was recorded in thirteenth-century deeds. There was a *Vildene Wey* or a *Fyldenewey* in Sherbourne.[223] The course of this road appears to have been eastwards through Hatton and Grove Park in Budbrooke. (A map of 1721, drawn before the enlargement of the park to its modern extent, shows Grove Park Lane running east from Nun Old Common[224], after which it turned southwards to run through the eastern side of Sherbourne parish across the Avon to become the modern A429 through Barford.) Apparently neither Budbrooke nor Sherbourne was in the Feldon, as the road had not reached its destination when it passed through them. Yet we know from the sixteenth-century survey of Budbrooke that Budbrooke was not in the Woodland either. This evidence suggests that there were parts of Warwickshire which were neither Arden nor Woodland nor Feldon. The conclusion is reinforced by the course of the other routes.

Another *Fildeneford*, in Stoneleigh,[225] may have been the starting point for a route which was called *Le ffildenewey* in Bubbenhall,[226] *fildenewey* in Cubbington,[227] and *ffildenewey* in Long Itchington.[228] The course of this road is very significant for the regional divisions of Warwickshire. It suggests that a sizeable part of the south of the county, at least as far as Long Itchington, was not in the Feldon.

The north-eastern corner of the county also seems to have been outside the Feldon. *le Fildeneweye* in Ryton in Bulkington[229] may have been the road which ran through Wolvey as the *Fildenewey* into Leicestershire.[230] Fieldenway was recorded as a field-name on an estate map for Wolvey in 1794 (see Fig. 84).[231] A *feldenewey* ran through Bilton and Toft in Dunchurch.[232]

A road called *Fildenestrete*[233] was recorded in the thirteenth century in Alspath (in Meriden) and earlier as *fildenestret*.[234] Its course is unknown, but it might have become the modern A45 through Coventry, another long-distance route.

The dichotomy between the use of Arden and Woodland in place-names and the use of Feldon in road-names and crossing points is striking. It implies that people in the former looked to the latter as an important place. The association of Feldon and roads is not unique to Warwickshire. For example, there was a *fildene stret* in Bengeworth on the eastern side of Evesham in Worcestershire.[235] There were a *Fildenewey* and a *Fildenbrige* in Old Wardon in Bedfordshire.[236] However, the *Fildenewoda* of Broadfield in Hertfordshire shows that *feld* was used in other types of compound.[237] Its survival as a district name appears to be exclusive to Warwickshire and probably owes much to the continuing interest of topographers and historians in the regional contrasts in the county.

The Feldon seems to have been in the very south of the county, roughly corresponding to that part south and east of the Avon which was in the diocese of Worcester and therefore presumably in the kingdom of the Hwicce. It might be suggested that it was the name of another Anglo-Saxon *regio*, like the *Stoppingas*, but the frequency of Feldon elsewhere in the midlands argues against its use as a distinctive name for a political territory. It is more likely to have been a purely topographical term. The hills around the edge of the Warwickshire Feldon, also within it (as at Winderton in Brailes), and the presence of woodland in the later medieval period, together with some minor names derived from *wald*, all provide suitable topographical contexts for the formation of the name.

In summary, Feldon may be used as evidence of open country, Arden of high ground and Woodland as self-explanatory. They did not cover the whole of Warwickshire. The Avon was certainly not the boundary between them. Of the three regional names, only the Arden can be presumed to have been in use throughout the early medieval period. Feldon may not have come into use before, say, the seventh or eighth centuries or even later. Woodland may have been adopted as a regional name only in the later medieval period. These names therefore do not provide evidence of the distribution of woodland in the early medieval period. Their association with the presence or absence of woodland in the early modern period is potentially misleading.

In contrast, the boundaries of parishes and townships, rather than of regions, may be very significant in their relationship with woodland.

Intercommoning in woods

The location of many of Warwickshire's woods on the boundaries of parishes or townships is apparent from later medieval records. In some cases a wood in such a position can be shown to have adjoined the wood of another parish or township. There were some notable concentrations of adjoining woods, such as those on the boundaries of Honiley, Kenilworth, Balsall, Haseley and Wroxall, of Rowington, Baddesley Clinton and Wroxall, of Kingsbury, Freasley and Baddesley Ensor, and of Binley, Brandon and Brinklow. In such cases it was not unusual, in north and west Warwickshire, for the tenants of two adjoining parishes to enjoy common rights in both woods. The woods, albeit shared, were distinct.

168

Examples of intercommoning in woods have been found between Rowington and Shrewley, Packington and Kinwalsey, Freasley in Polesworth and Kingsbury, Castle Bromwich in Aston and Yardley in Worcestershire, Widney in Solihull and Knowle, Stoneleigh and Kenilworth, Kenilworth and Ashow, Alne and Kinwarton, Allesley and Coventry, Stoneleigh and parts of Coventry (although here the woods were not obviously contiguous by the later medieval period), Balsall and Berkswell, Rudfen in Kenilworth and Berkswell, Westwood in Stoneleigh and Berkswell, Spernall and Little Alne in Aston Cantlow, and Spernall and Morton Bagot.[238]

When, and in what circumstances, these links were formed, is potentially crucial to the history of woodland in the early medieval period. Intercommoning could have been a way of avoiding the labour of creating and maintaining stock-proof boundaries between adjacent woods, although such boundaries would have been necessary between the woods and adjoining arable land, and also within the woods to protect the regrowth of any underwood from grazing. It can also be suggested that intercommoning arose when two settlements which were discrete entities came under joint lordship. Alternatively, the custom may have originated at a time when the woods were a single wood serving more than one settlement within a larger territory and may have been so strong and so highly valued that it was maintained even when the territory was fragmented and the wood divided between the constituent settlements. It could also be suggested that the custom of intercommoning pre-dated the formation of woodland and that the woods in which it was practised were secondary woods which had developed on areas of common pasture at a time when they were grazed less intensively than before.

In some of the cases cited above, the intercommoning is matched by administrative links which are arguably early medieval in origin. In Chapter One it was explained that ecclesiastical parish boundaries are thought to perpetuate early medieval land units. As noted earlier in this chapter, Yardley was part of Aston parish. Kenilworth was a member of Stoneleigh, Allesley of Coventry.[239] Kinwalsey was a detached part of the parish of Hampton-in-Arden, being divided from it by Great Packington, whose church was claimed as a chapel of Bickenhill church.[240] The parish of Hampton-in-Arden also included Balsall and Nuthurst, and at one stage Hampton's church claimed Alspath church.[241] Balsall's position between Berkswell and Berkswell's chapelry of Barston suggests that Berkswell and Barston were also part of an early medieval territory with its administrative centre at Hampton-in-Arden.[242] These relationships suggest that in other cases intercommoning may be a pointer to former administrative links of which no other trace remains.

However, some of the links crossed known early medieval territorial boundaries. There was intercommoning not only between Berkswell and Balsall but also between Berkswell and Westwood in Stoneleigh (but not in the rest of Stoneleigh's common woods) and between Berkswell and Rudfen in Kenilworth. Any tenurial link between Berkswell on the one hand and Stoneleigh and Kenilworth on the other

must pre-date 1086, when Stoneleigh and Kenilworth were held by the king and Berkswell by the Count of Meulan.[243] There are no known ecclesiastical links to indicate earlier tenurial links. Indeed, as has already been pointed out, Berkswell seems to have been attached to Hampton-in-Arden rather than to Stoneleigh. It may be significant that Berkswell's tenants' common rights were confined to a particular wood within Stoneleigh and did not extend to other common woods in that parish. Perhaps they dated from a period before, as suggested above, *Armele*, *Crattele* and *Dolle* became woods.

Morton Bagot's intercommoning in Spernall's woods crossed the boundary of the early medieval territory of Wootton Wawen. In the thirteenth century Robert Bagod, lord of Morton Bagot, surrendered to John Durvassal, lord of Spernall, his common rights in the wood of Spernall. In the agreement no reference was made to any common rights exercised by tenants.[244] It could therefore be suggested that the common rights arose from a period of common lordship. Domesday Book recorded that Morton and Spernall, albeit under different overlords, were each held by someone called Hugh,[245] arguably the same person. Hugh, or a predecessor or successor in the lordship, could have introduced the practice for his own animals. However, this argument loses force in the face of two other deeds which testify to the surrender of common rights in the woods and lands of Spernall by John of Greenhill (in Morton Bagot) and Thomas Rufus of Little Alne (in Aston Cantlow).[246] These were presumably freehold tenants. Moreover, Aston Cantlow was not in the same lordship as Spernall in 1086.[247] Nor is there any suggestion of ecclesiastical links between Spernall and Morton Bagot.

It could therefore be suggested that the intercommoning between the woods of Morton Bagot and Spernall pre-dated the formation of the territory of Wootton Wawen. That territory is thought to have been part of a larger territory which included Alcester in the Romano-British period and possibly for some time afterwards.[248] The two relict road and field boundary systems identified in the Wootton Wawen area extended beyond the presumed early medieval territory. The later of the two road systems was so regular in its layout as to be arguably part of planned, public development during the Romano-British period; such development must have taken place over a unified territory.[249]

The Romano-British period and the centuries immediately following it form plausible contexts for the exercise of intercommoning between Morton Bagot and Spernall. Whether the intercommoning took place over land which was at that time wooded is another matter. As suggested above, it cannot be assumed that the woods over which common rights were exercised in the later medieval period had always been woodland. They might have been secondary woodland which was formed after the Romano-British period, perhaps on areas already used as common pasture.

Primary and secondary woodland: the fifth and sixth centuries

In some other parts of England archæology has provided evidence that certain areas of later medieval woodland had been densely settled in the Romano-British period and were therefore largely secondary woodland.[250] However, where the archæological evidence is of scattered, possibly industrial, settlement, it may point to economic activity within a wood or on the edge of a wood whose extent had altered over the centuries.[251]

In Warwickshire archæological investigation has concentrated very much on known or inferred Romano-British habitation sites, especially towns, and on rescue excavations. There has been relatively little of the systematic field survey which has been undertaken in other counties, such as Northamptonshire, or even at parish level, as at Hanbury in Worcestershire.[252] Even using field survey techniques, it would be difficult to show that any of Warwickshire's medieval woodland overlay Romano-British settlements or fields, because medieval records rarely give precise information about the exact location and extent of medieval woods. Medieval wood banks are not a reliable substitute, because such banks were associated with coppice woods or coppice compartments within wood pasture, and cannot be a guide to the full extent of wood pasture before clearance or encoppicing. Moreover, when a wood was converted to arable or pasture any boundary bank could have been levelled. It certainly cannot be assumed that the early modern boundaries of woods equate to those in the later medieval period; several of Warwickshire's extant woods which are thought to have existed in the medieval period include areas of ridge and furrow denoting former arable land.[253]

Archæological investigation in Glasshouse Wood, in the parish of Ashow, has shown it to be secondary woodland. It contains the site of a Romano-British dwelling and also of apparent Romano-British fields. The dwelling is thought to have been deserted towards the end of the Romano-British period and the adjoining land seems to have become woodland thereafter.[254] Glasshouse Wood was known as Cookes grove in 1597.[255] The name suggests that a wood had existed in the medieval period, though not necessarily of the same size as in 1597. There was certainly woodland in the vicinity in the later medieval period (see Chapter Three).

Oakley Wood, south of Warwick in the parish of Bishop's Tachbrook, includes, within the wood bank, earthworks which have been attributed to an Iron Age hillfort, but this identification has been disputed and the nature of the earthworks is unresolved.[256] A thirteenth-century deed,[257] which described land called *Pleystowe* (a name surviving in the modern Plestowes Farm) in Barford as abutting on to the heath towards the wood of *Occle* to the east, suggests that Oakley Wood extended to the boundary between Bishops Tachbrook and Barford. The earthworks, therefore, though enclosed within the great woodbank, may have been originally peripheral to an area of early medieval woodland which was not enclosed until a later date. Moreover, as suggested above in the discussion about the meaning of *leah*,

Oakley may have been the name of an area of secondary woodland, possibly one adjacent to an older wood.

If, as argued in this chapter, field-names including the word wold or holt indicate sites of woodland which lost its trees during the early medieval period, they preserve the sites of early medieval woods without later accretions. Therefore any records of pre-medieval cultivation or settlement on such sites would suggest that the wolds were, in part at least, secondary woodland. The sites of wolds in Warwickshire which it has been possible to identify from later field-names are, with one exception, free of any known evidence of pre-medieval cultivation or settlement. However, there has been no large-scale field survey in Warwickshire and the location of an apparent Bronze Age barrow on the edge of Ichington Holt by the boundary with Kington in Chesterton does suggest that at least part of Itchington's wold was secondary woodland.[258] Field surveys of Warwickshire's wolds not currently under grass, to establish whether they were cultivated during the Romano-British period or during the centuries immediately following, could contribute significantly to the debate about the extent to which secondary woodland developed between the Romano-British and early medieval periods.[259]

Topographical analysis in relation to fields in the Wootton Wawen area will be discussed in more detail in the following chapter, but also provides a context for the history of Warwickshire's woods. The technique has been used to show the survival of pre-medieval rectilinear frameworks of roads and boundaries over the greater part of the area, leading to the conclusion that much of the land has been in more or less continuous agricultural use since at least the Romano-British period.[260] In these circumstances there could not have been great, undivided tracts of woodland. However, topographical analysis does not show whether the pockets of land in which neither of the two pre-medieval field systems of the area has been traced were woodland, moor or pasture, leave alone whether any woodland was primary or secondary. It is possible that primary woodland did survive in parts, but equally possible that the field systems were disrupted by the development of secondary woodland after the Romano-British period. In and around Spernall Park and Morton Common (the presumed area of later medieval woodland) the Roman field systems have indeed been interrupted, but whether by secondary woodland or other post-Roman developments, is unknown. Moreover, a combination of topographical analysis and documentary evidence for one part of this area opens up the possibility that pre-medieval field boundaries could have survived the growth of secondary woods. This possibility has been discounted quite recently, on the basis that most field-boundaries were probably without ditches.[261] The example discussed below questions that assumption.

The area in and around the present Merryman's Farm in Ullenhall presents an interesting combination of topographical and documentary evidence which has potentially significant implications for the technique of topographical analysis and for the history of medieval woodland. As explained in Chapter Three, a twelfth-century grant of part of the wood of Ullenhall indicated that it included substantial earthworks in the form of three great ditches (*cum tribus magnis fossatis*).[262] From their proximity to Botley, named in the grant as bordering the wood, these can be identified as Hobditch and two connected banks, which had associated ditches and are at the latest of early post-Roman date and possibly of Iron Age origin.[263] This is rare evidence of the precise site of medieval woodland which was secondary in origin, for the woodland must have developed after the earthworks were constructed. The western earthwork, the general trend of the river valley, and the road along the valley formed a loosely rectilinear framework which could have influenced the boundaries in the immediate area at any time.[264] Therefore the boundaries on Merryman's Farm, within the area of the medieval wood, could have been inserted when the trees disappeared. However, some of the boundaries continue beyond the immediate area of Merryman's Farm and follow the dominant alignment of the Wootton Wawen boundary system, which is of pre-medieval origin.[265]

On first consideration, Merryman's Farm appears to present examples of the way in which some boundaries identified by topographical analysis as part of a pre-medieval boundary system can post-date that system. However, the great western earthwork must have preceded the woodland, and, presumably because of its size, was preserved within Ullenhall's medieval wood to re-emerge at a later date. It is possible that the tree cover of the wood was sparse enough to allow other, lesser, boundary ditches or banks, notably those whose alignment continued northwards across the river, to survive for re-use in the later medieval field system. The suggestion advanced in this study, that some, if not much, medieval woodland was open and used as pasture, thus allowing the survival of some pre-existing boundaries, makes an important contribution to the latter argument. It may reconcile the development of secondary woodland in Ullenhall with the survival, on the same site, of a significant number of apparently pre-medieval field boundaries. More generally, it suggests that there might have been more regrowth of woodland in parts of England after the Romano-British period than the practitioners and advocates of topographical analysis have identified hitherto.

Alongside this possibility is the evidence presented above for a pre-medieval origin for the later medieval custom of intercommoning in woods and for the woods themselves. If the intercommoning had originated on pasture it would suggest a substantial growth of secondary woodland at some time after the custom originated. It would also imply that pre-medieval common pasture was uniformly allowed to revert to woodland, instead of some being preserved as pasture. The association between common grazing rights and later medieval woods and wolds is so strong that the balance of the argument may be in favour of a pre-medieval origin for woods in which intercommoning was practised.

The debate about the relative proportions of primary and secondary woodland in the early medieval period highlights the lack of evidence for the fifth and sixth centuries. The only datable evidence for the distribution of woodland in north and west Warwickshire in the early medieval period comes from the early eighth century, in relation to Nuthurst and Wootton Wawen. English place-name elements cannot be applied to a period before Old English was in general use. There were pagan Anglo-Saxon cemeteries in the valley of the Avon from the beginning of the sixth century, but from phonological criteria it seems that British speech persisted in south Staffordshire, near the Warwickshire border at Hints (a British name) in the second half of the sixth century and around Lichfield as late as the mid-seventh century.[266] The date of the adoption of the Old English language in north and west Warwickshire is uncertain, but there may well have been a period of two centuries after the end of the Romano-British period before English place-names were introduced, giving plenty of time for the formation of secondary woodland. The three Warwickshire names thought to contain the British word for wood, *ceto*, cannot therefore be taken to refer to Romano-British woods; they may refer to secondary woodland formed between the end of Roman rule and the adoption of English place-names.

Conclusions

The questions about primary and secondary woodland, as with those about the precise amounts of woodland in different parts of Warwickshire at different stages in the early medieval period, have no certain answers. Nonetheless, they should be asked. The tentative answers given to them show that much of the evidence on which views of the county's early medieval topography have been based hitherto is capable of different interpretation. New interpretations owe something to the careful examination of detailed evidence from the later medieval period. They also owe much to recent archæological research and current thinking about early medieval settlement, which will be discussed at greater length in the following chapter.

The detailed evidence has shown pretty conclusively that there was significantly more woodland in Warwickshire before 1086 than in the later medieval period. It has also modified some of the traditional views about the topographical divisions within Warwickshire. The broad distinction between the areas on either side of the Avon in the later medieval period may have been less marked in, say, the eighth century. Detailed research has not solved the difficulties involved in interpreting the evidence of place-names, but it has confirmed the importance of such evidence and has contributed to the case for continuing review. In particular there is a need for more work on minor topographical place-names. This study has also highlighted the need for much more archæological investigation and topographical analysis in Warwickshire.

Despite the imperfections of the evidence, enough new information has emerged about woodland in Warwickshire to prompt questions about the implications for other aspects of the early medieval topography of the region. The next chapter will consider in particular the relationship between the distribution of woodland and regional variation in rural topography.

1 *English Historical Documents c.500-1042* (ed. D. Whitelock, second edition, 1979), pp. 4-10.
2 P. Sims-Williams, 'The Settlement of England in Bede and the Chronicle', *Anglo-Saxon England*, 12 (1983), pp. 1-41; *idem*, 'Gildas and the Anglo-Saxons', *Cambridge Medieval Celtic Studies*, 6 (Winter, 1983), pp. 1-30; J. Campbell, 'Bede', ed. T. Dorey, *Latin Historians* (1966), pp. 159-90, see p. 172; Brooks, 'The creation and early structure of the kingdom of Kent'; B. Yorke, 'The Jutes of Hampshire and Wight and the origins of Wessex', in ed. Bassett, *The Origins of Anglo-Saxon Kingdoms*, pp. 84-96.
3 Sawyer, *Anglo-Saxon Charters*, passim; Gelling, *Signposts to the Past*, p. 208; Whitelock, *English Historical Documents*, pp. 3, 374-5; S. Keynes, *The Diplomas of King Aethelred 'The Unready': A study in their use as historical evidence* (1980), p. 1.
4 For summaries of the position nationally and locally, see, for example, J. Campbell, *The Anglo-Saxons* (1982), Chapters One and Two; C. Hills, 'The archaeology of Anglo-Saxon England in the pagan period: a review', *Anglo-Saxon England*, 8 (1979), pp. 297-329; P.H. Sawyer, *From Roman Britain to Norman England* (1978); C.C. Taylor, *Village and Farmstead* (1983).
5 Gelling, *Signposts to the Past*, passim; *idem*, *Place-Names in the Landscape*, passim; Sawyer, *From Roman Britain to Norman England*, pp. 150-63.
6 See, for example, Stenton, *Anglo-Saxon England*, p. 43; for an acknowledgement of how recent the change has been Dyer, *Hanbury*, p. 12.
7 Taylor, *Village and Farmstead*, Chapters 6 and 7.
8 Dyer, *Hanbury*, pp. 15-18.
9 N. Higham, *Rome, Britain and the Anglo-Saxons* (1992), passim; Taylor, *Village and Farmstead*, Chapters 6 and 7; P.J. Drury and W. Rodwell, 'Settlement in the later Iron Age and Roman periods', ed. D.G. Buckley, *Archaeology in Essex to A.D. 1500*, C.B.A. Research Report 34 (1980), pp. 59-75; T. Williamson, 'Sites in the Landscape: approaches to the post-Roman settlement of south-eastern England', *Archaeological Review from Cambridge*, 4.1 (1985), pp. 51-64; *idem*, 'Parish boundaries and early fields: continuity and discontinuity', *Journal of Historical Geography*, 12.3 (1986), pp. 241-48; H. Harke, 'Finding Britons in Anglo-Saxon graves', *British Archaeology*, 10 (December, 1995), p. 7.
10 M.G. Welch, 'Rural settlement patterns in the Early and Middle Anglo-Saxon periods', *Landscape History*, 7 (1985), pp. 13-25, especially pp. 13-14; J.N.L. Myres, *The English Settlements*, Volume 1B in the Oxford History of England (1986).
11 G. Crawford, 'Wasperton, Warwickshire. Excavation of gravel site', *West Midlands Archaeology*, 24 (1981), pp. 121-29; *idem*, 'Excavations at Wasperton: 3rd interim report', *West Midlands Archaeology*, 26 (1983), pp. 15-27; P. Wise, 'Wasperton', *Current Archaeology*, 126 (1991), pp. 256-59.
12 Bassett, *The Wootton Wawen Project: interim report no. 4*, pp. 14-21.
13 S.R. Bassett, personal communication.
14 S.R. Bassett, 'Churches in Worcester before and after the conversion of the Anglo-Saxons', *The Antiquaries Journal*, LXIX, Part II (1989), pp. 225-56; *idem*, 'Church and diocese in the West Midlands: the transition from British to Anglo-Saxon control', in ed. J. Blair and R. Sharpe, *Pastoral Care Before the Parish* (1992), pp. 13-40.
15 Whitelock, *English Historical Documents*, p. 369; *Victoria History of the County of Stafford*, Vol. III (ed. M.W. Greenslade, 1970), p. 174.
16 Initially by G.B. Grundy, 'Saxon Charters of Worcestershire', *TBAS*, LII and LIII (1927, 1928), pp. 1-183 and 18-131 respectively, and more recently in Hooke, *Anglo-Saxon Landscapes of the West Midlands: the Charter Evidence* and *idem*, *Worcestershire Anglo-Saxon Charter-Bounds*, Studies in Anglo-Saxon History II (1990).
17 For examples of groves, *ibid*., pp. 205-7, 254, 261-4, 284-6, 311-4, 359-60, 368-70, 377-83.
18 *ibid*., pp. 397-400.
19 *ibid*., pp. 120-1.
20 References to published transcriptions or translations of these charters and to comments upon them are given in Sawyer, *Anglo-Saxon Charters*. The enumeration of the charters and dates given in that work are as follows: 64 - Shottery, Nuthurst (699x709); 1278 - Nuthurst (872); 1177 - Ingon (704x709); 120 - Hampton Lucy (781); 1252 - Stratford-upon-Avon (699x717); 1257 - Stratford, Sture and Hampton Lucy (781); 1388 - Bishopton, Warwick (1016); 1358 - Clopton (988); 1421 - Luddington (bounds only); 94 - Wootton Wawen (716x737); 1307 - Aspley and *Teodeces leage* (963); 720 - Duddeston (963); 1536 - Austrey (1002x1004); 588 - Wormleighton (956); 1574 - Wormleighton (bounds only); 937 - Wormleighton and Farnborough (990x1006); 61 - Shipston-on-Stour (764x775); 1573 - Shipston-on-Stour (bounds only); 1310 - Alveston (966); 1334 - Tiddington in Alveston (969); 1318 - Tiddington in Alveston (977); 1350 - Tiddington and Alveston (985); 751 - Bickmarsh in Welford-on-Avon (967); 773 - Kineton (969); 892 - Southam, Ladbroke and Radbourn (998); 898 - Long Itchington, Arley (1001); 911 - Little Compton, Studley (1005); 967 and 973 - Myton in Warwick (1033-34); 1098 and 1099 - Coventry (1043x1053); 1407 - Weston-on-Avon (1053x1056).
21 Sawyer, *Anglo-Saxon Charters*, no. 79; H.P.R. Finberg, *The Early Charters of the West Midlands* (second edition, 1972), p. 88.
22 Gover, Mawer and Stenton, *Place-Names of Warwickshire*, p. 123 for the bounds of Arley.
23 D. Hooke, 'The Oldberrow Charter and boundary clause', *West Midlands Archaeological News Sheet*, 21 (1978), pp. 81-3; D. Hooke and D. Marshall, *The Arrow Valley Project. 2. Oldberrow, A Parish Survey*, University of Birmingham, Department of Geography, Occasional Publication Number 30 (1994), pp. 13-20; Gover, Mawer and Stenton, *Place-Names of Warwickshire*, pp. 282 (Kineton), 144-5 (Southam), 135 (Ladbroke and Radbourn).
24 For a readily accessible interpretation of the bounds, Gover, Mawer and Stenton, *Place-Names of Warwickshire*, pp. 133-4.
25 Birch, *Cartularium Saxonicum*, Vol III (1893), no. 1182.
26 Hooke, *The Anglo-Saxon Landscape: the kingdom of the Hwicce*, p. 205.
27 Birch, *Cartularium Saxonicum*, Vol I, nos. 239 and 241 (pp. 332-3, 335-6) for Hampton Lucy; *ibid*., p. 178 for Ingon. For a discussion about the identity of Ingon, see P. Sims-Williams, 'Cuthswith, seventh-century abbess of Inkberrow, near Worcester, and the Wurzburg manuscript of Jerome on Ecclesiastices', *Anglo-Saxon England*, 5 (1976), pp. 1-21, see p. 12.
28 *RBW*, p. 276.
29 Sawyer, *Anglo-Saxon Charters*, numbers 576, 720, 1388.
30 Birch, *Cartularium Saxonicum*, Vol. I, no. 123; on the date of the boundary clause, Cox, 'The Place-Names of the Earliest English Records', p. 66, cited in Hooke, 'Village Development in the West Midlands', p. 143.
31 Hooke, *The Anglo-Saxon Landscape*, pp. 204, 57.
32 Birch, *Cartularium Saxonicum*, Vol. I, no. 157.
33 As in A. Sharer, *Die angelsachsische Konigsurkunde im 7. und 8. Jahrhundert*, Veroffentlichung des Institutes fur Osterreichische Geschichtsforschung, XXVI (1982), pp. 176-8, which attributes the charter to a later rather than an earlier date within the years 718-37.
34 Bassett, *Wootton Wawen Project: interim report no. 4*, p. 21; W. Cooper, *Wootton Wawen: its history and records* (1936), p. 4; Hooke, *Anglo-Saxon Landscapes of the West Midlands: the Charter Evidence*, p. 165.
35 Birch, *Cartularium Saxonicum*, Vol. I, nos. 191, 247 and Sawyer, *Anglo-Saxon Charters*, no. 123.
36 Birch, *Cartularium Saxonicum*, Vol. I, no. 303 and Brooks, 'The creation and early structure of the kingdom of Kent', p. 70.
37 Latham, *Revised Medieval Latin Word-List*, p. 417.
38 S.R. Bassett, *The Wootton Wawen Project: interim report no. 7*, University of Birmingham (1989), p. 3; *idem*, personal

communication; Gover, Mawer and Stenton, *Place-Names of Warwickshire*, p. 217.

39 See Chapter Three under Wootton Wawen.

40 Finberg, *The Early Charters of the West Midlands*, p. 88.

41 Hooke, 'The Oldberrow Charter and boundary clause' includes the boundary clause of *Teodeces leage* on p. 83; for a variation to the suggested northern boundary of Oldberrow, Hooke and Marshall, *The Arrow Valley Project. 2. Oldberrow*, pp. 13-20.

42 *ibid.*

43 Gelling, *Place-Names in the Landscape*, p. 196, suggests that *holt* describes a wood with a single or dominant species of tree.

44 S.B.T., DR37/853.

45 Roberts, *Settlement, Land Use and Population*, Figure 44. For the tithe award, W.C.R.O., CR328/53.

46 Sawyer, 'English Medieval Settlement: New Interpretations', p. 4; Gelling, *Signposts to the Past, passim*.

47 For an explicit recognition of the difference, Dyer, *Hanbury*, p. 1.

48 Gelling, *Place-Names in the Landscape*, developed an interest begun in *idem, Signposts to the Past*.

49 This account of the development of Old English place-name studies is based on Gelling, *Signposts to the Past*, Chapter 5 (pp. 106-29) and addenda, pp. 253-5.

50 Gelling, *Signposts to the Past*, p. 88.

51 *ibid.*, map on p. 91, as modified in M. Gelling, *The West Midlands in the Early Middle Ages* (1992), p. 57.

52 *ibid.* and Gelling, *Signposts to the Past*, p. 92.

53 *ibid.*, p. 93.

54 *ibid.*, pp. 83-5.

55 *ibid.*, p. 93.

56 M. Gelling, 'Why Aren't We Speaking Welsh?', ed. W. Filmer-Sankey, *Anglo-Saxon Studies in Archaeology and History 6* (1993), pp. 51-6, explains that the British origin of these two names had been rejected as late as 1982 because "it seemed questionable whether there could ever have been an oak forest extending along the eastern part of Warwickshire" and that the reservation had been subsequently "removed by a better understanding of Warwickshire geography".

57 For the source of this name, *Dugdale*, Vol. I, p. 227, taken from the original, B.L., Cotton Vitellius A i, f. 44. (*VCH*, Vol. VI, p. 36 translates *nemus* as grove.) Dr. Gelling, personal communication, has kindly confirmed that *munechet* is a "distinct possibility" for a *ceto* name, but, in the absence of mountains or great hills in Binley, is unable to throw any light on the element *mune*.

58 Gelling, *West Midlands in the Early Middle Ages*, Chapter 3 and p. 53.

59 *ibid.* and Gelling, *Signposts to the Past*, pp. 22, 88.

60 Sawyer, 'English Medieval Settlement: New Interpretations', p. 1.

61 C. Johansson, *Old English Place-Names and Field-Names containing leah* (Stockholm, 1975), p. 28.

62 See, for example, Gover, Mawer and Stenton, *Place-Names of Warwickshire*, pp. 123 (Arley), 144-45 (Southam); Hooke, 'The Oldberrow Charter and boundary clause'; for later medieval field names see the parish studies in Chapter Three.

63 H.S.A. Fox, 'Approaches to the adoption of the Midland system', in ed. T. Rowley, *The Origins of Open Field Agriculture* (1981), pp. 64-111, see pp. 89-90.

64 Sawyer, 'English Medieval Settlement: New Interpretations', p. 4; Gelling, *Signposts to the Past*, p. 126.

65 Taylor, *Village and Farmstead*, pp. 104-5, 111, 122-3.

66 M. Gelling, 'The Evidence of Place-Names I' in ed. P.H. Sawyer, *English Medieval Settlement* (1976), pp. 110-21, see p. 111.

67 Gelling, *Place-Names in the Landscape*, p. 7 and *passim*.

68 *ibid.*, Chapter Six.

69 For example, Skipp, *The Origins of Solihull*, p. 8.

70 Gelling, *Place-Names in the Landscape*, pp. 198-9; Johansson, *Old English Place-Names and Field-Names containing leah*, p. 31.

71 Gelling, *Place-Names in the Landscape*, p. 199.

72 *ibid.*, pp. 198-9.

73 Gelling, *The West Midlands in the Early Middle Ages*, p. 14.

74 See Chapter Two.

75 Hooke, *Anglo-Saxon Landscapes of the West Midlands: the Charter Evidence*, p. 154; *idem*, 'The Anglo-Saxon Landscape', in ed. T.R. Slater and P.J Jarvis, *Field and Forest: an historical geography of Warwickshire and Worcestershire* (1982), pp. 79-103, see p. 85.

76 Gelling, *Place-Names in the Landscape*, p. 234 and Chapter Six.

77 Hooke, *Worcestershire Anglo-Saxon Charter-Bounds, passim*; *leah* is repeatedly translated as "wood (or glade/clearing)". In addition, the possibility that in some cases it could have become a proper name by the time the boundary clause was written is overlooked, notably on p. 399, where *leah* is said to denote an area of woodland when it could have been part of a proper name for that area of land.

78 Everitt, *Continuity and Colonization: the evolution of Kentish settlement*, pp. 30-31, 54; Witney, 'The Woodland Economy of Kent', pp. 22-7.

79 Rackham, *Trees and Woodland in the British Landscape* (second edition), p. 56.

80 Gelling, *Place-Names in the Landscape*, p. 198.

81 *ibid.*, p. 206.

82 For woods called *lee* in Hampton-in-Arden, B.R.L., Wingfield Digby MSS., A1/2. A3, A4, A5, Sutton Coldfield, P.R.O., C 133/86/1, Nuneaton, B.L., Add. Ch. 48,491, and Canley, S.B.T., DR18/1/838. *Le T(h)acheley*, P.R.O., E 164/21, f. 11v, copy in W.C.R.O., MI409 and S.B.T., DR10/223. For Oakley Wood and *Bradlegh* see Appendix 1 under Bishops Tachbrook and Offchurch; the suffix to Oakley, W.C.R.O., CR1908/104/1 and CR1908/105/3. For Stoneleigh, B.L., Harley 3650, f. 76, copy in W.C.R.O., MI 392/1; *SLB*, p. 4; S.B.T., DR10/1017.

83 Rackham, *History of the Countryside*, p. 83.

84 For example, P.R.O., E 40/4380, see *Calendar of Ancient Deeds*, A4380.

85 Gelling, *Place-Names in the Landscape*, p. 197.

86 Sutton Coldfield's minor place-names including hurst: Echelhurst, M.MSS., Mi M 134/9; Brockhurst, B.R.L., 348,028; Ramshurst, B.R.L. 348,039; Langleyhurst, W.C.R.O., Z75/3. Minor place-names including *leah*: Wyndley, M.MSS, Mi M 134/1; Roughley - no medieval record located; Langley, Walmley, *Ravennsley* and *Wylnerdesleye*, B.L., Add. MS. 28,024, f. 101, copy in W.C.R.O., MI 177; *Wytelee*, M.MSS., Mi D 3949/1 and B.R.L. 348,041-2; *la lee*, P.R.O., C 133/86/1.

87 A. Everitt, 'River and wold. Reflections on the historical origin of regions and pays', *Journal of Historical Geography*, 3.1 (1977), pp. 1-19; D. Hooke, 'Early Cotswold Woodland', *Journal of Historical Geography*, 4.4 (1978), pp. 333-41; A. Everitt, 'The wolds once more', *Journal of Historical Geography*, 5.1 (1979), pp. 67-71; T.R. Slater, 'More on the wolds', *Journal of Historical Geography*, 5.2 (1979), pp. 213-8; Gelling, *Place-Names in the Landscape*, pp. 222-7.

88 H.S.A. Fox, 'The People of the Wolds in English Settlement History' in ed. M. Aston, D. Austin and C. Dyer, *The Rural Settlements of Medieval England* (1989), pp. 77-101.

89 Gelling, *Place-Names in the Landscape*, p. 223.

90 For the latter view, Everitt, 'River and wold', p. 11; *idem*, 'The wolds once more', p. 68; Slater, 'More on the wolds', p. 217. For the former view, Gelling, *Place-Names in the Landscape*, p. 222.

91 *ibid.*, p. 224.

92 C. Dyer, 'Dispersed Settlements in Medieval England. A Case Study of Pendock, Worcestershire', *Medieval Archaeology*, XXXIV (1990), pp. 97-121, see p. 108.

93 D. Hall, 'The Late Saxon Countryside: Villages and their Fields', in ed. D. Hooke, *Anglo-Saxon Settlements* (1988), pp. 99-122, see pp. 109-10, 112-3.

94 *Dugdale*, Vol. I, p. 18.

95 Fox, 'The People of the Wolds', p. 79.

96 *ibid.*, p. 81.

97 The change from wold to holt is well documented in deeds dated 1620 relating to Ladbroke, W.C.R.O., CR 1849/2, and Southam, W.C.R.O., CR1248/bundle 141/7; for the local dialect, Gover, Mawer and Stenton, *Place-Names of Warwickshire*, p. 144.

98 C.C. Dyer and C.J. Bond, *Compton Murdak. Deserted Medieval Settlement and its Historical and Archæological Context* (1994), section 4.1.

99 S.B.T., DR10/2606.

100 S.B.T., DR98/278.

101 P.R.O., E 164/21, f. 248r, copy in W.C.R.O., MI 409.

102 W.C.R.O., L1/34; P.R.O., E 41/517.

103 The bounds of Southam and Ladbroke, with Radbourn, are attached to a charter dated 998, printed in *The Crawford Collection of Early Charters and Documents* (ed. A.S. Napier and W.H. Stevenson, 1895), no. 8. The bounds of Kineton are attached to a charter dated 969, printed in Birch, *Cartularium Saxonicum*, Volume III, no. 1229 and in translation in Whitelock, *English Historical Documents*, pp. 563-4. Two sets of bounds survive for Wormleighton, in Birch, *Cartularium Saxonicum*, nos. 946 and 947. Commentaries on all these bounds are given in Gover, Mawer and Stenton, *Place Names of Warwickshire*, pp. 135, 275, 282.

104 This charter, dated to 716-37, survives only in a later copy, but is regarded as authentic, see Sawyer, *Anglo-Saxon Charters*, no. 94, and Sharer, *Die Angelsachsische Konigsurkunde*, pp. 176-8.

105 Birch, *Cartularium Saxonicum*, Vol. I, nos. 191, 247, 303; Sawyer, *Anglo-Saxon Charters*, no. 123; Brooks, 'The creation and early structure of the kingdom of Kent', p. 70.

106 On another example of *haeme* in Warwickshire, see Gelling, 'The place-name volumes for Worcestershire and Warwickshire: a new look', p. 70.

107 See above, in the section on the evidence of early medieval charters, also Chapter Three.

108 On Wolverton's *waldfeld*, *BD*; S.B.T., ER103/2 (map).

109 Gelling, *Place-Names in the Landscape*, p. 225.

110 Fox, 'The People of the Wolds', pp. 82-5.

111 For *Shyrewolt*, S.B.T., DR37/853, and *Sherwold*, S.B.T., DR37/box 74. For the *scir holtes weg*, see above, in the discussion on charters.

112 Gelling, *Place-Names in the Landscape*, pp. 223, 225, 227; Everitt, 'The wolds once more', p. 68.

113 Fox, 'The People of the Wolds', p. 82.

114 Chapter Three for Hatton and Budbrooke; *Book of Seals*, no. 260 (B.L., Cott. Ch. xxix 90) for Pailton.

115 *DB*, 238d; *FF*, Vol. I, no. 159.

116 S.B.T., DR37/2116; Staffs. R.O., D641/1/4V/2; P.R.O., E 40/7220; B.L., Add. Ch. 48,162; W.C.R.O., CR1284/72/2; W.C.R.O., CR1886/222 and B.L., Cotton Caligula A xiii, ff. 64, 112, 120; Northamptonshire R.O., Spencer MSS. 1559; P.R.O., CP 25/1/243/21; S.B.T., DR98/867 and B.L., Cotton Vitellius A i, f. 81; S.B.T., DR37/2804 and Northamptonshire R.O., D4137 and D1116; W.C.R.O., CR2026/12, survey of Rectory of Withybrook, 1595.

117 Ford, *The Pattern of Settlement in the Central Region of the Warwickshire Avon*, p. 144.

118 Lichfield Joint Record Office, D30/N6.

119 Fox, 'The People of the Wolds', pp. 92, 94.

120 Hall, 'The late Saxon Countryside: Villages and their Fields', pp. 99-122.

121 W.C.R.O., CR1248/bundle 141/7; I owe this reference to Mr. Charles Ivin.

122 For Southam, see maps of 1775 and 1778 (W.C.R.O., CR927/1 and CR8/184. For Ladbroke, W.C.R.O., Z358. Other examples can be found in the enclosure award for Wolvey, with plan, dated 18th June, 1797, which includes land "in the Wolds" covering 193 acres, 2 roods and 9 perches (W.C.R.O., CR1124/1). Itchington Holt in Bishop's Itchington included over 86 acres in the tithe award (W.C.R.O., CR569/135).

123 M. Gelling, 'Some notes on Warwickshire place-names', *TBWAS*, 86 (1974), pp. 59-79, see p. 79.

124 Gelling, *Place-Names in the Landscape*, p. 191.

125 Kenilworth, P.R.O., JUST 1/954, rot 64r; Shrewley, Ryland, *Records of Rowington*, pp. 124-5; Brinklow, S.B.T., DR10/117 and DR37/box 114.

126 Frith Wood in Amington in Tamworth, Lichfield Joint Record Office, D/W/1851/10/3; *ffrithbrok* by Coundon and Whoberley, P.R.O., E 164/21, f. 6r, copy in W.C.R.O., MI 409, and C.R.O., BA/B/A/19/1 and BA/B/A/54/13; *la Frid* in Tanworth-in-Arden, S.B.T., DR37/43; *le ffyrthe* in Coughton, W.C.R.O., CR1998/box 35/bundle K; *frith* in Wolvey, Leicestershire R.O., DE2559/106.

127 Gelling, *Place-Names in the Landscape*, pp. 208-9, 324.

128 B.L., Add. MS. 28,024, ff. 103v-104r, copy in W.C.R.O., MI 177; S.B.T., DR18/1/260; S.B.T., DR37/box 115; B.L., Add. Roll 49,760; B.R.L., Wingfield Digby MSS., A108.

129 P.R.O., E 315/41/99.

130 Gover, Mawer and Stenton, *Place-Names of Warwickshire*, pp. 217, 19; in *ibid.*, p. 364, 'olt' in Bishop's Itchington is translated as *holt*, not *wold*.

131 Gelling, *Place-Names in the Landscape*, pp. 192-3; Gover, Mawer and Stenton, *Place-Names of Warwickshire*, p. 209.

132 Gelling, *Place-Names in the Landscape*, p. 193.

133 For example, Wolverton, see map in S.B.T., ER103/2.

134 Gelling, *Place-Names in the Landscape*, p. 227.

135 *RBW*, p. 243.

136 Gelling, *Place-Names in the Landscape*, p. 229; Gover, Mawer and Stenton, *Place-Names of Warwickshire*, pp. 290-1; S.B.T., DR10/258.

137 *RBW*, pp. 254-5.

138 Kingswood in Wroxall, S.B.T., DR3/48, 50; in Tamworth, *Collections for a History of Staffordshire*, William Salt Archaeological Society, Part I, Vol. V (1884), p. 88; in Stoneleigh, S.B.T., DR18/1/696; P.R.O., LR 2/185.

139 Gover, Mawer and Stenton, *Place-Names of Warwickshire*, pp. 190-1, 242-3, 265-6.

140 Smith, *English Place-Name Elements*, Part II, p. 188.

141 Gelling, *Signposts to the Past*, p. 128.

142 Birch, *Cartularium Saxonicum*, Vol. I, no. 157.

143 Gelling, *Place-Names in the Landscape*, p. 227.

144 M. Gelling, *The Place-Names of Shropshire - Part One: The Major Names of Shropshire* (1990), pp. 325-6.

145 *ibid.*, p. 326.

146 Gelling, *Place-Names in the Landscape*, p. 227.

147 Smith, *English Place-Name Elements*, Part I, p. 31.

148 *ibid.*, p. 244.

149 Gelling, *Place-Names of Shropshire*, p. 326.

150 *VCH*, Vol. VI, p. 167, for Leek Wootton church and its dependent chapels; for Wootton Wawen, see below.

151 The three hundredal centres identified to date are Wootton in Oxfordshire (*Victoria History of the County of Oxford*, Vol. XI (1983), p. 259); Wotton (*sic*) in Surrey (*Victoria History of the County of Surrey*, Vol. III, pp. 154-64); and Wootton-under-Edge in Gloucestershire (R. Atkyns, *The Ancient and Present State of Gloucestershire* (republished 1974), p. 853 states that Berkeley Hundred had been called Wootton Hundred).

152 Bassett, *Origins of Anglo-Saxon Kingdoms*, *passim*; on Wootton Wawen, *idem*, 'In search of the origins of Anglo-Saxon kingdoms', p. 18.

153 *ibid.*, p. 19. This view has been stongly disputed; see, for example, D. Rollason, 'the ecclesiastical context', ed. H.S.A. Fox, *The Origins of the Midland Village*, papers prepared for a

174

discussion session at the Economic History Society's annual conference, Leicester, April, 1992, pp. 73-90.

154 Bassett, *Origins of Anglo-Saxon Kingdoms*, pp. 23-4.

155 Bassett, 'Churches in Worcester before and after the conversion of the Anglo-Saxons', p. 230 and footnotes.

156 S.R. Bassett, personal communication. I am indebted to Dr. Bassett for sharing his views on the early medieval status of Wootton Wawen and Leek Wootton which have informed this discussion about the place-name Wootton.

157 *VCH*, Vol. VI, p. 167.

158 In addition to the three hides in *Optone* in 1086 the hidage assessments of other places within the later medieval parish of Leek Wootton were: Ashow (two), Bericote (two), Milverton (two less one virgate), Woodcote (two), Lillington (four and a half), Leamington (two), Cubbington (ten) - *DB*, 238b, 241c, 241d, 239d, 240c, 239b, 238d, 242b.

159 B.L., Harley 3650, ff. 36-7, copy in W.C.R.O., MI 392/1.

160 S.R. Bassett, personal communication.

161 See Chapter Three, under Kenilworth and Leek Wootton.

162 Gover, Mawer and Stenton, *Place-Names of Warwickshire*, pp. 191, 266; Gelling, *Place-Names in the Landscape*, p. 325.

163 *VCH*, Vol. VIII, p. 423.

164 S.R. Bassett, personal communication.

165 Bassett, 'In search of the origins of Anglo-Saxon kingdoms', p. 6.

166 Wager, *Early Medieval Land Units in the Birmingham Area*, pp. 177-81.

167 Slater, 'The Origins of Warwick', pp. 1-13; S.R. Bassett, personal communication.

168 Gelling, *Place-Names in the Landscape*, pp. 2, 188.

169 W.J. Ford, 'Some Settlement Patterns in the Central Region of the Warwickshire Avon', in ed. Sawyer, *Medieval Settlement: Continuity and Change*, pp. 274-94, see p. 282.

170 *ibid.*, pp. 279-80; the theory of long-distance transhumance within the Hwiccan kingdom has been accepted by Sawyer, *From Roman Britain to Norman England*, pp. 146-7, by Hooke, *Anglo-Saxon Landscapes of the West Midlands: the Charter Evidence*, p. 149, and, more recently, by Gelling, *West Midlands in the Early Middle Ages*, p.13.

171 Ford, 'Some Settlement Patterns', pp. 279-80.

172 See Chapter Three, under Lapworth.

173 *VCH*, Vol. V, p. 132.

174 *HR*, pp. 165-7, 169.

175 Ford, 'Some Settlement Patterns', p. 279.

176 *Taxatio Ecclesiastica* (Record Commission, 1802), p. 242.

177 Ford, *The Pattern of Settlement in the Central Region of the Warwickshire Avon*, p. 44.

178 *Valor Ecclesiasticus*, Vol. III (Record Commission, 1817), p. 82.

179 Finberg, *Early Charters of the West Midlands*, p. 177.

180 Bassett, 'The administrative landscape of the diocese of Worcester', pp. 162-3.

181 H.S.A. Fox, "Introduction: transhumance and seasonal settlement', ed. *idem*, Seasonal Settlement, Vaughan Paper 39, University of Leicester Department of Adult Education (1996), pp. 1-23, see pp. 7-9.

182 For a summary of such views, see Dyer, 'The Retreat from Marginal Land', pp. 55-7 and references given there.

183 *Itinerary of John Leland*, Parts I-III, p. xxi.

184 *ibid.*, Parts IV and V, p. 47.

185 Gelling, *West Midlands in the Early Middle Ages*, pp. 57-8.

186 Gover, Mawer and Stenton, *Place-Names of Warwickshire*, pp. 11-12.

187 P.R.O., SC 8/269/13404.

188 Roberts, *Settlement, Land Use and Population*, p. 82.

189 *ibid.*, p. 87.

190 *ibid.*, pp. 89-90.

191 Rackham, *Ancient Woodland*, p. 177 refers to the popular belief, but disputes its origin, for which see the following paragraph; for the thirteenth song of Polyolbion dealing with Warwickshire and the Arden see ed. R. Hooper, *The Complete Works of Michael Drayton*, Vol. II (1876), p. 144.

192 See the petition from the tenants of Stoneleigh *en Arderne* to the king c.1290, complaining about enclosure and assarting of woodland in Stoneleigh *cuntre le usage de Arderne* - P.R.O., SC 8/269/13404

193 See, for example, Dyer, 'The Retreat from Marginal Land', p. 55; Hilton, *The Social Structure of Rural Warwickshire in the Middle Ages*, p. 11. See also the precision of E. Shirley, *Deer and Deer Parks* (1867), p. 159, footnote.

194 See, for example, Roberts, *Settlement, Land Use and Population*, *passim*; Gelling, *West Midlands in the Early Middle Ages*, p. 13, where it is stated that "Arden was a forest in the literal sense"; Watkins, 'The Woodland Economy of the Forest of Arden', p. 19, where it is stated that "most of Warwickshire lying to the north of the Avon Valley was covered by the Forest of Arden".

195 For example, Higham, *Rome, Britain and the Anglo-Saxons*, p. 79.

196 Roberts, *Settlement, Land Use and Population*, p. 88.

197 Rackham, *Ancient Woodland*, p. 177.

198 *Monasticon*, Vol. V, p. 482.

199 *ibid.*

200 *Inquisitions ad quod dampnum*, No. CXLVIII; *Dugdale*, Vol. II, p. 1104.

201 See Chapter Three, under Kenilworth.

202 W. Camden, *Britain* (translated into English by P. Holland, 1610), p. 561, 565; *Dugdale, passim*.

203 *Dugdale*, Vol. I, p. vi.

204 Camden, *Britain*, p. 561.

205 *Dugdale*, Vol. I, pp. 372, 113, Vol. II, pp. 1130, 957, 1083.

206 *FF*, Vol. I, p. 190; *BD*, W.C.R.O., CR1243/7.

207 Gover, Mawer and Stenton, *Place-Names of Warwickshire*, p. 217.

208 W.C.R.O., L2/86.

209 P.R.O., SC 12/16/22.

210 W.C.R.O., CR895/80/1.

211 Camden, *Britain*, p. 565.

212 P.R.O., SC 12/16/22.

213 See Dyer and Bond, *Compton Murdak*, section 2.5.

214 Gelling, *Place-Names in the Landscape*, pp. 235-7.

215 *ibid.*, p. 241.

216 Hooke, *Worcestershire Anglo-Saxon Charter-Bounds*, p. 176, citing Tengstrandt, *A Contribution to the Study of Genitival Composition in Old English Place-Names* (Uppsala, 1940), pp. 99-105.

217 Hooke, *The Anglo-Saxon Landscape: the kingdom of the Hwicce*, p. 205.

218 *BD*.

219 W.C.R.O., CR1911/12.

220 Gover, Mawer and Stenton, *Place-Names of Warwickshire*, p. 15; the existence of long-distance routeways has been noted in relation to alleged transhumance within the Hwiccan kingdom by Hooke, *Anglo-Saxon Landscapes of the West Midlands: the Charter Evidence*, p. 149.

221 Gover, Mawer and Stenton, *Place-Names of Warwickshire*, p. 9 and W.C.R.O., CR284/1.

222 *BD*.

223 S.B.T., DR98/776.

224 W.C.R.O., CR895/19.

225 Gover, Mawer and Stenton, *Place-Names of Warwickshire*, p. 15.

226 C.R.O., BA/D/K/13/3.

227 P.R.O., E 315/37/56.

228 *BD*.

229 Gover, Mawer and Stenton, *Place-Names of Warwickshire*, pp. 8-9.

230 P.R.O., E 326/8950.

231 W.C.R.O., CR1124/7.

232 B.L., Cotton Caligula A xiii, ff. 65, 76, 79.

233 S.B.T., DR10/534.

234 B.R.L., 608,881.

235 Hooke, *Anglo-Saxon Landscapes of the West Midlands: the Charter Evidence*, p. 149.

236 *Cartulary of the Abbey of Old Wardon*, Bedfordshire Historical Record Society, XIII (1930), pp. 227, 230.

237 *ibid.*, p. 289.

238 For Rowington and Shrewley, *Reading Abbey Cartularies*, Vol. I, pp. 456-7; Packington and Kinwalsey, B.L., Add. MS. 47,677, ff. xxiij-xxv, copy in W.C.R.O., MI 392/2; Freasley and Kingsbury, P.R.O., JUST 1/1316, rot 4d; Castle Bromwich and Yardley, P.R.O., JUST 1/955, rot 4r; Widney and Knowle, P.R.O., JUST 1/1245, rot 7r; Stoneleigh and Kenilworth, *SLB*, p. 101; Kenilworth and Ashow, S.B.T., DR10/516; Alne and Kinwarton, P.R.O., JUST 1/955, rot 6r; Allesley and Coventry, P.R.O., JUST 1/955, rot 10d; Stoneleigh and Coventry, *SLB*, p. 101; Balsall and Berkswell, P.R.O., JUST 1/1283A, rot 7d; Rudfen and Berkswell, P.R.O., JUST 1/955, rot 14d; Stoneleigh and Berkswell, *SLB*, p. 101; Spernall and Little Alne, W.C.R.O., CR1998/box 42/AA7/1-2; Spernall and Morton Bagot, W.C.R.O., CR1998/box 42/AA2 and AA5/1-3.

239 For Kenilworth and Stoneleigh, *DB*, 238b; Allesley and Coventry, *VCH*, Vol. VI, p. 4.

240 W.C.R.O., CR328/22 (Hampton-in-Arden tithe award); B.L., Add. MS. 47,677, f. xviii, copy in W.C.R.O., MI 392/2.

241 W.C.R.O., CR328/22; B.L., Add. MS. 47,677, ff. xxx, xxxiiij, copy in W.C.R.O., MI 392/2.

242 *VCH*, Vol. IV, pp. 24, 33.

243 *DB*, 238b, 240b, 224a-b.

244 W.C.R.O., CR1998/box 42/AA2.

245 *DB*, 242d, 243c.

246 W.C.R.O., CR1998/box42/AA5/1-3 and AA7/1-2.

247 *DB*, 244a.

248 Bassett, *Wootton Wawen Project: interim report number 4*, pp. 18-9.

249 *ibid.*, p. 19.

250 Taylor, *Village and Farmstead*, p. 121; for a local example, Dyer, *Hanbury*, p. 17.

251 B. Bellamy, 'Anglo-Saxon dispersed sites and woodland at Geddington in the Rockingham Forest, Northamptonshire', *Landscape History*, 16 (1994), pp. 31-7.

252 See volumes of the *West Midlands Archaeological News Sheet* continued by *West Midlands Archaeology*; *Transactions of the Birmingham and Warwickshire Archaeological Society*; and Warwickshire County Council's Sites and Monuments Record; Royal Commission on Historical Monuments (England), *An Inventory of the Historical Monuments in the County of Northampton*, Vols. I-VI (1975-1985); S.R. Bassett and C.C. Dyer, 'Hanbury, Hereford and Worcester. Documentary and Field Survey SO 96 64', *West Midlands Archaeology*, 23 (1980), pp. 88, 90-91, and 24 (1981), pp. 73-78. The Edge Hill Project, a voluntary initiative working in co-operation with the Warwickshire Sites and Monuments Record, has recently started a systematic field survey in the parish of Tysoe; the aim is to extend the survey in due course to adjacent parishes.

253 Examples include Hampton Wood in Hampton Lucy, Rough Hill Wood in Sambourne, Kingsbury Wood.

254 E. Willacy and R. Wallwork, 'Exploratory Excavations at a Romano-British site in Glasshouse Wood, Kenilworth, 1971', *TBWAS*, 88 (1976-7), pp. 71-81.

255 Estate map, copy in W.C.R.O., Z141(U).

256 Warwickshire County Council's Sites and Monuments Record.

257 P.R.O., E315/52/125.

258 For access to the Warwickshire County Council's Sites and Monuments Record I am indebted to Ms. E. Jones, Site and Monuments Record Officer. The Bronze Age round barrow is described in number WA811 in the Record.

259 A small start is being made as part of the field survey in Tysoe being undertaken by the Edge Hill Project, a voluntary initiative working with the Warwickshire Sites and Monuments Record.

260 Bassett, *Wootton Wawen Project: interim report number 4*, pp. 15-21.

261 Higham, *Rome, Britain and the Anglo-Saxons*, p. 131.

262 In the Stone Priory cartulary, B.L., Cotton Vespasian E xxiv, f. 4.

263 Bassett, *Wootton Wawen Project: interim report no. 4*, pp. 21-23; *idem, Wootton Wawen Project: interim report no. 5*, pp. 21-25.

264 *idem*, personal communication.

265 *ibid.*

266 Gelling, *Signposts to the Past*, pp. 100-1.

Chapter Six

WOODLAND AND REGIONAL VARIATIONS IN TOPOGRAPHY

Introduction

Regional differences in Warwickshire have been recognised for centuries. Indeed, the regional variety of Warwickshire's woodland has been fundamental to this study, wbhich has shown that there were regional variations in woodland in the early as well as in the later medieval period and that the degree of variation seems to have changed over time. Although the evidence has been used to modify extreme views about the amounts of woodland which were present in different parts of the county in the later medieval period, it does confirm the presence of far more woodland in the north and west of Warwickshire than in the south and east. Insofar as woodland is concerned, regional diversity is at least as old as Domesday Book, even allowing for that document's imperfections. The situation during the five or six centuries preceding the Norman Conquest is much more difficult to assess, but there are certainly pointers to regional variations, albeit unquantifiable, in amounts of woodland.

The research for this study was prompted by doubts about the adequacy and accuracy of some published studies[1] in the light of new thinking about English topographical history. It concentrated firstly on seeking to define the extent and nature of the woodland of medieval Warwickshire. As it progressed, it was stimulated by a desire not only to find the evidence for that definition but also to seek answers to the questions raised by the evidence. This chapter considers why there were such regional differences in the distribution and management of Warwickshire's woodland, when they first appeared and to what extent they could be explained by research into, and theories about, regional variation elsewhere in England. As the evidence for Warwickshire was analysed it seemed that it might make a small contribution towards the continuing process of understanding the history of the English countryside.

Woodland is only one indicator of regional variation in topography. In the lowland zone a broad distinction has been drawn, at least since the sixteenth century, between open or 'champion' areas and woodland areas. An alternative name for the former, the 'planned countryside', reflects the presence of great open fields and compact villages in the medieval period and the enclosure of those fields and other common land in the modern period. Another name for the latter, the 'ancient countryside', implies more continuity in topographical features, and is associated with scattered dwellings, linked by winding lanes, amidst small areas of irregular open fields and enclosed crofts interspersed with woods.[2] Topographical studies have revealed infinite variety within this broad distinction and combinations of different types of field system and settlement pattern within a locality. To convey the richness of that variety, and its economic, social and cultural dimensions, scholars often use the French word *pays*.[3]

Warwickshire is often regarded as a microcosm of these contrasts and variations. The relationship between the presence or absence of woodland and typical field and settlement patterns, within Warwickshire and nationally, has been the subject of several studies.[4] A presumed link between the disappearance of woodland and an increase in cultivation has long been axiomatic to studies of medieval settlement. Indeed, uneven distribution of settlement and population has often been taken as the main reason for the division of lowland England between woodland and champion regions. However, more recent studies of the later medieval period have shown that, whilst increases in population led to more land under cultivation and more dwellings, these developments took place within a variety of field systems and settlement patterns.[5] Interdisciplinary studies, to which archæological discoveries have been crucial, have shown that many parts of England were intensively settled earlier than was previously thought and that their subsequent topographical history displayed much regional and local variety.[6]

The results of these topographical studies have altered previous theories about the origins of certain aspects of regional variation. They have dealt mainly with the extent of cultivation, the organisation of fields and the distribution of dwellings. With some notable exceptions,[7] which have concentrated on the contributions of woodland to local society and economy, woodland has been of peripheral interest inasmuch as its disappearance has been used simply as an indicator of extended agriculture consequent on expanding settlement. However, recent topographical research may have other implications for the history of woodland.

This chapter will summarise recent research into regional differences, concentrating on the search for some explanation of them, or at least for an indication of when they first emerged. It will examine not only field systems and settlement patterns but also what is known about types of land use. It will then consider the implications of the research for the history of woodland. Finally, it will relate the findings of recent research to Warwickshire, and suggest how the distribution of different types of woodland might inform future research into medieval topography.

The summary begins with the debate about the origins of one of the most striking and well-known aspects of the medieval English countryside, open fields, for that research encompasses many of the arguments which have been advanced in trying to determine the origins of regional differences.

Field systems and open fields

The history of field systems and particularly of open fields has been one of the most popular, enduring and controversial subjects in English topographical studies.[8] It has been vexed by problems of definition. It has been complicated by attempts to explain simultaneously both the phenomenon of open fields and the geographical distribution of different field systems.

Some scholars have treated as open fields any fields in which several people held unfenced or unditched strips of land, regardless of the size of the fields and the way in which strips were distributed within and amongst them. Others have followed a narrower definition, classifying as open fields that type of subdivided field called the 'Midland system'. They have regarded this system as distinctive enough to place it in a category of its own and to seek a special explanation of its origins.

Many parishes or townships in the midlands, north-east and parts of southern England had in the later medieval and early modern periods two, or three, great fields, which together occupied most of the parish or township. Each field contained groups of strips, generally called furlongs. Tenants held intermingled strips which were distributed evenly between the fields so that each year one field could be left fallow whilst ensuring that each tenant could cultivate a fair proportion of his land. The fallow field provided a large area of common grazing. There could be flexible cropping within fields, but the common grazing of a whole, fallow field on a regular basis was strictly regulated by the tenants acting communally. Common grazing could be found in other types of open fields, but this might be seasonal or not closely regulated; annual fallowing of an entire field occupying a half or a third of the township's arable was the key feature of the system. For this reason some have preferred the term 'common fields'.[9] This term was used in the later medieval period, although it has been described as "very rare" before the end of the fourteenth century.[10] The fields of other open-field systems were smaller and, despite being more numerous, occupied in total less of the land. The strips of land held by individuals might form compact holdings in one or two fields, rather than being evenly divided between all the fields in the township.

Establishing the chronology of field systems does not in itself reveal the reasons for the particular forms which developed, but is a pre-requisite to a search for those reasons. In the last two decades debate over the chronology of the Midland system has been transformed by archæological research. Some widespread and thorough surveys of known former open fields in Northamptonshire have shown that the furlongs were laid out over old field boundaries and former settlement sites. The pottery which was found on the settlement sites showed that they had been abandoned before wheel-made pottery became common from c.900. It seems, therefore, that the farmland of Northamptonshire must have been reorganised from about the late ninth century onwards. The new open fields seem to have been altered after their formation, with long furlongs, over a mile in length, being subsequently divided into the much shorter furlongs which are familiar from earthworks of ridge and furrow surviving in the English countryside. The frequent correlation between the numbers of tenants' holdings in the later medieval period and the hidages attributed to manors in Domesday Book has been used to argue that the reorganisation had taken place before 1086. Open fields were located around villages, which seem to have replaced a dispersed settlement pattern.[11] Similar research has been undertaken elsewhere in the East Midlands and in Yorkshire, with like results, although in some areas, such as Holderness, it is considered that the reorganisation did not take place until the eleventh or twelfth century.[12]

The archæological research finally disposed of the old assumption that open-field systems were brought to England by Anglo-Saxon immigrants in the fifth and sixth centuries, or were developed by such settlers in the process of communal land clearance on arrival in an allegedly thickly wooded country. Continental research had already shown that the Midland system was not to be found there at the time of the migrations to Britain.[13] As explained in the previous chapter, archæological research also led to the conclusion that English-speaking immigrants came to a land which was already occupied and cultivated by a native British-speaking population. The immigrants' linguistic dominance is thought to have been achieved by their political, social and cultural influence rather than by numerical superiority, for, although there were probably many immigrants, they appear nonetheless to have been greatly outnumbered by the native population. The cultural evidence, in the form of pagan burials, is strongest in the east of England, although there are significant gaps in the distribution of such cemeteries in south-east England.[14] Over much of south-east England the large open fields of the Midland system are absent or not a typical feature.

Archæological research has not made the same advances in tracing the chronology of the smaller, irregular, open or common fields which existed in the later medieval period. Much that has been written about these fields lacks the information which systematic field survey might provide.[15] However, as it is generally believed that subdivided fields of various types were almost ubiquitous in the early medieval period,[16] it can be suggested that the small, irregular, open fields familiar from later medieval documents had early medieval origins and preceded the large open fields, which replaced them in some townships. If this chronological sequence is accepted it suggests that the factors which precipitated the development of two large, open fields in some townships were absent in whole or in part from townships whose irregularly subdivided fields escaped reorganisation. In that case some regional differences must have preceded the regular open fields of the Midland system.

Much attention has been paid to the process by which the Midland system emerged as well as the reasons for its creation. The archæological evidence is against the theory of evolution which was once propounded.[17] One of the distinctive characteristics of large, regular, open fields, communal regulation by the users, has also been used to argue against an evolutionary development and thus supports the conclusions drawn from archæological evidence.[18]

It has been claimed that the very characteristics of the system point to a demand for grazing combined with a shortage of permanent pasture as the key factors in its development.[19] It has been argued that permanent pasture was reduced by conversion to arable land, and by the loss of access to local or detached areas of wood pasture, until what remained was inadequate in quantity and difficult to fence and control. This theory assumes that large open fields were formed from existing areas of arable or pasture rather than by expanding agriculture over other land. It therefore regards the absence of large areas of surplus land, in the form of heath, moor, marsh or woodland, as a precondition for the adoption of the Midland system. It implies that there were regional differences in topography in lowland England before open fields appeared. The logical conclusion is that open fields may have intensified regional differences but did not initiate them.

It has also been claimed that a demand for additional arable or pasture would not have been enough in itself to persuade independent peasants voluntarily to surrender their freedom. It has been argued instead that where arable and pasture were in short supply the introduction of large open fields was stimulated or facilitated by strong local lordship. It has also been suggested that such lordship was an indirect influence on the organisation of field systems. By imposing heavy duties or dues lords may have encouraged farmers to grow more grain and impelled them into communal action, including the maximum efficiency in the use of animals for ploughteams, to maximise production.[20]

It has been both argued, and disputed,[21] that strong lordship, in the form of townships under the control of a single lord and with relatively few freeholders, was more characteristic of regions where open fields predominated in the later medieval period. Conversely, 'woodland' regions have been associated with a preponderance of freehold tenants cultivating enclosed fields and engaged also in non-agricultural occupations.[22] However, there were high proportions of free tenures in parts of eastern England with open fields, such as Lincolnshire.[23] In Hertfordshire and north-west Essex there were relatively few freeholders, yet these regions were not characterised by great open fields.[24] In the absence of detailed information about most individual townships a few hundred years before Domesday Book was compiled, it is difficult for the proponent of either argument to prove the case. Records of free tenants in Domesday Book have been used as evidence of regional variation in society by 1086, but it has also been shown that Domesday Book was not consistent in its records of tenants and that entries for some counties, such as Staffordshire, seem to have omitted some groups of tenants.[25]

External influences may have affected the precise form of the reorganisation of fields. The uniformity of the system, especially the distribution of tenants' holdings within the fields and furlongs in a regular order, suggests that its replication may have followed the spread of an idea. The early medieval period demonstrates the power of ideas in other aspects of its history, such as the influence of the Church and the development of the institution of kingship. It is therefore possible that the idea of reorganising small,

subdivided fields into large, regular, open fields, may have originated in one particular place or territory and spread because the characteristics of the system met the perceived agricultural needs of other places.

It has been suggested that the history of a region's social structure might have been a decisive factor in the development of open fields.[26] It has been claimed that in some regions, particularly in the south-east, East Anglia and western England, a relatively peaceful transition from Romano-British government to the English kingdoms protected the kin-based society which characterised Iron Age and Roman Britain, whereas in other regions that social structure was weakened during phases in the process whereby English-speaking people gained political control. In the midlands and north-east, for example, the political process was allegedly more violent and more disruptive of the existing social order, creating a situation in which those who cultivated the land lost much independence as local lordship developed and increased the burdens on them.

The relationship between the alleged instability of early medieval society and the origins of the Midland field system remains a subject of debate. However, the nature of early medieval society is fundamental to the history of field systems in another respect. The very existence of subdivided fields is usually attributed to the custom of partible inheritance. If two-field systems were formed by reorganising irregularly subdivided fields, the strips of the new system can be interpreted as perpetuating the consequences of repeated division of land between all the children of a landholder. It is therefore necessary to explain not only the decision to reorganise by creating two common fields but also the existence of subdivided fields in the first place.

The origins of partible inheritance are therefore crucial to the history of field systems. It is not known whether the custom was common before the early medieval period, whether subdivided fields represented a constant process of amalgamation and redistribution of land according to individual patterns of marriage and fertility, or whether partible inheritance replaced other customs which had favoured land holdings in the form of groups of discrete fields or crofts. With the results of archæological research and topographical analysis, it can no longer be argued that all enclosed fields were restricted to land which was cleared in the centuries after the development of open fields. Rather it is necessary to accept the possibility that some may have predated open fields and may even have been inherited from the Romano-British period. In the absence of evidence for the organisation of cultivation in Romano-British fields,[27] this possibility is conjectural. However, if there were such continuity, it would be necessary to consider whether medieval enclosed fields had ever been subdivided and, if they had, why the subdivision had not been maintained.

The history of field systems has been overshadowed by the search for the origins of one particular system, open fields. The available evidence, which is far from adequate, and the theories advanced suggest that open fields, in all their variety, were the product of particular combinations of circumstances. Persistent as many historians have been, it is difficult to sustain an argument for a single cause or explanation. This study does not attempt to offer the definitive explanation which has eluded so many others. However, research into regional variations in field systems can help in the interpretation of the evidence for woodland.

That research confirms the existence of an ancient countryside, albeit with regional variations in its history, in which land had been divided and fields laid out long before the later medieval period and in which the definition of individual woods could have had a similar chronology. It also suggests that the formation of regular open fields followed and intensified existing regional variations in topography, which could have included variable amounts of woodland. Furthermore, it assumes that this and other field systems were divided between individual farming families who cultivated the particular portion of land allocated to them. This tradition of what in later centuries could be called peasant farming has implications for the division and use of other types of land.

Settlement

This study has already referred to the association, in the later medieval period, between certain types of field system and settlement pattern. Medieval settlement has been divided into two broad types, nucleated and dispersed. Nucleated settlement has been equated to villages, and dispersed settlement to scattered farmsteads or hamlets. Studies of medieval settlement have revealed that within these two very broad types there was considerable variety.

In the later medieval period villages were the usual form of settlement in regions where open fields predominated and, as already indicated, seem to have been formed as part of the reorganisation of fields. The creation of large open fields in Northamptonshire was accompanied by the abandonment not only of individual settlements but also of a dispersed settlement pattern.[28] A similar development has been discerned in the fieldwork which followed the extensive excavations at Wharram Percy in Yorkshire and set the results of those excavations in their topographical context.[29] The ground plans of villages in some parts of England are so regular as to suggest a complete replanning as a single event. Others, such as those in Northamptonshire, are irregular, suggesting that smaller nuclei of settlement expanded, or moved, and coalesced; some groups of dwellings within a village might have been built to a regular plan in the process of settlement growth or shift. Detailed research into village plans and sites often reveals a process of successive changes over many centuries.[30] The inhabitants of some parishes were concentrated in a single village; other parishes had a central village and several hamlets, each of which seems to have had its own field system.

Settlement patterns in regions or parishes where open fields were absent, or were small and irregular, were complex, not only in their forms but also in their history. Settlement could be entirely dispersed or could include a mixture of villages and scattered farmsteads. The sites of individual dwellings were changed, but often perpetuated dispersal.

Archæological research in certain counties has shown that dispersed settlement was the typical form of rural habitation during the Iron Age and Romano-British periods and that it persisted, though not necessarily at the same density or on the same sites, during the first few centuries of the early medieval period.[31] In Essex, scattered dwellings continued as the main form of habitation throughout the medieval period, but in Northamptonshire they were largely replaced by a pattern of villages and hamlets. Dispersed settlement is no longer thought to be exclusively, or even mainly, a consequence of 'late' settlement or 'colonization' in woodland. However, the precise forms of the dispersal displayed considerable variations, regionally and locally, which appear to be linked with particular phases of settlement. Three examples of the detailed research which has been undertaken illustrate the point.

The chalky boulder-clay plateau which extends north-eastwards from Hertfordshire through north-west Essex into Suffolk and south Norfolk lacks the large open fields of the 'Midland system' but otherwise displays a variety of field systems and settlement patterns. Medieval settlement around greens and commons was more frequent in the north and east of the area.[32] On the claylands of east Suffolk[33] such a settlement pattern is thought to have begun in the ninth or tenth century, long after the abandonment of Romano-British dwellings in the area, and to have continued through to the thirteenth century. The lines of Roman roads survive intermittently on the claylands, indicating continuity of use of some of the land despite the inferred absence of dwellings for several centuries. The settlements which developed around the greens and commons are described as secondary in contrast with primary settlements on the valley gravels.[34] Settlement on the claylands and in the valleys below was dispersed.

Bedfordshire has a mixture of both villages and scattered settlements. In central and north-east Bedfordshire archæological research has identified extensive Romano-British settlement. However, the dispersed settlement pattern cannot be attributed simply to a continuation of a Romano-British pattern nor to an expansion of settlement over wood or waste during the early medieval period. There are well-researched cases of settlement expanding in the twelfth century in a dispersed pattern over former arable land as part of a reorganisation of settlement which accompanied an expansion of cultivation over former woodland nearby. Therefore dispersed settlement which can be attributed to the later medieval period is not necessarily to be associated directly with the sites of former woods. It has been suggested that similar conclusions might be reached if systematic surveys were undertaken in other counties.[35]

Hanbury in Worcestershire is on the edge of the wooded area of the county. It was characterised by extensive, dispersed settlement in the Romano-British period, but few of the Romano-British sites correspond to known medieval dwellings. The latter were also scattered over the parish, but many were built around 'ends' or 'greens'. The dwellings around the former were mostly customary tenures, those around the latter freeholdings, suggesting that they belonged to different phases of settlement.[36] No archæological investigation has been undertaken to establish the chronology of either type of site in this instance, but the Bedfordshire research described above points to a similar association between particular types of tenure and phases of settlement.[37]

Before the introduction of open fields and associated villages there is no evidence of the regional variation in settlement patterns which is familiar from the later medieval period. However, it cannot be inferred that regional variety was unknown. The apparent universality of dispersed settlement was not necessarily matched by uniformity of field systems. As in the later medieval period, dispersed settlement could have coexisted with subdivided fields of irregular form or with enclosed fields held in discrete blocks and cultivated as a single unit. For the Romano-British period and the centuries immediately following, demonstrable regional differences may have taken the form of diversity in land use.

Land use

Land use may be defined narrowly as intensive human use principally for agriculture and settlement. More widely, it may also cover undeveloped land with natural resources exploited to some extent by the local population.

There are parts of England for which there is evidence of continuous, relatively intensive, use of land since the Romano-British period. Large areas, covering many square miles, were divided on a rectilinear basis. Local layouts of roads and field boundaries follow common alignments dating from the Romano-British period or earlier. The technique used to discover this boundary framework, topographical analysis, has been applied fairly widely in Essex and East Anglia and also in parts of south-east England, Lincolnshire, Staffordshire and Warwickshire.[38] The antiquity of the patterns has been deduced from their relationship to known Roman roads superimposed upon them. The practitioners of topographical analysis have been careful to acknowledge that many of the surviving boundaries within these frameworks may be later insertions.[39] However, the survival of the general orientation indicates continuity of human regulation of land division.

The converse does not hold. Rectilinear systems of land division dating from the Romano-British period could have been replaced by new systems, such as open fields, without any interruption to the overall level of economic activity.[40] It is also conceivable that road and boundary layouts which pre-dated the rectilinear systems and which in some areas were not replaced by them, or by later land divisions, survive in parts of the English countryside.

Evidence for the continuity of roads and boundary alignments suggests the proportion of land in agricultural use as distinct from the type of agriculture practised on it. It says little about the allocation, management or cultivation of that land or about the precise location of dwellings. Persistence of boundary alignments should not obscure the amount of adaptation which could have occurred within them to meet demographic, economic and social changes. Systems of land division do not help in defining relative proportions of arable and pasture. The search for the origins of regional differences in the medieval countryside has been hampered by lack of knowledge not only about the types of field systems which preceded open fields (whether large or small) but also about the kind of agriculture practised in them.

There has been some recognition of the need to establish the nature of agricultural activity during the Romano-British period in order to assess claims that such activity declined subsequently. Widely and sparsely distributed scatters of pottery sherds are usually thought to indicate manuring of arable land. However, they do not show whether the land was cultivated continuously throughout the Romano-British period or rotated between arable and pasture either in the short-term or long-term. In short, population density and field systems identified from pottery scatters do not show how intensively land was cultivated nor for how long any intensive cultivation lasted.[41] It is only from documentary records that we know that the later open fields of a two-field system were used as pasture, not arable, for half the time and can calculate the apparent yields for crops; written records are not available to show how fields were used before the later medieval period.[42]

The taxation imposed by the Roman government to support its army and other public expenditure meant that at rural level the Romano-British economy must have been organised above the level of subsistence to meet the government's demands. Hence levels of production and types of land use were not influenced simply by levels of population. The inferred continuity of some Romano-British institutions into the early medieval period, combined with contacts with the Continent, would also have exerted some influence on the rural economy and hence on land use.

It has been claimed that archæological evidence shows that any unevenness in the general decline in population levels and settlement activity either during or after the Romano-British period did not necessarily match regional topographical differences in the medieval period. It has therefore been argued that the regional variation familiar from the later medieval period must have developed during the early medieval period.[43] This argument is based on an implicit and unsustainable assumption that topographical differences depend wholly on the amount of land in use, rather than on the type of agriculture practised on that land or on ways of organising agricultural production. It also implies a knowledge about population levels which does not exist.[44]

A need for pasture has been identified as one of the principal determinants of the Midland system of open fields. It has been suggested that this need might have been prompted by taxation and trading rather than by local increases in population.[45] A predominantly pastoral economy might have evolved in other regions in other circumstances. There could have been different types of pastoral farming, as there were in Warwickshire in the later medieval period, when the north and west were characterised by cattle-grazing and the south and east by sheep-rearing.[46] Changes in proportions of arable and pasture could have been as great, or even greater, in areas where large-scale reorganisation of fields was absent than in areas where open fields were introduced. Evolutionary developments could have been as significant for the appearance of the countryside as wholescale reorganisation. There could have been pre-medieval differences in land use which made for regional variation independently of field systems and settlement patterns.

Soil types have often been regarded as crucial to land use. Locally, this may have been the case, if sufficient surplus land was available for choices to be made. However, it has been questioned whether soil types were influential on a regional scale.[47] For example, it has been pointed out that much of the traditional 'champion' area of south and east Warwickshire is covered with grey clay soils which elsewhere might not be regarded as so favourable for cultivation as other soil types.[48]

Variation in land use between the lowland and highland zones of Britain has been attributed largely to climate. The north and west of Britain, the 'highland zone', contains the island's mountains and much of its high ground; it is exposed to westerly winds which bring rain off the Atlantic Ocean. It has been argued that the highland zone was less populous and less economically prosperous even before the Roman occupation of Britain and that the development of Romano-British economy and society accentuated the difference.[49] The climatic argument may be applicable to a lesser degree to parts of the lowland zone which are on higher ground and catch more rain than the valleys and plains.

The territorial organisation behind agricultural production could have influenced the type, as distinct from the amount, of land use. As described in Chapter Four, early medieval territories have been traced through surviving pre-Conquest charters, those hundredal boundaries which appear to have been relatively undisturbed, and medieval ecclesiastical links. Occasionally, place-name evidence hints either at agricultural specialisation within those territories or at dues in kind owed to a central place by dependent settlements. Rye might have been produced or rendered by Ryton, sheep by Shipton, milk and butter by herds at Hardwick. It has been suggested that rulers of such territories had no equivalent of later medieval demesne land but relied wholly on produce rendered by the inhabitants of dependent settlements.[50] Whether these people cultivated the land as extended families, in wider collaborative groups or as individuals, whether they worked under the direction of the territorial ruler or on their own initiative, are all unknown factors. Moreover, the local specialities need not have been the only products of these places.

The theory assumes that there were defined land units within larger territories. Some scholars regard scattered settlements based on units of land equivalent to the later medieval townships as the basic units of rural organisation, which remained relatively static as the larger units into which they were grouped were amalgamated or divided at different stages in their histories.[51] Others have interpreted the evidence from pre-Conquest charters or from topographical analysis as indicating that the boundaries of townships were defined when larger territories fragmented. It has also been

suggested that the sub-division of fields may have been related to this fragmentation.[52] If the latter suggestion is accepted then it is necessary to explain why the apparently late delineation of township boundaries in some other regions was not accompanied by the creation of open fields.[53] It is possible that the truth lies somewhere between the two theories, that fission might have occurred broadly along the lines of pre-existent units within the territory but that the boundaries of these units might have been adjusted or defined more precisely during the fission or even modified subsequently.

Theories about the origins of townships are largely silent about the history of smaller landholdings which might have contained far fewer acres than a township. It has been acknowledged that the numbers of inhabitants and the distribution of their dwellings within such townships are unknown.[54] The assumption that the fields of a township were cultivated in individual portions by peasant farmers has implications for the organisation and use of that land.

The various factors which could have affected land use are relevant to the distribution of woodland. It is in this context that the debate about the amounts of woodland in the Romano-British and early medieval periods and the relationship between woodland distribution and other regional variations in topography should be considered.

Regional variety in woodland

Given that woodland developed to cover most of lowland England in the post-glacial period, its subsequent uneven distribution is arguably one of the earliest manifestations of regional variation attributable to human intervention. All too little is known about the precise chronology of the prehistoric disappearance of trees from large areas of land and still less about any regional or local variations in the incidence of that disappearance. However, the loss of trees has been attributed to the encouragement of grazing and to the development of agriculture. From the evidence of pollen analysis, stratigraphy and archæology it has been deduced that at least half the land had been taken into cultivation by the end of the Romano-British period.[55] It is therefore possible that there have been regional differences in amounts of woodland for two thousand years or more.

It has been suggested that types of soil might have determined the loss or retention of woodland in prehistory and that until the Romano-British period agriculture and settlement were concentrated on lighter soils.[56] Similar arguments have been applied to the medieval period.[57] However, as explained in Chapter One, comparisons between regions within the midlands have shown that similar, heavy, clay soils had markedly different amounts of woodland in the later medieval period.[58] It is therefore logical to allow for some disregard of soil types in prehistory. As woodland originally covered almost the whole of lowland England it must have been located on both fertile and poor soils. Trees may have disappeared through over-grazing rather than through deliberate clearance and the over-grazing may have had no regard to soil type. Where trees were felled and grubbed out, however, the area of land to be cleared might well have been decided by the fertility of the soil or its adaptability to cultivation. The type of land use, arable or pastoral, could therefore have been very significant. It could have influenced the way in which some of the country's woodland disappeared and the distribution of the woodland which remained.

The debate about medieval regional variations in woodland has concentrated on the amounts of woodland inherited from the Romano-British period and on the extent to which secondary woodland developed on former agricultural land during the early medieval period. In the light of the findings of archæological research it has been claimed that the distribution of woodland at the end of the Romano-British period was not fundamentally different from that of 1086. The evidence of Old English place-names has been used in support of this claim; the distribution of certain place-name elements has been matched more or less to the incidence of woodland recorded in Domesday Book.[59] It may also be significant that the pottery industries which flourished throughout most of the Romano-British period, and which required good supplies of wood for firing, were associated with regions which had plenty of woodland in the later medieval period.[60]

Other scholars have drawn different conclusions from comparing the amounts of woodland recorded in Domesday Book with the archæological record of Romano-British settlement. They hold that there must have been significant growth of secondary woodland in the fifth and sixth centuries,[61] or even in later centuries.[62] They point to archæological evidence of Romano-British settlements in areas of later medieval woodland. In addition, some of the known roads and rectilinear boundary frameworks of Romano-British or earlier date are interrupted in places which are suspected of having, or known from documentary evidence to have had, woodland in the later medieval period.[63]

The evidence needs to be very precise to sustain the latter argument. The absence of relict boundaries from part of an area may be due to the presence of woodland there when the boundary framework was first laid out, or to the development of secondary woodland at a later date, or to a combination of both. The Romano-British land divisions might have accommodated areas of woodland which were inherited from the Iron Age and did not expand beyond their original boundaries within the rectilinear framework until the creation of a later medieval park or the growth of secondary woodland after c.1350. Even the development of secondary woodland in the centuries immediately after the end of Roman rule might have involved marginal expansion of an area of woodland which was part of the original land division. In addition, smaller patches of woodland could have developed without disturbing the pattern; some fields, including former settlement sites, could have been allowed to revert to scrub and then to woodland whilst others remained in agricultural use.

Some secondary woodland which grew in such circumstances might have adjoined older woods. In later centuries the latter might have been cleared in preference to the former, so that the surviving woodland occupied a different site from its predecessor. Such a process of woodland shift would have resembled the phenomenon of settlement shift.

In apparent contrast to the argument for significant amounts of secondary woodland, it has been claimed that "the idea of widespread regeneration of the woodland in the fifth and sixth centuries is a myth".[64] The research on which the claim is based acknowledges that there is evidence of some regeneration, especially in the highland zone, as well as of more continuity than was once thought.[65] The key is the definition of "widespread"; should it be interpreted as meaning 'frequent' or 'common', without specifying the quantities of wood involved, or does it refer to extensive tracts of woodland? Growth of secondary woodland might have occurred frequently, over the whole country or selectively in some regions, without covering very large areas of land.

There are flaws in the debate over the amounts and distribution of woodland. One is the propensity to draw general conclusions from local examples. Only much more extensive field surveys and much more pollen analysis and related botanical research can hope to bridge the gap. There are problems in these areas of research. Pollen evidence is rarely closely dated, even when it has survived to be recovered,[66] and field survey depends on identifying the exact boundaries of medieval woods before c.1350. As will be apparent from Chapter Three, the latter have been very difficult to define in Warwickshire. It is dangerous to assume that the known sizes of woods in the sixteenth or seventeenth century can be equated to the extent of medieval woodland, for it is possible that medieval woods were enlarged by the growth of secondary woodland after c.1350.

The second problem arises from the belated recognition that there is no simple equation between growth in population and in settlement and the loss of woodland.[67] The implications of this recognition have yet to exert a general influence on references to woodland in topographical studies. Hitherto interest has concentrated on amounts of woodland, on woodland clearance and woodland preservation in the later medieval period, and on the management of later medieval demesne woods.[68] There has also been a bias towards the post-Conquest history of particular woods for which there is a fair amount of documentary evidence. One of the foremost scholars of medieval woods has explicitly declined to speculate on amounts of woodland in the eighth century as distinct from the eleventh and has concentrated on historical ecology, the history of the vegetation of individual woods, particularly those still extant.[69] Most regional accounts deal with woods in which common rights were disputed, woods within royal forests,[70] and the demesne woods which appear in manorial and associated records.[71] These accounts portray the history of the management of woodland as an inexorable, albeit gradual, spread of enclosed, coppiced woods in private ownership at the expense of open woods in which many local inhabitants had common rights. This trend has been described as largely complete by c.1250.[72] There have been no systematic regional surveys of the nomenclature and management of medieval woodland.

Regional differences in woodland may reflect factors which have been described as relevant to field systems, such as settlement, social structure and land use.[73] These factors may help to explain why some woods were large and used in common and others were small and apparently held by individual lords or tenants, why some were shared by several settlements and others reserved to the inhabitants of one township, why some were managed as pasture and others to produce underwood and timber, why both kinds could be found within the same township and why some townships apparently had no woodland at all. Once the possible influences behind such diversity are acknowledged regional variations in woodland become as potentially interesting as regional diversity in field systems.

Regional variations in woodland might have pre-dated the medieval period and been intensified during the decline in economic activity which arguably followed the collapse of Roman rule. There might have been a greater increase in secondary woodland in some regions than in others. In the latter, for example, a decline in arable production might have led to increased grazing rather than to the growth of secondary woodland. The importance of pastoral farming which was allegedly behind the Midland system of open fields has further implications for the distribution and management of woodland. Over-grazing can reduce woodland to waste. The assertion that "common woodland usually, given time, degenerated to treeless pasture"[74] begs the question why some areas of wood pasture survived for centuries after other areas of woodland disappeared. An increased demand for pasture might have been responsible for loss of woodland in some regions in the early medieval period. Settlements which concentrated on grain production, or at least had a system of mixed farming which did not make extensive use of woods for pasture, might have retained more common woodland than those in regions which at that time were predominantly pastoral.

The close association between specific settlement patterns, field systems and quantities of woodland which is apparent in the medieval period might have emerged only as regional variation intensified. Nonetheless, pre-medieval variation in amounts of woodland may have been a pre-condition for subsequent developments, whose precise nature and occurrence depended on other factors. In addition, regional differences in types of woodland, which at the beginning of the medieval period might have been already in existence, or increasing, or emerging, may be related to factors which influenced the later divergence in field and settlement patterns.

The distribution of groves, which may be very relevant to this argument, has been sorely neglected. Groves allowed intensive production of wood. Where they were in the vicinity of dwellings, they offered a convenient supply of wood for fuel and other purposes without the labour and tedium of collecting and transporting it from a distant wood. The advantages of groves could have been realised as soon as individual woods were separated from the wildwood and

subjected to human management. Their disadvantages lay in the expense and labour involved in keeping them enclosed, in fencing and ditching them to protect the new growth from browsing animals. If the advantages outweighed the disadvantages, why were groves largely absent from many places in England? If the disadvantages predominated, why were groves to be found at all and particularly in places which also had common woods? The answers to these questions involve a number of considerations.

The enclosure of an area of woodland, or the growth of secondary woodland, to form a grove implies a social structure and landholding arrangements which allow such developments, economic circumstances which favour them, and a conscious decision to effect enclosure or allow land to revert to woodland. If no local lord had the authority to enclose or the will to exercise that authority, common woodland could have lost its trees by default, especially if pastoral farming led to over-grazing. The presence or absence of demesne groves may reflect the history of local lordship, the point at which a lord had enough authority to appropriate an enclosed wood from an existing land unit or to enclose some common woodland. It may also reflect the relative scarcity of woodland in the neighbourhood and exceptional pressure upon that woodland. The absence or presence of tenants' groves might reflect not only the degree to which there was a need to conserve and manage woodland for fuel but also the relative dependence or independence of peasants in managing the land which they held. If arable land was cultivated in individual family units it is theoretically possible that woodland could have been divided in the same way, at least for the production of fuel, even if small, individual areas of wood pasture might have been impractical to manage.

Neither of the two studies which included descriptions of tenants' groves in the Chilterns[75] sought parallels elsewhere to explain the phenomenon, and it has attracted little subsequent attention from historians of the countryside and rural settlement. Yet this study of Warwickshire's woodland has shown a distribution of groves for which there is no obvious, simple explanation, but which appears to have a partial relationship to other regional variations. Research into the history of the countryside of medieval England, in particular the origins of regional variations, might, if extended into Warwickshire, help to explain the diversity of woodland there. The groves of Warwickshire may provide a new dimension to the history of regional variation.

Regional variations in Warwickshire: fields and settlements

Discussion of the origins of regional variations in Warwickshire is hampered by the very limited amount of field survey and related archæological research into rural settlements and field systems in the county.[76] The only method available in these circumstances is to argue by analogy, using other evidence to define the nature of Warwickshire's medieval topography as far as possible and then comparing the result with other regions where field survey and related archæology have been practised on a large scale. A recent survey of medieval settlement in the West

Midlands, including Warwickshire, which used pre-Conquest charters, place-names, and a small amount of archæological information, demonstrates the potential of this approach.[77] It is possible to supplement the evidence with the results of topographical analysis of part of Warwickshire.

As Warwickshire adjoins Northamptonshire it seems likely that a comparable pattern of open fields and villages in the former might have had similar origins to that in the latter. Large, open fields with compact villages can be inferred from later medieval records for a number of townships in south and east Warwickshire.[78] In some cases, such as Fenny Compton, the descriptions in medieval deeds of small parcels of land divided between two fields refer to the boundaries of more than one adjoining place, showing that the fields extended to the edge of the township and were presumably large open fields of a typical two-field system.[79] The Warwickshire examples do not constitute proof that the county's open fields pre-dated the Conquest. Even if there were archæological evidence of dispersed settlement in the early medieval period, it could be argued that settlement sites could have been abandoned to cultivation centuries before open fields were formed. Nonetheless, it remains possible that, as in Northamptonshire, open fields may have replaced smaller fields and scattered dwellings from the ninth century onwards, and long before they were recorded in the thirteenth century.

The research in Northamptonshire has not argued for universal continuity of agricultural activity and settlement since the Romano-British period. It has surmised the regrowth of wood on the claylands where, despite thorough surveys, no archæological evidence of dwellings from the early centuries of the medieval period has been found, and has inferred from later field-names the clearance of woodland to extend certain open-field systems.[80] Excavation has shown in a few instances that the boundaries of some medieval furlongs followed earlier ditches. The consequent possibility of a direct link between Romano-British fields and some medieval furlongs allows at least some continuity of land use throughout the Romano-British and medieval periods to be postulated, albeit with reservations.[81]

If an analogy between Northamptonshire and Warwickshire is sound, then presumably dispersed settlements and associated small fields preceded open, two-field systems in south and east Warwickshire. There is a little evidence to support this presumption. Occasional chance discoveries of concentrations of Romano-British pottery point to some small, dispersed, rural settlements, a pattern which may be emerging already in the early stages of field survey in Tysoe, and some archæological investigation of later medieval settlement sites has revealed Romano-British occupation.[82] Aerial photography revealed a dispersed settlement pattern on the river gravels of the Avon valley,[83] although aerial photography depends on suitable soils and sites for cropmarks and cannot of itself determine the age of those marks. Old English habitative place-names incorporating *worth*, *cot*, *tunstall*, and *tun* which have been found within medieval open field systems have also been used as evidence

of former dispersed settlement in south and east Warwickshire.[84]

A possible Romano-British framework for the boundary alignments of medieval open fields in south and east Warwickshire can be argued by comparison with some of the results of research in Northamptonshire. Moreover, in the Avon valley, excavations at Wasperton have unearthed a Romano-British field system whose alignment has persisted into the modern period.[85] An early medieval origin has been suggested for the grid pattern of roads and boundaries in Grandborough. If Grandborough's two open fields[86] postdated the early medieval period, they were presumably formed within existing boundary alignments.[87]

The suggestion that political disturbance in the early medieval period weakened social structures to the point where lords could impose a complete reorganisation of field systems is difficult to pursue in relation to the evidence for Warwickshire. It is not known whether Anglo-Saxon culture spread through social contacts or through political change. Nor is it known whether the postulated accretion of small territories to form kingdoms in the early medieval period occurred peacefully or with some disruption and violence. However, there is a marked regional variation in Anglo-Saxon culture in Warwickshire.

The distribution of pagan burials in the Anglo-Saxon cultural tradition is limited to the south and east of the county, particularly the Avon valley. The burials excavated at Wasperton indicated, by the way in which burials respected previous interments and by the relatively small number of graves containing typical Anglo-Saxon jewellery, that the owners of these artefacts were integral members of a local community with diverse cultures.[88] Pagan Anglo-Saxon burials have been found only in the southern parts of the county. They became sparse by the late sixth century and none attributable to the seventh century has been found in the region. This distribution has been interpreted as marking the extent of Anglo-Saxon immigration to the point at which, influenced by the native population, the immigrants or their descendants changed their burial practices.[89] The geographical distribution of these burials along main river valleys and their immediate hinterland has been taken to reflect immigrants' migration routes. Rather it may reflect relative prosperity within the region, with the most powerful of the people characterised by those cultural practices choosing to take over the richest lands in the region, arguably those in fertile river valleys. Did the area of the Avon valley and south Warwickshire therefore attract cultural change because it was more prosperous? Was it more prosperous because it was more intensively cultivated, having far less woodland and pasture? Or was its prosperity based on livestock rearing? Was it stimulated by population levels or by other economic and social factors, such as a concentration of economic activity in particular areas after the end of Roman rule?

Although distinctive regional differences in field systems and settlement patterns seem to have developed during the early medieval period, field systems and settlement patterns were not the only determinants of regional variation. As explained earlier in this chapter, uniform systems of land division could have supported diverse types of agriculture and land use. This line of argument is strengthened by research in the Alne and Arrow valleys of Warwickshire, an area which has been described as a topographical extension of the middle and lower Avon valley.[90]

It has long been recognised that in the later medieval period north and west Warwickshire was characterised either by irregular open fields with a mixture of villages and dispersed settlement or by dispersed settlement and field systems where tenants held small fields or crofts in severalty and where open fields were confined to a small area, as in the south of Tanworth-in-Arden,[91] or were absent altogether, as in Packwood.[92] In north and west Warwickshire, as in the Chilterns, a dispersed settlement pattern has been attributed to a gradual clearance of woodland and waste during the medieval period, particularly after the Conquest.[93] However, the recent research in other regions of England which was described earlier in this chapter suggests that some dispersed settlement patterns may have much earlier origins, even if they were expanded and modified by medieval developments.[94] There is evidence of such origins in at least one part of Warwickshire.

As explained in the previous chapter, the technique of topographical analysis which has been used in some recent settlement studies has been applied to the Wootton Wawen area of Warwickshire. Two roughly rectilinear systems of roads and field boundaries have been identified, one of demonstrably early Romano-British or even pre-Roman origin and the other of probable Romano-British rather than later date. The former extended into the southern part of Tanworth-in-Arden and into much of Nuthurst, Lapworth and Rowington.[95] Whilst several roads belonging to the later system were superimposed on the earlier there was virtually no overlap between the field boundaries of the two systems. Most traces of the later system are found on higher ground. They are so regular and extensive that they have been interpreted as the results of an extension or reorganisation of agriculture during the Romano-British period under the direction of public authorities. They are aligned on a predominantly north-west/ south-east axis. The projected course of a principal road in the second system runs from Metchley Roman forts in Edgbaston to the river crossing at Stratford-upon-Avon, suggesting that the system's alignment reflected military or administrative needs.

The perpetuation of the boundaries of the two pre-medieval field systems in and around Wootton Wawen shows that the area has been subject to continuous human regulation of land use since the establishment of those systems. Whatever changes were made in the organisation of fields and other land during the medieval period were by way of adaptations to the pre-medieval systems of land division. The medieval period did not see the creation of a new landscape but the evolution of an old. In the centre of Wootton Wawen the boundary alignments of the earlier of the two pre-medieval systems are extensively preserved. In the later medieval period this was an area of open fields.[96] The boundaries of the medieval furlongs were not necessarily those of the

Romano-British fields, but they were laid out within the old framework, respecting its orientation.

The alignment of the earlier of the two pre-medieval field systems was also perpetuated in Tanworth-in-Arden, although not to the same density as in the centre of Wootton Wawen. Research into the later medieval topography of Tanworth has identified only one small area of irregular open fields in the south of the parish.[97] Agriculture elsewhere in the parish, including the rest of the area covered by the pre-medieval system, seems to have been practised in enclosed fields or crofts. Whilst some of Tanworth's crofts were formed from woodland and waste in the later medieval period, a larger proportion than has been presumed hitherto, and particularly those within the pre-medieval boundary alignments, may have remained in some kind of agricultural use, albeit with modifications, since the Romano-British period.

The locations of the different types of later medieval field within Wootton Wawen and Tanworth do not correspond neatly to one or other of the two pre-medieval systems of land division nor to areas in which pre-medieval systems can or cannot be traced. However, the largest area of open-field land seems to have coincided with the greatest concentration of pre-medieval boundary alignments. On this basis it might be suggested that the strongest evidence for continuity of cultivation is associated with subdivided rather than with enclosed fields.

The pre-medieval alignments of field boundaries in the Wootton Wawen area suggest that other enclosed field systems in north and west Warwickshire may have been formed within a framework of similar antiquity. However, the absence of the Wootton Wawen road and relict field boundary systems north of Tanworth, Lapworth and Rowington is an obstacle to developing this argument, unless topographical analysis were to reveal the existence of separate road and field boundary layouts on a different axis, but demonstrably as old as those in Wootton Wawen.[98]

The survival of at least a few known and important Roman roads, such as Watling Street, provides a minimum of continuity. On the north-eastern edge of Warwickshire there seems to have been tenurial continuity, if nothing more, in the land unit which was centred on the Romano-British settlement of *Venonæ* and whose early medieval extent, arguably centred on Claybrooke in Leicestershire, has been traced through later medieval ecclesiastical and tenurial links. The land unit straddled the county boundary with Leicestershire across Watling Street and included the Warwickshire townships of Copston, Wibtoft and Willey.[99]

The available evidence for the history of medieval topography in parts of Warwickshire and comparisons with similar field systems elsewhere suggest that some regional variation in field systems probably arose during the early medieval period but that other topographical diversity may date from the Romano-British period or earlier. It is possible, therefore, that regional differences in Warwickshire's woodland preceded the variation in field systems.

Warwickshire's woodland and regional variations in rural topography

In the previous chapter it was concluded that place-names indicated some kind of regional variation in Warwickshire's woodland dating at least from the early medieval period. This conclusion was based mainly on the distribution of surviving field-names incorporating *leah*, *hyrst* and *wald*. All these words for woodland were in common use as place-name elements well before the ninth century. The survival of far fewer minor names ending in -ley and -hurst in south and east Warwickshire than in the north and west of the county may reflect the original distribution of such names when English came to be spoken locally. If this is the case, regional variety in woodland preceded the development of large, regular open fields which, in Northamptonshire at least, is thought to date from the late ninth century.

The regional variety in Warwickshire's woodland seems to have corresponded roughly to the regional differences in field-systems. It could be argued therefore that the smaller amount of woodland in south and east Warwickshire was not only a context but also a pre-condition for the development of open fields. This conclusion is compatible with the theory that the two-field Midland system was a method of increasing pasture in areas which had lost most of their permanent pasture and had little or no surplus woodland which could be converted to pasture. However, the history of some of Warwickshire's wolds requires a refinement of the theory and of the conclusions which have been drawn from research in Northamptonshire.

In the previous chapter minor place-names incorporating wold and the tradition of common pasture on some of Warwickshire's wolds in the later medieval period were used to suggest that for some time during the early medieval period the wolds were woodland, at least some of which was managed as wood pasture. The word *wald* is thought to have fallen out of common use for woodland after c.800 and its preservation in minor names suggests that the places concerned probably lost their trees before the ninth century. This prompts the question why trees disappeared from the wolds at this time.

Reference was made in the previous chapter to a suggestion that the disappearance of trees from Warwickshire's wolds was in some way associated with the development of open fields. If open fields were a response to a shortage of land, particularly for pasture, then it would have been logical to clear the wolds, for arable or pasture, before resorting to a wholescale reorganisation of field systems. The suggestion that wolds lost their trees by c.800 fits this chronology. However, it does not explain why, once they had lost their trees, some wolds in Warwickshire remained as separate areas of common pasture rather than being absorbed into a system which combined common pasture with open fields.

The separate identity of Warwickshire's wolds casts doubt on the assumptions about the chronology of woodland clearance in Northamptonshire. It has been deduced, on the basis of furlong patterns, that some areas of woodland in Northamptonshire were cleared after, rather than before,

open fields were created and were then added to those fields.[100] The assumption is that the clearance of woodland in Northamptonshire was related directly to conversion to agriculture. However, the fate of the wolds as discrete areas could have been independent of the loss of trees.

Intercommoning between townships, discussed in the previous chapter, would have prevented a common wold which was shared between townships from being divided and absorbed into the respective fields of those townships. This obstacle could have been overcome if and when those involved found some way of extinguishing the intercommoning rights. Where such rights were maintained the wold remained as common pasture separate from the common fields. As explained above, the survival of the term wold suggests that the trees disappeared before the ninth century, that is, before open fields are thought to have been created. Even where intercommoning was extinguished on the wolds there might have been a considerable gap between the loss of the trees and the extinction of common rights with a subsequent conversion to arable production. Moreover, the loss of the trees might have been the result of over-grazing rather than deliberate clearance. A link between the transformation of the wolds and the development of large-scale open fields may therefore be more complex than has been assumed hitherto.

The existence of common rights over several wolds in Warwickshire suggests that pasture was a highly valued type of land use. The very survival of these wolds as discrete areas indicates that in those townships common grazing over open fields supplemented an existing source of pasture on the wolds, although it might also have replaced some permanent pasture which had not been part of the wolds. The history of Warwickshire's wolds therefore not only supports the theory that the need for pasture was a crucial pre-condition for the creation of open fields but also suggests that those fields reflected an emphasis on, if not a shift to, pastoral farming.

The concentration of wolds in south and east, rather than in north and west, Warwickshire seems to be a highly significant regional variation. It was suggested earlier in this chapter that a concentration on pastoral farming in some regions might have led to over-grazing and the loss of trees from wood pasture. Alternatively, pastoral farming might have been universally practised, but with differing effects on the countryside according to the amount of pasture available in a particular region as well as the demand for it. The size of the wolds of Warwickshire in relation to the size of the parishes or townships to which they were attached suggests that, whilst wolds may have covered several hundred acres, they did not form such a large proportion of the land units to which they belonged as did woodland in many places in north and west Warwickshire.

The history of Warwickshire's wolds supports the suggestion that intensification of demand for pasture may not have been due simply, perhaps not even principally, to growth in population. Indeed, an expanding population might have been expected to stimulate arable, rather than pastoral, farming. Earlier in this chapter reference was made to the suggestion that the growth of towns, trade and taxation were amongst the economic factors which should be considered in trying to explain the changes in the early medieval countryside, and this suggestion has been related specifically to the development of open fields.[101] Open-field agriculture may have been established in many places in south and east Warwickshire not because they were "pasture-starved",[102] an argument difficult to sustain in face of the survival of several wolds as extensive areas of common grazing, but because open fields, like the wolds, offered grazing suitable for large-scale animal husbandry[103] instead of the more limited pasture needed for subsistence farming. One can speculate that here, indeed, may lie the explanation of the regional name Feldon, derived from a noun originally associated with open land used as pasture rather than with arable fields.[104]

The distribution of Warwickshire's wolds also suggests some modification to the theory that Warwickshire's wolds were an extension of the Northamptonshire wolds into the eastern fringe of Warwickshire and formed with them a region which was distinct from both woodland and champion districts.[105] The presence of individual areas called wolds throughout most of south and east Warwickshire, a traditional 'champion' region, warns against an exclusive association between the term wold and a special kind of regional topography.

The evidence for early medieval woodland considered in the previous chapter produced little information about groves. It did not add anything to the discussion about their origins and their distribution. However, studies of regional variation in field systems, settlement patterns and land use can advance our understanding of this type of woodland. The groves themselves may contribute something to the wider debate.

It was suggested in the previous chapter that the origins of some groves may be closely linked to the history of townships and their field systems. In the later medieval period many demesne groves were named after parishes or townships. The chronology of these groves may relate to the origins of the delineation of land units which became later medieval townships.

In the discussion about land use earlier in this chapter it was noted that some, perhaps many, later medieval townships may have been even older land units than the early medieval territories of which they were components. This theory raises the possibility that the woods and groves attached to those townships were also pre-medieval in origin. The contrary view, that townships originated in the fission of early medieval territories, suggests that groves may have acquired independent identities during that process of fission, by the subdivision of a wood which had belonged to the territory as a whole or by the formation of secondary woodland.

This study of Warwickshire's woodland makes the latter argument more difficult to sustain. Wolds tended to adjoin each other, but the same cannot be said of groves. As noted in the previous chapter, groves were not usually located near wolds or by the groves of neighbouring townships. They offer no evidence to support the postulated subdivision of

blocks of early medieval woodland between townships, and secondary woodland is unlikely to have been formed at a time when other woods seem to have disappeared. The association between groves and townships may therefore be an argument in support of the theory that many townships had delineated their own areas of woodland, and therefore had their own identity, long before the fission of the early medieval territories into which they were grouped.

It is notable that several demesne groves were situated in townships which were dependent parts of an ecclesiastical parish whose central settlement did not have such a grove:- Bishopton and Clopton in Stratford-upon-Avon, Langley, Kington, Songar, Bearley and Offord in Wootton Wawen, Asthill, Horwell, Bigging, Shortley, Harnall, and Hawkesbury around Coventry, Bascote and possibly Stoneythorpe[106] in Long Itchington. A reconstruction of early medieval territorial affiliations in Warwickshire might produce further examples. It is even possible to speculate that the absence of a grove from the central place reflected the reliance of the rulers of these presumed early territories on renders from dependent settlements rather than on home production of wood.

The organisation of agriculture within townships is pertinent to the origins of the later medieval tenants' groves. If fields were cultivated in the early medieval period in a similar way to that documented in the later medieval period, by peasants each working an individual portion of land, then theoretically some of those individual early medieval landholdings could have included woodland as well as arable land. If large open fields were preceded by irregularly subdivided fields or small undivided crofts, it is also theoretically possible that small groves could have been scattered amongst those fields or crofts as they appear to have been in some parishes in north and west Warwickshire in the thirteenth century. They could have been swept away during the reorganisation of the fields and crofts into large, regular open fields.

There are no minor place-names to suggest the former existence of tenants' groves in south and east Warwickshire. However, small groves could easily disappear without trace. Comparisons of fifteenth-century documents and nineteenth-century maps (in Tanworth-in-Arden, Packwood and Beaudesert, for example) show how completely later medieval groves could disappear, leaving not even a field-name to mark their former sites. (The survival of a few of the many groves recorded in Tanworth-in-Arden seems to have been due to the development of the Archer estates from the holdings of fellow-tenants and the policy of keeping some woods in hand for direct exploitation.) If known later medieval groves could disappear so readily, within a shorter space of time and without a fundamental reorganisation of the local field system, small early medieval groves would have been much more vulnerable during a complete replanning of the fields.

It is therefore possible that in the early medieval period, before the introduction of large, regular open fields, there were small groves attached to some of the landholdings within the townships of south and east Warwickshire. One of them might have been attached to the land which became the later medieval demesne. Alternatively, during the reorganisation of the fields, the local lord might have decided, for each township, to take one of the small groves into his control. In the absence of systematic archæological investigation into settlement patterns in Warwickshire, and given the lack of early medieval documentary evidence, this theory is extremely speculative, but the current state of knowledge about regional variations in field systems and settlement patterns in other counties does at least allow it to be advanced as a possibility. There is another possible, though much later, parallel in north and west Warwickshire. In Chapter Four it was suggested that some demesne groves in north and west Warwickshire might have originated as the groves of substantial freeholders and have been promoted to demesne status as manors proliferated in the later medieval period.

Alternatively, and on an equally speculative basis, it can be suggested that the widespread loss of trees and the definition of remaining woodland in south and east Warwickshire might have occurred at a time when local lords were strong enough to establish a monopoly over the enclosure of hitherto common woodland. Tenants' groves may always have been absent from most of that part of the county and may have developed in north and west Warwickshire only during later centuries.

There is evidence of a multiplicity of medieval groves in one township in south Warwickshire, Ratley. Groves extant in the twelfth century and a field-name point to at least three groves there. One of these was called *cnihtegraue*, the retainer's grove,[107] arguably the pre-Conquest equivalent of the grove of a small later medieval manor. The *doddesgrove* of neighbouring Radway[108] also suggests woodland associated with a person rather than a township. Parallels can be drawn between the terrain and quantities and types of woodland found in Ratley and similar features in some townships in north and west Warwickshire. However, the nature and nomenclature of Ratley's woodland offer no further clues to the period when the self-contained groves attained separate identities. The history of Ratley's groves, if it were known, might resemble the origins of the groves of north and west Warwickshire.

Each of the theories advanced above must account for the uneven distribution of later medieval groves within north and west Warwickshire. Demesne groves were absent from most manors and tenants' groves were concentrated in certain parishes. Tenants' groves were associated with parishes or townships which had plenty of woodland in the later medieval period, but not all places which had large areas of woodland had tenants' groves. Were such groves absent from some parishes in north and west Warwickshire for the same reasons that they were absent from most of south and east Warwickshire? Did they disappear during changes to the countryside which occurred during the early medieval period? Or were they always absent from these parishes because of a different social structure, or a different chronology of land development and settlement in those places? The distribution of groves suggests that there is no simple association between medieval crofts and irregular open fields, and groves. Why, for example, were there no tenants' groves amongst the crofts of Sutton Coldfield and only one recorded in the neighbouring Erdington? Did the settlement pattern there and in some other parishes belong to a different phase in the history of the countryside from the enclosed fields and dispersed settlement of Tanworth-in-Arden?

Theories must also account for the coexistence of tenants' groves and common woods. Where groves were confined to the lord's demesne, common woods presumably survived to meet the needs of peasants for both fuel and pasture. However, rights to estovers and common pasture in woods can be found in places with numerous tenants' groves, such as Tanworth-in-Arden.[109] Where groves and hedges around their crofts provided individual peasants with fuel, why did common rights persist? As many holdings in north and west Warwickshire, even some in Tanworth, did not include groves, it seems that common woods continued to meet a real demand either as a principal or supplementary source of pasture and wood. Tenants who also had their own groves must have enjoyed the best of both woods!

These questions about the distribution of tenants' groves suggest that the evolution of field systems and settlement patterns in north and west Warwickshire was varied and complex. Much more research is needed into the topographical history of the county in the light of studies of other regions of lowland England. The nature and history of Warwickshire's woodland could provide a new dimension to such research. Different types of woodland might hold the key to the chronology of enclosed field systems or to the degree of change in the medieval countryside. A combination of historical and archæological research into the medieval settlement history of parishes and townships with a significant number of groves and of parishes or townships with plenty of woods but few or no groves might produce enough evidence of apparently common factors to test alternative theories.

One theory seeks to relate tenants' groves to enclosed or small and irregularly subdivided fields inherited from the early medieval period. The other associates them with enclosed fields formed during woodland clearance during the later medieval period. If the weight of evidence in one region supported one of these theories, analogies might then be drawn for other regions which were characterised by similar types of woodland but where research had not been undertaken.

The view of the heart of the Arden as an area of 'late' settlement[110] would point to the development of groves as contemporaneous with that settlement. The results of topographical analysis in parts of what has been described as the core of the Arden (Tanworth, Packwood, Knowle, Baddesley Clinton, Wroxall, and Forshaw in Solihull)[111] compel a reappraisal of this argument. Instead of being exclusively attendant on 'late' settlement, some groves at least may be indicators of relict pre-medieval land division and a social structure associated with the persistence of dispersed settlement. Evidence of continuity in use of the land combined with a likely pre-English name for the region may be more than mere coincidence. Dr. Roden's study of the Chiltern field systems and woodland was undertaken before the technique of topographical analysis was widely applied, so it is not known whether that region, with its pre-English name and tenants' groves, also retained pre-medieval road and field boundary alignments.[112]

As explained in the previous chapter, even where the survival of pre-medieval boundary systems has been demonstrated the field boundaries within them may not be as old as the original systems; they may have been inserted later in conformity with the main framework. An area of woodland bounded by roads of Romano-British origin could have been cleared for cultivation in the medieval period, with the new field boundaries following the existing boundary alignments in the area. Part of the woodland could have been spared, enclosed and preserved as a grove. It is possible, therefore, that whilst later medieval tenants' groves existed within an old boundary system their delineation may have been of more recent origin. There is no direct evidence of the formation of groves during the twelfth and thirteenth centuries; indeed, in some places characterised by extensive woodland clearance in those centuries they are conspicuous by their absence. However, they may have been typical of an early medieval, rather than Romano-British, phase of woodland definition. In some places a number of early medieval groves may have multiplied during the later medieval period.

The distribution of different types of woodland in the later medieval period may thus be the cumulative result of developments which shaped and sharpened regional differences. Regional variation in woodland seems to have preceded regional variation in field and settlement patterns. The possibility that the variation was of type as much as of quantity may point to factors which also influenced the diversification of both field systems and settlement patterns.

The association between plentiful woodland and enclosed fields may have become gradually stronger during the medieval period. The greater variety of woodland in north and west Warwickshire may reflect both the quantity of woodland and a complex topographical history. Medieval woodland may be more than a simple indicator of broad regional variation. Its nature and history may also help to refine some of the current theories about social, economic and topographical history in rural England. Different types of woodland may serve as pointers to aspects of continuity or change in the medieval countryside and consequently to the factors which made for stability or development. They may be as important in answering questions about the history of the countryside as different types of field and settlement.

1 See, for example, Hilton, *Social Structure of Rural Warwickshire in the Middle Ages*, pp. 11-12; Harley, 'Population trends and agricultural developments from the Warwickshire Hundred Rolls of 1279', pp. 9, 12; Roberts, *Settlement, Land Use and Population*, p. 146.

2 For these terms, Rackham, *History of the Countryside*, pp. 4-5.

3 Dyer, *Hanbury*, p. 1.

4 Williamson, 'Explaining Regional Landscapes', pp. 5-6; Dyer, 'The Retreat from Marginal Land', pp. 55-7 and the works cited there.

5 Williamson, 'Explaining Regional Landscapes', *passim*.

6 For a summary of the research, *ibid*.

7 For example, Birrell, 'Common Rights in the Medieval Forest'; Watkins, 'The Woodland Economy of the Forest of Arden'.

8 For helpful summaries of the debate, to which the following paragraphs are indebted, see Williamson, 'Explaining Regional Landscapes', pp. 6-7; N. Higham, 'Settlement, land use and Domesday ploughlands', *Landscape History*, 12 (1990), pp. 33-44, see pp. 34-5.

9 J. Thirsk, 'The Origins of the Common Fields', *Past & Present*, 33 (April, 1966), pp. 142-7 insists upon the use of the term 'common fields'.

10 J. Titow, 'Medieval England and the Open-Field System', *Past & Present*, 32 (December, 1965), pp. 86-102, see p. 96. Warwickshire has an example from 1252 - *le Communchaump* in Offchurch, P.R.O., CP 25/1/244/23 - and at least one fourteenth-century example, in an inquisition post mortem dating from 1352 and referring to Long Itchington, *in communibus campis*, P.R.O., C 135/120/11.

11 D.N. Hall, 'The origins of open-field agriculture - the archæological fieldwork evidence', in ed. T. Rowley, *The Origins of Open Field Agriculture* (1981), pp. 22-38; *idem*, 'Late Saxon Topography and Early Medieval Estates', ed. Hooke, *Medieval Villages*, pp. 61-9, especially pp. 63-4 and 66.

12 Williamson, 'Explaining Regional Landscapes', p. 6; Higham, 'Settlement, land use and Domesday ploughlands', p. 34.

13 Williamson, 'Explaining Regional Landscapes', p. 6.

14 *ibid.*, p. 11.

15 For example, ed. A.R.H. Baker and R.A. Butlin, *Studies of Field Systems in the British Isles* (1973), *passim*; Skipp, 'The Evolution of Settlement and Open-field Topography in North Arden'.

16 Williamson, 'Explaining Regional Landscapes', p. 6.

17 For the evolutionary theory, J. Thirsk, 'The Common Fields', *Past & Present*, 29 (December, 1964), pp. 3-25.

18 B. Campbell, 'Commonfield Origins - The Regional Dimension', in Rowley, *The Origins of Open-Field Agriculture*, pp. 112-29, see pp. 119-29.

19 Fox, 'Approaches to the Adoption of the Midland System'; *idem*, 'The Agrarian Context', in ed. *idem*, *The Origins of the Midland Village* (papers prepared for a discussion session at the Economic History Society's annual conference, Leicester, April, 1992), pp. 36-72.

20 *ibid.*; Williamson, 'Explaining Regional Landscapes', p. 7; on the use of ploughteams, Higham, 'Settlement, land use and Domesday ploughlands', especially pp. 35-6.

21 Campbell, 'Commonfield Origins', p. 128, makes the claim; Williamson, 'Explaining Regional Landscapes', p. 8, disputes it.

22 For a summary of the social structure traditionally associated with 'woodland' regions and for qualifications based on a west midlands example, Dyer, *Hanbury*, pp. 48-9 and the references cited there.

23 Williamson, 'Explaining Regional Landscapes', p. 8.

24 T. Williamson, 'Settlement Chronology and Regional Landscapes: The Evidence from the Claylands of East Anglia and Essex', in ed. Hooke, *Anglo-Saxon Settlements*, pp. 153-75, see p. 174.

25 J.F.R. Walmsley, 'The *Censarii* of Burton Abbey and the Domesday population', *North Staffordshire Journal of Field Studies*, 8 (1968), pp. 73-80.

26 Williamson, 'Explaining Regional Landscapes', pp. 10-12.

27 See C. Taylor, *Fields in the English Landscape* (1975), Chapters 4 and 5, also p. 67 and p. 94; P.J. Fowler, 'Agriculture and rural settlement', in ed. D.M. Wilson, *The Archæology of Anglo-Saxon England* (1978), pp 23-48, see pp. 26, 44.

28 Hall, 'The Late Saxon Countryside'.

29 M.W. Beresford and J.G. Hurst, 'Wharram Percy: a Case Study in Microtopography', in ed. Sawyer, *English Medieval Settlement*, pp. 52-85, see especially p. 84; J.G. Hurst, 'The Wharram Research Project: Problem Orientation and Strategy 1950-1990', in ed. Hooke, *Medieval Villages*, pp. 201-4, see especially p. 204.

30 For example, C.C. Taylor, 'Polyfocal settlement and the English village', *Medieval Archaeology*, 21 (1977), pp. 189-93; C.J. Bond, 'Medieval Oxfordshire Villages and their Topography: a Preliminary Discussion', in ed. Hooke, *Medieval Villages*, pp. 101-23.

31 Hall, 'The Late Saxon Countryside'; see also T. Williamson, 'The development of settlement in north-west Essex: the results of recent field survey', *Essex Archæology and History*, 17 (1986), pp. 120-32.

32 Williamson, 'Settlement Chronology and Regional Landscapes: The Evidence from the Claylands of East Anglia and Essex', see especially pp. 153-6.

33 Warner, *Greens, Commons and Clayland Colonization*, pp. 9-12.

34 *ibid.*, p. 15.

35 A.E. Brown and C.C. Taylor, 'The origins of dispersed settlement; some results from fieldwork in Bedfordshire', *Landscape History*, 11 (1989), pp. 61-81.

36 Dyer, *Hanbury*, pp. 15-18, 36-41.

37 Brown and Taylor, 'The origins of dispersed settlement', pp. 69, 72, 76-7, 79.

38 For Essex, W. Rodwell, 'Relict Landscapes in Essex', in ed. H.C. Bowen and P.J. Fowler, *Early Land Allotment*, British Archæological Reports (British Series) 48 (1978), pp. 89-98; Drury and Rodwell, 'Late Iron Age and Roman settlement'; T. Williamson, 'The Roman countryside: settlement and agriculture in N.W. Essex', *Britannia*, 15 (1984), pp. 225-30; for East Anglia, *idem*, 'Early Co-axial Field Systems on the East Anglian Boulder Clays', *Proceedings of the Prehistoric Society*, 53 (1987), pp. 419-31; for south-east England, Higham, *Rome, Britain and the Anglo-Saxons*, pp. 130, 132; for Lincolnshire, S.R. Bassett, 'Beyond the edge of excavation: the topographical context of Goltho', in ed. H. Mayr-Harting and R.I. Moore, *Studies in Medieval History Presented to R.H.C. Davis* (1985), pp. 21-39; for Staffordshire, *idem*, 'Medieval Lichfield. A Topographical Review', *Transactions of the South Staffordshire Archæological and Historical Society*, XXII (1980-81), pp. 93-121, see pp. 95-8; for Warwickshire, *idem*, *The Wootton Wawen Project: interim report no. 4*, pp. 15-21.

39 For example, Williamson, 'Early Co-axial Field Systems', pp. 425-7.

40 *ibid.*, p. 420.

41 M. Fulford, 'The Landscape of Roman Britain: A Review', *Landscape History*, 12 (1990), pp. 25-31, see p. 27.

42 Taylor, *Fields in the English Landscape*, p. 67.

43 Williamson, 'Explaining Regional Landscapes', p. 9.

44 See, for example, P. Salway, *Roman Britain* (1981), pp. 542-4.

45 Fox, 'The Origins of the Midland Village', pp. 64-6; P.J. Fowler, 'Farming in the Anglo-Saxon landscape: an archæologist's review', *Anglo-Saxon England*, 9 (1981), pp. 263-80, see especially p. 273 ff.

46 A. Watkins, 'Cattle Grazing in the Forest of Arden in the Later Middle Ages', *Agricultural History Review*, 37 (1989), pp. 12-25, see p. 13.

47 As in Williamson, 'Explaining Regional Landscapes', p. 7 and Dyer, *Hanbury*, pp. 10-11.

48 *ibid.*, p. 10.

49 Higham, *Rome, Britain and the Anglo-Saxons*, Chapter Two, especially pp. 37-9.

50 R. Faith, 'Estates, demesnes and the village', in ed. Fox, *The Origins of the Midland Village*, pp. 11-35.

51 For example, Fox, 'The Agrarian Context', pp. 38-9; Blair, *Early Medieval Surrey*, pp. 24-30.

52 For example, Williamson, 'Parish boundaries and early fields', p. 247; D. Hooke, 'Early forms of open-field agriculture in England', in ed. U. Sporrong, *The Transformation of Rural Society, Economy and Landscape*, Papers from the 1987 meeting of the Permanent European Conference for the Study of the Rural Landscape, (University of Stockholm), pp. 143-51, see especially p. 151.

53 Williamson, 'Parish boundaries and early fields' is based on research in Norfolk and Suffolk, where large-scale open fields were absent.

54 Hooke, *Anglo-Saxon Landscapes of the West Midlands: the Charter Evidence*, p. 105.

55 Rackham, *Ancient Woodland*, Chapter 8, see especially pp. 97, 104-6.

56 *ibid.*, p. 105; *idem, Trees and Woodland in the British Landscape* (second edition), p. 35.

57 See, for example, R.H. Hilton, *A Medieval Society* (second edition, 1983), p. 13.

58 Dyer, *Hanbury*, pp. 10-11; Williamson, 'Explaining Regional Landscapes', p. 7.

59 Rackham, *History of the Countryside*, p. 84; *idem, Ancient Woodland*, p. 131.

60 Fulford, 'The Landscape of Roman Britain', p. 29.

61 For example, Dyer, 'The Retreat from Marginal Land', pp. 52-3.

62 Higham, *Rome, Britain and the Anglo-Saxons*, p. 79.

63 Williamson, 'Early Co-axial Field Systems', p. 427.

64 Fulford, 'The Landscape of Roman Britain', p. 30.

65 M. Bell, 'Environmental Archæology as an Index of Continuity and Change in the Medieval Landscape', ed. Aston, Austin and Dyer, *The Rural Settlements of Medieval England*, pp. 269-86, see pp. 274-6, 286; Higham, *Rome, Britain and the Anglo-Saxons*, pp. 77-9.

66 Fulford, 'The Landscape of Roman Britain', p. 29.

67 Williamson 'Explaining Regional Landscapes', p. 10.

68 For example, Roden, 'Woodland and its Management in the Medieval Chilterns'; Rackham, *Trees and Woodland in the British Landscape* (second edition), see especially p. 55; Witney, 'The Woodland Economy of Kent'.

69 Rackham, *History of the Countryside*, p. 9; *idem, Ancient Woodland*, p. viii and *passim*.

70 For example, Birrell, 'Common Rights in the Medieval Forest'.

71 For example, Witney, 'The Woodland Economy of Kent', pp. 33-5.

72 Rackham, *Trees and Woodland in the British Landscape* (second edition), pp. 39, 55, 62-3.

73 Williamson, 'Explaining Regional Landscapes', p. 10, approaches this view, although the statements that "woods *sensu stricto* were, in general, private manorial property" and that there was "an early tendency" for wooded waste to be held in severalty in woodland regions do not square with the evidence from Warwickshire.

74 *ibid.*

75 Vollans, 'The Evolution of Farm-Lands in the Central Chilterns'; Roden, *Studies in Chiltern Field Systems*, see especially pp. 91, 127, 183, 255, 314, 350, 354-5. The permission of the Librarian of the University of London to cite the latter work is gratefully acknowledged.

76 There has been a full survey of Admington, for which see C. Dyer's summary in the Medieval Settlement Research Group's Annual Report 10 (1995), p. 42, but this parish was not part of the Domesday county. There has been some field-walking in Barston and in the east of Sutton Coldfield under the auspices of the Birmingham and Warwickshire Archæological Society. A group of volunteers has recently started field survey in Tysoe parish and it is hoped to extend this in due course to adjacent parishes.

77 Hooke, 'Village Development in the West Midlands'.

78 The list in H.L. Gray, *English Field Systems* (1915), p. 31 is supplemented by Tate, 'Enclosure Acts and awards relating to Warwickshire', p. 56. During the research into the woodland of

medieval Warwickshire, records of two open fields have been found in relation to Tysoe (P.R.O., E 315/48/115), Napton (W.C.R.O., CR1248/71/20-2, CR1248/72/2, CR1248/73/4), Shuckburgh (W.C.R.O., CR1248/70/2, CR1248/71/2-4, CR1248/68/7), Stretton-on-Fosse (P.R.O., E 326/4843, 4835, 4817), Bishop's Itchington (W.C.R.O., CR1886/Cupboard 4/Top shelf/CAR/1), Fenny Compton (W.C.R.O., L1/1, 2, 4, 5, 12), Grandborough (P.R.O., E 315/378, f. 12r), Harbury, (B.L., Add. MS., 47,677, f. lxxiii), Hodnell (B.L., Add. Chs. 48,154, 48,161), Ratley (P.R.O., E 326/11626), Hampton Lucy (*RBW*, p. 263), Stratford-upon-Avon (*RBW*, p. 243), Dassett (P.R.O., E 315/378, f. 7r), Ettington (W.C.R.O., CR229/box 18/3/1-2), Aston Cantlow (P.R.O., C 263/2/1), Farnborough (Staffs. R.O., D593/A/1/8), Sawbridge (Cambridge University Library, Add. 3021, f. 447); Binton, (P.R.O., E 315/45/39, 177). For Compton Verney, Dyer and Bond, *Compton Murdak*.

[79] For the deeds relating to Fenny Compton, W.C.R.O., L1/1, 2, 4, 5, 12.

[80] Hall, 'The Late Saxon Countryside', pp. 100-1, 109-10.

[81] C.C. Taylor and P.J. Fowler, 'Roman Fields into Medieval Furlongs', in ed. Bowen and Fowler, *Early Land Allotment*, pp. 159-62.

[82] Ford, 'Some Settlement Patterns in the Central Region of the Warwickshire Avon', p. 286; C.J. Bond, 'Deserted Medieval Villages in Warwickshire: A Review of the Field Evidence', *TBWAS*, 86 (1974), pp. 85-112, see p. 88.

[83] G. Webster and B. Hobley, 'Aerial Reconnaissance over the Warwickshire Avon', *Archæological Journal*, 121 (1964), pp. 1-22.

[84] Ford, 'Some Settlement Patterns', p. 286; for an example of *tunstall*, Dyer and Bond, *Compton Murdak*.

[85] Bassett, *The Wootton Wawen Project: interim report no. 4*, p. 21.

[86] See the Register of Chacombe Priory, P.R.O., E 315/378, f. 12r.

[87] N.W. Alcock, 'Grandborough - a problem in topography', *Warwickshire History*, Vol. 1, No. 4 (Autumn, 1970), pp. 23-7.

[88] Gelling, *West Midlands in the Early Middle Ages*, pp. 30-48; Wise, 'Wasperton', p. 258.

[89] Bassett, 'Church and diocese in the West Midlands', pp. 15-16.

[90] Bassett, *Wootton Wawen Project: interim report no. 4*, p. 21.

[91] Roberts, *Settlement, Land Use and Population*, fig. 48.

[92] P.R.O., E 164/21, ff. 204r-206r, copy in W.C.R.O., MI 409.

[93] See, for example, Hilton, *Social Structure of Rural Warwickshire*, p. 11.

[94] Williamson, 'Explaining Regional Landscapes', especially pp. 8-10.

[95] Bassett, *Wootton Wawen Project: interim report no. 4*, pp. 16-21.

[96] S. Bassett, *The Wootton Wawen Project: interim report no. 2*, (University of Birmingham, 1984), pp. 8-9.

[97] Roberts, *Settlement, Land Use and Population*, Figures 44, 48; however, there was ridge and furrow elsewhere in the parish, over part of the area enclosed in the later Ladbroke Park, see Tasker, *The Nature of Warwickshire*, p. 30.

[98] S.R. Bassett, personal communication.

[99] C. Phythian Adams, *Continuity, Fields and Fission: The Making of a Midland Parish*, University of Leicester Department of English Local History Occasional Papers, Third Series, number 4 (1978), see in particular pp. 4-5, 24-31. The description of the natural resources of the area in the tenth century is based on an attribution of a pre-Conquest charter which Dr. Gelling has shown to be mistaken, see her review in *TBWAS*, 90 (1980), pp. 85-6. I am indebted to Dr. S.R. Bassett for drawing my attention to that review, which unfortunately seems to have been overlooked by Squires and Jeeves, *Leicestershire and Rutland Woodlands Past and Present*, p. 23. However, the minor names in holt in Wibtoft and Willey (see the account of wolds in Chapter Five above) indicate the presence of woodland in the early medieval period, at least on the Warwickshire side of Watling Street.

[100] Hall, 'The Late Saxon Countryside', p. 110.

[101] Fox, 'The Agrarian Context', pp. 64-6.

[102] *ibid.*, p. 55.

[103] On the importance of large areas of grazing for flocks of sheep, *ibid.*, p. 57.

[104] On the change in the meaning of the word *feld* at about the time open fields were introduced, *ibid.*, pp. 58-9.

[105] Fox, 'The people of the wolds', *passim*.

[106] The name "The Grove Close or Grounds" appears on a map of the Stoneythorpe estate dated 1754 (W.C.R.O., CR1470/Box 2) and in a deed of 1621 (W.C.R.O., CR1470/box 2/bundle 7), but no medieval or sixteenth-century record of woodland has been found, hence the hesitation over the existence of a medieval grove.

[107] For Ratley's groves, see Chapter Two and the references cited there, notably S.B.T, DR10/1406, ff. 203-23; P.R.O., E 326/11626, E 329/234.

[108] S.B.T., DR10/1457.

[109] B.L., Add. MS. 28,024, f. 98, copy in W.C.R.O., MI 177.

[110] For example, Hilton, *Social Structure of Rural Warwickshire*, pp. 11-12.

[111] Roberts, *Settlement, Land Use and Population*, p. 86.

[112] Dr. Roden's thesis was completed in 1965. For the origin of Chiltern, E. Ekwall, *The Concise Oxford Dictionary of English Place-Names* (fourth edition, 1960), p. 104.

Chapter Seven

CONCLUSIONS: CONTINUITY AND CHANGE

Aims and objectives: the results

This concluding chapter assesses how far the research has achieved the aims and objectives which were set out in the introduction. It will then consider whether, in the light of the study's conclusions, the woods of medieval Warwickshire can be seen as relatively permanent features in a changing countryside.

Chapter Two achieved the first objective of the study by effectively disposing of the assertion that Warwickshire south and east of the Avon was "woodless" in 1086. In the process it was shown that the *silva* of Domesday Book was probably wood pasture, and that the Domesday survey seems to have omitted Warwickshire's groves, with the accidental exception of that in Lighthorne. The evidence for woodland in south and east Warwickshire during the later medieval period and in 1086 implies that the two distinct traditions of woodland management, coppicing and pasture, existed by the eleventh century. These conclusions were foreshadowed in the author's earlier research into the history of Hampton Wood and are confirmed by this wider study.

Chapters Three and Four dealt with the woodland of north and west Warwickshire in the later medieval period. The woodland of the Avon valley below Stratford-upon-Avon resembled that south and east of the river in its nature and distribution. Further north and west there was much more woodland than in the south and east, both in 1086 and subsequently. The theory that most of the woodland lost in this area during the thirteenth century was wood pasture is certainly supported by cases in the king's courts. There is evidence of assarting in the twelfth century, but not in enough detail to pursue the argument that the woodland lost then was also mainly wood pasture rather than coppice woods, although the circumstantial evidence from Stoneleigh does point to that conclusion. The association between assarting and wood pasture may simply reflect the strong tradition of common pasture in the region. The loss of woodland, which may have been caused as much or more by over-grazing as by deliberate clearance, appears to have involved a change in land use rather than the settlement of new territory. There was expansion of settlement, but the use of the word 'colonization', which has been applied so often to topographical change in north and west Warwickshire in the later medieval period, is inappropriate. Even before this change, the large amounts of Domesday *silva* may have combined trees and grass to form areas of woodland which were relatively open and accessible, rather than dense and forbidding.

The widespread distribution of *silva* in north and west Warwickshire in 1086 does not allow Domesday Book to be used as evidence of two separate traditions of woodland management in this part of the county. However, the existence of several groves in the twelfth century makes it possible to suggest that both coppicing and wood pasture were practised in the region at an earlier date. The research demonstrates the variety of woodland in the later medieval period - woods, outwoods and common woods, groves and hays. Tenants' groves were concentrated in certain parishes; neglected in most previous historical studies, they show that later medieval woods were not necessarily common or restricted to lords.

In view of the paucity of documentary evidence for the early medieval period it is not surprising that it has proved much more difficult to estimate the amounts of woodland in Warwickshire during that period. The level and chronology of the formation of secondary woodland also remain uncertain. However, critical examination of the evidence of place-names, particularly minor names including *wold*, *leah* and *hyrst*, has led to the conclusion that there were significant amounts of woodland in south and east Warwickshire in the early centuries of the period, although apparently still less than in the north and west of the county. Warwickshire's later medieval wolds were in all probability former woods, which arguably lost their trees during the early medieval period, but the place-name element *leah* may reflect as much an increase as a reduction in woodland. Despite careful consideration of possible meanings, the significance of the appellatives Grafton and Wootton have proved elusive.

The results of topographical analysis in the Wootton Wawen area are very relevant to the study. They show that this part of north and west Warwickshire did not have a continuous, dense cover of wood during the early medieval period, but they do not exclude the presence of woodland. Some secondary woodland may have developed alongside woods which existed in the Romano-British period, but the exact quantities of woodland and degrees of change in both the Romano-British and early medieval periods remain unknown. The tradition of intercommoning in adjoining woods belonging to parishes or townships which had no known tenurial links or ecclesiastical affiliations may point to a pre-medieval origin for such common pasture and hence for the woods in which it was practised. Alongside the potential antiquity of many woods and rights of common pasture there may have been an equally strong, separate tradition of enclosed coppice woods called groves.

Chapter Six developed the theme of regional variation by considering the origins of different types of woodland in the context of field systems, settlement patterns and land use. Regional variation in amounts of woodland appears to have preceded regional variation in field and settlement patterns. The suggested link between Warwickshire's wolds and the creation of open fields may be complex. The distribution of different types of woodland in the later medieval period may be the cumulative result of earlier developments which sharpened regional variation. The history of Warwickshire's medieval woodland may make a small contribution to research into the development of regional topography. The different types of woodland may have developed during different periods and as a consequence of diverse social and economic conditions. They may serve as pointers to the incidence and chronology of continuity or change in the countryside.

Continuity and change in the distribution of woodland

Continuity and change[1] have been recurring themes in recent studies of the English countryside. They run through this study, reflected in most of the aims and objectives set out in the introductory chapter. Those aims were inspired partly by the concept of woods as some of the most enduring features in the English countryside. The idea that many English woods are very old and that woodland has been relatively stable since at least the thirteenth century, by which time coppicing had been established in most woods,[2] associates woodland with continuity rather than with change. Therefore one of the aims of this study was to compare and draw conclusions from the known extent and distribution of coppice woods and wood pasture in the early and later medieval periods respectively. In particular it was intended to test the theory that the former were relatively permanent in comparison with wood pasture and to assess the degree of change in the rural topography of Warwickshire, especially its woodland.

The prehistory of English topography is certainly one of change. Over several millennia from the Neolithic period onwards a naturally wooded country became a mixture of arable, pasture, meadow, heath, moor, marsh and wood.[3] This study has been concerned with the levels of change and continuity in woodland during the medieval period. Much of the Romano-British countryside was densely settled. The research has therefore tried to assess how much woodland existed c.400 in that part of lowland England which became Warwickshire, and how the quantities, distribution and types of woodland might have changed during the following thousand years.

Students of the history of English rural topography during the last two or three hundred years will be aware of the great changes which have occurred as the result of Parliamentary enclosures, urbanisation and the intensification of agricultural production. The propensity for change, arguably accelerated by modern technology, is a salutary reminder of the potential for change during the much longer period covered by this study.

Research has shown that many woods in eastern England which were recorded in the thirteenth century can be matched to woods in the modern countryside.[4] By analogy with woods which were named in some of the boundary descriptions which were attached to early medieval charters, later medieval woods are thought to have been already very old in the thirteenth century. Their inferred stability has been contrasted with other changes in the medieval countryside, implying that, in comparison with woods, many other features were relatively transient.

Woodland before c.1250 has been regarded as far less stable, much of the *silva* recorded in Domesday Book having disappeared during the intervening 160 years.[5] The emphasis on change in this study of Warwickshire's woodland could be attributed therefore to the attempt to deal with the whole of the medieval period. However, the account of woods in south and east Warwickshire in Chapter Two and in north and west Warwickshire in Chapter Three show that there was a real regional difference in the amount of change in the later medieval period, as measured by the survival rate of the county's later medieval woods after c.1250.

After Chapter Two had disposed of the alleged lack of woodland in south and east Warwickshire it traced the subsequent fate of those medieval woods for which there was documentary evidence. It was found that a large proportion of them survived into the nineteenth or twentieth century. There was little evidence of pasture in them, the woods of Long Compton, Whichford and Thornton in Ettington being exceptions.[6] Continuity rather than change characterised the woodland of the region from 1086 to c.1500. Several changes occurred after 1500. They involved the growth rather than the loss of woodland. Indeed, in the south and east of Warwickshire significant amounts of the surviving woodland are post-medieval.

The decline of arable production, the depopulation of some settlements and the importance of country estates surrounded by parkland or by countryside adapted for hunting presumably provided the context for new woodland. Chapter Two revealed the development of Chesterton Wood from a small medieval grove to a wood of over one hundred acres. The modern Bowshot Wood adjoining the Fosse Way seems to be largely secondary woodland; the map drawn in 1728 of the manors of Walton (in the parish of Wellesbourne) shows the land covered by the modern wood as areas of trees called Friz hill Copse and Brake, Compton Peece, Brake, and New Copse.[7] Wellesbourne Wood itself expanded in the eighteenth or early nineteenth century. Between 1735 and 1848[8] it acquired Wood Hill Plantation, Red Hill Plantation, Brake Hill Plantation and Green Hill Plantation.

Substantial amounts of post-medieval woodland are by no means unusual. They are not a development peculiar to south and east Warwickshire. It has been estimated that only one third of Britain's modern woodland covers sites which have been continuously wooded since the later medieval period.[9] The statement that most of the surviving woodland in western Arden is old established[10] should therefore be treated with caution. For example, Ladbroke Park in Tanworth-in-Arden included the site of the medieval messuage,[11] whilst parts of the adjoining Windmill Naps and Tyler's Grove lie over the ridge and furrow of former cultivation.[12] In Chapter Three it is argued that much of Keresley's remaining woodland probably originated as secondary woodland during the fifteenth and sixteenth centuries. There are several other examples of secondary woods formed during the modern period, such as Siden Hill Wood in Hampton-in-Arden,[13] Rook Wood in Maxstoke,[14] and Wilkinson's Grove in Astley.[15] There is a lack of earlier documentary records for many seventeenth- or eighteenth-century woods which may reflect a late origin rather than documentary deficiencies.

In north and west Warwickshire change predominated throughout the later medieval period as well as subsequently. The individual parish and township studies in Chapter Three, where much space is devoted to discussions about the likely sites of former woods and groves, contain ample evidence of the loss of medieval woodland in the north and west of the county after as well as before c.1250. Much of the lost woodland appears to have been wood pasture, which has a much less stable ecology than coppice woods. However, whilst coppice woods or groves may have been more stable during the twelfth and thirteenth centuries, tenants' groves proved to be very vulnerable after the medieval period. Numerous fields called wood or grove testify to former woodland which disappeared during or after the medieval period. Other later medieval woods have left no trace in the modern countryside. It is often impossible to find on eighteenth- and nineteenth- century maps the minor field- and place-names which, if they had survived from the medieval period, could have at least pointed to the former sites of medieval woods.

Some woods survived the changes to the medieval countryside only to be destroyed in the nineteenth and twentieth centuries. Replanting with conifers, which can effectively destroy a deciduous wood, was widespread after the Second World War. Ettington Grove, Haywood in Baddesley Clinton, much of Oakley Wood in Bishop's Tachbrook, Blackwell Wood in Kenilworth, part of Arley Wood and Brandon, Weston, and Wetherley Woods are examples; the partial replanting of Cubbington Wood may yet be redeemable. Replanting has occurred very recently in some of Warwickshire's surviving medieval woods, such as Austy Wood in Wootton Wawen, Mockley Wood by Ullenhall and Songar Grove in Claverdon. Urbanisation and industrialisation accounted for much destruction in the north of the county; Chelmsley Wood is a sad, post-war example.

The relative stability of woodland in south and east Warwickshire since 1086 does not seem to have applied to that region in earlier centuries. Continuity appears in relict features rather than in extant woods. There is strong evidence to indicate that the wolds of Warwickshire had been woodland in the early medieval period. Pasture rights on the wolds of south and east Warwickshire survived long after the trees had disappeared. Medieval field-names including *hurst* and *leah* testify to the loss of woodland during the medieval period. Once the wolds and hursts had lost their trees, the balance changed to favour continuity, presumably a reflection of the smaller amounts of woodland and their consequent scarcity value.

It could be suggested that the disappearance of trees from the wolds of Warwickshire was evidence of the relative instability of wood pasture as against coppice woods in the south and east of the county. However, it was argued in Chapter Five that some of the wolds might have retained their trees to become later medieval woods, such as those in Bubbenhall, Princethorpe, Ryton, Stretton-on-Dunsmore,

Wappenbury, Whichford, Long Compton, and Wolford. None of these was ever called a grove in any surviving document. Compton and Whichford Woods certainly had a tradition of pasture in the later medieval period and there was common pasture in some woodland in Princethorpe;[16] most of the other woods were too poorly documented to produce evidence of their management. It is suggested in Chapter Five that wold ceased to be the common word for a wood after many wolds had lost their trees and that the old name stuck to the treeless pastures whilst wolds which had retained their trees came to be called woods.

Although many of the groves recorded for south and east Warwickshire in the later medieval period have survived, it is possible that several others were lost in the early medieval period. Some were certainly lost in the later medieval period. At least one of Ratley's groves was asserted in the twelfth century and records of assarts in Birdingbury suggest that Birdingbury's grove met the same fate. There was a furlong (*culturam*) called *Barndegrove* in Princethorpe.[17] There is therefore no conclusive evidence that all the woods which were lost in south and east Warwickshire were wood pasture.

Recent research into continuity and change in other topographical features has partially illuminated one of the main unresolved questions of this study, the origin of groves. The continuity of use of the land in some parts of the region since the Romano-British period provides a context in which coppicing could have been practised throughout the medieval period and in which different types of woodland could have coexisted. The discussion about the origins of open fields, nucleated settlements and land use in Chapter Six shows that the regional variation in the distribution and types of woodland in the later medieval period might have been strongly influenced by earlier variations in the level of change and continuity in the countryside. There was a potential for some continuity through evolutionary change in topographical features within a relatively stable framework of boundaries. Certain features in the later medieval countryside might have been very old. The reorganisation of some field systems to create open fields implied a greater degree of change. Nonetheless, even where large open fields were formed, pre-medieval boundary alignments could persist. In some cases, features on the margins of those fields, including woods, may have been relatively undisturbed.

In Chapter Six it is concluded that regional variation may have been intensified, rather than initiated, by particular combinations of continuity and change in the early medieval period. Particular types of woodland may have developed or disappeared during different periods in certain regions of the countryside. For example, tenants' groves seem to have been confined to north and west Warwickshire, but were present in quantity only in a minority of parishes there. Their uneven distribution may point to distinct phases in the history of the countryside or to a local diversity of social structure and to consequently varying levels of continuity and change in particular regional topographies.

The woodland of medieval Warwickshire was not stable. During at least part of the medieval period there was significantly more woodland than there is now. Many woods were lost after c.1250 as well as before. Those which survive, and which can be shown to have been medieval and not later, secondary woodland, are relatively scarce relict features in a changed and changing countryside. They may have had a better survival rate than many other topographical features - they are not as rare as "unimproved", and consequently flower-filled, meadows have become in the last fifty years - but this fact should not obscure the changes and losses which have occurred. A study which began with an interest in woods as possible exemplars of continuity in the English countryside has become a history of woodland as part of the changing topography of rural Warwickshire.

Whilst some continuity can be found in boundaries and field-names, it is change which predominates in the appearance of the Warwickshire countryside. The underlying geology of hill and vale is unaltered and the countryside seems to have been more or less densely inhabited for the last two millennia and more. However, its modern aspects must differ substantially in detail from the views which would have been encountered during the medieval period. The balance between arable, pasture, meadow, heath, moor and wood has changed. Even in areas which remain predominantly rural, much woodland, heath and moor have been lost in the last thousand years. In some parishes modern hedged fields have replaced the open fields of the later medieval period; in others the fields may always have been enclosed but have changed in shape and size. Medieval field boundaries may have looked very different to modern hedges. Modern roads may follow very different courses to medieval routes. Both the sites of dwellings and their architecture have undergone marked changes. Modern pesticides and fertilisers have destroyed the beautiful wild flowers of fields, meadows and pastures and the rich variety of insects, birds and animals which lived in them. It is a countryside in which one often has to search for physical traces of medieval topographical history. Careful research is then needed to show the place of any physical remains in that history.

For these reasons the woodland of medieval Warwickshire needs to be approached through history and archæology.[18] However, the ecology of extant medieval woods in Warwickshire, like other physical remains and other evidence used in this study, has a contribution to make, if it is interpreted with care.

Continuity and change in the management and appearance of woods

Even where the evidence for continuity of woodland from the medieval period is strong, precise topographical reconstruction is impossible. The appearance of woodland is influenced by aspects of human management which cannot be traced through archæological evidence or map analysis and which are rarely mentioned in documents. Medieval documents do not describe the appearance of a wood. Dr. Rackham has drawn attention to a fifteenth-century painting of huntsmen in a wood, but this is of Flemish origin.[19] A sketch of fields and a small wood in Hampshire dates from

the early sixteenth century and cannot be presumed to picture the scene in earlier centuries.[20] As has been explained in Chapter Four, wood pasture with widely scattered timber trees and little underwood presents a very different aspect to a coppice wood, with or without standard trees.

The situation is somewhat analogous to field systems. Even if they can be traced, their visual impact on the medieval countryside is not always clear. Were they bounded by ditches, banks, fences, low hedges, or tall hedges with timber trees? Different types of bounds must have had a profound effect on the appearance of the countryside. There are occasional clues as to the nature of field boundaries. The hedges along Arrow's lanes must have been tall and thick to hide murderers lying in wait for their victim in 1381.[21] It appears that much of the wood and timber surveyed in Tanworth-in-Arden c.1500 was to be found in hedgerows.[22] As far as timber is concerned, this impression is confirmed for north and west Warwickshire by many of the surveys prepared in the reign of Henry VIII prior to royal grants of former monastic possessions or other lands which had been acquired by the Crown.[23] In some manors in south and east Warwickshire these 'particulars for grants' show that timber was in short supply in the early sixteenth century.[24] However, the management practices reflected in these surveys may have been different to those prevailing in earlier centuries.

There is some information pertinent to the appearance of a few of Warwickshire's woods in the fourteenth and fifteenth centuries. If upwards of 24,000 faggots (bundles of underwood) were taken out of the woods of Wedgnock Park in 1425-6[25] then those woods must have been coppiced at regular intervals and would have been fairly open and light. Coppicing is also documented for Withycombe Wood in 1448,[26] Mockley Wood in Ullenhall in 1401,[27] Wodehurst in Middleton in 1385,[28] Bigging Grove in Coventry in 1460,[29] and *Wodlondsgrove, Charlecote grove, blakemore grove, kyntlondgrove* and *Barford grove* in Tanworth-in-Arden in the early sixteenth century.[30] Two examples are given in Appendix 6. However, whilst these documents may refer to timber trees amongst the underwood, they do not tell us whether these trees grew within or alongside the coppiced areas, nor how densely they were spaced. Records of sales of wood also do not indicate for how long the woods had been subject to organised, intensive coppicing. Management practices may have been very different in earlier centuries, with consequent effects on the appearance of the woods.

Sixteenth-century legislation may provide some evidence for management practices. In 1543 "An Acte for the preservacion of Woodes" provided that in any coppices felled after twenty-four years growth or less twelve "standills or storers of Oke", or, if necessary, other suitable trees, should be left in each acre to develop as timber and should not themselves be felled until their girth measured ten inches at three feet above the ground.[31] Apart from the possibility that the Act may have introduced a higher density of timber trees than had been the norm and that it might have been honoured more in the breach than in the observance, it cannot be taken as evidence of management practices several centuries earlier. The evidence for coppicing cited above comes mostly from agreements for the sale of wood which include requirements for enclosing coppiced woods, but most of these documents date from the fifteenth century. As explained in Chapter Four, one has to keep an open mind about the appearance of Warwickshire's medieval woods and groves.

These points may be illustrated by the present differences between two ancient woods in Warwickshire. In Hampton Wood the Warwickshire Wildlife Trust reintroduced coppicing about forty years after the Wood, including its mature timber trees, had been felled, grazed and then neglected so that it became overgrown. Coppicing has been concentrated in the parts of the Wood where there seems to be the least damage from grazing, and is being extended over part of the secondary woodland. The coppiced areas are now light and open, each with some timber trees, none of very great age. The Wood may give a good impression of a medieval coppice with standards, a wood where the emphasis was on underwood rather than timber and where timber was cut before it had reached full maturity, a wood full of the wildlife encouraged by traditional management.

Underwood is still cut in the woods of Long Itchington and Ufton, but parts of those woods have a high density of mature oaks, many of which have grown tall to reach the light and have few side branches. These oaks may be the product of eighteenth- or nineteenth-century management for timber as much as for underwood and of a deliberate policy of promoting oak.[32] They may not reflect management practices in earlier centuries. Even if oaks were promoted to the same density in medieval woods they were probably felled at an earlier stage in their growth, for the timber used in many buildings after the thirteenth century did not come from great trees.[33] It was possible for forty-seven oaks to be taken out of Itchington Wood in 1385-6,[34] but they may have been much smaller and more sparsely distributed than their modern successors. Certainly the reference in the charter of 1001[35] to the high oak in the middle of *wulluht graf* suggests that it was a distinguishing feature and that high oaks were not common in the Wood in the early eleventh century.

It is much more difficult to find modern examples of wood pasture which might help towards an understanding of the nature of medieval woods in which common pasture rights were recorded. It appears that large areas of woodland in north and west Warwickshire in the later medieval period were wood pasture. Medieval wood pasture was unstable. Much of it became waste during the later medieval period and was therefore more susceptible to clearance. Those areas which survived became mainly treeless commons, many of which were enclosed during the eighteenth and nineteenth centuries. Some parkland was an enclosed, specialist form of wood pasture. Medieval parks rarely survive, and early modern parks were in a different tradition. Sutton Park originated as a medieval park. Much of it is now, and may have been previously, grassland, heath and marsh rather than woodland. Thanks to mainly traditional management over the centuries, this remarkable relict, rich in wildlife, may resemble (apart from the odd conifer plantation) parts of the Warwickshire countryside at some time during the medieval period. Stoneleigh's wood pasture probably covered an area over three times the size of Sutton Park.

Hampton Wood and the woods of Long Itchington and Ufton are predominantly a mixture of hazel and ash underwood and oak standards. Hampton Wood also has an area of English elm, which can become invasive and change the ecology of a wood.[36] Warwickshire's surviving medieval woods are mainly of hazel, ash and maple. They are rarely dominated by a single species of tree. There are no woods characterised chiefly by beech, hornbeam, elm or alder. At least four later medieval woods were named after birches.[37]

The variety which specialised woods bring to the countryside is exemplified in Dr. Rackham's evocative description of lime woods in blossom.[38] Piles Coppice is Warwickshire's sole surviving example of a wood predominantly of small-leaved lime. As pointed out in Chapter Five, some minor place-names testify to the former presence of lime woods. They are found in north and west Warwickshire rather than in the south and east of the county. The regional variation in the quantities of woodland in medieval Warwickshire might therefore have been complemented by a regional variation in woodland ecology. Such variation occurs elsewhere in England and is thought to reflect variety in the composition of the original wildwood.[39] Pollen analysis, if available from enough sites, could provide more information on this point.

Of the ground flora in Warwickshire's medieval woods there is not a hint. The records of medieval woods were all made, directly or indirectly, for economic reasons. The beauty of spring flowers in coppice woods was utterly irrelevant, as were the typical flowers in meadows, pastures and cornfields. Hampton Wood and Ufton Wood have many plants in common, but in different proportions. Both have plenty of bluebells, but Hampton Wood is a primrose wood, whereas Ufton Wood, whilst it has some primroses, is carpeted with celandines and wood anemones in the early spring. Woods which were open to common pasture may have had a very different ground flora, depending on the intensity of grazing. Someone walking through the hursts of Sutton Park today encounters layers of dead holly and oak leaves turning to leaf mould underfoot, with none of the spectacular displays of spring flowers to be found in ancient coppice woods, but where grazing was regulated alongside coppiced enclosures spring flowers could have flourished.

A rich ground flora is usually associated with ancient woods, but is not a certain indicator of primary woodland. Secondary woodland can acquire the ground flora of an adjacent primary wood, although differences may persist for centuries. In Hampton Wood primroses, bluebells and yellow archangel appear on the ridge and furrow which was within the Wood by 1736, but wood anemones have not spread in the same way. Yet the ridge and furrow on the northern edge of Kingsbury Wood is covered with wood anemones, which may have spread from Edge Hill Wood, where they are also found in abundance and which is probably on the site of the medieval wood of Kingsbury. Certain plants combined with a generally rich flora may thus indicate that medieval woodland existed in the vicinity, even if the surviving woodland was formed at a later date. Some secondary woodland may not have adjoined existing woodland and may never have developed the fine ground flora which is thought to derive ultimately from prehistoric wildwood. A limited ground flora may also be the result of management practices, past or present. Therefore the absence of plants associated with ancient woodland does not necessarily mean that the wood in question is post-medieval. For example, whilst there are medieval records of a grove in Ettington which presumably occupied part at least of the site of the modern Ettington Grove, the modern Grove has been largely replanted with conifers, and even the remaining deciduous part lacks an understorey and spring flowers.

Relict flora of former woods may linger in hedgerows to point to the sites of these woods. Bluebells grow on the verges near the presumed site of Offord Wood. A patch of red campion, also a flower of ancient woods, can be seen by the road between Edge Hill and Kineton; is this the ghost of a wood which disappeared over a thousand years ago?

An appreciation of ecological history is essential to a full awareness of the possible nature of regional variation in Warwickshire. Amounts of woodland and the layout of fields cannot in themselves describe the appearance of the countryside. The impoverishment of the English countryside since the Second World War makes it even more difficult for younger generations of historians to imagine the colours and variety which were familiar to people who knew the countryside before the widespread use of pesticides and artificial fertilizers helped to destroy much of its pre-war beauty. The work of the Warwickshire Wildlife Trust and other organisations involved in nature conservation has helped to save some of the remaining unspoilt sites. Woods such as Hampton Wood and Ryton Wood are precious, irreplaceable sites of historical value as well as nature reserves.

It must always be remembered that the modern appearance of woods may be different from the medieval realities and also that there could have been much change during the medieval period. With this in mind, surviving medieval woods, especially those where coppicing has been continued or reintroduced, can lead to a better understanding of historical records. Combined with careful interpretation of the available documentary evidence, they illuminate, even if they cannot tell, the history of the woodland of medieval Warwickshire.

[6] For Long Compton and Whichford, B.L., Egerton MS. 3724, f. 80; for Thornton, P.R.O., JUST 1/952, rot 4d.

[7] W.C.R.O., CR750/1.

[8] Compare the estate map of 1735, W.C.R.O., CR611/715/2, and tithe map of 1848, W.C.R.O., CR569/259.

[9] Rackham, *Ancient Woodland*, p. ix, citing G.F. Peterken, 'Habitat conservation priorities in British and European woodlands', *Biological Conservation*, 11 (1977).

[10] Roberts, *Settlement, Land Use and Population*, p. 143.

[11] P.R.O., DL 29/642/10427 under Tanworth.

[12] Tasker, *The Nature of Warwickshire*, p. 30.

[13] This wood does not appear on a map of 1812, W.C.R.O., Z151, being a copy of P.R.O., MPEE/84.

[14] The area covered by this wood was not woodland in 1767, W.C.R.O., Z149(L).

[15] This wood appears as a band of trees in W.C.R.O., CR764/107, dating from after 1807; there was no wood in this spot in 1696, W.C.R.O., CR136/M12, M9.

[16] For Whichford Wood and Compton Wood, B.L., Egerton MS., 3724, f. 80. For Princethorpe, P.R.O., JUST 1/952, rot 5r.

[17] W.C.R.O., CR314/1, 9.

[18] This study deliberately takes a different approach to that in Rackham, *Ancient Woodland*, which is avowedly a study in historical ecology, see p. viii.

[19] *ibid*., p. 15 and frontispiece.

[20] P.D.A. Harvey, 'The documents of landscape history: snares and delusions', *Landscape History*, 13 (1991), pp. 47-52, see p. 50.

[21] P.R.O., JUST 1/973, rot 3d, "*iacendo in sepibus cuiusdam venelle apud Arwe*".

[22] L.D.W. Smith, 'A survey of building timber and other trees in the hedgerows of a Warwickshire estate, c.1500', *TBWAS*, 90 (1980), pp. 65-73.

[23] In the P.R.O., class E 318, Particulars for Grants. See, for example, E 318/21/998 (Aston Cantlow, Tanworth-in-Arden, Butlers Marston, Preston Bagot, Haselor); E 318/21/1121 (Claverdon, Bearley, Wolverton, Norton Lindsey).

[24] For example, P.R.O., E 318/5/144 (Dunchurch, Long Lawford, Newbold); E 318/18/874 (Halford).

[25] W.C.R.O., CR1886/487.

[26] P.R.O., E 164/22, ff. cxxxii-cxxxiii, copy in W.C.R.O., Z251(Sm).

[27] King's College, Cambridge, WOW/128.

[28] M.MSS., Mi D 4525/2.

[29] C.R.O., 468/15.

[30] S.B.T., DR37/1071, 1084, 1086, 1090, 1091.

[31] *Statutes of the Realm*, Vol. III (1817), pp. 977-80.

[32] For the deliberate promotion of oak timber in woods and the consequent lack of general appreciation of the variety in types of woodland, Rackham, *Ancient Woodland*, pp. 16-18.

[33] Rackham, *History of the Countryside*, p. 87.

[34] P.R.O., SC 6/1041/12 (under accounts for Ladbroke).

[35] S898; Rackham, *History of the Countryside*, p. 79.

[36] *ibid*., p. 106.

[37] *Birchgrove* in Beausale, *BD*, box 137; *Bircheleia* in Hampton-in-Arden, B.R.L., A1/2, 4 and in Brinklow, S.B.T., DR10/39, 191; *Netherbirches* in Ashow, P.R.O., E 210/5693, E 326/459, 497, 3471; *Birchenehurst* in Tanworth-in-Arden, S.B.T., DR37/box 82.

[38] Rackham, *Ancient Woodland*, p. 238.

[39] *ibid*., p.99; *idem, History of the Countryside*, pp. 102-6.

[1] The phrase appears in the title of ed. P.H. Sawyer, *Medieval Settlement: Continuity and Change* (1976). Its relevance will be apparent in the many works cited in this chapter.

[2] Rackham, *History of the Countryside*, p. 85.

[3] Rackham, *Ancient Woodland*, Chapter 8; *idem, Trees and Woodland in the British Landscape* (second edition), pp. 26-35.

[4] *ibid*.

[5] Rackham, *Trees and Woodland in the British Landscape* (second edition), p. 55.

Appendix 1: Gazetteer of recorded medieval* woods in Warwickshire

Wood	Date and reference	Comments
Alcester		

Wood	Date and reference	Comments
apud Alencestr' de bosco domini regis	1238, *Curia Regis Rolls*, XVI, no. 149c.	
in boscis de Alenc'... de dono Willelmi Botereus et Petri filii Herberti .. de vasto boscorum illorum	1262, *Calendar of Close Rolls, 1261-4*, p. 58	in the Forest of Feckenham
wood of Walter de Beauchamp	1291, *Calendar of Close Rolls, 1288-96*, pp. 173-4.	licence to bring 60 acres into cultivation, the wood being within the Forest of Feckenham
super Hurstam	n.d., ?13th C., W.C.R.O., CR1886/61.	not stated whether it was woodland
Copyc called Astlens hurste *=Astlyns Hurst* *?=Asplinhurst Coppice* *=Asplinshurst Wood*	1573, W.C.R.O., CR1886/box 105/1629 1614, W.C.R.O., CR1886/box411/1 1639, W.C.R.O., CR1886/box411/2 1754, W.C.R.O., CR1886/M9.	
hanginge well *=Hanging Well Coppice*	1614, W.C.R.O., CR1886/box411/1 1754, W.C.R.O., CR1886/M9.	
copyc called old parke	1573, W.C.R.O., CR1886/box 105/1629.	by Astlens hurst coppice
Luttulwodefeld	1466-7, W.C.R.O., CR1886/166a.	pasture in 1466-7.
Buldewode	1466-7, W.C.R.O., CR1886/166a.	pasture in 1466-7.
copec vocata Brokehulle cowpyce	1466-7, W.C.R.O., CR1886/166a	
copec vocata kyttevalettelowe *?= a coepiece called kytferret*	1466-7, W.C.R.O., CR1886/166a. 1578, W.C.R.O., CR1886/box 106/1649.	near to the Ridgeway
boscus voc' le Waste	1504-5, W.C.R.O., CR1886/183	timber cut there
Buttras coppyes *=Buttress Coppice*	1355, W.C.R.O., CR1998/box 35/bundle K 1754, W.C.RO., CR1886/M9	deed gave permission to enclose the coppice the modern Butlers Coppice
The priory grove	1544, P.R.O., E 318/19/984	parcel of a pasture called Priors Close, a common wood of 3 acres
A Coppice adioyning to a wood called Oversley Parke	1544, P.R.O., E 318/19/984	2½ acres of underwood of ash, beech, maple and thorn
The priors hacking	1544, P.R.O., E 318/19/984	6 acres, a parcel of waste ground adjoining Sombourne Heath
The hckyng	1544, P.R.O., E 318/19/984	2 acres, a common wood
Coughton grove	1614, W.C.R.O., CR1886/TN1	in King's Coughton, Alcester
Pryors woode	1598, W.C.R.O., CR1886/box 108/1688	part of Beauchamps Court waste, including a lodge, warren

Allesley

Wood	Date and reference	Comments
Boscum de Asschawe *=boscus qui vocatur Asshawe* *=Boscus separalis que vocatur Hasshauwe* *=grossus boscus vocatus Assheshawe*	1208, P.R.O., CP 25/1/242/8 1317, C.R.O., BA/B/A/107/4 1325, P.R.O., C 134/91/27 1392, P.R.O., DL 43/14/3	 by Whaburley and Coundon containing 50 acres, a demesne wood 37 acres, 1 rood, 8 perches
boscum .. qui vocatur holifast *=boscus grossus vocatus holyfast* *=hollifax* *=Hollyfast*	1305, C.R.O., BA/B/A/47/10 1392, P.R.O., DL 43/14/3 1626, W.C.R.O., CR623/box 14 1668, B.R.L., 241,400	demesne wood of John de Hastings containing 30 acres, 1 rood 52 acres, 2 roods, 24 perches coppice or spring wood
boscus forinsecus separalis que vocatur Bolewellschauwe	1325, P.R.O., C 134/91/27	8 acres, a demesne wood

---

* Some woods for which the earliest known record dates from the sixteenth century have been included where it seems likely that the wood existed in the medieval period (i.e. before 1500). Parks have been included where there is evidence that they contained woodland.

boscus separalis que vocatur estendmor	1325, P.R.O., C 134/91/27	5 acres, a demesne wood, no underwood but pasture
=boscus grossus vocatus Estendemore	1392, P.R.O., DL 43/14/3	18½ acres, 16 perches
boscus separalis que vocatur suffagegroue	1325, P.R.O., C 134/91/27	2 acres, a demesne wood
=grossus boscus vocatus suffagegroue	1392, P.R.O., DL 43/14/3	3 acres, 2 roods, 21 perches
pomerium iuxta aulam	1325, P.R.O., C 134/91/27	5 acres, a demesne wood
=grossus boscus vocatur Orchard	1392, P.R.O., DL 43/14/3	15 acres, 12 perches
parcus	1250-1, *SLB*, p. 175	
=parcum	1279, *HR*, p. 85	300 acres
=parcus	1325, P.R.O., C 134/91/27	no underwood, used for cattle
=parcus inclusus	1392, P.R.O., DL 43/14/3	100 acres of great wood
boscum forinsecum	1279, *HR*, p. 85	40 acres
gravam	1279, *HR*, p. 85	containing 1 rood of land formerly common pasture which had been enclosed to the harm of the neighbourhood
grove called Netherfyney	1326, S.B.T., DR10/1	
Haukesty wodes	1396-7, S.B.T., ER1/65/455	
?=grovam iacentem in hawxtiende	1530, B.R.L., 328,923	"Bandland [h]is wood"
?=grove at Hawkesty end	1626, W.C.R.O., CR623/box 14	surrendered by William Tallis
?=2 woods in Hauxtie End	1654, W.C.R.O., CR299/42	in tenure of William Meigh
?=coppice in Hauxtie End	1668-9, W.C.R.O., CR299/49/1-2	near Hawkes End
?=Meigh's Wood	1842, W.C.R.O., CR569/3	
grouam vocatam le Moserddeswod	1411, E 164/21, f. 11v	in Corley in 1410-11
?=Muzzards Wood	1840, W.C.R.O., CR569/3	
two groves called the Byches	1441-2, S.B.T., DR98/699c	near the lane to *Hallye ffaste*
one grove callyd ley loughton	1441-2, S.B.T., DR98/699c	at wall hill near the lane to *Hallye ffaste*
hunygrove	1467-8, W.C.R.O., CR623/box 1	
le Chirchegreve	1423, W.C.R.O., DR564/I(a)/493	
?=little groave in Alleysley called Churches groave	1600, WC.R.O., DR564/I(a)/506	containing 2 acres less 5 perches
=Trinity Church grove	1627, W.C.R.O, DR564/I(a)/507	a croft "sometymes a grove", 4 acres
a grove with a pasture and meadow pleck called Nine Acres	1486, S.B.T., DR10/394	adjoining Barnesley field
peciam grossi bosci vocatam huddeslond	1392, P.R.O., DL 43/14/3	2 acres, ½ rood
?=unius grove sive pasture vocate huddes	1585, B.R.L, 328,926	
Grove in Elkyns	1572, W.C.R.O., CR1150	in the Rydinges ende, east of Birchley Hall
?=Elkins Wood	1840, W.C.R.O., CR569/3	15 acres, 1 rood, 33 perches, location fits that of 1572

Alne

bosco et plano ad Alnam pertinentibus	c.1169, Royce, *Landboc*, Vol. I, p. 184	
bosco nostro de Alna	c.1240, Royce, *Landboc*, Vol. II, pp. 530-1	an assart there, around *parvam Asseberne*
boscum de Alne	1316, W.C.R.O., CR1886/292	by *Newlond*
una grava	1435, Royce, *Landboc*, Vol. II, pp. 562-3	part of *Borrowardes*

Alspath - see Meriden

Alvecote - see Shuttington

Alveston

wudu	966, Birch, *Cartularium Saxonicum*, Vol. III, no. 1182	

Amington - see Tamworth

Ansley

in Bosco de Anestleye	1246-7, P.R.O., JUST 1/952, rot 40r	
boschum meum qui iacet inter duos dictos campos *=unum Boscum quondam Henrici Lilleburne*	n.d., ?13th C., P.R.O., E 315/41/20 1413, P.R.O., E 212/93	granted by Robert Walkelin to Henry de Lilleburne approval given to grant to Arbury Priory - ?in the vicinity of Priest Fields on modern maps
boscum vocatum Astonestray	1411, Bartlett, *Manduessedum Romanorum*, p. 141	by a pasture called *Ley Lawndes*
boscum vocatum Monewod	1411, Bartlett, *Manduessedum Romanorum*, p. 141	by *Monewod-Hall-Felde*

Ansty

de bosco de Anesty *?=de bosco de Anesty* *?=in bosco de Anesty*	1254, P.R.O., KB 26/154 1256, P.R.O., CP 25/1/244/24 1261-2, P.R.O., JUST 1/954, rot 57d	claim for estovers there half granted to Coventry Priory, with permission to assart
medietatem bosci sui de Anesty	1411 for 1349-59, P.R.O., E 164/21, f. 202v	belonging to Richard Stanappe
parcum de Ansty *?=The grove alias the Parke*	1411, P.R.O., E 164/21, rots 54v-56r c.1600, W.C.R.O., CR285/56	

Arley

medietatem Bosci *?=Arley Wood*	1202-3, P.R.O., CP 25/1/242/6 1839, W.C.R.O., CR569/8	?corresponding in part to the present Wood

Arrow (see also Oversley)

boscum suum de Arewe *?=ad boscum* *?=wood of Arue* *?=wood of Arewe*	1229, *Calendar of Close Rolls, 1227-31*, p. 187 1261-2, P.R.O., JUST 1/954, rot 48d 1326, *Calendar of Close Rolls, 1323-7*, p. 557 1333, *Calendar of Patent Rolls, 1330-4*, p. 406	of William de Camvill' and within the forest of Feckenham belonging to Robert Burdet licence to Robert Burdet to impark it
bosco Stephani de Ragele	1238, <u>Curia Regis Rolls</u>, XVI, no. 149c	?in Ragley

Ashorne - see Newbold Pacey

Ashow

boscum de Esseho *?=bosci de essehou*	1200, *Pipe Roll Society*, Vol. L (new series XII), p. 184 n.d., ?13th C., P.R.O., E 210/3697	
boscum forinsecum	1279, *HR*, p. 110	of William de Simely
boscum inclusum	1279, *HR*, p. 110	of William de Simely
boscum *?=in illo bosco qui vocatur Thyckethorne* *=Bosc' de Thikethorn* *=Thickthorn Wood*	1279, *HR*, p. 110 1316, B.L., Add. MS. 47,677, f. cxlv 1478, S.B.T., DR18/30/15/1 1597, W.C.R.O., Z141/(U)	of the Prior of Kenilworth held by Kenilworth Priory the modern Thickthorn Wood
boscum quod vocatur Le ho *=bosco meo de Hoo* *?=How grove*	n.d., ?13th C., S.B.T., DR18/1/54 1301, P.R.O., LR 14/229 1597, W.C.R.O., Z141/1(U)	next to meadow and water called *Esseswyle* belonging to Geoffrey le Symyli
le Birches/Nether(e)-birches *=totius bosci del Netherbyrches*	n.d., P.R.O., E 326/497, 459, 3471, E 210/6517, E 315/51/73 1324, P.R.O., E 210/5693	divided from Ho Hill by an assart
bosco meo qui vocatur Wydenhey	1301, P.R.O., LR 14/229	belonging to Geoffrey le Symyli
graua	1375, P.R.O., E 210/5451	
unam gravam	1431, S.B.T., DR18/1/59	granted to John Alryche

bosco in Byricoth *?=boscum .. inclusum ad modum* *parci* *?=Buricote Grove* *=Bery Coate grove*	c.1235, S.B.T., DR10/14 1279, *HR*, p. 106 1500, S.B.T., DR18/30/24/45 1597, W.C.R.O., Z141/1(U)	granted with the ditch (*fossato*) in Bericote
moppesgroue	1389, P.R.O., SC 2/207/77	in Bericote

Astley

unus parcus .. alius parcus	1300, P.R.O., C 133/98/32	of Andrew de Astley
le cause Grove	1394-5, W.C.R.O., CR136/C150	
le howspole *?=How Pool Wood*	1394-5, W.C.R.O., CR136/C150 1696, W.C.R.O., CR136/M9	bark sold there
silua Thome Becche	1394-5, W.C.R.O., CR136/C150	
unam gravam sive copiam silue *vocata gallo' feilde alias hawts* *grove* *?=Haut's Wood*	1587, W.C.R.O., CR136/C170 1696, W.C.R.O., CR136/M9	
grova vocata Slades grove	1587, W.C.R.O., CR136/C170	

Aston (see also Erdington)

claus de bosco de lozdgynssehull *?=Losells Wood*	1532, B.R.L., 413,517 1758, B.R.L., 371,055	the name appears also as lozeshull in the same document ?= Lozells
Waiswode *?=vastu .. vocatur Wasshewode*	1326, Staffs. R.O., D1287/6/18 1440, Staffs. R.O., D1287/6/18	no indication that it had trees at this date; presumably in the area of Washwood Heath
Le Wode	1363, B.R.L., 19,868	in Castle Bromwich, near the road to Coleshill
Lettelfeld atte Wode	1360, P.R.O., E 40/11983	in Castle Bromwich
boscus .. vocatus le spring	1548-9, Staffs. R.O., D641/1/2/288	in Castle Bromwich
unam grauam bosci apud holebrok	1331, B.R.L., 19,836	inclosed by a hedge and ditch (*sepe et fossato*)
parte unius graue vocatur le *Coniger*	1539, B.R.L., 347,879	perhaps on the site of Coneygrove in 1759 (B.R.L., 148,157)
boscum	1261-2, P.R.O., JUST 1/954, rot 28d	of Adam Bacon in Water Orton
Witton Wood	1469, B.R.L., 347,863	?on the site of Witton Common

Aston Cantlow

de parco *=parcus* *=parcus* *=?parcus vocatur Shelfhull* *=parcum de Shelfhull*	1254, P.R.O., C 132/17/15 1273, P.R.O., C 133/2/7 1345, P.R.O., C 135/41/19 1392, P.R.O., DL 43/14/3 1467-8, W.C.R.O., CR623/box 1	152 acres, with underwood and pannage 161 acres of great wood (*gross' bosc'*)
Astongrove *=Groua vocata Astone Grove* *=Aston Grove*	1467-8, W.C.R.O., CR623/box 1 1539-40, P.R.O., SC 6/Hen VIII/5694 1776, W.C.R.O., CR882	 the modern Aston Grove

Atherstone

boscus	n.d., *Select Documents Abbey of Bec*, (ed. Chibnall), p. 103	nuts and pannage there
the owtewoodes *=Atherstone Outwoods*	1547, W.C.R.O., L2/86 c.1740, W.C.R.O., Z323/1	

Atherstone-on-Stour

quatuor acris bosci	1497-8, P.R.O., CP 25/1/248/74	

Austrey

Avon Dassett

Baddesley Clinton

in defensa que vocatur haywde =*bosco qui vocatur Haywodeparc*	c.1200, S.B.T., DR3/1 c.1300, S.B.T., DR3/11	presumably approximates to the modern Haywood
outwode *?=in communi bosco*	c.1300, S.B.T., DR3/13 1429, S.B.T., DR3/785	distinct from the enclosed wood
Gilberdeshurne *?=tribus grovis* *?=Gilberdesgrove in Gilberdeslond* *?=Gilberts Coppice*	1325, S.B.T., DR3/34 1336, S.B.T., DR3/66-7 various dates, S.B.T., DR3/53-6, 66-7, 69, 86, 89, 104-5, 115, 134-5, 163-4, 170, 195-6, 344, 289-90 1699, W.C.R.O., Z234	a piece of woodland between Grenefeld and Haywood in *Gilberdeslond*
Geggegroue =*Geggegrove* =*unum virgultum vocatum Geges Grove* =*Geg grove* =*Gay Grove*	1329, S.B.T., DR3/48 1407, S.B.T., DR3/158-9 1465, S.B.T., DR3/793 1593, *BD*, 22/45/37 1699, W.C.R.O., Z234	 14 acres now part of the modern Haywood
groua =*grauam quondam Rogeri Chetewynde* *?=Chatings*	1356, S.B.T., DR3/93 1376, S.B.T., DR3/111 1699, W.C.R.O., Z234	near Haywood and Geggegrove
unum grovettum .. quondam fuit duo crofta et pars unius crofte videlicet Bromecroft, Pappeley croft et pars de Lediscroft =*duas parcellas bosci vocatas Broumesgrove* =*Brounesgrove* =*una grova....vocata Bromesgrove* =*Bromesgrove*	c.1422, S.B.T., DR3/183 1435, S.B.T., DR3/787 1444-5, S.B.T., DR3/800 n.d., 15th C., S.B.T., DR3/807 1596, S.B.T., DR3/339	between Haywood and the road from Baddesley to Warwick; the crofts were not woodland in 1330 - see S.B.T., DR3/51 next to Haywood by *Greenefyelde* alias Bromescroft - a piece of ground by 1597 - S.B.T., DR3/481
Dodgrove	1422-3, S.B.T., DR3/184	by a close called Chetewyns
Newenhamesgrove =*field with a grove called Newlonde*	1346-7, S.B.T., DR3/80 1339, S.B.T., DR3/71	
Birchy grove =*Birchengrove* =*Birchyngrove* =*Graua vocata Birchyngrove*	1429, S.B.T., DR3/785 1444, S.B.T., DR3/241 1446, S.B.T., DR3/245 1462-3, P.R.O., DL 29/463/7551	 land of the Duchy of Lancaster a wood of the Duchy of Lancaster
Barlowes grove *?=gravam apud morreylane*	1532, S.B.T., DR3/302 1491, S.B.T., DR3/795	by *Birchingrove* - S.B.T., DR3/303 held by Robert Barlowe
tylhous groue dyche =*Tylhouse grove* *?=Clay Pitts grove* *?=Clay Pitts Coppice*	1478, S.B.T., DR3/794 1503, S.B.T., DR3/289-90 1639, S.B.T., DR3/395-7 1699, W.C.R.O., Z234	 *Tilhouse* was associated with land called *Clepittes* in 1628 - S.B.T., DR3/391
duo graue adiacencia *?=Long Grove* =*Sideses Coppice*	1429, S.B.T., DR3/203-4 1606, S.B.T., DR3/354 1699, W.C.R.O., Z234	between Haywood park and the waste of Baddesley and the park and road to Temple Balsall, granted to John Mayell land called Males is recorded in 1699 by Sideses Coppice, near Haywood and the waste
Whitlesgrove =*Whitleys grove*	1456-7, S.B.T., DR3/804 n.d., 15th C., S.B.T., DR3/807	 by the common of Baddesley
Grovam Henrici Somerlane	n.d., 15th C., S.B.T., DR3/807	by Newlond
una Grova	1451-2, S.B.T., DR3/803	between the manor and the millpond ?= plot no. 170 on the tithe award
una Grova	1451-2, S.B.T., DR3/803	by *le Sprynges* and the land called *magyndey* next to the manor ?= plot no. 156 on the tithe award
Rowington Coppice	1593, S.B.T., DR3/334	shown on map of 1699 - W.C.R.O., Z234

Farthyngsgrove	1549, S.B.T., DR3/309	a meadow in 1568 - S.B.T., DR3/319

Baddesley Ensor

ad boscum de Baddesle	n.d., ?13th C., Staffs. R.O., D593/A/1/10/10	near to the new assart in Freasley
a parcell of Woode callyd the grove	1532, P.R.O., E 303/7/121	

Baginton

grava	c.1130-61, B.L., Harley 3650, f. 19	between the boundary with Stoneleigh and the park, i.e. presumably the grove marked on the tithe map by the river Sowe
?=gravam	1279, *HR*, p. 55	
?=gravam	c.1280, C.R.O., 39/6	
Estgrava	c.1130-61, B.L., Harley 3650, ff. 19, 29-30	
=Estgrava	n.d., B.L., Add. MS., 47,677, f. cl.	near the river Avon
?=Astegrove	1529, P.R.O., E 303/18/519	
?=Ashe Grove	1544-5, P.R.O., LR 2/181	
millegroue	1469-71, S.B.T., DR10/2220	
=mylgrove	1529, P.R.O., E 303/18/519	
=Mylle Grove	1544-5, P.R.O., LR 2/181	
Pipilgraue	1313, C.R.O., 39/19	by *Smethelowe*; whether woodland not stated
placea prati et bosci vocata le Lount	1350, S.B.T., DR10/24	presumably by the Lunt
whitmore copies	1529, P.R.O., E 303/18/519	?=modern Whitmoor Wood
=Whytmore Copies	1544-5, P.R.O., LR 2/181	
kingsclieff	1529, P.R.O., E 303/18/519	
potters pyttes	1529, P.R.O., E 303/18/519	
Estwod	n.d., 12th C., *SLB*, pp. 8, lviii	associated with Baginton, but not stated to be in Baginton

Balsall

in bosco nostro de Belesale	n.d., early 13th C., P.R.O., E 210/5586	pannage and assarts there
?=Balsall Wood	1538, W.C.R.O., CR112/Ba.188/2	a great common wood of at least 350 acres, ?= Balsall Wood/Common on enclosure
Le Merewod	1322, *Calendar of Close Rolls, 1318-1323*, p 588	? by Meer End, part of Balsall Common on enclosure
park	1538, W.C.R.O., CR112/Ba.188/2	277 acres
Frogmoor	1538, W.C.R.O., CR112/Ba.188/2	described as a young wood, it probably became the present Frogmoor Wood
le Netherwood	1538, W.C.R.O., CR112/Ba.188/2	
priests park	1540, P.R.O., E 315/361	41 acres, probably the present Priests Park Wood
Dopkyns grove	1538, W.C.R.O., CR112/Ba.188/2	
nemus operabile apud Chedleswich	c.1135-61, B.R.L., Wingfield Digby MSS., A1/2, A3, A4, A5	presumably in Chadwick

Barcheston

Broade Grove furlong	n.d., ?15th C., W.C.R.O., CR580/1	no evidence of the grove itself

Barford

subtus bosco de persele	n.d., 13th C., B.L., Harl. Ch. 46 A 30	by the great meadow of Barford, presumably Westham
=una acra bosci .. in Perceleye	1316, P.R.O., JUST 1/968, rot 14d	*Perceleygrove* next to Hampton Episcopi (i.e. Hampton Lucy)
spinam que vocatur Cutteleyron	1326, P.R.O., E 326/2921	

Barston

park and wood	1199, *Calendar Rotuli Chartorum*, 16 (cited in *VCH*, Vol. IV, p. 23)	
Barston park	1540-1, P.R.O., E 315/361	a common wood, 8 acres
Escott Wood	1540-1, P.R.O., E 315/361	a common wood, north of the river

Barton-on-the-Heath

boscum de Berton	1233, *Curia Regis Rolls*, XV, no. 910	separated by a field from Compton
Bosco suo de Barton	1246-7, P.R.O., JUST 1/952, rot 37d	

Baxterley

le Owtewode de Baxterley	1497-8, P.R.O., E 315/283, f. 20	

Bearley

totam grauam *=totam grauam meam quam pater meus adquisiuit de geri* *?=Graua de Burleia* *?=graua Johannis* *?=Burleye grove* *=Burleygrove*	n.d., *Formulare*, no. DCLX n.d. (before 1216), P.R.O., E 326/8453 n.d., 13th.C., P.R.O., E 315/43/155 n.d. P.R.O., E 315/45/106 1317, S.B.T., DR98/786 1439 and 1461, S.B.T., DR10/2429 and DR38/1429	by Pathlow near Pathlow; a road led from the grove to Clopton of John de Burleia? this seems to have been enlarged to become the seventeenth-century grove of 160 acres (S.B.T., DR38/44-5)

Beaudesert

trescentas acras bosci infra magnum parcum *=boscus infra magnum parcum*	1326, B.L., Cott. Ch. xxvii 137 1419-20, M.MSS., Mi M 124	
a grove within lymseys	1463, P.R.O., E 40/9087	
a groue within the seyd Penkes	1463, P.R.O., E 40/9087	

Beausale

Scortwode *?=vastum de Schortwode*	1209, P.R.O., CP 25/1/242/8 n.d., 13th C., B.R.L., Keen 26	reference also to the heath of Shortwood
la Birchesgrave *?=boscum inclusum*	n.d., 13th C., S.B.T., DR10/33; 1342-3, B.R.L., Keen 26; 1392-3, *BD*, box 139 1316, P.R.O., C 134/49	

Bedworth

le Northwode *=bosco et pastura vocatis Northwod* *=bosco vocato Northwod*	1270, P.R.O., E 326/388 1383, *Formulare*, no. CCIX 1440, W.C.R.O., CR136/C107	included *karwellemor* - W.C.R.O., CR136/C109; common pasture - W.C.R.O., CR136/C126
le Suthwode	1270, P.R.O., E 326/388	common pasture - W.C.R.O., CR136/C126
in bosco meo de Bedewrth *= bosco que vocatur le Hook* *?=the towns end Hook*	n.d., 13th C., P.R.O., E 326/3608 1702, W.C.R.O., CR432/box 29	of Isabel de Turville, by the furlong called *Thelichte*; alternative name in the endorsement part of Cattels wood
in bosco ospitalis sancti Johannis quod vocatur le Oxewodde	1333, P.R.O., E 326/10778	
in bosco qui vocatur Calvecroft	1275-6, P.R.O., E 326/11258	this adjoined the two woods below
boscum Thome filii petri de monte	1275-6, P.R.O., E 326/11258	see above

boscum qui fuit quondam Roberti michel	1275-6, P.R.O., E 326/11258	see above
?=Great Marshalls Wood	1633-4, P.R.O., E 178/5689	owned by Robert Fisher in 1633-4
?=Sir Clement Fisher's wood	1696, W.C.R.O, CR136/M9	
a little grove called Botts grove	1538, P.R.O., E 303/17/219	belonging to the Charterhouse of Coventry
=grove called Botts grove	c.1600-20, S.B.T., DR91/2	
=Close called Botts Grove or little Wood	1698, W.C.R.O., CR410/box 25	part of Walesend farm

Bentley

[parts of woods]	12th C., *VCH*, Vol. IV, p. 211; *Dugdale*, Vol. II, p. 1048	given by Walter de Camvile to Merevale Abbey
park of Bentley	1240, *Calendar of Close Rolls, 1237-42*, p. 221	of Maud de Camvile
	n.d., W.C.R.O., CR136/C707	of Nicholas de Astley
=parco de Benteleye	1484, *Calendar of Patent Rolls, 1476-85*, p. 479	
=Bentley Wood	1543-4, B.R.L., 168,242	
=Bosco vocato Bentley parke		
partem ducentarum acrarum bosci	1267, P.R.O., KB 26/176, rots 18r, 35r	claimed by the widow of Robert Curzun
Hoare Parke	1614, S.B.T., ER3/2546	

Berkswell

in bosco meo de berkeleswell	n.d., S.B.T., DR18/1/181	of Nigel de Mundeville/Mandeville
=bosco meo de Bercleswell	n.d., B.L., Harley 3650, f. 27	ditto
partem illam que dicitur Bernet	n.d., B.L., Harley 3650, f. 27	part of the wood of Berkswell
?=le bernet	n.d., S.B.T., DR18/1/181	by *Whithames ruding, Widenhay*
?=boscus qui vocatur Le Bernet	1316, P.R.O., C 134/49, 51	
?=copicium domini vocatum Bernett	1455-6, P.R.O., SC 6/1038/2	with spring or underwood
?=le Bernet	1480-1, P.R.O., DL 29/642/10422	by *le longfeld*
?=bearnet	c.1555, P.R.O., E 36/167	a demesne wood
?=lord's wood called Bernett	1613, W.C.R.O., MR21/2	by Cotmans fields; for the suggested location see text and map
boscus dicti Comitis qui vocatur Haskoresmore/le haueskesmore/ hauekaresmore	c.1303-10, B.L., Add. MS. 28,024, ff. 80-1	In 1758 (no. 1962 in the Merevale MSS) Hawkers Moore Farm was described as formerly a coppice wood
?=hawkars more	c.1555, P.R.O., E 36/167	a demesne wood
suboscus del Broderedyng	1316, P.R.O., C 134/51	
suboscus de yesterhuyrne	1316, P.R.O., C 134/51	
boscus qui vocatur Rounderuding	1316, P.R.O., C 134/49	
=le Roundrudyng	1480-1, P.R.O., DL 29/642/10422	
=Rounde Riddinge	c.1555, P.R.O., E 36/167	a demesne wood
boscus qui vocatur le Rooclos	1316, P.R.O., C 134/49	
?=quadam Copicia vocata Ruffe Closse	1547, B.R.L., 168,255	
?=The Rowghe Close	c.1555, P.R.O., E 36/167	a demesne wood
?=Rough Close Wood	1782, W.C.R.O., CR299/80	
in bosco vocato Wastewode	1455-6, P.R.O., SC 6/1038/2	by Westwood in Stoneleigh on enclosure in 1808 - W.C.R.O., CR172/1-2
?=Westwood/ wast wood	c.1555, P.R.O., E 36/167	
Bechewode	1455-6, P.R.O., SC 6/1038/2	presumably the modern Beechwood
?=bechewood	c.1555, P.R.O., E 36/167	called a common wood c.1555
le blakehale	1480-1, P.R.O., DL 29/642/10422	
=Blakehale	1555, P.R.O., E 36/167	a common wood, ?by Black Hole
c.30 tenants' groves	1555, P.R.O., E 36/167	a few named - see below
pastura vocata Twychefield cum una graua .. adiacente	1480-1, P.R.O., DL 29/642/10422	
?=cuiusdam copicie vocate Twychelwood	1547, B.R.L., 168,255, m. 43	?see Twitchell on tithe map
Walsall groves	1486, S.B.T., DR10/394	

groves called nedor Fenn' and over Fenn	1486, S.B.T., DR10/394	
grovam .. vocatam goodyge *?=Goodinge grove or Goodens Grove*	1555, P.R.O., E 36/167 1614, W.C.R.O., MR21/2	next to *Beeachende* by Beechewood House
Ryders Grove *?=Ryding Grove* *?=Redding Coppice alias Slibberslade grove*	1555, P.R.O., E 36/167 1665, W.C.R.O., MR21/5 1638, W.C.R.O., B.R.L., 276,818	by Claypitt fields presumably became Slipperslide Wood, see modern maps
Waldyff Wode *?=Waldwood* *?=Wallywood* *?=Waldiewood or Walden Wood*	1489, S.B.T., DR18/30/24/24 1555, P.R.O., E 36/167 1612, W.C.R.O., MR21/2 1627, B.R.L., 276,809	in Cornest End by Walden fields
Morecote Wood *=Morecote Wood*	1538, W.C.R.O., CR112/Ba.188/2 1605, W.C.R.O., CR2440/1/2-3	'grounds', not wood

Bevington - see Salford

Bickenhill

Haregrave	1240, P.R.O., CP 25/1/243/19	reference to permission to assart and enclose land there
in Bosco quod vocatur Echles	1271-2, P.R.O., CP 25/1/244/29	in Marston Culy; the name of the wood can be read as *Echles* or *Ethles*
apud Lyndon boscus *?= Lyndon wode*	1446-7, P.R.O., SC 11/819 1464, W.C.R.O., CR1911/12	in Lyndon

Bidford

Billesley

Bilton

Binley

boscum forinsecum	1279, *HR*, p. 128	held by the Abbot of Coombe
boscum forinsecum	1279, *HR*, p. 129	
partem illam nemoris mei de Billneia *?=quartem partem nemoris me ab occidentale parte* *?=the westwode* *=the west wood* *=west wood*	n.d., 12th C., B.L., Cotton Vitellius A i, f. 42 n.d., ?12th C., B.L., Cotton Vitellius A i, f. 43 1538, P.R.O., E 303/16/39 c.1550, S.B.T., DR37/box 114 1565-6, S.B.T., DR10/2224	 by the convent pool common wood associated with New Close Wood in 1823- W.C.R.O., D34
partem nemoris mei quod dicitur munechet	n.d., 12th C., B.L., Cotton Vitellius A i, f. 44	
bosco incluso qui vocatur Shortwode in Bilneye	1334, Bodleian Library, MS Top. Warks C8	?near the waste of Sowe called Shortwood
Binley Wood *?=Binley Common Wood*	?c.1580, M.MSS., Mi M 232 1823, W.C.R.O., D34	by the great coppice in Brandon
a Wood or copies called the newe closse *=Neweclose Copes* *?=New Close Wood*	1538, P.R.O., E 303/16/36 c.1550, S.B.T., DR37/box 114 1823, W.C.R.O., D34	in Wood Grange, by Brandon Heath presumably corresponding to the present New Close Wood
A Grove in Bynley called Comeners Grove *?=Gardners Wood* *=Buttons Wood*	1538, P.R.O., E 303/16/57 1746, Bodleian Library, Craven 320	leased to John Gardener and Elene his wife map shows it to occupy the same area as the modern Buttons Wood
Bynley Copies *?=coppis of Sir John Haringtons*	c.1550, S.B.T., DR37/box 114 n.d., t. Eliz., M.MSS., Mi M. 232	?= Piles Coppice; Sir John Harington's lands came to the Craven family and his coppice adjoined Brandon, as does Piles Coppice

Binton

quandam grovam sive Copesium bosci	1546, W.C.R.O., CR114A/104/1	by *six hadlonds*, in the tenure of John Draper
wood	1554-5, W.F. Noble, *History of Binton* (1879) p. 182 (W.C.R.O., CR2776/1)	20 acres, no name
Townsend grove or Yelvesgrove & Well grove	1625, Noble, *History of Binton*, p. 187	3 *grovets* in 1632-3, Noble, History of Binton, p. 429

Birdingbury

grauam	n.d., B.L., Add. Ch. 48,031	
?=parue graue	n.d., B.L., Add. Ch. 48,029	
?=in le grove infra sepe	1392, P.R.O., DL 43/14/3	arable land
?=pasture called the Grove	1476, W.C.R.O., CR1998/box 45/GG7	

Birmingham

a lytell wod or grove called Wyatts Feld	1529, B.R.L., 94,314	contained 4 acres, all oaks
i pastura sive boscus vocatus le Worston	1529, B.R.L., 94,314	

Bishop's Itchington

Bishop's Tachbrook - see Tachbrook

Bourton on Dunsmore

Brailes

quedam grava	1268, P.R.O., C 132/35/13	
?=groua	1413-4, B.R.L.,167,904	
?=quidam boscus	1316, P.R.O., C 134/49, 51	36 acres
?=Brayles Wode	1479-80, P.R.O., DL 29/642/10421	
=Brayles Wod	1543, B.R.L., 168,216	20 acres
?=The Lawne Woode	c.1585, W.C.R.O., CR3231	map shows the wood, at Grove End (there was a medieval park, ?hence the name Lawne)
?=subter Boscum	1631, B.R.L., 167,910	*apud le Grove End*
?=Brayles Wood	1692, B.R.L., 168,052	40 acres

Brandon

Boscum & Brueram de Braundon	1226, P.R.O., CP 25/1/244/15	separated from the wood of *Burlegh* (in Brinklow) by heath
boscum forinsecum	1279, *HR*, p. 52	40 acres of wood
bosco meo	1366, M.MSS., Mi D 3956	
great coppisse in the parke	1571, M.MSS, Mi Da 94	107 acres (perch of 18 feet)
the litle coppisse	1571, M.MSS, Mi Da 94	37 acres 1 rood (perch of 18 feet)
Standinge Wood	1582, M.MSS, Mi Da 94	

Brinklow (see also Coombe)

in bosco meo de Burchtleio	c.1150, S.B.T., DR10/191	?=Birchley Wood
?=bosco meo de Brinkalaue	c.1170-86, S.B.T., DR10/37-8	
?=de nemore meo de Brincalawa quod dicitur Burhtleia	c.1170-82, S.B.T., DR10/39	given to the Abbey of Coombe
bosco suo de Brinkele	1206, *Curia Regis Rolls*, Vol. IV, pp. 205-6	of the abbot of Coombe
=Bosco excluso de Burlegh	1226, P.R.O., CP 25/1/244/15	of the Abbey of Coombe, separated by heath from the wood and heath of Brandon
a copie made out of part of Bourtley	1500-1, S.B.T., DR10/117	
?=Byrtley Copies	c.1550, S.B.T., DR37/ box 114	

Brynkelowe Copice	c.1550, S.B.T., DR37/ box 114	
grove called morse grove	1538, P.R.O., E 303/16/86	by a close called Armeley in Brinklow field; closes called grove were by Harmley close in 1838, W.C.R.O., MB Bri

Broom - see Bidford

Bubbenhall

quendam boscum	1279, *HR*, p. 90	
quamdam partem forinseci bosci	1391, P.R.O., E 149/60/16	
Bubnell Spryng *?= Mr. Bromley's Spring Wood*	1548-9, N.W. Alcock, *Warwickshire Grazier and London Skinner* (1981), pp. 156, 175 1726, W.C.R.O., Z414(U)	= the modern Bubbenhall Wood
Bubbenhill woodde alias Bubbenhill copyes	1580, W.C.R.O., Z542/2/5	a demesne wood, 98 acres, 2 perches with the shrubbes (see below)
Bubbenhill shrubbes *=le Shrubbes wood* *=Shrubbs Wood*	1580, WC.R.O., Z542/2/5 1639, S.B.T., DR18/30/6/1 1726, W.C.R.O., Z413, Z414(U)	see above adjacent to Ryton Wood

Budbrooke

de nemore eiusdem ville	late 12th C., P.R.O., E 164/22, f. ix	of Budbrooke or Hampton Curlieu?
quidam boscus	1290-1, P.R.O., SC 12/14/87	in the manor of Budbrooke
boscum qui vocatur Wegenok	1316, P.R.O., C 134/47/18	in the manor of *la Graue*
grova	1316, P.R.O., C 134/47/18	described as a wood, next to the capital messuage of the manor of *la Graue*
Blusardesgrove/ Blesardsgrove/ Blysardesgrove	1408-25, W.C.R.O., CR895/8/4, 10, 11, 12, 13, 14	
[acre of wood in Hampton Curly]	1507, P.R.O., E 315/34/148	
parsonage grove	1589-90, W.C.R.O., CR895/80/1	by the church; the site of the manor lay east of the church
The Grove	1589-90, W.C.R.O., CR895/80/1	of 5 acres, part of Parkers holding at the wold
copice in Judde feilds	1589-90, W.C.R.O., CR895/80/1	

Bulkington

boscum forinsecum	1277, P.R.O., C 133/17/5	in Weston
parcus	1299, P.R.O., C 133/90/2	in Weston
de bosco domini *?=boscum Prioris Sancti Johannis Jerusalem* *=boscum .. de Bernangle*	1380, P.R.O., SC 2/207/33 1411, P.R.O., E 164/21, f. 54v 1411, P.R.O., E 164/21, f. 55r	in Barnacle in Barnacle

Burmington

Burton Dassett

grove	1497, Northants. R.O., Temple (Stowe), box 4/bundle 1a/1	by the *mese* [dwelling]

Burton Hastings

centum acras terre bosci pasturis	16th C., Leadam, *Domesday of Inclosures*, p. 451	in *Shyrford*, i.e. Shelford

Butlers Marston

Caldecote

quidam boscus separalis *?=boscum de Caldecote* *?=Calcotte wood* *?=Cawlcote Wood* *?=Caldecote Wood*	1364, P.R.O., C 135/181/16 1378-9, B.L., Add. Roll 49,721 1538, B.L., Add Ch. 48,775 1543, W.C.R.O., Z364(Sm) 1839, W.C.R.O., CR569/57	
in quadam placia bosci	1261-2, P.R.O., JUST 1/954, rot 10d	about ten acres, common pasture for pigs there

Caludon

Boscum Walteri de Couentre in Caludun *=Boscum quondam Walteri de Couentre* *?=boscum de Calwedon .. bosco de Caloudon*	n.d., 13th C., C.R.O., BA/H/H/163/1 and 2 n.d., 13th C., C.R.O., BA/H/H/163/3 n.d., B.L., Harley 4748, f. 4	a meadow of Walter de Couintre lay between the wood and river Sowe
Boscum forincecum de Calowdon	1461, S.B.T., DR10/2460	
wood called *Newhewen* *=boscis de [Dedmor &] Newhewen* *=Newhewen*	1385, *Calendar of Inquisitions Miscellaneous*, Vol. IV, no. 299 1425, P.R.O., C 139/16/12 1443, S.B.T., DR10/2446 1461, S.B.T., DR10/2460	under Wyken? by *lyttilstoblyfeldes*?
wood of the manor called *Dedemoor* *=boscis de Dedmor [& Newhewen]*	1385, *Calendar of Inquisitions Miscellaneous*, Vol. IV, no. 299 1425, P.R.O., C 139/16/12	
La graue in Stub[bi]feld	1338-53, B.L., Add. MS. 37,671, f. 23	xvii acres
park	1262, *FF*, Vol. I, no. 835	80 acres in 1316, P.R.O., C 134/97/5

Canley

Grava	n.d., ?13th C., S.B.T., DR18/1/850	
in bosco .. qui vocatur la lee	1270, S.B.T., DR18/1/838	
schortwode	n.d., c.1285, S.B.T., DR18/1/847	

Castle Bromwich - see Aston

Chadshunt

Chapel Ascote - see Radbourn

Charlecote

a thicket of trees .. called .. Thelesford-grove *=Grove ibidem vocate Thellesford grove*	1543, *Dugdale*, Vol. I, p. 501, citing Pat. 35 H.8, p. 8 1544, P.R.O., E 318/22/1212	adjoining the site of Thelsford Priory containing 7 acres

Chesterton

unam gravam inclusam *?=La grave* *?=quadam parte bosci* *?=sub bosco* *?=v acre subbosci* *?=le Wode* *?=quidam boscus inclusus* *?=boscum* *?=the wode* *?=unam parcellam bosci vocatam le grove* *?=one woode or copice called Chesterton grove*	1279, *HR*, p. 235 1272-1307, S.B.T., DR98/245 1293, P.R.O., E 152/4, m. 15 1287, S.B.T., DR98/266 1300, P.R.O., C 133/93/24 1345, S.B.T., DR98/373 1353, P.R.O., C 135/123/5 1441-2, B.R.L., 295,194 1474, S.B.T., DR98/519 1508, Northants. R.O., Spencer MSS. 1491; S.B.T., DR98/540 1568, S.B.T., DR98/938	containing ten acres of underwood by the *overlete* and *Netherlete*

Chilvers Coton

sexaginta acrarum bosci ..in Cheluredescote	1221, P.R.O., CP 25/1/243/11	of William de Ses, one third claimed as dower
?=Seyzwode	n.d., ?13th C., W.C.R.O., CR136/C744a	?remnant in the modern Seeswood, 12 acres in
=le Sceswode	1394-5, W.C.R.O., CR136/C150	1713, W.C.R.O., CR764/104/1
dimidium boscum unum videlicet le hudell	n.d., ?c.1200, P.R.O., E 315/39/17	This confirms a grant recorded in *Dugdale*, Vol. II, p. 1074, as having been made to Arbury Priory in the reign of Henry II
=boscum cum terra quod vocatur hudeles	n.d., ?13th C., W.C.R.O., C136/C716	
Nemore .. de Herwardeshay	1234, W.C.R.O., CR136/C145	
=cum Bosco qui vocatur Hewardeshay	1253-4, W.C.R.O., CR136/C717	granted by Thomas son of Saery de Stoke to Thomas de Astley
=Boscum .. qui vocatur Herewardeshey	n.d., 13th C., W.C.R.O., CR136/C725	given to Arbury Priory by Andrew de Astley
?=woode growyng within the New parke	1491, P.R.O., E 303/17/241	
=the new parke	1587, W.C.R.O., CR136/C341	a spring wood (CR136/C361)
in Bosco	1261-2, P.R.O., JUST 1/954, rot 27d	of Isman de Sutlegh
?=bosco suo de Chelverescote	n.d., W.C.R.O., CR136/C300	of John de Sudleye, next to *Horselebrok*
?=Boscum Domine de la Graue	1316, B.L., Add. Ch. 48,068	near the road from Astley and the *horsleybroc*
?=boscum meum forinsecum	1321-2, W.C.R.O., CR136/C747 & n.d., W.C.R.O., CR136/C410	of John de Sudleye by the wood called *le kedyng*
?=boscum meum vocatum le Outewode	1468, W.C.R.O., CR136/C420a	of Ralph Boteler, lord of Sudeley
=Coton Outwoods	1606, W.C.R.O., CR136/C1098	
a Nemore quod quondam fuit Roberti de Camera	1284, W.C.R.O., CR136/C724	
boscum qui vocatur le kedyng	n.d., ?13th C, W.C.R.O., CR136/C410	belonging to Arbury Priory
?=Kyddings	1587, W.C.R.O., CR136/C341	
=Springkiddinges	1597, W.C.R.O., CR764/104/1	
=Spring Kidding Wood	1807, W.C.R.O., CR764/107	
grave	n.d., ?13th C, W.C.R.O., CR136/C731	of William Loteman
una grava que appellatur Odenegreven	1296, W.C.R.O., CR136/C729, C739	
una placea bosci mei que vocatur malynnusmor	1319, W.C.R.O., CR136/C746	
=unam gravam	1332, W.C.R.O., CR136/C756a	part of *modymanneslond*
=una grava bosci vocata malynesmor	n.d., ?14th C, W.C.R.O., CR136/C777	part of *modymannyslond*
boscum	1319, W.C.R.O., CR136/C746	of William de la sclade
placia bosci que vocatur le Wardemor	1337, W.C.R.O., CR136/C759	
?=una grava	1356, P.R.O., E 326/3731	held by William Warde
boscum	1337, W.C.R.O., CR136/C759	of William Postely, by *Wardemor*
boscum	1337, W.C.R.O., CR136/C759	of Edith le Warde, by *Wardemor*
grava vocata holemore	1375, W.C.R.O., CR136/C776	
grava bosci iuxta le jolassche	1371, W.C.R.O., CR136/C775	
bosco adiacente vocato Nythtynggalegroue	1392, W.C.R.O., CR136/C786	next to *Greysacre*
lez haunche	1481, W.C.R.O., CR136/C309	wood
=great haunche, little haunch, Haunch Wood	c.1700, W.C.R.O., CR136/M10-M11	
grove vocata woodcocks grove	1532, W.C.R.O., CR440/12	on western edge of Griff, in Carringtons Closes
=Woodcocks grove	ante 1537-8, W.C.R.O., CR136/C1250	- W.C.R.O., CR136/M18, M95, M96
temple park grove	1516, W.C.R.O., CR136/C798	a grove of underwood
the kyngesffeld grove	1516, W.C.R.O., CR136/C798	

Wrights grove or the spring wood =Wrights Grove now Lago's Ruff =Largoes Ruff =Dagleys Wood	1536, P.R.O., E 315/404 post 1610, W.C.R.O., CR136/172a 1681, W.C.R.O., CR764/104/4 n.d., W.C.R.O., CR136/M94, M97A	
Schypeleyes grove ?=Shipley Wood	1538-9, W.C.R.O., CR136/C313 18th C., W.C.R.O., CR319/13	field-name

Church Lawford

cum separali Grova in loco super dunesmore heth vocato le Stode	1538-9, P.R.O., SC 6/Hen VIII/3737	? name perpetuated in fields called Steads, VCH, Vol. VI, plate facing p. 148, copy in W.C.R.O., Z8/7-8

Churchover

uno Graveto ibidem crescente vocato le greite park =Grove or Wodde called the great parke	1535, P.R.O., E 303/16/82 1537, P.R.O., E 303/16/60	

Claverdon

nemus ?=in bosco de Claverdona ?=bosco meo de Clauerdon	1123, P.R.O., E 164/22, f. xii 1184-93, Reading Abbey Cartularies, Vol. I, no. 582 c.1196, W.C.R.O., CR133/1	 ?towards Langley of Waleran earl of Warwick
graua .. iuxta suhangra grangia =in grauam de Suangre/Soengre =Songar groue =Songar Grove	n.d., ?c.1216, BD n.d., ?13th C., BD 1545, P.R.O., E 318/21/1121; BD 1827, W.C.R.O., CR1663/20	presumably the modern Songar Grove
Kinghemegraue	n.d., ?13th C., King's College, WOW/110	near the wood of Halestowe (Austy)
sirhoulte	n.d., 13th C., P.R.O., E 315/38/41	not called a wood, but described as part of assarts
Birchurst	n.d., 13th C., Reading Abbey Cartularies, p. 429	not called a wood
Langle grove	n.d., ?16th-17th C., W.C.R.O., CR895/18	a wood, still wood in 1695, B.R.L., Keen 48
snelles graue	n.d., ?13th C., BD	in Langley or Edstone

Clifton upon Dunsmore

Coleshill

boscum qui vocatur Chelemundesheia =bosco meo in Chelmondeshay	1200, P.R.O., CP 25/1/242/4 n.d., 13th C., B.R.L., Wingfield Digby MSS., A46	presumably approximating to Chelmsley Wood
Boscum qui vocatur Witemor	1200, P.R.O., CP 25/1/242/4	
Boscum de Hoppele	1200, P.R.O., CP 25/1/242/4	
boscum a quercu que vocatur quercus Castelli usque ad Lutleshaie vurende, & inde usque [ad] Wirsetemede ..&..ad Bromwiche Blakeleg	1200, P.R.O., CP 25/1/242/4	Bromwiche is presumably Castle Bromwich, indicating the approximate location of part of the wood
Boryateswode	1437-8, Staffs. R.O., D641/1/2/269	leased by the lord of Sheldon
de bosco de Beltesley =boscum quod vocatur Beltesley =bosco de beltesleye	1261-2, P.R.O., JUST 1/954, rot 53r 1402, B.R.L., Wingfield Digby MSS., A433 n.d., P.R.O., E 326/10722	 associated with Aldcotenhale
[wood in] Alcotenhall	1492, Calendar Inquisitions Post Mortem, Henry VII, Vol, II, p. 802	20 acres ?= modern Alcott Wood
le Ruydyng in the ladywode =Lady Wood	1351, B.R.L., Wingfield Digby MSS., A258 1495, P.R.O., SC 11/683	see modern field called Lower Ladywood, W.C.R.O., Z436(U) and P.G. 3354
una graua	1367, B.R.L., Wingfield Digby MSS., A333	

Compton - see Fenny Compton, Long Compton

Compton Verney

Coombe (Fields)

In bosco de Cumbe	1261-2, P.R.O., JUST 1/954, rot 58d	
?=Combe woods	c.1550, S.B.T., DR37/box 114	
wood or copies lying next unto the	1537, P.R.O., E 303/16/55	in Smite
seid hill feild called hill parke or		
hell parke		
=hill parke copice	1620, Bodleian, Craven 71	
=Hill Park	1823, W.C.R.O., D34	
Swynstie grove	1538, P.R.O., E 303/16/36	in Wood Grange in Coombe
=Swynstie grove	c.1550, S.B.T., DR37/box 114	2 acres
the Fryth	1538, S.B.T., DR10/117	
=the Frythe	1538, P.R.O., E 303/16/36	near the grange pool in Wood Grange
=Frythe wood	c.1550, S.B.T., DR37/box 114	*?=the modern High Wood*
=Frithwood	1620, Bodleian Library, Craven 71	

Corley

grauam	1260, S.B.T., DR10/217	of Henry Jaumbe
=Jaumbe Wode	1323, B.R.L., 348,005	by *Jaumbefeld, tynfelde, dawe felde*
=Geambewode	1394 for 1391, *Calendar of Close Rolls, 1392-96*, p. 209	*?=fields called Jane Wood in the tithe award,* W.C.R.O., CR569/75
=Geambe Wood	1429, C.R.O., BA/D/D/49/5	by *dawefelde*
grave in Thachele	c.1261, S.B.T., DR10/223	belonging to the priory
=unam grouam vocatam le Thacheley	1411, P.R.O., E 164/21, f. 11v	belonging to Coventry Cathedral Priory
unam grauam que vocatur Wallehawinge	n.d., 13th C., Bodleian Library, Queen's College 2337	
graua Johannis de filungele in cornleya	n.d., 13th C., Bodleian Library, Queen's College 2337	
grauam Radulfi Wodecot or Wodecoc	n.d., 13th C., Bodleian Library, Queen's College 2337	
?=le Wodcokksgroue	1411, P.R.O., E 164/21, f. 11v	in south-east corner of Corley, near Muzzards
=gravam .. vocatam woodcoxe	1561, W.C.R.O., CR136/C708	grove
medietatem unius graue vocate Papurismor	1338, C.R.O., BA/D/D/49/3	*?by Whetefield and Wattemor*
grove	1394 for 1391, *Calendar of Close Rolls, 1392-96*, p. 209	adjacent to a field called *Phelipstokkynge*
grove	1394 for 1391, *Calendar of Close Rolls, 1392-96*, p. 209	adjacent to a meadow called *Horsley*
grouam vocatam le Falkewod	1411, P.R.O., E 164/21, f. 11v	part of the wood in Corley, the rest in Fillongley parish - see tithe map
parua groua	1411, P.R.O., E 164/21, f. 11v	by two fields called *le monkesfeld*
Maisterwode	1394 for 1391, *Calendar of Close Rolls, 1392-96*, p. 209	with a field called *Maisterlonde*
=silvam vocatam le maysterswod	1411, P.R.O., E 164/21, f. 11v	
unius grave in Corley iuxta Syserslone	1418-9, W.C.R.O., CR136/153	
?=the Sycers grove	1688, W.C.R.O., CR1371	see tithe map
grove called Tomkyns	1537, S.B.T., DR10/237	
grove called Jerves	1537, S.B.T., DR10/237	
grova sive clauso vocato Blocksyche	1561, W.C.R.O., CR136/C708	
Quarrell woode	1607, Staffs. R.O., D1287/6/20	a field-name

Coughton

bosco suo	1238, *Curia Regis Rolls*, Vol. XVI, no.149C	of Simon de Coughton
?=in bosco meo de coctun	n.d., c.1241, W.C.R.O., CR1886/15	of Simon lord of Coughton
?=boscum meum	n.d., W.C.R.O., CR1998/J2/32	in Wyke, of Robert son of Simon Bruly of Coughton
?=le Wykewode	1430, W.C.R.O., CR1998/box35/K	in the park of the lord
=le Wykewode	1500, S.B.T., DR5/2192	
?=a copice called neither weeke copice	1599-1600, W.C.R.O., CR1998/box 61/folder4/16	30 acres ?=wood in Coughton Park: map c.1695, W.C.R.O., CR1998/7
nemore meo de coctun	n.d., c.1241, W.C.R.O., CR1886/15	of Simon lord of Coughton
bosco meo de coctune	n.d., c.1241, W.C.R.O., CR1886/62	of Alexander lord of Kinwarton
nemore meo de coctune	n.d., c.1241, W.C.R.O., CR1886/62	of Alexander lord of Kinwarton
Bradegraua	n.d., 13th C., W.C.R.O., CR1998/box 34/B6	not called a wood

Coundon

In Bosco de Cundulme	1246-7, P.R.O., JUST 1/952, rot 41r	
?=quendam boscum forinsecum	1279, *HR*, p. 126	
?=Coundulmewode	ante 1411, P.R.O., E 164/21, f. 187r	
?=vastum de Coundulne quondam nemus de Coundulne	1411, P.R.O., E 164/21, f. 4r	of Coventry Cathedral Priory, by *Herneiswast* and *Bradnokkwast*, near *Holifast* in Allesley
?=in bosco de Coundon	1533, P.R.O., LR 2/181	land there
una graua cum quodam parroco bosci in Coundulme	1347, C.R.O., BA/B/A/44/12	of Adam Boydon
Gravam....vocatam Foulesmore	1407, C.R.O., BA/B/A/48/9	by *le Reynaldesfeld* and *hobbecroft* and
=unam grauam vocatam le Fowlesmore	1411, P.R.O., E 164/21, f. 3v	*lewynthyng* - see plot no. 106 in enclosure award, W.C.R.O., QS75/36
graua/groua	1411, P.R.O., E 164/21, f. 5r	by *Gefreyfeld*, *Boydonlane*, *Normansgrene*, held by John Hoore
graua	1411, P.R.O., E 164/21, f. 4v	held by William Staunton, near *Julyansfelde*, *Poukelane*, *Brounshull* and *Northfelde*
?=Copicia sive Grova	1574, W.C.R.O., CR299/89/5	on the southern boundary of *Brouneshill*
harpers grove	1593, C.R.O., BA/D/A/20/1	near Coundon Green to the north
=harpers grove	c.1600, S.B.T., DR91/2	near Coundon Green
=Tarletons or Harpers Grove	1649, W.C.R.O., CR299/89/8	near Coundon Brook
Grave que vocatur Brademore	n.d., Bodleian Library, MS. Top. Warks, C8	
?=Bradmoore Coppice	1668, W.C.R.O., CR1097/87	
Stronges Grove	1574, W.C.R.O., CR299/89/5	

Coventry (see also Allesley, Coundon, Caludon, Exhall, Foleshill, Keresley, Sowe, Stivichall, Willenhall)

in bosco meo	1204-8, Coss, *Early Records*, p. 23	
?=de bosco Coventre	n.d., 13th C., *LC*, no. 439	
?= in forinseco bosco de Covintr'	1243, *Calendar of Close Rolls Henry III, 1243-7*, p. 46	
?=Boscum de Couentre	1244, P.R.O., CP 25/1/243/20	
?=in Bosco de Couentre	1260, P.R.O., KB 26/164, rot 25d; 1261-2, P.R.O., JUST 1/954, rot 13d	
Haselwode	1297, C.R.O., BA/D/H/26/2	
=Haselwode	1315, C.R.O., BA/B/Q/20/7	
=Hasilwood	c.1392, *SLB*, p. 101	
=boscum intrincecum de Hasilwod	1411, P.R.O., E 164/21, ff. 52v-53r	
boscum forinsecum de Bernet	1411, P.R.O., E 164/21, f. 52v	
Boscum de Spanna	1208, P.R.O., CP 25/1/242/8	presumably in Spon
?=boscum liulfe spone	c.1200-14, C.R.O., BA/H/H/55/1	separated by a moor from Asshawe (for Asshawe see under Allesley)

grauam .. inclusam	1279, *HR*, p. 123	in Horwell
?=una graua	1439, W.C.R.O., DR564/I(a)/437	at *le Horewelle*, between common pasture called *hethsale* and pasture called *middelwode*
?=placea bosci vocata littel horewell	1373, W.C.R.O., DR564/I(a)/429	by Hearsall
hastel Groue	1351, W.C.R.O., DR564/I(a)/418	for the likely site of this wood, see Chapter Three
=le Asthull Grove	1354, W.C.R.O., DR564/I(a)/419	
=Gravam de Hastlehull	1388, C.R.O., 468/350	
=Graua de Asthull	1488, C.R.O., 468/361	
=Asthull Grove	1462, P.R.O., DL 29/463/7551	wood sold by the duchy of Lancaster
in bosco qui dicitur middelwode	n.d., 13th C., W.C.R.O., DR564/I(a)/403	for the likely site of this wood, see Chapter Three
?=campo qui dicitur middelwode	n.d., 13th C., W.C.R.O., DR564/I(a)/405	
?= pastura vocata middelwode	1439, W.C.R.O., DR564/I(a)/437	by Horwell (see above)
alnetum	1210-43, *LC*, no. 237	by the mill of Bisseley
Grauam que vocatur Shortele	1262, P.R.O., CP 25/1/244/26	
=grouam dicti Shortley	1350, *LC*, no. 257	
boscum de Pynneley	n.d. and 1237, *LC*, nos. 439, 379	by Stifford Mill
=wood	1251, *Calendar of Patent Rolls, 1247-58*, p. 100	licence to impark granted to Geoffrey de Langley
=boscum	1279-80, *HR*, p. 148	held by Walter de Langley
=boscum de Pynleye	1347, C.R.O., BA/B/P/431/5 and 1357, C.R.O., BA/B/P/431/6	by *Stiffordmulne*
le Growe (sic) Johannis de Langel'	1315, C.R.O., BA/H/H/375/1	?=*Luttelgraue* - see below
=le Groue Johannis de Longeleye	1317, C.R.O., BA/H/H/375/2	
=Grovetu	1343, C.R.O., BA/B/P/431/4	
una grava que vocatur Luttelgraue	1347, C.R.O., BA/B/P/439/7	
..boscum qui vocatur Luttelgraue		
=una groua que vocatur Lutelgroue iuxta Shirebourne inter Bussheleymulne et le Neuwemulne	1351, C.R.O., BA/B/P/137/13	
?=parua groua	1357, C.R.O., BA/B/P/441/1	near the garden of the Carmelites
?=Grouam iuxta Busheleymulne que vocatur Langeleeygroue	1368, C.R.O., BA/B/P/440/5	
=Langley/Longgeley grove	1393, C.R.O., BA/B/P/14/5	next to the chapel of St. Anne
?=Sent Anne grove	1423, C.R.O., BA/A/A/3/1	pasture by Charterhouse in 1733, C.R.O., BA/D/A/47/1
=graue Gilde Sancte Trinitatis de Couentre vocate langeleygrove	1487, C.R.O., BA/B/A/86/1	separated by *Parkefeld* and *Wriggesden* from *Baronsfeld*
alder grove	1241, *LC*, no. 305	
?=Plategroue	c.1235-43 and mid-13th C., *LC*, nos. 350, 418	by the bridge of *Alreneford* and the mill of Whitley
?=Plategrevam	1280, *LC*, no. 527	leased with the mill at *Alreneford*
?=unam parcellam terre vocatam Plattegreve	1386, S.B.T., DR10/687	in the fields of Pinley
?=groua	1476, S.B.T., DR10/489	by Alderford Mill
wood of Joel Berenger	1243-53, *Calendar of Inquisitions Miscellaneous*, Vol. I, no. 478	in Whitley
grove	1243-53, *Calendar of Inquisitions Miscellaneous*, Vol. I, no. 478	in Whitley
grouam .. vocatam Closegroue quam laici vocant Fukkersgroue	1411, P.R.O., E 164/21, ff. 2r, 42v	in Radford, by *Barkersfelde*
groua vocata le priestmore	1411, P.R.O., E 164/21, f. 3r	in Whitmore park
grouam in Whitmore que vocatur le Bradmore	1411, P.R.O., E 164/21, f. 3r	
una grova vocata Synklers grove	1539-40, P.R.O., LR 2/181	in Whitmore
grauam vocatam le connyng'	1411, P.R.O., E 164/21, f. 62v	in Priorsharnale
?=graua	1355, Bodleian Library, MS. Top. Warks. C8, p. 48	in the priory's manor, by *Gosfordfeld*
una Groua in Harenhale	1348, C.R.O., BA/H/H/293/9	
?=harnale Groue	1453, C.R.O., 468/360	

totam terram meam .. que vocatur le Harperswode .. & virgulto	t. John, B.L., Cotton Vitellius A i, f. 49	
?=harpereswode	1327, C.R.O., 468/316	
?=unum Boscum vocatum Harperesgroue	1378, C.R.O., 468/139	
=Harperesgrove	1379, C.R.O., 468/87	*ad le Netherplace* in Stoke
?=una Graua in Byggyng iuxta Stoke que vocatur harpersgrove	1400, C.R.O., 468/53	
corbynsgroue	1379, C.R.O., 468/87	*ad le Netherplace* in Stoke
Shukkeburghgroue	1379, C.R.O., 468/87	*ad le Netherplace* in Stoke
Biggeng Grove	1456, C.R.O., 468/215	
=Byggyng Grove	1460, C.R.O., 468/15	

Cubbington

Grauam	1220-2, P.R.O., E 210/318	the relationship to the Foot Grove and the Horse Grove of 1768 (W.C.R.O., CR1218/19/1), the Town grove of 1651 (B.R.L., 86,005) and Everton's grove of 1750 (B.R.L., 193,175) is unknown
?=gravam inclusam	1279, *HR*, p. 154	
?=le Grove de Cobynton	1377, S.B.T., DR18/1/698	
billingesgroue	1273, P.R.O., E 210/4582; n.d., P.R.O., E 210/9112, E 315/31/34, E 315/48/71	
?=Billinsgrove	1651, B.R.L., 86,005	

Curdworth

illam partem nemoris sui que est inter filum aque de Ebroc & filum aque de Tama .. usque ad divisas de Erdinton	n.d., 12th C., J. Nichols, *The History and Antiquities of the County of Leicester*, Vol. I, Part II (1813), Appendix XVII, p. 79	given to the canons of St. Mary de Pre, Leicester, as part of their manor of Berwood
=Berewod Scilicet de tota illo bosco qui est inter Ebroc & Bredestret usque ad Goseforth	1224, P.R.O., CP 25/1/243/13	deed dealt with 24 acres of wood
?=ccc acre bosci		
?=in bosco de Berwode	n.d., Nichols, *History of Leicester*, Vol. I, Part II, Appendix XVII, p. 79	
boscis suis de Cruddeworth [et Pedimor]	1288, B.L., Add. MS. 28,024, f. 102	of Thomas de Ardern (Peddimor in Sutton Coldfield)
bossco meo in hullesmor	n.d., Staffs. R.O., D1287/6/18/5	of Thomas de Ardern
place de sonn boys en le manoir de Donton .. nome Clapschawe	?1313, B.L., Add. MS. 28,024, f. 103	of Ralph de Gorges
una grova vocata Dernshawe	1514, S.B.T., DR18/1/260	in Dunton
boscum vocatum Ardernewode	c. 1300, B.R.L., Wingfield Digby MSS., A101	in Minworth

Dassett - see Burton Dassett

Dorridge - see Knowle

Dunchurch

Edgbaston

Edstone - see Wootton Wawen

Elmdon

quadraginta acris bosci & pasture	1314, P.R.O., JUST 1/969, rot 2d	common pasture there

Erdington

boscum forinsecum *?=bosco domini Henrici de* *Erdington .. ad boscum .. Willi* *clerici .. inter boscum Abbatis &* *Conventus Leycestri*	1282, P.R.O., C 133/32 1309, Staffs. R.O., D1287/6/20/21	adjacent to land called *Clerkeshey* by *Langeleyemor*; for the wood of the abbot and convent of Leicester see Berwood under Curdworth
?=centum acre bosci	1433, P.R.O., C 139/63	of Thomas Erdynton
?=Berewode	1442, B.R.L., 347,860	
=lord's wood .. called berewodde	1541, B.R.L., 347,879	
=Berwood	1760, B.R.L., 292,886	
boscum	1246-7, P.R.O., JUST 1/952, rot 14d	of William Maunsel, who held that part of Erdington which became Pype manor (*VCH*, Vol. VII, p. 64)
?=boscum domini de Berewode	1413, 1417, M.MSS., Mi M 129/1	of the earl of Warwick, who had acquired the Pype manor (*ibid.*)
?=pypewode	1442, B.R.L., 347,860	next to *le Foxholen in Berewode*
?=Boscum .. in Pyp	1259, P.R.O., KB 26/162, rot 32r	of Henry de Pyrie
una grova vocata dwerffeshole	1462-3, B.R.L., 347,913	?by land called dwarfhole meadow and hills in 1655, B.R.L., 349,825
=una grava vocata dwerffeholes *grove*	1543, B.R.L., 347,879	by a blade mill
Olifast	1525, B.R.L., 347,876	
holyfast	1541, B.R.L., 347,879	
?=Hollyfast	1802, B.R.L., 1382/1, 3	

Ettington - see also Thornton

grauam	n.d., (1246-59), W.C.R.O., CR229/box 18/3/1-2	in the manor of Lower Ettington
?=sa graue	1278, *Rotuli Parliamentorum*, Vol. I, p. 2	wood cut down and sold
?=Etington grove	1550-1, W.C.R.O., CR229/box 18 /3/36	wood growing there
=Eatington Grove	1795, W.C.R.O., CR229/117/9	in Lower Ettington
a grove of Ashe Tees .. called *Nollandes grove*	1653, W.C.R.O., D19/418	in Upper Ettington

Exhall (by Alcester)

Exhall (by Coventry)

in bosco de Eccleshal *=in bosco de Eccleshale*	1246-7, P.R.O., JUST 1/952, rot 40d 1261-2, P.R.O., JUST 1/954, rot 57d	
boscus de Sydenhale/ *Sydenhalewode* *=Sydnall woode*	1411, P.R.O., E 164/21, f. 18r c.1600, S.B.T., DR91/2	shared with Foleshill
Presteswodend	1411, P.R.O., E 164/21, f. 18r	?a reference to Sowe wood
grove	n.d., 13th C., P.R.O., E 326/1225	to go to Bedworth church on the death of Robert de Craft
?=graua	n.d., 13th C., P.R.O., E 326/5806	of Philip de Turvillle, parson
?=Parsonage Grove	c.1600, S.B.T., DR91/2	probable location, W.C.R.O, CR1175
grauam	1446, W.C.R.O., DR564/I(a)/476	of John Ruydyng
unam paruam grouam in Hughern	1411, P.R.O., E 164/21, f. 15r	held by William de Wymeswold, near *Welcrofte* - see tithe map
grauam suam	1411, P.R.O., E 164/21, f. 189v	held by William chaplain of Corley
boscus .. vocatus le calverhey/ *grouam .. vocatam le Calverhey/* *boscum de Calverhey*	1411, P.R.O., E 164/21, ff. 12r, 12v	by the manor of Newland, belonging to Coventry Cathedral Priory
le Corleygroue	1411, P.R.O., E 164/21, f. 12r	belonging to Coventry Cathedral Priory, in the manor of Newland between *le Connyngg* and *le* *park*
boscum vocatum le Connyngg	1411, P.R.O., E 164/21, f. 12r	in the manor of Newland
boscus inclusus vocatus le zonghok	1411, P.R.O., E 164/21, f. 12r	in the manor of Newland

Robinst grove *?=Grouette ... vocate Robyns* *Grove*	1528, P.R.O., E 303/17/216 1538-9, P.R.O., SC 6/Hen.VIII/3738	leased by Charterhouse in Charterhouse lands
=Robins grove	1546-7, P.R.O., E 318/22/1190	
Roberts grove	1544, P.R.O., E 318/6/201	of Coventry Cathedral Priory

Farnborough

Fenny Compton

Fillongley

boscus inclusus	1313, P.R.O., C 134/31/1	held by the Marmion family
Bircheleyheye *=birchelehay* *=a woodde cauled Birchleyhey* *=Birchley hey*	1361, C.R.O., BA/D/D/50/2 1435-6, Bodleian Library, Trinity College 84, f. 14 n.d., 15th/16th C., W.C.R.O., CR1886/3370 1533-4, S.B.T., DR10/1409, f. 290	presumably approximating to the modern Birchley Hays Wood
le Falkewod *=Falkewoode* *=Fauke woodd* *=falkewood*	1411, P.R.O., E 164/21, f. 11v 1474, C.R.O., BA/D/D/50/3 n.d., 15th/16th C., W.C.R.O., CR1886/3370 1533-4, S.B.T., DR10/1409, f. 290	by Corley, see Fork Wood Field in Wood End
silua de Hawerdyn *?=Harden Wood* *=Harding Wood*	n.d., 15th C., Bodleian Library, Trinity College 84, f. 57 1698, S.B.T., DR18/3/20/17 1767, W.C.R.O., Z149(L)	
quadam placia bosci .. in graua .. *vocata le Holowegreuen* *?=one grove called hollye greves*	1317, Northants. R.O., Th. 1495 1577, S.B.T., DR18/1/274	in Old Fillongley In Old Fillongley, between the road from Maxstoke to Fillongley church and *wyde feilde*, and described as a piece of gound by 1637 (S.B.T., DR18/1/304)
slad' grove *?=sladen groue* *=Sladen grove*	1408-9, Bodleian Library, Trinity College 84, f. iii n.d., 15th/16th C., W.C.R.O., CR1886/3370 1598, W.C.R.O., CR2981 (uncatalogued)	
grove of William Snelle	1485, S.B.T., DR18/10/46/3/1	by *Walkys*
albones grove *?=Almonds grove*	n.d., 15th/16th C., W.C.R.O., CR1886/3370 1663, W.C.R.O., CR562/3	
Cotterells grove	n.d., 15th/16th C., W.C.R.O., CR1886/3370	
pertre grove	n.d., 15th/16th C., W.C.R.O., CR1886/3370	?became the later Pear Tree Wood
the herst in marbrooks	n.d., 15th/16th C., W.C.R.O., CR1886/3370	
lawrance cookes woodde	n.d., 15th/16th C., W.C.R.O., CR1886/3370	
the Water Woodde	n.d., 15th/16th C., W.C.R.O., CR1886/3370	
shetthawnce	n.d., 15th/16th C., W.C.R.O., CR1886/3370	*?=schutehaunch* in Meriden
Carters Woodde	n.d., 15th/16th C., W.C.R.O., CR1886/3370	by *wrechboulls lands*
hesell hurst	n.d., 15th/16th C., W.C.R.O., CR1886/3370	in *wrechboulls lande*
hye asche groue	n.d., 15th/16th C., W.C.R.O., CR1886/3370	
Churchford Grove	1598, W.C.R.O., CR2981 (uncatalogued)	

Foleshill

bosco Comitis de folkeshull *=Boscum Comitis* *=bosco domini Comitis* *=bosco qui vocatur Erleswode* *?=vasto meo quod vocatur* *Erleswode* *=Herleswode*	1231-2, P.R.O., JUST 1/951A, rot 3r c.1240-50, C.R.O., BA/B/Q/20/2 n.d., 13th C., Bodleian, Queen's College, 2339 n.d., 13th C., Bodleian, Queen's College, 2348 n.d., 13th C., M.MSS., Mi. D 4007 1411, P.R.O., E 164/21, f. 202r	

boscum domini Willielmi de la Souche *?=boscum .. vocatum le Hay*	1327, M.MSS., Mi D 4011 1411, P.R.O., E 164/21, f. 22r	of Lord le la Souche, by *Boyswast* and *le Hoo*
boscum quod Stephanus modursone tenuit	1327, M.MSS., Mi D 4011	
bosco dicti domini le moubray qui vocatur Randulnesmore	1411, P.R.O., E 164/21, f. 202r	next to *Herleswode*
dame agnes groue *=damagnesgrove* *=Dame Agnys grove*	1411, P.R.O., E 164/21, f. 19r 1478-9, B.R.L., 168,237 1538-9, P.R.O., SC6/Hen.VIII/3737	see Agnes Grove on tithe map - W.C.R.O., CR569/105
unam grouam	1411, P.R.O., E 164/21, f. 19r	held by Henry Wolf, by Dame Agnes grove, Whitmore park
groua/graua *?=Beech waste coppice*	1411, P.R.O, E 164/21, ff. 19v, 44r 1544, P.R.O, E 318/22/1175	in *le Beches*, next to *Hasilwod*, opposite Whitmore park, and by the *Bechewast*
St. Cleeres grove *=Clare grove*	1639, 1660, and 1688, C.R.O., BA/D/A/22/1, 2, 3 1714, C.R.O., BA/D/A/22/4	belonging to Sir Thomas White's Charity - see Clare's Grove on tithe map - W.C.R.O., CR569/105
le Groue	1405, C.R.O., BA/G/F/33/2	by *Walleforlong*, *Goldyfeld* and *Grendonfeld* in Foleshill

Frankton - see Thurlaston

Freasley - see Polesworth

Fulbrook

Grafton

grauam que vocatur Kingesgraue *?=the Grove*	1247, P.R.O., CP 25/1/243/21 1740, B.R.L., 247,148-9	?see field-names in Grove in the enclosure award, W.C.R.O., QS75/47

Grandborough

Grendon

in bosco de Grendon *=in bosco meo de Grendona*	1221, *Rolls of the Justices in Eyre*, p. 373; 1261-2, P.R.O., JUST 1/954, rot 51d n.d., ?13th C., M.MSS., Mi D 4022	between Watling Street and a water-course descending through *Haselhurst*
communiam de Grendon vocatam Grendon outewoddys *?= Grendon Common*	1564, B.R.L., 193,151 1722, Staffs. R.O., D1176/A/39/11	
grounde or springe woods called Grendon ley	1567, William Salt Library, H.M. Chetwynd bundle 95	
le Wyndmulnegraue	n.d., ?13th C., William Salt Library, H.M. Chetwynd, bundle 3	

Halford

Hampton-in-Arden (see also Balsall, Baddesley Clinton, Nuthurst)

siluulam de birchleia et hespelea	1154-79, B.R.L., Wingfield Digby MSS., A1/2, 4	?in the vicinity of Birchleyes Coppice and Aspleys Coppice; held by Robert the Archdeacon
siluulam de la lea *?= Leawood*	1154-79, B.R.L., Wingfield Digby MSS., A1/2, A4, A10 1588-9, P.R.O., SC 12/26/67	held by Robert the Archdeacon pasture by 1591, P.R.O., E 178/2347
boscum	n.d., 12th C., B.L., Cott. Ch. xi 35	part of the lands of Robert the Archdeacon
alneto *?=Alneto*	1184-1205, B.L., Add. Ch. 21,416 1299, S.B.T., DR37/2170	towards the bridge of *Bradeford* near to river Blythe and Packington

illud boscum vocatum Parkersmor ?=coppice called Parkars More ?=Parkers Moore Coppice	1376, P.R.O., SC 2/207/31 1591, P.R.O., E 178/2347 1649, B.R.L., 511,984	37 acres in 1591 (?wood acres) 43 acres in 1649
Kynweysey/Kynesey grove	1566, W.C.R.O., CR650; 1569, W.C.R.O., CR669	adjoining a close called Kynweysey, between a common lane to the west and Kinoldsey Hall to the east
Abbats Lawghton woode or grove	1566, W.C.R.O., CR650; 1569, W.C.R.O., CR669	in Kinwalsey, by a common lane on the north, another on the east

Hampton on the Hill - see Budbrooke

Hampton Lucy

de bosco, sub bosco ?= boscus inclusus qui vocatur le Park =Hampton Wode	c.1170, RBW, p. 277 1353, P.R.O., E 152/91 1453, Worcs. R.O., 001:9, BA 2636 164 92178a	arguably partly preserved in the present Hampton Wood
Ingon groves	1552-3, S.B.T., ER3/261	

Harborough Magna

Harbury

Hartshill

boscum qui vocatur Suthhaye =le Sowthay	1276, P.R.O., C 133/14/2 1376, B.L., Harl. Roll Y 13	enclosed, ?part of the present Hartshill Hayes willows cut there
boscum qui vocatur le Hokehaie	1276, P.R.O., C 133/14/2	enclosed, ?part of the present Hartshill Hayes
boscum qui vocatur le Neuhaye	1276, P.R.O., C 133/14/2	common pasture in the wood, ?part of the present Hartshill Hayes
Wasto meo in Boso [sic] de Hardredishull	1296, Bartlett, Manduessedum Romanorum, p. 137	common land
Le hay ?=sylve vocate Hardreshull Hay	1376, B.L., Harl. Roll Y 13 1403, Bartlett, Manduessedum Romanorum, p. 149	trees cut there next to the manor and vill (manerium et villam) of Hartshill
in quadam Groua	1376, B.L., Harl. Roll Y 13	little oaks and ashes cut there

Haseley

Boscum de Le clos ?=boscum quod vocatur Haseley clos ?= boscus clausus ?= Haseley Close Coppice = Haseley Close Coppice	1312, B.R.L., Keen 72 1351, B.R.L., 304,288 1316, P.R.O, C 134/49 ?c.1534, BD 1627 and 1648, BD, box 138 and 22/45/39	with Cokeyesruding alias Sloley adjacent in 1431 (B.R.L., Keen 72), next to land of Sloley in 1351 100 acres in 1627, still wood in 1648
Russelegrove	1339-40, B.L., Add. MS. 28,024, f. 69	
copies vocat' luscom groue	1392-3, BD	within the park - see Luscomb field-names in 1841, tithe map, W.C.R.O., CR569/125
Grova vocata le Conynger =apud le conyng'e	1423-4, BD 1394-5, BD	wood produced there both years
copie callede Lynen Drapers =grove called Lyn Drapers	ante 1588, BD 1593, BD	
Horne grove =horn grove	ante 1588, BD 1593, BD	said to be in Hatton in 1593, but see field-name in Haseley in 1841, W.C.R.O., CR569/125
unam grovam ?=unius grove in Haseley nuper .. Johannis Shakespere	1536-7, P.R.O., E 315/404 1546-7, B.R.L., 168,255	part of Wroxall priory's lands

Haselor

westgraf *?=West grove* *=le Weste Grove* *=Hemings Wood otherwise West Grove*	n.d., pre-1066, *S64* 1534, P.R.O., E 303/18/502 1544, P.R.O., E 318/21/998 1767, W.C.R.O., QS75/56	?=modern Westgrove
undecim acras bosci mei de Widecombe & middlegroue & Rowheya	n.d., 12th C., P.R.O., E 164/22, f. cxxv	for further details of two of these as separate woods see below
wode at haselore cald Withicombe *= uno bosco ...Wythecombe* *=one severall wood...called Wythycombe Grove*	1448, P.R.O., E 164/22, f. cxxxvi 1544, P.R.O., E 318/21/998 1544-5, P.R.O., LR 2/181	presumably approximating to the modern Withycombe Wood
middelgroue	1447-8, P.R.O., E 164/22, f. cxxxii	near *barlicheweye*
in bosco de Upton *coopertum bosci* *?=sexaginta acris bosci .. in Upton* *?=Upton Wood*	1221, *Rolls of the Justices in Eyre*, p. 331 n.d., P.R.O., E 164/22, f. cxxiiid 1314, P.R.O., CP 25/1/245/42 1537, W.C.R.O., CR1998/box 45/ GG7	60 acres
Rolveswode *?=Roles wood* *?=Rolls Wood Piece*	1364, *Calendar of Close Rolls, Edward III*, Vol. XII, pp. 71-2 1626, W.C.R.O., D19/475 1862, W.C.R.O., EAC/068/1	part of the wood of Upton pasture adjoining Oversley Wood
une grave in defenso	1316, P.R.O., C 134/46/14	?=Westgrove (see above)
Maisterswoode *?=masters wood* *=Red Hill Wood*	1465-6, B.R.L., 168,238 1626, W.C.R.O., D19/475 1791, W.C.R.O., CR114/114A	belonging to the Knights Hospitallers' manor of Grafton, but in Haselor
wood of the Hermytage	1544, *VCH*, Vol. III, p. 109	
a woode ... called Clynchames Copies	1537, W.C.R.O., CR1998/box 45/ GG7	by Upton Wood and Buttelers Hill
Shrowdehill *?=Shroud Hill Coppice*	1607, W.C.R.O., CR1998/box 82/1-26 1619, W.C.R.O., CR1998/box 71(1)	adjoining Oversley Park/Wood
Coppice springe Wood or Woodground .. called .. Awcocks Arbor	1619, W.C.R.O., CR1998/box 71(1)	presumably the modern Alcocks Arbour
Walsinghams Coppice *?=half a woode in Upton called Rowe marshe*	1619, W.C.R.O., CR1998/box 71(1) 1537, W.C.R.O., CR1998/box 45/ GG7	in Upton, granted to the Walsynghams in 1537

Hatton - see also Beausale, Shrewley

communionem boschi mei	n.d., ?12th C., P.R.O., E 315/47/129	wood of Hugh son of Richard
quadraginti acre bosci *?=unius bosci; le boys qest appelle Weggenok Deyuyle* *=Deyvilwode; Devylewodehende; Develwode*	1267, P.R.O., KB 26/176, rots 4d, 27r 1342, B.L., Add. MS. 28,024, ff. 68-9, 70 1398-9; 1400-1; 1425-6, W.C.R.O., CR1886/475, 481, 487	claimed by the widow of Roger de Eyuill in the western part of Wedgnock Park
sub graua prioris de Stodeleye *=Graua Prioris de Stodleye*	n.d., ?13th C., *BD* 1324, *BD*	
graua	1309, P.R.O., E 40/8284	of Richard de Boreford, near *Wowelondes* and *Redhulfeld*
Honyley hurne *?=Coppice Wood .. called .. Honiley Hyorne*	1394-5, W.C.R.O., CR1886/474 1627, *BD*, box 138	adjacent to Wedgnock Park 16 acres, in Hatton parish
Grouiculum *?=unam grovam vocatam Nether Countelowe* *?=Grenis grove*	1439, S.B.T., DR37/2183 1504, S.B.T., DR37/2190 1516, P.R.O., E 40/3952	between the road from Warwick to Haseley, *reddylfylde* and *mayel countelow*

Henley-in-Arden

grauam	c.1275, S.B.T., DR37/2199	of John Golafre

Hill (see Church Lawford)

Hillmorton

Hodnell (including Chapel Ascote)

Honiley

medietatem bosci mei de Nutehurst	n.d., 13th C., B.L., Cott. Ch. xxiii 15-16	granted to Richard Peche by Henry de Bereford
?=peaches owtewoode	1581, P.R.O., LR 2/185	
boscum Hugonis filii Willielmi	n.d., 13th C., B.L., Cott. Ch. xxiii 15-16	
boscum illum	n.d., 13th C., B.L., Cott. Ch. xxiii 15	by *Warkedich* and ditch of earl of Warwick
Will Richard & Dowrye groves *=a coppice heretofore part of the* *coppice called Will Richards* *Coppice and Dowry Grove*	1588, S.B.T., DR18/3/25/9 1742, W.C.R.O., CR1311/18/1	

Honington

Hunningham

Idlicote

graua	1527, P.R.O., E 303/17/268	?=present Idlicote Grove

Ilmington

ii bosci vocati thorngrove...hasyll *grove*	1446-7, P.R.O., SC 11/819	in Lark Stoke, Gloucestershire (Lark Stoke was in Ilmington parish)
?=le grove	1456, W.C.R.O., CR1911/9	
?=haselgrove and	1464, W.C.R.O., CR1911/12	
Thornedon Grove	1472, W.C.R.O., CR1911/13	in Stoke, ashes and willows in 1472

Ipsley

bosco Henrici Hubaud	1270-1, P.R.O., E 32/229, m. 8	

Itchington -see Bishop's Itchington and Long Itchington

Kenilworth

boscum	c.1124, B.L., Harley 3650, f. 9	
?=boscum nostrum de Odybern	c.1221-c.1250, *Formulare*, pp. 377-8	
=bosco qui vocatur Odybern	1235-58, B.L., Add. MS., 47,677, f. cxxvii	
=boscum de Odybarn	1478, S.B.T., DR18/30/15/1	
=A wood...Odybourn sprynge	1545, P.R.O., E 318/21/1143	20 acres, with timber
?=boscum	1279, *HR*, p. 48	160 acres
nemus ad parcum suum et ad *inforestandum*	c.1125, B.L., Add. MS. 47,677, ff. ccclix-ccclx	presumably became part of the park and chase
[in aliis boscis meis preter] haiam *=haya/haia/haiam*	1124-5, B.L., Harley 3650, f. 2 1236, 1238, 1241-2, *Calendar of Close Rolls* *Henry III, 1234-7*, p. 303 and *Calendar of* *Close Rolls, Henry III, 1237-42*, pp. 50, 78, 105, 302, 373, 385, 443	
in Bosco de Kenillewurth	1231-2, P.R.O., JUST 1/951A, rot 4r	identity of wood uncertain - see Chapter Three
?= in bosco/ in forinseco bosco *regis de Kenill'*	1235-7, *Calendar of Close Rolls Henry III,* *1234-7*, pp. 96, 292, 502, 507	
?= in bosco de Kenillewurth extra *hayam*	1242, *Calendar of Close Rolls Henry III, 1237-* *42*, p. 385	
?=in Bosco de Kenilwrth	1246-7, P.R.O., JUST 1/952, rot 42d	

in forinceco bosco	1388-9, P.R.O., DL 29/463/7539; 1438-9, DL 29/463/7540; 1439-40, DL 29/463/7541	despite numerous references the identity of this wood is uncertain -see Chapter Three
in bosco qui vocatur La Fryd *=le Fryth* *=le Fryth*	1261-2, P.R.O., JUST 1/954, rot 64r 1279, *HR*, p. 44 1322, S.B.T., DR10/516	alias Kingswood, divided into coppices by 1581, P.R.O., LR2/185
nemus	n.d., ?12th C., B.L., Harley 3650, f. 9	granted to Robert Franciscus, associated with Blackwell and Wridefen
nemoris ipsorum canonicorum de Blackwell *?=Boscum de Blakwell Wodde* *=Blackwell Wood*	c.1200, B.L., Harley 3650, f. 59 1537-8, P.R.O., SC 6/Hen.VIII/ 3736 1545, P.R.O., E 318/16/743	presumably approximates to the modern Blackwell Wood
alnetum	n.d., 12th C., B.L., Harley 3650, f. 8	in Blackwell or Wridefen
Rynselcopies *=Ryncoles copies* *=Ruynsull copys* *=copiciam in Rynshill* *=Boscus modo .. hoggs parke ..* *Runsill Cops*	1383, *John of Gaunt's Register*, Camden 3rd Series, LVII, nos. 880, 885 1388-90, P.R.O., DL 29/463/7539 1400-1, W.C.R.O., CR1886/475 1444-5, P.R.O., DL 29/463/7545 1591, W.C.R.O., CR576/1	see map of 1692 (W.C.R.O., CR143A), when no longer wood
pasturam que vocatur Burtoneswode	n.d., B.L., Add. MS. 47,677, f. xv	?name refers to William de Borton, Prior of Kenilworth in 3 Henry III
le Novel Coupys *?=Newcopyes*	1381, *John of Gaunt's Register*, Camden 3rd Series LVI, no. 609 1470-1, P.R.O., DL 29/463/7558	within the castle park
le Copies de Assho *?=Ashoe coppice*	1440-1, P.R.O., DL 29/463/7542 1581, P.R.O., LR 2/185	part of Kingswood or the Frith
i gravam inclausam	1279, *HR*, p. 49	held of the Priory by a tenant
duobus grauis siue virgultis in villa de Kenelworth que vocantur magnum Maney & paruum Maney	1362, P.R.O., C 54/200, m 23d	associated with the manor of Milburn in Stoneleigh
Pykynggesgroue	n.d., B.L., Add. MS. 47,677, f. cxxxvi	by *Homedewe*, under the Abbey
cum grava que vocatur Parrok	n.d., B.L., Add. MS., 47,677, f. xv	in Wridefen
kyngesgraue	1438-9, P.R.O., DL 29/463/7540	a croft
alstors grove *?=Allesters Grove als. Preists Grove*	1589-90, P.R.O., SC 12/27/36 1649, P.R.O., E 317/15	
Thornton Wood *=Thornton Wood* *=Henry Eaves Coppice*	1581, P.R.O., LR 2/185 1591, W.C.R.O., CR576/1 1694, W.C.R.O., Z421(Sm)	270 acres, within the Chase

Keresley

grauam *?=alterius Grouetti ibidem vocati Bennetts leez*	1411, P.R.O., E 164/21, ff. 11, 44 1541-2, P.R.O., E 318/1/18	given by Elias Buns to Coventry Cathedral Priory, held by Benet
groua vocata le Hardeshull	1411, P.R.O., E 164/21, f. 8v	by *Wilkefelde*
paruam grouam	1411, P.R.O., E 164/21, f. 7r	part of *le Wesyndenthyng*
groua	1411, P.R.O., E 164/21, f. 10r	in *le Bernecroft*
unius Grouetti .. vocati thevestake	1541-2, P.R.O., E 318/1/18	two and a half acres
Cokeshote groue	1541-2, P.R.O., E 318/1/18	
unius Grouetti vocati Stripegrouewood	1541-2, P.R.O., E 318/1/18	1 acre, 3 roods
halyerd copy *?=a little grove called Hall Yard* *?=Hall Yard Wood*	1520-6, Queen's College, 4 F 12a 1700, Queen's College, 4 F 72 1846, W.C.R.O., CR569/84	8 acres
pykhorn *=Pikthorn* *?=Pike Horn Wood*	1520-6, Queen's College, 4 F 12a 1700, Queen's College, 4 F 72 1846, W.C.R.O., CR569/84	5 acres a little grove
gret bonson; lytyll bonson copy *?=Bunson Wood*	1520-6, Queen's College, 4 F 12a 1587, Queen's College, 4 F 8	30 acres and 6 acres respectively between new dike and *fivefeild*

masons copy	1520-6, Queen's College, 4 F 12a	3 acres
long acre	1520-6, Queen's College, 4 F 12a	12 acres
houndhyll copyes	1520-6, Queen's College, 4 F 12a	4 acres
Symons Grove	1681, C.R.O., 468/229; W.C.R.O., D19/493	4 acres 20 perches, by a wood called Goldfarme, Longfeild and Tomfeild
Sisley grove alias Poultneys grove	1667, B.R.L., 294,034	close or pasture ground by Sisley fields and Yeild Wood

Kineton

King's Newton - see Seckington

Kingsbury

in bosco meo	c.1180, c.1200, M.MSS., Mi D 4059, 4515	of John de Bracebruge, ?in Kingsbury or Hurley
boscum de Kinsebur'	n.d., 13th C., Staffs. R.O., D593/A/1/10/10	by *boscum de Fres* (Freasley)
in bosco de Hornle	1261-2, P.R.O., JUST 1/954, rot 52r	
?=in quodam Bosco	1261-2, P.R.O., JUST 1/954, rot 21r	in Hurley, 60 acres, assarted
?=in Hurlewode	n.d., 13th C., M.MSS., Mi D 4041	above *Resehul*
quadraginta acris bosci	1411, P.R.O., CP 25/1/248/68	40 acres, in *Plumptonfeldes*
in bosco domini apud le Clyfe in le spryng'	1419, B.L., Egerton Roll 8621	? in the area of the later Thistlewood
placeam bosci	n.d., Staffs. R.O., D1287/6/37	*apud Holsti*

Kingston - see Chesterton

Kington - see Claverdon

Kinwarton

Knowle

in bosco de la knolle	1285, P.R.O., JUST 1/958, rot 31r	
=in bosco de Cnolle	1294-5, WA, 27,694	
?=Knollewode	1400-1, P.R.O., SC 6/1039/21	waste there
=Knollewode	1408-9, P.R.O., SC 6/1040/1	reference to lime trees
?=in bosco forinseco	1293, WA, 27,692	
=le Outwode	1355-6, P.R.O., SC 6/1039/19	
=Knolleoutwode	t. Hen. IV, WA, 620	common pasture
Chessetewode	1293, WA, 27,692	
=Chassetwode	1406-7, P.R.O., SC 6/1039/22	*lyndes* there
=unus boscus forinsecus vocatus Chessetwod	t. Hen. IV, WA, 620	common pasture
=Chassetwode	1408-9, P.R.O., SC 6/1040/1	reference to lime trees
=Chessett wood Coppice. ...adoiyneing...the wast called Chessett wood	1637, W.C.R.O., CR1886/2363	the coppice was between Bakers Lane (see modern maps) and the waste called Chessett wood
in uno bosco quod vocatur Derruge	c.1279-90, P.R.O., JUST 1/1245, rot 7r	
=Derrig/derrich	1293, WA, 27,692	
=unus clausus bosci Derrech	t. Hen. IV, WA, 620	
=coppice or grove of wood called Dorydge	1556, W.C.R.O., CR1886/2252	50 acres
=Dorredge Wood'	1576, P.R.O., Ward 2/39/1461/82	
=Dorridge Coppice	1605, P.R.O., LR 2/228	
unus alius clausus bosci vocatus Newclos	t. Hen. IV, WA, 620	
?=grauam vocatam Newcloswode	1400-1, P.R.O., SC 6/1039/21	
=newcroswode [sic] alias dicte Nicholswode	1532, P.R.O., SC 2/207/47	pasture in 1532
=New Clos or Nicklis Wood	1605, P.R.O., LR 2/228	pasture in 1605

unus clausus bosci vocatus Rowlemor	t. Hen. IV, WA, 620	
unus clausus bosci in Briddeslond ?=*grava* called *Briddesmor*	t. Hen. IV, WA, 620 1276, *Calendar of Inquisitions Miscellaneous*, Vol. I, no. 2200	10 acres by the priory of Henwood (across the river from Knowle)
i graua bosci	1448-9, WA, 621	held by John Hogges
graua vocata Bromlesgraue	1386-7, WA, 27,711	
Jacknetts Wodde	1542, P.R.O., LR 2/185	
ii grovas in Rotteyrew	1542, P.R.O., LR 2/185	3 acres

Ladbroke

Langley - see Claverdon

Lapworth

boscum de Lawurde ?=woods of Lapworth ?=*apud lappworth boscus*	n.d., ?late 12th C., *Reading Abbey Cartularies*, no. 617 1221, *Reading Abbey Cartularies*, no. 575 1446-7, P.R.O., SC 11/819	part of the Bishopton lands
totum boscum de Lappewurde quod vocatur Bissopeswude =*unum boscum qui vocatur Bissop Wude* =*le forein bois de Bysswode*	1197, ed. D.M. Stenton, *The Great Roll of the Pipe...1197*, Pipe Roll Society, new series viii (1931) p. 178 1252, *RBW*, p. 471 1375, B.L., Add. Ch. 14,006	presumably surviving in part in the modern Bushwood
Kyngeswode =*Boscum* =*Kynteswoode*	1279, HR, pp. 165-7, 169, 280 1381, P.R.O., E 315/43/216 1418, P.R.O., E 40/4271	manorial link with Wellesbourne in Kingswood still wood in 1418
Wolvernewode =*Wulvurenewude* =*Wolfernewode* =*Wolfurnwode*	n.d., 13th C., P.R.O.; E 40/4264 n.d., 13th C., P.R.O., E 40/4660 1350, P.R.O., E 40/4655 1446-7, P.R.O., SC 11/819	reference to waste of reference to assart of two fields with a meadow a close
graua	1364, P.R.O., E 40/4246	next to *le Harperesfeld*
grauam	1408, P.R.O., E 40/4416	adjoining land called *Nevewast*
& una graua [in]..Gorstyfeldes	1456-7, S.B.T., DR37/2251	granted by Roger Childe to John porsons; by *le Jovoteslond*, road to Birmingham, lane to Henley and *le Longefeld*
Bromon grove ?=*a certeyne ground called the grove*	1500-1, B.R.L., 437,896 1586, P.R.O., E 41/124	8 acres of wood, in the manor of Brome alias Bromon part of Brome Hall and lands
une groue que est appelle la petite park	1369, S.B.T., DR37/2247	
groues	1369, S.B.T., DR37/2247	listed as appurtenances to the manor

Lawford -see Church Lawford, also Long Lawford in Newbold on Avon

Lea Marston

Blacggreue	n.d., 13th C., M.MSS., Mi D 4169, 4174, 4177	?place-name or wood
la graue	1316, M.MSS., Mi D 4196	
Bayondewode ?=*apud yondwode*	1316, M.MSS., Mi D 4196 1574, B.R.L., Norton 182	?=beyond the wood by *middlefeilde*
Lee Wode ?=*boscum vocatum le leewode*	1478, B.R.L., Norton 92 1497-8, P.R.O., E 315/283, f. 5	
le Hammes Wode ?=*a wode within the neder hamys*	1472, B.R.L., Norton 89 1540, B.R.L., Norton 128	?near the modern Hams Hall

Leamington Hastings

Leamington Priors

Leek Wootton - see also Woodcote

Lighthorne

una Graua	1086, *DB*, 243b	2 furlongs long by 20 perches wide
?=i graua	1316, P.R.O., C 134/51	containing six acres
=groua	1390-1, S.B.T., DR98/672b	
=groua	1400-1, S.B.T., DR98/676a	produced rods for *le Watellyngs*
paruum spinetum	1301, P.R.O, C 133/100/1	?=the grove
=unum spinetum clausum	1316, P.R.O., C 134/49	
forinseco bosco	1398-9, S.B.T., DR98/674a	
?=in bosco	1401-2, S.B.T., DR98/675	

Lillington

Long Compton

bosco suo de Compton	1251-2, B.L., Eg. MSS., 3724	
?=boscum	1279, *HR*, p. 318	
?=boscus	1292-97, P.R.O., E 352/94, rots 25d-26d	wood enclosed after cutting
?=Cumptone Wode	1477, Castle Ashby MSS., no. 460	
boscum	1279, *HR*, p. 318	two woods are mentioned in the *HR*.
?=Yerdeley	1477, Castle Ashby MSS., no. 460	described with *Cumptone Wode* (see above) as
		underwoods (*subboscis*) and *siluas*

Long Itchington

x acras subbosci	1305, P.R.O., C 133/119/5	location of underwood not given
?=boscus separale	1347, P.R.O., C 135/83/25	
?=Ichinton Wode	1385-6, P.R.O., SC 6/1041/12	47 oaks cut there
?=Long Itchington Wood	1687, S.B.T., DR18/25/Bn.72	may include part of the park
a grove	1466, Walsall Local History Centre, 276/63	providing *fyrebote, housebote, haybote*, in Bascote

Long Lawford - see Newbold on Avon

Longdon - see Solihull

Loxley

Luddington - see Stratford-upon-Avon

Lyndon - see Bickenhill

Mancetter - see also Ansley, Atherstone, Hartshill

bosco	1231, *Curia Regis Rolls*, Vol. XIV, nos. 1105, 1630	
?=de bosco de Mancester	1232, P.R.O., CP 25/1/243/17	
?=boscus forinsecus	1234, P.R.O., CP 25/1/243/18	?=outwood of Mancetter
?=centu & quadraginta acris bosci.. in manecestr'	1315, P.R.O., CP 25/1/245/42	
=outwood of Mancetter	1538, P.R.O., E 303/18/444	by the outwood of Oldbury
in bosco de Harmeleg'	1232, P.R.O., CP 25/1/243/17	
?= in parco suo de Armele	1234, P.R.O., CP 25/1/243/18	
boscum de Crumpeleg'	1234, P.R.O., CP 25/1/243/18	between *Merestrete, Warlauwesmede*, Coventry way, and the ancient foss between *Crumpeleg* and the meadow of the villeins of Mancetter

Marston - see Butlers Marston, Lea Marston, Priors Marston, and, for Marston Jabbett, Bulkington

Marton

Maxstoke

unus boscus forinsecus	1295, P.R.O., C 133/73/2	
=forinsecum Boscum	1325-6, Bodleian Library, Trinity MS. 84, f. clxxiii	by a field called *blaklond*
?=le Outewode	1346, *Calendar of Close Rolls, 1346-9*, p. 84	imparked on building of the castle
Byrchenemor	1347, S.B.T., DR18/3/35/3	described as a plot of wood ground
the Oldfeld	1347, S.B.T., DR18/3/35/3	described as a plot of wood ground
i grove bosci	1402-3, Bodleian Library, Trinity MS. 84, f. lii	
?=grova terre & bosci	1419, P.R.O., E 40/621; B.R.L. Keen 92	by the highway from Coventry to Maxstoke and Coleshill
parcelle terre & bosci vocate le maysse	1437-8, Staffs. R.O., D641/1/2/269; 1486-7, W.C.R.O., CR2981/ uncatalogued	
halmonswode	1437-8, Staffs. R.O., D641/1/2/269	pasture
=halomeswode	1486-7, W.C.R.O., CR2981/ uncatalogued	pasture, stated to be within the park
Erleswode	1437-8, Staffs. R.O., D641/1/2/269	pasture
monwode	1437-8, Staffs. R.O., D641/1/2/269	a field, ? in Astley
Gilmor	n.d., 15th C., Bodleian Library, Trinity MS. 84, f. 57	
?=Gilmore Wood	1690, S.B.T., DR18/3/20/4	see map of 1767, W.C.R.O., Z149
Brodmor	1435-6, Bodleian Library, Trinity MS. 84, f. 14 1690, S.B.T., DR18/3/20/4	
?=Breadmoor Wood		see map of 1767, W.C.R.O., Z149
Hichwood	1521-2, S.B.T., ER1/63/280, f. 71	?=modern Heach Wood
Bethnally Wood	1521-2, S.B.T., ER1/63/280, f. 71	
Combys Wood	1521-2, S.B.T., ER1/63/280, f. 71	
Clarkffylde Wood	1521-2, S.B.T., ER1/63/280, f. 71	
Priors Grove	1521-2, S.B.T., ER1/63/280, f. 71	
Cowpers Wood	1521-2, S.B.T., ER1/63/280, f. 71	
?=Coopers Grove	18th C., W.C.R.O., Z309/2(U)	

Merevale

in quodam bosco quod continet centum acras	1260, P.R.O., JUST 1/953, rot 4r	common pasture there
?=meryvall outwode	1437-8, Staffs. R.O., D641/1/2/269	(listed under Atherstone)

Meriden, including Alspath

in bosco meo	?1162-73, G. Barraclough, *The Charters of the Anglo-Norman Earls of Chester*, Record Society of Lancashire and Cheshire, CXXVI, 1988, p. 173	the text of the document is described as "extremely corrupt", but probably representing "a genuine transaction"; the earl allowed the grantee to put forty pigs in the wood
?=communem boschum	n.d., B.R.L., 608,881	
?=bosco de allespath	n.d., B.R.L., 608,882	an assart there granted by petrus albus to William Waldgiue
=in bossco de alisspathe	n.d., 13th C., S.B.T., DR10/534	
?=bosco meo de Alespath	n.d., B.R.L., 608,879	of Alexander de bikenhul
?=Bosco meo de Allespath	c.1240-50, C.R.O., BA/D/K/10/2; n.d., S.B.T., ER1/63/293	of Gilbert de Segrave
illud bosscum	c.1240, C.R.O., BA/D/K/10/1	bought of petrus alba of Alspath by Gerard, son of William de Alspath
?=wood of William de Alspath	1308, De Banco Roll 173, m. 233, cited in *VCH*, Vol. IV, p. 151	
nemoris Ricardi de Kinton	n.d., S.B.T., DR10/534	by or in the wood of Alspath
partem bosci que vocatur schutehaunch	n.d., B.R.L., 608,881	bought by Richard de Kinton of Peter le blund (?=alba, see above) *juniore*
?=Shewte haunche	1533-4, S.B.T., DR10/1409, f. 291	
=Coppice wood or grove called .. Scotthaunce alias Shoutehaunce	1555, W.C.R.O., CR669/bundle G	adjoined Jeningswood on the south

bosco de Horn =*the hornewod*	n.d., S.B.T., ER1/63/297 1513, William Salt Library, H.M. Chetwynd, bundle 8	see Horn Wood on modern maps still wood in 1513, pasture in 1614 (W.C.R.O., CR669/bundle G)
Boscum quod Radus de finunglia tenuit	1202, P.R.O., CP 25/1/242/6	in Alspath, near *Hocwei*
medietatem bossci mei ..iacentem iuxta le Wallegrene	1316, S.B.T., DR10/543	granted by Richard Pagge of Alspath to Stephen de Cleybrock
unum croftum .. cu bosco adiacente	1316, S.B.T., DR10/544	granted by William Jordan to Stephen de Cleybrock
grove que vocatur Ormesgreva	1323-4, S.B.T., ER1/63/294	
cuiusdam bosci que nuper fuit Rogeri Bukmore in Alspathe	1401, P.R.O., E 315/31/235	
unam grauam ex dono Gerardi de Waldeyve *?=unius groue*	1411, P.R.O., E 164/21, f. 48v 1546-7, B.R.L., 168,255, m. 14	belonging to Coventry Cathedral Priory
unam grovam vocatam Whittgroue *?=a grove called Margerie Grove* =*oon litle grove there* *?=Close .. called Megge wood* =*Megge wood close* *?=Close .. called Magg Grove* *?=Meggrove*	1452, C.R.O., 54/27 1528, C.R.O., 9/1 1546, C.R.O., BA/D/K/10/24 1581, C.R.O., BA/A/A/2/2 1630-1, C.R.O., 54/69 1652, C.R.O., BA/D/K/10/26 1656, 1668, W.C.R.O., Finch Knightley 3/3/11, 13 (list of papers at Packington Hall)	in Meriden, granted by John Braylis to Margaret his wife part of a messuage in Alspath called Breylles in Braiiles lands by lodge green - 6 acres by lodge green - 6 acres by lodge green and associated with the tenement called Braylis, may be marked by the field called Grove in Pisford's lands on map of 1789, W.C.R.O., CR2381. north of the lane from Meriden to Fillongley
grovam vocatam Chirchegrave *?=Awselie Church Grove* *?=Church wood*	1455, W.C.R.O., CR669/bundle G 1531, W.C.R.O., CR299/207 1587, W.C.R.O., Finch Knightley 3/3/8 (list of papers at Packington Hall)	by *Taylllereslond* and *Oldworthyng*
clausuram terre & bosci .. *Dyberodyng* =*a close of wood called dyve ruddyng* *?=unam Grovam vocatam Dyve Ryddyng*	1408, P.R.O., E 329/222 1454, P.R.O., E 326/8944 1550, B.R.L., 249,976	between Alspath and Packington see Dive Reddings on the border with Packington, north of Church Wood in 1789, W.C.R.O., CR2381
unam paruam Grovam vocatam *Chauntre grove* *?=Chantrie grove* *?=Chantry Wood*	1550, B.R.L., 249,976 1587, Finch Knightley 3/3/8 (list in W.C.R.O.) c.1795, W.C.R.O., CR2381	by a grove called Dyve Ryddyng (see above)
grove in Alspath ..voc' shafts *Sprynge* *?=the Shaftes* *?=Grovam vocatam Shaftes*	1523-7, S.B.T., DR10/1777 1531, W.C.R.O., CR299/207 1603, B.R.L., 277,121	described as a wood -?later Meriden Shafts
Withie Grove	1531, W.C.R.O., CR299/207	map, 1789, W.C.R.O., CR2381
Hanch Wood	1531, W.C.R.O., CR299/207	map, 1789, W.C.R.O., CR2381
Cokshot Woode	1531, W.C.R.O., CR299/207	
Farris Grove	1531, W.C.R.O., CR299/207	
Ballis Grove	1531, W.C.R.O., CR299/207	map, 1789, W.C.R.O., CR2381
Bakers Grove	1531, W.C.R.O., CR299/207	
Benetts spryng	1513, William Salt Library, H.M. Chetwynd bundle 8	
the reught/row lesue	1513, William Salt Library, H.M. Chetwynd bundle 8	
millyscent wood	1597, S.B.T., DR10/560	?= modern Millison's Wood

Middleton

in bosco de Middelton =*in boscum de Middelton* =*bosco de Midilton* ?=*boscum* ?=*in bosco domini* ?=*quidam boscus forinsecus* =*in bosco forinseco*	1221, *Roll of the Justices*, p. 373 1231-2, P.R.O., JUST 1/951A, rot 6r 1249, M.MSS., Mi D 4310 n.d., M.MSS, Mi D 4253 1308, M.MSS., Mi M 131/4 1313, P.R.O., C 134/34/14 1315, M.MSS., Mi M 131/9	in common
bosscum meum quod vocatur le Lindes ?=*Wastum quod vocatur le Lindes* =*vasto nostro vocato Le Lyndes*	n.d., 13th C., M.MSS., Mi D 4255 n.d., 13th C., M.MSS., Mi D. 4265 1333, M.MSS., Mi D. 4382	on the heath of *Turteleye*
bosscum meum quod vocatur sokone =*boscum meum quod vocatur la soken* ?=*wastum meum quod vocatur la soken* ?=*assartum meum quod vocatur la sokone*	n.d., 13th C., M.MSS., Mi D 4277, 4328 n.d., 13th C., M.MSS., Mi D 4291 n.d., 13th C., M.MSS., Mi D 4270 n.d., 13th C., M.MSS., Mi D 4299	near to *drybrok* and *le spires*, ?= The Spires on map of 1865, M.MSS., Mi 2 P 5A
alnetum	1286, M.MSS., Mi D 4317	of Richard de *scheldon*
in alto bosco ?=*pastura vocata le Henwode*	1297, M.MSS., Mi D 4323 1454-5, M.MSS., 5/167/102	?=the high wood ?in the vicinity of Hanwoods on map of 1865, M.MSS., Mi 2 P 5A
siluam que vocatur Wodehurst =*le clos de Wodehurst* =*i boscus forincicus vocatus Wodyshurst*	1299, M.MSS., Mi D 4325 1385, M.MSS., Mi D 4525/2 1419-20, M.MSS., Mi M 124	contained oaks, maples and crabs
in bosco vocato Wallehede ?= *ii parcelle bosci forinseci vocate le Wallehede*	1387, M.MSS., Mi M 131/29 1419-20, M.MSS., Mi M 124	
ii parcelle bosci vocate Swarthale close	1419-20, M.MSS., Mi M 124	*Swarthalheth* was by *Wodehurst* in 1385, M.MSS., Mi D 4525/2
i boscus vocatus Sharpenok	1419-20, M.MSS., Mi M 124	

Milverton

Mollington

Monks Kirby

totum boscum meum qui dicitur La Grave =*le Groue*	1302, B.L., Cott. Ch. xxix 90 1403, B.L., Eg. Ch. 6160	in Pailton - see modern Grove wood in tithe award, W.C.R.O., CR569/150

Moreton Morrell

grova de moorton	1425-6, P.R.O., SC 6/1040/7	wood taken from there for Lighthorne, ?present Moreton Wood

Morton Bagot

in bosco de Morton	1227, *Curia Regis Rolls*, XIII, no. 273	?in the vicinity of the later Morton Waste/Common

Napton

Newbold on Avon

viginti acris bosci ?=*le groue/growe*	1368, P.R.O., JUST 1/1472, rot 22d 1484-94, P.R.O., SC 11/685-8	belonging to a free-holding in Newbold herbage sold there

illam partem spineti que est apud occidentem	n.d., B.L., Cotton Caligula A xiii, f. 133	in Long Lawford, given to Pipewell Abbey by Roger de Stuteville
=medietas predicti spineti	1210, B.L., Cotton Caligula A xiii, f. 145	
de graua mea que appellatur Blachenurd ab augmento quod antea habebant de Rogero de stuteuill	n.d., B.L., Cotton Caligula A xiii, ff. 144-5; P.R.O., E 315/53/189	granted to Pipewell Abbey by Roger Pantolf, ?part of the *spinetum* above
=totum spinetum de Blakethirne usque ad Caldewell	n.d., B.L., Cotton Caligula A xiii, f. 148	

Newbold Pacey

lytell grove	1585, *Ecclesiastical Terriers*, Vol. II, p. 15	in Ashorne

Newnham Regis

Newnham - see Aston Cantlow

Newton Regis - see Shuttington

Norton Curlieu - see Budbrooke

Norton Lindsey

Nuneaton

magno bosco	ante 1477, J. Nichols, *The History and Antiquities of the county of Leicester*, Vol. I, Part II (1815), Appendix XVII	belonging to Gaufridus de Turvilla, in Stockingford
bosco de Newhay	ante 1477, Nichols, *History and Antiquities of the county of Liecester*, Vol. I, Part II, App. XVII	of Stephen de Segrave, in Stockingford
bosco .. qui vocatur Netlebeddesmoor	n.d., P.R.O., E 326/1882	in Stockingford
campo qui vocatur Godsalmes Wode	1290, B.L., Add. Ch. 49,069	in Stockingford
all his woods	t. Stephen, *Dugdale*, Vol. II, p.1066	of Robert Fitz Jocelin
?=illo campo qui vocatur silua Jocelini	n.d., ?c. 1290, B.L., Add. Ch. 49,071	in Stockingford
?=[land] in bosco Jocelini	n.d., P.R.O., E 326/8008	
in bosco de Eton	1285, P.R.O., JUST 1/958, rot 33d	
bosco vocato le Hanche	1368-9, B.L., Add. Roll 49,711	?=the later Hanch Wood
?=le Hanche	1369-70, B.L., Add. Roll 49,712; 1400-1, B.L., Add. Roll 49,759; 1406-7, B.L., Add. Roll 49,762	
?=Spring or Grove called hanche	1543, W.C.R.O., Z364 (Sm)	30 acres in 1543
Joneswode	1377-8, B.L., Add. Roll 49,720	presumably on the site of closes called John's Wood in tithe award, W.C.R.O., CR569/184
=Jonuswode	1401-2, B.L., Add. Roll 49,760	
	1405-6, B.L., Add. Roll 49,763	
	1406-7, B.L., Add. Roll 49,762	
?=Johnnyswood	1543, W.C.R.O., Z364 (Sm)	
Boscum quod vocatur le lee	n.d., ?13th C., B.L., Add. Ch. 48,491	by Caldecote Wood - B.L. Add. Rolls 49,760, 49,762, also by Hartshill park; relationship to *overle, nethurle, middelle* and *Neusonle* not clear
=in bosco vocato le lee [or] le lee	various from 1370 - B.L., Add. Rolls 49,713, 49,715, 49,717-9, 49,721-2, 49,751, 49,760, 49,762-3	
?=Great Ley wood	1542, B.L., Add Ch. 48,791, 48,793	
le lee superior	1331-2, B.L., Add. Roll 49,727	
?=overle	1406-7, B.L., Add. Rolls 49,762, 49,765	
middelle	1401-2, B.L., Add. Roll 49,760	
Nethurle	1401-2, B.L., Add. Roll 49,760	
	1406-7, B.L., Add. Rolls 49,762, 49,765	

boscum vocatum Neusonle =Neusonle	1369-70, B.L., Add. Roll 49,712 1401-2, B.L., Add. Roll 49,760	
Newewode =boscum vocatum le Neuwode =le Neuwode	1370-1, B.L., Add. Roll 49,713 1372-3, B.L., Add. Roll 49,715 1374-5, 1380-1, 1407, B.L., Add. Rolls 49,717, 49,722, 49,765	next to the wood called le lee near Wedyntonbrugge, B.L. Add. Roll 49,765
in Neutakenhyn =le Neutakenhin ?=grove called new taken Inne	1331-2, B.L., Add. Roll 49,727 1380-1, 1386-8, 1401-2, 1405-6, 1406-7, 1407, B.L., Add. Rolls 49,722, 49,751, 49,760, 49,763, 49,762, 49,765 1538, B.L., Add. Ch. 48,776	underwood there in 1331-2
in bosco vocato le Neunomenyn ?=Neunemenhin ?=pastura bosci vocati le Neunomnhin	1372-3, B.L., Add. Roll 49,715 1374-5, B.L., Add. Roll 49,717 1401-2, B.L., Add. Roll 49,760	relationship with Neutakenhin uncertain - both appear in the same account roll - B.L., Add. Roll 49,760
boscum vocatum le merilinde wode	1374-5, 1375-6, 1401-2, 1405-6, 1406-7, B.L., Add. Rolls 49,717, 49,719, 49,760, 49,763, 49,762	
le hackyng	1369-70, 1374-5, 1400-1, 1401-2, 1405-6, 1406-7, B.L., Add. Rolls 49,712, 49,717-8, 49,759, 49,760, 49,763, 49,762	near Merilindewode - B.L., Add. Rolls 49,759, 49,763
le hywod ?=in alto bosco ?=in bosco vocato le Hiwode =in bosco vocato hywode	1331-2, B.L., Add. Roll 49,727 1374-5, B.L., Add. Roll 49,718 1375-6, B.L., Add. Roll 49,719 1400-1, 1401-2, 1405-6, B.L., Add Rolls 49,759, 49,760, 49,763	
in le heyewode =le heywode	1374-5, B.L., Add. Roll 49,717 1401-2, B.L., Add. Roll 49,760	
bosco vocato Haliwellesich	1372-3, B.L., Add. Roll 49,715	
Le Outwode	1406-7, 1407, B.L., Add. Rolls 49,762, 49,765	next to Jonuswode, Merilindewode and hardecnol
boscum vocatum le hardecnol	1401-2, B.L., Add. Roll 49,760	by the Outwode and wood called lee B.L., Add. Rolls 49,765, 49,763
in bosco vocato Hanchemor	1400-1, B.L., Add. Roll 49,759	by le Hanche, B.L., Add. Roll 49,760
bosco vocato Blakewater	1407-8, B.L., Add. Roll 49,765	presumably by Blackwatergate
in boscum vocatum Wisshawe ?=Wyshawe	1401-2, B.L., Add. Roll 49,760 1543, W.C.R.O., Z364(Sm)	in 1543 this was a field-name attached to land within the precinct of the manor up to barre grene
boscum vocatum le Clos subtus villa de Eton	1378-9, B.L., Add. Roll 49,721	
iuxta boscum de le Temple	1397-9, B.L., Add. Roll 49,757	
bosco de Horston =boscum vocatum horston wode =the wode/boscum ?=unius crofti vocati horston wood =Whoreston Wood	1372-3, 1386-8, B.L., Add. Rolls 49,715, 49,751 1401-2, B.L., Add. Roll 49,760 1408-9, B.L., Add. Roll 49,403 1557, B.R.L., 347,953 1690, W.C.R.O., CR136/C704	In 1408-9 by longeleies, lancotegate and the field of Attleborough, B.L., Add. Roll 49,403
Comiteswoode =Countes Wood	1541, B.L., Add. Ch. 48,790 1543, W.C.R.O., Z364(Sm)	pasture in 1543, between barre pool, water mill, Blackwater field and tamefield
Hyrdmanys grove =hardemans grove	1543, W.C.R.O., Z364(Sm) 1557, B.R.L., 347,953	next to the Myddylpoole
Spryngwood grove	1552, B.L., Add. Ch. 48,819	

Nuthurst

Hnuthyrste	699-709, S64	place-name
campo vocato Lynthurst	1357, 1360, S.B.T., DR37/2285a/50, 52	by Myddle Fielde and Sandie Croft in 1568, S.B.T., ER1/67/565
unam grauam vocatam Systelyes groue	1420, S.B.T., DR37/2285a/69	
Gunnild grove	1428, S.B.T., DR37/2285a/73	

le grove	1476, B.R.L., Wingfield Digby MSS., A615	in pasture and land called *Oldenutthurste* with Bayard' Croft
Yondrewod	1336, S.B.T., DR37/2285a/36	?=beyond the wood
a coppis called Ketles graves	1597, B.R.L., 277,427	

Offchurch

boscus inclusus vocatus Bradlegh	1411, P.R.O., E 164/21, f. 207v	

Oldbury

partem nemoris ex Sutest de Aldeburia *=nemus Hugonis*	c.1129-48, S.B.T., ER1/64/342-4	no statement that the wood was in Oldbury or in Hartshill or Mancetter adjoining
Byrcheley grove	1541, P.R.O., E 318/20/1077	2½ acres
Grove called the more	1541, P.R.O., E 318/20/1077	3½ acres, ?modern Moor Wood
a grove	1541, P.R.O., E 318/20/1077	5 acres, held by Richard Baresolde
[3] parcells of wood in oldebury comen *?=the Outwoods of Oldebery*	1541, P.R.O., E 318/20/1077 1538, P.R.O., E 303/18/444, 431	15½ acres of wood by the outwood of Mancetter
the Newecopie	1538, P.R.O., E 303/18/444	by the outwood

Oversley

park *=in parco domini* *=parcus* *?=Oversley park woods* *=park*	1283, *Calendar of Inquisitions Post Mortem*, Vol II, no 529 1319, S.B.T., DR5/2246 c.1320, S.B.T., DR5/2246b 1600, S.B.T., DR5/2356 1747, W.C.R.O., CR1998/M12	 hazel rods cut there 387 acres, 1½ perches, with pasture, pannage and underwood map shows area of c.380 acres, about half of which is covered by the present Oversley Wood
Budeleye	1318, S.B.T., DR5/2245 1319, S.B.T., DR5/2246 c.1320, S.B.T., DR5/2246b 1332, S.B.T, DR5/2249 1387-8, S.B.T., DR5/2255	 trees cut there one of the three woods in the manor near to the field of Oversley
Holewegrove *?=Hoghwegrove* *?=Holuwegroue*	1318, S.B.T., DR5/2245 c.1320, S.B.T., DR5.2246b 1332, S.B.T., DR5/2249	 one of the three woods in the manor ? near to Highway Ground
Caluhul *=Calwohull*	1319, S.B.T., DR5/2246 c.1320, S.B.T., DR5/2246b	 one of the three woods in the manor
in bosco domini *?=boscus separalis*	c.1332, 1353-4, 1385, S.B.T, DR5/2249, 2250, 2251 1334, P.R.O., C 135/38/31	 of William le Boteler

Oxhill

Packington, Great

forinseco bosco de Pakynton *?=bosco de Pakynton* *?=Packington comen*	n.d, ?13th C., B.L., Add. MS. 47,677, ff. xxiii, xxlv n.d., ?13th C., B.L., Add. MS. 47,677, ff. xxii, xxiii 1544, P.R.O., E 318/10/434	the outwood is marked on a map of 1777, copy in W.C.R.O., Z301/1(U) 13 acres of wood there
boscum Ailgmeshey/ Ailyhmehey *?=Agmondeshill* *?=groves called Admondes hill*	n.d., ?13th C., B.L., Add. MS. 47,677, ff. xxiv, xxv 1521, S.B.T., ER1/63/280 1547, W.C.R.O., Finch Knightley 1/14 (list of papers at Packington Hall)	described as part of the foreign wood described as wood

Great Close Wood *=Close Wood*	1536, W.C.R.O., Finch Knightley 1/2 (list of papers at Packington Hall); 1544, P.R.O., E 318/10/434 1761, W.C.R.O., Z314(Sm)	70 acres in 1544
New hewe wood	1536, W.C.R.O., Finch Knightley 1/2 (list of papers at Packington Hall); 1544, P.R.O., E 318/10/434	20 acres in 1544
Newe parke wood	1544, P.R.O., E 318/10/434	36 acres
Olde parke wood	1544, P.R.O., E 318/10/434	20 acres
lyttel grove	1547, W.C.R.O., Finch Knightley 1/14 (list of papers at Packington Hall)	

Packington, Little

in bosco de Pakinton Pigot	n.d., ?13th C., Staffs. R.O., D1287/6/18/28	

Packwood

nemus de pacwda et ecclesia illic constructa	c.1183, S.B.T., DR10/258	not clear whether the church was built in the place called Packwood or in its wood
boscum forinsecum	1279, *HR*, p. 180 1411, P.R.O., E 164/21, f. 204r	
parcum inclusum *?=magnum boscum vocatum le Parke*	1279, *HR*, p. 180 1411, P.R.O., E 164/21, f. 204r	
cum tribus grovis vocatis Lusterley Groves	1411, P.R.O., E 164/21, f. 204r	?near to modern listelowe in the north of the parish - see tithe award, W.C.R.O., CR328/33
grava apud Pakwode vocata Cooksetegroue	1398, C.R.O., 54/40	underwood sold there
graua; grauam; grauis	1411, P.R.O., E 164/21, ff. 204r-206r	17 groves in all, held by tenants; timber belonged to the lord
grove at the head of lyghtfelde	1519, B.R.L., Keen 104; S.B.T., DR12/4	see Grove field-name in the Light Fields on map of 1723, copy in W.C.R.O., Z230(L)

Pailton - see Monks Kirby

Pillerton Priors and Pillerton Hersey

Pinley - see Coventry and Rowington

Polesworth

in bosco de Polleswrth	1285, P.R.O., JUST 1/958, rot 31d	
boscus	1285, P.R.O., C 133/41/5	in Pooley
boscum quem vendidi & boscum quem retinui *?=boscum de Fres'*	n.d., 13th C., Staffs. R.O., D593/A/1/10/10; *Select Cases in the Court of King's Bench under Edward I*, Vol. II (ed. Sayles), pp. 97-112	Freasley's wood, which had been divided, was the subject of much dispute; it adjoined the wood of Kingsbury
boscum de Stotefoldeshay *=bosco curie sue vicino qui vocatur Stodfoldeshay*	n.d., 13th C., Staffs. R.O., D593/A/1/10/10	in Freasley
sexaginta acris bosci *?=part of quinquaginta & una acras bosci*	1300-1, P.R.O., JUST 1/1320, rot 10d 1302, William Salt Library, H.M. Chetwynd Bundle 3	in Dordon
mosegrauehull	n.d., ?13th C., William Salt Library, H.M. Chetwynd Bundle 3	? a place-name or a grove on a hill, ? near Hoo Hill in Dordon
Newe taken in coppice	1545, P.R.O., E 318/11/499	12 acres
Sheldon coppice	1545, P.R.O., E 318/11/499	2 acres
Lytwood coppice	1545, P.R.O., E 318/11/499	6 acres
Parke wood	1545, P.R.O., E 318/11/499	15 acres
Bearley wood	1545, P.R.O., E 318/11/499	8 acres
m'hay	1545, P.R.O., E 318/11/499	3 acres of wood there

Echylls common	1545, P.R.O., E 318/11/499	trees there
Bucketts coppice	t. Henry VIII, P.R.O., E 318/15/710	3 acres
More coppice	t. Henry VIII, P.R.O., E 318/15/710	1 acre

Preston Bagot

cum quodam bosco *?=graua*	?1221-38, B.L., Cotton Vespasian E xxv, f. 71 1226-38, B.L., Cotton Vespasian E xxv, f. 71	dates from <u>Reading Abbey Cartularies</u>, pp. 444-5; both deeds involve Simon Bagot and lands associated with a mill

Princethorpe

in quodam bosco	1246-7, P.R.O., JUST 1/952, rot 5r	common rights there, ?=present Princethorpe Great Wood

Priors Hardwick

Priors Marston

Radbourn

Radford - see Coventry

Radford Semele

Viginti Acras bosci *?=le Grove*	1514, B.L., Add. MS. 47,677, ff. lxi, lxii 1537-8, P.R.O., SC6/Hen VIII/ 3736	wood sold there

Radway

in doddesgrove	1308-9, S.B.T., DR10/1457	small branches (*Ramuscul'*) sold there

Ratley

unam grauam que vocatur cnihtegraue	n.d., 12th C., S.B.T., DR10/1406, f. 203	
=unam grouam que vocatur knicthegraue	n.d., 12th C., S.B.T., DR10/1406, f. 206	permission to assart included
=essarta de knictegraue	1184-1204/5, P.R.O., E 326/11626	
=essarta de chnictgraue	n.d., ?c.1200, S.B.T., DR10/1406, ff. 210-13; P.R.O., E 329/234	
?=Nygrove	1612, B.L., Add. Roll 43,001	
sub bosco qui vocatur estlee	n.d., ?12th C., S.B.T., DR10/1406, f. 208	
?=grauam de estleia	n.d., S.B.T., DR10/1406, f. 209	
=graua sua de estlee	n.d., P.R.O., E 329/234	
=Astley groue	n.d., ?14th C., S.B.T., DR18/1/596	near Hornton and Fleet meadow
Heigrauemore	n.d., 12th C., S.B.T., DR10/1406, ff. 210-13; P.R.O., E 329/234, E 326/11626	place-name which may not refer to an extant grove

Rowington

boscum de Rochinton'	?late 12th C., *Reading Abbey Cartularies*, no. 617	
?=Rowenton Wood	1457-8, S.B.T., DR3/805	in the northern part of Rowington, towards Baddesley Clinton
=boscum vocatum Rowyngton Wood	1491, S.B.T., DR3/795	
=Rowington Woodde	1606, P.R.O., LR 2/228	
communionem .. in bosco abbatis de Aspeleia	1150, *Reading Abbey Cartularies*, no. 614	
?=Boscum Domini Regis ibidem vocatum Asple Wood	1543-4, P.R.O., E 315/457	
=Aspeley Wood	1582, S.B.T., DR473/291, ff. 10, 11, 14, 19, 20	on the south-east side of Rowington, near Shrewley

bosco de Pinnele *?=vasto vocato Pynleywodde*	c.1220, W.C.R.O., CR284/1 1481, W.C.R.O., CR1008/32	
Eweruge *?=Overuge*	1221, Reading Abbey Cartularies, no. 575 1491, 1509, W.C.R.O., CR1008/36, 43	a wood ?a place-name, near *Brommesgrove* in Lapworth
Inwode	1252, *Reading Abbey Cartularies*, no. 622	?by modern Inwood End
una parua gravenett spinossa	1537, *BD* (under Hatton)	2 acres, south of a close called Park Field

Rugby

Ryton - see Bulkington

Ryton-on-Dunsmore

aisiamentis nemoris mei *?=in nemore de Ruton/Ruitun* *?=boscum forinsecum* *?=boscum de Ruytone*	n.d., ?12th C., Cambridge University Library, Add 3021, f.238 1231-2, P.R.O., JUST 1/951A, rot 3d 1279, *HR*, p. 151 1335, W.C.R.O., CR350/3	? presumably part survives in the modern Ryton Wood

Salford

boscum ipsius prioris de Salford *?=bosco de Woluedone* *=boscum suum de Woluedon* *=the said Wode ycalled Woluendon*	1237, *Curia Regis Rolls*, Vol. XV, no. 36 1270-71, P.R.O., E 32/229, rots 2r, 4d n.d., B.L., Add. MS. 47,677, f. clxxxi 1433, B.L., Add. MS. 47,677, f. clxx	The wood of Wolvedon seems to have been divided into coppices by the late sixteenth century - see below
Old Close Coppice; *Rough Hill Coppice;* *Coldepittes Coppice*	1580 for 1576, B.R.L., 167,733	enclosed together with a hedge and containing 134 acres, these woods belonged to Kenilworth Abbey (formerly Priory); from the location of Rough Hill, these woods matched the site of Wolvedon
essarto de Biuintonesgraue *=?Barne Grove*	n.d., B.L., Harley 3650, f. 77; B.L., Add. MS. 47,677, ff. clxiiii, clxxii 1580, B.R.L. 167,733	presumably in (Wood) Bevington, belonging to Kenilworth Priory formerly of Kenilworth Abbey
Pikersale Coppice	1580, B.R.L. 167,733	formerly of Kenilworth Abbey
Bury Coppice	1531, P.R.O., E 303/17/293	belonging to St. John's College
quatuor acris bosci ...in Abbot Saldford	1314, P.R.O., CP 25/1/245/42	
sex acris bosci & brusseti	1316, P.R.O., JUST 1/968, rot 13d	in Abbot's Salford (as distinct from Salford Priors)

Sambourne

in bosco de Saundburn *=in siluis de Somburn* *=bosco suo de sunburn*	1231-2, P.R.O., JUST 1/951A, rot 2r 1261-2, P.R.O., JUST 1/954, rot 49r 1280, P.R.O., E 32/231, rot 11d	of the Abbot of Evesham, ?=Rough Hill Wood (see below)
boscum vocatum Roughehill	1574, S.B.T., DR5/2368	presumably approximating to the present Rough Hill Wood
copicie .. vocate hicocks *=copeciam tenementi sui vocatam hicocks alias Whelers*	1480, S.B.T., DR5/2358 1482, S.B.T., DR5/2358	held by Johanna mulleward
copeciam	1480, S.B.T., DR5/2358	held by Edward hubawde
copeciam apud Adamsforlonge	1480, S.B.T., DR5/2358	?in Newland in 1515/6, S.B.T., DR5/2360
copecie sue apud pighell in Pullesore *?=Pilsors wood*	1490, S.B.T., DR5/2358 1574, S.B.T., DR5/2368	held by Thomas Morgan next to Rough Hill Wood
copecie in le Newlond	1489, S.B.T., DR5/2360	held by Agnes Burstan
copecie .. apud le Newlond & le Thomefeld *=copeciam suam apud hethlane ende in le Newlond'*	1490, S.B.T., DR5/2358 1502, S.B.T., DR5/2360	held by Beche held by Thomas Beche

copeciam in pastura vocata Brodeclosse	1511, S.B.T., DR5/2360	held by Johanna Taylor
copeciam in hyckfylds	1512, S.B.T., DR5/2360	held by John Robyns; ?in Newland in 1515-6, S.B.T., DR5/2360
copeciam .. apud Dunstallhey	1512, S.B.T., DR5/2360	held by Richard Barker
copeciam iuxta tenementum	1512, S.B.T., DR5/2360	tenement belonged to Thomas Spack
copecias vocatas Tomsfyld' Newlond' Coppice =copeciam in Tomsfeld .. copeciam in Newlande	1512, 1514, S.B.T., DR5/2360	held by William and Elizabeth Shyngler
copeciam vocatam parkefylds copys	1513, S.B.T., DR5/2361	held by William Style
copeciam suam	1513, S.B.T., DR5/2361	held by William Sale

Seckington (including King's Newton)

in Bosco...in Kynges Neuton	1261-2, P.R.O., JUST 1/954, rot 8r	belonging to Thomas of Edensor and Hugh de Meynill
?=medietas cuiusdam bosci forinseci	1285, P.R.O., C 133/41/5	in King's Newton, of Thomas de Endesore
?=quidam boscus	1285, P.R.O., C 133/41/6	in King's Newton, of Philip de Meignyll

Sheldon (including Lyndon)

boscum	1346, B.R.L., 431,125	of John Haumond, near to the river Cole and the lord's waste
Briyateswode	1437-8, Staffs. R.O., D641/1/2/269	pasture
Boryate Wode *boriyateswode*	1443-4, Staffs. R.O., D641/1/2/270 1464-5, Staffs. R.O., D641/1/2/274 1455-6, B.R.L., 168,236	?in Coleshill, ?=*Briyateswode* above
lyndonnewode	1437-8, Staffs. R.O., D641/1/2/269	pasture
Gerardsgrove	1437-8, Staffs. R.O., D641/1/2/269	
the lyne outwood	1567, B.R.L., 431,160	near Poole field in Lyndon
wood called the ladie wood	1567, B.R.L., 431,160	in Lyndon, near *Tailers more*, *masons land* and the *lyne outwood*

Sherbourne

Shilton

Shrewley

in bosco de Scraveleia *=boscum de Schreueleye* *?=vastum de Screueleye*	1150, *Reading Abbey Cartularies*, no. 614 n.d., 13th C., *BD*, box 160 n.d., 13th C., *BD*, box 160	common pasture there by *le kyngesfeld* by *le kyngesfeld*
bosco qui vocatur le Frith	1206, *Curia Regis Rolls*, Vol. IV, p. 228	contained 12 acres by the perch of wood (*perticam bosci*)
duos clausos bosci	1316, P.R.O., C 134/47/14	
graua	n.d., 13th C., 1317, *BD*, box 160	associated with *kyngesfeld*
Fylylode groue	1433, *BD*, box 160	by *Welmorefeld* and *Cowzmorefeld*
Shrewley groue	1594, *BD*, box 160	7 acres in 1627, *BD*, box 138

Shuckburgh

Shustoke

boscum meum/ bosco meo *?=Boscum de Scustok*	?c.1231-48, W.C.R.O., Z551/4(Sm.); n.d., 13th C., B.R.L., Keen 54, P.R.O., E 40/9877 n.d., 13th C., B.R.L., Keen 54	of William de Esseby
la Coppedegraveforlong	1329-30, B.R.L., Keen 54	presumably referring to a nearby grove
Brograve *?=in bosco de broggraue*	n.d., 13th C., B.R.L., Keen 54 n.d. (c.1300), Merevale MSS., nos. 1326, 1371	by the field of Blythe and the park of Shustoke

Shuttington

in bosco de Shytyngton	1285, P.R.O., JUST 1/958, rot 31d	
Aukote Wode ?=Alvecote woode ?=Alvecote Woods [and] Alvecott Springwood	1366, Staffs. R.O., D593/A/1/23/4 1578-9, P.R.O., LR 2/185 1718, Staffs. R.O., D948/4/4/19	divided into two coppices and "the greate woode" the Springwood may be the Spring Coppice on the first edition of the one-inch O.S map
Copnell woode ?=Copnell Coppice	1578-9, P.R.O., LR 2/185 1718, Staffs. R.O., D948/4/4/19	100 acres

Snitterfield

Coldwellhull	1306, Gover, Mawer and Stenton, *Place-Names of Warwickshire*, p. 224	a wood
The Bushes	1560, S.B.T., DR38/1435-6	for the medieval period see text

Solihull

Bosco del Lee	c.1270-95, S.B.T., DR37/2337	
le Rouwode ?=one wood called Rowe woode	1331, P.R.O., C 146/996 1601, S.B.T., DR37/box 116	parts were later called Paynes land, W.C.R.O., CR1998/box72 and S.B.T., DR37/2613, Harpers Land, S.B.T., DR473/4, *Bruckfeildes*, W.C.R.O., CR299/286
Collemoreswod	1349, P.R.O., C 146/2960	
clauso bosco ?=le clos ?=Closse wood ?=Clowes Wood	1268-98, S.B.T., DR37/147 1310, P.R.O., E 326/3642 1580, S.B.T., DR37/1420 1632, W.C.R.O., CR1886/9424	of Sir Nicholas de Oddingesel, near to the waste of Tanworth and Longley heath of Forshaw, by the earl of Warwick's wood (in Tanworth) next to *Pert Greves* in Tanworth in the manor of Forshaw, by the boundary of Solihull next to *New Fallinge* Wood in Tanworth
Solihull Woods ?=Solyhull Wood =Solyhull wood =one common called Solyhull wood	1495, B.R.L., 427,740 1595, W.C.R.O., CR1998/box 72 1601, S.B.T., DR37/box 116 1606, S.B.T., DR37/box 116	opposite Yardley Woods 400 acres 400 acres
wood of Longdon ?=wast wood of the abbotte of westminster lying nye to ...Hynewode	c.1155, *Dugdale*, Vol. II, p. 950 ?1500 or 1524, P.R.O., Req. 2/4/361	Longdon was part of Knowle manor, held by Westminster Abbey
Sowthaye cum Grova adiacente ?=Sowthey alias Sowthey Coppice	1431-71, S.B.T., DR37/box 76 1540, S.B.T., DR37/2557	in Longdon, see fields called Coppice by Southay in the tithe award
terras, prata, grauas vocata copperedyng	1412, *BD*	in Longdon - see fields called Cop Ridding in the tithe award
depewall grove =depewall growe	1441, S.B.T., DR37/box 109/6 c.1500, S.B.T., DR37/box 74/30	east of Shelley Green, by *flouddeyatts feylde*
Herynggesgroue	n.d., ?15th C., S.B.T., DR37/box 116	?attached to lands called *Herryngs* in Olton
bosco vocato [.....]ardesgroue ?=Churchyarde Coppice	1368, P.R.O., C 146/10192 1585, B.R.L., 324,101	near *le Whitefeld*, leased by William atte Chircheyard; manuscript is torn

Songar - see Claverdon

Southam

Sowe

tocius bosci	1200, P.R.O., CP 25/1/242/3	
?=bosco de Sowe	1203, *Curia Regis Rolls*, Vol. II, p. 278	disputed between de Loges family and the Prior of Coventry
?=bosci forinseci	*HR*, pp. 141, 143	divided between the Prior and Richard de Loges
?= de bosco nostro de Sowe	n.d., C.R.O., BA/B/A/94/1	
?=a bosco qui vocatur Schortwode	n.d., ?late 13th C., C.R.O., BA/H/H/344/2	
=a bosco qui vocatur Schortwod	1411, P.R.O., E 164/21, f. 57r	
=Sowe Woodewast quod nos vocamus Schortwod	1411, P.R.O., E 164/21, f. 54v	
Wardesgrove	c.1250, C.R.O., BA/B/A/93/1	
bosco dicti domini le moubray qui vocatur Randulnesmore	1411, P.R.O., E 164/21, f. 202r	next to Earlswood
graua	1411, P.R.O., E 164/21, f. 58r	annexed to Hawkesbury manor
?=Grove vocate .. Hawkesbury grove	1538-9, P.R.O., SC 6/Hen VIII/ 3737	
=Hawkesbury Grove	1581, C.R.O., BA/A/A/2/2	by *Calvecrofte*
=Hauxbury Grove	c.1600, S.B.T., DR91/2	near Alderman's Green
groua	1411, P.R.O., E 164/21, ff. 45v, 199v	in Attoxhale, part of *Erneysplace*
=Grove	1538-9, P.R.O., SC 6/Hen VIII/ 3737	
duo grouae simul adiacentes	1411, P.R.O., E 164/21, f. 58v	belonging to *Bagotplace* next to *Ernesplace*
grauam	1411, P.R.O., E 164/21, f. 46r	in *le Wodend*, given to the Priory by William Bagot or William Suivet
Woldegroue	1411, P.R.O., E 164/21, f. 57r	
Graua	1422, C.R.O., BA/B/A/99/14	attached to a tenement of Thomas langhurst

Spernall

totum Boscum meum de Spernouera cum pertinentiis sic clausum est quod vocatur Les oueres Et la meregraue	n.d., c.1238, W.C.R.O., CR1998/box 42/CC2	Morgroves Coppice appears to have become the modern Morgons Coppice, see W.C.R.O., CR1998/20/1 and 2
?=morrgrove copyse	1549, W.C.R.O., CR1998/box 42/DD2	The field-name Nowers, adjoining Spernall Park (W.C.R.O., CR1094) may record the
=Moregrove	1589, W.C.R.O., CR1998/box43	location of *Les oueres*
coppieswoode called nunwoode	1542, P.R.O., E 318/10/446	of the Priory of Cokehill, 15 acres
?=Nun Coppice or Nunwood	1716, S.B.T., DR5/1255	90 acres (contrasted with 25 c.1695, see map in W.C.R.O., CR1998/M15)
helwood	1549, W.C.R.O., CR1998/box 42/DD2	described as a close of wood

Stivichall

Grovam [called] *Mertones Grove & Edmundus Grove*	1418, S.B.T., DR10/710-3	by *le Heye*, *Heylane* and *le Hallefelde*, formerly held by Edmund Horde and John Merton
i paruo grouetto	1425, P.R.O., SC 12/16/45	held with the *Hethmylne*
?=parvo grovetto vocato le hale	1429, S.B.T., DR10/2436b	ditto
?=hethmylgrove	1480-2, S.B.T., DR10/2474	
=una Graua vocato hethmyll grove	1488, S.B.T., DR10/2484	
?=Milnegrove	1498, S.B.T., DR10/738	
?=Hingolds grove	1556, S.B.T., DR10/780	between *Hethemylne* and another mill

Stoneleigh

de bosco Stanleie	n.d., 12th C., B.L., Harley 3650, f. 6	assarts there
bruillum de Wethele	1204, *SLB*, pp. 23-4 1244-5, *FF*, Vol. I, no. 618	separate from the *boscum* of Wethele (see below)
boscum de Wethele	1290, S.B.T., DR18/1/705	presumably approximates to Waverley Wood
bosco de Bradley	1377, S.B.T., DR18/1/698	?=fields called Bradley in 1597 (W.C.R.O., Z324(Sm))
graua	c.1175-1224, B.L., Add. MS. 47,677, f. cxxxix	by *Sprottochford* in Stareton

in bruillo de Eacheles	c.1155, *SLB*, pp. 15-6	presumably approximates to the Echells Wood
?=boscum qui dicitur Eacheles	n.d., *SLB*, p. 15	of 1597 (W.C.R.O., Z324(Sm)), the site of the
?=Echells woode	1556, S.B.T., DR18/30/24/109	modern National Agricultural Centre
Eyresgrove	n.d., pre-1392, *SLB*, p. 126	?near the Avon and Echells Wood
locus nemorosus	1204, *SLB*, p. 24	at *Burystede* in Cryfield
?=bosco de Burystede	n.d., pre-1392, *SLB*, p. 220	
Westwode	n.d., 13th C., S.B.T., DR18/1/831	in the north-west of the parish
=bosco suo de Westwod'	1250, *Calendar of Close Rolls, 1247-51*, p. 339	
	1279, *HR*, pp. 66, 73	
=Westwode	1290, S.B.T., DR18/1/705	one of three common woods
=boscum de Westwode		
partem bosci qui vocatur Crattel'	c.1221-50, *Formulare*, no. 684	adjoining Odybarn Wood in Kenilworth
=bosco nostro de Crateley	1235-58, S.B.T., DR18/1/926	
=Crattele	13th C., B.L., Harley 3650, f. 76	
=Crattele	1279, *HR*, pp. 66, 73	one of three common woods
Dolle	13th C., B.L., Harley 3650, f. 76	
=Dolle	1279, *HR*, pp. 66, 73	one of three common woods
=in bosco de Dalle	1271, *SLB*, p. 39	
=boscum de Dalle	1277, *SLB*, p. 42	
=boscum de Dauley	n.d., 13th C., S.B.T, DR10/1017	by Canley
Armele	13th C., B.L., Harley 3650, f. 76	pannage and herbage there, so presumably a wood
vasti nostri in kingeswode	c.1293-1310, P.R.O., E 210/8066	on the road from Berkswell to Coventry, ?=area
=vasto quod dicitur Kingeswod	1326, S.B.T., DR18/1/696	between Tile Hill and Allesley Brook, see map
		of 1767, copy in W.C.R.O., Z142(L)
in nemore de Flychamstede	c.1130, B.L., Add. MS. 47,677, f. cccxli	grant for a hermitage there
grova quodam Nicholai Malyn	n.d., pre-1392, *SLB*, p. 207	in Fletchamstead
grove	1468, S.B.T., DR10/1189	by *Hethsale, Guphillfurthe* and *Whaburley*
in bosco .. qui vocatur la lee	1270, S.B.T., DR18/1/838	in Canley
Graua	n.d., 13th C., S.B.T., DR18/1/850	part of a holding in Canley
schortwode	n.d., c.1285, S.B.T., DR18/1/847	in Canley
grauam monachorum	n.d., ?13th C., P.R.O., E 210/201	in Hurst
?=The Groue	1597, W.C.R.O., Z324(Sm)	in Hurst
Bordell	1387, P.R.O., E 326/3958	a wood near the road from Kenilworth to
?=one wood called Bardells	1600, W.C.R.O., CR561/2; 1639, S.B.T., DR18/10/27/1	Westwood, ?= the present Broadwells Wood
groveta	n.d., pre-1392, *SLB*, p. 214	at *Battereswast* in Hurst
Helwenin in Boscho	n.d., c.1235, S.B.T., DR10/1079	?by the wood of Armeley or Dalle
?=Harlewyngrove	n.d., pre-1392, *SLB*, p. 217	?=Upper Grove by Wainbody Wood
bosc' de Taselhulle	n.d., pre-1392, *SLB*, p. 163	in Cryfield, ?by the present Tocil Wood
?=Towsall Wood alias Towsall Grove	1615, S.B.T., DR18/10/41/3	(Potters Field Coppice in 1767 - W.C.R.O., Z142(L)
parco de Crulefeld scilicet le Monkeshay	1307, *SLB*, p. 127	
=parco vocato Monkeshay	n.d., pre-1392, *SLB*, p. 220	
=herbag' bosci vocati Monkes Heyes	c.1538, S.B.T., DR18/1/733	in Cryfield, see map of 1767, copy in W.C.R.O., Z142(L)
clausum bosci de Thornhale	n.d., pre-1392, *SLB*, p. 221	in Cryfield
graua bosci vocata le Conynger	n.d., pre-1392, *SLB*, p. 150	
una parua Graua	1438, P.R.O., SC 2/207/79	belonging to *jakyard* in Cryfield
quemdam Copicium apud le hore nok	1481, S.B.T., DR18/30/24/17	
persones Grove	1501, S.B.T., DR18/30/24/50	
una groua .. ad partem occidentalem prati vocata Holbroke	1499, B.L., Lansdowne 200, ff. lxiv-lxv	
=unius groue iacentis ex parte occidentali de Holdebroke meade	1544, P.R.O., E 318/4/106	
?=Holbrooke grove	1536, S.B.T., DR18/10/55/7	

una grova et una pastura cum certis terris arabilibus vocatis diraunts	1499, B.L., Lansdowne 200, ff. lxiv-lxv	
=*unius groue .. cum certis terris arrabilis vocatis dyraunts*	1544, P.R.O., E 318/4/106	
?=*Durham Tys*	1535, S.B.T., DR18/1/972a	
?=*Derhams grove*	1597, W.C.R.O., Z139/2(U)	
una acra alneti	1346, P.R.O., E 210/8333	in Finham
two groves	t. Henry I, *SLB*, p. 121	in Fynburghe
?=*Cole hanche groue.. Fynburye groue*	1544, P.R.O., E 318/23/1281	in Stoneleigh Grange
herbag' bosci vocati Rough Knolls	c.1538, S.B.T., DR18/1/733	presumably approximating to the present Rough Knowles Wood
groua vocata Joletts	c.1538, S.B.T., DR18/1/733	in Milburn
?=*Milbourne Groue*	1597, W.C.R.O., Z139/2(U)	
in clausura vocata Grimes wodd	1535, P.R.O., SC 12/3/35	in Milburn Grange, located by Greg Poole Grove in 1597, W.C.R.O., Z139/1(U)
=*Grymeswod*	c.1538, 1559, 1578, S.B.T, DR18/1/733, 1061, 1070	
Cannocks grove	1511, S.B.T., DR18/3/47/47	
Helynhul Grove	1529, S.B.T, DR10/1194	by Helynhull Grange c.1542, S.B.T, DR10/1468
Daniell Grove	1529, S.B.T., DR10/1194	
grove in Emyng & Sloberdes	1536, S.B.T., DR18/1/970	
?=*Slowe Beards grove*	1597, W.C.R.O., Z139/2(U)	
Lawles grove	1562, S.B.T., DR18/30/24/128	
=*Lawles grove*	1597, W.C.R.O., Z139/1(U)	
Kyngs grove	1546, S.B.T., DR10/764	
Bawdewyns Grove	1522, S.B.T., DR10/997	

Stratford-upon-Avon

Grava, Cloptonegrove	1280, S.B.T., ER3/235/1-6; 1272-1307, S.B.T., ER3/236-8, 240	?place-name, ?also wood-name, on the boundary with Snitterfield in 1439, S.B.T., DR10/2429, may have become Park Wood in Clopton
?=*a certen Grove called Clopton Grove*	1604, S.B.T., DR150/2/1	
in Bosco de Bisschopeton	1231-2, P.R.O., JUST 1/951A, rot 9d	
=*in bosco de Bissopeston*	1233, *Curia Regis Rolls*, Vol. XV, no.12	
?=*le groue*	1413-4, W.C.R.O., CR1911/14	in Bishopton, producing wood
xl acres of wode	1514, S.B.T., P54/14	in Ruin Clifford

Stretton Baskerville

Stretton on Dunsmore

viginti & quatuor acris bosci & Brueri	1285, P.R.O., JUST 1/958, rot 1r	in Stretton *super Dunnesmor* =?part of the eighteenth-century Stretton Wood alias Burnthurst, maps, W.C.R.O., Z414(U), Z8/22

Stretton on Fosse

virgulto Willielmi filii Roberti de Stratton	n.d., P.R.O., E 326/4812	For the noun *virgultum* in relation to woodland see Chapter One. In this case the noun *virgata*, virgate, appears in the same deed, implying a distinction between the two.

Studley

nemus de Haia	1201, S.B.T., ER1/61/19	
nemus Roberti filii Willielmi	1201, S.B.T., ER1/61/19	
bosco de Gorcota	n.d., S.B.T., ER1/61/26	in Old Gorcote, by Great Alne
=*bosco de gorgota*	n.d., ?13th C., *BD*	*ad grossam alnam*

Ladygrove =*Ladigroue*	1374-5, S.B.T., ER1/61/26 1375, *BD*; n.d., P.R.O., E 40/9136	in a field in Gorcot called *le Hayfeld*
alder wood	1328 for12th C., *Calendar of Charter Rolls,* *1327-41*, pp. 60-1	between *Stretford* and *Wasford*, ?=Studley Alders in 1820-1, W.C.R.O., CR1094
parcus =*boscus vocatus Stoodleypark*	1296, P.R.O., C 133/76/4 1419-20, M.MSS., Mi M 124	
totum dimidium bosci de *Mappelbarowe*	1369, P.R.O., E 41/375	acquired by Peter de Montfort from Peter Corbyson in Studley
in bosco....qui vocatur Gorcotemor	n.d., ?13th C., *BD*	belonging to Peter de Woluardinton
Graungecumb Wood	1560, B.R.L., 167,486-7	in Skilts Park, B.R.L., 167,405, 167,446

Sutton Coldfield

unum parcum & unam liberam *Hayam in defensione* ?=*quidam parcus inclusus*	ante 1153, *Dugdale*, Vol. II, pp. 909-10 1316, P.R.O., C 134/49, 51	
in Bosco de Sutton ?=*In Nemore meo de Sutton ad La* *Withemore*	c.1237, B.R.L., 348,039 ante 1242, B.R.L., 348,037	?by modern Withy Hill
quidam boscus qui vocatur La Lee =*bosco separabile qui vocatur La* *Lee*	1298, P.R.O., C 133/86/1 1316, P.R.O., C 134/51	contained fifty acres associated with the park
forinseci bosci	1316, P.R.O., C 134/49, 51	
hullewode =*boscum de Hullewode* = *in bosco domini in hillwood*	1313, B.L., Add. MS. 28,024, f. 103 1480, *Ministers' Accounts*, p. 32 1518, M.MSS., Mi M 134/20	presumably marked by the modern place-name Hill Wood in the north of the parish, by Hill Village
clausum vocatum Sidehaleheye ?=*copic' de Syndenhamhey* ?=*coppice called Sydnall haye*	1316, P.R.O., C 134/49 1480, *Ministers' Accounts*, p. 35 1581, M.MSS., Mi Da 87	?marked by the modern place-name Signal Hayes in Walmley 30 acres of pasture, land, wood, furze and vert
boscum vocatum hauckesnest ?=*copic' de Hawkenest*	1334, B.R.L., 348,022 1480, *Ministers' Accounts*, p. 35	near Langley, ?marked by the field-names on the enclosure award (W.C.R.O., QS75/111) near Reddicap Heath rather than north of Peddimor Hall
bosco domini apud Echelhurst ?=*eychylhurst coppys* =*copicia vocata Echilhurste*	1427, M.MSS., Mi M 134/9 1519, M.MSS., Mi M 134/21 1581, M.MSS., Mi Da 87	presumably near the modern Eachelhurst Common near Ebroke
bosco domini vocato hawkeshurst	1427, M.MSS., Mi M 134/9	?in error for Hawkesnest
Lyndrich Copies	1480, *Ministers' Accounts*, p. 37	presumably near Lindridge Road/Pool
Reddewey coppes	1480, *Ministers' Accounts*, p. 31	
coppice called wythenhill	1581, M.MSS., Mi Da 87	34 acres of land, pasture, furze and vert, presumably by Withy Hill
boscis suis de [Cruddeworth &] *Pedimor*	1288, B.L., Add. MS. 28,024, f. 102	presumably near Peddimor Hall and Curdworth
boscum Johannis Gamel vocatum *Greveokus* ?=*boscum Galfridi Gamel*	1339, Staffs. R.O., D1287/6/19/53 1331, Staffs. R.O., D1287/6/19/54	by the field of *Wyginghull* (modern Wiggins Hill) and not far from the highway between Minworth and Curdworth
copicium .. vocatum Rowmore	1504-5, P.R.O., SC 6/Hen VII/865	
unius copicii in Hillewode vocati *Rowlee*	1507-8, P.R.O., SC 6/Hen VII/1345	

Tachbrook

partem bosci mei Acleœ *boscum de Occle* =*boscum suum qui vocatur Oklie* =*bosco de Okele* =*boscum domini de Okeleye* =*Okeley woodde* =*Oakly Wood*	1161-82, *Formulare*, pp. 245-6 n.d., ?13th C., P.R.O., E315/52/125 1296-1321, B.L., Add. MS. 28,024, f. 63 1360, S.B.T., DR10/2593 1364, S.B.T., DR10/2597 1573, W.C.R.O., CR1908/104/1, CR1908/105/1-3 1710, W.C.R.O., CR1886/M28	by the road leading to Barford near Pleystowe permission to impark by the road to London approximating to the present wood

wood called *Morton Close*	1609, S.B.T., DR3/528	*Merton close* in 1573 (W.C.R.O., CR1908/105/3), now part of Oakley Wood
wood called *Wiggerland wood* alias *Wiggerland coppice*	1609, S.B.T., DR3/528	*Wyggerlande Close* in 1573 (W.C.R.O., CR 1908/105/3), presumably relates to the modern Wiggerland Wood
la Le Grove =*la Lee Grove* =*grauam* =*Leafeild Grove*	n.d., P.R.O., E 326/1917 1337-8, B.L., Add. MS. 28,024, f. 5 1415, W.C.R.O., CR26/A/XVI 1596, W.C.R.O., CR1886/7097	 by *le leefelde* pasture by 1596
the grove	1549-50, W.C.R.O., CR1908/207	in Tachbrook Mallory, by Banfurlonge, ?=The Grove north of the manor house on map of 1710, W.C.R.O., CR1886/M28

Tamworth

tercia pars totius Bosci de Aminton =*Boscum* ?=*in bosco meo de Amynton*	1214, P.R.O., CP 25/1/242/9 1304, P.R.O., JUST 1/965, rot 1d 1319, Staffs. R.O., D593/A/1/22/10	the third towards Alvecote, ? including the later Frith Wood in Great Amington, with common pasture of Henry de Bray
boscum de Stretfordlee	1446, B.R.L., Norton 67	?=Lea Wood Parke, 1673, S.B.T., DR76/2/21 and park of 1810, copy map in W.C.R.O., Z212/2
bosco nostro quod vocatur Kyngeswode ?=*vasto meo de kyngeswod* ?=*Kings Wood*	1281-1305, *Collections for a History of Staffordshire*, Part I, Vol. V (1884), p. 88 n.d., B.R.L., 480,682 1793, Yates's map of Warwickshire	given to Burton Abbey by Margery de Styveschale belonging to William de meygnill, by *Farleybroc* and *Depmor* adjoining Polesworth north of Watling Street

Tanworth-in-Arden

bosco meo de Tanworth =*boscum Comitis Warr'* =*Le Urleswode* =*in bosco vocato Erlswode* ?=*magnum Nemus* ?=*boscus forinsecus*	c.1196, W.C.R.O., DR133/1 1311, S.B.T., DR37/352 1339, S.B.T., DR37/546 1399-1400, S.B.T., DR37/box 107/8 1229-c.1239, S.B.T., DR37/64 1316, P.R.O., C 134/49, 51	of the earl of Warwick presumably approximating to the modern Earlswood Common by the road to *Calvesleya*
nemus	1153-84, S.B.T., DR37/1	in Monkspath
boscum de Chesewick	c.1270-80, S.B.T., DR37/211	by *mallelond* and the heath
boscum .. qui vocatur Calvermor	c.1300-10, S.B.T., DR37/306	of Richard de Folewode, by *Pynkemor* and *Ruycroft*
medium bosci ?=*quadam placea bosci*	1332, S.B.T., DR37/499 1364, S.B.T., DR37/702	of Roger de Middelmor, by *le heye* of Edmund de Middelmor, by *le heye*
unam placeam bosci ?=*quodam bosco*	1364, S.B.T., DR37/702 1380, S.B.T., DR37/756	granted to Simon Waryng, near the piece of wood of Edmund de Middelmor and *le Heye* held by Simon Waryng of Thomas Archer
placeam bosci mei in magno bosco meo in Toneworth que .. vocatur le heyeholt	1345, S.B.T., DR37/593	of William de Folwod
uno bosco vocato le Shawe	1347, S.B.T., DR37/box 115	held by Letitia and Edmund de Middelmor, in Monkspath
unam parcellam bosci	1368, S.B.T., DR37/720	3 acres, of the Middelmor family
boscum Henrici simondes	1368, S.B.T., DR37/720	by the wood of John de Folewode and the road to *Foschawe*
a bosco Johannis de Folewode	1368, S.B.T., DR37/720	by the wood of Henry simondes and the road to *Foschawe*
una placea bossi .. vocata Berefordewode	1388, S.B.T., DR37/785	by the wood of John de Foluwode and the road to *Foschawe*
Contesclos	1380-81, 1389-90, 1399-1400, 1412-3, S.B.T., DR37/box 107/2, 4, 8, 25	wood etc. sold there, presumably Countess Coppice of the tithe award, W.C.R.O., CR328/53

boscum .. vocatum le Newenehewene	1375, S.B.T., DR/box 82, m. 3	of William de Catesby
boscum vocatum Birchenehurst	1375, S.B.T., DR/box 82, m. 3	of William de Catesby
in Watlond in bosco domini *?=a Wode called Watland*	1381, S.B.T., DR37/box 109/2s) 1441, S.B.T., ER1/1/13	
Newefallynge *=Newefalling* *=parcella bosci vocata* *Newefallyng* *=Newefallynge*	1377-8, 1385-6, 1389-90, 1399-1400, S.B.T., DR37/box 107/1, 3, 4, 8 1418-9, S.B.T., DR37/box108/31 1419-20, S.B.T., DR37/box 108/32 1429-30, S.B.T., DR37/box 108/41	presumably corresponds to the later Newfalling Coppice - see tithe award, W.C.R.O., CR328/53
boscum comitis Warr' vocatum le Sarehurst	1452, S.B.T., DR37/956	by *Rudescroftes, Rowecrofts* and *Roseland*
the grete wode *?=Fulwods Woode*	1448, S.B.T., DR37/949 1495, S.B.T., DR37/1057	of the Fulwoods a great wood by the manor of Fulwode
200 acres of wood in *Le Lee*	1495, S.B.T., DR37/1031	
Lutlesgrovehei	c.1200-10, S.B.T., DR37/24	in the area of the common fields north-east of the present village
La Bottedegrave	c.1210-1220, S.B.T., DR37/35	by *stokimede* and *cocsuteford*
La Grave Bodde *?=grove*	c.1229-c.1239, S.B.T., DR37/55 1342, S.B.T., DR37/580	by *Budlond* on the north-west edge of the common fields in *Boddelond*
graua	c.1270-80, S.B.T., DR37/185	bought of Simon de Manecestre
parvam grauam Ricardi de la sponne *?=sponne grove* *?=too groves caulde spon grove*	c.1270-80, S.B.T., DR37/185 1441, S.B.T., DR37/box109/6 c.1500, S.B.T., DR37/box 74/30	adjacent to the *graua* above perhaps included the grove bought of Simon de Manecestre
grauam Ricardi de la coppe *?=grove in coppefeld*	c.1270-80, S.B.T., DR37/191 1422, S.B.T., DR37/877	
grave...iuxta boscum Ricardi de folewode que vocatur calvermor *?=the Grove*	c.1300-10, S.B.T., DR37/306 1448, S.B.T., DR37/949	also near *Pynkemor* and *Ruycroft* in *Cowlesowe*, near *Ricroft, Calvermore, Pynkemorecroft*, part of the Fulwoods' lands
grauam Henrici de Sydenhale	c.1300, S.B.T., DR37/320	*?=Ilshawgrove* (see below)
quadam crava [sic]	1309, S.B.T., DR37/349	by the land of Henry Elys and the road from Brown's house of *Haukesawebroc*, i.e. in north-east
gravam que vocatur Watmor	c.1320, S.B.T., DR37/407	
quadam grava	1321, S.B.T., DR37/415	enfeoffed by Roger le Rede
grauam Reginaldi de Berkeswell	1326, S.B.T., DR37/460	between *Stokyng* and *Apulton*
illam grauam que fuit quondam Johannis Gilbert .. cum vivario de Cherlecote *?=Charlecotte growe*	1328, S.B.T., DR37/466 1497-8, S.B.T., DR37/box 74/12	 = approximating to the modern Chalcot Wood, see sketch map c.1500, S.B.T., DR37/box 74/20
unam gravam que fuerit Johannis atte berne *?=berns growe*	1348-9, S.B.T., DR37/box 109/3 c.1500, S.B.T., DR37/box 74/20	 near *Charlecotte growe* on map
unum campum cum graua	1329, S.B.T., DR37/box 109/2e)	of William le Archer
unum campum cum graua que vocatur tappe g's	1329, S.B.T., DR37/box 109/2e)	
boscum vocatum Tylhous groue	1374, S.B.T., DR37/box 82, being a copy of P.R.O., E 40/6610	presumably approximating to the modern Tylers Grove
una graua & mora .. in Oldecrowunhal	1379, S.B.T., DR37/775	between Cheswick and Ilshaw
Grauam vocatam Willingus grove	1385, S.B.T., DR37/771	land called *Hickelond Willing* was in *Fenshawe*, S.B.T., DR37/149

Ylsshawegroue =*Ilshawgrove*	1390, S.B.T., DR37/794 1483, S.B.T., DR37/1021	between *Haukeshawbroke* and *Ilshawebroke* and between *Ilshawheth* and the river Blythe
Wawmondes grove	1395-6, S.B.T., DR37/box 107/6	
grouam vocatam Newefallyng	1398, S.B.T., DR37/822	elsewhere called simply *Newfallynge* (see above)
una groua	1398, S.B.T., DR37/822	in *Putfeld*, by *Newefallynge*
grauam vocatam Teythberne	1406, S.B.T., DR37/838	by *Clerkeslonde*, *Blakefeld* and the road from Tanworth church
Rankegrove	1418-9, 1420-1, S.B.T., DR37/box 108/31, 34	variously called a parcel of wood and a coppice
una groua vocata symkyns groue	1407, S.B.T., DR37/840	by *Schepkotefeld*; from its position it is probably *Shepcotre groue*
Colinsgraue *?=grove .. sometime one Thomas Collyns*	1417, S.B.T., DR37/864 c.1500, S.B.T., DR37/box 74/17	near a moor called *swansdiche*
duobus grouis	1417, S.B.T., DR37/864	one of the two was *Colinsgraue* (above)
Fulvordesgrove	1429-30, S.B.T., DR37/box 108/41	
duabus gravis	1478, S.B.T., DR37/1018	by *Stockyng* and *Blakemor*
Blakemore grove =*a grove of blakemore*	1509, S.B.T., DR37/1086 c.1500, S.B.T., DR37/box 74/16	by *Peryll*, *Stockyng* and *Henfylde*, probably one of the *duabus gravis* above
Berfordgrove *?= grove in Barfardslond*	1484, S.B.T., DR37/1026 c.1500, S.B.T., DR37/box 74/16	
a grove cauld arcursgrevos	c.1500, S.B.T., DR37/box 74/16	near *blakemore*, *pyryhyll*, *bancroft*, *stockyng* and *hemfeld*
Shepcotre groue =*scheppecott grove*	1473, S.B.T., DR37/997 c.1500, S.B.T., DR37/box 74/16	by *Apulton seuerrell* and *Pyryhull* by *Wheytteddych*, *appulton severall*, *wygenhall*, *pyrryhyll*, *stockyng*, *hemfeld*
a growe	c.1500, S.B.T., DR37/box 74/30	by *hyfeyld* and *Cottulmosheth*
a lyttul grove	c.1500, S.B.T., DR37/box 74/30	by the *nethur pooll*
archers growe	c.1500, S.B.T., DR37/box 74/30	
a grove betweyn the gret porteweye and a ground of barburrs	c.1500, S.B.T., DR37/box 74/30	
a grove of moorrs and archerrs	c.1500, S.B.T., DR37/box 74/30	
a wode called Watland *?=Wattelonde grove*	1441, S.B.T., ER1/1/13 c.1500, S.B.T., DR37/box 74/16	associated with *Charlecottegrove*
grova' *?=grove callyd Wodlond grove*	1446, S.B.T., DR37/box 74/4 1502, S.B.T., DR37/1071	in *le Wodelond*
a growe caulde goosfoot	c.1500, S.B.T., DR37/box 74/24	at the end of *pen croftus*, see Goosefoot on tithe map
Wyndmyll grove *?=grove in Wyndmylnefylde*	c.1500, S.B.T., DR37/box 74/17 1520, S.B.T., DR37/1100	
a grove	c.1500, S.B.T., DR37/box 74/17	by springwell lane, the bounds of Tanworth and Nuthurst, stapletons
Kyntlondgrove	1515, S.B.T., DR37/1090	
a grove and a medo caulde greryns	1506, S.B.T., DR37/box 74/29	
Smythus pooll with the grove	1506, S.B.T., DR37/box 74/29	
Grove vocate monkespathmore	1446, S.B.T., DR37/box 74/6	presumably in Monkspath

Thelsford -see Charlecote

Thornton

quodam bosco que continet x acras *?=grava domini*	1246-7, P.R.O., JUST 1/952, rot 4d 1431, W.C.R.O., CR1911/6	common pasture there, ?became the Thornton Wood of 1765, map in W.C.R.O., CR711

Tysoe - see also Westcote

virgulto	n.d., B.L., Cott. Roll XIII 6, item 1	for comments on the meaning of *virgultum* see Chapter One

Ufton

wulluht graf	1001, *S*989	on the boundary of Itchington
?=quendam boscum	1279, *HR*, p. 158	of Coventry Cathedral Priory
?=sub paruo bosco/ sub bosco/ sub bosco Thome de Wauton	c.1284, P.R.O., E 164/21, f. 85r	
?=boscum	1313, P.R.O., E 164/21, f. 100r	of Coventry Cathedral Priory
?=unus boscus	1411, P.R.O., E 164/21, f. 212r	of Coventry Cathedral Priory
?=Ufton Wood	1556, Balliol College C.1.20	

Ullenhall

quandam partem Nemoris mei de Olehale	n.d., 12th C., B.L., Cotton Vespasian E xxiv, f. 4	granted by Robert son of Nicholas [earl] of Stafford to Stone Priory, by Botley and including three great ditches (*cum tribus magnis fossatis*)
virgulto	n.d. ?13th C., King's College, WOW/87	conveyed with a croft, messuage and *orto* in *hulehale*, near the heath of the lord of Wootton, *haueruge* and the road going to Tanworth
Eylys grove	1565, King's College, S53	

Upton -see Haselor and Ratley

Walton - see Wellesbourne

Wappenbury

Boscum de Wappenbir'	1208-9, P.R.O., CP 25/1/242/8	presumably approximates to the present Wappenbury Wood
?=in the Wode of Wappenbury .. Wappenbury Wode	1493-1500, B.R.L., Keen 133	
?=the hye wood in Wapenbury	1549, Alcock, *Warwickshire Grazier and London Skinner*, p. 178	

Warmington

Warwick - see also Woodcote

quodam boscum .. qui vocatur parcus de Wegenok	1321, P.R.O., SC 6/1040/24	park subsequently much enlarged, see Chapter Three
in bosco ipsius Roberti in Stokehull	1251, P.R.O., CP 25/1/244/23	held by Robert le Megre
?=megurwode	1394-5, W.C.R.O., CR1886/474	described as a coppice, P.R.O., E164/22, f. 329
=copicium vocatum megrewode	1425-6, W.C.R.O., CR1886/487	lists tens of thousands of faggots sold
?=Margarewoode	1576, W.C.R.O., CR1886/BB185	
xii acras Bosci in Wodelawe	1261-2, P.R.O., JUST 1/954, rot 20r	
?=Wodelowegrove	1398-9, W.C.R.O., CR1886/481	adjacent to Wedgnock Park
?=groua/grova	1430, W.C.R.O., CR26/W16-17	in manor of Woodlowe
=Grovam de Woddelowe	1458, W.C.R.O., CR26/XXXII	by *Fernyfeld*
the lowe grove	1573, W.C.R.O., CR1886/4849	a Grove or Coppice of wood by the *looe* lane, belonging to Anthony Stoughton, who acquired the lands of St. John's Hospital (*VCH*, Vol. VIII, p. 444)
?=Mr. Stoughton's grove	1658, W.C.R.O., CR26/1(2) bundle B/27	
grova	1422-3, W.C.R.O., CR1886/485	in *Gybbeclyfe*, i.e. Guy's Cliff
?=Gyclyff Grove	1483, P.R.O., DL 29/643/10439	
Prior's Grove	1546, W.C.R.O., CR26/1	a field-name amongst former lands of St. Sepulchre's Priory
Dame Royse grove	post 1425, P.R.O., E 164/22, f. 329	in Wedgnock Park, St. Mary's parish
le newewode	post 1425, P.R.O., E 164/22, f. 329	in Wedgnock Park, St. Mary's parish
le Mechelcopice	1425-6, W.C.R.O., CR1886/487	in Wedgnock Park
valett vocat' Kylyngworthhurne	1401-2, W.C.R.O., CR1886/482	wood sold there in 1401-2
wood of Fernhill	1555, P.R.O., C 147/233	adjoining Wedgnock Park
=woods called Fernehill	1602, W.C.R.O., CR1886/2584	

Wasperton

Water Orton - see Aston

Weddington

in bosco de Wetington	1231-2, P.R.O., JUST 1/951A, rot 6r	presumably related to the Weddington Wood of the tithe award, W.C.R.O., CR569/258

Weethley

in bosco de Wylee	1221, *Roll of the Justices In Eyre*, p. 333	
?=in bosco .. in Wyleg	1261-2, P.R.O., JUST 1/954, rot 9r	of John d'Abitot
?=quinquaginta acris bosci	1288, P.R.O., JUST 1/1278, rot 2r	of Alex d'Abitot
?=Whetheley coppice	1543-4, P.R.O., E 318/15/683	formerly of Evesham Abbey

Welford on Avon

Wellesbourne

graua	c.1190-91, W.C.R.O., DR1911/17	
?=in Graua de Welleburne	1247, P.R.O., CP 25/1/243/21	grant of an acre of wood in the grove
?=grava de Wellesburn	1261-2, M.MSS., Mi D 3933	
?=in bosco de Welleburn	1285, P.R.O., JUST 1/958, rot 38d	presumably approximates to part of the modern Wellesbourne Wood
una Graua vocata Chadley	1469-70, B.L., Add. Roll 44,559	underwood farmed out there
?=Chedley grove	1483, S.B.T., DR18/30/15/4	presumably near the modern Chadley Farm

Westcote (in Tysoe)

| le bosco domini in Westcote | 1498, Castle Ashby MSS. No. 579, copy in W.C.R.O., MI 167/1 | The wood on Edge Hill south of King John's Lane is called The Grove |
| ?=the grove | n.d., ?15th/16th C., Magdalen College, Westcote 112 | |

Weston on Avon (part only - Milcote)

Weston by Cherington

Weston under Wetherley

nemus .. Boscum	n.d., 13th C., P.R.O., E 326/6029	
?=inter duos boscos	n.d., 13th C., P.R.O., E 315/44/216	
?=boscum	1279, *HR*, p. 162	belonging to Arbury Priory
?=Weston Wode	ante 1392, *SLB*, pp. 102, 248	

Wetherley - see Stoneleigh

Whatcote

Whichford

in Bosco suo de Wicheford	1246-7, P.R.O., JUST 1/952, rot 22r; *ibid.*, CP 25/1/243/21	of Reginald de moy'am, presumably approximating to the present Wood
?=in bosco de Whichford	1247, B.L., Egerton MS. 3724, f. 63	of Reginald de Mohun
?=boscum suum de Wicheford	1251-2, B.L., Egerton MS. 3724, f. 80	Reginald de Mohun obtained agreement to impark this wood
?=boscum clausum	1279, *HR*, p. 297	of John de Moun
?=ad boscum de Whicheford	1379-80, Gloucestershire R.O., D1099/M31/46	

Whitacre

| de Bosco | 1261-2, P.R.O., JUST 1/954, rot 14r | in Nether Whitacre, of Egidius son of Nicholas |
| in Bosco domini | 1498, W.C.R.O., CR440/1 | belonging to the Priory of St. John of Jerusalem |

Whitchurch

Whitley - see Coventry and Wootton Wawen

Whitnash

Wibtoft and Willey

Wiggins Hill - see Sutton Coldfield

Willenhall

exitum bosci prioris de Couintre in territorio de Willenhal	c.1220, B.L., Cotton Vitellius A i, f. 165	adjoining lands of Coombe Abbey
?=in bosco de Wylenhal	1221, *Roll of the Justices in Eyre*, p. 408	
?=boscum forinsecum	1279, *HR*, p. 121	of Coventry Cathedral Priory
?=in bosco ipsius prioris de Wylenhale	1279, *HR*, p. 121	tenants had reasonable estovers there
?=bosco dicti Prioris videlicet in bosco de Wylenhal	1334, Bodleian Library, MS Top. Warks., C8	
?=wynell wood	t. Elizabeth, M.MSS., Mi M 232	by Woolseyes heath and Brandon

Willoughby

Wishaw

quidam boscus forinsecus	1326, P.R.O., C 134/102/6	
boscum de moxhull	n.d., ?13th C., M.MSS., Mi D 4300	presumably approximating to fields called
?=de bosco in territorio de moxhul	1253, B.R.L., 348,028	Moxhull Wood in the Wishaw tithe award
?=una pastura vocata moshull wode	1428, W.C.R.O., MR1/Folder 1	(W.C.R.O., CR328/58)
?=moxhull wode	1505, W.C.R.O., MR1/Folder 1	
i boscus vocatus [..]ikmore	n.d., ?c.1500, M.MSS., 6/170/73	survey endorsed Wishaw, but may be in Sutton Coldfield
unum boscum domini vocatum Blacmore	n.d., ?c.1500, M.MSS., 6/170/73	

Withybrook

Witton - see Aston

Wixford - see Oversley

Wolfhampcote

Wolford

medietatem totius bosci ... Nemoris	1225, P.R.O., CP 25/1/243/13	meadow was between the gate of the wood and the old pool (*vivarium*)
?=in quodam bosco domini ibidem vocato Wolfordwod	1464-5, Staffs. R.O., D641/1/2/274	of the earl of Stafford, in Wolford Magna, presumably approximating to the present
=Wolfordewode	1504-5, P.R.O., SC 6/Hen VII/867	Wolford Wood

Wolston

Wolverton

Wolvey

alneto	n.d., 13th C., B.L., Cotton Vitellius A i, ff. 88, 92	
?=partem alneti	n.d., ?13th C., Leicestershire R.O., DE2559/105	
?=alnetum	1437-8, Staffs. R.O., D641/1/2/269	

Wood Bevington - see Salford

Woodcote

unam grauam que est inter duas Wudechotes	1153-84, W.C.R.O., CR26/A/I	
unum paruum Grouetum *?=una Grova vocata Pavysgrove*	1412, P.R.O., E 326/5441 1458, W.C.R.O., CR26/XXXII	in Over Woodcote, formerly of William Pavy in Woodcote
Grovam vocatam Boseworthgrove .. *Grouam de Boseworth*	1458, W.C.R.O., CR26/XXXII	annexed to Woodcote and Woodloes in 1462-3. W.C.R.O., CR556/212

Woodlowe - see Warwick

Wootton Wawen - see also Bearley, Beaudesert, Claverdon, Preston Bagot, Ullenhall

In bosco meo de halestou *=boscum de halewestowe* *=le Halstowe* *=boscum domini vocatum halstowode* *=boscum domine vocatum halstowe* *=Boscum domini .. vocatum hallestowe .. hallestowewode*	n.d., Wootton Wawen Priory cartulary, copy in W.C.R.O., MI 332, f. 2 n.d., 13th C., W.C.R.O., CR712/2 1437-8, Staffs. R.O., D641/1/2/269 1449-50, Staffs. R.O., D641/1/2/272 1455-6, B.R.L., 168,236; 1464-5, Staffs. R.O., D641/1/2/274 1467-8, Staffs. R.O., D641/1/2/276	presumably approximates to the present Austy Wood; other references can be found in accounts after 1467-8
quidam boscus vocatus Forwod	1419-20, M.MSS., Mi M 124	20 acres of land. The place-name survives by Wootton Hill Farm
decem acras bosci .. in Maheus Forwode *?=diverse parcelle bosci in mayowes*	1326, B.L., Cott. Ch. xxvii 137 1419-20, M.MSS., Mi M 124	 5 acres, ?related to the present May's Wood
bosco/boscus *Molkeley Wode* *=Molkeley Wode* *?=Mockley Wood*	1341-2, P.R.O., E 372/187 1401, King's College, WOW/56 1445, King's College, WOW/128 1565, King's College, S53	presumably approximates to the present Mockley Wood in Aspley
in bosco ipsorum de Offewrth *?=Ufford [wood]* *=Offordwod* *=my ladies wod at Wawenswotton called Offordwod* *=Boscum domini vocatum Offordwode* *=boscum domini vocatum Offordewode*	1246-7, P.R.O., CP 25/1/243/21 1386, Staffs. R.O., D641/1/2/3 1464-5, Staffs. R.O., D641/1/2/274 1464-6, Staffs. R.O., D641/1/2/275 1467-8, Staffs. R.O., D641/1/2/276 1506-7, P.R.O., SC 6/Hen VII/868	of John de Staunton and his wife of the earls of Stafford, probably in the area of the Wootton Park shown on the estate map of 1736, W.C.R.O., DR195/28; other references can be found in accounts after 1467-8
Offord Grove *=Offordgrove* *=Offordgrove*	1467-8, Staffs. R.O., D641/1/2/276 1504-5, P.R.O., SC 6/Hen VII/867 1506-7, P.R.O., SC 6/Hen VII/868	distinct from Offord Wood, see field called Grove in 1736, W.C.R.O., DR195/28
le lytulgroue	1386, Staffs. R.O., D641/1/2/3	?= Offord Grove
Lyhtewode	1246-7, P.R.O., CP 25/1/243/21	In Offord
unius Grove Willielmi Harewell armigeri vocate Lucy[es Wood] *=Lucyes Wood*	1449-50, King's College, WOW223 1505, B.L., Add. Ch. 49,116	wood sold there; manuscript torn
Shortgrove	1449-50, King's College, WOW223	wood sold there; presumably it became the Short Grove on the east side of Austy Wood

Wormleighton

Grovam	1387, Northamptonshire R.O., Spencer MSS., 216	

Wroxall

bosco	1141, *Monasticon*, Vol. IV, pp. 90-92	adjoining Rowington
altum nemus	1141, *Monasticon*, Vol. IV, p. 92	in Nunneley
cent acres de Boys en Wroxhale *trois centz acres du boys .. en .. Wroxhale*	c.1312-22, P.R.O., SC 8/68/3357 n.d., P.R.O., SC 8/152/7586	
le Kingeswode	1329, S.B.T., DR3/48, 50	described as waste - for location see map of Baddesley Clinton, copy in W.C.R.O., Z234
unam grauem	1327-8, P.R.O., SC 11/697	held by Thomas atte Lynde
graua	1327-8, P.R.O., SC 11/697	held by Nicholas Scoti
graua	1327-8, P.R.O., SC 11/697	held by William Adam
graua	1327-8, P.R.O., SC 11/697	held by Roger Adam
graua	1327-8, P.R.O., SC 11/697	held by Robert Benet
grauem	1327-8, P.R.O., SC 11/697	held by Thomas de Kylcote
grauem	1327-8, P.R.O., SC 11/697	held by William Rolnes
grauem	1327-8, P.R.O., SC 11/697	held by Richard Miller
duas grovas bosci	1425-6, S.B.T., DR37/box 112	
lythnys Grove le holte Grove Tofts alias dict' Taffs Grove	1542, W.C.R.O., CR113/Wr3	

Appendix 2: Evidence of woodland in Warwickshire south and east of the River Avon in the later medieval period

A. Places in south and east Warwickshire with no *silva* in Domesday Book but with woods recorded in the later medieval period

(i) pre-1350

Place	Wood/grove	Earliest reference	Comments
Barford	*sub bosco de persele* *una acra bosci...in Perceleygrove*	n.d. ?13th C., B.L., Harl. Ch. 46 A 30 1316, P.R.O., JUST 1/968, rot 14d.	The location of *Perceleygrove* is uncertain. Next to Hampton Episcopi, (Hampton Lucy) it may have been west or east of the Avon.
Lower Ettington	*graua'* *sa grave*	1246-59, W.C.R.O., CR229/box 18/3/1-2 Rotuli Parliamentorum, Vol. I (Record Commission), p. 2.	This record refers to wood being taken from the grove.
Thornton (in Ettington)	*gravam domini* *de comuna pasture sue in quodam bosco que continet x acras* *?=le Grove* *?=i boscus vocatus thor'grove*	1431, W.C.R.O. CR1911/6 1246-7, P.R.O., JUST 1/952, rot 4d 1456, W.C.R.O., CR1911/8 1446-7, P.R.O., SC 11/819	?= the modern Thornton Wood (see map of 1765 - W.C.R.O., CR711)
Lighthorne	*una Graua* *i graua que continet vi acras* *paruu spinetu* *?= unum spinetum clausum* *de forinceco bosco*	1086, *DB* 1316, P.R.O., C 134/51 1301, P.R.O., C 133/100/1 1316, P.R.O. C 134/49 1398-9, S.B.T., DR98/674a	
Chesterton	*la grave* *?= unam grauam inclusam* *sub bosco*	1272-1307, S.B.T., DR98/245 1279, *HR* 1287, S.B.T., DR98/266	12 acres
Tachbrook	*partem bosci mei Acleæ* *?=boscum suum qui vocatur Oklie* *la Le[e] Grove* *=Grava vocata Lee Grove*	1161-82, *Formulare*, pp. 245-6 1296-1321, B.L., Add. MS. 28,024, f. 63 n.d. (?13th C.), P.R.O., E 326/1917 1337-8, B.L., Add. MS. 28,024, f. 69	presumably partly surviving in the present Oakley Wood Lea Field was taken into Castle Park, Warwick (see tithe map, W.C.R.O., CR569/252)
Long Itchington	*boscum* *?=boscus separale* *?=Ichynton Wode*	1260, P.R.O., JUST 1/953, rot 7d 1347, P.R.O., C 135/83/25 1385-6, P.R.O., SC 6/1041/2	of Robert de Pynkeney presumably approximating to the present wood of Long Itchington
Ufton	*wulluht grafe* *?=boscum* *?=boscum/unus boscus*	1001, *S898* 1279, *HR*, p. 158 1411 for 1313, P.R.O., E 164/21, ff. 100r, 212r.	arguably the present wood. 89 acres in 1411.
Weston-under-Wetherley	*spinetum* *nemus* *=?Weston Wode*	1086, *DB* 1279, *HR* *SLB*, pp. 248, 102	presumably approximating to the present wood
Cubbington	*grauam* *?=graua inclusa* *?=le Grove de Cobynton* *billin'grove*	1220-2, P.R.O., E 210/318 1280, S.B.T., DR18/31/3 1377, S.B.T., DR18/1/698 1273, P.R.O., E 210/4582	Relationship to the present Cubbington Woods is not clear. Billinsgrove, 1651, B.R.L., 86,005
Bericote in Ashow	*boscum cum fossato bosci* *moppesgroue*	c.1235, S.B.T., DR10/14 1389, P.R.O., SC 2/207/77	suggests that Bericote Grove was enclosed by this date the record is of a blocked ditch adjacent to the grove
Barton-on-the-Heath	*boscum de Berton*	1233, Curia Regis Rolls Vol XV, no. 910	by the boundary with Compton
Tysoe	*virgulto*	n.d., B.L., Cott. Roll XIII 6, item 1	For the meaning of *virgultum* see Chapter One

Ratley	*unam grauam que vocatur Cnihtegraue sicut bradeweie diuidit sub bosco qui vocatur estlee*	S.B.T., DR10/1406, p. 203.	the Old English name suggests a pre-Conquest existence (see text) this wood presumably survived as the early modern Ashley Wood
	=graua sua de Estlee	S.B.T., DR10/1406, p. 208 P.R.O., E 329/234	
Radway	*doddesgrove*	1308-9, S.B.T., DR10/1457	sale of small branches (*ramuscul'*)
Great Wolford	*nemoris*	1225, *FF*, Vol. I, no. 351	presumably related to the present wood
Stretton-on-Fosse	*virgulto*	n.d., P.R.O., E 326/4812	For the meaning of *virgultum* see Chapter One
Birdingbury	*grauam*	n.d. (?13th C.), B.L., Add. Ch. 48,031	
	in superiore parte parue graue	n.d. (?13th C.), B.L., Add. Ch. 48,029	
Long Lawford	*Illam partem spineti que est apud occidentem*	n.d., B.L., Cotton Caligula A xiii, f. 133	
	?=medietas predicti spineti	1210, B.L., Cotton Caligula A xiii, f. 145	
	?=de graua mea que appellatur blachenurd	*ibid.*, ff. 144-5, and P.R.O., E 315/53/189	
	?=totum spinetum de Blakethirne usque ad Caldewell	n.d., B.L., Cotton Caligula A xiii, f. 148	
(ii) 1350-1400			
Wormleighton	*Grauam*	1387, Northants. R.O., Spencer MSS., no. 216	
(iii) 1401-1500			
Offchurch	*unus boscus inclusus vocatus Bradlegh*	1411, P.R.O., E 164/21, f. 207v	
Moreton Morrell	*in grova de moorton*	1425-6, P.R.O., SC 6/1040/7	possibly the modern Moreton Wood
Bascote in Long Itchington	*A grove*	1466, Walsall Local History Centre, 276/63	
Westcote in Tysoe	*le bosco domini in Westcote*	1498, Castle Ashby MSS. 579, copy in W.C.R.O., MI 167/1	?= the later Westcote Grove, south of King John's Lane
Burton Dassett	*grove*	1497, Northants. R.O., Temple (Stowe), box 4/bundle 1a/1	situated north-west of the manor house and church - see N.W. Alcock, Warwickshire Grazier and London Skinner 1532-1555 (British Academy, 1981) pp. 28, 38

251

B. Places in south and east Warwickshire with *silva* in Domesday Book

Place	Later medieval woodland	Date and reference	Comments
Bubbenhall	*quamdam partem forinseci bosci*	1391, P.R.O., E 149/60/16	presumably related to the Bubbenhall Wood recorded on enclosure - W.C.R.O., Z413(Sm)
Ryton-on-Dunsmore	*aisiamentis nemoris mei* *?=quendam boscum forinsecum* *?=boscum de Ruytone*	n.d., 12th C., Cambridge University Library, Add 3021, ff. 238-9 1279, *HR*, p. 151 1335, W.C.R.O., CR350/3	the earliest reference is to the wood of Henry de Arderne; the present Ryton Wood presumably perpetuates the medieval wood
Stretton-on-Dunsmore	*bosci* *bosco*	1285, P.R.O., JUST 1/958, rot 1r 1246-7, P.R.O., JUST 1/952, rot 5r	24 acres of wood in Stretton in Princethorpe
Wappenbury	*Boscum*	1208, P.R.O., CP 25/1/242/8	presumably related to the present wood
Lillington	-	-	
Southam	-	-	
Wasperton	-	-	
Wellesbourne	*graua* *?=Welleburne Grove* *?=grava de Wellesburn* *?=in bosco de Welleburne* *una Grava vocata Chadley*	n.d. (13th C.), W.C.R.O., CR1911/17 1247, *FF*, Vol. I, no. 664 1261-2, M.MSS., Mi D 3933 1285, P.R.O., JUST 1/958, rot 38d 1469-70, B.L., Add. Roll 44,559	?part of the present wood belonging to Kenilworth Priory, presumably by the modern Chadley
Walton	-	-	Walton Grove is shown on a map of 1728 (W.C.R.O., CR750/1)
Pillerton Hersey	-	-	
Brailes	*grava* *?=quidam boscus*	1268, P.R.O., C 132/35/13 1316, P.R.O., C 134/49, 51	presumably the wood at Grove End in 1631 (B.R.L., 167,910); an estate map c.1585 (W.C.R.O., CR3231) shows 'The Lawne Woode' there
Whichford	*Bosco suo de Wicheford* *?=boscum suum de Wicheford includere & parcum suum inde construere*	1246-7, P.R.O., JUST 1/952, rot 22r 1251-2, B.L., Egerton MSS. 3724, f. 80	presumably related to the present wood
Long Compton	*bosco suo de Compton* *?=boscus* *?=Cumptone Wood* *Yerdeley*	1251-2, B.L., Egerton MSS., 3724, f. 80 1296-7, P.R.O., E 352/94, rot 26 1477, Castle Ashby MSS., 460, copy in W.C.R.O., MI 167/1 *ibid.*	=?part of the present Long Compton Woods enclosed for the regrowth of wood presumably by the present Yardley
Waverley/ Wetherley in Stoneleigh	*boscum de Wethele* *boscus de Bradley*	pre-1392, *SLB*, p. 25 pre-1392, *SLB*, p. 248	? part of present Waverley Wood ? in the area of fields called Bradley (see map of 1597, copy in W.C.R.O., Z141(U))

C. References to groves in the modern period as woods or as field-names in south and east Warwickshire

Place	Grove/grove name	Earliest reference	Comments
Church Lawford	*cum separali Grova in loco super dunesmore heth vocato le Stode*	1538-9, P.R.O., SC 6/Hen VIII/3737	?perpetuated in field-names of Stead, *VCH*, Vol. VI, plate facing p. 148.
Radford Semele	*le Grove*	1537-8, P.R.O., SC 6/Hen VIII/3736	wood sold there
Newbold Pacey	*lytell grove*	1585, Ecclesiastical Terriers, Vol II, p. 15	in Ashorne
Stoneythorpe in Long Itchington	Grove Close	1754, W.C.R.O., CR1470/box 2	Map shows a rectangular block of trees in the close
Tachbrook Mallory	the Grove ?=grove	t. Henry VIII, P.R.O., SC 11/917 1549-50, W.C.R.O. CR1908/207	a grove can be see on a map of 1710, when it had trees , W.C.R.O., CR1886/M28
Idlicote	*graua*	1527, P.R.O., E 303/17/268	presumably related to the present Idlicote Grove
Whitchurch	Old Grove	1635, Ecclesiastical Terriers, Vol. II, pp. 169, 170	
Warmington	The Grove	1613, W.C.R.O., CR404/12	a close in 1613
Barcheston	Brode Grove furlong The Grove	n.d. (?15th C.), W.C.R.O., CR580/1 1807, W.C.R.O., CR580/41/2	no indication that there was a wood a close in 1807
Milverton	Grove Close	1805, W.C.R.O., QS75/77	

Appendix 3: Place-names suggestive of woodland in Warwickshire south and east of the River Avon in the early medieval period: minor place names apparently including *leah* and *hyrst*

A. Minor place-names apparently including *leah*

Place	Name	Date and reference
Alveston	*Newfrethesley*	1490, B.L., Add. Ch. 58,836
Barford	*persele*	n.d. (13th. C.), B.L., Harl. Ch. 46 A 30
	borseley	1574, W.C.R.O., CR1886/fifth shelf/BB634
	Ridowle	
Brailes	*Cademoreley*	n.d., B.L., Add. MS. 47,677, f. ccvij
Clifton-on-Dunsmore	*Cotenleye*	n.d. (?13th. C.), W.C.R.O., CR1886/222
Compton Verney	Heyle	1738, W.C.R.O., Z228/2(U)
Cubbington	*Colltleye*	1341, P.R.O., E 210/4443
	Cubbele	n.d., (?13th. C), P.R.O., E 210/8793
	Sohrtele	n.d., (?13th. C), P.R.O., E 210/9112
Dunchurch - Thurlaston	Foxley	1717, W.C.R.O., Z8/1
Frankton	*Armeley*	1411, P.R.O., E 164/21. f. 217
	Wakeley	1840, W.C.R.O., CR569/121A
Grandborough	*kytle*	1406, B.L., Add. Ch. 73,416
	Cottelehul	n.d., P.R.O., E 315/378
	Baggeleforlong	n.d., P.R.O., E 315/378
	Cosseleforlong	n.d., P.R.O., E 315/378
	Blakeley	18th C., W.C.R.O., CR1709/320/3
Kineton	*yerdeley*	1440-1, W.C.R.O., CR1886/263
	hawksley	1733, W.C.R.O., QS9/11, mm. 15-16
Ladbroke	*cherchelee*	1374, P.R.O., SC 12/16/27
Long Compton	*Yerdeley*	1477, Castle Ashby MSS., no. 460, copy in W.C.R.O., MI 167/1
Loxley	*Locheslei*	1086, DB
Milverton	Hockley	1805, W.C.R.O., QS75/77
Offchurch	*Bradlegh*	1411, P.R.O., E 164/21, f. 207
Princethorpe	Handley	1763, W.C.R.O., CR829/140
	Ratley	
Priors Hardwick or Marston	Tilley	1602, B.R.L., 437,934
	Holdele	n.d., P.R.O., E 40/9001
Radford Semele	Crawley	1843, W.C.R.O., CR569/195
Ratley	*Rotelei*	1086, DB
	Estlee	n.d. (?c.1200), P.R.O., E329/234
Rugby	Rowley	1718, W.C.R.O., D19/681
Ryton	Hayle Coppice	1608, W.C.R.O., CR2981
	Knightley	1735, W.C.R.O., CR155
	barbelee	n.d., (?c.1200), P.R.O., E 329/234
Stoneleigh (S.E. of Avon)	*Bradele*	1377, S.B.T., DR18/1/698
	Wethele	1204, SLB, pp. 23-4
Stratford-upon-Avon, Ruin Clifford	*Rokesly*	1599, S.B.T., ER1/72
Tachbrook	*Acle*	1161-82, Formulare, pp. 245-6
	Lee	13th. C., P.R.O., E 326/1917, 5907, 5972, 8474-76, 8616, 9308, and E315/20/49, E 315/36/108, E 315/41/86, E 315/48/255, E329/19
Wappenbury	Birchley	1668, W.C.R.O., CR1097/87
Wellesbourne	*Graua voc Chadley*	1469-70, B.L., Add. Roll 44,559
Weston-under-Wetherley	Rattley	1668, W.C.R.O., CR1097/87
Whitchurch	Cresly	1725, W.C.R.O., Z145(U)
Wimpstone (in Whitchurch)	Checkley	1869, W.C.R.O., QS75/127

B. Minor place-names apparently including *hyrst*

Place	Name including *hyrst*	Date and reference
Alveston	The Hurst	1772, W.C.R.O., QS75/1
Brailes	*hurst*	n.d., B.L., Add. MS. 47,677, f. ccviii
Cubbington	*greathurst*	n.d., 13th. C., P.R.O., E 210/5389
Dassett	*le Hurst*	1343, S.B.T., DR98/161
Dunchurch - Toft	*tonmonnehurst*	n.d., P.R.O., E 326/10316
Harbury	*lanerhurst*	n.d., B.L., Add. MS. 47,677, f. lxxiij
Hodnell	*hurst*	n.d., P.R.O., E 40/4393
	esthurst	n.d., B.L., Cott. Vitell. XVIII, f. 71
	?=Asthurst	n.d., B.L., Add. Ch. 48,159
	?=Hasthurst	n.d., B.L., Add. Ch. 48,153
	Hardehurst	n.d., B.L., Add. Ch. 48,153
Kineton - Combrook	*The hurst*	n.d., ?14th. C., W.C.R.O., CR1886/2373
	The drey hurste	
Princethorpe	Longhurst	1763, W.C.R.O., CR829/140
Priors Hardwick or Marston	Redhurste	1602, B.R.L., 437,934
	appel hurst	n.d. (?t. R. II), P.R.O., SC 12/40/106
Radbourne	*condeshurst*	n.d., B.L., Cott. Vitell., A i, f. 123
	semaldehurst	n.d., B.L., Cott. Vitell., A i, f. 124
Ratley	*astbroceshurst*	?14th. C., S.B.T., DR18/1/596
Stretton-on-Fosse	*Hurst*	1199, *FF*, Vol. I, no. 36 (mistakenly identified as Stretton-on-Dunsmore)
Stretton-on-Dunsmore	Burnd hurst	1608, W.C.R.O., CR2981
Tachbrook	*Bromhurst*	1161-82, *Formulare*, pp. 245-46
	ffroghilhurst	1569, B.R.L., 432,692
Tysoe	*lambersthurst*	1443-4, Staffs. R.O., D641/1/2/270
	lamcoteshurst	1465-6, Staffs. R.O., D641/1/2/274
		?= field called Lamperts Husk in the mid-eighteenth century, W.C.R.O., MI 167/8, being a copy of books of reference to Warwickshire estate maps at Castle Ashby, and Z275(Sm), being copies of the maps
Wolston	*Ravenshurst*	c.1340, P.R.O., SC11/696

Appendix 4: The wolds of Warwickshire

Place	Wold	Date, reference and comments
Bulkington	*le Wold*	n.d., P.R.O., E 40/4317 - by *Russyigorin*
Marston Jabett	*in Valdo, super Waldum, in Waldo*	n.d., 12th./13th. C., B.L., Cotton Vitell. A i, ff. 95, 97, 98, 103
Wolvey	*in Waldo, in inferiori Waldo, Netherewolt*	n.d., ?13th. C., B.L., Cotton Vitell. A i, ff. 88, 92
Wibtoft	*le Wolde, the Wolde*	1323, B.L., Add. Ch. 49,145
Withybrook	*Waldum, Waldo, Wold*	n.d., 13th. C., B.L., Cotton Vitell, A i, ff. 75, 80, 81
Monks Kirby	*sorthewold*	n.d., P.R.O., E 210/8794
	Shortewold	n.d., P.R.O., LR 14/349
Pailton in Monks' Kirby	*lowold, lo Heywold*	n.d., ?13th. C., B.L., Eg. Ch. 6151
Churchover and Coton	*de Waldo de Cotes & de Waldo de Wauere*	1223, B.L., Cotton Vitell. A i, f. 115
Newton in Clifton-on-Dunsmore	*Schortwold*	n.d., 13th. C. B.L., Add. MS. 47,677, ff. cccxxiiij, cccxxv
Little Lawford in Newbold-on-Avon	*Waldefurlong, Fletenwold*	1348, W.C.R.O., CR162/113
Wolston	*in alta Wolden*	t. Edward III, P.R.O., SC 11/696
Walsgrave-on-Sowe	*le Wold, ye Woldeweye, Le Woldhale*	1338-9, P.R.O., SC 12/16/42
Ryton-on-Dunsmore	*woldford*	1497, W.C.R.O., MR19
Southam	*le Waud*	1262, W.C.R.O, L1/34
	Valdo de Suham	1231, B.L., Cott. Vitell. A i, f. 32
	Waldwei	1206-7, *FF*, Vol. I, no. 159
	Southam wold	1603, W.C.R.O., CR1849/2
	the olde	n.d., 16th. C., *BD*
Ladbroke	*Wold*	1374, P.R.O., SC 12/16/27
	Ladbrooke Walde = Ladbrooke olte	1620, W.C.R.O., CR1849/2
	the olt	1639, copy map, W.C.R.O., Z358
Napton	*la Wolde*	n.d., W.C.R.O., CR1284/71/18
Radbourn	*in Waldo*	n.d., 12th./13th. C., B.L., Cotton Vitell. A i, f. 121
Priors Marston	*waldfurlong*	1355, Northants. R..O., Spencer MSS. 1559
Priors Hardwick	*Olden*	1602, B.R.L., 437,934
Shuckburgh	*Waldfurlong*	1317-8, P.R.O., SC 2/207/69
Wormleighton	*longwoldfurlong*	1522, Northants. R.O., Spencer MSS., court roll 226
Ufton	*Grenwold*	1411, P.R.O,. E 164/21, f. 85
	le longewold	1313, P.R.O., E 164/21, f. 100
Harbury	*cum toto Waldo*	n.d., ?13th. C., B.L., Add. MS. 47,677, f. lxxv
Bishop's Itchington	*le Wold*	1246, Staffordshire Historical Collections (1924), no. 195
Chadshunt	*Chaddesdon Wold*	1495, S.B.T., DR10/2606
	Woldweye	1350, S.B.T., DR10/2587
Gaydon	*Gaydon Wold*	1495, S.B.T., DR10/2606
	Geadon Woulds	1697, S.B.T., DR98/1817 - map, adjacent to Kingston and Itchington Holt
Kingston in Chesterton	*comuna in pastura que vocatur le Wold*	1310, 1314, S.B.T., DR98/278, 370
	woldfurlong	n.d., ?13th. C., S.B.T., DR98/240, 326a
Compton Verney	*Compton Wolde LetleWolde*	t. Henry III, S.B.T., DR98/6
Kineton	*Kingemewold*	c.1260-70, Magdalen College, Oxford, Westcote 23. Adjoined Westcote in Tysoe
	?=Holt	1778, S.B.T., DR98/1825, map shows holt names in east of the parish
Tysoe	*le Templewolde*	1265-78, Magdalen College, Oxford, Westcote 33
Warmington	*the Holt*	1654, W.C.R.O., D19/757
Leamington Priors	*the Wold*	1483, S.B.T., DR18/30/18/5 - a common parcel of land
Whitnash	*le Wolde*	1321, W.C.R.O., CR1908/177/6

Budbrooke	*le Wolde*	1405-6, W.C.R.O., CR895/8/3
	the Wold	1590, W.C.R.O., CR895/80/1
	wold	1788, W.C.R.O., CR895/101, map showing name north of Grove Park
Hatton	*Le Nunnewolde*	n.d., ?13th. C., *BD* =? modern Nunhold
	Nunwold	1590, W.C.R.O., CR895/80/1
Snitterfield	*wald*	1240, *FF*, Vol. I, no. 569
	walda	1315, S.B.T., ER2/397
Wolverton	*Wold, la Wolde*	n.d., 13th. C., P.R.O., E 326/5928 and 6310

Appendix 5: Hays

Parish or township	Hay	Date and reference
Ansley	*Ansteley hey, Oxhey*	1505, Bartlett, Manduessedum Romanorum, p. 141; 1535, P.R.O., C 146/9980
Aston (Castle Bromwich)	hay	1199, *FF*, Vol. I, no. 64
Baddesley Clinton	*Haywde*	c.1200, S.B.T., DR3/1
Birmingham	*le Heye*	1293, B.R.L., 660,292
Brandon	*le haye/hey*	1470, M.MSS., Mi M 128/3
Chilvers Coton	*Nemore de Herewardeshay* *Boscum...qui vocatur Herewardeshay*	1234, W.C.R.O., CR136/C145 n.d. (?13th C.), W.C.R.O., CR136/C725
Coleshill	*Chelemundesheia*	1200, *FF*, Vol. I, no. 73
Corley	*le Hay* *in territorio haye*	c.1250, S.B.T., DR10/216 n.d. (mid. 13th C.), S.B.T., DR10/215
Coughton	*viride qui vocatur le heye*	n.d. (13th C.), W.C.R.O., CR1998/box 34/B6
Donnelie	*haia*	1086, *DB*, 240a
Erdington	*le Heye*	1282, P.R.O., E 210/8735
Foleshill	*boscum..vocatum le Hay*	1411, P.R.O., E 164/21, f. 22r
Hampton-in-Arden	*omnes haias*	n.d., (12th C.), B.R.L., Wingfield Digby MSS., A1/2
Hartshill	*boscum qui vocatur Suthhaye...boscum qui vocatur le Hokehaie...boscum qui vocatur le Neuhaye*	1276, P.R.O., C 133/14/2
Haselor	*Rowheya*	n.d. (?12th C.), P.R.O., E 164/22, f. cxxv
Hatton	*Hactonhaye*	n.d. (13th C.), P.R.O., E 40/6947
Kenilworth	*haia*	c.1130-5, B.L., Add. MS. 47,677, f. cxxiii
Kingsbury	*totam haiam que est inter tama & lacu* *la haie*	n.d. (?12th C.), B.L., Cott. Ch. xxv 25 n.d. (?12th C.), B.L., Cott. Ch. xxii 2
Lea Marston	*heyam de merston*	n.d. (?13th C.), M.MSS., Mi D 4163
Middleton	*le hay* *le Haye*	1375, M.MSS., Mi M 131/27 1387, M.MSS., Mi M 131/29
Monks' Kirby - Easenhall Monks' Kirby - Street Ashton	*le heye* *le Hay*	1317, P.R.O., E 210/9000 ?1428-9 or 1491-2, P.R.O., SC 11/685; 1493-4, P.R.O., SC 11/688
Nuneaton	*bosco de Newhay*	*ante* 1477, Nicholls, History of Leicester, Vol. I, Part I, p. 82.
Packington (Great)	*Ailyhmehey*	B.L., Add. MS. 47,677, f. xxv
Polesworth	*le dordonhey*	1564, B.R.L., 193,151
Polesworth (Freasley)	*boscum de Stotefoldeshay*	n.d. (13th C.), Staffs. R.O., D593/A/1/10/10
Solihull	*le heye* *Sowthaye* *=Sowthey* *Holteheye*	n.d. (13th C.), P.R.O., C146/1732 n.d., S.B.T., DR37/box 76 1540, S.B.T., DR37/2557 1355, P.R.O., C146/1136, by *la Rouwode*
Stivichall	*Le Hey*	n.d., S.B.T., DR10/1406, p. 111
Studley	*nemus de Haia*	1201, S.B.T., ER1/61/19
Sutton Coldfield	*unam liberam Hayam in defensione*	*ante* 1153, *Dugdale*, Vol. II, pp. 909-10
Tanworth-in-Arden	*le heye* *le heyeholt*	1364, S.B.T., DR37/702 1345, S.B.T., DR37/593
Tysoe	*la haye*	1443-4, Staffs. R.O., D641/1/2/270
Wroxall	*haya*	1327-8 for 12th C., Ryland, Records of Wroxall Abbey, p. 19

Appendix 6: Management of two coppice woods in Warwickshire in the mid-fifteenth century

I. Withycombe Wood, Haselor, 1448 (source - Register of St. Mary's Collegiate Church, Warwick, P.R.O., E164/22, ff. cxxxii-iii, copy in W.C.R.O., Z251(Sm))

"Haselore - Indentura vendicionis bosci ibidem vocati Withicombe anno xxvii Regis Henrici sexti

"Thys endenture made at Warrewyk the xx day of decembre the xxvii yere of kyng Harry the sixthe betwene the deane & chapitre of the collage of Warrewyk on the one part, Richard Ruttour & John Ruttour of Newenham withinne the parrissh of Aston cantelow & Wylliam Perkyns of Haselore on the othere part. Wytnessethe that the seyd Rychard Ruttour John Ruttour and Willyam perkyns have boght of the seyd Dean & Chapitre alle the tymber and underwode that growethe in theire wode at Haselore cald Wythicombe to haven hyt & to fallen hit be the grounde The parcell of wode there cald the persones wode With alle the bordures therof And also alle the bordures of the seyde Withicombe that ys to sey the stake rewe & alle that growethe withoute the stake rewe to the seyd deane & Chapitre wholly reserued. And the seyd Richard John & William shule haue dayes of owtying of the seyde wode cald Withycombe from the day of the makyng of these endenture, Unto the feste of the natiuite of seynt John the Baptist that shalle ben in the yere of our Lord Jesu a MCCCCLI. With fre entree & issue in to the seyde Wythicombe to falle & to carie in due tymes as here folewethe That ys to sey they shulle falle and do falle feyre & kyndely for the growing ayein almanere wode except ook euery yere duryng the seyd terme from seynt Andrewes day, Un to the furst day of Maii & no lengere. And ooke unto the laste day of Maii & no lengere And they shul carie & do carie euery yere duryng the seyde terme from Allehalewentide unto the feste of the natiuite of seynt John Baptiste & no lengere Allewey forseye & accorded that the forseyde Richard John & Wylliam shule save & do save alle the yonge spryng that shall growe in the seyd Wode calde Withicombe duryng the seide terme from biting brekyng & tredyng doune of manne and beste & cariage that shulle come or be broght in to the seide Wode cald Withicombe at ony tyme by the forseyde Richard John & William or by ony of hem or by ony othere persone in theire name or auctorite durynge the forseyd terme. And that almanere of wode & tymber that may be found fald & ligging among the quik spring in the seyde Withicombe after the feste of the Natiuite of seint John Baptist in ony yere duryng the seyde terme be forfet & lost from the forseide buyers & to be had & disposed be the seyde Deane & Chapitre as theym shall beste seme. Also the seyde buyers shule kepe the closure abowte the seyd Wode cald Withicombe at their costes during the seide terme. And in the ende of the same terme theishule leve alle the seide closure wel & competently made and repared. And the forseyd Richard John & William shule paye wele & truly to the seide Deane & Chapitre for the forseid wood & tymber thus to hem sold - l. li. vi s. viii d. Wherof they have payed in hande the day of the asseallyng of these endentures xxvi li. xiii s. iiiid. And they shule pay althe remanent the seconday of Nouembere next coming after the date of these endentures that ys to sey xxiii li. xiii s. iiii d. And in caas that they fayle of the payment of the seyd xxiii li. xiii s. iiii d the seconde day of Nouembre a fore seide, that then they shule forfete & lese alle the wode & tymber that at that tyme shalle be found growing or falde withinne the forseyd Wode calde Withycombe to the use & profitz of the seyde Deane & Chapitre And also that theforeseid Richard John & William shule welle & truly kepe & parfourme alle the forseid Couenauntz as they belonge to theire part they haue found these boroghes that ys to sey John alkok of Aston cantelowe, John Webbe of the same toune, John fremanne of alcestre & John Mase of rovn alne. Weche boroghes buthe bounden in an obligacion under theire sealles euery of hem in xl marcs sterling to the seyd deane & Chapitre for the suretee of this bargeyn the weche they shule pay to the seyd Deane & Chapitre yf the forseyd buyers breke ony of their forsaid Covenauntz. And the forseyd deane & Chapitre shule warrante the sale of the forseid wode cald Withicombe to the forseyd Buyers therof in maner & fourme as ys above seyde. Into witnesse of alle that is above wreten the forseid parties to these endentures either partye to others parte have set theire sealles at Warrewyk the day & the yere a boue seyde."

II. Bigging Grove, Coventry, 1460 (source, C.R.O., 468/15)

"This endenture made be twene Nicolas Dylcok on that oon party And John Seman on that other party Wynessethe that the said Nicolas hathe let & to ferme sette to the said John a Close yn Byggyng called Cley Pyttes And a Grove called Byggyng Grove to have and to hold the said Close & Grove to the said John & his assignes from the fest of Mighelmas last past unto the end of terme of xxvi yere next comyng yeldyng yerely to the said Nicolas his heyres & his assignes yerely atte fest of Myssomer A Rose Floure yyf hit be asked And hit shalle be levefulle to the said John & his assignes to hakke hewe & Carriawey alle maner Wode growyng in the said Grove duryng the saide terme except Appultrees & Crabtrees And the said Nicolas the said Close & Grove to the said John & his assignes duryng the said terme A yenst alle menne shalle Warant & defende And the said John grauntyth that the said Nicolas shalle have and ocupye the Joystment of the said Wode duryng the said terme not hurtyng the Sprynge growyng or to growe duryng the said terme in the same Wode And the said John Seman shalle close the said Closse & Grove havyng alle the woode growyng there a boughte the bordurs of the said Close and Grove And Where the said Nicolas ys bounden to the said John in A obligacion of x li. to be payed to the same John atte fest of Crystenmas next comyng the same John grauntythe by this present wrytyng yyf he peseabully enjoy the said Close & Grove as a bove ys rehersyd duryng the said terme Without interupcion or disturbance of the said Nicolas or of any other person than the said John grauntith that the said obligacion be voyde & of no vertu In to Wytnesse of the which thyng the forsaid partyes to these endentours theire sealys haue putt chaungeably yeven at Couentre the iiii Day of October The yere Raynyng of kyng Herr' the vi Aftur the conquest the xxxix"

BIBLIOGRAPHY

Manuscript Sources

These are described under their respective repositories, which are listed in alphabetical order by title.

Within each repository the manuscripts are listed alphabetically by place or, in the case of records covering several places, by the estate which included those places. When an individual document within an estate collection can be attributed to a single place, listing by place has been preferred, so that listing by estate has been confined mainly to cartularies or registers and account rolls. Estates under which such references will be found include the earldoms of Warwick and Stafford, the Bishopton, Catesby, Leigh and Mohun estates, the ecclesiastical estates of Coventry Cathedral Priory, Chacombe Priory, Maxstoke Priory, Merevale Abbey, Pipewell Abbey, Stoneleigh Abbey and Kenilworth Priory and the accounts of dissolved religious houses kept by the Crown. Listing has been by class of record instead of place for three classes of document in the Public Record Office, the Assize rolls, the King's Bench rolls, and the Forest Proceedings, as they covered many places in Warwickshire.

The dates of documents have been printed in italics, to distinguish them from the numbers which form part of the repositories' references for documents. Medieval documents which are undated (n.d.) are usually from the twelfth or thirteenth century.

The descriptions of documents are brief. The general term 'deed' has been used to cover a wide variety of documents recording the permanent or temporary transfer of property rights.

Balliol College

A list of documents relating to the College's ownership of the manor of Ufton is kept in W.C.R.O.

Ufton deed, *1556*, C.1.20

Berkeley Castle (via Gloucestershire Record Office)

Claverdon deed, *1312*, GC1888
Ullenhall deed, *1194*, SC 38

Birmingham Reference Library, Archives Department

Allesley deeds, *1530*, 328,923; *1585*, 328,926; *1668*, 241,400
Alspath deeds, n.d., 608,879, 608,881, 608,882; *1550*, 249,976; *1603*, 277,121
Aston (Castle Bromwich) deeds, *n.d. - 14th. C.*, 19,801-74
Aston rental, *1532*, 413,517
Aston estate maps, *1758*, 371,055; *1759*, 148,157
Aston deed, *1539*, 347,879
Aston court roll, *1469*, 347,863
Beausale deeds, *13th C. -1342-3*, Keen 26 (under Haseley)
Berkswell deeds, *1627*, 276,809; *1638*, 276,818
Bickenhill deed, *1642*, 193,194
Birmingham transcript of survey, *1529*, 93,314
Birmingham deed, *1293*, 660,292
Brailes accounts, *1413-4*, 167,904

Brailes deeds, *1543*, 168,216; *1631*, 167,910; *1692*, 168,052; *1724*, 168,204
Brinklow deeds, *1351-1410*, Keen 40A
Chesterton document relating to law proceedings, *c.1605*, 272,820
Chesterton accounts, *1441-2*, 295,194
Claverdon (Langley) deed, *1695*, Keen 48
Coleshill deeds, Wingfield Digby MSS., *n.d. - 1461*, A21, A24/1, A30, A31, A38, A45, A46, A47, A51, A72, A76, A91, A92, A108, A258, A333, A388, A433, A519, A589
Coleshill deed, *1557*, 321,104
Corley deeds, *1323*, 348,005; *1435*, 348,009
Coventry Cathedral Priory accounts, *1478-9*, 168,237
Cubbington deeds, *1651*, 86,005; *1750*, 193,175
Curdworth - see under Minworth below
Erdington rental, *1462-3*, 347,913
Erdington court rolls, *1350*, 347,854; *1442*, 347,860; *1461-70*, 347,863; *1525*, 347,876; *1539-43*, 347,879
Erdington survey, *1655*, 349,825
Erdington draft estate map, *1760*, 292,886
Erdington enclosure award (with Witton), *1802-4*, 1382/1, 3
Grafton and Haselor accounts, *1465-6*, 168,238
Grafton estate map, *1740*, 247,148-9
Grendon court roll, *1564*, 193,151
Hampton-in-Arden deeds, n.d., Wingfield Digby MSS., A1/2, A3, A4, A5
Hampton-in-Arden survey, *1649*, 511,984
Haseley deeds, *1312-1431*, Keen 72; *1351*, 304,288
Haselor accounts, *1465-6*, 168,238
Keresley deed, *1667*, 294,034
Lapworth deed, *1500-1*, 437,896
Lea Marston deeds, *1472*, Norton 89; *1478*, Norton 92; *1574*, Norton 182
Maxstoke deed, *1419*, Keen 92
Merevale Abbey lands survey, *1543-4*, 168,242
Meriden - see under Alspath above
Minworth deed, n.d., Wingfield Digby MSS., A101
Monastic lands (former) accounts, *1547*, 168,255
Nuneaton survey, *1557*, 347,953
Nuthurst deeds, *1476*, Wingfield Digby MSS., A615; *1594*, 277,430; *1597*, 277,427
Packwood deed, *1519*, Keen 104
Polesworth deed, *1564*, 193,151
Priors Hardwick/Priors Marston terrier, *1602*, 437,934
Salford crown lease of woods, *1580*, 167,733
Sheldon deeds, n.d., 431,122; *1346*, 431,125; *1567*, 431,160
Sheldon tithe map, *1840*, TM2/14
Sheldon enclosure award, *1813*, MS 1382/6
Shustoke deeds, *1312*, 429,351; n.d., Keen 54; *1330*, Keen 118
Solihull deed, *1585*, 324,101
Stafford earldom accounts, *1455-6*, 168,236
Studley deeds, *1560*, 167,486-7; *1596*, 167,446; *1605*, 167,405
Sutton Coldfield deeds, n.d., 348,037, 348,039; *1253*, 348,028; *1321*, 348,041-2; *1344*, 348,022
Tamworth deeds, n.d., 480,682; *1446*, Norton MSS. 67
Upton (in Ratley) estate map, *1774*, 307,947 (copy in W.C.R.O., Z202)
Wappenbury petition, n.d. (presumably *1493-1500*), Keen 133
Warwick St. Nicholas, copy of enclosure award of 1773, *1787*, 353,352
Witton estate map, *1759*, 305,520
Yardley court roll, *1495*, 427,740

260

Bodleian Library, Oxford

Binley estate map, *1746*, Craven 320
Binley, Brinklow and Coombe deed, *1620*, Craven 71
Coombe Abbey and Binley accounts, *1623-44*, Craven 78
Coombe manor Parliamentary survey, *1652*, Craven 6
Corley, Keresley, Exhall and Foleshill deeds, n.d., Queen's College, 2337, 2339, 2348, 2376
Maxstoke Priory Register, MS. Trinity College 84 (copy in W.C.R.O., MI 272)
Ufton map, *1695* and survey, *1672*, Balliol College 68/252 (copies in W.C.R.O., Z181(U))
Collection of copy MSS. for Warwickshire, MS. Top, Warks C8

British Library

A list of cartularies is followed by a list of other documents arranged alphabetically by place.

Beauchamp cartulary, Add. MS. 28,024 (copy in W.C.R.O., MI 177)
Coombe Abbey cartularies, Cotton Vitell. A i, Cotton. Vitell. XVIII
Kenilworth cartularies, Harl. MS. 3650, Add. MS. 47,677 (copies in W.C.R.O., MI 392)
Knights Hospitallers lease book, Lansdowne 200
Mohun cartulary, Egerton MS. 3724 (copy in W.C.R.O., MI 144)
Pipewell Abbey cartulary, Cotton Caligula A xiii
Reading Abbey cartulary, Cotton Vespasian E xxv
Segrave feodary, Add. MS 37,671
Segrave cartulary, Harley 4748
Stone Priory cartulary, Cotton Vespasian E xxiv

Alspath deed, *1348*, Add. Ch. 8398
Alveston deed, *1490*, Add. Ch. 58,836
Barford deed, n.d., Harl. Ch. 46 A 30
Beaudesert deed, *1326*, Cott. Ch. xxvii 137
Birdingbury deeds, n.d., Add. Chs., 48,029, 48,031, 53,105; *1363*, 48,451
Brandon estate maps, *c.1630*, Add. MS. 48,181 (copy of first map in W.C.R.O., Z203(U))
Chilvers Coton deed, *1316*, Add. Ch. 48,068
Grandborough deed, *1406*, Add. Ch. 73,416
Hampton-in-Arden deeds, n.d., Cott. Ch. xi 35, Add. Ch. 21,416
Hartshill rental, n.d., Cott. Ch. iv 52
Hartshill court roll, *1376*, Harl. Roll Y 13
Hodnell deeds, n.d., Add. Chs. 48,153, 48,159, 48,161, 48,162; *1276*, Add. Ch. 48,154
Honiley deeds, n.d., Cott. Ch. xxiii 15 and 16
Kingsbury deeds, n.d., Cott. Ch. xxii 2, Cott. Ch. xxii 3, Cott. Ch. xxv 25
Kingsbury court roll, *1419*, Egerton Roll 8621
Kingsbury rental, n.d., Egerton Roll 8618
Lapworth deeds, n.d., Harl. Ch. 86 E 27; *1375*, Add. Ch. 14,006
Nuneaton deeds, (Aston Manuscripts, most of which have been copied on to microfilm in Nuneaton Library), n.d., Add Chs. 48,491, 49,070, 49,071; *1290*, 49,069; *1538*, 48,776; *1538*, 48,775; *1541*, 48,790; *1542*, 48,791; *1543*, 48,793; *1550*, 48,806; *1552*, 48,819; *1574*, 48,918
Nuneaton valor, *1539*, Add. Roll 49,457
Nuneaton rentals, *1325*, Add. Roll 49,464; *1335*, Add Roll 49,466

Nuneaton accounts, Add. Rolls (copies in Nuneaton Library) *1331-2*, 49,727; *1368-9*, 49,711; *1369-70*, 49,712; *1370-1*, 49,713; *1372-3*, 49,715; *1374-5*, 49,717; *1374-5*, 49,718; *1375-6*, 49,719; *1377-8*, 49,720; *1378-9*, 49,721; *1380-1*, 49,722; *1386-7*, 49,751; *1397-8*, 49,757; *1402-3*, 49,759; *1401-2*, 49,760; *1406-7*, 49,762; *1405*, 49,763; 1406-7, 49,765; *1408-9*, 49,403
Pailton deeds, n.d., Eg. Ch. 6151; *1302*, Cott. Ch. xxix 90; *1403*, Eg. Ch. 6160
Preston Bagot deed, n.d., Cott. Ch. xxvii 134
Ratley deed, n.d. (*12th.C.*), Harl. Ch. 45 C 47
Ratley terrier, *1612*, Add. Roll 43,001
Shustoke deed, *1447*, Cott. Ch. xii 33
Shenstone (Staffordshire) and Sutton Chase deed, *1229-42*, Add. Ch. 20,468
Snitterfield accounts, *1430-1*, Egerton Roll 8624
Stivichall map, *1787*, Add. MS. 41,477 (copy in S.B.T., PR63)
Tysoe copies of deeds, n.d., Cott. Roll XIII 6
Wellesbourne accounts, *1469-70*, Add. Roll 44,559
Wibtoft deed, *1323*, Add. Ch. 49,145
Wootton Wawen deeds, *1326*, Cott. Ch. xxvii 137; *1505*, Add. Ch. 49,116

Cambridge University Library

Thorney Abbey cartulary, Vol. 2, Add. 3021

Castle Ashby - see Warwickshire County Record Office

Coventry Record Office

Allesley and Coundon deeds, *1361-4*, BA/B/A/19/1-2; *1347*, BA/B/A/44/12; *1300-1305*, BA/B/A/47/3-11; *1407*, BA/B/A/48/9; *c.1300-1358*, BA/B/A/54/1, 11, 12, 13; *1305*, BA/B/A/55/1-10; *1317*, BA/B/A/107/4; *1360*, BA/B/P/260/1; *1343*, BA/B/P/357/1; *1336*, BA/B/P/401/2; *1332*, BA/B/P/451/8; *1593*, BA/D/A/20/1
Alspath deeds, *1528*, 9/1; *1542*, 54/27; *1546*, BA/D/K/10/24; *1581*, BA/A/A/2/2; *1630-1*, 54/69; n.d., BA/D/K/10/1-2; *1546*, BA/D/K/10/24; *1652*, BA/D/K/10/26
Asthill evidence relating to a dispute over tithes, n.d., (*?16th.C*), 17/10/2
Baginton deeds, *c.1280*, 39/6; *1298*, 39/8; *1313*, 39/19
Bubbenhall deed, *1323*, BA/D/K/13/3
Caludon deeds, n.d., BA/H/H/163/1-3
Corley deeds, *1338*, BA/D/D/49/3; *1429*, BA/D/D/49/5
Coundon deeds - see above under Allesley
Coventry deeds, n.d., BA/H/H/55/1; *1297*, BA/D/H/26/2; *1315*, BA/B/Q/20/7; *1315*, BA/H/H/375/1; *1317*, BA/H/H/375/2; *1343*, BA/B/P/431/4; *1347*, BA/B/P/439/7; *1347*, BA/B/P/431/4, 5; *1347*, BA/B/P/439/7; *1348*, BA/H/H/293/9; *1351*, BA/B/P/137/13; *1357*, BA/B/P/431/6; *1357*, BA/B/P/441/1; *1368*, BA/B/P/440/5; *1393*, BA/B/P/14/5; *1423*, BA/A/A/3/1; *1487*, BA/B/A/86/1; *1580*, BA/B/P/432/1; *1610*, BA/G/D/1/1
Coventry deed (including Asthill), *1729*, 101/1/262
Coventry (Drapers' Company) deeds, *1327-1460*, 468/15, 53, 59, 87, 139, 169, 215, 316, 350, 360, 361; volume of surveys and maps, *1759*, 1573/19/1-2; copy of survey and maps, *1803*, 1573/19/3-4
Fillongley deeds, *1361*, BA/D/D/50/2; *1474*, BA/D/D/50/3

Foleshill deeds, n.d., BA/B/Q/20/2; *1405*, BA/G/F/33/2; *1639-1714*, BA/D/A/22/1-4

Meriden - see Alspath

Packwood deed, *1398*, 54/40

Sowe deeds, n.d., BA/B/A/41/1, BA/H/H/344/2, BA/B/A/93/1, BA/B/A/94/1; *1422*, BA/B/A/99/14; *1581*, BA/A/A/2/2/

Devon Record Office

Birdingbury accounts, *1397-8*, 248 M/M6

Gloucestershire Record Office (see also Berkeley Castle)

Alne court roll, *1361-2*, D678/99

Sutton-under-Brailes accounts, *1291-2, 1304-5, 1323-4, 1377-8, 1379-80*, D1099/M31/9, 23, 40, 44, 46

Hereford and Worcester Record Office, St. Helen's Branch (Worcester)

Bishopric of Worcester, Hampton [Lucy] court roll, *1453*, 001:9 BA 2636 164 92178a; Hampton [Lucy] account rolls, *1376-7* and *1392-3*, 009:1 BA 2636 163 92161 and 92169

Calendar of Manuscripts at Madresfield Court

John Rylands University Library of Manchester

The Bromley Davenport Manuscripts (abbreviated to *BD* in this study) have not been fully indexed. The collection consists mainly of deeds, with some medieval accounts and modern estate records. They are accessible by place. Copies of the map of Bubbenhall and of the accompanying enclosure award in 1726 are in W.C.R.O., Z414(U) and Z413(Sm).

King's College, Cambridge

The College acquired the lands of Wootton Wawen Priory. The records include medieval deeds, account and court rolls and early modern surveys.

Wootton Wawen deeds, n.d., WOW/87, 90, 94, 95, 110; *1285*, WOW/52; *1401*, WOW/56; *1445*, WOW/128

Wootton Wawen surveys, *1565*, S53; *1736*, S44 (copies in W.C.R.O., MI 176)

Wootton Wawen accounts, *1449-50*, WOW223

Leicestershire Record Office

Claybrooke (Wibtoft) tithe award, *1845*, Ti/70/1 (DE76)

Willey estate map, *1805*, (DG28) DE66 box 2209

Wolvey deeds, n.d., and *1226*, DE2559/105, 106

Lichfield Joint Record Office

Amington estate map, n.d. (? nineteenth century), D/W/1851/10/3

Bishopric of Coventry and Lichfield, estate accounts, *1305-6*, D30/N6

Magdalen College, Oxford

Tysoe deed, n.d., Westcote 33

Westcote notes and evidences, n.d., Westcote 112

Westcote deed, n.d., Westcote 23, 56

Merevale Hall

A microfilm copy of the catalogue of the manuscripts kept at Merevale Hall is in

Warwickshire County Record Office, MI 211.

Atherstone map of outwood, n.d., uncatalogued

Berkswell deeds, *1708*, nos. 1901, 1945; *1722*, no. 1494; *1758*, nos. 1962A&B

Shustoke deeds, n.d. (catalogued as *c.1300*), nos. 1326, 1371

Northamptonshire Record Office

Burton Dassett deed, *1497*, Temple (Stowe), box 4/bundle 1a/1

Chesterton deed, *1508*, Spencer MSS. 1491

Fillongley deed, *1317*, Th.1495

Priors Marston deed, *1355*, Spencer MSS. 1559

Wolfhampcote deeds, *1344*, D4137; *1416*, D1116

Wormleighton court rolls, *1387-1522*, Spencer MSS. rolls 216, 226

University of Nottingham

The documents consulted are all from the Middleton Manuscripts (M. MSS.).

Brandon court roll, *1470*, Mi M 128/3

Brandon surveys, *1571 - c.1580*, Mi M 232

Brandon deeds, *1366*, Mi D 3956; *1582*, Mi Da 94

Coleshill deed, *1520*, Mi D 3980

Erdington court rolls, *1413-17*, Mi M 129/1, 3

Foleshill deeds, n.d., Mi D 4007; *1327*, Mi D 4011

Grendon deeds, n.d., Mi D 4021, 4022, 4027, 4028

Kingsbury deeds, n.d., Mi D 4041, 4054, 4059, 4515; *1240-1*, Mi D 4070, 4071; *1300*, Mi D 4020/1; *1331*, Mi D 4091; *1332*, Mi D 4094

Kingsbury copy rental, *1527-8*, Mi M 130/47B

Kingsbury court roll, *1514*, Mi M 130/2

Lea Marston deeds, n.d., Mi D 4163, 4169, 4174, 4177; *1316*, Mi D 4196

Middleton deeds, n.d., Mi D 4253, 4255, 4265, 4270, 4271, 4277, 4291, 4299, 4300, 4306, 4328; *1249*, Mi D 4310; *1286*, Mi D 4317; *1297*, Mi D 4323; *1299*, Mi D 4325; *1333*, Mi D 4382; *1333*, Mi D 4384; *1352*, Mi D 4413; *1385*, Mi D 4525/2

Middleton copy of assize proceedings, *1247*, Mi Da 84/4

Middleton manorial survey, *1419-20*, Mi M 124

Middleton accounts, *1454-5*, 5/167/102; court rolls, *1308*, Mi M 131/4; *1315*, Mi M 131/9; *1375*, Mi M 131/27; *1387*, Mi M 131/29

Middleton rentals, Mi M 175, 206, 207

Middleton survey of demesne lands, *1605*, Mi M 237/1

Middleton estate map and key, *1865*, Mi 2 S10, Mi 2 P5A

Studley survey, *1419-20*, Mi M 124

Sutton Coldfield rental, n.d., Mi Da 84/41

Sutton Coldfield deeds, n.d., Mi D 3949/1; *1581*, Mi Da 87

Sutton Coldfield court rolls, *1411-1519*, Mi M 134/1, 3, 9, 20, 21

Sutton Coldfield (manor of Berefford including Wiggins Hill) survey, n.d., 6/170/73

Wellesbourne deed, *1261-2*, Mi D 3933

Wootton Wawen manorial survey, *1419-20*, Mi M 124

Public Record Office

The classes of record which have been consulted are listed below, followed by the individual references in alphabetical order according to the place, estate (for example, the earldom of Warwick, Stoneleigh Abbey) or subject (e.g. Assize Rolls, Forest Proceedings, Monastic Accounts) to which they refer.

C 53: Chancery: Charter Rolls
C 54: Chancery: Close Rolls
C 81: Chancery: Ancient Petitions
C 132: Chancery: Inquisitions Post Mortem, Series I, Henry III
C 133: Chancery: Inquisitions Post Mortem, Series I, Edward I
C 134: Chancery: Inquisitions Post Mortem, Series I, Edward II
C 135: Chancery: Inquisitions Post Mortem, Series I, Edward III
C 136: Chancery: Inquisitions Post Mortem, Series I, Richard II
C 137: Chancery: Inquisitions Post Mortem, Series I, Henry IV
C 138: Chancery: Inquisitions Post Mortem, Series I, Henry V
C 139: Chancery: Inquisitions Post Mortem, Series I, Henry VI
C 140: Chancery: Inquisitions Post Mortem, Series I, Edward IV
C 141: Chancery: Inquisitions Post Mortem, Series I, Richard III
C 142: Chancery: Inquisitions Post Mortem, Series I, Henry VII
C 146: Chancery: Ancient Deeds, Series C
C 147: Chancery: Ancient Deeds, Series CC
C 148: Chancery: Ancient Deeds, Series CS
C 263/2: Chancery: Exemplifications
CP 25: Court of Common Pleas: Feet of Fines
DL 29: Duchy of Lancaster: Ministers' Accounts
DL 43: Duchy of Lancaster: Rentals and Surveys
E 13: Exchequer: Exchequer of Pleas: Plea Rolls
E 32: Justices of the Forest: Records formerly in the Treasury of the Receipt of the Exchequer
E 36: Exchequer: Treasury of Receipt: Miscellaneous Books
E 40: Exchequer: Ancient Deeds, Series A
E 41: Exchequer: Ancient Deeds, Series AA
E 42: Exchequer: Ancient Deeds, Series AS
E 106: Exchequer: Extents of Alien Priories
E 149: Exchequer: Inquisitions Post Mortem, Series I
E 152: Exchequer: King's Remembrancer: Enrolments of Inquisitions
E 164: Exchequer: King's Remembrancer: Miscellaneous Books, Series I
E 178: Exchequer: King's Remembrancer: Special Commissions of Enquiry
E 210: Exchequer: Ancient Deeds, Series D
E 211: Exchequer: Ancient Deeds, Series DD
E 212: Exchequer: Ancient Deeds, Series DS
E 303: Exchequer: Augmentations Office: Conventual Leases
E 315: Exchequer: Augmentations Office: Miscellaneous Books
E 318: Exchequer: Augmentations Office: Particulars for Grants of Crown Lands
E 326: Exchequer: Ancient Deeds, Series B
E 327: Exchequer: Ancient Deeds, Series BX
E 328: Exchequer: Ancient Deeds, Series BB
E 329: Exchequer: Ancient Deeds, Series BS
E 352: Exchequer: Pipe Office: Chancellor's Rolls
E 364: Exchequer: Pipe Office: Foreign Accounts Rolls
E 372: Exchequer: Pipe Office: Pipe Rolls
JUST 1: Assize Rolls
KB 26: Curia Regis Rolls
LR 2: Exchequer: Land Revenue: Miscellaneous Books
LR 14: Exchequer: Land Revenue: Ancient Deeds, Series E

LR 15: Exchequer: Land Revenue: Ancient Deeds, Series EE
Req. 2: Court of Requests
SC 2: Special Collections: Court rolls
SC 6: Special Collections: Ministers' Accounts
SC 8: Special Collections: Ancient Petitions
SC 11: Special Collections: Rentals and Surveys [General Series]: Rolls
SC 12: Special Collections: Rentals and Surveys [General Series]: Portfolios
Sta Cha: Court of Star Chamber Proceedings
Ward 2: Court of Wards and Liveries: Deeds and Evidences

Assize rolls, *1231-2*, JUST 1/951A; *1246-7*, JUST 1/952; *1260*, JUST 1/953; *1261-2*, JUST 1/954; *1272*, JUST 1/955; *1284-5*, JUST 1/958; *1295-8*, JUST 1/964; *1303-7*, JUST 1/965; *1306-7*, JUST 1/966; *1314-8*, JUST 1/968; *1314-9*, JUST 1/969; *1329-30*, JUST 1/970; *1380-1*, JUST 1/973; *1274-7*, JUST 1/1228; *1275-7*, JUST 1/1231; *1276-8*, JUST 1/1237; *1278-88*, JUST 1/1245; *1287-8*, JUST 1/1278; *1287-8*, JUST 1/1279; *1288-9*, JUST 1/1283A, 1283B; *1299-1300*, JUST 1/1316; *1301-2*, JUST 1/1320; *1328-41*, JUST 1/1400; *1364-9*, JUST 1/1472; *1395-8*, JUST1/1508
Abbots Salford deed, *1314*, CP 25/1/245/42
Alcester particulars for grants, *1544*, E 318/19/984
Allesley rental, *1298-1300*, SC 11/679
Allesley inquisition post mortem, *1325*, C 134/91/27
Allesley, Birdingbury and Fillongley survey, *1392*, DL 43/14/3
Alspath deeds, *1202*, CP 25/1/242/6; *1401*, E 315/31/235; *1454*, E 326/8944; *1408*, E 329/222
Alvecote and Shuttington enclosure award, *1805*, E 13/1187 (copy in W.C.R.O., MI 141)
Amington deed, *1214*, CP 25/1/242/9
Ansley deeds, n.d., E 315/41/20; *1413*, E 212/93; *1535*, C 146/9980
Ansty deed, *1256*, CP 25/1/244/24
Arley deed, *1202-3*, CP 25/1/242/6
Ashow deeds, n.d., E 210/3697, 7497; E 326/459, 497, 3471; E 315/51/73; *1301*, LR 14/229; *1324*, E 210/5693; *1327-8*, E 210/6517; *1340*, E 315/47/115; *1375*, E 210/5451
Ashow court rolls, *1389-1439*, SC 2/207/77, 79
Ashow lease of woods, *1537*, E 303/17/285
Astley inquisition post mortem, *1300*, C 133/98/32
Aston Cantlow inquisitions post mortem, *1254-1436*, C 132/17/15, C 133/2/7, C 135/41/19, C 139/76
Aston Cantlow deed, *1395-6*, C 263/2/1
Aston Cantlow survey (with Allesley, Bubbenhall, etc.), *1392*, DL 43/14/3
Aston Cantlow accounts, *1539-40*, SC 6/Hen VIII/5694
Atherstone-on-Stour deed, *1497-8*, CP 25/1/248/74
Baddesley Ensor lease, *1532*, E 303/7/121
Baginton lease, *1529*, E 303/18/519
Baginton Star Chamber evidence, *1447*, Sta.Cha.2/XX152
Balsall deed, n.d., E 210/5586
Balsall surveys, *1540*, E 315/361 (with Barston) (copy in W.C.R.O., Z146/3); *1581*, LR 2/185 (copy in W.C.R.O., MI 295)
Barford deeds, n.d., E 315/52/125; *1326*, E 326/2921
Bearley deeds, n.d., E 210/7462, E 315/41/265, E 315/43/155, E 315/45/106, E 326/772, 8453; *1249*, E 326/4566
Beaudesert deed, *1467*, E 40/9087; *1442-3*, E 315/41/99
Beausale (and Honiley) deed, *1209*, CP 25/1/242/8

Bedworth deeds, n.d., E 326/3608, E 315/35/232, E326/10790; *1270*, E 326/388; *1275-6*, E 326/11258; *?1282*, E 326/11257B; *1287*, E 326/10773; *1315*, E 326/11652; *1333*, E 326/10778

Bedworth memorandum of deeds, n.d., E 326/12950

Bedworth lease, *1538*, E 303/17/219

Bedworth special inquisition *1633-4*, E 178/5689

Berkswell inquisition post mortem, *1325*, C 134/90/16

Berkswell survey, *1553*, E 36/167

Berkswell accounts, *1455-6*, SC 6/1038/2

Bickenhill deeds, *1240*, CP 25/1/243/19; *1271-2*, CP 25/1/244/29

Binley leases, *1538*, E 303/16/36, 39, 57, 80

Binley particulars for grant, *1547*, E 318/38/2042

Binton deeds, n.d., E 315/37/213; E 315/40/21, 193; E 315/41/88, 149; E 315/44/218, 223; E 315/45/5, 39, 177, 201; E 315/46/156; E 315/47/233, 259; E 315/48/209; E 315/49/135; E 315/50/111, 125, 261; E 315/52/245

Bishopric of Worcester inquisition post mortem, *1353*, E 152/91

Bishop's Tachbrook (Tachbrook Mallory) terrier, n.d. (t. Hen. VIII), SC 11/917

Bishopton lands rental, *1446-7*, SC 11/819

Brinklow (and Brandon) deed, *1226*, CP 25/1/243/15

Brinklow lease, *1538*, E 303/16/86

Bubbenhall inquisition post mortem, *1391*, E 149/60/16

Bubbenhall lease, *1371*, E 42/219

Bubbenhall and Ladbroke accounts, *1385-6*, SC 6/1041/12

Budbrooke extent, *1290-1*, SC 12/14/87

Budbrooke inquisition post mortem (manor of La Grave), *1316*, C 134/47/18

Budbrooke deed, *1507*, E 315/34/148

Bulkington deed, E 40/4317

Bulkington (Weston-in-Arden) inquisitions post mortem, *1277*, C 133/17/5; *1299*, C 133/90/2

Bulkington (Barnacle) court roll, *1380*, SC 2/207/33

Caludon inquisitions post mortem, *1316*, C 134/97/5; (with Weston iuxta Cherington), *1425*, C 139/16/12

Castle Bromwich deed, *1360*, E 40/11983

Catesby family accounts, *1385-6*, SC 6/1041/2

Caldecote inquisition post mortem, *1364*, C 135/181/16

Chacombe Priory Register, E 315/378

Chesterton inquisition, *1293*, E 152/4

Chesterton inquisitions post mortem, *1300*, C 133/93/24; *1353*, C 135/123/5

Chilvers Coton deeds, n.d., E 326/1464, 3964; E 315/39/17; *1241*, E 315/38/89; *1356*, E 326/3731; *1221*, CP 25/1/243/11

Chilvers Coton lease, *1491*, E 303/17/241

Chilvers Coton (Arbury Priory) accounts, surveys and rentals, E 315/400; E 315/404

Churchover leases, *1535-7*, E 303/16/82, 60

Claverdon inquisition post mortem, *1325*, C 134/90/16

Claverdon deeds, n.d., E 315/38/41; E 315/39/13; E 326/1107, 4883, 11416

Claverdon (Songar) particulars for grants, *1545*, E 318/21/1121

Coleshill deed, *1200*, CP 25/1/242/4

Coleshill deed, n.d., E 326/10722

Coleshill survey, *1495*, SC 11/683

Coombe leases, *1537-8*, E 303/16/55, 36

Coughton confirmation of grant, *1241*, C 53/34

Coughton Forest proceedings, *1270-1*, E 32/229

Coventry deeds, *1208*, CP 25/1/242/8; *1244*, CP 25/1/243/20; *1262*, CP 25/1/244/26

Coventry Cathedral Priory Register, E 164/21 (copy in W.C.R.O., MI 409)

Cubbington deeds, n.d., E 315/31/34, E 315/37/56, E 315/48/71, E 210/5389, 8793, 9112; *1220-2*, E 210/318; *1273*, E 210/4582; *1341*, E 210/4443

Curdworth deed, *1224*, P.R.O., CP 25/1/243/13

Dunchurch (Toft) deed, n.d., E 326/10316

Elmdon deed, n.d., C 146/2025

Erdington inquisitions post mortem, *1282*, C 133/32; *1433*, C139/63

Erdington deed, *1282*, E 210/8735

Exhall (by Coventry) deeds, n.d., E 326/1225, 5806

Exhall (by Coventry) lease, *1528*, E 303/17/216

Exhall (by Coventry) particulars for grants, *1544*, E 318/6/201; *1546-7*, E 318/22/1190

Fillongley inquisitions post mortem, *1313*, C 134/13/1; (with Allesley) *1325*, C 134/91/27; *1436*, C 139/76

Foleshill particulars for grants, *1544*, E 318/22/1175

Forest Proceedings, *1261-1280*, E 32/227-231, *1300-1*, E 32/255

Fulbrook inquisition post mortem, *1478*, C 140/67

Grafton deed, *1247*, CP 25/1/243/21

Grafton particulars for grants, *1545*, E 318/20/999

Grandborough deed, n.d., E 315/378

Halford particulars for grants, *1545*, E 318/18/874

Hampton-in-Arden court roll, *1376*, SC 2/207/31

Hampton-in-Arden rental, *1588-9*, SC 12/26/67

Hampton-in-Arden inquisition, *1591*, E 178/2347

Hampton-in-Arden estate map, *1812*, MPEE/84 (copy in W.C.R.O., Z151)

Hampton-in-Arden lease, *1613*, LR 15/2/68

Hampton Lucy grant, *1549*, C 54/463

Hampton Lucy particulars for grant, *1557*, E 318/41/2191

Hartshill inquisition post mortem, *1276*, C 133/14/2

Haselor (Upton) deed, *1314*, CP 25/1/245/42

Haselor inquisition post mortem, *1316*, C 134/46/14

Haselor lease, *1534*, E 303/18/502

Haselor particulars for grants, *1544*, E 318/21/998

Hatton deeds, n.d., E 315/47/129; E 40/6377, 6947; *1309*, E 40/8284; *1516*, E 40/3952

Hatton King's Bench case, *1267*, KB 26/176, rots 4d, 27r

Hodnell deeds, n.d., E 40/4393, 7220

Honiley deed, *1209*, CP 25/1/242/8

Idlicote lease, *1527*, E 303/17/268

Inkberrow (Worcestershire) accounts, *1539-40*, SC 6/Hen VIII/5694

Kenilworth accounts, *1388-9*, DL 29/463/7539; *1438-9*, DL 29/463/7540; *1439-40*, DL 29/463/7541; *1440-1*, DL 29/463/7542; *1444-5*, DL 29/463/7545; *1446-7*, DL 29/463/7546; *1448-9*, DL 29/463/7547; *1460-1*, DL 29/463/7548; *1461-2*, DL 29/463/7549; *1461-2*, DL 29/463/7550; *1462-3*, DL 29/463/7551; *1463-4*, DL 29/463/7552; *1464-5*, DL 29/463/7553; *1465-6*, DL 29/463/7554; *1465-6*, DL 29/463/7555; *1468-9*, DL 29/463/7556; *1469-70*, DL 29/463/7557; *1470-1*, DL 29/463/7558; *1470-1*, DL 29/463/7559; *1471-2*, DL 29/463/7560; *1472-3*, DL 29/463/7561; *1474-5*, DL 29/463/7562; *1482-3*, DL 29/463/7563

Kenilworth petitions, *c.1324-5*, SC 8/55/2750, C 81/129/7129; *c.1322*, SC 8/161/8023

Kenilworth surveys, *c.1545*, SC 12/16/22; *1581*, LR 2/185 (copy in W.C.R.O., MI 295)

29/642/10424; *1491-2*, DL 29/642/10427; *1493-4*, DL 29/642/10428; *1496-7*, DL 29/642/10429; *1504-5*, SC 6/Hen VII/865; *1507-8*, SC 6/Hen VII/1345; *1510-11*, SC 6/Hen VIII/3683

Warwick earldom valor, *1526-7*, SC 12/16/47

Warwick earldom deed, *1555*, C 147/233

Weethley particulars for grants, *1543-4*, E 318/15/683

Wellesbourne deed, *1247*, CP 25/1/243/21

Weston-under Wetherley deeds, n.d., E 326/6029, E 315/44/216

Whichford deed, *1246-7*, CP 25/1/243/21

Wishaw inquisition post mortem, *1326*, C 134/102/6

Wolford deed, *1225*, CP 25/1/243/13

Wolston survey, n.d. (t. Edw. III), SC 11/696

Wolverton deeds, n.d., E 326/5928, 6310

Wolvey deed, *1342*, E 326/8950

Woodcote deed, *1412*, E 326/5441

Wootton Wawen inquisitions post mortem, *1337*, C 135/51/7; (Aspley) *1372*, C 135/224/4

Wootton Wawen deeds, *1246-7*, CP 25/1/243/21; n.d., E 315/32/107; E 315/48/125; E 315/49/41; E 326/5809; *1442-3*, E 315/41/99

Wootton Wawen survey of lands of alien priories, *1341-2*, E 372/187

Wootton Wawen (Offord) particulars for grants, *1543-4*, E 318/3/81

Wroxall petitions, n.d., SC 8/68/3357, SC 8/152/7586

Wroxall rental, *1327-8*, SC 11/697

The Queen's College, Oxford

Survey of Keresley's demesne woods, *1520-26*, 4 F 12a

Keresley leases, *1587*, 4 F 8; *1700*, 4 F 72

Shakespeare Birthplace Trust, Stratford-upon-Avon

Allesley deeds, *1326*, DR10/1; (copy), *1396-7*, ER1/65/455

Allesley survey of lands of William Nilder, *1441-2*, DR98/699c

Allesley (with Berkswell) will, *1486*, DR10/394

Alspath and Meriden deeds, n.d., DR10/531, 534; *1316*, DR10/543, 544; *c.1523-7*, DR10/1777; *1597*, DR10/560; (copies) n.d., ER1/63/293, 297; *1323-4*, ER1/63/294

Ashow deeds, n.d., DR18/1/54; *1431*, DR18/1/59

Asthill deeds, n.d., DR10/457; *1555*, DR10/781; *1573* and *1620*, DR10/421, 439-40

Baddesley Clinton deeds, *c.1200-1639*, DR3/1, 5, 11, 13, 14, 16-19, 21, 34, 40, 48, 50, 51, 53-6, 66, 67, 69, 71, 80, 86, 89, 93, 103, 104, 105, 111, 115, 134, 135, 158, 159, 163, 164, 170, 183, 184, 195, 196, 203, 204, 241, 245, 289, 290, 302, 303, 304, 309, 334, 336, 339, 344, 354, 357, 380, 391, 395-7; *1812*, DR422/34-35

Baddesley Clinton account rolls, *1442-58*, DR3/799, 800, 801, 802, 803, 804, 805

Baddesley Clinton court rolls, *1409-91*, DR3/781, 783, 785, 787, 793, 794, 795

Baddesley Clinton rental, n.d., DR3/807

Baginton deed, *1350*, DR10/24

Baginton accounts, *1423-6*, DR10/2119b; *1469-70*, DR10/2220

Bearley deed, *1317*, DR98/786; see also under Snitterfield

Beausale deed, n.d., DR10/33

Bentley deed, *1614*, ER3/2546

Bericote deed, *c.1235*, DR10/14

Berkswell deed, n.d., DR18/1/181

Berkswell (with Allesley) will, *1486*, DR10/394

Binley court roll, *1565-6*, DR10/2224

Bishop's Tachbrook deed, *1609*, DR3/528; for court rolls see under Coventry and Lichfield bishopric

Brinklow deeds, n.d., DR10/37-42, 191; *1262*, DR10/48; *1272*, DR10/49; *1500*, DR10/11

Brinklow survey of Coombe Abbey lands and woods, *c.1550*, DR37/box 114

Bubbenhall court roll, *1639*, CR18/30/6/1

Chesterton and Kington deeds, n.d., DR98/240, 245; *1287*, DR98/266; *1310*, DR98/278; *1314*, DR98/370; *1322*, DR98/300; *1330*, DR98/326a; *1344*, DR98/371; *1345*, DR98/373; *1474*, DR98/519; *1491*, DR98/540; *1520*, DR98/551; *1538*, DR98/577; *1568*, DR98/938

Chesterton lease, *1537*, DR98/573

Chesterton book of receipts and payments, *1632-3*, DR98/1708

Chesterton estate maps, n.d. (*18th. C.*) DR98/1823; *1697*, DR98/1817 (Kingston)

Claverdon estate survey, *1791*, DR473/28

Clopton deeds, *1279-80*, ER3/235/1-6; n.d., ER3/236-8, 240; *1604*, DR150/2/1

Compton Verney deed, n.d., DR98/6

Coombe Abbey deed, *1500*, DR10/117

Coombe Abbey survey of lands and woods, *c.1550*, DR37/box 114

Corley deeds, n.d., DR10/215, 216, 218, 219, 221, 222, 223; *1260*, DR10/217; *1537*, DR10/237

Coughton rentals, *1483-1500*, DR5/2191-2; *1571-2*, DR5/2196

Coundon survey (with parts of Bedworth, Exhall, Sowe), *c.1600*, DR91/2

Coventry and Lichfield bishopric estates court rolls, *1350*, DR10/2587; *1360*, DR10/2593; *1364*, DR10/2597; *1495*, DR10/2606

Coventry Cathedral Priory, Coventry Hundred Roll, *1280*, DR18/31/3

Coventry Cathedral Priory confirmation of grants, *c.1183*, DR10/258

Coventry deeds, *1386*, DR10/687; *1573* and *1620*, DR10/421, 439-40

Coventry (Pinley) deeds, *1383*, DR10/479; *1476*, DR10/489

Coventry (Stivichall) court rolls, *1443*, DR10/2446; *1461*, DR10/2460

Cubbington deed, *1377*, DR18/1/698

Curdworth (Dunton) deed, *1514*, DR18/1/260

Farnborough deed, *1375*, DR37/2116

Fillongley deeds, *1485*, DR18/10/46/3/1; *1577*, DR18/1/274; *1637*, DR18/1/304; *1698*, DR/18/3/20/17;

Gregory Leger Book, DR10/1409

Hampton-in-Arden deed, *1299*, DR37/2170

Hatton deeds, *1439*, DR37/2183; *1540*, DR10/2190

Henley-in-Arden deed, n.d., DR37/2199

Honiley rental, *1588*, DR18/3/25/9

Ingon deed, *1553*, ER3/261

Kenilworth petition, *1322*, DR10/516

Kenilworth Priory court rolls, *1478*, DR18/30/15/1; *1483*, DR18/30/15/4; *1483*, DR18/30/18/5; *1529-30*, DR18/30/15/11

Kineton estate map, *1778*, DR98/1825

Kingston (in Chesterton) estate map, *1697*, DR98/1817

Kington (in Claverdon) estate survey, *1575*, DR18/3/23

Langley court roll, *1383*, DR18/30/18/1

Lapworth deeds, *1369*, DR37/2247; *1456-7*, DR37/2251

Leamington Priors court roll, *1483*, DR18/30/18/5

Lighthorne accounts, *1389-90*, DR98/672a; *1390-1*, DR98/672b; *1392-3*, DR98/672d; *1395-6*, DR98/674; *1398-9*, DR98/674a; *1401-2*, DR98/675; *1400-1*, DR98/676

Lighthorne estate map, n.d. (*18th. C.*), DR98/1821

Lillington court roll, *1483*, DR18/30/15/5

Long Itchington estate map, *1687*, DR18/25/Bn.72

Maxstoke, translation of deed of *1347*, DR18/3/35/3

Maxstoke survey of woods, *1521-2*, ER1/63/280, f. 71

Maxstoke deed, *1690*, DR18/3/20/4

Meriden draft lease, *1597*, DR10/560

Nuthurst deeds, n.d., DR37/2285a/1, 8, 9, 22, 23; *1336*, DR37/2285a/36; *1357*, DR37/2285a/50; *1360*, DR37/2285a/52; *1420*, DR37/2285a/69; *1428*, DR37/2285a/73

Oldbury (in Mancetter) deed (copy), n.d., ER1/64/342

Oversley survey, *c.1320*, DR5/2246b

Oversley court rolls, *1318*, DR5/2245; *1319*, DR5/2246; *1332*, DR5/2249; *1353-4*, DR5/2250; *1385*, DR5/2251

Oversley abstract of court rolls, *1600-1740*, DR5/2356

Oversley accounts, *1387-8*, DR5/2255

Packington deed (copy), *1521*, ER1/63/280

Packwood deed, *1519*, DR12/4

Ratley cartulary, DR18/1/596

Ratley estate map, *1728*, DR18/25/Bn.38

Rowington survey, *1582*, DR473/291

Sambourne court rolls, *1480-1516*, DR5/2357-2363; *1574*, DR5/2368; *1598*, DR5/2387

Sherbourne deed, n.d., DR98/776

Snitterfield accounts, *1439*, DR10/2429; *1461*, DR38/1429

Snitterfield deeds, *1309*, ER2/396; *1315*, ER2/397; (with Bearley) *1668*, DR38/44, 45, 56; (with Bearley) *1692*, DR38/65; (with Bearley) *1816*, DR38/152

Snitterfield court rolls, *1560*, DR38/1434-6; *1672*, DR38/1477

Snitterfield valuation, *1765*, ER1/140

Solihull deeds, n.d., DR37/2337; *1431-71*, DR37/box 76; *1540*, DR37/2557; *1580*, DR37/1420; abstract of deeds, *1583* and *1604*, DR37/2574

Solihull surveys, *1601*, *1606*, DR37/box 116

Spernall deed, *1716*, DR5/1255

Stivichall deeds, *1418*, DR10/710-3; *1498*, DR10/738; *1556*, DR10/780

Stivichall accounts, *1480-2*, DR10/2474

Stivichall court rolls, *1488*, DR10/2484

Stivichall rental, *1429*, DR10/2436b

Stivichall surveys, *c.1580-90*, DR10/1786; *1787*, DR10/1431, with copy of map at PR63

Stoneleigh Abbey cartulary (fragment), DR10/1406

Stoneleigh deeds, n.d., DR10/258, 1017, 1079, 1299, 1300, 1762; DR18/1/831, 847, 850, 926; *1279*, DR10/459; *1546*, DR10/764; *1522*, DR10/997; *1468*, DR10/1189; *1529*, DR10/1194; *1571*, DR10/1212; *1326*, DR18/1/696; *1377*, DR18/1/698; *1290*, DR18/1/705; *1560*, DR18/1/745; *1270*, DR10/838; *1536*, DR18/1/970; *1535*, DR18/1/972a; *1559*, DR18/1/1061; *1578*, DR18/1/1070; n.d., DR18/1/1127, 1130; *1295*, DR18/1/1131; *1294*, DR18/1/1133; n.d., DR18/1/1137-9; *1313*, DR18/1/1140-4; *1327*, DR18/1/1147; *1536*, DR18/10/55/7; *1615*, DR18/10/41/3

Stoneleigh memorandum on common pasture, *1526*, DR10/1459

Stoneleigh accounts (copy), *1536*, DR18/1/733

Stoneleigh rental, *1556*, DR18/30/24/109

Stoneleigh court rolls, *1477*, DR18/30/24/13; *1481*, DR18/30/24/17; *1489*, DR18/30/24/24; *1500*, DR18/30/24/45; *1501*, DR18/30/24/50

Stoneleigh and Ashow certificate of survey and valor of woods, *1562*, DR18/30/24/128

Stoneleigh sales of woods, *1680*, DR18/3/28/4; *1688-97*, DR18/3/52/24, 26, 30, 31; *1687-9*, DR18/25/Bn.72

Stoneleigh conveyance of Cryfield, *1639*, DR18/10/27/1

Stoneleigh memorandum concerning lands in Cannock, Hurst and Stivichall, *1545-1627*, DR18/3/47/47

Stoneleigh legal papers relating to Wainbody/Cannock, *1622*, DR18/3/45/2

Stoneleigh copy of inquisition post mortem, n.d., DR10/1457

Stoneleigh estate map, *1766*, DR18/25/Bn.77

Stratford-upon-Avon (Ruin Clifford) deed, Clopton Cartulary (copy), *1514*, P54/14; see also under Clopton

Stratford-upon-Avon (Ruin Clifford) map (copy), *1599*, ER1/72

Studley deeds (copies), *1201*, ER1/61/19; n.d., ER1/61/26

Studley deed, *1640*, DR33/16

Studley survey, *1719*, DR36/2

Sutton Coldfield accounts, *1433-4*, BRT1/3/180

Tamworth particular of manor, *1673*, DR/76/2/21

Tanworth-in-Arden surveys, rentals and plans, *c.1432-c.1519*, DR37/box 74/1, 4, 6, 12, 16, 17, 19, 20, 22, 23, 24, 25, 26, 28, 29, 30; DR37/box 115

Tanworth-in-Arden surveys and map, *c.1500*, DR36/box 74/20

Tanworth-in-Arden accounts, *1377-1456*, DR37/boxes 107-8

Tanworth-in-Arden court rolls, including extracts, *?1290-1591*, DR37/box 109

Tanworth-in-Arden legal papers, t. Henry VI- Elizabeth I, DR37/box 82

Tanworth-in-Arden deeds, n.d., DR37/1, 24, 35, 43, 55, 64, 185, 191, 211, 306, 320, 407; *1309*, DR37/349; *1311*, DR37/352; *1321*, DR37/415; *1326*, DR37/460; *1328*, DR37/466; *1332*, DR37/499; *1339*, DR37/546; *1342*, DR37/580; *1345*, DR37/593; *1364*, DR37/702; *1368*, DR37/720; *1380*, DR37/756; *1385*, DR37/771; *1379*, DR37/775; *1388*, DR37/785; *1390*, DR37/794; *1398*, DR37/822; *1406*, DR37/838; *1407*, DR37/840; *1410*, DR37/853; *1417*, DR37/864; *1422*, DR37/877; *1448*, DR37/949; *1452*, DR37/956; *1473*, DR37/997; *1478*, DR37/1018; *1483*, DR37/1021; *1484*, DR37/1026; *1495*, DR37/1031, 1057; *1502*, DR37/1071; *1506*, DR37/1084; *1509*, DR37/1086; *1515*, DR37/1090; *1516*, DR37/1091; *1520*, DR37/1100; *1544*, DR37/1277; *1555*, DR37/1322; *1441*, ER1/1/13

Tanworth-in-Arden map of part of parish, n.d., DR134/8

Warwick estate survey, *1582*, DR473/291

Willoughby deed, n.d., DR98/867

Wolfhampcote deed, *1310*, DR37/2804

Wolverton estate map, *1820*, ER103/2

Woodcote deed, *1633*, DR3/534

Woodlow deed (St. Sepulchre's, Warwick), *1588*, DR37/2763

Wootton Wawen (Edstone) deeds, *1360-1*, DR37/3012-4

Wroxall rental, *1425-6*, DR37/box 112

Staffordshire County Record Office

Amington deeds, n.d., D593/A/1/22/3; *1319*, D593/A/1/22/10; *1366*, D593/A/1/23/4

Corley deed, *1607*, D1287/6/20

Curdworth deeds, n.d., D1287/6/18/5

Dordon and Grendon estate map, *1722*, D1176/A/39/11

Erdington deed, *1309*, D1287/6/20/21

Farnborough deeds, n.d., D593/A/1/8

Freasley, Lilleshall Abbey cartulary, D593/A/1/10/10

Grandborough rental, n.d., D641/1/4V/2

Kingsbury deed, n.d., D1287/6/37

Packington deed, n.d., D1287/6/18/28

Saltley deeds, *1444*, D1287/6/15/36; *1326*, D1287/6/18/43; *1440*, D1287/6/18/47

Shustoke deed, n.d., D593/A/1/24/1

Shuttington deed, *1718*, D948/4/4/19

Stafford earldom estates survey, *1385-6*, D641/1/2/3

Stafford earldom accounts, *1437-8*, D641/1/2/269; *1443-4*, D641/1/2/270; *1444-5*, D641/1/2/271; *1449-50*, D641/1/2/272; *1450-1*, D641/1/2/273; *1464-5*, D641/1/2/274; *1467-8*, D641/1/2/276; *1497-8*, D641/1/2/277

Sutton Coldfield and Curdworth deeds, n.d., D1287/6/18/5; *1339*, D1287/6/19/53; *1331*, D1287/6/19/54

Walsall Local History Centre

Bascote lease, *1466*, 276/63

Warwickshire County Record Office

The Office holds a large number of private collections, including large deposits from the Warwick Castle archives, the Newdigate family and the Throckmorton family, as well as records of public provenance, such as the tithe and enclosure awards. It has also obtained copies of many other records from both public repositories and private collections; those on microfilm are prefixed with the letters MI or P.G. and those in the form of photostats with the letter Z.

Alcester accounts, *1466-7*, CR1886/166a; *1504-5*, CR1886/183

Alcester deeds, n.d., CR1886/28, 61; *1317*, CR1886/81; *1355*, CR1998/K; *1563*, CR1886/box 417/96; *1573*, CR1886/box 105/1629; *1578*, CR1886/box 106/1649; *1598*, CR1886/box 108/1688; *1641*, CR1886/box 416/3; *1614*, CR1886/box 416/37/2; *1678*, *1706* and *1724*, CR1886/box 417/92

Alcester estate map, *1754*, CR1886/M9

Allesley accounts (with Aston Cantlow), *1467-8*, CR623/box 1

Allesley deeds (Holy Trinity) *1423-1627*, DR564/Ia/493, 506-7

Allesley deeds, *1572*, CR1150; *1654*, CR299/42; *1668-9*, CR299/49/1

Allesley survey, *1626*, CR623/box 14

Allesley tithe award, *1840*, CR569/3

Allesley estate map, *1808*, CR1709/75/10

Alne deed, *1316*, CR1886/292

Alne estate map (with Spernall), *c.1695*, CR1998/M15

Alne tithe award, *1838-41*, CR569/4

Alspath deed, *1555*, CR669/bundle G

Alveston enclosure award, *1772*, QS75/1

Ansley estate maps, *1759*, CR1169/36; *1869-70*, CR2755/1

Ansty estate map, *c.1600*, CR285/56

Ansty tithe award, *1850*, CR569/7

Arley tithe award, *1839*, CR569/8

Arrow estate map, *c.1800*, CR114A/190

Arrow estate map (Ragley), n.d., CR114/RagIII/6/ii, iii

Arrow tithe award, *1849*, CR569/9

Ashow tithe award, *1839*, CR569/13

Astley accounts, *1394-5*, CR136/C150

Astley deed, *1587*, CR136/C170

Astley estate maps, *1696*, CR136/M12, M9; n.d., CR764/107

Aston Cantlow accounts (with Allesley), *1467-8*, CR623/box 1

Aston Cantlow estate map, *1776*, CR882

Atherstone survey, *1547*, L2/86

Atherstone estate maps, *1763*, P8; *1848*, (copy in P.R.O., MPE 992), Z206/1-3(U)

Baddesley Clinton estate map (copy), *1699*, Z234

Baddesley Clinton tithe award, *1847*, CR328/2

Baddesley Ensor tithe award, *1849*, CR328/3

Baginton tithe award, *1841*, CR569/15

Balsall survey of the manor, *1538*, CR112/Ba.188/2

Balsall Common enclosure award, *1802*, QS75/52

Balsall estate maps, *1759-80*, CR621/5-8

Barcheston list of lands, n.d., (*?15th C.*), CR850/1

Barcheston lease, *1807*, CR580/41/2

Barford deed (with Walton), *1555*, CR133/30

Barford survey, *1574*, CR1886/Fifth Shelf/BB.634

Barford estate maps, *1810*, P30; (Westham), *c.1853*, CR1616/1

Barston map of Escott Wood, *1818*, CR1775

Barston tithe award, *1840*, CR328/4

Bearley estate maps, *c.1775*, CR611/607; *1867*, P48

Bearley deed, *1680*, CR611/653

Beaudesert tithe award, *1839*, CR569/23

Bedworth deeds, n.d., CR136/C109, C126; *1340*, CR136/C111a; *1440*, CR136/C107; *1696*, CR299/83/1; *1698*, CR410/box 25; *1702*, CR432/box 29

Bedworth sketch map, *1695*, CR764/104/4

Bedworth tithe award, *1840*, CR569/24

Bentley deed, n.d., CR136/C707

Bentley survey, *1759*, CR1169/36

Bentley estate maps (copies), *1740-2* and n.d., Z323/2, 3(U)

Bentley tithe award (with Shustoke), *1840*, CR328/42

Berkswell court roll, *1612-4*, MR21/2; *1665*, MR21/5

Berkswell enclosure award, *1808*, QS75/12/4-8 and CR172/1-2

Berkswell glebe terriers, *1612*, DR72A/1; *1635-82*, DR72A/2; *1690*, DR72A/5; *1701*, DR72A/6; *1734*, DR72A/7; *1705*, DR72A/8; *1711*, DR72A/9; *1736-1832*, DR72A/13-29

Berkswell tithe award, *1841*, CR569/29

Berkswell deeds, *1605*, CR2440/1/2-3; *1706*, CR299/136/1A-B; *1782*, CR299/80

Bickenhill deeds, *n.d. -1457*, CR593/1-126

Bickenhill tithe award, *1837*, CR328/6

Binton deeds, *1546*, CR114A/104/1; (including Binton Grove) *17th-19th C.*, CR912

Binley estate maps, *1778*, CR8/184; *1821-3*, D34

Binley deed, *1739*, CR8/47

Birdingbury deed, *1476*, CR1998/box 45/GG7

Bishop's Itchington - cartulary of Precentor of Lichfield Cathdral, n.d. (*?15th. C.*), CR1886/Cupboard 4/Top shelf/CAR/1

Bishop's Itchington tithe award, *1838*, CR569/135

Bishop's Tachbrook survey (Tachbrook Mallory), *1549-50*, CR1908/207

Bishop's Tachbrook deeds, *1573*, CR1908/104/1, CR1908/105/1-3

Bishop's Tachbrook estate map, *1710*, CR1886/M28

Bishopton estate accounts, *1413-4*, CR1911/14

Bishopton estate roll of evidences (referring to earlier documents), *1446-7*, CR1911/17

Bishopton court roll, *1464*, CR1911/12

Bishopton Hill Farm sale particulars, EAC/138; CR2433/31/125

Brailes estate map, *c.1585*, CR3231.

Brandon and Bretford tithe award, *1849*, CR569/274

Brinklow estate map, *1838*, MB Bri

Bubbenhall accounts (copy), *1580*, Z542//2/5 (original in the Bodleian Library)

Bubbenhall copy of estate map, *1726*, Z414(U) and related enclosure award, Z413(Sm) (original in the John Rylands University Library of Manchester)

Budbrooke accounts, *1403-1435*, CR895/8/2, 3, 4, 5, 10, 11, 12 ,13, 14, 19

Budbrooke survey, *1589-90*, CR895/80/1

Budbrooke rentals and surveys, *1592-1788*, CR895/18

Budbrooke estate maps, *1721*, CR895/19; *1788*, CR895/101

Caldecote tithe award, *1839*, CR569/57

Chadshunt tithe award, *1838*, CR569/60

Chesterton (Kingston) map, *1697* (copy), Z228(U)

Chilvers Coton deeds, n.d., CR136/C300, C410, C716, C725, C731, C734, C744a, C777; *1234*, CR136/C145; *1253-4*, CR136/C717; *1284*, CR136/C724; *1296*, CR136/C729; *1296*, CR136/C739; *1319*, CR136/C746; *1321-2*, CR136/C747; *1332*, CR136/C756a; *1337*, CR136/C759; *1341*, CR136/C760-C761; *1371*, CR136/C775; *1375*, CR136/C776; *1392*, CR136/C786; *1468*, CR136/C420a; *1481*, CR136/C309; *1516*, CR136/C798; *1532*, CR440/12; *1538-9*, CR136/C313; *1587*, CR136/C341; *1600*, CR136/C361; *1606*, CR136/C1098; *1610*, CR136/172a

Chilvers Coton description of bounds, n.d., CR136/C1139

Chilvers Coton rentals, n.d., CR136/C1250; *1601-2*, CR136/C1030

Chilvers Coton accounts (with Astley), *1394-5*, CR136/C150

Chilvers Coton surveys, *1685*, CR136/V13; *1681-5*, CR136/V122; (with Bedworth), *1702*, CR432/box 29; *1597-1713*, CR764/104/1

Chilvers Coton maps, n.d., CR136/M10, M11, M18, M83A, M94, M95, M96, M97A, CR319/13; *1681*, CR764/104/4; *1807*, CR764/107

Claverdon tithe award, *1838*, CR569/65

Clifton-on-Dunsmore (Newton) deed, n.d., CR1886/222

Coleshill plan of parish (copy), *1843-4*, Z436(U); Parish Records Survey Book (copy), *1845*, P.G. 3354

Compton Verney map (copy), *1738*, Z228/2(U)

Corley deeds, *1561*, CR136/C708; *1688*, CR1371

Corley rent roll (with Astley), *1418-9*, CR136/153

Corley tithe award, *1839*, CR569/75

Coughton deeds, n.d., CR1886/15, 62, CR1998/A1/3, CR1998/A4/3 ,CR1998/B2, CR1998/B3, CR1998/B6, CR1998/F1, CR1998/G3, CR1998/J2/32, 34; *1339*, CR1998/G7; *1355*, *1430*, CR1998/K; *1569*, CR1886/1582

Coughton maps, *1695*, CR1998/M7; *1746*, CR1998/M29; *1754*, CR1886/M9; *1838-9*, CR1998/M23-M24

Coughton accounts, *1599-1600*, CR1998/box 61/folder4/16.

Coughton, King's - see Alcester

Coundon deeds, *1574*, CR299/89/5; *1649*, CR299/89/8; *1668*, CR1097/87

Coundon and Keresley enclosure award, *1848*, QD75/36

Coventry, St. Michael and St. John tithe award, *1846*, CR569/86

Coventry, Holy Trinity tithe award, *1848*, CR569/81

Coventry deeds (Holy Trinity Guild), n.d., DR564/I(a)/402, 403, 405; *1351*, DR564/I(a)/418; *1354*, DR564/I(a)/419; *1373*, DR564/I(a)/429; *1439*, DR564/I(a)/437; *1446*, DR564/I(a)/476; *1593*, DR564/I(a)/440; *1599*, DR564/I(a)/441

Coventry (Holy Trinity Guild) volume of maps, CR1709/192

Coventry (Drapers' Company) volume of maps, CR929/2

Craven estate volume of surveys and maps, *1778*, CR8/184; estate maps, *1821-3*, D34

Cubbington enclosure award, *1768*, CR1218/19/1

Curdworth (Dunton) tithe award, *1846*, CR328/13

Dosthill tithe award, *1839*, CR328/26

Ettington deeds, *1246-59*, CR229/box 18/3/1-2; *1550-1*, CR229/box 18/3/36; *1653*, D19/418; estate map, *c.1795*, CR229/117/9 and 11

Exhall (by Coventry) estate map, *1829*, CR1175

Exhall (by Coventry) tithe award, *1847*, CR569/98

Fenny Compton deeds, n.d., L1/1, 2, 4, 5, 12

Fillongley list of woods, n.d., CR1886/3370

Fillongley deeds, *1598*, CR2981 (uncatalogued); *1663*, CR562/3

Fillongley tithe award, *1843*, CR569/102

Foleshill tithe award, *1841*, CR569/105

Frankton tithe award, *1840*, CR569/121A

Freasley tithe award, *1849*, CR328/38

Grafton enclosure award, *1814*, QS75/47

Grandborough terrier of fields, n.d. (*18th. C.*), CR1709/320/3

Grendon tithe award, *1848*, CR328/18

Grendon arbitration award, *1571*, CR762/35

Hampton-in-Arden estate map (copy), *1812*, Z151

Hampton-in-Arden tithe award, including Balsall, *1841*, CR328/22

Hampton Lucy estate map and survey, *1736*, L6/1035-6

Hampton Lucy tithe award, *1846*, CR569/122

Hartshill and Ansley enclosure award, *1808-11*, CR491

Haseley deed (referring to Hatton), *1457*, CR1243/7

Haseley tithe award, *1841*, CR569/125

Haseley estate map (with Hatton), *1728*, P43

Haseley survey (with Hatton), *1727*, CR611/214

Haselor deeds, *1537*, CR1998/box 45/GG7/1-6; *1607*, CR1998/box 82/1-26; *1619*, CR1998/box 71(1); *1626*, D19/475; *1791*, CR114/114A

Haselor estate map and sales particulars, *1862*, EAC/068/1

Haselor enclosure award, *1767*, QS75/56

Hatton estate map and survey, *1728*, P43

Hatton survey (with Haseley), *1727*, CR611/214

Hatton tithe award, *1841*, CR569/126

Hatton enclosure award (with Haseley and Wroxall), *1835*, QS75/57

Honiley court roll (copy), *1694*, Z421(Sm)

Honiley deed, *1742*, CR1311/18/1

Hurley enclosure award, *1822*, CR416/8

Ilmington (Lark Stoke) court roll, *1472*, CR1911/13

Kenilworth survey, *1591*, CR576/1

Kenilworth estate map, *1692*, CR143A

Kenilworth tithe award, *1849*, CR569/139

Keresley deeds, *1681*, DR468/229, D19/493

Keresley enclosure award (with Coundon), *1848*, QS75/36

Keresley tithe award, *1847*, CR569/84

Kineton rental, *1440-1*, CR1886/263

Kineton copy of survey, n.d., CR1886/2373

Kineton enclosure award (Little Kineton), *1733*, QS9/11

Kingsbury tithe award, *1847*, CR328/27; enclosure award (Hurley), *1822*, CR416/8

Kingswood enclosure award, *1808*, QS75/70

Kinwalsey deeds, *1566-8*, CR650; *1569*, CR669

Knowle deeds, *1556*, CR1886/2252; *1637*, CR1886/2363

Knowle estate map, *1816*, CR982

Knowle enclosure award, *1820*, CR487

Ladbroke deed, *1620* (copy), CR1849/2

Ladbroke estate map (copy), *1639*, Z358 (original in Derby Borough Library, Palmer-Morwood collection)

Lapworth deed, *1569*, CR1008/43

Lapworth tithe award, *1843*, CR328/30

Langley enclosure award, *1835*, QS75/28

Lee (in Bishop's Tachbrook) deeds, *1415*, CR26/A/XVI; *1596*, CR1886/7097

Leek Wootton tithe award, *1846*, CR569/277

Leigh estate maps (copies), *1597*, Z139/1-2(U), Z141/1(U); *1766-9*, Z142(L); *1766-71*, Z149(L)

Lighthorne tithe award, *1844*, CR569/157

Lillington enclosure award, *1730*, QS9/11

Long Compton deed, *1477*, list of Castle Ashby MSS., no. 460

Lyndon court roll, *1464*, CR1911/12

Mancetter park estate map, *1775*, CR258/340

Maxstoke tithe award, *1846*, CR328/31

Maxstoke estate map (copy), n.d., Z309/2(U) (original at Packington Hall)

Meriden (see also Alspath) deeds, *1531*, CR299/207; *1455-1614*, CR669/bundle G; *1587*, list of Finch-Knightley papers at Packington Hall, 3/3/8; *1656-68*, list of Finch-Knightley papers at Packington Hall, 3/3/11, 13

Meriden estate maps, *1789*, CR2381; n.d., Z309/2(U)

Meriden survey (copy), n.d., MI 367/4

Milverton enclosure award, *1805*, QS75/77

Minworth estate maps (copies), *1589*, Z567(U)

Monks' Kirby tithe award, *1842*, CR569/141

Moreton Morrell tithe award, *1846*, CR569/171

Moreton Morrell estate map (copy), *1767*, Z140/2(U)

Morton Bagot estate maps, *1820-1*, CR1094

Napton deeds, n.d., CR1284/71/18-21, CR1284/72/2, CR1248/73/4; *1393*, CR1284/71/22

Newbold-on-Avon (Little Lawford) lease, *1348*, CR162/113

Nuneaton tithe award, *1842*, CR569/184

Nuneaton and Stockingford enclosure award, *1806*, QS75/83

Nuneaton survey (copy), *1543*, Z364(Sm)

Nuneaton deed, *1690*, CR136/C704

Nuthurst tithe award, *1839*, CR328/24

Offchurch tithe award, *1846-8*, CR569/187

Oldbury estate map, *1728*, CR604

Oversley estate map, *1747*, CR1998/M12; map of Oversley Lodge Farm, *1872*, CR1998/M27

Packington tithe award, CR328/22

Packington deeds, list of Finch-Knightley papers at Packington Hall, *1536*, 1/2; *1547*, 1/14; n.d. (*13th.C.*), Bundle J/2/71; copies of deeds of various dates, Bundle J/2/88

Packington estate map (copy), *1777*, Z301/1(U)

Packington estate survey, *1761*, Z314(Sm)

Packington estate map and survey (copies), *1818*, Z296(U), Z313(Sm)

Packwood enclosure award, *1819*, QS75/85

Packwood tithe award, *1839*, CR328/33

Packwood estate map (copy), *1723*, Z230(L)

Pailton tithe award, *1842*, CR569/150

Pinley deeds, *c.1220*, CR284/1; *1481*, CR1008/32

Princethorpe deeds, n.d., CR314/1, 9

Princethorpe enclosure award (copy), *1763*, CR829/140

Princethorpe map of intended wood (copy), n.d. (*c.1763*), Z8/14

Radford Semele tithe award, *1843*, CR569/195

Ratley deeds, *1669-1848*, CR45/1

Ratley estate maps, *1791*, CR620/1; *1808*, CR45/bn3/1

Rowington deeds, *1491*, CR1008/36; *1509*, CR1008/43; *1522*, CR1008/45; *1707*, CR1008/107

Rowington tithe award, *1849*, CR569/197

Rowington enclosure award (with Bushwood), *1824*, QS75/92

Rugby deed, *1718*, D19/681

Ryton-on-Dunsmore deeds, *1335*, DR350/3; *1608*, CR2981 (not catalogued)

Ryton-on-Dunsmore court roll, *1497*, MR19

Ryton-on-Dunsmore terrier, *1735*, CR155

Salford Priors estate map, *1749*, CR1296.

Sambourne estate map, *1746*, CR1998/M11

Shilton tithe award, *1843-4*, CR569/202

Shuckburgh deeds, n.d., CR1248/70/2, CR1248/71/2-4; *1498*, CR1248/68/7

Shustoke deeds, n.d., Z551/4-5(Sm) (copies of deeds in a private collection); *1632-67*, CR1184/box 1

Shustoke tithe award, *1840*, CR328/42

Shustoke estate map (copy), *1703*, Z646/10(U)

Snitterfield tithe award, *1840*, CR569/206

Solihull deeds, *1595*, CR1998/box 72; *1632*, CR1886/9424; *1666*, CR299/288/2; *1719*, CR299/195/1A; *1742-60*, CR1291/100/1-6

Solihull survey (Forshaw), *1652*, CR645/19

Solihull enclosure award, *1843*, QS75/102

Solihull tithe award, *1837*, CR328/44

Solihull sketch map of Longdon and Henwood, n.d., CR1886/2372

Songar estate map, *1826*, CR449/1/3

Southam deeds, *1262*, L1/34; *1603*, CR1849/2; *1620*, CR1248/bundle 141/7

Southam estate maps, *1775*, CR927/1; *1778*, CR8/184

Sowe tithe award, *1844*, CR569/207

Spernall deeds, n.d., CR1998/box 42/CC2, CR1998/box 42/AA7/1-2, CR1998/box 42/AA2, CR1998/box 42/AA5/1-3; *1549*, CR1998/box 42/DD2; *1589*, CR1998/box 43

Spernall estate map, *c.1695*, CR1998/M15

Spernall tithe award, *1839*, CR569/208

Stafford earldom accounts in Maxstoke MSS., CR2981 (uncatalogued)

Stivichall estate map (copy), *1775*, Z279(Sm)

Stoke tithe award, *1842*, CR569/209

Stoneleigh, copies of estate maps, *1597*, Z139/1-2(U), Z141(U); *1766-7*, Z142(L)

Stoneleigh abstract of Cryfield deeds, CR561/2

Stoneleigh tithe award, *1843*, CR569/213

Stoneton (Northants.) estate map (copy), *1634*, Z176/1/1

Stoneythorpe (in Long Itchington) deed, *1621*, CR1470/box 2/bundle 7

Stoneythorpe (in Long Itchington) estate map, *1754*, CR1470/box 2

Stretton-on-Dunsmore deed, *1608*, CR2981 (not catalogued)

Studley enclosure award, *1824*, QS75/110

Studley tithe award, *1845*, CR569/235

Sutton Coldfield enclosure award, *1851*, QS75/111

Sutton Coldfield deed (copy), *1316*, Z75/3

Tamworth estate map (copy), *1810*, Z212/2

Tanworth-in-Arden tithe award, *1839*, CR328/53

Thornton (in Ettington) court rolls, *1431-56*, CR1911/6, 8

Thornton (in Ettington) estate map, *1765*, CR711

Thurlaston estate map (copy), *1717*, Z8/1

Tysoe estate map (copy), *1765-71*, Z275(Sm)

Tyose court roll (copy), *1498*, microfilm of Castle Ashby MSS., MI167/1, roll 579

Ufton estate map and survey (copies), *1695*, *1672*, Z181(U) (originals in Bodleian Library, Balliol College, 68/252)

Ufton tithe award, *1844*, CR569/249

Walton deeds, n.d., CR133/1; *1551*, CR133/30

Walton estate map, *1728*, CR750/1

Wappenbury, Weston-under-Wetherley survey, *1668*, CR1097/87

Wasperton accounts, *1382-3*, CR2238/1

Warmington deeds, *1613*, CR404/12; *1654*, D19/757

Warwick (see also Woodcote and Woodlowe) estate accounts, *1394-5*, CR1886/474; *1398-9*, CR1886/481; *1400-1*, CR1886/475; *1401-2*, CR1886/482; *1422-3*, CR1886/485; *1425-6*, CR1886/487

Warwick grant (St. Sepulchre's Priory), *1546*, CR26/1

Warwick survey, *1576*, CR1886/BB185

Warwick estate maps of Wedgnock Park, *1682*, CR1886/M3; *1750*, CR1886/M5; *1760*, CR1886/M312; *1774*, CR1886/M4; *1788*, CR1886/M24A

Warwick estate maps including Lee (copies), *1690*, Z204/2(U), *1743*, Z327/1(U)

Warwick survey of Wedgnock Park, late sixteenth century, CR1886/2593

Warwick survey of Wedgnock, *1602*, CR1886/2584

Warwick survey, *1575*, CR1886/Cupboard 4/18

Warwick estate receipts and payments, *1614-5*, CR1886/box 411/1; *1643-4*, CR1886/box 411/5; *1664*, CR1886/box 411/48

Weddington tithe award, *1840*, CR569/258

Weethley tithe award (part of Kinwarton), *1839*, CR569/140

Wellesbourne estate map, *1735*, CR611/715/2

Wellesbourne tithe award, *1848*, CR569/259

Wellesbourne Hastings and Newbold Pacey map of common fields, *1733*, CR750/2

Whitacre court roll, *1498*, CR440/1

Whitnash deed, *1321*, CR1908/177/6

Wishaw court rolls, *1428* (copy), MR1/Folder 1; *1507*, MR2/Folder 13

Wishaw tithe award, *1845*, CR328/58

Whichford Wood map, *1817*, CR1635/410

Wolvey enclosure award, *1797*, CR1124/1

Woodcote deeds, n.d., CR26/1(1)bundle A/I; *1437*, CR26/1(1)bundle A/W18; *1439*, CR26/1(1)bundle A/W20; *1658*, CR26/1(2)/bundle B/27

Woodcote rental, *1458*, CR26/XXXII

Woodcote sketch map, c.*1815*, CR1709/320/6

Woodcote and Woodlowe estate map, *1711*, CR217/1

Woodlowe lease, *1430*, CR26/W16-17

Woodlowe accounts, *1462-3*, CR556/212

Woodlowe deed, *1573*, CR1886/4849

Wootton Wawen tithe award, *1842*, CR569/278

Wootton Wawen deeds, n.d., CR712/2; *1384*, CR712/8

Wootton Wawen estate maps (copy), *1736*, CR195/28; (Edstone), *1827*, CR1663/20

Wootton Priory cartulary entries relating to Wootton Wawen Priory (copy - original with the Abbey of Conches), MI 332

Wroxall grant, *1542*, CR113/Wr3

Wroxall estate survey, *1714*, CR113/197

Westminster Abbey

The Abbey held the manor of Knowle, which included some land in the parish of Solihull.

Knowle survey, n.d. (t. Henry IV), 620

Knowle rentals, *1448-9*, 621; n.d., 63,959

Knowle grant, *1292*, 3,246

Knowle accounts, *1293*, 27,692; *1293-4*, 27,693; *1294-5*, 27,694; *1298-9*, 27,695; *1301-2*, 27,699; *1304-5*, 27,704; *1386-7*, 27,711

Longdon (in Solihull) lease, *1373*, 607

William Salt Library, Stafford

Bishopric of Coventry and Lichfield accounts, *1472-3*, Salt Roll 335 (1)

Dordon and Grendon deeds, *1302*, *1315*, H.M Chetwynd, bundle 3

Grendon deed, *1567*, H.M. Chetwynd, bundle 95

Meriden deed, *1513*, H.M. Chetwynd, bundle 8

Printed Sources

These are listed in alphabetical order by title.

Abstract of the bailiffs' accounts of the monastic and other estates in the county of Warwick under the supervision of the Court of Augmentation for the year ending at Michaelmas, 1547 (ed. W.B. Bickley, Dugdale Society, II, 1923)

An Accurate Map of the County of Warwick Divided into its Hundreds (T. Jefferys, n.d., c.1787)

The Beauchamp Cartulary Charters 1110-1268 (ed. E. Mason, Pipe Roll Society, New Series, XLIII, 1971-73)

Bracton on the Laws and Customs of England, Volume Three (S.E. Thorne, 1977)

Calendar of Ancient Deeds

Calendar of Charter Rolls

Calendar of Charters and Documents relating to Selborne and its Priory preserved in the Muniment Room of Magdalen College, Oxford (ed. W.D. Macray, Hampshire Record Society, 1891)

Calendar of Close Rolls

Calendar of Inquisitions Post Mortem

Calendar of Inquisitions Miscellaneous

Calendar of Letters and Papers of Henry VIII

Calendar of Patent Rolls

W. Camden, *Britain* (translated into English by P. Holland, 1610)

Cartularium Saxonicum (ed. W. de G. Birch, 3 vols., 1885-93)

Cartulary of the Abbey of Old Wardon (Bedfordshire Historical Record Society, XIII, 1930)

The Cartulary of the Knights of St. John of Jerusalem in England, Part 2 Prima Camera Essex (ed. M. Gervers, British Academy Records of Social and Economic History, New Series, 23, 1996)

The Charters of the Anglo-Norman Earls of Chester c.1071-1237 (ed. G. Barraclough, The Record Society of Lancashire and Cheshire, CXXVI, 1988)

Charters of the Honour of Mowbray 1107-1191 (D.E. Greenway, British Academy Records of Social and Economic History, new series, i, 1972)

Chertsey Cartularies (Surrey Record Society, Vol II, part 1, 1958)

Collections for a History of Staffordshire (William Salt Archaeological Society)

The Crawford Collection of Early Charters and Documents (ed. A.S. Napier and W.H. Stevenson, 1895)

Curia Regis Rolls

Descriptive Catalogue of the Charters and Muniments...at Berkeley Castle (I.H. Jeayes, Bristol, 1892)

Domesday Book. 23. Warwickshire (ed. J. Morris, 1976) (abbreviated to *DB* in references)

Domesday Book. 14. Oxfordshire (ed. J. Morris, 1978)

Domesday Book. 16. Worcestershire (ed. J. Morris, F. and C. Thorn, 1982)

The Domesday of Inclosures 1517-18, Volume II (ed. I.S. Leadam, Royal Historical Society, 1897)

The Early Records of Medieval Coventry (ed. P.R. Coss, 1986)

Ecclesiastical Terriers of Warwickshire Parishes (ed. D.M. Barratt, 2 vols., Dugdale Society, XXII, 1955 and XXVII, 1971)

English Historical Documents c.500-1042 (ed. D. Whitelock, second edition, 1979)

English Historical Documents Volume Three 1189-1327 (ed. H. Rothwell, 1975)

Formulare Anglicanum (ed. T. Madox, 1702) (abbreviated to *Formulare* in references)

The Great Roll of the Pipe for the Ninth Year of the Reign of King Richard The First. Michaelmas 1197. (Pipe Roll 43) (ed. D.M. Stenton, Pipe Roll Society, new series, VIII, 1931)

The History and Antiquities of the County of Leicester, Vol. I, Part II (J. Nichols, 1815, republished 1971)

Inquisitions ad quod dampnum

The Itinerary of John Leland in or about the years 1535-1543 (ed. L. Toulmin Smith, 11 parts, 1907-10)

John of Gaunt's Register, 1379-1383 (ed. J.C. Lodge and R. Somerville, 2 vols. Camden Third Series, LVI-LVII, 1937)

The Kenilworth Cartulary (ed. C. Watson, University of London Ph. D. thesis, c.1968, copy in W.C.R.O., MI 238)

The Knights Hospitallers in England (ed. L.B. Larking, Camden Society, LXV, 1857)

Landboc sive registrum monasterii beatae mariae virginis et sancti cenhelmi de Winchelcumba (ed. D. Royce, 2 vols., 1892-1903)

The Langley Cartulary (ed. P.R. Coss, Dugdale Society, XXXII, 1980) (abbreviated to *LC* in references)

The Manuscripts of the late Reginald Rawdon Hastings, Vol. I (Historical Manuscripts Commission, 1928)

A Map of Warwickshire Drawn from an Actual Survey taken in the Years 1787-1788-1789 by Willm. Yates & Sons (1793)

Medieval deeds of Bath and District (ed. B.R. Kemp, Somerset Record Society, 73, 1974)

Ministers' Accounts of the Warwickshire Estates of the Duke of Clarence, 1479-80 (ed. R.H. Hilton, Dugdale Society, XXI, 1952)

Monasticon Anglicanum (W. Dugdale, ed. J. Caley, H. Ellis, and B. Bandinel, 6 vols., 1849) (abbreviated to *Monasticon* in references)

Reading Abbey Cartularies, Vol I (ed. B.R. Kemp, Camden Fourth Series, Vol. 31, 1986)

'Some Records of Northill College, No. II', (C.G. Chambers, Bedfordshire Historical Record Society, Vol 2, 1914, pp. 111-125)

Records of Rowington, Vol. I (J.W. Ryland, 1896)

Records of the Templars in England in the Twelfth Century (B.A. Lees, 1935)

Records of Wroxall Abbey and Manor, Warwickshire (J.W. Ryland, 1903)

Red Book of Worcester (4 parts, ed. M. Hollings, Worcestershire Historical Society, 1934-50) (abbreviated to *RBW* in references)

Registrum Malmesburiense, (ed. J.S. Brewer and C.T. Martin, Rolls Series, Vol II, 1880, reprinted 1965)

Registrum sive Liber irrotularius et consuetudinarius Prioratus Beatae Mariae Wigorniensis (ed. W.H. Hale, Camden, 91, 1865)

Rolls of the Justices in Eyre for Gloucestershire, Warwickshire, and Staffordshire, 1221, 1222 (ed. D.M. Stenton, Selden Society, LIX, 1940)

Rotuli Parliamentorum (6 vols., Record Commission, no date)

Rotuli Parliamentorum Anglie Hactenus Inediti MCCLXXIX-MCCCLXXIII, (ed. H.G. Richardson and G. Sayles, Camden, Third Series, LI, 1935)

Select Cases in the Court of King's Bench under Edward I, Vol. II (ed. G.O. Sayles, Selden Society, LVII, 1938)

Select documents of the English lands of the Abbey of Bec (ed. M. Chibnall, Camden, Third Series, LXXIII, 1951)

Sir Christopher Hatton's Book of Seals (ed. L.C. Loyd and D.M. Stenton, 1950) (abbreviated to *Book of Seals* in references)

Statutes of the Realm (11 vols., 1810-28)

The Stoneleigh Leger Book (ed. R.H. Hilton, Dugdale Society Publications, XXIV, 1960) (abbreviated to *SLB* in references)

Taxatio Ecclesiastica (Record Commission, 1802)

Valor Ecclesiasticus (Record Commission, 1817)

Walter of Henley and other treatises on estate management and accounting (ed. D. Oschinsky, 1971)

Warwickshire Feet of Fines (ed. F.C. Wellstood, 3 vols., Dugdale Society, XI, 1932, XV, 1939, and XVIII, 1943) (abbreviated to *FF* in references)

The Warwickshire Hundred Rolls of 1279-80: Stoneleigh and Kineton Hundreds (ed. T. John, British Academy, Records of Social and Economic History, New Series XIX, 1992) (abbreviated to *HR* in references)

Secondary works: books (including theses and typescripts/manuscripts)

G.W.O. Addleshaw, *The Beginnings of the Parochial System*, St. Anthony's Hall Publications No. 3 (third edition, 1970)

G.W.O. Addleshaw, *The Development of the Parochial System from Charlemagne (768-814) to Urban II (1088-1099)*, St. Anthony's Hall Publications No. 6 (second edition, 1970)

D.M.K. Agutter, *Meriden: Its People and Houses* (1990)

N.W. Alcock, *Warwickshire Grazier and London Skinner 1532-1555: The account book of Peter Temple and Thomas Heritage*, British Academy Records of Social and Economic History, New Series, IV (1981)

ed. M. Aston, D. Austin, and C. Dyer, *The Rural Settlements of Medieval England* (1989)

R. Atkyns, *The Ancient and Present State of Gloucestershire* (1712, republished 1974)

ed. A.R.H. Baker and R.A. Butlin, *Studies of Field Systems in the British Isles* (1973)

B. Bartlett, *Manduessedum Romanorum: Being the History and Antiquities of the Parish of Manceter [including the hamlets of Hartshill, Oldbury, and Atherstone], and also of the adjacent parish of Ansley, in the County of Warwick* (1791)

S.R. Bassett, *The Wootton Wawen Project: interim report no. 2* (University of Birmingham, 1984)

S.R. Bassett, *The Wootton Wawen Project: interim report no. 3* (University of Birmingham, 1985)

S.R. Bassett, *The Wootton Wawen Project: interim report No. 4* (University of Birmingham, 1986)

S.R. Bassett, *The Wootton Wawen Project: interim report No. 5* (University of Birmingham, 1987)

S.R. Bassett, *The Wootton Wawen Project: interim report no. 7* (University of Birmingham, 1989)

S.R. Bassett, *The Wootton Wawen Project: interim report no.8* (University of Birmingham, 1990)

ed. S. Bassett, *The Origins of Anglo-Saxon Kingdoms* (1989)

G.R. Beard, *Soil Survey Record No. 81: Soils in Warwickshire V: Sheet SP27/37 (Coventry South)* (1984)

J.J. Belton, *The Story of Nuthurst cum Hockley Heath, Warwickshire* (1948)

Birmingham City Council Planning andArchitecture Department, *Archaeology in Sutton Park* (leaflet, no date)

J. Blair, *Early Medieval Surrey: Landholding, Church and Settlement before 1300* (1991)

ed. H.C. Bowen and P.J. Fowler, *Early Land Allotment*, British Archæological Reports (British Series), 48 (1978)

J. Campbell, *The Anglo-Saxons* (1982)

C.R. Cheney, *Handbook of Dates for Students of English History* (Royal Historical Society, London, 1978)

P.R. Coss, *Lordship, knighthood and locality: A study in English society c.1180-c.1280* (1991)

P. Colebourn, *Hampshire's Countryside Heritage: Ancient Woodland* (Hampshire County Council, 1983)

W. Cooper, *Wootton Wawen: its history and records* (1936)

County of Warwick, yearbook for 1865

H.C. Darby, *Domesday England* (1977)

ed. H.C. Darby and E.M.J. Campbell, *The Domesday Geography of South-east England* (1962)

H.C. Darby and I.B. Terrett, *The Domesday Geography of Midland England* (second edition, 1971)

G.R.C. Davis, *Medieval Cartularies of Great Britain: a short catalogue* (1958)

W. Dugdale, *The Antiquities of Warwickshire* (second edition, 2 vols., 1730)

G.H. Dury, *The Face of the Earth* (fourth edition, 1976)

C. Dyer, *Lords and Peasants in a Changing Society: The Estates of the Bishopric of Worcester 680-1540* (1980)

C. Dyer, *Hanbury: Settlement and Society in a Woodland Landscape*, University of Leicester Department of English Local History Occasional Papers, Fourth Series, Number 4 (1991)

C. Dyer, *Everyday Life in Medieval England* (1994)

C. Dyer and C.J. Bond, *Compton Murdak. Deserted Medieval Settlement and its Historical and Archæological Context* (typescript, 1994)

E. Ekwall, *The Concise Oxford Dictionary of English Place-Names* (fourth edition, 1960)

ed. A.M. Emmet and J. Heath, *The Moths and Butterflies of Great Britain and Ireland*, Vol. 7, Part 1 (1990)

F.G. Emmison, *Archives and Local History* (1966)

A.M. Everitt, *Continuity and Colonization: the evolution of Kentish settlement* (1986)

H.P.R. Finberg, *The Early Charters of the West Midlands* (second edition, 1972)

W.J. Ford, *The Pattern of Settlement in the Central Region of the Warwickshire Avon* (M.A. thesis, University of Leicester, 1973)

ed. H.S.A. Fox, *The Origins of the Midland Village* (papers prepared for a discussion session at the Economic History Society's annual conference, Leicester, April, 1992)

M. Gelling, *Signposts to the Past*, (1978, second, revised edition, 1988)

M. Gelling, *Place-Names in the Landscape* (1984)

M. Gelling, *The Place-Names of Shropshire - Part One: The Major Names of Shropshire* (1990)

M. Gelling, *The West Midlands in the Early Middle Ages* (1992)

J.E.B. Gover, A. Mawer and F.M. Stenton, *The Place-Names of Warwickshire* (1936)

H.L. Gray, *English Field Systems* (1915)

ed. H.E. Hallam, *The Agrarian History of England and Wales, Volume II, 1042-1350* (1988)

J.B. Harley, *Maps and the Local Historian* (1972)

J.B. Harley, *Ordnance Survey Maps: a descriptive manual* (1975)

C.R. Hart, *The Hidation of Northamptonshire*, University of Leicester Department of English Local History Occasional Papers, Second Series, Number 3 (1970)

L.C. Hector, *The Handwriting of English Documents* (second edition, 1966, reprint, 1988)

N. Higham, *Rome, Britain and the Anglo-Saxons* (1992)

R.H. Hilton, *Social Structure of Rural Warwickshire in the Middle Ages*, Dugdale Society Occasional Paper 9 (1950)

R.H. Hilton, *A Medieval Society* (second edition, 1983)

D. Hooke, *Anglo-Saxon Landscapes of the West Midlands: The Charter Evidence*, British Archæological Reports (British Series), 95 (1981)

D. Hooke, *The Anglo-Saxon Landscape: the kingdom of the Hwicce* (1985)

ed. D. Hooke, *Medieval Villages: A Review of Current Work*, Oxford University Committee for Archæology No. 5 (1985)

ed. D. Hooke, *Anglo-Saxon Settlements* (1988)

D. Hooke, *Worcestershire Anglo-Saxon Charter-Bounds*, Studies in Anglo-Saxon History II (1990)

D. Hooke and D. Marshall, *The Arrow Valley Project 1. Morton Bagot, a parish survey, Part 1. The Landscape, a topographical survey* (University of Birmingham, Department of Geography Occasional Publication Number 24, 1987)

D. Hooke and D. Marshall, *The Arrow Valley Project 2. Oldberrow, A Parish Survey* (University of Birmingham, Department of Geography Occasional Publication Number 30, 1994)

W.G. Hoskins, *The Making of the English Landscape* (1955)

W.G. Hoskins, *Local History in England* (second edition, 1972)

C. Johansson, *Old English Place-Names and Field-Names containing leah* (Stockholm, 1975)

S. Keynes, *The Diplomas of King Aethelred 'The Unready': A study in their use as historical evidence* (1980)

R.E. Latham, *Revised Medieval Latin Word-List* (1965)

R.E. Latham, *Dictionary of Medieval Latin from British Sources*, (1975-continuing)

ed. R. Lea, *Scenes from Sutton's Past* (1989)

R. Lean and D.P. Robinson, *Warwickshire: Inventory of Ancient Woodland* (Nature Conservancy Council, 1989)

F.W. Maitland, *Domesday Book and Beyond* (1897)

R. Morris, *The church in British archaeology*, C.B.A. Research Report 47 (1983)

P. Murray and S. Carrington, *Flora and Fauna Survey 1979-80* (Warwickshire College of Agriculture)

J.N.L. Myres, *The English Settlements*, Volume 1B in the Oxford History of England (1986)

W.F. Noble, *History of Temple Grafton, Bidford and Binton From the National Archives in the British Museum and Public Record Office* (manuscript, 1879, in W.C.R.O., CR2776/1)

R. Oliver, *Ordnance Survey Maps: a concise guide for historians* (1993)

The Compact Edition of the Oxford English Dictionary (1971)

C. Page and R. Page, *Snitterfield: the 1766 enclosures* (typescript, 1977, copies in W.C.R.O., CR1784, and S.B.T., 87.2)

C. Phythian Adams, *Continuity, Fields and Fission: The Making of a Midland Parish*, University of Leicester Department of English Local History Occasional Papers, Third Series, number 4 (1978)

O. Rackham, *Hayley Wood: Its History and Ecology* (1975)

O. Rackham, *Ancient Woodland: its history, vegetation and uses in England* (1980)

O. Rackham, *The Ancient Woodland of England: The Woods of South-East Essex* (1986)

O. Rackham, *The History of the Countryside* (1986)

O. Rackham, *Trees and Woodland in the British Landscape* (1976, second, revised edition, 1990)

D. Roden, *Studies in Chiltern Field Systems*, (University of London Ph. D. thesis, 1965)

B.K. Roberts, *Settlement, Land Use and Population in the western portion of the Forest of Arden, Warwickshire, between 1086 and 1350: A Study in Historical Geography* (University of Birmingham Ph. D. thesis, 1965)

ed. T. Rowley, *The Origins of Open-Field Agriculture* (1981)

Royal Commission on Historical Monuments (England), *An Inventory of the Historical Monuments in the County of Northampton*, Vols. I-VI (1975-1985)

P. Salway, *Roman Britain* (1981)

G.E. Saville, *Oversley: Some of its History: Part I*, Alcester and District Local History Society Occasional Paper No. 28 (1982)

P.H. Sawyer, *Anglo-Saxon Charters: An annotated list and bibliography* (1968)

ed. P.H. Sawyer, *Medieval Settlement: Continuity and Change* (1976)

P.H. Sawyer, *From Roman Britain to Norman England* (1978)

ed. P.H. Sawyer, *English Medieval Settlement* (1979)

ed. P. Sawyer, *Domesday Book: A Reassessment* (1985)

B. Schumer, *The Evolution of Wychwood to 1400: Pioneers, Frontiers and Forests*, University of Leicester Department of English Local History Occasional Papers, Third Series, number 6 (1984)

A. Sharer, *Die angelsachsische Konigsurkunde im 7. und 8. Jahrhundert*, Veroffentlichunge des Institutes fur Osterreichische Geschichtsforschung, XXVI (1982)

E. Shirley, *Deer and Deer Parks* (1867)

V.H.T. Skipp, *Discovering Bickenhill* (1963)

V.H. Skipp, *Greater Birmingham* (1980)

V. Skipp, *The Origins of Solihull* (second, revised, edition, 1984)

ed. T.R. Slater and P.J. Jarvis, *Field and Forest: an historical geography of Warwickshire and Worcestershire* (1982)

A.H. Smith, *English Place-Name Elements*, Parts I and II (1956)

A Squires and M. Jeeves, *Leicestershire and Rutland Woodlands Past and Present* (1994)

F.M. Stenton, *Anglo-Saxon England* (third edition, 1971)

W.B. Stephens, *Sources for English Local History* (1981)

A. Tasker, *The Nature of Warwickshire* (1990)

C. Taylor, *Fields in the English Landscape* (1975)

C.C. Taylor, *Village and Farmstead* (1983)

A.E. Trueman, *Geology and Scenery in England and Wales* (revised edition, 1972)

Victoria History of the County of Oxford

Victoria History of the County of Staffordshire

Victoria History of the County of Surrey

Victoria History of the County of Warwickshire

S.J. Wager, *Early Medieval Land Units in the Birmingham Area: An Historical Study* (University of Birmingham M. Phil. thesis, 1988)

S.G. Wallsgrove, *Kenilworth 1086-1756* (1991)

P. Warner, *Greens, Common and Clayland Colonization: The Origins and Development of Green-side Settlement in East Suffolk*, University of Leicester Department of English Local History Occasional Papers, Fourth Series, Number 2 (1987)

J. West, *The Administration and Economy of the Forest of Feckenham during the Early Middle Ages*, (University of Birmingham thesis, 1964)

ed. E.G. Wheler-Galton, *Pinley Priory and Manor: documents concerning Pinley Priory* (typescript, c.1930, in W.C.R.O., CR2310/1)

W.A.D. Whitfield, *Soil Survey Record No. 19: Soils in Warwickshire 1: Sheet SP36 (Leamington Spa)* (1974)

W.A.D. Whitfield and G.R. Beard, *Soil Survey Record No. 25: Soils in Warwickshire II: Sheet SP05 (Alcester)* (1975)

W.A.D. Whitfield and G.R. Beard, *Soil Survey Record No. 45: Soils in Warwickshire III: Sheets SP47/48 (Rugby West/Wolvey)* (1977)

W.A.D. Whitfield and G.R. Beard, *Soil Survey Record No. 66: Soils in Warwickshire IV: Sheet SP29/39 (Nuneaton)* (1980)

W.A.D. Whitfield, *Soil Survey Record No.101: Soils in Warwickshire VI: Sheet SP 25/35 (Stratford-upon-Avon East)* (1986)

T. Williamson and L. Bellamy, *Property and Landscape* (1987)

J. Woodall, *From Hroca to Anne* (1974)

Secondary works: articles

N. Adams, 'The Judicial Conflict over Tithes', *English Historical Review*, LII (1937), pp. 1-22

N.W. Alcock, 'Grandborough - a problem in topography', *Warwickshire History*, Vol. 1, No. 4 (Autumn, 1970), pp. 23-7

L. Barnett and C. Emms, 'Des. Res. to let', *Warwickshire Wildlife*, 97 (Winter 1997), p. 7

S.R. Bassett, 'Medieval Lichfield. A Topographical Review', *Transactions of the South Staffordshire Archæological and Historical Society*, XXII (1980-81), pp. 93-121

S.R. Bassett and C.C. Dyer, 'Hanbury, Hereford and Worcester. Documentary and Field Survey SO 96 64', *West Midlands Archaeology*, 23 (1980), pp. 88, 90-1; *ibid.*, 24 (1981), pp. 73-8

S.R. Bassett, 'Beyond the edge of excavation: the topographical context of Goltho', ed. H. Mayr-Harting and R.I. Moore, *Studies in Medieval History Presented to R.H.C. Davis* (1985), pp. 21-39

S. Bassett, 'In search of the origins of Anglo-Saxon kingdoms', ed. *idem, The Origins of Anglo-Saxon Kingdoms* (1989) pp. 3-27

S.R. Bassett, 'Churches in Worcester before and after the conversion of the Anglo-Saxons', *The Antiquaries Journal*, LXIX, Part II (1989), pp. 225-56

S.R. Bassett, 'Church and diocese in the West Midlands: the transition from British to Anglo-Saxon control', in ed. J. Blair and R. Sharpe, *Pastoral Care Before the Parish* (1992), pp. 13-40

S. Bassett, 'The administrative landscape of the diocese of Worcester in the tenth century', in ed. N. Brooks and C. Cubitt, *St. Oswald of Worcester: Life and influence* (1996), pp. 147-73

M. Bell, 'Environmental Archæology as an Index of Continuity and Change in the Medieval Landscape', ed. M.Aston, D.Austin and C.Dyer, *The Rural Settlements of Medieval England* (1989) pp. 269-86

B. Bellamy, 'Anglo-Saxon dispersed sites and woodland at Geddington in the Rockingham Forest, Northamptonshire', *Landscape History*, 16 (1994), pp. 31-7

M.W. Beresford, 'The economic individualism of Sutton Coldfield', *TBAS*, 64 (1941-42), pp. 101-8

M.W. Beresford and J.G. Hurst, 'Wharram Percy: a Case Study in Microtopography', ed. P.H. Sawyer, *English Medieval Settlement* (1979), pp. 52-85

J. Birrell, 'Common Rights in the Medieval Forest: Disputes and Conflicts in the Thirteenth Century', *Past & Present*, 117 (1987), pp. 22-49

J. Blair, 'Secular Minster Churches in Domesday Book', ed. P. Sawyer, *Domesday Book: A Reassessment* (1985), pp. 104-142

C.J. Bond, 'Deserted Medieval Villages in Warwickshire: A Review of the Field Evidence', *TBWAS*, 86 (1974), pp. 85-112

C.J. Bond, 'Medieval Oxfordshire Villages and their Topography: a Preliminary Discussion', in ed. D Hooke, *Medieval Villages: A Review of Current Work*, Oxford University Committee for Archæology No. 5 (1985) pp. 101-23

C.N.L. Brooke, 'Rural Ecclesiastical Institutions in England: the search for their origins', *Settimane di Studio del Centro Italiano di Studi Sull' alto Medioevo*, XXVIII (1982), Vol. 2, pp. 685-711

N. Brooks, 'The creation and early structure of the kingdom of Kent', ed. S. Bassett, *The Origins of Anglo-Saxon Kingdoms* (1989), pp. 55-74

A.E. Brown and C.C. Taylor, 'The origins of dispersed settlement; some results from fieldwork in Bedfordshire', *Landscape History*, 11 (1989), pp. 61-81

B. Campbell, 'Commonfield Origins - The Regional Dimension', ed. T. Rowley, *The Origins of Open-Field Agriculture* (1981), pp. 112-29

J. Campbell, 'Bede', ed. T. Dorey, *Latin Historians* (1966), pp. 159-60

G. Crawford, 'Wasperton, Warwickshire. Excavation of gravel site', *West Midlands Archaeology*, 24 (1981), pp. 121-29

G. Crawford, 'Excavations at Wasperton: 3rd interim report', *West Midlands Archaeology*, 26 (1983), pp. 15-27

B. Cox, 'The Place-Names of the Earliest English Records', *Journal of the English Place-Name Society*, 8 (1975-6), pp. 12-66

R. Dace, 'The Foundation and Endowment of Wroxall Priory', *Warwickshire History*, Vol. VII, No. 3, Summer, 1991, pp. 75-9

P.J. Drury and W, Rodwell, 'Settlement in the later Iron Age and Roman periods', ed. D.G. Buckley, *Archaeology in Essex to A.D. 1500*, C.B.A. Research Report 34 (1980), pp. 59-75

C.C. Dyer, 'A Small Landowner in the Fifteenth Century', *Midland History*, Vol. I, no. 3 (Spring, 1972), pp. 1-14

C. Dyer, 'English Peasant Buildings in the Later Middle Ages (1200-1500)', *Medieval Archaeology*, 30 (1986), pp. 19-45

C. Dyer, 'The Retreat from Marginal Land: The Growth and Decline of Medieval Rural Settlements', in ed. M. Aston, D. Austin, and C. Dyer, *The Rural Settlements of Medieval England* (1989), pp. 45-57

C. Dyer, 'Dispersed Settlements in Medieval England. A Case Study of Pendock, Worcestershire', *Medieval Archaeology*, XXXIV (1990), pp. 97-121

C. Dyer, 'The Hidden Trade of the Middle Ages: evidence from the West Midlands of England', *Journal of Historical Geography*, 18 (1992), pp. 141-57.

C. Dyer, 'Admington. SP200460', *Medieval Settlement Research Group, Annual Report* 10 (1995), p. 42

A.M. Everitt, 'The making of the agrarian landscape of Kent', *Archaeologia Cantiana*, XCII (1976), pp. 1-31

A. Everitt, 'River and wold. Reflections on the historical origin of regions and pays', *Journal of Historical Geography*, 3.1 (1977), pp. 1-19

A. Everitt, 'The wolds once more', *Journal of Historical Geography*, 5.1 (1979), pp. 67-71

R. Faith, 'Estates, demesnes and the village', in ed. H.S.A. Fox, *The Origins of the Midland Village*, (papers prepared for a discussion session at the Economic History Society's annual conference, Leicester, April, 1992), pp. 11-35

W.J. Ford, 'Some Settlement Patterns in the Central Region of the Warwickshire Avon', ed. P.H. Sawyer, *Medieval Settlement: Continuity and Change* (1976), pp. 274-94

P.J. Fowler, 'Agriculture and rural settlement', ed. D.M. Wilson, *The Archæology of Anglo-Saxon England* (1978), pp 23-48

P.J. Fowler, 'Farming in the Anglo-Saxon landscape: an archæologist's review', *Anglo-Saxon England*, 9 (1981), pp. 263-80

H.S.A. Fox, 'Approaches to the adoption of the Midland system', ed. T. Rowley, *The Origins of Open-Field Agriculture* (1981), pp. 64-111

H.S.A. Fox, 'The People of the Wolds in English Settlement History', ed. M. Aston, D. Austin and C. Dyer, *The Rural Settlements of Medieval England* (1989), pp. 77-101

H.S.A. Fox, 'The Agrarian Context', ed. *idem*, *The Origins of the Midland Village* (papers prepared for a discussion session at the Economic History Society's annual conference, Leicester, April, 1992), pp. 36-72

H.S.A. Fox, 'Introduction: transhumance and seasonal settlement', ed. *idem*, *Seasonal Settlement*, Vaughan Paper 39, University of Leicester Department of Adult Education (1996), pp. 1-23

M. Freeman, 'Whichwood Forest, Oxfordshire: An Episode in its Recent Environmental History', *Agricultural History Review*, 45 (1997), pp. 137-48

M. Fulford, 'The Landscape of Roman Britain: A Review', *Landscape History*, 12 (1990), pp. 25-31

M. Gelling, 'Some notes on Warwickshire place-names', *TBWAS*, 86 (1974), pp. 59-79

M. Gelling, 'The Evidence of Place-Names I', ed. P.H. Sawyer, *English Medieval Settlement* (1976), pp. 110-21

M. Gelling, review of C. Phythian-Adams, *Continuity, Fields and Fission: The Making of a Midland Parish*, University of Leicester Department of English Local History Occasional Papers, Third Series, number 4 (1978), in *TBWAS*, 90 (1980), pp. 85-6

M. Gelling, 'The place-name volumes of Worcestershire and Warwickshire: a new look', ed. T.R. Slater and P.J. Jarvis, *Field and Forest: an historical geography of Warwickshire and Worcestershire* (1982), pp. 59-78

M. Gelling, 'Why Aren't We Speaking Welsh?', ed. W. Filmer-Sankey, *Anglo-Saxon Studies in Archaeology and History 6* (1993), pp. 51-6

G.B. Grundy, 'Saxon Charters of Worcestershire', *TBAS*, Vols. LII, LIII (1927, 1928), pp. 1-183 and 18-131 respectively

D.N. Hall, 'The origins of open-field agriculture - the archæological fieldwork evidence', ed. T. Rowley, *The Origins of Open-Field Agriculture* (1981), pp. 22-38

D. Hall, 'Late Saxon Topography and Early Medieval Estates', ed. D. Hooke, *Medieval Villages: A Review of Current Work*, Oxford University Committee for Archæology No. 5 (1985), pp. 61-9

D. Hall, 'The Late Saxon Countryside: Villages and their Fields', ed. D. Hooke, *Anglo-Saxon Settlements* (1988), pp. 99-122

H. Harke, 'Finding Britons in Anglo-Saxon graves', *British Archaeology*, 10 (December, 1995), p. 7

J.B. Harley, 'Population Trends and Agricultural Developments from the Warwickshire Hundred Rolls of 1279', *Economic History Review*, second series, xi (1958-9), pp. 8-18

P.D.A. Harvey, 'The documents of landscape history: snares and delusions', *Landscape History*, 13 (1991), pp. 47-52

N. Higham, 'Settlement, land use and Domesday ploughlands', *Landscape History*, 12 (1990), pp. 33-44

C. Hills, 'The archaeology of Anglo-Saxon England in the pagan period: a review', *Anglo-Saxon England*, 8 (1979), pp. 297-329

R.H. Hilton, 'A Study in the Pre-history of English Enclosure in the Fifteenth Century', reprinted in *idem, The English Peasantry in the Later Middle Ages* (1975), pp. 161-73

M. Hodder, 'Earthwork Enclosures in Sutton Park, West Midlands', *TBWAS*, 89 (1978-79), pp. 166-70

D. Hooke, 'The Oldberrow Charter and boundary clause', *West Midlands Archaeological News Sheet*, 21 (1978), pp. 81-3

D. Hooke, 'Early Cotswold Woodland', *Journal of Historical Geography*, 4.4 (1978), pp. 333-41

D. Hooke, 'The Anglo-Saxon Landscape', ed. T.R. Slater and P.J Jarvis, *Field and Forest: an historical geography of Warwickshire and Worcestershire* (1982), pp. 79-103

D. Hooke, 'Village Development in the West Midlands', ed. *idem, Medieval Villages: A Review of Current Work*, Oxford University Committee for Archæology No. 5 (1985), pp. 125-54

D. Hooke, 'Early forms of open-field agriculture in England', ed. U. Sporrong, *The Transformation of Rural Society, Economy and Landscape*, Papers from the 1987 meeting of the Permanent European Conference for the Study of the Rural Landscape (University of Stockholm), pp. 143-51

D. Hooke, 'Pre-Conquest Woodland: its Distribution and Usage', *Agricultural History Review*, 37 (1989), pp. 113-29

D. Hooke, 'Reconstructing Anglo-Saxon landscapes in Warwickshire', *TBWAS*, 100, pp. 99-116

D. Hooke and R. Taylor, 'The Augustinian priory of Studley, Warwickshire', *TBWAS*, 98 (1993-94), pp. 73-90

J.G. Hurst, 'The Wharram Research Project: Problem Orientation and Strategy 1950-1990', ed. D Hooke, *Medieval Villages: A Review of Current Work*, Oxford University Committee for Archæology No. 5 (1985) pp. 201-4

D Morfitt, 'Ecology of the Moor: A Threatened "Ancient" Landscape - Hawkhurst Moor and Rough Close Wood', *Berkswell Miscellany*, Vol. III (1987) (no page numbers)

D. Morfitt, 'Oliver Rackham views Warwickshire woodland', *Warwickshire Wildlife*, 74 (Warwickshire Nature Conservation Trust, September, 1990)

O. Rackham, 'Neolithic Woodland Management in the Somerset Levels: Garvin's, Walton Heath, and Rowland's Tracks', ed. J.M. Coles, B.J. Orme, F.A. Hibbert, G.J. Wainwright, C.J. Young, *Somerset Levels Papers*, 3 (1977)

D. Roden, 'Woodland and its Management in the Medieval Chilterns', *Forestry*, 41 (1968), pp. 59-71

W. Rodwell, 'Relict Landscapes in Essex', ed. H.C. Bowen and P.J. Fowler, *Early Land Allotment*, British Archæological Reports (British Series), 48 (1978), pp. 89-98

B.K. Roberts, 'A Study of Medieval Colonization in the Forest of Arden', *Agricultural History Review*, 16 (1968), pp. 101-13

B.K. Roberts, 'North-West Warwickshire: Tanworth-in-Arden', ed. R.A. Skelton and P.D.A. Harvey, *Local Maps and Plans from Medieval England* (1987), pp. 317-28

B.K. Roberts, 'Field Systems of the West Midlands', ed. A.R.H. Baker and R.A. Butlin, *Studies of Field Systems in the British Isles* (1973), pp. 181-231

B.K. Roberts, 'Village forms in Warwickshire: a preliminary discussion', ed. T.R. Slater and P.J. Jarvis, *Field and Forest: an historical geography of Warwickshire and Worcestershire* (1982), pp. 125-46

D. Rollason, 'The ecclesiastical context', ed. H.S.A. Fox, *The Origins of the Midland Village*, (papers prepared for a discussion session at the Economic History Society's annual conference, Leicester, April, 1992), pp. 73-90

P.H. Sawyer, 'Medieval English Settlement: New Interpretations', ed. P.H. Sawyer, *English Medieval Settlement* (1979), pp. 1-8

P. Sawyer, 'Domesday Studies since 1886', ed. Sawyer, *Domesday Book: A Reassessment*, pp. 1-4

P. Sims-Williams, 'Cuthswith, seventh-century abbess of Inkberrow, near Worcester, and the Wurzburg manuscript of Jerome on Ecclesiastices', *Anglo-Saxon England*, 5 (1976), pp. 1-21

P. Sims-Williams, 'The Settlement of England in Bede and the Chronicle', *Anglo-Saxon England*, 12 (1983), pp. 1-41

P. Sims-Williams, 'Gildas and the Anglo-Saxons', *Cambridge Medieval Celtic Studies*, 6 (Winter, 1983), pp. 1-30

V. Skipp, 'The Evolution of Settlement and Open-Field Topography in North Arden down to 1300', ed. T. Rowley, *The Origins of Open-Field Agriculture* (1981), pp. 162-83

T.R. Slater, 'More on the wolds', *Journal of Historical Geography*, 5.2 (1979), pp. 213-8

T.R. Slater, 'The Origins of Warwick', *Midland History*, VIII (1983), pp. 1-13

L.D.W. Smith, 'A survey of building timber and other trees in the hedgerows of a Warwickshire estate, c.1500', *TBWAS*, 90 (1980), pp. 65-73

W.E. Tate, 'Enclosure Acts and Awards relating to Warwickshire', *TBAS*, LXV (1943, 1944)

C.C. Taylor, 'Polyfocal settlement and the English village', *Medieval Archaeology*, 21 (1977), pp. 189-93

C.C. Taylor and P.J. Fowler, 'Roman Fields into Medieval Furlongs', ed. H.C. Bowen and P.J. Fowler, *Early Land Allotment*, British Archæological Reports (British Series), 48 (1978), pp. 159-62

C.S. Taylor, 'The Origin of the Mercian Shires', ed. H.P.R. Finberg, *Gloucestershire Studies* (1957), pp. 17-51

J. Thirsk, 'The Common Fields', *Past & Present*, 29 (December, 1964), pp. 3-25

J. Thirsk, 'The Origins of the Common Fields', *Past & Present*, 33 (April, 1966), pp. 142-7

H. Thorpe, 'The Lord and the Landscape', *TBAS*, 80 (1962), pp. 38-77

J. Titow, 'Medieval England and the Open-Field System', *Past & Present*, 32 (December, 1965), pp. 86-102

D. Tracey, 'Within the Pale - the story of Berkswell Park', *Berkswell Miscellany*, Vol. IV (1988), pp. 7-9

E.C. Vollans, 'The Evolution of Farm-Lands in the Central Chilterns in the twelfth and thirteenth centuries', *Transactions of the Institute of British Geographers*, 26 (1959), pp. 197-238

J.F.R. Walmsley, 'The *Censarii* of Burton Abbey and the Domesday population', *North Staffordshire Journal of Field Studies*, 8 (1968), pp. 73-80

A. Watkins, 'Cattle Grazing in the Forest of Arden in the Later Middle Ages', *Agricultural History Review*, 37 (1989), pp. 12-25

276

A. Watkins, 'The Woodland Economy of the Forest of Arden in the Later Middle Ages', *Midland History*, XVIII (1993), pp. 19-36

A. Watkins, 'Merevale Abbey in the late 1490s', *Warwickshire History*, Vol. IX, No. 3 (1994), pp. 87-104

M.G. Welch, 'Rural settlement patterns in the Early and Middle Anglo-Saxon periods', *Landscape History*, 7 (1985), pp. 13-25

G. Webster and B. Hobley, 'Aerial Reconnaissance over the Warwickshire Avon', *Archæological Journal*, 121 (1964), pp. 1-22

M. Welch, 'The kingdom of the South Saxons: the origins', ed. S. Bassett, *The Origins of Anglo-Saxon Kingdoms* (1989), pp. 75-83

E. Willacy and R. Wallwork, 'Exploratory Excavations at a Romano-British site in Glasshouse wood, Kenilworth, 1971', *TBWAS*, 88 (1976-7), pp. 71-81.

T. Williamson, 'The Roman countryside: settlement and agriculture in N.W. Essex', *Britannia*, 15 (1984), pp. 225-30

T. Williamson, 'Sites in the Landscape: approaches to the post-Roman settlement of south-eastern England', *Archaeological Review from Cambridge*, 4.1 (1985), pp. 51-64

T. Williamson, 'Parish boundaries and early fields: continuity and discontinuity', *Journal of Historical Geography*, 12.3 (1986), pp. 241-8

T. Williamson, 'The development of settlement in north-west Essex: the results of recent field survey', *Essex Archæology and History*, 17 (1986), pp. 120-32

T. Williamson, 'Early Co-axial Field Systems on the East Anglian Boulder Clays', *Proceedings of the Prehistoric Society*, 53 (1987), pp. 419-31

T. Williamson, 'Explaining Regional Landscapes: Woodland and Champion in Southern and Eastern England', *Landscape History* 10 (1988), pp. 5-13

T. Williamson, 'Settlement Chronology and Regional Landscapes: The Evidence from the Claylands of East Anglia and Essex', ed. D. Hooke, *Anglo-Saxon Settlements*, (1988), pp. 153-75

P. Wise, 'Wasperton', *Current Archaeology*, 126 (1991), pp. 256-9

K.P. Witney, 'The Woodland Economy of Kent, 1066-1348', *Agricultural History Review*, 38, Part I (1990), pp. 20-39

B. Yorke, 'The kingdom of the East Saxons', *Anglo-Saxon England*, 14 (1985), pp. 1-36

B. Yorke, 'The Jutes of Hampshire and Wight and the origins of Wessex', ed. S. Bassett, *The Origins of Anglo-Saxon Kingdoms* (1989), pp. 84-96

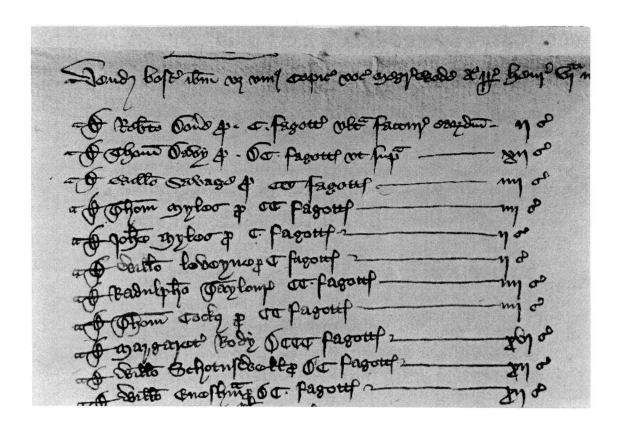

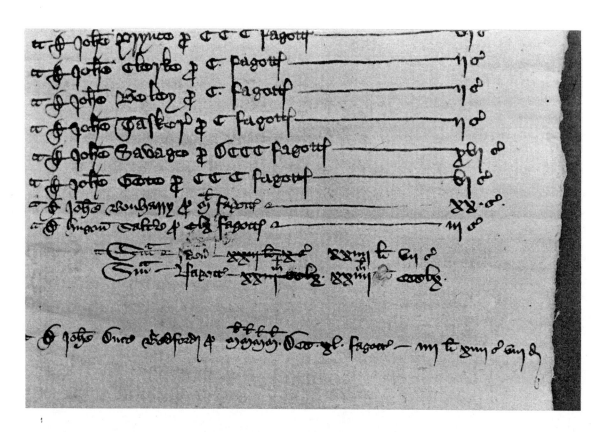

Figure 86: Extracts from list of firewood sold in Megrewode, 1425-6 (W.C.R.O., CR1886/487)

This paper list is attached to the account roll for Wedgnock Park in 1425-6. The photographs show the beginning and end of the list, which records in Latin the sale of 24,360 faggots (spelt fagotts - bundles of firewood) sold at two shillings a hundred and also a sale to the Duke of Bedford, who held the manor of Fulbrook, a few miles to the south.
Reproduced by kind permission of Warwickshire County Record Office

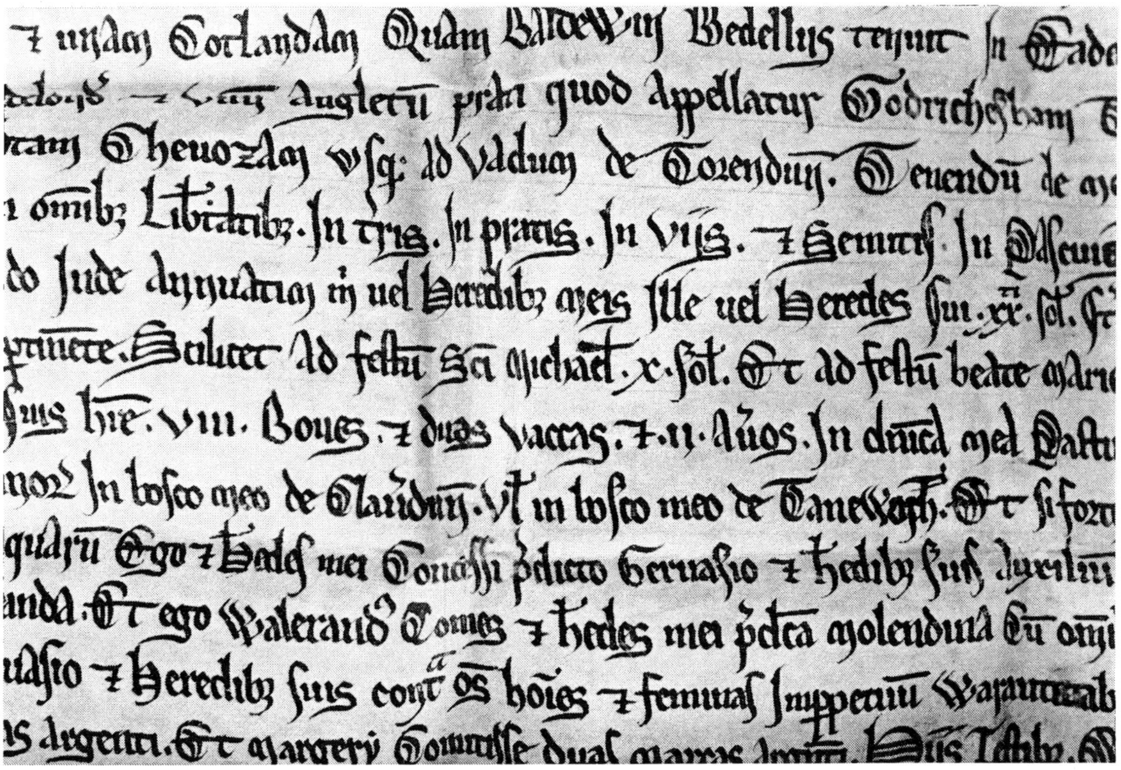

Figure 87: Deed, Walton, c.1196 (W.C.R.O., CR133/1)

The grant (in Latin) by Waleran, earl of Warwick, concerns mills in Walton (by Wellesbourne) and Barford. This extract shows, in the fifth line from the bottom, a reference to the earl's wood (bosco) of Claverdon or his wood in Tanworth, where (timber) supports were to be provided for the mills.
Reproduced by kind permission of Warwickshire County Record Office

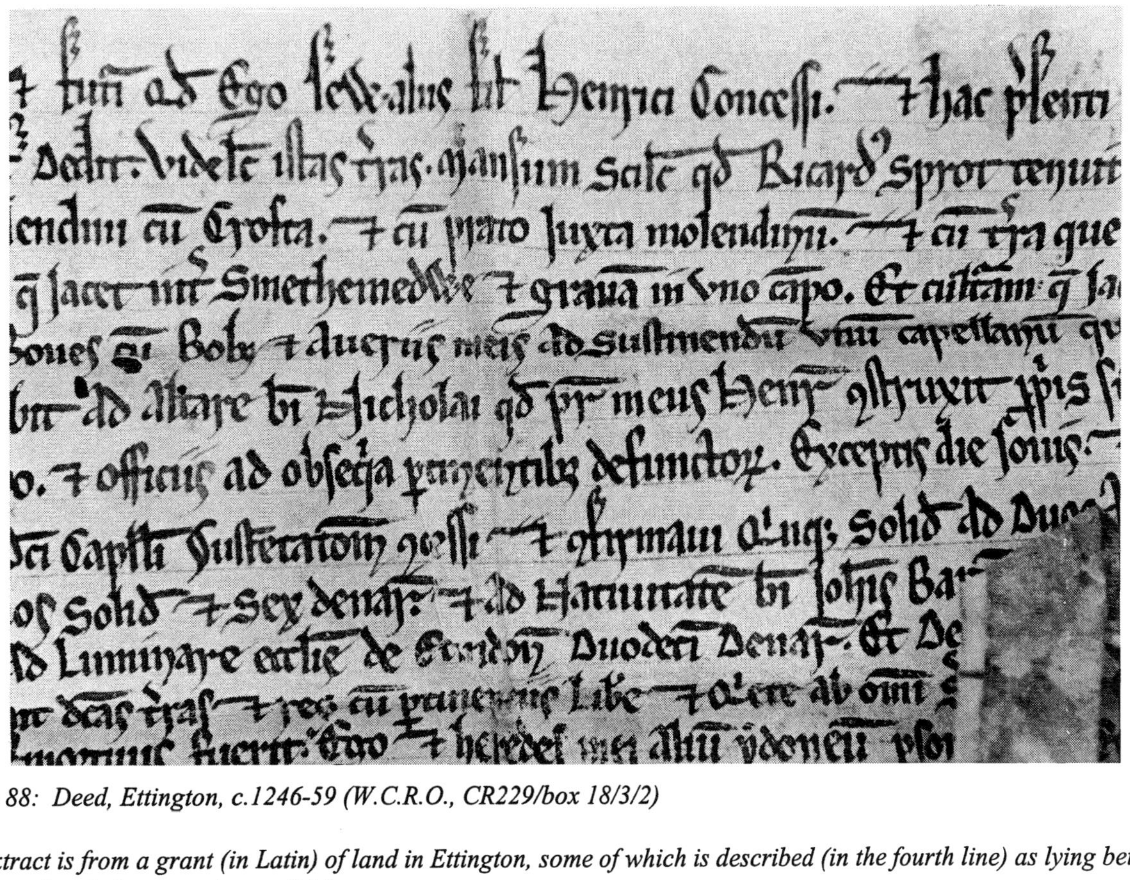

Figure 88: Deed, Ettington, c.1246-59 (W.C.R.O., CR229/box 18/3/2)

This extract is from a grant (in Latin) of land in Ettington, some of which is described (in the fourth line) as lying between Smethemedwe & the grove in one field.
Reproduced by kind permission of Warwickshire County Record Office

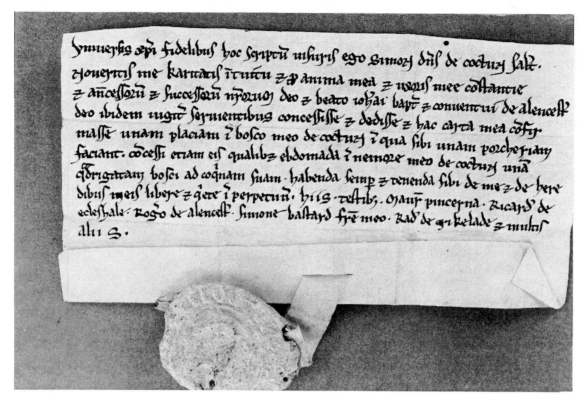

Figure 89: Deed, Coughton, c.1241 (W.C.R.O., CR1886/15)

Simon, lord of Coughton, grants a place in the wood (bosco) of Coughton for a pigsty and a wagon load of wood for the Abbey's kitchen every week in the wood (nemore) of Coughton.
Reproduced by kind permission of Warwickshire County Record Office

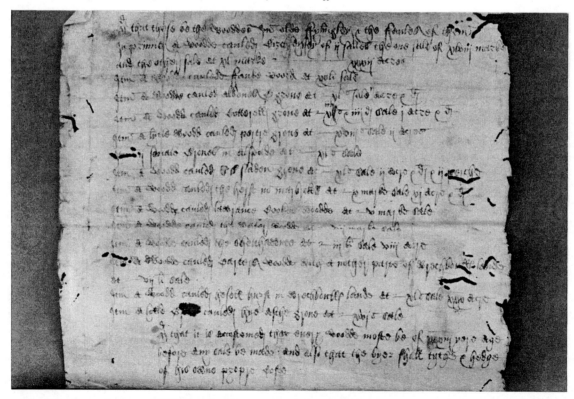

Figure 90: List of woods cut in Old Fillongley (W.C.R.O., CR1886/3370)

This list is in English, and probably dates from the fifteenth or early sixteenth century. It names several woods and gives details of the "Faules" or fellings of these woods.
Reproduced by kind permission of Warwickshire County Record Office